P9-CDD-622

Media and Cultural Studies
KeyWorks

Looking forward
to many discussions
& lots of coffee
Love,
Gabor

KEYWORKS IN CULTURAL STUDIES

As cultural studies powers ahead to new intellectual horizons, it becomes increasingly important to chart the discipline's controversial history. This is the object of an exciting new series, KeyWorks in Cultural Studies. By showcasing the best that has been thought and written on the leading themes and topics constituting the discipline, KeyWorks in Cultural Studies provides an invaluable genealogy for students striving to better understand the contested space in which cultural studies takes place and is practiced.

Media and Cultural Studies

KeyWorks

Edited by

Meenakshi Gigi Durham and Douglas M. Kellner

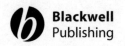
Blackwell
Publishing

© 2001 by Blackwell Publishing Ltd
except for editorial material and organization © 2001 by Meenakshi Gigi Durham and
Douglas M. Kellner

350 Main Street, Malden, MA 02148-5020, USA
108 Cowley Road, Oxford OX4 1JF, UK
550 Swanston Street, Carlton, Victoria 3053, Australia

All rights reserved. No part of this publication may be reproduced, stored in a
retrieval system, or transmitted, in any form or by any means, electronic, mechanical,
photocopying, recording or otherwise, except as permitted by the UK Copyright,
Designs, and Patents Act 1988, without the prior permission of the publisher.

First published 2001 by Blackwell Publishing Ltd
Reprinted 2002, 2003 (twice), 2004

Library of Congress Cataloging-in-Publication Data

  Media and Cultural studies: keyworks / edited by Meenakshi Gigi Durham
    and Douglas Kellner.
        p. cm.—(Keyworks in cultural studies; 2)
    Includes bibliographical references and index.
    ISBN 0–631–22095–X (alk. paper)—ISBN 0–631–22096–8 (alk. paper)
    1. Mass media and culture.   2. Popular culture.   I. Durham, Meenakshi Gigi.
  II. Kellner, Douglas, 1943- III. Series.
  P94.6 .M424 2001
  302.23—dc21

                                                                    00-060798

A catalogue record for this title is available from the British Library.

Set in 10 on 12.5 pt Galliard
by Kolam Information Services Pvt. Ltd, Pondicherry, India
Printed and bound in the United Kingdom
by TJ International Ltd, Padstow, Cornwall

For further information on
Blackwell Publishing, visit our website:
http://www.blackwellpublishing.com

Contents

Adventures in Media and Cultural Studies: Introducing the KeyWorks

Douglas M. Kellner and Meenakshi Gigi Durham

Few would disagree with the claim that media and culture today are of central importance to the maintenance and reproduction of contemporary societies. Societies, like species, need to reproduce to survive, and culture cultivates attitudes and behavior that predispose people to consent to established ways of thought and conduct, thus integrating individuals into a specific socioeconomic system. Forms of media culture such as television, film, popular music, magazines, and advertising provide role and gender models, fashion hints, life-style images, and icons of personality. The narratives of media culture offer patterns of proper and improper behavior, moral messages, and ideological conditioning, sugar-coating social and political ideas with pleasurable and seductive forms of popular entertainment. Likewise, media and consumer culture, cyberculture, sports, and other popular activities engage people in practices which integrate them into the established society, while offering pleasures, meanings, and identities. Various individuals and audiences respond to these texts disparately, negotiating their meanings in complex and often paradoxical ways.

With media and culture playing such important roles in contemporary life, it is obvious that we must come to understand our cultural environment if we want control over our lives. Yet there are many approaches to the study of media, culture, and society in separate disciplines and academic fields. Often critics take a single perspective and use a specific method and theory to understand, make sense of, interpret, or criticize media and cultural texts. Others eschew all methodological and theoretical critical strategies in favor of empirical description and analysis.

We would advocate the usefulness of a wide range of theoretical and methodological approaches to the study of media, culture, and society, yet we do not believe that any one theory or method is adequate to engage the richness, complexity, variety, and novelty displayed in contemporary constellations of rapidly proliferating cultural forms and new media. We have therefore assembled what we consider some "*KeyWorks*" of current theories and methods for the study of the abundance and diversity of culture and media in the present age. The texts we have chosen are "Key" because we believe that the perspectives and theorists which we have included in this volume are among the most significant and serviceable for engaging the forms and influences of contemporary media and culture.

The texts in this reader provide "keys" which help unlock the domain of meaning, value, politics, and ideology in familiar forms of cultural artifacts and practices. They furnish openings which enable critical readers to see cultural texts and phenomena in a new light, generating insight into the sometimes hidden production processes and ideological constraints of media culture. Key theories and methods help unlock and unveil structural codes and organizing conventions of media texts, their meanings and values, and often contradictory social and political effects. Understanding culture critically also provides insight into the ways that media and culture construct gender and role models, and even identities, as the populace come to pattern their lives on the celebrities and stars of media culture. These readings are also "key" in that they open new theoretical directions and formulations of culture and society; at the time of their writing, they presented inventive and sometimes revolutionary new directions in the study of media and culture.

The texts selected are "works" in that their methods and theories enable media literate readers to engage in the activity of analysis, interpretation, criticism, and making sense of their cultural and social worlds and experiences. The theories and methods presented provide tools for critical vision and practice, helping to produce active creators of meaning and interpretation, rather than merely passive audiences. The *KeyWorks* thus empower those who wish to gain skills of media literacy, providing instruments of criticism and interpretation. They provide essential elements of becoming intelligent and resourceful cultural subjects, discriminating readers, and creative users and producers of contemporary culture.

Thus, the texts assembled in this book can help cultural consumers to become critics and creators. Our introduction will accordingly attempt to demonstrate how the diverse approaches and texts that we have assembled provide valuable keys to cultural criticism and interpretation, helping to produce more competent and discriminating critics. We discuss below how the specific groupings of the *KeyWorks* provide different approaches to the study of media and culture and point to the contributions and limitations of each perspective. In this introduction, we accordingly furnish overviews of each distinctive way of seeing and engaging culture and media. More detailed presentation of the theorists and critics we have chosen, together with explications of the key concepts, theories, and methods selected, will head each of the five parts we have delineated.

Theory/Method/Critique: A Multiperspectival Approach

There is *only* a perspective "seeing", *only* a perspective "knowing"; and the *more* affects we allow to speak about one thing, the more complete will our "concept" of this thing, our "objectivity," be.

(Friedrich Nietzsche)

Our opening discussion will give the reader a sense of current debates and issues within cultural and media theory, emphasizing which issues and controversies are of crucial importance in the contemporary era. Our narrative will track salient developments in the study of culture and media, supplying a mapping of the prevailing thickets of theories and methods which have proliferated especially since the 1960s. Indeed, to pursue our *KeyWorks* metaphor, each perspective provides an opening into the complex terrain of contemporary media and culture, furnishing access to understanding the world in which we live. Each "key" will open doors to new domains, such as ideology, the politics of representations, and cultural studies. They provide novel ways of seeing and understanding the flora and fauna of images, symbols, and messages through which we wander, trying to make sense and give shape to our lives.

The terrain of contemporary culture, however, is so vast, the maze of theories so complex, and the debates over media and culture so intense and convoluted that we have necessarily had to choose some perspectives and theorists to the exclusion of others. In fact, there are many forms of media that saturate our everyday lives and the cultural change of the current technological revolution is so turbulent that it is becoming increasingly difficult to map the transformations and to keep up with the cultural discourses and theories that attempt to make sense of it all. Culture today is both ordinary and complex, encompassing multiple realms of everyday life. We – and many of the theorists assembled in this volume – employ the term "culture" broadly to signify types of cultural artifacts (i.e., TV, CDs, newspapers, paintings, opera, journalism, cyberculture, and so on), as well as discourses about these phenomena. Since culture is bound up with both forms, like film or sports, and discourses, it is both a space of interpretation and debate as well as subject matter and domain of inquiry. Theories and writings like this introduction are themselves modes of culture, spaces that attempt to make sense of particular phenomena and subject matter, and a part of a contemporary cultural field.

A theory is a way of seeing, an optic, that focuses on a specific subject matter. The Greek word *theoria* signifies perspective and vision which centers upon specific topics, processes, and attributes, as a theory of the state focuses on how the government works. Theories are also modes of explanation and interpretation that construct connections and illuminate sociocultural practices and structures, thus helping to make sense of our everyday life, as an analysis of how Microsoft dominates the computer software field would indicate what particular issues are at stake. Thus, cultural and social theories are descriptive and interpretive; they highlight specific topics, make connections, contextualize, provide interpretations, and offer explanations. There is also a narrative component to theory as in Adam Smith's or Karl Marx's theories of capitalism which tell of the origin and genesis of the market economy, as well as describing how it works and in Marx's case offering a critique and proposals of revolutionary transformation.

All social theories are thus perspectives that center attention on phenomena and their connections to the broader society and a wide range of institutions, discourses, and practices. As optics, or ways of seeing, they illuminate part of the social and cultural field, but may ignore or leave in darkness other dimensions. Consequently, constantly expanding one's theoretical perspectives and horizons helps to illuminate multiple dimensions of our cultural environment, providing richer and more complex understandings of our sociocultural life. Multiplying theories and methods at one's disposal helps to grasp the diverse dimensions of an object, to make more and better connections, and thus provide richer and more comprehensive understanding of cultural artifacts or practices under scrutiny.

It is therefore our conviction that no one approach contributes *the* key to cultural and media criticism, that all given theories and methods have their limitations as well as strengths, their blindspots as well as illuminating perspectives. Hence, in our view, no one theory, method, or thinker dispenses privileged access to the truth of our culture and society; there is no magical formula or hermeneutic key to unlock the hidden secrets of cultural meaning and effects. Rather, we believe that the categories, theories, and texts presented in *KeyWorks* provide tools for making sense of our life, or – to switch the metaphor – weapons of critique which enable individuals to engage in discriminating practice in distinct contexts.

Furthermore, some of the theoretical perspectives offered will furnish useful material for some tasks, while others will prove more valuable for different projects. Someone might choose, for instance, to do a feminist reading of a cultural text, while at another time the category of race or class may be most salient to one's critical intentions. Analyses will necessarily often involve the confluence of these and other vectors. Likewise, one critical exercise might focus on the ideology of the text and the ways that texts legitimate and reproduce dominant forms of oppression, while another reading might emphasize the ways that specific texts resist dominant institutions and ideologies – or show how certain texts both legitimate and contest the established culture and society at the same time and are thus markedly ambiguous.

Viewing culture from political economy, from the perspective of analysis of the system of production and distribution, may disclose how the culture industries reproduce the dominant corporate and commercial culture, excluding discourses and images that contest the established social system. Closer reading of media texts can reveal a wealth of meanings, values, and messages, often contradictory. Examining how people engage cultural texts, however, may reveal that audiences refuse dominant meanings and offer their own, sometimes surprising, interpretations. Conjoining production/text/audience perspectives can thus help provide a more complex sense of how culture and media actually operate in everyday life.

It is our conviction that competent and critical cultural consumers and commentators need to be able to examine media, culture, and society from a variety of perspectives, in order to cultivate critical vision and understanding of the nature and effects of cultural production and the artifacts with which we interact. Each new approach, each new theory, equips the budding critic with a different way of seeing and interpreting, thus creating more diverse perspective for understanding media and culture. Thus, the many concepts, theories, and methods embedded in the texts in *KeyWorks* will enable readers themselves to engage in cultural and media criticism, and consequently to become competent critics and consumers.

The texts and approaches we have chosen for *KeyWorks* are foundational in the sense that they provide building-blocks for constructing analyses, interpretations, and criticisms of cultural texts and the societies in which they originate and operate. Most of the selections are "radical" in the sense that they go to the roots of the situation (the meaning of the Latin term *radix*), showing, for example, how media and culture are grounded in a social system and its conflicts. All of the perspectives we have selected are "sociological" in the sense that they show, in varying ways, how media and cultural texts are rooted in a particular system of political economy such as capitalism, or in the dominant media and cultural forms of a particular social order based on relations of domination and subordination in the arenas of gender, race, and class. The roots of media and cultural texts are consequently embedded in social reproduction and conflict, part and parcel of our social life.

The theorists and writings chosen accordingly provide critical understandings and interpretations of media and culture, showing how they are often constructed to serve specific social interests and functions – and yet can be read, enjoyed, and interpreted in a multiplicity of ways. We conceive of *KeyWorks* as a toolkit that enables individuals to produce their own understandings, meanings, and critiques of contemporary culture, media, and society. We will try to make these often complex perspectives on media and culture accessible and to make our text "user-friendly" by, first, explaining in the sections that follow the key concepts and methods deployed in the leading competing approaches to the study of media and culture, and by introducing the theorists presented in our reader. At the beginning of each part, we provide more detailed contextualizing of both the particular topics through which we have organized the collection and the theorists and texts chosen. While the book was designed to be employed in classroom situations, we also hope that enterprising readers will use it on their own to become more competent cultural consumers and critics; hence, we also hope that it will prove valuable to people who wish to educate themselves in the theories and methods of cultural and media criticism. Consequently, we begin with discussion of the origins and meanings of some key concepts to begin the trek toward a more empowering cultural and media literacy that will enable people to make better sense of their world and to become more competent actors within it.

Culture, Ideology, and Hegemony

The ideas of the ruling class are in every epoch the ruling ideas; i.e., the class which is the ruling *material* force of society, is at the same time its ruling *intellectual* force. The class which has the means of material production at its disposal has control at the same time over the means of mental production, so that thereby, generally speaking, the ideas of those who lack the means of mental production are subject to it.

(Karl Marx and Friedrich Engels)

Contemporary criticism has forced students and teachers to see that there are no innocent texts, that all artifacts of the established culture and society are laden with meaning, values, biases, and messages. There is no pure entertainment that does not contain representations – often extremely prejudicial – of class, gender, race, sexuality, and myriad social categories and groupings. Cultural texts are saturated with social meanings, they generate political effects, reproducing or opposing governing social institutions and relations of domination and subordination. Culture can also embody specific political discourses – liberal, conservative, oppositional, or mixed – advancing competing political positions on issues such as the family and sexuality, masculinity or femininity, or violence and war. Cultural representations thus often transcode major political discourses and perspectives presenting, for instance, an array of positions on topics such as sexuality, the state, or religion.

Culture in today's societies thus constitutes a set of discourses, stories, images, spectacles, and varying cultural forms and practices that generate meaning, identities, and political effects. Culture includes artifacts such as newspapers, television programs, movies, and popular music, but also practices like shopping, watching sports events, going to a club, or hanging out in the local coffee shop. Culture is ordinary, a familiar part of everyday life, yet special cultural artifacts are extraordinary, helping people to see and understand things they've never quite perceived, like certain novels or films that change your view of the world. We would hope that some of the challenging theoretical texts included here will provide new understandings of culture and media.

The concept of *ideology*, for example, forces readers to perceive that all cultural texts have distinct biases, interests, and embedded values, reproducing the point of view of their producers and often the values of the dominant social groups. Karl Marx and Friedrich Engels coined the term "ideology" in the 1840s to describe the dominant ideas and representations in a given social order. On their analysis, during the feudal period, ideas of piety, honor, valor, and military chivalry were the ruling ideas of the hegemonic aristocratic classes. During the capitalist era, values of individualism, profit, competition, and the market became dominant, articulating the ideology of the new bourgeois class which was consolidating its class power. Today, in our high-tech and global capitalism, ideas that promote globalization, new technologies, and an unrestrained market society are becoming the prevailing ideas – conceptions that further the interests of the new governing elites in the global economy.

As we note below, feminists, multiculturalists, and members of a wide range of subordinate groups detected that ideologies also reproduced relations of domination in the arenas of gender, race, ethnicity, sexuality, and further domains of everyday life. Feminists, for example, criticized sexist ideologies that advanced the domination of women by men and social institutions and practices that propagated male supremacy. Racist ideologies were criticized that furthered the subordination of specific races and ethnicities. In a broad sense, therefore, ideologies reproduce social domination, they legitimate rule by the prevailing groups over subordinate ones, and help replicate the existing inequalities and hierarchies of power and control.

Ideologies appear natural, they seem to be common sense, and are thus often invisible and elude criticism. Marx and Engels began a critique of ideology, attempting to show how ruling ideas reproduce dominant societal interests serving to naturalize, idealize, and legitimate the existing society and its institutions and values. In a competitive and atomistic capitalist society, it appears natural to assert that human beings are primarily self-interested and competitive by nature, just as in a communist society it is natural to assert that people are cooperative by nature. In fact, human beings and societies are extremely complex and contradictory, but ideology smoothes over conflicts and negative features, idealizing human or social traits such as individuality and competition, which are elevated into governing conceptions and values.

For classical Marxism, the ruling classes employ intellectuals and cultural producers who both produce ideas that glorify the dominant institutions and ways of life, and propagate these governing ideas in cultural forms such as literature, the press, or in our day film and television. The concept of ideology thus makes us question the naturalness of cultural texts and to see that prevailing ideas are not self-evident and obvious, but are constructed, biased, and contestable. This notion makes us suspicious and critical, putting into question regnant ideas which often serve the interests of governing groups. Moreover, the more one studies cultural forms and representations, the more one sees the presence of ideologies that support the interests of the reigning economic, gender, race, or social groups, who are presented positively and idealized, while subordinate groups are often presented negatively and prejudicially.

The Italian Marxian thinker Antonio Gramsci developed these ideas further, arguing that diverse social groups attained "hegemony," or dominance, at different times through inducing the consent of the majority of subaltern, or subordinate, groups to a given socio-political constellation. He points out that while the unity of prevailing groups is usually created through the state (as in the American revolution, or unification of Italy in the nineteenth century), the institutions of "civil society" also play a role in establishing hegemony. Civil society, in this discourse, involves institutions of the church, schooling, the media and forms of popular culture, among others. It mediates between the private sphere of personal economic interests and the family and the public authority of the state, serving as the locus of what Habermas described as "the public sphere."

For Gramsci, societies maintained their stability through a combination of "domination," or force, and "hegemony," defined as consent to "intellectual and moral leadership." Thus, social orders are founded and reproduced with some institutions and groups violently exerting power and domination to maintain social boundaries and rules (i.e., the police, military, vigilante groups, etc.), while other institutions (such as religion, schooling, or the media) induce consent to the dominant order through establishing the hegemony, or ideological dominance, of a distinctive type of social order (i.e., market capitalism, fascism, communism, and so on). In addition, societies establish the hegemony of males and certain races through the institutionalizing of male dominance or the rule of a specific race or ethnicity over subordinate groups.

Hegemony theory for Gramsci involves both analysis of current forces of domination and the ways that particular political forces achieved hegemonic authority, *and* the delineation of counterhegemonic forces, groups, and ideas that could contest and overthrow the existing hegemony. An analysis, for instance, of how the conservative regimes of Margaret Thatcher in Britain and Ronald Reagan in the United States in the late 1970s and early 1980s won power would dissect how conservative groups

gained dominance through control of the state, and the use of media, new technologies, and cultural institutions such as think tanks and fund-raising and political
action groups. Explaining the Thatcher–Reagan conservative hegemony of the 1980s
would require analysis of how conservative ideas became dominant in the media,
schools, and culture at large. It would discuss how on a global level the market rather
than the state was seen as the source of all wealth and solution to social problems,
whereas the state was pictured as a source of excessive taxation, overregulation, and
bureaucratic inertia.

A cultural hegemony analysis would thus show how particular media, technology,
or institutions contributed to a broader socio-political domination by forces such as
fascism, communism, or market capitalism. A Gramscian theory would also discuss
how a hegemonic social order is always contested by counterhegemonic forces, such
as when during the 1980s conservative rule was contested and in part overthrown
during the 1990s with a resurgence of liberalism and social democratic movements
and regimes, as well as an upsurge of oppositional social movements. Such analysis,
however, would also have to show how the more liberal hegemonic groups
compromised with the dominant conservative forces, whereby liberal democrats like
Bill Clinton, or social democrats like Tony Blair, would themselves take conservative
positions in curbing welfare, cutting social spending, or unleashing military intervention.

Hegemony theory thus calls for historically specific socio-cultural analysis of particular contexts and forces, requiring dissection of how culture and a variety of social
institutions from the media to the university facilitate broader social and political
ends. Analyses of hegemony emphasize that a wide array of cultural institutions
function within social reproduction including the church, schools, traditional and
elite culture, sports, and the entertainment media. The approach requires social
contextualization of all ideas, representations, and cultural forms; it enjoins seeing
societies as a locus of social contestation between competing groups who seek
dominance and who manipulate reigning institutions and culture to promote their
ends.

Theories of hegemony and ideology were further developed by a group of thinkers
who were organized around the Frankfurt Institute for Social Research in the 1930s.
Their core members were Jewish radicals and so they went into exile to the United
States after Hitler's rise to power. Establishing themselves in a small institute in New
York affiliated with Columbia University, they developed analyses of the culture
industries which had emerged as key institutions of social hegemony in the era
they called state-monopoly capitalism. Max Horkheimer, Theodor W. Adorno,
Herbert Marcuse, and Walter Benjamin, who was loosely affiliated with the Institute
for Social Research, analyzed the new forms of corporate and state power during a
time in which giant corporations ruled the capitalist economies and the might of the
state grew significantly under the guise of fascism, Russian communism, and the state
capitalism of Roosevelt's New Deal which required a sustained government response to the crisis of the economic Depression in the 1930s. In this conjuncture,
ideology played an increasingly important role in inducing consent to a diversity of
social systems.

To a large extent, the Frankfurt School inaugurated critical studies of mass communication and culture, showing how the media were controlled by groups who employed them to further their own interests and domination. They were the first social theorists to see the importance of what they called the "culture industries" in the reproduction of contemporary societies, in which so-called mass culture and communications stand in the center of leisure activity, are important agents of socialization, mediators of political reality, and should thus be seen as primary institutions of contemporary societies with a variety of economic, political, cultural, and social effects.

Having experienced the rise of fascism and fascist use of the media in Germany in the 1930s, they noted during their exile in the United States how the culture industry was controlled by predominant capitalist economic interests and functioned to reproduce the established market society and democratic polity. The Frankfurt School developed a critical and transdisciplinary approach to cultural and communications studies, combining critique of political economy of the media, analysis of texts, and audience reception studies of the social and ideological effects of mass culture and communications. They coined the term "culture industries" to signify the process of the industrialization of mass-produced culture and the commercial imperatives which drove the system. The critical theorists analyzed all mass-mediated cultural artifacts within the context of industrial production, in which the commodities of the culture industries exhibited the same features as other products of mass production: commodification, standardization, and massification. The culture industries had the singular function, however, of providing ideological legitimation of the existing capitalist societies and of integrating individuals into the framework of the capitalist system.

Furthermore, the critical theorists investigated the cultural industries in a political context as a form of the integration of the working class into capitalist societies. The Frankfurt School were one of the first neo-Marxian groups to examine the effects of mass culture and the rise of the consumer society on the working classes who were to be vehicles of revolution in the classical Marxian scenario. They also analyzed the ways in which the culture industries were stabilizing contemporary capitalism and accordingly sought new strategies for political change, agencies of social transformation, and models for human emancipation that could serve as norms of social critique and goals for political struggle.

Thus, in their theories of the culture industries and critiques of mass culture, the Frankfurt School were the first to systematically analyze and criticize mass-mediated culture and communications within critical social theory. Their approach suggests that to properly understand any specific form of media or culture, one must understand how it is produced and distributed in a given society and how it is situated in relation to the dominant social structure. The Frankfurt School thought, for the most part, that media culture simply reproduced the existing society and manipulated mass audiences into obedience.

One of their members, however, Walter Benjamin, had a more optimistic and activist view of the potential of media, such as film, to promote progressive political ends than his colleagues Horkheimer and Adorno. In "The Work of Art in the Age of

Mechanical Reproduction," Benjamin argued that film, sports, and other forms of mass entertainment were creating a new kind of spectator, able to critically dissect cultural forms and to render intelligent judgment on them. For Benjamin, the decline of the aura of the work of art – the sense of originality, uniqueness, and authenticity – under the pressures of mechanical reproduction helped produce a public able to more actively engage a wide range of cultural phenomena. He argued that, for instance, the spectators of sports events were discriminating judges of athletic activity, able to criticize and analyze games, athletes, strategies, and so on. Likewise, Benjamin postulated that the film audiences as well can become experts of criticism and ably dissect the construction, meanings, and ideologies of film.

Benjamin saw that politics were being aestheticized in the contemporary era, deploying techniques of mystification and cultural manipulation to produce media spectacles to gain mass assent to specific political candidates and groups. He was one of the first to dissect the new public spheres that were emerging in the period when the fascist party and state used organs of public communication such as film, radio, or political rally to promote their ends. Moreover, Benjamin's work is also important for focusing on the technology of cultural reproduction, seeing the changes in new media techniques, and carrying out political critique while calling for democratic transformation of media technology and institutions.

A second-generation member of the Frankfurt School, Jürgen Habermas, grew up under German fascism, found it repellent, and undertook life-long investigations of contemporary society and culture in part motivated by desire to prevent the recurrence of a rebirth of fascism. After studying with Horkheimer and Adorno in Frankfurt in the 1950s, Habermas investigated in his early work the ways that a new public sphere emerged during the time of the Enlightenment and the American and French revolutions, and how it promoted political discussion and debate. Habermas's concept of the public sphere described a space of institutions and practices between private and public interests. The public sphere mediated for Habermas between the domains of the family and the workplace – where private interests prevail – and the state which often exerts arbitrary forms of power and domination. What Habermas called the "bourgeois public sphere" consisted of the realm of public assemblies, pubs and coffee houses, literary salons, and meeting halls where citizens gathered to discuss their common public affairs and to organize against arbitrary and oppressive forms of social and public authority. The public sphere was nurtured by newspapers, journals, pamphlets, and books which were read and discussed in social sites such as pubs and coffee houses.

Habermas notes that newspapers were initially commercial sheets that disseminated "news" (i.e., what was novel and contemporary), but then were transformed into instruments of political debate under the pressures of the American and French revolutions and the organization of political groups to revolutionize society. Yet newspapers also fell prey to commercial imperatives and often put profit and business interests above political opinion, selling advertising and papers via tabloid sensationalism and entertainment rather than disseminating political information and ideas. On the other hand, as the society became more dominated by mass media, powerful corporations came to control major institutions such as newspapers, radio, film, and television. These arms of the culture industry served the interests of the media conglomerates and the corporations and advertisers who financed them. Thus, in this conjuncture, the public sphere was colonized by big media which came to dominate public life and which recast the public sphere from a locus of information and debate to a site of manipulation by corporate powers.

In retrospect, the theorists discussed so far articulate ascending stages of modern Western societies. While Habermas's theory of the public sphere describes the early phase of liberal bourgeois society, Marx and Engels analyze the consolidation of the class rule of the bourgeoisie and hegemony of capitalism during the mid-nineteenth century. Gramsci in turn presents the transition from liberal capitalism to fascism in Italy in the 1930s, whereas the work of Horkheimer and Adorno can be read as an articulation of a theory of the state and monopoly capitalism which became dominant throughout the world during the 1930s. This era constituted a form of "organized capitalism," in which the state and mammoth corporations managed the economy and in which individuals submitted to state and corporate control.

The period is often described as "Fordism" to designate the system of mass production and the homogenizing regime of capital which sought to produce mass desires, tastes, and behavior. The culture industries discussed by Horkheimer and Adorno were thus the form of cultural organization parallel to Fordism as a mode of industrial production. Just as American automobiles were produced on assembly lines according to a well-organized plan and division of labor, so too were film, broadcasting, magazines, and assorted forms of media culture generated according to types and with a well-organized division of labor.

The decades following World War II were thus a period of mass production and consumption characterized by uniformity and homogeneity of needs, thought, and behavior constituting a "mass society" and what the Frankfurt School described as "the end of the individual." No longer was personal thought and action the motor of social and cultural progress; instead, gigantic organizations and institutions overpowered individuals. The period corresponds to the staid, ascetic, conformist, and conservative world of corporate capitalism that was dominant in the 1950s with its organization men, its conspicuous consumption, and its mass culture.

During this period, mass culture and communication were essential in generating the modes of thought and behavior appropriate to a highly organized and homogenized social order. Thus, the Frankfurt School theory of "the culture industries" articulates a vital historical shift to an epoch in which mass consumption and culture were indispensable to producing a consumer society based on uniform needs and desires for mass-produced products and a mass society based on social organization and conformity. It is culturally the time in the United States of strongly controlled network radio and television, insipid "top forty" pop music, glossy Hollywood films, national magazines, largely conservative newspapers, and other mass-produced cultural artifacts. Its analogue in Europe, the Soviet Communist bloc, and other sectors where state-controlled broadcasting prevailed, was a system of broadcasting intended to reproduce the dominant culture or state ideology, thus serving as an instrument of social integration and conformity.

Of course, media culture was never as massified and homogeneous as in the Frankfurt School model, and one could argue that the analysis was flawed even during its time of origin and influence and that other models were preferable (such as those of Walter Benjamin, Sigfried Kracauer, Ernst Bloch and others of the Weimar generation and, later, British cultural studies, as we suggest below). Yet the original Frankfurt School theory of the culture industry articulated the important social roles of media culture during a particular socio-historical epoch and provided a model, still of use, of an exceedingly commercial and technologically advanced culture that promotes the needs of dominant corporate interests, plays a principal role in ideological reproduction, and enculturates the populace into the dominant system of needs, thought, and behavior.

Following the lines of this narrative, we will argue throughout this introduction that the subsequent forms of cultural and media analysis respond to developments within Western capitalist societies from the end of World War II until the present. Cultural theories analyze historical metamorphosis and novelties, and thus articulate socio-historical conditions, practices, and transformations. Theories provide maps of social orders and tools to understand and transform them. The proliferation of theories in the past two decades itself highlights increasing differentiation and fragmentation of Western societies during an epoch of intense social struggle and turbulent change. Accordingly, we will map the vicissitudes of theory in the post-World War II conjuncture in the remainder of this introduction, providing an overview of the emergence of leading theories, methods, and themes within the terrain of media and cultural studies.

Social Life and Cultural Studies

> But certainly for the present age, which prefers the sign to the thing signified, the copy to the original, fancy to reality, the appearance to the essence, ... illusion only is sacred, truth profane. Nay, sacredness is held to be enhanced in proportion as truth decreases and illusion increases, so that the highest degree of illusion comes to be the highest degree of sacredness.
>
> (Ludwig Feuerbach)

Culture is produced and consumed within social life. Thus, particular cultural artifacts and practices must be situated within the social relations of production and reception in which culture is produced, distributed, and consumed in order to be properly understood and interpreted. Contextualizing cultural forms and audiences in historically specific situations helps illuminate how cultural artifacts reflect or reproduce concrete social relations and conditions – or oppose and attempt to transform them. The foundational writings which we discussed in the previous section provide concepts for situating culture and media within distinctive social and historical contexts. Likewise, in our introduction, we are positioning the emergence of theories of media and culture within determinate socio-historical circumstances and are thus engaging in social contextualization ourselves.

After World War II, the consumer society emerged throughout the Western world. Whereas the primary US corporations were developing systems of mass production and consumption in the 1920s (which saw the rise of media industries such as broadcasting, advertising, and mass publications to promote consumer goods), the 1930s Depression and then World War II prevented the introduction of the consumer society. The Frankfurt School, living in exile in the United States, were among the first to theorize this new configuration of society and culture in their critique of the culture industry, the integrative role of mass consumer society, and the new values and personality structures being developed. By the 1950s, theorists throughout the more evolved capitalist countries were producing theories of consumption, the media, and the changed conditions of everyday life to respond to the changes and transformations in the emergent consumer and media society.

In the United States, marketing research for big corporations and advertising agencies took up broadcasting research and out of this process a certain model of "mass communication" studies emerged. Paul Lazarsfeld and his colleagues at the Princeton Radio Research Institute, which included Frankfurt School member T. W. Adorno, began researching which programs audiences regularly tuned into, studied audience taste, and accordingly advised corporations concerning consumer demand for broadcasting product and what sort of programming was most popular. Hence, mass communication research emerged as an off-shoot of consumer research in the 1940s and 1950s, producing a tradition of empirical study of the established forms of culture and communications.

Rapid modernization in France after World War II and the introduction of the consumer society in the 1950s provoked much debate and contributed to constructing a variety of discourses on the media and consumer society in France, inspiring Roland Barthes, Henri Lefebvre, Guy Debord, Jean Baudrillard, and their contemporaries to develop novel analyses of the emerging forms of society and culture. It was clear that the consumer society was multiplying images, spectacles, and new cultural forms and modes of everyday life. The leading French theorists of the period attempted to explain, make sense of, and in many cases criticize the novelties of the era.

Roland Barthes applied the new theories of structuralism and semiology to make sense of the expansion of media culture and its important social functions. Structuralism was developed in the 1950s by the French anthropologist Claude Lévi-Strauss to articulate the basic structures of culture and society. Semiology, created earlier in the century by the Swiss linguist Ferdinand de Saussure, analyzed the fundamental rules, codes, and practices of language usage. In the hands of Barthes, semiology assumed that society and culture were texts that could be analyzed for their structures, significance, and effects.

Barthes' *Mythologies* employed both methods to analyze the codes and meanings embedded in artifacts of popular culture ranging from wrestling to soap ads, while dissecting their social functions. The "mythologies" Barthes studied functioned to naturalize and eternalize the historically contingent forms of French bourgeois culture that he analyzed. In his famous reading of a picture of a Black African soldier saluting the French flag, for example, Barthes claimed that the image erased the horrors of French imperialism, presenting a sanitized portrait of a French soldier that made it appear natural that an African should salute the French flag and exhibit the proper signs of military behavior and French national allegiance.

French theorist Louis Althusser applied the structuralist and semiological theories to the study of culture and ideology in his writings of the 1970s. Beginning with Marx's thesis that the mode of production determines the character of social, intellectual, and cultural life, Althusser saw ideology as an effect of the structure of society, a force in which economic, political-legal, and ideological practices were interrelated to shape social consciousness. In Althusser's version of "structural Marxism," "ideological state apparatuses" (schooling, media, the judiciary, etc.) "interpellated" individuals into preconceived forms of subjectivity that left no space for opposition or resistance. On this account, subjects were constructed as self-centered individuals, men or women, members of a specific class, and were induced to identify with the roles, behavior, values, and practices of the existing state capitalist society. Combining Marxism and structuralism, Althusser thus analyzed how individuals were incorporated into specific social systems and functioned to reproduce contemporary capitalist societies.

A very different historical and cultural approach to the study of media and culture was developed in North America in the 1950s and 1960s by Marshall McLuhan. In his distinguished and influential work *Understanding Media*, McLuhan described a paradigm shift from earlier print culture to the new media culture. Whereas print culture, McLuhan argued, produced rational, literate, and individualist subjects, who followed the linear and logical form of print media in thought and reasoning, the new media culture produced more fragmentary, non-rational, and aestheticized subjects, immersed in the sights, sounds, and spectacles of media such as film, radio, television, and advertising. The new media culture was, McLuhan argued, "tribal," sharing collective ideas and behavior. It was generating a new global culture and consciousness that he believed would overcome the individualism and nationalism of the previous modern era.

McLuhan aroused a generation to take seriously media as an active agent of fundamental historical change and media culture as an important terrain of study. In his groundbreaking work *Society of the Spectacle*, Guy Debord described the proliferation of commodities and the "immense accumulation of spectacles" that characterized the new consumer society. Grocery, drug, and department stores were exhibiting a dazzling profusion of commodities and things to purchase which in turn were celebrated in advertising campaigns that inscribed the new consumer items with an aura of magic and divinity. The media themselves are spectacles in Debord's sense, with MTV, for example, broadcasting a collage of dazzling music videos, ads, and sequences that attempt to capture the dynamics and attractions of contemporary youth culture. Films provide larger than life spectacle replete with special effects, snappy editing, and intense sound.

Hence, the "society of the spectacle" refers to a media and consumer society, organized around the consumption of images, commodities, and spectacles. In our day, malls, the cyberspectacle of the Internet, and emerging virtual reality devices proliferate the realm of the spectacle, providing new relevance to Debord's analysis.

Moreover, the "society of the spectacle" also refers to the vast institutional and technical apparatus of contemporary societies which produce commodities and media events. The concept encompasses all the means and methods ruling powers employ, outside of direct force, which subject individuals to societal manipulation, while obscuring the nature and effects of operations of domination and subordination. Under this broader definition, the education system and the institutions of representative democracy, as well as the endless inventions of consumer gadgets, sports, media culture, and urban and suburban architecture and design are all integral components of the spectacular society. Schooling, for example, involves sports, fraternity and sorority rituals, bands and parades, and various public assemblies that indoctrinate individuals into dominant ideologies and practices. Contemporary politics is also saturated with spectacles, ranging from daily "photo opportunities," to highly orchestrated special events which dramatize state power, to TV ads and image management for prepackaged candidates during election campaigns.

In the post-World War II conjuncture, the spectacle became globalized as corporations such as Coca-Cola and Pepsi, sundry national automobile corporations, IBM and the nascent computer industry, and subsequently McDonald's, Nike, Microsoft, and a cornucopia of global products circulated throughout the world. Ariel Dorfman and Armand Mattelart record the response of Third World activists to the saturation of their Latin American culture with products from the Walt Disney corporation. In their controversial *How to Read Donald Duck*, they provide critical dissection of the meanings, messages, and ideologies in artifacts as seemingly harmless as comic books. The authors explain that these popular comics contained a wealth of images and stories that naturalized capitalism and imperialism, much like the "mythologies" which Barthes criticized in France.

Critical approaches to society and culture were thus proliferating throughout the world by the 1960s. All of the theories we have discussed so far can be seen as providing models of media and cultural studies, but the school of cultural studies that has become a global phenomenon of great importance over the last decade was inaugurated by the University of Birmingham Centre for Contemporary Cultural Studies in 1964. Under its director Richard Hoggart, and his successor Stuart Hall who directed the Centre from 1968 to 1979, the Birmingham groups developed a variety of critical perspectives for the analysis, interpretation, and criticism of cultural artifacts, combining sociological theory and contextualization with literary analysis of cultural texts. The now classical period of British cultural studies from the early 1960s to the early 1980s adopted a Marxian approach to the study of culture, one especially influenced by Althusser and Gramsci. Through a set of internal debates, and responding to social conflicts and movements of the 1960s and the 1970s, the Birmingham group came to concentrate on the interplay of representations and ideologies of class, gender, race, ethnicity, and nationality in cultural texts, especially concentrating on media culture. They were among the first to study the effects of newspapers, radio, television, film, and other popular cultural forms on audiences. They also explored how assorted audiences interpreted and deployed media culture in varied ways and contexts, analyzing the factors that made audiences respond in contrasting manners to media artifacts.

From the beginning, British cultural studies systematically rejected high/low culture distinctions and took media culture seriously, thus surpassing the elitism of dominant literary approaches to culture. Likewise, British cultural studies overcame the limitations of the Frankfurt School notion of a passive and manipulated audience in their conceptions of an active audience that creates meanings and the popular. Reproducing the activism of oppositional groups in the 1960s and 1970s, the Birmingham School was engaged in a project aimed at a comprehensive criticism of the present configuration of culture and society, attempting to link theory and practice to orient cultural studies toward fundamental social transformation. British cultural studies situated culture within a theory of social production and reproduction, specifying the ways that cultural forms served either to further social control, or to enable people to resist. It analyzed society as a hierarchical and antagonistic set of social relations characterized by the oppression of subordinate class, gender, race, ethnic, and national strata. Employing Gramsci's model of hegemony and counter-hegemony, British cultural studies sought to analyze "hegemonic," or ruling, social and cultural forces of domination and to seek "counterhegemonic" forces of resistance and contestation.

British cultural studies aimed at a political goal of social transformation in which location of forces of domination and resistance would aid the process of political change. From the beginning, the Birmingham group was oriented toward the crucial political problems of their age and milieu. Their early spotlight on class and ideology derived from an acute sense of the oppressive and systemic effects of class in British society and the movements of the 1960s against class inequality and oppression. The work of the late 1950s and early 1960s Williams/Hoggart/Hall stage of cultural studies emphasized the potential of working-class cultures, and then in the 1960s and 1970s began appraising the potential of youth subcultures to resist the hegemonic forms of capitalist domination. Unlike the classical Frankfurt School (but similar to Herbert Marcuse), British cultural studies looked to youth cultures as providing potentially new forms of opposition and social change. Through studies of youth subcultures, British cultural studies demonstrated how culture came to constitute distinct forms of identity and group membership and appraised the oppositional potential of diverse youth subcultures.

Cultural studies came to center attention on how subcultural groups resist dominant forms of culture and identity, creating their own style and identities. Individuals who conform to hegemonic dress and fashion codes, behavior, and political ideologies thus produce their identities within mainstream groups, as members of particular social groupings (such as white, middle-class conservative Americans). Individuals who identify with subcultures, such as punk or hip hop, look and act differently from those in the mainstream, and thus create oppositional identities, defining themselves against standard models.

In the 1970s and 1980s, British cultural studies continued to develop and successively appropriated emerging analyses of gender, race, sexuality, and a wide range of critical theories. They created ways to examine and critique how the established society and culture promoted sexism, racism, homophobia, and additional forms of oppression – or helped to generate resistance and struggle against domination and injustice. This approach implicitly contained political critique of all cultural forms that promoted oppression, while positively affirming texts and representations that produced a potentially more just and egalitarian social order.

Developments within British cultural studies have thus been in part responses to contestation by a multiplicity of distinct groups which have produced new methods and voices within cultural studies (such as a variety of new feminisms, gay and lesbian studies, many multiculturalisms, critical pedagogies, and projects of critical media literacy). Hence, the center and fulcrum of British cultural studies at any given moment was determined by the struggles in the sociohistorical conjuncture at that time and their major work was thus conceived as political interventions. Their studies of ideology and the politics of culture directed the Birmingham group toward analyzing cultural artifacts, practices, and institutions within existing networks of power. In this context, they attempted to show how culture both provided tools and forces of domination and resources for resistance and opposition. This political optic valorized studying the effects of culture and audience use of cultural artifacts, which provided an extremely productive focus on audiences and reception, topics that had been neglected in most previous text-based methods. Yet recent developments in the field of cultural studies have arguably vitiated and depoliticized the enterprise, as we shall note in the conclusion to the Introduction.

British cultural studies, then, in retrospect, emerges in a later era of capital following the stage of state and monopoly capitalism analyzed by the Frankfurt School, into a more variegated and conflicted cultural formation. The forms of culture described by the earliest phase of British cultural studies in the 1950s and early 1960s articulated conditions in an era in which there were still significant tensions in Britain and much of Europe between an older working-class-based culture and the newer mass-produced culture whose models and exemplars were the products of American culture industries. The initial stage of cultural studies developed by Richard Hoggart, Raymond Williams, and E. P. Thompson attempted to preserve working-class culture against the onslaughts of mass culture produced by the culture industries. Thompson's historical inquiries into the history of British working-class institutions and struggles, the defenses of working-class culture by Hoggart and Williams, and their attacks on mass culture were part of a socialist and working-class-oriented project which assumed that the industrial working class was an agent of progressive social change and that it could be mobilized and organized to resist the inequalities of the existing capitalist societies and work for a more egalitarian one. Williams and Hoggart were deeply involved in schemes of working-class education and oriented toward socialist working-class politics, seeing their form of cultural studies as an instrument of progressive social change.

The initial critiques in the first wave of British cultural studies of Americanism and mass culture in Hoggart, Williams, and the Birmingham School paralleled to some extent the earlier critique of the Frankfurt School, yet celebrated a working class that the Frankfurt School saw as defeated in Germany and much of Europe during the period of fascism, and which they never saw as a strong resource for emancipatory social change. The early work of the Birmingham School was continuous with the radicalism of the first wave of British cultural studies (the Hoggart–Thompson

–Williams "culture and society" tradition). The post-1980s work inspired by British cultural studies became global in impact and responded to the new cultural and political conditions described in postmodern theory which we discuss below.

As we shall see, many forms of the study of culture and media preceded and accompanied the development of British cultural studies. In the following sections, we will observe examples of North American cultural studies and developments within the field throughout the world. We will also present a range of perspectives, often critical of the Frankfurt School, British cultural studies, and the other theories that we have so far examined. Next, however, we will introduce an approach to media and culture which focuses on the system and practices of production and distribution. This "political economy" perspective is sometimes taken as antithetical to cultural studies, and representatives of each position often attack each other, claiming their approach is superior. We, however, will argue that cultural studies and political economy viewpoints can be integrated, and that both are key parts of a more inclusive critical theory.

Political Economy

> The anatomy of civil society is to be sought in political economy.
>
> (Karl Marx)

A political economy approach to media and culture centers more on the production and distribution of culture than on interpreting texts or studying audiences. The references to the terms "political" and "economy" call attention to the fact that the production and distribution of culture takes place within a specific economic and political system, constituted by relations between the state, the economy, social institutions and practices, culture, and organizations such as the media. Political economy thus encompasses economics and politics, and the relations between them and the other central structures of society and culture. With regard to media institutions, for instance, in Western democracies, a capitalist economy dictates that cultural production is governed by laws of the market, but the democratic imperatives mean that there is some regulation of culture by the state. There are often tensions within a given society concerning which activities should be governed by the imperatives of the market, or economics, alone and how much state regulation or intervention is desirable to assure a wider diversity of broadcast programming, or the prohibition of phenomena agreed to be harmful (such as cigarette advertising or pornography).

Political economy highlights that capitalist societies are organized according to a dominant mode of production that structures institutions and practices according to the logic of commodification and capital accumulation. Cultural production and distribution is accordingly profit- and market-oriented in such a system. Forces of production (such as media technologies and creative practice) are shaped according to dominant relations of production (such as the profit imperative, the maintenance of hierarchical control, and relations of domination). Hence, the system of production (e.g., market or state-oriented) is important, as suggested below, in determining what sort of cultural artifacts are produced and how they are consumed. Thus, "political economy" does not merely pertain solely to economics, but to the relations between the economic, political, technological, and cultural dimensions of social reality. The structure of political economy links culture to its political and economic context and opens up cultural studies to history and politics. It refers to a field of contestation and antagonism and not an inert structure as caricatured by some of its opponents.

Political economy should also discern and analyze the role of technology in cultural production and distribution, seeing, as with McLuhan, how technology and forms of media structure economic, social, and cultural practices and forms of life. In our era, the proliferation of new technologies and multimedia – ranging from computers to CD-ROMs to new types of digitized film – call attention to the key role of technology in the economy and everyday life and make clear that technological and economic factors are often deeply interconnected. In a time of technological revolution, the role of technology is especially important and so political economy must engage the dominant forms of technology in its analysis.

In the present stage of capitalist hegemony, political economy grounds its approach within empirical analysis of the actual system of cultural production, investigating the constraints and structuring influence of the dominant capitalist economic system and a commercialized cultural system controlled by powerful corporations. Inserting texts into the system of culture within which they are produced and distributed can help elucidate features and effects of the texts that textual analysis alone might miss or downplay. Rather than their being antithetical approaches to culture, political economy can contribute to textual analysis and critique. The system of production often determines what type of artifacts will be produced, what structural limits there will be as to what can and cannot be said and shown, and what kind of audience effects cultural artifacts may generate.

Study of the codes of television, film, or popular music, for instance, is enhanced by examining the formulas and conventions of media culture production. These cultural forms are structured by well-defined rules and conventions, and investigation of the production of culture can help elucidate the codes actually in play. Because of the demands of the format of radio or music television, for instance, most popular songs are three to five minutes, fitting into the structure of the distribution system. Because of their control by giant media corporations oriented primarily toward profit, film and television production in America is dominated by specific genres such as talk and game shows, soap operas, situation comedies, action/adventure shows, and so on. This economic factor explains why there are cycles of certain genres and sub-genres, sequelmania in the film industry, crossovers of popular films into television series. Seeing how competition for audiences decides what shows are produced also helps explain why there is homogeneity in products constituted within systems of production with established generic codes, formulaic conventions, and well-defined ideological boundaries.

Furthermore, one cannot really discern the role of the media in events such as the Gulf War without analyzing the production and political economy of news and information, as well as the actual text of the Gulf War and its reception by its audience. Or, one cannot fully grasp the Madonna phenomenon without discussing her marketing strategies, her political environment, her cultural artifacts, and their effects. Likewise, in appraising the full social impact of pornography, one needs to be aware of the sex industry and the production process of, say, pornographic films, and not just the texts themselves and their effects on audiences.

In addition, study of political economy can help ascertain the limits and range of political and ideological discourses and effects. Study of television and politics in the United States, for instance, suggests that takeover of the television networks by leading transnational corporations and communications conglomerates was part of a "right turn" within American society in the 1980s, whereby powerful corporate groups won control of the state and the mainstream media. For example, during the 1980s all three networks were taken over by leading corporate conglomerates: ABC was purchased by Capital Cities, NBC merged with GE, and CBS was bought by the Tisch Financial Group. Both ABC and NBC sought corporate mergers and this motivation, together with other benefits derived from Reaganism, might well have influenced them to downplay criticisms of Reagan and to generally support his conservative programs, military adventures, and simulated presidency.

In the current conjuncture which is exhibiting a crossing of boundaries and synergy between information and entertainment industries, there have been significant mergers between the immense corporations. Previous forms of entertainment are rapidly being absorbed within the Internet, and the computer is coming to be a major household appliance and source of entertainment, information, play, communication, and connection with the outside world. As clues to the immensity of the transformation going on, and as indicators of the syntheses of information and entertainment in the emerging infotainment society, one might reflect on the massive mergers of the primary information and entertainment conglomerates that have taken place in the United States during the past few years which have seen the most extensive concentration and conglomeration of information and entertainment industries in history, including:

Time Warner and Turner	$7.5 billion
Disney/Capital Cities/ABC	$19 billion
NBC and Microsoft	$20 billion
Viacom and CBS	$37 billion

Dwarfing all previous information/entertainment corporation mergers, Time Warner and America On-Line (AOL) proposed a $163.4 billion merger in January 2000. These fusions bring together corporations involved in TV, film, magazines, newspapers, books, information data bases, computers, and other media, suggesting a coming implosion of media and computer culture, of entertainment and information in a new communications/infotainment society. The merger mania is now global in scale, pointing to an ever-more intricately connected global economy. In 1999, the US company MCI negotiated a $37 billion amalgamation with WorldCom, which topped British Telecommunications and GTE offers, and then bought Sprint for

$115 billion; in a $72 billion merger of two regional telephone companies, SBC Communications Inc. and Ameritech formed the largest Bell operating company; the German telecommunications firm Mannesmann bought Orange for $33 billion, and shortly thereafter Vodafone Airtouch, the world's leading mobile-phone company, announced a hostile bid for Mannesmann, initially for a record $117 billion which they increased as the weeks went by to $178.7 billion when the merger was sealed in February 2000 (earlier in the year Vodafone absorbed Airtouch Communications for $60 billion). In addition, telecommunications companies have been buying cable television systems with At&T purchasing TCI in 1998 for $60.9 billion while acquiring MediaOne for $63.1 billion in 1999.

The corporate media, communications, and information industries are frantically scrambling to provide delivery for the wealth of information, entertainment, and further services that will include increased Internet access, cellular telephones and satellite personal communication devices, and computerized video, film, and information on demand, as well as Internet shopping and more unsavory services such as pornography and gambling. Thus, study of the political economy of media can be immensely useful for describing the infrastructure of the media, information, and communications industry and their effects on culture and society. Yet political economy alone does not hold the key to cultural studies and, important as it is, it has limitations as a single perspective.

Some political economy analyses reduce the meanings and effects of texts to rather circumscribed and reductive ideological functions, arguing that media culture merely reflects the ideology of the ruling economic elite that controls the culture industries and is nothing more than a vehicle for the dominant ideology. It is true that media culture overwhelmingly supports capitalist values, but it is also a site of intense conflict between different races, classes, gender, and social groups. Thus, in order to fully grasp the nature and effects of media culture, one should see contemporary society and culture as contested terrains, and media and cultural forms as spaces in which particular battles over gender, race, sexuality, political ideology, and values are fought.

Indeed, as Susan Willis argues, political economy also involves domestic activities such as cleaning, child-rearing, shopping, and additional forms of consumption. She contends that activities of packaging, marketing, and display are important dimensions of the capitalist economy and that therefore study of consumption is as significant as production in constructing political economy. Moreover, Willis combines a political economy account with concrete cultural studies in her analyses of packaging, shopping, fashion, exercising, and other everyday activities.

In addition, as Jésus Martín-Barbero's work suggests, the political dimension of political economy involves state, nation, and people, as well as analysis of the economy. Martín-Barbero analyzes the way that popular classes produce their cultures out of a hybridized appropriation of local and traditional forms combined with new types of global culture. Local cultures are subjected to potentially homogenizing and destructive global forces, but groups and individuals can create new hybridized cultures of their own and resist corporate domination and homogenization. Discussing the mediations involved in the construction of national cultures, Martín-Barbero relates cultural forms to social movements such as populism whereby masses of people entered the political process for the first time through participation in a national culture. This development eventually helped produce new hybrid cultures as the global economy distributed transnational cultural forms and local cultures appropriated and mixed these and more traditional popular forms in complex ways.

Consequently, political economy today necessarily involves discussion of a new global capitalist world economy in an era marked by the fall of communism in 1989, technological revolution, and emergence of a "new economy" based on computer and communication networks. The term "globalization" is often deployed as a cover concept for the new world economy, but as Herbert Schiller argues, its continuities with the old world-system of market capitalism should not be ignored. In fact, globalization is a contested term with some identifying it with new forms of imperialism (and seeing it as predominantly negative), while others equate it with modernization and the proliferation of novel products, cultural forms, and identities. In fact, it is best to see it as an extremely complex and ambiguous phenomenon that contains both exciting and progressive forms such as the Internet, innovative terrains of cyberculture, and emergent economic and political actors and groups in the world economy – combined with the growing strength of transnational institutions, intensified competition on a global level, heightened exploitation, corporate downsizing, and greater levels of unemployment, economic inequality, and insecurity.

Globalization is connected with scientific, technological, and economic revolution which involves the advent of emergent forms of labor, politics, culture, and everyday life. The new global economy contains economic opportunities, openings for political transformation, and a wealth of innovative products and technologies which might improve the human condition. Yet it also threatens to increase divisions between the "haves" and the "have nots," deplete diminishing resources, undermine union and labor rights, and circulate new forms of war and terrorism. Hence, globalization is highly ambiguous, with both promising and threatening features.

Indeed, globalization is both creating new modes of cultural homogenization and proliferating cultural differences and hybridities. It is advancing the interests of major American and other transnational corporations, as well as providing openings for new economic forms and players. Global processes are producing emergent transnational institutions and forces, while challenging the state to strengthen its authority and regulatory powers. And as globalization comes ever more to the fore, the importance of the local is highlighted and dramatized.

The conception of political economy that we are thus proposing goes beyond traditional, sometimes excessively economistic approaches that focus on more strictly economic issues such as ownership, gate-keeping, and the production and distribution of culture. Instead, we are suggesting that it involves relations between economy and polity, culture and people, as well as the interconnection between production and consumption, distribution and use. Although some forms of political economy are reductive, focusing solely on the economic dimension, we believe that far richer notions of political economy are possible.

In addition, we would argue that both political economy and more sociologically and culturally oriented approaches to the study of media culture should be combined.

For some decades now, however, advocates of media and cultural studies based in textual or audience analysis have been at war with those who advocate a political economy optic. The hostility between political economy and cultural studies, in our view, reproduces a great divide within the field of communication and cultural studies between two competing approaches with different methodologies, objects of study, and, by now, bodies of texts that represent the opposing schools. This dichotomization pits social science-based approaches that take media and communications as their object against a humanities and text-based view that focuses on culture.

A largely textual approach centers on the analysis and criticism of texts as cultural artifacts, employing methods primarily derived from the humanities. The methods of political economy and empirical communications research, by contrast, utilize more social science-based research strategies, ranging from straight quantitative analysis to more qualitative empirical studies of specific cases or topics, structural analysis of media institutions, or historical research. Topics in this area include analysis of ownership patterns within the political economy of the media, empirical studies of audience reception and media effects, or structural analysis of the impact of media institutions in the economy, politics, or everyday life.

Thus, the seemingly never-ending hostility between political economy and cultural studies replicates a bifurcation within the fields of communications and culture between competing paradigms. In our view, the divide is an artificial one, rooted in an arbitrary academic division of labor. These conflicting approaches point to a splintering of the field of media communications into specialized sub-areas with competing models and methods, and, ironically, to a lack of communication in the field of communications. The split reproduces an academic division of labor which – beginning early in the century and intensifying since the end of World War II – followed the trend toward specialization and differentiation symptomatic of the capitalist economy. The university has followed this broader trend which some theorists equate with the dynamics of modernity itself, interpreted as a process of ever-greater differentiation and thus specialization in all fields from business to education. This trend toward specialization has undermined the power and scope of cultural and media studies and should be replaced, as we are arguing, by a more transdisciplinary position.

Moreover, in the present configuration of the emergence of a new global economy, a critical cultural and media studies needs to grasp the global, national, and local systems of media production and distribution. In the 1960s, critics of the global capitalist system described the domination of the world economy by transnational – mostly American and European – corporations as "imperialism" or "neo-imperialism," whereas its supporters celebrated "modernization." Today, the term "globalization" is the standard term used to describe the hegemonic global economy and culture. One of the features of globalization is the proliferation of new voices and perspectives on culture and society and the politicization and contestation of forms of culture previously taken for granted. In a global culture, the proliferation of difference and novel actors are part of the landscape and the question of representation becomes intensely politicized and contested, as we see in the next section.

The Politics of Representation

Representation in the mediated "reality" of our mass culture is in itself Power.
(Larry Gross)

Whereas political economy approaches to the media and culture derive from a social sciences tradition, analysis of the politics of representation in media texts derives from a humanities-based textual approach. Earlier, mass communication approaches to media content ranged from descriptive content analysis to quantitative analysis of references, figures, or images in media texts. The more sophisticated methods of textual analysis, however, emerged from more advanced understandings of texts, narratives, and representation, as well as the contributions of critical concepts such as ideology and hegemony.

The idea that all cultural representations are political is one of the major themes of media and cultural theory of the last few decades. In the 1960s, feminist, African-American, Latino, gay and lesbian, and disparate oppositional movements attacked the stereotypes and biased images of their groups. These critiques of sexism, racism, homophobia, and other biases made it clear that images and representations are never innocent or pure, that they contain positive, negative, or ambiguous depictions of diverse social groups, that they can serve pernicious interests of cultural oppression by positioning certain groups as inferior, thus pointing to the superiority of dominant social groups. Studies of representations of women or blacks on American television, for instance, would catalogue negative potrayals and show how they produce sexism or racism, or would champion more positive ones.

Early interventions in the politics of representation concentrated primarily on "images of" particular social groups, decrying negative images and affirming more constructive ones. The limitations of such approaches were quickly apparent and already by the 1970s more sophisticated analyses began emerging of how texts position audiences, of how narratives, scenes, and images produce biased representations. There emerged, then, more sophisticated understanding of how textual mechanisms help construct social meanings and representations of specific social groups. Exclusions of groups such as Latinos, as well as negative stereotypes, were thus emphasized, as were the ways framing, editing, subtexts, and the construction of pictorial images produced culturally loaded and biased representations of subordinate groups. The narratives of media culture were scrutinized to discern how certain (usually socially dominant) forces were represented more affirmatively than subordinate groups, and there was a search for narratives and representations that more positively rendered social types that had been excluded or negatively presented in mainstream culture (i.e., various ethnic groups, gays and lesbians, or members of the deaf community).

The turn toward audiences in the 1980s, as we have noted, also created more complex notions of the construction of meaning by stressing how audiences could perform oppositional readings, reacting negatively to what they perceived as prejudiced representations of their own social groups, thus showing themselves to be active creators of meaning, and not just passive victims of manipulation. Reading culture was thus seen as a political event, in which one looked for negative or positive representations, learned how narratives were constructed, and discerned how image and ideology functioned with media and culture to reproduce either social domination and discrimination, or more positive social change.

The debates over the politics of representation and how best to analyze and criticize offensive images of subordinate groups provided a wealth of insights into the nature and effects of culture and media. Culture was now conceived as a field of representation, as a producer of meaning that provided negative and positive depictions of gender, class, race, sexuality, religion, and further key constituents of identity. The media were thus seen as potent creators of role models, gender identity, norms, values, and appropriate and inappropriate behavior, positioning audiences to behave in diverging ways. Audiences, however, were eventually able to perceive themselves as active and creative, able to construct meanings and identities out of the materials of their culture.

Culture and identity were thus regarded as constructed, as artificial, malleable, and contestable artifacts and not as natural givens. Representations in turn were interpreted not just as replications of the real, reproductions of natural objects, but as constructions of complex technical, narrative, and ideological apparatuses. The emphasis on the politics of representation called attention to media technologies, as well as narrative forms, conventions, and codes. It was determined that formal aspects of media texts, such as framing, editing, or special effects could help construct specific representations and that various technologies produced different products and effects.

In addition, the growing emphasis on the active role of audiences from the 1980s to the present suggested that people could creatively construct cultural meanings, contest dominant forms, and create alternative readings and interpretations. Audiences could be empowered to reject prejudicial or stereotyped representations of specific groups and individuals, and could affirm positive ones. The politics of representation thus focused on both encoding and decoding, texts and audiences, and called for more critical and discriminating responses to the products of media production.

Thus, cultural representations were perceived to be subject to political critique, and culture itself was conceived as a contested terrain. Film, television, music, and assorted cultural forms were interpreted as an arena of struggle in which representations transcode the discourses of conflicting social movements. Beginning in the 1960s, alternative representations of gender, race, class, the family, the state, the corporation, and additional dominant forces and institutions began appearing in a sustained fashion. More complex and engaging representations of women, for instance, transcoded the critiques of negative stereotypes and sexist representations, as well as the demand for more active and positive representations. Calls for alternative voices and the creation of oppositional subcultures were met by increased cultural production by women, people of color, sexual minorities, and others excluded from cultural debate and creation. Giving voice to alternative visions, telling more complex stories from the perspective of subordinate groups, and presenting works of marginalized people shook up dominant systems of cultural production and representation. The process created more variety and diversity, but also intensified cultural resistance as a backlash against oppositional groups of women, people of color, gays and lesbians, and, therefore, various marginalized subcultures inevitably began.

The Postmodern Turn and New Media

It seems that to talk seriously about postmodernism today, one is still by definition being defensive. This is because postmodernism has become everybody's favorite *bête noire*, while at the same time not only generously providing something solid to argue against, when so many other things have been "melting in the air," but also, in some mysterious way, being a concept in the right place at the right moment. Postmodernism has therefore served the function of shifting the paradigms in cultural studies and sociology, doing that kind of intellectual work which inevitably provokes controversy and protest, all the more so when what seems to be at stake are precisely those terms like history, society and politics that have given substance and direction to the kind of work we do as teachers and researchers and the reasons why we do it.

(Angela McRobbie)

The notion of the postmodern implies a fundamental rupture in culture and history. It suggests that there are important changes in the economy, society, culture, the arts, and our everyday life which require new theories, ways of perceiving the world, and forms of discourses and practice. Yet as the above quote indicates, postmodernism is extremely controversial with discourses and practices of the "post" attracting some and repelling others.

To make sense of the bewildering variety of uses of the family of terms within the field of the postmodern, we would propose distinguishing between modernity and postmodernity as epochs or stages of history; modernism and postmodernism as developments within art; and modern and postmodern theory as opposed modes of theoretical discourse and intellectual orientations toward the world. In terms of the narrative of our introduction, a postmodern turn in culture and society would correspond to an emergent stage of global capitalism, characterized by new multimedia, exciting computer and informational technology, and a proliferation of novel forms of politics, society, culture, and everyday life.

From this perspective, postmodern theorists such as Jean Baudrillard, Jean-François Lyotard, Michel Foucault, Fredric Jameson, Celeste Olalquiaga, Angela McRobbie, Mark Poster, and others are attempting to engage the new technologies, the emergent forms of culture and identity, the innovative modes of theory and discourse, and the ascendent forms of global capitalism that are shaping the contemporary era. Just as previous theories and methods responded to the new historical conditions of their era, so too do the new postmodern theories attempt to engage novel and original contemporary conditions. But just as previous theories and methods had their limitations and blindspots, postmodern theory also has its omissions and deficiencies. Hence, we would caution our readers, who are perhaps eager to embrace the latest theories and approaches, to be alert to drawbacks, as well as the benefits of the postmodern turn.

French theorist Jean Baudrillard was one of the first to engage the novel forms of culture in theorizing the modes of simulation and hyperreality by which he described the emergent media and cyberspaces of the new technologies. While he was prescient in perceiving the importance of emergent forms of culture and fields of cultural experience, by declaring "the end of political economy" and by claiming that simulation, hyperreality, and nascent modes of media and computer culture are autonomous organizing forces of the contemporary world, he forfeits insight into the connections between new technologies and forms of culture and the restructuring of global capitalism.

North American cultural theorist Fredric Jameson, by contrast, in his famous article "Postmodernism, or the Cultural Logic of Late Capitalism," interprets the new forms of postmodern culture within the context of contemporary capitalism, thus connecting the economy and culture. For Jameson, postmodernism is a form of culture appropriate to the glitzy surfaces, glossy culture of image and spectacle, and high-intensity emphasis on appearance, style, and look found in contemporary consumer and media culture. Theorizing postmodernism, for Jameson, requires understanding the new forms of global capitalism and culture that are emerging of which postmodernism is a symptomatic form.

Seen in retrospect, the cultural populism, the turn to the audience, and the fetishism of the popular that emerged in British cultural studies during the 1980s and 1990s can be read as part of a postmodern turn in cultural studies which corresponds to a new stage of consumer and global capitalism. The Frankfurt School described a mass society and culture that sought to incorporate individuals into a more homogenized culture, controlled by big corporations, the state and centralized media. By contrast, the current form of consumer capitalism is more fragmented, specialized, aestheticized and eroticized, and celebratory of difference, choice, and individual freedom than the previous stage. Celeste Olalquiaga, for example, points out the similarities between strategies of postmodernism, advertising, and popular art forms such as kitsch – all icons of a new consumer and media culture.

The postmodern turn has generated a great variety and diversity of new forms of cultural studies and approaches to the study of media and culture. At their most extreme, postmodern theories erase the economic, political, and social dimensions of cultural production and reception, engage in a new form of cultural and technological determinism, indulge in theoreticist blather, and renounce the possibility of textual interpretation, social criticism, and political struggle. In a more dialectical and political version, postmodern theory is used to rethink cultural criticism and politics in the contemporary era. In addition, postmodern theory can be effective in calling attention to innovative configurations and functions of culture, as it charts the trajectories and impacts of new technologies, the emergent global economy and culture, and the novel political terrain and movements without losing sight of questions of political power, domination, and resistance. In addition, some versions of postmodern theory provide extremely useful transdisciplinary perspectives, as did the

Frankfurt School, British cultural studies, feminist, and diverse critical theories at their best.

Concluding Remarks

Despite their dissimilarity, many of the theories and methods that we have discussed in this introduction, ranging from the Frankfurt School to British cultural studies to French postmodern theory, are transdisciplinary in terms of their metatheory and practice. Standard academic approaches are discipline-oriented with English departments typically analyzing cultural forms as literary texts, Sociology departments focusing on the social dimension of culture, Political Science departments highlighting the politics of culture, and so on. By contrast, transdisciplinary perspectives subvert existing academic boundaries by combining social theory, cultural analysis, and political critique. Such transdisciplinary theory requires knowledge of a multiplicity of methods and theories which we have indeed attempted to assemble in our reader.

While our multiperspectivist approach might suggest to the reader a liberal pluralist tolerance of disparate theories and methods, we want to advance more systematic and critical perspectives. Against pluralism and eclecticism, we believe that it is important to challenge the established academic division of labor and to develop a transdisciplinary approach that contests both the bifurcation of the field of media and cultural studies and the society that produces it. A transdisciplinary media and cultural studies will thus overcome the boundaries of academic disciplines and will combine political economy, social theory and research, and cultural criticism in its project which aims at critique of domination and social transformation.

Such a transformative venture must also engage the new cultural, political, and social forms of the present era. Confronting new technologies, multimedia, and modes of experience such as cyberspace creates a variety of challenges for media and cultural studies, ranging from the need to chart the emergent cultural terrains and experiences to producing new literacies to analyze and evaluate these spheres and their forms. Since media and culture are themselves a type of pedagogy, one needs to create a counterpedagogy to question and critically analyze the often distorted forms of knowledge, misinformation, deceptive images, and seductive spectacles of the media and consumer society. Cultivating critical media literacy to analyze intelligently contemporary forms of culture calls for advancement of a new postmodern pedagogy that takes seriously image, spectacle, and narrative, and thus promotes visual and media literacy, the ability to read, analyze, and evaluate images, stories, and spectacles of media culture. Yet a postmodern pedagogy is concerned to develop multiple literacies, to rethink literacy itself in relation to new technologies and new cultural forms, and to create a cultural studies that encompasses a wide array of fields, texts, and practices, extending from popular music to poetry and painting to cyberspace and multimedia such as CD-ROMs.

The particular pedagogy employed, however, should be contextual, depending on the concrete situation, interests, and problems within the specific site in which cultural studies is taught or carried out. Yet the pedagogy must address salient general issues. Media culture is produced in a context of asymmetries of race, class and gender and concrete relations of domination and subordination that must be accounted for in any critical analysis. For us, a postmodern pedagogy does not elide or occlude issues of power; rather, it allows for a contemporary understanding of current social and cultural configurations of culture, power, and domination. Thus, while the distinctive situation and interests of the teachers, students, or critics help decide what precise artifacts are engaged, what methods will be employed, and what pedagogy will be deployed, the socio-cultural environment in which cultural production, reception, and education occurs must be scrutinized as well.

Hence, a new cultural and media studies would productively engage postmodern theory and new interpretive discourses and methods while maintaining important traditional goals such as cultivating literacy, critical thinking, and the art of interpretation. We are currently living in a proliferating image and media culture in which new technologies are changing every dimension of life from the economy to personal identity. In a postmodern media and computer culture, fresh critical strategies are needed to read cultural texts, to interpret the conjunctions of sight and sound, words and images, that are producing seductive cultural spaces, forms, and experiences. This undertaking also involves exploration of the emergent cyberspaces and modes of identities, interaction, and production that is taking place in the rapidly exploding computer culture, as well as exploring the new public spaces where myriad forms of political debate and contestation are evolving. Yet engaging the new forms of culture requires using the tools and insights already gained, rather than simply rejecting all "modern" concepts and theories as irrelevant to the emergent "postmodern" condition. As we have argued, adequately understanding new postmodern phenomena requires contextualization in terms of the way that new cultural artifacts are produced by the dominant mode of production and are used to reproduce – or contest – existing figurations of class, race, gender, and other forms of power and domination.

Indeed, a future-oriented cultural and media studies should look closely at the development of the entertainment and information technology industries, the mergers and synergies taking place, and the syntheses of computer and media culture that are being planned and some already implemented. A global media- and cyberculture is our life-world and fate and we need to be able to chart and map it accordingly to survive the dramatic changes currently taking place and the even more transformative novelties of the rapidly approaching future.

Part I

Culture, Ideology, and Hegemony

Introduction to Part I

This section contains a set of key texts which introduce some of the fundamental concepts of cultural and media criticism. For the theorists whom we have selected here, culture always arises in specific historical situations, serving particular socio-economic interests and carrying out important social functions. For Marx and Engels, the cultural ideas of an epoch serve the interests of the ruling class, providing ideologies that legitimize class domination. We have selected a famous text on ideology written for their unpublished work *The German Ideology* in 1845. Here, for the first time, Marx and Engels presented their materialist theory of history whereby material interests and class struggles are conceived as the ruling forces of history – as opposed to the actions of great individuals, ideas and cultural forces, or political events such as elections and wars.[1]

The economic base of society for Marx and Engels consisted of the forces and relations of production in which culture and ideology are constructed to help secure the dominance of ruling social groups. This influential "base/superstructure" model considers the economy the base, or foundation, of society, and cultural, legal, political, and additional forms of life are conceived as "superstructures" which grow out of and serve to reproduce the economic base. Many of the theorists in this book develop, revise, and in some cases contest this model, attempting to theorize, for example, more precisely how culture and media function within contemporary societies and everyday life.

For the Italian Marxist theorist Antonio Gramsci, the ruling intellectual and cultural forces of the era constitute a form of *hegemony*, or domination by ideas and cultural forms which induce consent to the rule of the leading groups in a society. Gramsci's example in his *Prison Notebooks*, from which we reproduce a selection defining his concept of hegemony, is Italian fascism which supplanted the previous liberal bourgeois regime in Italy through its control of the state and multiplied, often repressive, influence over schooling, the media, and other cultural, social, and political institutions. Gramsci himself was imprisoned for his opposition to Mussolini's fascist regime and while in prison he sketched out criticism of the ways that fascism became the ruling force in Italy, an analysis through which he produced more general accounts of how ruling social groups and institutions attain social dominance or hegemony.[2]

Gramsci defined ideology as the ruling ideas which present the "social cement" that unifies and holds together the dominant social order. He described his own "philosophy of praxis" as a mode of thought opposed to ideology, which includes, among other things, a critical analysis of ruling ideas. In a short section from his "Cultural Themes: Ideological Material (1985)," Gramsci notes that in his day the press was the dominant instrument of producing ideological legitimation of the existing institutions and social order, but that many other institutions such as the Church, schools, and different associations and groups also played a role. He called for sustained critique of these institutions and the ideologies that legitimize them, accompanied by creation of counter institutions and ideas that would produce alternatives to the existing system.

Members of the Institute for Social Research, established in the 1920s in Frankfurt, produced some of the first critical perspectives on mass culture and communication in their famous studies of the culture industries.[3] T. W. Adorno's analyses of popular music and culture (1941, 1978 [1932], 1982, 1989, and 1991), Leo Lowenthal's studies of popular demagogues, literature, and magazines (1949, 1957, and 1961), Hedda Herzog's studies of radio soap operas (1941), and the perspectives and critiques of mass culture developed in Horkheimer and Adorno's famous study of the culture industries (1972, and Adorno 1991) provide many examples of the value of what became known as the "Frankfurt School" approach.

Victims of European fascism, the members of the Institute for Social Research experienced first hand the ways that the Nazis used the instruments of mass culture to induce submission to fascist culture and society. While in exile in the United States, the group came to believe that American media culture was also highly ideological and that it worked to promote the interests of US capitalism. Controlled by giant corporations, the culture industries were organized according to the structures of mass production, churning out products that generated a highly commercial system of culture which in turn sold the values, life-styles, and institutions of American capitalism.

The work of the Frankfurt School provided what Paul Lazarsfeld (1941), one of the originators of modern communications studies, called a critical approach, which he distinguished from the "administrative research," which served the interests of dominant corporations or institutions. The views of Adorno, Lowenthal, and other members of the inner circle of the Institute for Social Research were contested by Walter Benjamin, an idiosyncratic theorist loosely affiliated with the Institute. Benjamin, writing in Paris during the 1930s, discerned progressive aspects in new technologies of cultural production such as photography, film, and radio. In "The Work of Art in the Age of Mechanical Reproduction" (1969), Benjamin noted how new mass media were supplanting older forms of culture whereby the mass reproduction of photography, film, recordings, and publications replaced the emphasis on the originality and "aura" of the work of art in an earlier era. Freed from the the mystification of high culture, Benjamin believed that mass culture could cultivate more critical individuals able to judge and analyze their culture, just as sports fans could dissect and evaluate athletic activities. In addition, processing the rush of images of cinema created, Benjamin believed, subjectivities better able to parry the flux and turbulence of experience in industrialized, urbanized societies.

Himself a collaborator of the prolific German artist Bertolt Brecht, Benjamin worked with Brecht on films, created radio plays, and attempted to utilize the media as organs of social progress. In the essay "The Artist as Producer" (1999 [1934]), Benjamin argued that progressive cultural creators should "refunction" the apparatus of cultural production, turning theater and film, for instance, into a forum of political enlightenment and discussion rather than a medium of "culinary" audience pleasure. Both Brecht and Benjamin wrote radio plays and were interested in film as an instrument of progressive social change. In an essay on radio theory, Brecht anticipated the Internet in his call for reconstructing the apparatus of broadcasting from one-way transmission to a more interactive form of two-way, or multiple, communication (in Silberman 2000: 41ff.) – a form first realized in CB radio and then electronically mediated computer communication.[4]

Moreover, Benjamin wished to promote a radical cultural and media politics concerned with the creation of alternative oppositional cultures. Yet he recognized that media such as film could have conservative effects. While he thought it was progressive that mass-produced works were losing their "aura," their magical force, and were opening cultural artifacts for more critical and political discussion, he recognized that film could create a new kind of ideological magic through the cult of celebrity and techniques such as the close-up that fetishized certain stars or images via the technology of the cinema. Benjamin was thus one of the first radical cultural critics to look carefully at the form and technology of media culture in appraising its complex nature and effects. Moreover, he developed a unique approach to cultural history that is one of his most enduring legacies, constituting a micrological history of Paris in the eighteenth century, an uncompleted project that contains a wealth of material for study and reflection (see Benjamin 2000, and the study in Buck-Morss 1989).

Max Horkheimer and Theodor W. Adorno answered Benjamin's optimism in a highly influential analysis of the culture industry published in their book *Dialectic of Enlightenment*, which first appeared in 1948 and was translated into English in 1972. They argued that the system of cultural production dominated by film, radio broadcasting, newspapers, and magazines, was controlled by advertising and commercial imperatives, and served to create subservience to the system of consumer capitalism. While later critics pronounced their approach too reductive and elitist, it is important to note that Horkheimer and Adorno combine analysis of the system of cultural production, distribution, and consumption with analysis of the texts of the culture industry, and thus provide a model of a critical and multidimensional mode of cultural criticism that overcomes the divide between approaches that solely focus on political economy, texts, or audiences.[5]

In an encyclopedia article on the public sphere which we have included in *Key-Works*, the German social theorist Jürgen Habermas summarizes the ideas in his path-breaking book *The Structural Transformation of the Public Sphere*. Providing historical background to the triumph of what Horkheimer and Adorno described as the culture industry, Habermas notes how bourgeois society was distinguished by the rise of a public sphere which stood between civil society and the state and which mediated between public and private interests. For the first time in history, individuals and groups could shape public opinion, giving direct expression to their needs and interests while influencing political practice. The bourgeois public sphere made it possible to form a realm of public opinion that opposed state power and the dominant class forces that were coming to shape bourgeois society.

Yet Habermas also notes a transition from the liberal public sphere which originated in the Enlightenment and the American and French revolutions to a media-dominated public sphere in the current stage of what he calls "welfare state capitalism and mass democracy." This historical transformation is grounded in Horkheimer and Adorno's analysis of the culture industry, in which giant corporations have taken over the public sphere and transformed it from a site of rational debate into one of manipulative consumption and passivity. In this transformation, "public opinion" shifts from rational consensus emerging from debate, discussion, and reflection to the manufactured opinion of polls or media experts. For Habermas, the interconnection between the sphere of public debate and individual participation has thus been fractured and transmuted into that of a realm of political manipulation and spectacle, in which citizen-consumers ingest and absorb passively entertainment and information. "Citizens" thus become spectators of media presentations and discourse which arbitrate public discussion and reduce its audiences to objects of news, information, and public affairs. In Habermas's words: "Inasmuch as the mass media today strip away the literary husks from the kind of bourgeois self-interpretation and utilize them as marketable forms for the public services provided in a culture of consumers, the original meaning is reversed" (1989a: 171).

Habermas's critics, however, contend that he idealizes the earlier bourgeois public sphere by presenting it as a forum of rational discussion and debate when in fact certain groups were excluded. While the concept of the public sphere and democracy assume a liberal and populist celebration of diversity, tolerance, debate, and consensus, in actuality the bourgeois public sphere was dominated by white, property-owning males. As Habermas's critics have documented, working class, plebeian, and women's public spheres developed alongside the bourgeois public sphere to represent voices and interests excluded in this forum.[6]

Yet Habermas is right that in the period of the democratic revolutions a public sphere emerged in which for the first time in history ordinary citizens could participate in political discussion and debate, organize, and struggle against unjust authority. Habermas's account also points to the increasingly important role of the media in politics and everyday life and the ways that corporate forces have colonized this sphere, using the media and culture to promote their own interests.

In later sections, we will see how a variety of other groups have analyzed current configurations of culture, ideology, and hegemony and how the positions presented in this section have evolved in a variety of fashions and have been often sharply contested as new political and theoretical impulses and movements have come to the fore. Hence, whereas a critical cultural and media studies emerged in the 1960s during a time strongly influenced by Marxism, later theoretical formations would contest Marxian positions and generate a wide variety of approaches to culture and media.

Notes

1   *The German Ideology* is published in volume 5 of Karl Marx and Frederick Engels, *Collected Works* (New York: International Publishers). On Marxism, see Marx and Engels (1978). On the concept of ideology, see Thompson (1991).
2   See Gramsci (1971); on Gramsci, see Boggs (1984).
3   On the Frankfurt School theory of the cultural industries, see Horkheimer and Adorno (1972) and Adorno (1991); the anthology edited by Rosenberg and White (1957); the readers edited by Arato and Gebhardt (1982) and Bronner and Kellner (1989); the discussions of the history of the Frankfurt School in Jay (1971) and Wiggershaus (1994); and the discussion of the Frankfurt School Combination of social theory and cultural criticism in Kellner (1989).
4   Silberman (2000) collects a wealth of Brecht's texts on radio, film, and the construction of alternative media and culture. Enzensberger (1974) provides a highly influential updating of Brecht's and Benjamin's media activism in his call for a progressive media politics in the contemporary era.
5   For further discussion of the Frankfurt School culture industry analysis, see Kellner (1989 and 1997); for more primary texts on the debates between Benjamin and the Frankfurt School, see the collection in Bloch et al. (1977).
6   For a discussion of the first sets of critiques of Habermas's work on the public sphere see Hohendahl (1979); for a bibliography of writings on the topic, see Görtzen (1981); and for a set of contemporary English-language discussions of the work, after it was finally translated in 1989, see Calhoun (1992). To get a sense of the astonishingly productive impact of the work in encouraging research and reflection on the public sphere, see the studies in Calhoun (1992) and Habermas's "Further Reflections on the Public Sphere" (1992) that cite a striking number of criticisms or developments of his study.

References

Adorno, T. W. (with G. Simpson) (1941) "On Popular Music," *Studies in Philosophy and Social Science*, vol. 9, no. 1: 17–48.
——(1978 [1932]) "On the Social Situation of Music," *Telos*, 35 (Spring): 129–65.
——(1982) "On the Fetish Character of Music and the Regression of Hearing," in Arato and Gebhardt (1982: 270–99).
——(1989) "On Jazz," in Bronner and Kellner (1989: 199–209).
——(1991) *The Culture Industry.* London: Routledge. Arato, Andrew and Eike Gebhardt (1982) *The Essential Frankfurt School Reader.* New York: Continuum.
Benjamin, Walter (1969) "The Work of Art in the Age of Mechanical Reproduction," in *Illuminations.* New York: Shocken.
——(1999 [1934]) "The Artist as Producer," in Walter Benjamin, *Collected Writings*, vol. II. Cambridge, Mass.: Harvard University Press.
——(2000) *The Arcades Project.* Cambridge, Mass.: Harvard University Press.
Bloch, E. et al. (1977) *Aesthetics and Politics.* London: Verso.
Boggs, Carl (1984) *The Two Revolutions: Gramsci and the Dilemmas of Western Marxism.* Boston, Mass.: South End Press.

Bronner, Stephen and Kellner, Douglas (1989) *Critical Theory and Society: A Reader*. New York: Routledge.

Buck-Morss, Susan (1989) *The Dialectics of Seeing*. Cambridge, Mass.: MIT Press.

Calhoun, Craig (Ed.) (1992) *Habermas and the Public Sphere*. Cambridge Mass.: MIT Press.

Enzensberger, Hans-Magnus (1974) *The Consciousness Industry*. New York: Seabury.

Görtzen, R. (1981) *J. Habermas: Eine Bibliographie seiner Schriften und der Sekundärliteratur, 1952–1981*. Frankfurt.

Gramsci, Antonio (1971) "History of the Subaltern Classes," and "The Concept of 'Ideology,'" in *Selections from the Prison Notebooks of Antonio Gramsci*, 52–3, 57–8, 375–7. Edited and translated by Quintin Hoare and Geoffrey Nowell Smith. New York: International Publishers.

Gramsci, Antonio (1985) "Cultural Themes: Ideological material," in *Selections from Cultural Writings*, 389–90. Edited by David Forgacs and Geoffrey Nowell-Smith; translated by William Boelhower. London: Lawrence & Wishart.

Habermas, Jürgen (1989a) *The Structural Transformation of the Public Sphere*. Cambridge, Mass.: MIT Press.

——(1989b) "The Public Sphere: An Encyclopedia Article," in Bronner and Kellner 1989: 136–42.

——(1992), "Further Reflections on the Public Sphere" in Calhoun 1992: 421–61.

——(1998) *Between Facts and Norms*. Cambridge, Mass.: MIT Press.

Hertzog, Herta (1941), "On Borrowed Experience: An Analysis of Listening to Daytime Sketches," *Studies in Philosophy and Social Science*, vol. IX, no. 1: 65–95.

Hohendahl, Peter (1979) "Critical Theory, Public Sphere and Culture: Habermas and His Critics," *New German Critique*, 16 (Winter): 89–118.

Horkheimer, Max and T. W. Adorno (1972) *Dialectic of Enlightenment*. New York: Herder and Herder.

Jay, Martin (1971) *The Dialectical Imagination* (Boston, Mass.: Little, Brown).

Kellner, Douglas (1989) *Critical Theory, Marxism, and Modernity*. Cambridge and Baltimore: Polity and Johns Hopkins University Press.

——(1987) "Critical Theory and British Cultural Studies: The Missed Articulation," in *Cultural Methodologies*, edited by Jim McGuigan. London: Sage: 12–41.

Lazarsfeld, Paul (1941) "Administrative and Critical Communications Research," *Studies in Philosophy and Social Science*, vol. IX, no. 1: 2–16.

Lowenthal, Leo (1949) (with Norbert Guttermann) *Prophets of Deceit*. New York: Harper.

——(1957) *Literature and the Image of Man*. Boston, Mass.: Beacon Press.

——(1961) *Literature, Popular Culture and Society*. Englewood Cliffs, N.J.: Prentice-Hall.

Marx, Karl, and Friedrich Engels (1976), "The Ruling Class and the Ruling Ideas," in Karl Marx and Friedrich Engels, *Collected Works*, vol. 5, 59–62; translated by Richard Dixon. New York: International Publishers.

——(1978) *The Marx–Engels Reader*. New York: Norton.

Rosenberg, Bernard and David Manning White (Eds) (1957) *Mass Culture*. Glencoe, Ill.: The Free Press.

Silberman, Marc (Ed.) (2000) *Brecht on Film and Radio*. London: Methuen.

Thompson, John (1991) *Ideology and Modern Culture*. Cambridge: Polity Press.

Wiggershaus, Rolf (1994) *The Frankfurt School*. Cambridge: Polity Press.

1

The Ruling Class and the Ruling Ideas*

Karl Marx and Friedrich Engels

1. The Ruling Class and the Ruling Ideas: How the Hegelian Conception of the Domination of the Spirit in History Arose

[30] The ideas of the ruling class are in every epoch the ruling ideas: i.e., the class which is the ruling *material* force of society is at the same time its ruling *intellectual* force. The class which has the means of material production at its disposal, consequently also controls the means of mental production, so that the ideas of those who lack the means of mental production are on the whole subject to it. The ruling ideas are nothing more than the ideal expression of the dominant material relations, the dominant material relations grasped as ideas; hence of the relations which make the one class the ruling one, therefore, the ideas of its dominance. The individuals composing the ruling class possess among other things consciousness, and therefore think. Insofar, therefore, as they rule as a class and determine the extent and compass of an historical epoch, it is self-evident that they do this in its whole range, hence among other things rule also as thinkers, as producers of ideas, and regulate the production and distribution of the ideas of their age: thus their ideas are the ruling ideas of the epoch. For instance, in an age and in a country where royal power, aristocracy and bourgeoisie are contending for domination and where, therefore, domination is shared, the doctrine of the separation of powers proves to be the dominant idea and is expressed as an "eternal law".

The division of labour, which we already saw above (pp. [15–18])[a] as one of the chief forces of history up till now, manifests itself also in the ruling class as the division of mental and [31] material labour, so that inside this class one part appears as the thinkers of the class (its active, conceptive ideologists, who make the formation of the

---

[a] See *Karl Marx, Friedrich Engels: Collected Works*, vol. 5, 1976, pp. 44–8. – [Editor's note to that volume]

* *Karl Marx, Friedrich Engels: Collected Works*, vol. 5, *translated by Richard Dixon* (New York: International Publishers, 1976), pp. 59–62.

illusions of the class about itself their chief source of livelihood), while the others' attitude to these ideas and illusions is more passive and receptive, because they are in reality the active members of this class and have less time to make up illusions and ideas about themselves. Within this class this cleavage can even develop into a certain opposition and hostility between the two parts, but whenever a practical collision occurs in which the class itself is endangered they automatically vanish, in which case there also vanishes the appearance of the ruling ideas being not the ideas of the ruling class and having a power distinct from the power of this class. The existence of revolutionary ideas in a particular period presupposes the existence of a revolutionary class; about the premises of the latter sufficient has already been said above (pp. [18–19, 22–23]).[b]

If now in considering the course of history we detach the ideas of the ruling class from the ruling class itself and attribute to them an independent existence, if we confine ourselves to saying that these or those ideas were dominant at a given time, without bothering ourselves about the conditions of production and the producers of these ideas, if we thus ignore the individuals and world conditions which are the source of the ideas, then we can say, for instance, that during the time the aristocracy was dominant, the concepts honour, loyalty, etc., were dominant, during the domin- ance of the bourgeoisie the concepts freedom, equality, etc. The ruling class itself on the whole imagines this to be so. This conception of history, which is common to all historians, particularly since the eighteenth century, will necessarily come up against [32] the phenomenon that ever more abstract ideas hold sway, i.e., ideas which increasingly take on the form of universality. For each new class which puts itself in the place of one ruling before it is compelled, merely in order to carry through its aim, to present its interest as the common interest of all the members of society, that is, expressed in ideal form: it has to give its ideas the form of universality, and present them as the only rational, universally valid ones. The class making a revolution comes forward from the very start, if only because it is opposed to a *class*, not as a class but as the representative of the whole of society, as the whole mass of society confronting the one ruling class.[1] It can do this because initially its interest really is as yet mostly connected with the common interest of all other non-ruling classes, because under the pressure of hitherto existing conditions its interest has not yet been able to develop as the particular interest of a particular class. Its victory, therefore, benefits also many individuals of other classes which are not winning a dominant position, but only insofar as it now enables these individuals to raise themselves into the ruling class. When the French bourgeoisie overthrew the rule of the aristocracy, it thereby made it possible for many proletarians to raise themselves above the proletariat, but only insofar as they became bourgeois. Every new class, therefore, achieves domina- tion only on a broader basis than that of the class ruling previously; on the other hand the opposition of the non-ruling class to the new ruling class then develops all the more sharply and profoundly. Both these things determine the fact that the struggle to be waged against this new ruling class, in its turn, has as its aim a more decisive and

---

[b] See *Karl Marx, Friedrich Engels: Collected Works*, vol. 5, 1976, pp. 48–9 and 52–3. – [Editor's note to that volume]

more radical negation of the previous conditions of society than [33] all previous classes which sought to rule could have.

This whole appearance, that the rule of a certain class is only the rule of certain ideas, comes to a natural end, of course, as soon as class rule in general ceases to be the form in which society is organised, that is to say, as soon as it is no longer necessary to represent a particular interest as general or the "general interest" as ruling.

Once the ruling ideas have been separated from the ruling individuals and, above all, from the relations which result from a given stage of the mode of production, and in this way the conclusion has been reached that history is always under the sway of ideas, it is very easy to abstract from these various ideas "the Idea", the thought, etc., as the dominant force in history, and thus to consider all these separate ideas and concepts as "forms of self-determination" of the Concept developing in history. It follows then naturally, too, that all the relations of men can be derived from the concept of man, man as conceived, the essence of man, Man. This has been done by speculative philosophy. Hegel himself confesses at the end of the *Geschichtsphilosophie*[c] that he "has considered the progress of *the concept* only" and has represented in history the "true *theodicy*" (p. 446). Now one can go back again to the producers of "the concept", to the theorists, ideologists and philosophers, and one comes then to the conclusion that the philosophers, the thinkers as such, have at all times been dominant in history: a conclusion, as we see, already expressed by Hegel.

The whole trick of proving the hegemony of the spirit in history (hierarchy Stirner calls it) is thus confined to the following three attempts.

[34] No. 1. One must separate the ideas of those ruling for empirical reasons, under empirical conditions and as corporeal individuals, from these rulers, and thus recognise the rule of ideas or illusions in history.

No. 2. One must bring an order into this rule of ideas, prove a mystical connection among the successive ruling ideas, which is managed by regarding them as "forms of self-determination of the concept" (this is possible because by virtue of their empirical basis these ideas are really connected with one another and because, conceived as *mere* ideas, they become self-distinctions, distinctions made by thought).

No. 3. To remove the mystical appearance of this "self-determining concept" it is changed into a person – "self-consciousness" – or, to appear thoroughly materialistic, into a series of persons, who represent the "concept" in history, into the "thinkers", the "philosophers", the ideologists, who again are understood as the manufacturers of history, as the "council of guardians", as the rulers.[2] Thus the whole body of materialistic elements has been eliminated from history and now full rein can be given to the speculative steed.

This historical method which reigned in Germany, and especially the reason why, must be explained from its connection with the illusion of ideologists in general, e.g., the illusions of the jurists, politicians (including the practical statesmen), from the dogmatic dreamings and distortions of these fellows; this is explained perfectly easily from their practical position in life, their job, and the division of labour.

---

[c] G. W. F. Hegel, *Vorlesungen über die Philosophie der Geschichte*. – [Editor's note to *Collected Works*]

[d] This word is in English in the manuscript. – [Editor's note to *Collected Works*]

[35] Whilst in ordinary life every shopkeeper[d] is very well able to distinguish between what somebody professes to be and what he really is, our historiography has not yet won this trivial insight. It takes every epoch at its word and believes that everything it says and imagines about itself is true.

Notes

1. [Marginal note by Marx:] (Universality corresponds to 1) the class versus the estate, 2) the competition, world intercourse, etc., 3) the great numerical strength of the ruling class, 4) the illusion of the *common* interests, in the beginning this illusion is true, 5) the delusion of the ideologists and the division of labour.)
2. [Marginal note by Marx:] Man=the "thinking human spirit".

2

(i) History of the Subaltern Classes; (ii) The Concept of "Ideology"; (iii) Cultural Themes: Ideological Material

Antonio Gramsci

(i) History of the Subaltern Classes[*]

Methodological Criteria

The historical unity of the ruling classes is realised in the State, and their history is essentially the history of States and of groups of States. But it would be wrong to think that this unity is simply juridical and political (though such forms of unity do have their importance too, and not in a purely formal sense); the fundamental historical unity, concretely, results from the organic relations between State or political society and "civil society".[1]

 The subaltern classes, by definition, are not unified and cannot unite until they are able to become a "State": their history, therefore, is intertwined with that of civil society, and thereby with the history of States and groups of States. Hence it is necessary to study: 1. the objective formation of the subaltern social groups, by the developments and transformations occurring in the sphere of economic production; their quantitative diffusion and their origins in pre-existing social groups, whose mentality, ideology and aims they conserve for a time; 2. their active or passive affiliation to the dominant political formations, their attempts to influence the programmes of these formations in order to press claims of their own, and the consequences of these attempts in determining processes of decomposition, renovation or neo-formation; 3. the birth of new parties of the dominant groups, intended

* From *Selections from the Prison Notebooks of Antonio Gramsci*, ed. and trans. Quintin Hoare and Geoffrey Nowell Smith (New York: International Publishers, 1971), pp. 52–3, 57–8.

to conserve the assent of the subaltern groups and to maintain control over them; 4. the formations which the subaltern groups themselves produce, in order to press claims of a limited and partial character; 5. those new formations which assert the autonomy of the subaltern groups, but within the old framework; 6. those formations which assert the integral autonomy, . . . etc.[2]

The list of these phases can be broken down still further, with intermediate phases and combinations of several phases. The historian must record, and discover the causes of, the line of development towards integral autonomy, starting from the most primitive phases; he must note every manifestation of the Sorelian "spirit of cleavage".[3] Therefore, the history of the parties of the subaltern groups is very complex too. It must include all the repercussions of party activity, throughout the area of the subaltern groups themselves taken globally, and also upon the attitudes of the dominant group; it must include as well the repercussions of the far more effective actions (effective because backed by the State) of the dominant groups upon the subaltern groups and their parties. Among the subaltern groups, one will exercise or tend to exercise a certain hegemony through the mediation of a party; this must be established by studying the development of all the other parties too, in so far as they include elements of the hegemonic group or of the other subaltern groups which undergo such hegemony. . . .

The methodological criterion on which our own study must be based is the following: that the supremacy of a social group manifests itself in two ways, as "domination" and as "intellectual and moral leadership". A social group dominates antagonistic groups, which it tends to "liquidate", or to subjugate perhaps even by armed force; it leads kindred and allied groups. A social group can, and indeed must, already exercise "leadership" before winning governmental power (this indeed is one of the principal conditions for the winning of such power); it subsequently becomes dominant when it exercises power, but even if it holds it firmly in its grasp, it must continue to "lead" as well. . . .

(ii)   The Concept of "Ideology"*

"Ideology" was an aspect of "sensationalism", i.e. eighteenth-century French materialism. Its original meaning was that of "science of ideas", and since analysis was the only method recognised and applied by science it means "analysis of ideas", that is, "investigation of the origin of ideas". Ideas had to be broken down into their original "elements", and these could be nothing other than "sensations". Ideas derived from sensations. But sensationalism could be associated, without too much difficulty, with religious faith and with the most extreme beliefs in the "power of the Spirit" and its "immortal destinies", so that Manzoni,[4] even after his conversion and return to

---

* From *Selections from the Prison Notebooks*, pp. 375–7.

Catholicism, even at the time when he wrote the *Inni sacri*, continued to adhere in principle to the theory of sensationalism, until he learnt about the philosophy of Rosmini.[5]

How the concept of Ideology passed from meaning "science of ideas" and "analysis of the origin of ideas" to meaning a specific "system of ideas" needs to be examined historically. In purely logical terms the process is easy to grasp and understand.

It could be asserted that Freud is the last of the Ideologues, and that De Man is also an "ideologue". This makes the "enthusiasm" of Croce and the Croceans for De Man even more curious – or would if there wasn't a "practical" justification for their enthusiasm.[6] One should examine the way in which the author of the *Popular Manual* [Bukharin][7] has remained trapped in Ideology; whereas the philosophy of praxis represents a distinct advance and historically is precisely in opposition to Ideology. Indeed the meaning which the term "ideology" has assumed in Marxist philosophy implicitly contains a negative value judgment and excludes the possibility that for its founders the origin of ideas should be sought for in sensations, and therefore, in the last analysis, in physiology. "Ideology" itself must be analysed historically, in the terms of the philosophy of praxis, as a superstructure.

It seems to me that there is a potential element of error in assessing the value of ideologies, due to the fact (by no means casual) that the name ideology is given both to the necessary superstructure of a particular structure and to the arbitrary elucubrations of particular individuals. The bad sense of the word has become widespread, with the effect that the theoretical analysis of the concept of ideology has been modified and denatured. The process leading up to this error can be easily reconstructed:

1. ideology is identified as distinct from the structure, and it is asserted that it is not ideology that changes the structures but vice versa;
2. it is asserted that a given political solution is "ideological" – i.e. that it is not sufficient to change the structure, although it thinks that it can do so; it is asserted that it is useless, stupid, etc.;
3. one then passes to the assertion that every ideology is "pure" appearance, useless, stupid, etc.

One must therefore distinguish between historically organic ideologies, those, that is, which are necessary to a given structure, and ideologies that are arbitrary, rationalistic, or "willed". To the extent that ideologies are historically necessary they have a validity which is "psychological"; they "organise" human masses, and create the terrain on which men move, acquire consciousness of their position, struggle, etc. To the extent that they are arbitrary they only create individual "movements", polemics and so on (though even these are not completely useless, since they function like an error which by contrasting with truth, demonstrates it).

It is worth recalling the frequent affirmation made by Marx on the "solidity of popular beliefs" as a necessary element of a specific situation. What he says more or less is "when this way of conceiving things has the force of popular beliefs", etc. Another proposition of Marx is that a popular conviction often has the same energy as a material force or something of the kind, which is extremely significant. The analysis of these propositions tends, I think, to reinforce the conception of *historical bloc* in which precisely material forces are the content and ideologies are the form, though this distinction between form and content has purely didactic value, since the material forces would be inconceivable historically without form and the ideologies would be individual fancies without the material forces.

(iii)   Cultural Themes: Ideological Material*

A study of how the ideological structure of a dominant class is actually organized: namely the material organization aimed at maintaining, defending and developing the theoretical or ideological "front". Its most prominent and dynamic part is the press in general: publishing houses (which have an implicit and explicit programme and are attached to a particular tendency), political newspapers, periodicals of every kind, scientific, literary, philological, popular, etc., various periodicals down to parish bulletins. If this kind of study were conducted on a national scale it would be gigantic: one could therefore do a series of studies for one city or for a number of cities. A news editor of a daily newspaper should have this study as a general outline for his work: indeed, he should make his own version of it. Think of all the wonderful leading articles one could write on the subject!

The press is the most dynamic part of this ideological structure, but not the only one. Everything which influences or is able to influence public opinion, directly or indirectly, belongs to it: libraries, schools, associations and clubs of various kinds, even architecture and the layout and names of streets. It would be impossible to explain the position retained by the Church in modern society if one were unaware of the constant and patient efforts it makes to develop continuously its particular section of this material structure of ideology.[8] Such a study, done seriously, would be very important. Besides providing a living historical model of such a structure, it would accustom one to a more cautious and exact estimate of the forces acting in society. What resources can an innovative class set against this formidable complex of trenches and fortification of the dominant class? The spirit of scission,[9] in other words the progressive acquisition of the consciousness of its own historical personality, a spirit of scission that must aim to spread itself from the protagonist class to the classes that are its potential allies – all this requires a complex ideological labour, the first condition of which is an exact knowledge of the field that must be cleared of its element of human "mass".

* From Antonio Gramsci, *Selections from the Cultural Writings*, ed. by David Forgacs and Geoffrey Nowell Smith, trans. by William Boelhower (London: Lawrence and Wishart, 1985), pp. 389–90; © Lawrence and Wishart 1985.

Notes

1   For Gramsci's use of the term "civil society", see introduction to *State and Civil Society*, pp. 206–9.
2   The last three categories refer presumably to trade unions, reformist parties, and communist parties respectively.
3   See note 4 on p. 126.
4   Alessandro Manzoni (1785–1873), Italian novelist and poet, brought up on the ideas of the French and Italian Enlightenment but converted to Catholicism in or about 1810. His major work is the historical novel *I promessi sposi* (The Betrothed) (1827: revised and partly rewritten 1840) in which Enlightenment ideas co-exist uneasily with Catholic Quietism. The *Inni sacri* (Sacred Hymns, or Songs) date from 1812–22.
5   The most effective literary propagator of ideology was Destutt de Tracy 1754–1836), because of the ease and popularity of his exposition. Another was Dr. Cabanis with his *Rapport du Physique et du Moral*. (Condillac, Helvétius, etc., are more strictly speaking philosophers.) Link between Catholicism and ideology: Manzoni, Cabanis, Bourget, Taine (Taine is the *chef d'école* for Maurras and others of a Catholic tendency); also the "psychological novel" (Stendhal was a pupil of De Tracy, etc.). Destutt de Tracy's main work is the *Eléments d'Idéologie* (Paris, 1817–18). The Italian translation is more complete (*Elementi di Ideologia del Conte Destutt de Tracy*, translated by G. Compagnoni, Milan, Stamperia di Giambattista Sonzogno, 1819). In the French text a whole section is missing, I think the one on Love, which Stendhal knew and used from the Italian translation.
6   Henri De Man, Belgian Social-Democrat, was the author of a book *Au delà du Marxisme* ("Beyond Marxism"), frequently referred to and criticised in the *Quaderni* (see in particular MS, pp. 111–14). Croce's "practical" reason for enthusiasm for De Man lies in their shared opposition to revolutionary Marxism, although strictly speaking Crocean philosophy denies a serious theoretical role to ideological and instrumental thought such as De Man's.
7   For Gramsci's criticism of Bukharin's *Popular Manual*, see *Selections from the Prison Notebooks of Antonio Gramsci*, pp. 419–72.
8   In 1916 Gramsci had written of the array of titles in a Catholic bookshop window in Turin: "I admire and envy the priests who succeed in obtaining such visible results with their cultural propaganda. In reality, we do not pay much attention to this slow process of intellectual stagnation by the clergy. It is something impalpable, which slides along like an eel, limp, which does not seem solid, and yet it is like the mattress that resists cannonades better than the walls of Liège" (CT, p. 132; SM, pp. 39–40).
9   The term "scission" (sometimes translated as "cleavage") is drawn from Sorel, who wrote in the *Reflexions on Violence* (Chapter 6 § 1) of "the scission between classes, the basis of all socialism". It derives from his analogy between socialism and primitive Christianity. For Sorel, Christianity made a distinct "scission" or "rupture" from Judaism while at the same time inheriting its compatible elements. In the same way socialism, in its scission from capitalism, would keep the heritage both of capitalist science and technology and of the "morality of the producers" (i.e. the proletariat), formed through trade union solidarity and struggles (see *Le Système historique de Renan*, Paris 1905, p. 71). Compare Gramsci's statement of 1920: "Every revolution which, like the Christian and the Communist revolutions, comes about and can only come about through a stirring within the deepest and broadest popular masses, cannot help but smash and destroy the existing system of social organization" (SPWI, p. 331).

3

The Work of Art in the Age of Mechanical Reproduction*

Walter Benjamin

Our fine arts were developed, their types and uses were established, in times very different from the present, by men whose power of action upon things was insignificant in comparison with ours. But the amazing growth of our techniques, the adaptability and precision they have attained, the ideas and habits they are creating, make it a certainty that profound changes are impending in the ancient craft of the Beautiful. In all the arts there is a physical component which can no longer be considered or treated as it used to be, which cannot remain unaffected by our modern knowledge and power. For the last twenty years neither matter nor space nor time has been what it was from time immemorial. We must expect great innovations to transform the entire technique of the arts, thereby affecting artistic invention itself and perhaps even bringing about an amazing change in our very notion of art.[1]

(Paul Valéry, 'La Conquète de l'ubiquité")

Preface

When Marx undertook his critique of the capitalistic mode of production, this mode was in its infancy. Marx directed his efforts in such a way as to give them prognostic value. He went back to the basic conditions underlying capitalistic production and through his presentation showed what could be expected of capitalism in the future. The result was that one could expect it not only to exploit the proletariat with increasing intensity, but ultimately to create conditions which would make it possible to abolish capitalism itself.

The transformation of the superstructure, which takes place far more slowly than that of the substructure, has taken more than half a century to manifest in all areas of culture the change in the conditions of production. Only today can it be indicated what form this has taken. Certain prognostic requirements should be met by these statements. However, theses about the art of the proletariat after its assumption of

* From Walter Benjamin, *Illuminations* (New York: Schocken Books, 1969), pp. 217–51.

power or about the art of a classless society would have less bearing on these demands than theses about the developmental tendencies of art under present conditions of production. Their dialectic is no less noticeable in the superstructure than in the economy. It would therefore be wrong to underestimate the value of such theses as a weapon. They brush aside a number of outmoded concepts, such as creativity and genius, eternal value and mystery – concepts whose uncontrolled (and at present almost uncontrollable) application would lead to a processing of data in the Fascist sense. The concepts which are introduced into the theory of art in what follows differ from the more familiar terms in that they are completely useless for the purposes of Fascism. They are, on the other hand, useful for the formulation of revolutionary demands in the politics of art.

I

In principle a work of art has always been reproducible. Man-made artifacts could always be imitated by men. Replicas were made by pupils in practice of their craft, by masters for diffusing their works, and, finally, by third parties in the pursuit of gain. Mechanical reproduction of a work of art, however, represents something new. Historically, it advanced intermittently and in leaps at long intervals, but with accelerated intensity. The Greeks knew only two procedures of technically reproducing works of art: founding and stamping. Bronzes, terra cottas, and coins were the only art works which they could produce in quantity. All others were unique and could not be mechanically reproduced. With the woodcut graphic art became mechanically reproducible for the first time, long before script became reproducible by print. The enormous changes which printing, the mechanical reproduction of writing, has brought about in literature are a familiar story. However, within the phenomenon which we are here examining from the perspective of world history, print is merely a special, though particularly important, case. During the Middle Ages engraving and etching were added to the woodcut; at the beginning of the nineteenth century lithography made its appearance.

With lithography the technique of reproduction reached an essentially new stage. This much more direct process was distinguished by the tracing of the design on a stone rather than its incision on a block of wood or its etching on a copperplate and permitted graphic art for the first time to put its products on the market, not only in large numbers as hitherto, but also in daily changing forms. Lithography enabled graphic art to illustrate everyday life, and it began to keep pace with printing. But only a few decades after its invention, lithography was surpassed by photography. For the first time in the process of pictorial reproduction, photography freed the hand of the most important artistic functions which henceforth devolved only upon the eye looking into a lens. Since the eye perceives more swiftly than the hand can draw, the process of pictorial reproduction was accelerated so enormously that it could keep pace with speech. A film operator shooting a scene in the studio captures the images at the speed of an actor's speech. Just as lithography virtually implied the illustrated newspaper, so did photography foreshadow the sound film. The technical reproduction of sound was tackled at the end of the last century. These convergent endeavors made predictable a situation which Paul Valéry pointed up in this sentence: "Just as water, gas, and electricity are brought into our houses from far off to satisfy our needs in response to a minimal effort, so we shall be supplied with visual or auditory images, which will appear and disappear at a simple movement of the hand, hardly more than a sign" (*op. cit.*, p. 226). Around 1900 technical reproduction had reached a standard that not only permitted it to reproduce all transmitted works of art and thus to cause the most profound change in their impact upon the public; it also had captured a place of its own among the artistic processes. For the study of this standard nothing is more revealing than the nature of the repercussions that these two different manifestations – the reproduction of works of art and the art of the film – have had on art in its traditional form.

II

Even the most perfect reproduction of a work of art is lacking in one element: its presence in time and space, its unique existence at the place where it happens to be. This unique existence of the work of art determined the history to which it was subject throughout the time of its existence. This includes the changes which it may have suffered in physical condition over the years as well as the various changes in its ownership.[2] The traces of the first can be revealed only by chemical or physical analyses which it is impossible to perform on a reproduction; changes of ownership are subject to a tradition which must be traced from the situation of the original.

The presence of the original is the prerequisite to the concept of authenticity. Chemical analyses of the patina of a bronze can help to establish this, as does the proof that a given manuscript of the Middle Ages stems from an archive of the fifteenth century. The whole sphere of authenticity is outside technical – and, of course, not only technical – reproducibility.[3] Confronted with its manual reproduction, which was usually branded as a forgery, the original preserved all its authority; not so *vis à vis* technical reproduction. The reason is twofold. First, process reproduction is more independent of the original than manual reproduction. For example, in photography, process reproduction can bring out those aspects of the original that are unattainable to the naked eye yet accessible to the lens, which is adjustable and chooses its angle at will. And photographic reproduction, with the aid of certain processes, such as enlargement or slow motion, can capture images which escape natural vision. Secondly, technical reproduction can put the copy of the original into situations which would be out of reach for the original itself. Above all, it enables the original to meet the beholder halfway, be it in the form of a photograph or a phonograph record. The cathedral leaves its locale to be received in the studio of a lover of art; the choral production, performed in an auditorium or in the open air, resounds in the drawing room.

The situations into which the product of mechanical reproduction can be brought may not touch the actual work of art, yet the quality of its presence is always depreciated. This holds not only for the art work but also, for instance, for a land-scape which passes in review before the spectator in a movie. In the case of the art object, a most sensitive nucleus – namely, its authenticity – is interfered with whereas no natural object is vulnerable on that score. The authenticity of a thing is the essence of all that is transmissible from its beginning, ranging from its substantive duration to its testimony to the history which it has experienced. Since the historical testimony rests on the authenticity, the former, too, is jeopardized by reproduction when substantive duration ceases to matter. And what is really jeopardized when the historical testimony is affected is the authority of the object.[4]

One might subsume the eliminated element in the term "aura" and go on to say: that which withers in the age of mechanical reproduction is the aura of the work of art. This is a symptomatic process whose significance points beyond the realm of art. One might generalize by saying: the technique of reproduction detaches the repro-duced object from the domain of tradition. By making many reproductions it sub-stitutes a plurality of copies for a unique existence. And in permitting the reproduction to meet the beholder or listener in his own particular situation, it reactivates the object reproduced. These two processes lead to a tremendous shatter-ing of tradition which is the obverse of the contemporary crisis and renewal of mankind. Both processes are intimately connected with the contemporary mass movements. Their most powerful agent is the film. Its social significance, particularly in its most positive form, is inconceivable without its destructive, cathartic aspect, that is, the liquidation of the traditional value of the cultural heritage. This phenom-enon is most palpable in the great historical films. It extends to ever new positions. In 1927 Abel Gance exclaimed enthusiastically: "Shakespeare, Rembrandt, Beethoven will make films . . . all legends, all mythologies and all myths, all founders of religion, and the very religions . . . await their exposed resurrection, and the heroes crowd each other at the gate."[5] Presumably without intending it, he issued an invitation to a far-reaching liquidation.

III

During long periods of history, the mode of human sense perception changes with humanity's entire mode of existence. The manner in which human sense perception is organized, the medium in which it is accomplished, is determined not only by nature but by historical circumstances as well. The fifth century, with its great shifts of population, saw the birth of the late Roman art industry and the Vienna Genesis, and there developed not only an art different from that of antiquity but also a new kind of perception. The scholars of the Viennese school, Riegl and Wickhoff, who resisted the weight of classical tradition under which these later art forms had been buried, were the first to draw conclusions from them concerning the organization of perception at the time. However far-reaching their insight, these scholars limited themselves to showing the significant, formal hallmark which characterized percep-tion in late Roman times. They did not attempt – and, perhaps, saw no way – to show the social transformations expressed by these changes of perception. The conditions for an analogous insight are more favorable in the present. And if changes in the medium of contemporary perception can be comprehended as decay of the aura, it is possible to show its social causes.

The concept of aura which was proposed above with reference to historical objects may usefully be illustrated with reference to the aura of natural ones. We define the aura of the latter as the unique phenomenon of a distance, however close it may be. If, while resting on a summer afternoon, you follow with your eyes a mountain range on the horizon or a branch which casts its shadow over you, you experience the aura of those mountains, of that branch. This image makes it easy to comprehend the social bases of the contemporary decay of the aura. It rests on two circumstances, both of which are related to the increasing significance of the masses in contemporary life. Namely, the desire of contemporary masses to bring things "closer" spatially and humanly, which is just as ardent as their bent toward overcoming the uniqueness of every reality by accepting its reproduction.[6] Every day the urge grows stronger to get hold of an object at very close range by way of its likeness, its reproduction. Unmistakably, reproduction as offered by picture magazines and newsreels differs from the image seen by the unarmed eye. Uniqueness and permanence are as closely linked in the latter as are transitoriness and reproducibility in the former. To pry an object from its shell, to destroy its aura, is the mark of a perception whose "sense of the universal equality of things" has increased to such a degree that it extracts it even from a unique object by means of reproduction. Thus is manifested in the field of perception what in the theoretical sphere is noticeable in the increasing importance of statistics. The adjustment of reality to the masses and of the masses to reality is a process of unlimited scope, as much for thinking as for perception.

IV

The uniqueness of a work of art is inseparable from its being imbedded in the fabric of tradition. This tradition itself is thoroughly alive and extremely changeable. An ancient statue of Venus, for example, stood in a different traditional context with the Greeks, who made it an object of veneration, than with the clerics of the Middle Ages, who viewed it as an ominous idol. Both of them, however, were equally confronted with its uniqueness, that is, its aura. Originally the contextual integration of art in tradition found its expression in the cult. We know that the earliest art works originated in the service of a ritual – first the magical, then the religious kind. It is significant that the existence of the work of art with reference to its aura is never entirely separated from its ritual function.[7] In other words, the unique value of the "authentic" work of art has its basis in ritual, the location of its original use value. This ritualistic basis, however remote, is still recognizable as secularized ritual even in the most profane forms of the cult of beauty.[8] The secular cult of beauty, developed during the Renaissance and prevailing for three centuries, clearly showed that ritualistic basis in its decline and the first deep crisis which befell it. With the advent of the first truly revolutionary means of reproduction, photography, simultaneously with the rise of socialism, art sensed the approaching crisis which has become evident a century later. At the time, art reacted with the doctrine of *l'art pour l'art*, that is, with a theology of art. This gave rise to what might be called a negative theology in the form of the idea of "pure" art, which not only denied any social function of art but also any categorizing by subject matter. (In poetry, Mallarmé was the first to take this position.)

An analysis of art in the age of mechanical reproduction must do justice to these relationships, for they lead us to an all-important insight: for the first time in world history, mechanical reproduction emancipates the work of art from its parasitical dependence on ritual. To an ever greater degree the work of art reproduced becomes the work of art designed for reproducibility.[9] From a photographic negative, for example, one can make any number of prints; to ask for the "authentic" print makes no sense. But the instant the criterion of authenticity ceases to be applicable to artistic production, the total function of art is reversed. Instead of being based on ritual, it begins to be based on another practice – politics.

V

Works of art are received and valued on different planes. Two polar types stand out: with one, the accent is on the cult value; with the other, on the exhibition value of the work.[10] Artistic production begins with ceremonial objects destined to serve in a cult. One may assume that what mattered was their existence, not their being on view. The elk portrayed by the man of the Stone Age on the walls of his cave was an instrument of magic. He did expose it to his fellow men, but in the main it was meant for the spirits. Today the cult value would seem to demand that the work of art remain hidden. Certain statues of gods are accessible only to the priest in the cella; certain Madonnas remain covered nearly all year round; certain sculptures on medieval cathedrals are invisible to the spectator on ground level. With the emancipation of the various art practices from ritual go increasing opportunities for the exhibition of their products. It is easier to exhibit a portrait bust that can be sent here and there than to exhibit the statue of a divinity that has its fixed place in the interior of a temple. The same holds for the painting as against the mosaic or fresco that preceded it. And even though the public presentability of a mass originally may have been just as great as that of a symphony, the latter originated at the moment when its public presentability promised to surpass that of the mass.

With the different methods of technical reproduction of a work of art, its fitness for exhibition increased to such an extent that the quantitative shift between its two poles turned into a qualitative transformation of its nature. This is comparable to the situation of the work of art in prehistoric times when, by the absolute emphasis on its cult value, it was, first and foremost, an instrument of magic. Only later did it come to be recognized as a work of art. In the same way today, by the absolute emphasis on its exhibition value the work of art becomes a creation with entirely new functions, among which the one we are conscious of, the artistic function, later may be recognized as incidental.[11] This much is certain: today photography and the film are the most serviceable exemplifications of this new function.

VI

In photography, exhibition value begins to displace cult value all along the line. But cult value does not give way without resistance. It retires into an ultimate retrenchment: the human countenance. It is no accident that the portrait was the focal point of early photography. The cult of remembrance of loved ones, absent or dead, offers a last refuge for the cult value of the picture. For the last time the aura emanates from the early photographs in the fleeting expression of a human face. This is what constitutes their melancholy, incomparable beauty. But as man withdraws from the photographic image, the exhibition value for the first time shows its superiority to the ritual value. To have pinpointed this new stage constitutes the incomparable significance of Atget, who, around 1900, took photographs of deserted Paris streets. It has quite justly been said of him that he photographed them like scenes of crime. The scene of a crime, too, is deserted; it is photographed for the purpose of establishing evidence. With Atget, photographs become standard evidence for historical occurrences, and acquire a hidden political significance. They demand a specific kind of approach; free-floating contemplation is not appropriate to them. They stir the viewer; he feels challenged by them in a new way. At the same time picture magazines begin to put up signposts for him, right ones or wrong ones, no matter. For the first time, captions have become obligatory. And it is clear that they have an altogether different character than the title of a painting. The directives which the captions give to those looking at pictures in illustrated magazines soon become even more explicit and more imperative in the film where the meaning of each single picture appears to be prescribed by the sequence of all preceding ones.

VII

The nineteenth-century dispute as to the artistic value of painting versus photography today seems devious and confused. This does not diminish its importance, however; if anything, it underlines it. The dispute was in fact the symptom of a historical transformation the universal impact of which was not realized by either of the rivals. When the age of mechanical reproduction separated art from its basis in cult, the semblance of its autonomy disappeared forever. The resulting change in the function of art transcended the perspective of the century; for a long time it even escaped that of the twentieth century, which experienced the development of the film.

Earlier much futile thought had been devoted to the question of whether photography is an art. The primary question – whether the very invention of photography had not transformed the entire nature of art – was not raised. Soon the film theoreticians asked the same ill-considered question with regard to the film. But the difficulties which photography caused traditional aesthetics were mere child's play as compared to those raised by the film. Whence the insensitive and forced character of early theories of the film. Abel Gance, for instance, compares the film with hieroglyphs: "Here, by a remarkable regression, we have come back to the level of expression of the Egyptians.... Pictorial language has not yet matured because our eyes have not yet adjusted to it. There is as yet insufficient respect for, insufficient cult of, what it expresses."[12] Or, in the words of Séverin-Mars: "What art has been granted a dream more poetical and more real at the same time! Approached in this fashion the film might represent an incomparable means of expression. Only the most high-minded persons, in the most perfect and mysterious moments of their lives, should be allowed to enter its ambience."[13] Alexandre Arnoux concludes his fantasy about the silent film with the question: "Do not all the bold descriptions we have given amount to the definition of prayer?"[14] It is instructive to note how their desire to class the film among the "arts" forces these theoreticians to read ritual elements into it – with a striking lack of discretion. Yet when these speculations were published, films like *L'Opinion publique* and *The Gold Rush* had already appeared. This, however, did not keep Abel Gance from adducing hieroglyphs for purposes of comparison, nor Séverin-Mars from speaking of the film as one might speak of paintings by Fra Angelico. Characteristically, even today ultrareactionary authors give the film a similar contextual significance – if not an outright sacred one, then at least a supernatural one. Commenting on Max Reinhardt's film version of *A Midsummer Night's Dream*, Werfel states that undoubtedly it was the sterile copying of the exterior world with its streets, interiors, railroad stations, restaurants, motorcars, and beaches which until now had obstructed the elevation of the film to the realm of art. "The film has not yet realized its true meaning, its real possibilities . . . these consist in its unique faculty to express by natural means and with incomparable persuasiveness all that is fairylike, marvelous, supernatural."[15]

VIII

The artistic performance of a stage actor is definitely presented to the public by the actor in person; that of the screen actor, however, is presented by a camera, with a twofold consequence. The camera that presents the performance of the film actor to the public need not respect the performance as an integral whole. Guided by the cameraman, the camera continually changes its position with respect to the perform-ance. The sequence of positional views which the editor composes from the material supplied him constitutes the completed film. It comprises certain factors of move-ment which are in reality those of the camera, not to mention special camera angles, close-ups, etc. Hence, the performance of the actor is subjected to a series of optical tests. This is the first consequence of the fact that the actor's performance is presented by means of a camera. Also, the film actor lacks the opportunity of the stage actor to adjust to the audience during his performance, since he does not present his perform-ance to the audience in person. This permits the audience to take the position of a critic, without experiencing any personal contact with the actor. The audience's identification with the actor is really an identification with the camera. Consequently the audience takes the position of the camera; its approach is that of testing.[16] This is not the approach to which cult values may be exposed.

IX

For the film, what matters primarily is that the actor represents himself to the public before the camera, rather than representing someone else. One of the first to sense the actor's metamorphosis by this form of testing was Pirandello. Though his remarks on the subject in his novel *Si Gira* were limited to the negative aspects of the question and to the silent film only, this hardly impairs their validity. For in this respect, the sound film did not change anything essential. What matters is that the part is acted not for an audience but for a mechanical contrivance – in the case of the sound film, for two of them. "The film actor," wrote Pirandello, "feels as if in exile – exiled not only from the stage but also from himself. With a vague sense of discomfort he feels inexplicable emptiness: his body loses its corporeality, it evaporates, it is deprived of reality, life, voice, and the noises caused by his moving about, in order to be changed into a mute image, flickering an instant on the screen, then vanishing into silence. . . . The projector will play with his shadow before the public, and he himself must be content to play before the camera."[17] This situation might also be characterized as follows: for the first time – and this is the effect of the film – man has to operate with his whole living person, yet forgoing its aura. For aura is tied to his presence; there can be no replica of it. The aura which, on the stage, emanates from Macbeth, cannot be separated for the spectators from that of the actor. However, the singularity of the shot in the studio is that the camera is substituted for the public. Consequently, the aura that envelops the actor vanishes, and with it the aura of the figure he portrays.

It is not surprising that it should be a dramatist such as Pirandello who, in characterizing the film, inadvertently touches on the very crisis in which we see the theater. Any thorough study proves that there is indeed no greater contrast than that of the stage play to a work of art that is completely subject to or, like the film, founded in, mechanical reproduction. Experts have long recognized that in the film "the greatest effects are almost always obtained by "acting" as little as possible. . . ." In 1932 Rudolf Arnheim saw "the latest trend . . . in treating the actor as a stage prop chosen for its characteristics and . . . inserted at the proper place."[18] With this idea something else is closely connected. The stage actor identifies himself with the character of his role. The film actor very often is denied this opportunity. His creation is by no means all of a piece; it is composed of many separate performances. Besides certain fortuitous considerations, such as cost of studio, availability of fellow players, décor, etc., there are elementary necessities of equipment that split the actor's work into a series of mountable episodes. In particular, lighting and its installation require the presentation of an event that, on the screen, unfolds as a rapid and unified scene, in a sequence of separate shootings which may take hours at the studio; not to mention more obvious montage. Thus a jump from the window can be shot in the studio as a jump from a scaffold, and the ensuing flight, if need be, can be shot weeks later when outdoor scenes are taken. Far more paradoxical cases can easily be construed. Let us assume that an actor is supposed to be startled by a knock at the door. If his reaction is not satisfactory, the director can resort to an expedient: when the actor happens to be at the studio again he has a shot fired behind him without his being forewarned of it. The frightened reaction can be shot now and be cut into the screen version. Nothing more strikingly shows that art has left the realm of the "beautiful semblance" which, so far, had been taken to be the only sphere where art could thrive.

X

The feeling of strangeness that overcomes the actor before the camera, as Pirandello describes it, is basically of the same kind as the estrangement felt before one's own image in the mirror. But now the reflected image has become separable, transportable. And where is it transported? Before the public.[19] Never for a moment does the screen actor cease to be conscious of this fact. While facing the camera he knows that ultimately he will face the public, the consumers who constitute the market. This market, where he offers not only his labor but also his whole self, his heart and soul, is beyond his reach. During the shooting he has as little contact with it as any article made in a factory. This may contribute to that oppression, that new anxiety which, according to Pirandello, grips the actor before the camera. The film responds to the shriveling of the aura with an artificial build-up of the "personality" outside the studio. The cult of the movie star, fostered by the money of the film industry, preserves not the unique aura of the person but the "spell of the personality," the phony spell of a commodity. So long as the movie-makers' capital sets the fashion, as a rule no other revolutionary merit can be accredited to today's film than the promotion of a revolutionary criticism of traditional concepts of art. We do not deny that in some cases today's films can also promote revolutionary criticism of social conditions, even of the distribution of property. However, our present study is no more specifically concerned with this than is the film production of Western Europe.

It is inherent in the technique of the film as well as that of sports that everybody who witnesses its accomplishments is somewhat of an expert. This is obvious to anyone listening to a group of newspaper boys leaning on their bicycles and discussing the outcome of a bicycle race. It is not for nothing that newspaper publishers arrange races for their delivery boys. These arouse great interest among the participants, for the victor has an opportunity to rise from delivery boy to professional racer. Similarly, the newsreel offers everyone the opportunity to rise from passer-by to movie extra. In this way any man might even find himself part of a work of art, as witness Vertoff's *Three Songs About Lenin* or Ivens' *Borinage*. Any man today can lay claim to being filmed. This claim can best be elucidated by a comparative look at the historical situation of contemporary literature.

For centuries a small number of writers were confronted by many thousands of readers. This changed toward the end of the last century. With the increasing extension of the press, which kept placing new political, religious, scientific, professional, and local organs before the readers, an increasing number of readers became writers – at first, occasional ones. It began with the daily press opening to its readers space for "letters to the editor." And today there is hardly a gainfully employed European who could not, in principle, find an opportunity to publish somewhere or other comments on his work, grievances, documentary reports, or that sort of thing. Thus, the distinction between author and public is about to lose its basic character. The difference becomes merely functional; it may vary from case to case. At any moment the reader is ready to turn into a writer. As expert, which he had to become willy-nilly in an extremely specialized work process, even if only in some minor respect, the reader gains access to authorship. In the Soviet Union work itself is given a voice. To present it verbally is part of a man's ability to perform the work. Literary license is now founded on polytechnic rather than specialized training and thus becomes common property.[20]

All this can easily be applied to the film, where transitions that in literature took centuries have come about in a decade. In cinematic practice, particularly in Russia, this change-over has partially become established reality. Some of the players whom we meet in Russian films are not actors in our sense but people who portray *themselves* – and primarily in their own work process. In Western Europe the capitalistic exploitation of the film denies consideration to modern man's legitimate claim to being reproduced. Under these circumstances the film industry is trying hard to spur the interest of the masses through illusion-promoting spectacles and dubious speculations.

XI

The shooting of a film, especially of a sound film, affords a spectacle unimaginable anywhere at any time before this. It presents a process in which it is impossible to assign to a spectator a viewpoint which would exclude from the actual scene such extraneous accessories as camera equipment, lighting machinery, staff assistants, etc. – unless his eye were on a line parallel with the lens. This circumstance, more than any other, renders superficial and insignificant any possible similarity between a scene in the studio and one on the stage. In the theater one is well aware of the place from which the play cannot immediately be detected as illusionary. There is no such place for the movie scene that is being shot. Its illusionary nature is that of the second degree, the result of cutting. That is to say, in the studio the mechanical equipment has penetrated so deeply into reality that its pure aspect freed from the foreign substance of equipment is the result of a special procedure, namely, the shooting by the specially adjusted camera and the mounting of the shot together with other similar ones. The equipment-free aspect of reality here has become the height of artifice; the sight of immediate reality has become an orchid in the land of technology.

Even more revealing is the comparison of these circumstances, which differ so much from those of the theater, with the situation in painting. Here the question is: How does the cameraman compare with the painter? To answer this we take recourse to an analogy with a surgical operation. The surgeon represents the polar opposite of the magician. The magician heals a sick person by the laying on of hands; the surgeon cuts into the patient's body. The magician maintains the natural distance between the patient and himself; though he reduces it very slightly by the laying on of hands, he greatly increases it by virtue of his authority. The surgeon does exactly the reverse;

he greatly diminishes the distance between himself and the patient by penetrating into the patient's body, and increases it but little by the caution with which his hand moves among the organs. In short, in contrast to the magician – who is still hidden in the medical practitioner – the surgeon at the decisive moment abstains from facing the patient man to man; rather, it is through the operation that he penetrates into him.

Magician and surgeon compare to painter and cameraman. The painter maintains in his work a natural distance from reality, the cameraman penetrates deeply into its web.[21] There is a tremendous difference between the pictures they obtain. That of the painter is a total one, that of the cameraman consists of multiple fragments which are assembled under a new law. Thus, for contemporary man the representation of reality by the film is incomparably more significant than that of the painter, since it offers, precisely because of the thoroughgoing permeation of reality with mechanical equipment, an aspect of reality which is free of all equipment. And that is what one is entitled to ask from a work of art.

XII

Mechanical reproduction of art changes the reaction of the masses toward art. The reactionary attitude toward a Picasso painting changes into the progressive reaction toward a Chaplin movie. The progressive reaction is characterized by the direct, intimate fusion of visual and emotional enjoyment with the orientation of the expert. Such fusion is of great social significance. The greater the decrease in the social significance of an art form, the sharper the distinction between criticism and enjoyment by the public. The conventional is uncritically enjoyed, and the truly new is criticized with aversion. With regard to the screen, the critical and the receptive attitudes of the public coincide. The decisive reason for this is that individual reactions are predetermined by the mass audience response they are about to produce, and this is nowhere more pronounced than in the film. The moment these responses become manifest they control each other. Again, the comparison with painting is fruitful. A painting has always had an excellent chance to be viewed by one person or by a few. The simultaneous contemplation of paintings by a large public, such as developed in the nineteenth century, is an early symptom of the crisis of painting, a crisis which was by no means occasioned exclusively by photography but rather in a relatively independent manner by the appeal of art works to the masses.

Painting simply is in no position to present an object for simultaneous collective experience, as it was possible for architecture at all times, for the epic poem in the past, and for the movie today. Although this circumstance in itself should not lead one to conclusions about the social role of painting, it does constitute a serious threat as soon as painting, under special conditions and, as it were, against its nature, is confronted directly by the masses. In the churches and monasteries of the Middle Ages and at the princely courts up to the end of the eighteenth century, a collective reception of paintings did not occur simultaneously, but by graduated and hierarchized mediation. The change that has come about is an expression of the particular conflict in which painting was implicated by the mechanical reproducibility of paintings. Although paintings began to be publicly exhibited in galleries and salons, there was no way for the masses to organize and control themselves in their reception.[22] Thus the same public which responds in a progressive manner toward a grotesque film is bound to respond in a reactionary manner to surrealism.

XIII

The characteristics of the film lie not only in the manner in which man presents himself to mechanical equipment but also in the manner in which, by means of this apparatus, man can represent his environment. A glance at occupational psychology illustrates the testing capacity of the equipment. Psychoanalysis illustrates it in a different perspective. The film has enriched our field of perception with methods which can be illustrated by those of Freudian theory. Fifty years ago, a slip of the tongue passed more or less unnoticed. Only exceptionally may such a slip have revealed dimensions of depth in a conversation which had seemed to be taking its course on the surface. Since the *Psychopathology of Everyday Life* things have changed. This book isolated and made analyzable things which had heretofore floated along unnoticed in the broad stream of perception. For the entire spectrum of optical, and now also acoustical, perception the film has brought about a similar deepening of apperception. It is only an obverse of this fact that behavior items shown in a movie can be analyzed much more precisely and from more points of view than those presented on paintings or on the stage. As compared with painting, filmed behavior lends itself more readily to analysis because of its incomparably more precise statements of the situation. In comparison with the stage scene, the filmed behavior item lends itself more readily to analysis because it can be isolated more easily. This circumstance derives its chief importance from its tendency to promote the mutual penetration of art and science. Actually, of a screened behavior item which is neatly brought out in a certain situation, like a muscle of a body, it is difficult to say which is more fascinating, its artistic value or its value for science. To demonstrate the identity of the artistic and scientific uses of photography which heretofore usually were separated will be one of the revolutionary functions of the film.[23]

By close-ups of the things around us, by focusing on hidden details of familiar objects, by exploring commonplace milieus under the ingenious guidance of the camera, the film, on the one hand, extends our comprehension of the necessities which rule our lives; on the other hand, it manages to assure us of an immense and unexpected field of action. Our taverns and our metropolitan streets, our offices and furnished rooms, our railroad stations and our factories appeared to have us locked up hopelessly. Then came the film and burst this prison-world asunder by the dynamite of the tenth of a second, so that now, in the midst of its far-flung ruins and debris, we calmly and adventurously go traveling. With the close-up, space expands; with slow motion, movement is extended. The enlargement of a snapshot does not simply render more precise what in any case was visible, though unclear: it reveals entirely new structural formations of the subject. So, too, slow motion not only presents familiar qualities of movement but reveals in them entirely unknown ones "which, far from looking like retarded rapid movements, give the effect of singularly gliding, floating, supernatural motions."[24] Evidently a different nature opens itself to the camera than opens to the naked eye – if only because an unconsciously penetrated space is substituted for a space consciously explored by man. Even if one has a general knowledge of the way people walk, one knows nothing of a person's posture during the fractional second of a stride. The act of reaching for a lighter or a spoon is familiar routine, yet we hardly know what really goes on between hand and metal, not to mention how this fluctuates with our moods. Here the camera intervenes with the resources of its lowerings and liftings, its interruptions and isolations, its extensions and accelerations, its enlargements and reductions. The camera introduces us to unconscious optics as does psychoanalysis to unconscious impulses.

XIV

One of the foremost tasks of art has always been the creation of a demand which could be fully satisfied only later.[25] The history of every art form shows critical epochs in which a certain art form aspires to effects which could be fully obtained only with a changed technical standard, that is to say, in a new art form. The extravagances and crudities of art which thus appear, particularly in the so-called decadent epochs, actually arise from the nucleus of its richest historical energies. In recent years, such barbarisms were abundant in Dadaism. It is only now that its impulse becomes discernible: Dadaism attempted to create by pictorial – and literary – means the effects which the public today seeks in the film.

Every fundamentally new, pioneering creation of demands will carry beyond its goal. Dadaism did so to the extent that it sacrificed the market values which are so characteristic of the film in favor of higher ambitions – though of course it was not conscious of such intentions as here described. The Dadaists attached much less importance to the sales value of their work than to its uselessness for contemplative immersion. The studied degradation of their material was not the least of their means to achieve this uselessness. Their poems are "word salad" containing obscenities and every imaginable waste product of language. The same is true of their paintings, on which they mounted buttons and tickets. What they intended and achieved was a relentless destruction of the aura of their creations, which they branded as reproductions with the very means of production. Before a painting of Arp's or a poem by August Stramm it is impossible to take time for contemplation and evaluation as one would before a canvas of Derain's or a poem by Rilke. In the decline of middle-class society, contemplation became a school for asocial behavior; it was countered by distraction as a variant of social conduct.[26] Dadaistic activities actually assured a rather vehement distraction by making works of art the center of scandal. One requirement was foremost: to outrage the public.

From an alluring appearance or persuasive structure of sound the work of art of the Dadaists became an instrument of ballistics. It hit the spectator like a bullet, it happened to him, thus acquiring a tactile quality. It promoted a demand for the film, the distracting element of which is also primarily tactile, being based on changes of place and focus which periodically assail the spectator. Let us compare the screen on which a film unfolds with the canvas of a painting. The painting invites the spectator to contemplation; before it the spectator can abandon himself to his associations. Before the movie frame he cannot do so. No sooner has his eye grasped a scene than it is already changed. It cannot be arrested. Duhamel, who detests the film and knows nothing of its significance, though something of its structure, notes this circumstance as follows: "I can no longer think what I want to think. My thoughts have been replaced by moving images."[27] The spectator's process of association in view of these images is indeed interrupted by their constant, sudden change. This constitues the shock effect of the film, which, like all shocks, should be cushioned by heightened presence of mind.[28] By means of its technical structure, the film has taken the physical shock effect out of the wrappers in which Dadaism had, as it were, kept it inside the moral shock effect.[29]

XV

The mass is a matrix from which all traditional behavior toward works of art issues today in a new form. Quantity has been transmuted into quality. The greatly increased mass of participants has produced a change in the mode of participation. The fact that the new mode of participation first appeared in a disreputable form must not confuse the spectator. Yet some people have launched spirited attacks against precisely this superficial aspect. Among these, Duhamel has expressed himself in the most radical manner. What he objects to most is the kind of participation which the movie elicits from the masses. Duhamel calls the movie "a pastime for helots, a diversion for uneducated, wretched, worn-out creatures who are consumed by their worries . . . , a spectacle which requires no concentration and presupposes no intelligence . . . , which kindles no light in the heart and awakens no hope other than the ridiculous one of someday becoming a "star" in Los Angeles."[30] Clearly, this is at bottom the same ancient lament that the masses seek distraction whereas art demands concentration from the spectator. That is a commonplace. The question remains whether it provides a platform for the analysis of the film. A closer look is needed here. Distraction and concentration form polar opposites which may be stated as follows: A man who concentrates before a work of art is absorbed by it. He enters into this work of art the way legend tells of the Chinese painter when he viewed his finished painting. In contrast, the distracted mass absorbs the work of art. This is most obvious with regard to buildings. Architecture has always represented the prototype of a work of art the reception of which is consummated by a collectivity in a state of distraction. The laws of its reception are most instructive.

Buildings have been man's companions since primeval times. Many art forms have developed and perished. Tragedy begins with the Greeks, is extinguished with them, and after centuries its "rules" only are revived. The epic poem, which had its origin in the youth of nations, expires in Europe at the end of the Renaissance. Panel painting is a creation of the Middle Ages, and nothing guarantees its uninterrupted existence. But the human need for shelter is lasting. Architecture has never been idle. Its history is more ancient than that of any other art, and its claim to being a living force has significance in every attempt to comprehend the relationship of the masses to art. Buildings are appropriated in a twofold manner: by use and by perception – or rather, by touch and sight. Such appropriation cannot be understood in terms of the attentive concentration of a tourist before a famous building. On the tactile side there is no counterpart to contemplation on the optical side. Tactile appropriation is accomplished not so much by attention as by habit. As regards architecture, habit determines to a large extent even optical reception. The latter, too, occurs much less through rapt attention than by noticing the object in incidental fashion. This mode of appropriation, developed with reference to architecture, in certain circumstances acquires canonical value. For the tasks which face the human apparatus of perception at the turning points of history cannot be solved by optical means, that is, by contemplation, alone. They are mastered gradually by habit, under the guidance of tactile appropriation.

The distracted person, too, can form habits. More, the ability to master certain tasks in a state of distraction proves that their solution has become a matter of habit. Distraction as provided by art presents a covert control of the extent to which new tasks have become soluble by apperception. Since, moreover, individuals are tempted to avoid such tasks, art will tackle the most difficult and most important ones where it is able to mobilize the masses. Today it does so in the film. Reception in a state of distraction, which is increasing noticeably in all fields of art and is symptomatic of profound changes in apperception, finds in the film its true means of exercise. The film with its shock effect meets this mode of reception half-way. The film makes the cult value recede into the background not only by putting the public in the position of the critic, but also by the fact that at the movies this position requires no attention. The public is an examiner, but an absent-minded one.

Epilogue

The growing proletarianization of modern man and the increasing formation of masses are two aspects of the same process. Fascism attempts to organize the newly created proletarian masses without affecting the property structure which the masses strive to eliminate. Fascism sees its salvation in giving these masses not their right, but instead a chance to express themselves.[31] The masses have a right to change property relations; Fascism seeks to give them an expression while preserving property. The logical result of Fascism is the introduction of aesthetics into political life. The violation of the masses, whom Fascism, with its *Führer* cult, forces to their knees, has its counterpart in the violation of an apparatus which is pressed into the production of ritual values.

All efforts to render politics aesthetic culminate in one thing: war. War and war only can set a goal for mass movements on the largest scale while respecting the traditional property system. This is the political formula for the situation. The technological formula may be stated as follows: Only war makes it possible to mobilize all of today's technical resources while maintaining the property system. It goes without saying that the Fascist apotheosis of war does not employ such arguments. Still, Marinetti says in his manifesto on the Ethiopian colonial war: "For twenty-seven years we Futurists have rebelled against the branding of war as antiaesthetic.... Accordingly we state: ...War is beautiful because it establishes man's dominion over the subjugated machinery by means of gas masks, terrifying megaphones, flame throwers, and small tanks. War is beautiful because it initiates the dreamt-of metalization of the human body. War is beautiful because it enriches a flowering meadow with the fiery orchids of machine guns. War is beautiful because it combines the gunfire, the cannonades, the cease-fire, the scents, and the stench of putrefaction into a symphony. War is beautiful because it creates new architecture, like that of the big tanks, the geometrical formation flights, the smoke spirals from burning villages, and many others.... Poets and artists of Futurism!... remember these principles of an aesthetics of war so that your struggle for a new literature and a new graphic art... may be illumined by them!"

The manifesto has the virtue of clarity. Its formulations deserve to be accepted by dialecticians. To the latter, the aesthetics of today's war appears as follows: If the natural utilization of productive forces is impeded by the property system, the increase in technical devices, in speed, and in the sources of energy will press for an unnatural utilization, and this is found in war. The destructiveness of war furnishes proof that society has not been mature enough to incorporate technology as its organ, that technology has not been sufficiently developed to cope with the elemental forces of society. The horrible features of imperialistic warfare are attributable to the discrepancy between the tremendous means of production and their inadequate utilization in the process of production – in other words, to unemployment and the lack of markets. Imperialistic war is a rebellion of technology which collects, in the form of "human material," the claims to which society has denied its natural material. Instead of draining rivers, society directs a human stream into a bed of trenches; instead of dropping seeds from airplanes, it drops incendiary bombs over cities; and through gas warfare the aura is abolished in a new way.

"*Fiat ars – pereat mundus*," says Fascism, and, as Marinetti admits, expects war to supply the artistic gratification of a sense perception that has been changed by technology. This is evidently the consummation of "*l'artpourl'art*." Mankind, which in Homer's time was an object of contemplation for the Olympian gods, now is one for itself. Its self-alienation has reached such a degree that it can experience its own destruction as an aesthetic pleasure of the first order. This is the situation of politics which Fascism is rendering aesthetic. Communism responds by politicizing art.

Notes

1   Quoted from Paul Valéry, *Aesthetics*, "The Conquest of Ubiquity," translated by Ralph Manheim, p. 225. Pantheon Books, Bollingen Series, New York, 1964.

2   Of course, the history of a work of art encompasses more than this. The history of the "Mona Lisa," for instance, encompasses the kind and number of its copies made in the 17th, 18th, and 19th centuries.

3   Precisely because authenticity is not reproducible, the intensive penetration of certain (mechanical) processes of reproduction was instrumental in differentiating and grading authenticity. To develop such differentiations was an important function of the trade in works of art. The invention of the woodcut may be said to have struck at the root of the quality of authenticity even before its late flowering. To be sure, at the time of its origin a medieval picture of the Madonna could not yet be said to be "authentic." It became "authentic" only during the succeeding centuries and perhaps most strikingly so during the last one.

4   The poorest provincial staging of *Faust* is superior to a Faust film in that, ideally, it competes with the first performance at Weimar. Before the screen it is unprofitable to remember traditional contents which might come to mind before the stage – for instance, that Goethe's friend Johann Heinrich Merck is hidden in Mephisto, and the like.

5   Abel Gance, "Le Temps de l'image est venu," *L'Art cinématographique*, vol. 2, pp. 94 f, Paris, 1927.

6   To satisfy the human interest of the masses may mean to have one's social function removed from the field of vision. Nothing guarantees that a portraitist of today, when painting a famous surgeon at the breakfast table in the midst of his family, depicts his social function more precisely than a painter of the 17th century who portrayed his medical doctors as representing this profession, like Rembrandt in his "Anatomy Lesson."

7   The definition of the aura as a "unique phenomenon of a distance however close it may be" represents nothing but the formulation of the cult value of the work of art in categories of space and time perception. Distance is the opposite of closeness. The essentially distant object is the unapproachable one. Unapproachability is indeed a major quality of the cult image. True to its nature, it remains "distant, however close it may be." The closeness which one may gain from its subject matter does not impair the distance which it retains in its appearance.

8   To the extent to which the cult value of the painting is secularized the ideas of its fundamental uniqueness lose distinctness. In the imagination of the beholder the unique-ness of the phenomena which hold sway in the cult image is more and more displaced by the empirical uniqueness of the creator or of his creative achievement. To be sure, never completely so; the concept of authenticity always transcends mere genuineness. (This is particularly apparent in the collector who always retains some traces of the fetishist and who, by owning the work of art, shares in its ritual power.) Nevertheless, the function of the concept of authenticity remains determinate in the evaluation of art; with the secularization of art, authenticity displaces the cult value of the work.

9   In the case of films, mechanical reproduction is not, as with literature and painting, an external condition for mass distribution. Mechanical reproduction is inherent in the very technique of film production. This technique not only permits in the most direct way but virtually causes mass distribution. It enforces distribution because the production of a film is so expensive that an individual who, for instance, might afford to buy a painting no longer can afford to buy a film. In 1927 it was calculated that a major film, in order to pay its way, had to reach an audience of nine million. With the sound film, to be sure, a setback in its international distribution occurred at first: audiences became limited by language barriers. This coincided with the Fascist emphasis on national interests. It is more important to focus on this connection with Fascism than on this setback, which was soon minimized

by synchronization. The simultaneity of both phenomena is attributable to the depression. The same disturbances which, on a larger scale, led to an attempt to maintain the existing property structure by sheer force led the endangered film capital to speed up the development of the sound film. The introduction of the sound film brought about a temporary relief, not only because it again brought the masses into the theaters but also because it merged new capital from the electrical industry with that of the film industry. Thus, viewed from the outside, the sound film promoted national interests, but seen from the inside it helped to internationalize film production even more than previously.

10   This polarity cannot come into its own in the aesthetics of Idealism. Its idea of beauty comprises these polar opposites without differentiating between them and consequently excludes their polarity. Yet in Hegel this polarity announces itself as clearly as possible within the limits of Idealism. We quote from his *Philosophy of History*:

> Images were known of old. Piety at an early time required them for worship, but it could do without *beautiful* images. These might even be disturbing. In every beautiful painting there is also something nonspiritual, merely external, but its spirit speaks to man through its beauty. Worshipping, conversely, is concerned with the work as an object, for it is but a spiritless stupor of the soul....Fine art has arisen...in the church..., although it has already gone beyond its principle as art.

Likewise, the following passage from *The Philosophy of Fine Art* indicates that Hegel sensed a problem here.

> We are beyond the stage of reverence for works of art as divine and objects deserving our worship. The impression they produce is one of a more reflective kind, and the emotions they arouse require a higher test.... (G. W. F. Hegel, *The Philosophy of Fine Art*, trans., with notes, by F. P. B. Osmaston, vol. I, p. 12, London, 1920.)

The transition from the first kind of artistic reception to the second characterizes the history of artistic reception in general. Apart from that, a certain oscillation between these two polar modes of reception can be demonstrated for each work of art. Take the Sistine Madonna. Since Hubert Grimme's research it has been known that the Madonna originally was painted for the purpose of exhibition. Grimme's research was inspired by the question: What is the purpose of the molding in the foreground of the painting which the two cupids lean upon? How, Grimme asked further, did Raphael come to furnish the sky with two draperies? Research proved that the Madonna had been commissioned for the public lying-in-state of Pope Sixtus. The Popes lay in state in a certain side chapel of St. Peter's. On that occasion Raphael's picture had been fastened in a nichelike background of the chapel, supported by the coffin. In this picture Raphael portrays the Madonna approaching the papal coffin in clouds from the background of the niche, which was demarcated by green drapes. At the obsequies of Sixtus a pre-eminent exhibition value of Raphael's picture was taken advantage of. Some time later it was placed on the high altar in the church of the Black Friars at Piacenza. The reason for this exile is to be found in the Roman rites which forbid the use of paintings exhibited at obsequies as cult objects on the high altar. This regulation devalued Raphael's picture to some degree. In order to obtain an adequate price nevertheless, the Papal See resolved to add to the bargain the tacit toleration of the picture above the high altar. To avoid attention the picture was given to the monks of the far-off provincial town.

11 Bertolt Brecht, on a different level, engaged in analogous reflections: "If the concept of "work of art" can no longer be applied to the thing that emerges once the work is transformed into a commodity, we have to eliminate this concept with cautious care but without fear, lest we liquidate the function of the very thing as well. For it has to go through this phase without mental reservation, and not as noncommittal deviation from the straight path; rather, what happens here with the work of art will change it fundamentally and erase its past to such an extent that should the old concept be taken up again – and it will, why not? – it will no longer stir any memory of the thing it once designated."

12 Abel Gance, *op. cit.*, pp. 100–1.

13 Séverin-Mars, quoted by Abel Gance, *op. cit.*, p. 100.

14 Alexandre Arnoux, *Cinéma pris*, 1929, p. 28.

15 Franz Werfel, "Ein Sommernachtstraum, Ein Film von Shakespeare und Reinhardt," *Neues Wiener Journal*, cited in *Lu* 15, November, 1935.

16 "The film ... provides – or could provide – useful insight into the details of human actions.... Character is never used as a source of motivation; the inner life of the persons never supplies the principal cause of the plot and seldom is its main result." (Bertolt Brecht, *Versuche*, "Der Dreigroschenprozess," p. 268.) The expansion of the field of the testable which mechanical equipment brings about for the actor corresponds to the extraordinary expansion of the field of the testable brought about for the individual through economic conditions. Thus, vocational aptitude tests become constantly more important. What matters in these tests are segmental performances of the individual. The film shot and the vocational aptitude test are taken before a committee of experts. The camera director in the studio occupies a place identical with that of the examiner during aptitude tests.

17 Luigi Pirandello, *Si Gira*, quoted by Léon Pierre-Quint, "Signification du cinéma," *L'Art cinématographique, op. cit.*, pp. 14–15.

18 Rudolf Arnheim, *Film als Kunst*, Berlin, 1932, pp. 176 f. In this context certain seemingly unimportant details in which the film director deviates from stage practices gain in interest. Such is the attempt to let the actor play without make-up, as made among others by Dreyer in his *Jeanne d'Arc*. Dreyer spent months seeking the forty actors who constitute the Inquisitors' tribunal. The search for these actors resembled that for stage properties that are hard to come by. Dreyer made every effort to avoid resemblances of age, build, and physiognomy. If the actor thus becomes a stage property, this latter, on the other hand, frequently functions as actor. At least it is not unusual for the film to assign a role to the stage property. Instead of choosing at random from a great wealth of examples, let us concentrate on a particularly convincing one. A clock that is working will always be a disturbance on the stage. There it cannot be permitted its function of measuring time. Even in a naturalistic play, astronomical time would clash with theatrical time. Under these circumstances it is highly revealing that the film can, whenever appropriate, use time as measured by a clock. From this more than from many other touches it may clearly be recognized that under certain circumstances each and every prop in a film may assume important functions. From here it is but one step to Pudovkin's statement that "the playing of an actor which is connected with an object and is built around it ... is always one of the strongest methods of cinematic construction." (W. Pudovkin, *Filmregie und Filmmanuskript*, Berlin, 1928, p. 126.) The film is the first art form capable of demonstrating how matter plays tricks on man. Hence, films can be an excellent means of materialistic representation.

19   The change noted here in the method of exhibition caused by mechanical reproduction applies to politics as well. The present crisis of the bourgeois democracies comprises a crisis of the conditions which determine the public presentation of the rulers. Democracies exhibit a member of government directly and personally before the nation's representatives. Parliament is his public. Since the innovations of camera and recording equipment make it possible for the orator to become audible and visible to an unlimited number of persons, the presentation of the man of politics before camera and recording equipment becomes paramount. Parliaments, as much as theaters, are deserted. Radio and film not only affect the function of the professional actor but likewise the function of those who also exhibit themselves before this mechanical equipment, those who govern. Though their tasks may be different, the change affects equally the actor and the ruler. The trend is toward establishing controllable and transferrable skills under certain social conditions. This results in a new selection, a selection before the equipment from which the star and the dictator emerge victorious.

20   The privileged character of the respective techniques is lost. Aldous Huxley writes:

> Advances in technology have led . . . to vulgarity. . . . Process reproduction and the rotary press have made possible the indefinite multiplication of writing and pictures. Universal education and relatively high wages have created an enormous public who know how to read and can afford to buy reading and pictorial matter. A great industry has been called into existence in order to supply these commodities. Now, artistic talent is a very rare phenomenon; whence it follows . . . that, at every epoch and in all countries, most art has been bad. But the proportion of trash in the total artistic output is greater now than at any other period. That it must be so is a matter of simple arithmetic. The population of Western Europe has a little more than doubled during the last century. But the amount of reading – and seeing – matter has increased, I should imagine, at least twenty and possibly fifty or even a hundred times. If there were n men of talent in a population of x millions, there will presumably be 2n men of talent among 2x millions. The situation may be summed up thus. For every page of print and pictures published a century ago, twenty or perhaps even a hundred pages are published today. But for every man of talent then living, there are now only two men of talent. It may be of course that, thanks to universal education, many potential talents which in the past would have been still-born are now enabled to realize themselves. Let us assume, then, that there are now three or even four men of talent to every one of earlier times. It still remains true to say that the consumption of reading – and seeing – matter has far outstripped the natural production of gifted writers and draughtsmen. It is the same with hearing-matter. Prosperity, the gramophone and the radio have created an audience of hearers who consume an amount of hearing-matter that has increased out of all proportion to the increase of population and the consequent natural increase of talented musicians. It follows from all this that in all the arts the output of trash is both absolutely and relatively greater than it was in the past; and that it must remain greater for just so long as the world continues to consume the present inordinate quantities of reading-matter, seeing-matter, and hearing-matter.   (Aldous Huxley, *Beyond the Mexique Bay. A Traveller's Journal*, London, 1949, pp. 274 ff. First published in 1934.)

This mode of observation is obviously not progressive.

21 The boldness of the cameraman is indeed comparable to that of the surgeon. Luc
    Durtain lists among specific technical sleights of hand those "which are required in
    surgery in the case of certain difficult operations. I choose as an example a case from
    oto-rhinolaryngology; . . . the so-called endonasal perspective procedure; or I refer to the
    acrobatic tricks of larynx surgery which have to be performed following the reversed
    picture in the laryngoscope. I might also speak of ear surgery which suggests the precision
    work of watchmakers. What range of the most subtle muscular acrobatics is required from
    the man who wants to repair or save the human body! We have only to think of the
    couching of a cataract where there is virtually a debate of steel with nearly fluid tissue, or of
    the major abdominal operations (laparotomy)." – Luc Durtain, *op. cit.*

22 This mode of observation may seem crude, but as the great theoretician Leonardo has
    shown, crude modes of observation may at times be usefully adduced. Leonardo compares
    painting and music as follows: "Painting is superior to music because, unlike unfortunate
    music, it does not have to die as soon as it is born. . . . Music which is consumed in the very
    act of its birth is inferior to painting which the use of varnish has rendered eternal."
    (Trattato I, 29.)

23 Renaissance painting offers a revealing analogy to this situation. The incomparable devel-
    opment of this art and its significance rested not least on the integration of a number of
    new sciences, or at least of new scientific data. Renaissance painting made use of anatomy
    and perspective, of mathematics, meteorology, and chromatology. Valéry writes: "What
    could be further from us than the strange claim of a Leonardo to whom painting was a
    supreme goal and the ultimate demonstration of knowledge? Leonardo was convinced
    that painting demanded universal knowledge, and he did not even shrink from a theoret-
    ical analysis which to us is stunning because of its very depth and precision. . . ." – Paul
    Valéry, *Pièces sur l'art*, "Autour de Corot," Paris, p. 191.

24 Rudolf Arnheim, *loc. cit.*, p. 138.

25 "The work of art," says André Breton, "is valuable only in so far as it is vibrated by the
    reflexes of the future." Indeed, every developed art form intersects three lines of devel-
    opment. Technology works toward a certain form of art. Before the advent of the
    film there were photo booklets with pictures which flitted by the onlooker upon
    pressure of the thumb, thus portraying a boxing bout or a tennis match. Then there
    were the slot machines in bazaars; their picture sequences were produced by the turning of
    a crank.
      Secondly, the traditional art forms in certain phases of their development strenuously
    work toward effects which later are effortlessly attained by the new ones. Before the rise of
    the movie the Dadaists' performances tried to create an audience reaction which Chaplin
    later evoked in a more natural way.
      Thirdly, unspectacular social changes often promote a change in receptivity which will
    benefit the new art form. Before the movie had begun to create its public, pictures that
    were no longer immobile captivated an assembled audience in the so-called *Kaiserpanor-
    ama*. Here the public assembled before a screen into which stereoscopes were mounted,
    one to each beholder. By a mechanical process individual pictures appeared briefly before
    the stereoscopes, then made way for others. Edison still had to use similar devices in
    presenting the first movie strip before the film screen and projection were known. This
    strip was presented to a small public which stared into the apparatus in which the
    succession of pictures was reeling off. Incidentally, the institution of the *Kaiserpanorama*
    shows very clearly a dialectic of the development. Shortly before the movie turned the
    reception of pictures into a collective one, the individual viewing of pictures in these

swiftly outmoded establishments came into play once more with an intensity comparable
to that of the ancient priest beholding the statue of a divinity in the cella.

26   The theological archetype of this contemplation is the awareness of being alone with one's
God. Such awareness, in the heyday of the bourgeoisie, went to strengthen the freedom to
shake off clerical tutelage. During the decline of the bourgeoisie this awareness had to take
into account the hidden tendency to withdraw from public affairs those forces which the
individual draws upon in his communion with God.

27   Georges Duhamel, *Scènes de la vie future*, Paris, 1930, p. 52.

28   The film is the art form that is in keeping with the increased threat to his life which
modern man has to face. Man's need to expose himself to shock effects is his adjustment
to the dangers threatening him. The film corresponds to profound changes in the
apperceptive apparatus – changes that are experienced on an individual scale by the man
in the street in big-city traffic, on a historical scale by every present-day citizen.

29   As for Dadaism, insights important for Cubism and Futurism are to be gained from the
movie. Both appear as deficient attempts of art to accommodate the pervasion of reality by
the apparatus. In contrast to the film, these schools did not try to use the apparatus as such
for the artistic presentation of reality, but aimed at some sort of alloy in the joint
presentation of reality and apparatus. In Cubism, the premonition that this apparatus
will be structurally based on optics plays a dominant part; in Futurism, it is the premonition of the effects of this apparatus which are brought out by the rapid sequence of the
film strip.

30   Duhamel, *op. cit.*, p. 58.

31   One technical feature is significant here, especially with regard to newsreels, the propa-
gandist importance of which can hardly be overestimated. Mass reproduction is aided
especially by the reproduction of masses. In big parades and monster rallies, in sports
events, and in war, all of which nowadays are captured by camera and sound recording, the
masses are brought face to face with themselves. This process, whose significance need not
be stressed, is intimately connected with the development of the techniques of reproduction and photography. Mass movements are usually discerned more clearly by a camera
than by the naked eye. A bird's-eye view best captures gatherings of hundreds of thousands. And even though such a view may be as accessible to the human eye as it is to the
camera, the image received by the eye cannot be enlarged the way a negative is enlarged.
This means that mass movements, including war, constitute a form of human behavior
which particularly favors mechanical equipment.

4

The Culture Industry: Enlightenment as Mass Deception*

Max Horkheimer and Theodor W. Adorno

The sociological theory that the loss of the support of objectively established religion, the dissolution of the last remnants of precapitalism, together with technological and social differentiation or specialization, have led to cultural chaos is disproved every day; for culture now impresses the same stamp on everything. Films, radio and magazines make up a system which is uniform as a whole and in every part. Even the aesthetic activities of political opposites are one in their enthusiastic obedience to the rhythm of the iron system. The decorative industrial management buildings and exhibition centers in authoritarian countries are much the same as anywhere else. The huge gleaming towers that shoot up everywhere are outward signs of the ingenious planning of international concerns, toward which the unleashed entrepreneurial system (whose monuments are a mass of gloomy houses and business premises in grimy, spiritless cities) was already hastening. Even now the older houses just outside the concrete city centers look like slums, and the new bungalows on the outskirts are at one with the flimsy structures of world fairs in their praise of technical progress and their built-in demand to be discarded after a short while like empty food cans. Yet the city housing projects designed to perpetuate the individual as a supposedly independent unit in a small hygienic dwelling make him all the more subservient to his adversary – the absolute power of capitalism. Because the inhabitants, as producers and as consumers, are drawn into the center in search of work and pleasure, all the living units crystallize into well-organized complexes. The striking unity of microcosm and macrocosm presents men with a model of their culture: the false identity of the general and the particular. Under monopoly all mass culture is identical, and the lines of its artificial framework begin to show through. The people at the top are no longer so interested in concealing monopoly: as its violence becomes more open, so its power grows. Movies and radio need no longer pretend to be art. The truth that they are just business is made into an ideology in order to justify the rubbish they

* From Max Horkheimer and Theodor W. Adorno, *The Dialectic of Enlightenment* (New York: Continuum, 1995), pp. 120–67; English translation copyright © 1972 by Herder & Herder. Reprinted by permission of Continuum International Publishing Group Inc.

deliberately produce. They call themselves industries; and when their directors' incomes are published, any doubt about the social utility of the finished products is removed.

Interested parties explain the culture industry in technological terms. It is alleged that because millions participate in it, certain reproduction processes are necessary that inevitably require identical needs in innumerable places to be satisfied with identical goods. The technical contrast between the few production centers and the large number of widely dispersed consumption points is said to demand organization and planning by management. Furthermore, it is claimed that standards were based in the first place on consumers' needs, and for that reason were accepted with so little resistance. The result is the circle of manipulation and retroactive need in which the unity of the system grows ever stronger. No mention is made of the fact that the basis on which technology acquires power over society is the power of those whose economic hold over society is greatest. A technological rationale is the rationale of domination itself. It is the coercive nature of society alienated from itself. Automobiles, bombs, and movies keep the whole thing together until their leveling element shows its strength in the very wrong which it furthered. It has made the technology of the culture industry no more than the achievement of standardization and mass production, sacrificing whatever involved a distinction between the logic of the work and that of the social system. This is the result not of a law of movement in technology as such but of its function in today's economy. The need which might resist central control has already been suppressed by the control of the individual consciousness. The step from the telephone to the radio has clearly distinguished the roles. The former still allowed the subscriber to play the role of subject, and was liberal. The latter is democratic: it turns all participants into listeners and authoritatively subjects them to broadcast programs which are all exactly the same. No machinery of rejoinder has been devised, and private broadcasters are denied any freedom. They are confined to the apocryphal field of the "amateur," and also have to accept organization from above. But any trace of spontaneity from the public in official broadcasting is controlled and absorbed by talent scouts, studio competitions and official programs of every kind selected by professionals. Talented performers belong to the industry long before it displays them; otherwise they would not be so eager to fit in. The attitude of the public, which ostensibly and actually favors the system of the culture industry, is a part of the system and not an excuse for it. If one branch of art follows the same formula as one with a very different medium and content; if the dramatic intrigue of broadcast soap operas becomes no more than useful material for showing how to master technical problems at both ends of the scale of musical experience – real jazz or a cheap imitation; or if a movement from a Beethoven symphony is crudely "adapted" for a film sound-track in the same way as a Tolstoy novel is garbled in a film script: then the claim that this is done to satisfy the spontaneous wishes of the public is no more than hot air. We are closer to the facts if we explain these phenomena as inherent in the technical and personnel apparatus which, down to its last cog, itself forms part of the economic mechanism of selection. In addition there is the agreement – or at least the determination – of all executive authorities not to produce or sanction anything that in any way differs from their own rules, their own ideas about consumers, or above all themselves.

In our age the objective social tendency is incarnate in the hidden subjective purposes of company directors, the foremost among whom are in the most powerful sectors of industry – steel, petroleum, electricity, and chemicals. Culture monopolies are weak and dependent in comparison. They cannot afford to neglect their appeasement of the real holders of power if their sphere of activity in mass society (a sphere producing a specific type of commodity which anyhow is still too closely bound up with easygoing liberalism and Jewish intellectuals) is not to undergo a series of purges. The dependence of the most powerful broadcasting company on the electrical industry, or of the motion picture industry on the banks, is characteristic of the whole sphere, whose individual branches are themselves economically interwoven. All are in such close contact that the extreme concentration of mental forces allows demarcation lines between different firms and technical branches to be ignored. The ruthless unity in the culture industry is evidence of what will happen in politics. Marked differentiations such as those of A and B films, or of stories in magazines in different price ranges, depend not so much on subject matter as on classifying, organizing, and labeling consumers. Something is provided for all so that none may escape; the distinctions are emphasized and extended. The public is catered for with a hierarchical range of mass-produced products of varying quality, thus advancing the rule of complete quantification. Everybody must behave (as if spontaneously) in accordance with his previously determined and indexed level, and choose the category of mass product turned out for his type. Consumers appear as statistics on research organization charts, and are divided by income groups into red, green, and blue areas; the technique is that used for any type of propaganda.

How formalized the procedure is can be seen when the mechanically differentiated products prove to be all alike in the end. That the difference between the Chrysler range and General Motors products is basically illusory strikes every child with a keen interest in varieties. What connoisseurs discuss as good or bad points serve only to perpetuate the semblance of competition and range of choice. The same applies to the Warner Brothers and Metro Goldwyn Mayer productions. But even the differences between the more expensive and cheaper models put out by the same firm steadily diminish: for automobiles, there are such differences as the number of cylinders, cubic capacity, details of patented gadgets; and for films there are the number of stars, the extravagant use of technology, labor, and equipment, and the introduction of the latest psychological formulas. The universal criterion of merit is the amount of "conspicuous production," of blatant cash investment. The varying budgets in the culture industry do not bear the slightest relation to factual values, to the meaning of the products themselves. Even the technical media are relentlessly forced into uniformity. Television aims at a synthesis of radio and film, and is held up only because the interested parties have not yet reached agreement, but its consequences will be quite enormous and promise to intensify the impoverishment of aesthetic matter so drastically, that by tomorrow the thinly veiled identity of all industrial culture products can come triumphantly out into the open, derisively fulfilling the Wagnerian dream of the *Gesamtkunstwerk* – the fusion of all the arts in one work. The alliance of word, image, and music is all the more perfect than in *Tristan* because the sensuous elements which all approvingly reflect the surface of social reality are in principle embodied in the same technical process, the unity of which becomes its distinctive content. This process integrates all the elements of the production, from the novel (shaped with an eye to the film) to the last sound effect. It is the triumph of invested capital, whose title as absolute master is etched deep into the hearts of the dispossessed in the employment line; it is the meaningful content of every film, whatever plot the production team may have selected.

The man with leisure has to accept what the culture manufacturers offer him. Kant's formalism still expected a contribution from the individual, who was thought to relate the varied experiences of the senses to fundamental concepts; but industry robs the individual of his function. Its prime service to the customer is to do his schematizing for him. Kant said that there was a secret mechanism in the soul which prepared direct intuitions in such a way that they could be fitted into the system of pure reason. But today that secret has been deciphered. While the mechanism is to all appearances planned by those who serve up the data of experience, that is, by the culture industry, it is in fact forced upon the latter by the power of society, which remains irrational, however we may try to rationalize it; and this inescapable force is processed by commercial agencies so that they give an artificial impression of being in command. There is nothing left for the consumer to classify. Producers have done it for him. Art for the masses has destroyed the dream but still conforms to the tenets of that dreaming idealism which critical idealism balked at. Everything derives from consciousness: for Malebranche and Berkeley, from the consciousness of God; in mass art, from the consciousness of the production team. Not only are the hit songs, stars, and soap operas cyclically recurrent and rigidly invariable types, but the specific content of the entertainment itself is derived from them and only appears to change. The details are interchangeable. The short interval sequence which was effective in a hit song, the hero's momentary fall from grace (which he accepts as good sport), the rough treatment which the beloved gets from the male star, the latter's rugged defiance of the spoilt heiress, are, like all the other details, ready-made clichés to be slotted in anywhere; they never do anything more than fulfill the purpose allotted them in the overall plan. Their whole *raison d'être* is to confirm it by being its constituent parts. As soon as the film begins, it is quite clear how it will end, and who will be rewarded, punished, or forgotten. In light music, once the trained ear has heard the first notes of the hit song, it can guess what is coming and feel flattered when it does come. The average length of the short story has to be rigidly adhered to. Even gags, effects, and jokes are calculated like the setting in which they are placed. They are the responsibility of special experts and their narrow range makes it easy for them to be apportioned in the office. The development of the culture industry has led to the predominance of the effect, the obvious touch, and the technical detail over the work itself – which once expressed an idea, but was liquidated together with the idea. When the detail won its freedom, it became rebellious and, in the period from Romanticism to Expressionism, asserted itself as free expression, as a vehicle of protest against the organization. In music the single harmonic effect obliterated the awareness of form as a whole; in painting the individual color was stressed at the expense of pictorial composition; and in the novel psychology became more important than structure. The totality of the culture industry has put an end to this. Though concerned exclusively with effects, it crushes their insubordination and makes them subserve the formula, which replaces the work. The same fate is inflicted on whole and parts alike. The whole inevitably bears no relation to the details – just like the career of a successful man into which everything is made to fit as an illustration or a proof, whereas it is nothing more than the sum of all those idiotic events. The so-called dominant idea is like a file which ensures order but not coherence. The whole and the parts are alike; there is no antithesis and no connection. Their prearranged harmony is a mockery of what had to be striven after in the great bourgeois works of art. In Germany the graveyard stillness of the dictatorship already hung over the gayest films of the democratic era.

The whole world is made to pass through the filter of the culture industry. The old experience of the movie-goer, who sees the world outside as an extension of the film he has just left (because the latter is intent upon reproducing the world of everyday perceptions), is now the producer's guideline. The more intensely and flawlessly his techniques duplicate empirical objects, the easier it is today for the illusion to prevail that the outside world is the straightforward continuation of that presented on the screen. This purpose has been furthered by mechanical reproduction since the lightning takeover by the sound film.

Real life is becoming indistinguishable from the movies. The sound film, far surpassing the theater of illusion, leaves no room for imagination or reflection on the part of the audience, who is unable to respond within the structure of the film, yet deviate from its precise detail without losing the thread of the story; hence the film forces its victims to equate it directly with reality. The stunting of the mass-media consumer's powers of imagination and spontaneity does not have to be traced back to any psychological mechanisms; he must ascribe the loss of those attributes to the objective nature of the products themselves, especially to the most characteristic of them, the sound film. They are so designed that quickness, powers of observation, and experience are undeniably needed to apprehend them at all; yet sustained thought is out of the question if the spectator is not to miss the relentless rush of facts. Even though the effort required for his response is semi-automatic, no scope is left for the imagination. Those who are so absorbed by the world of the movie – by its images, gestures, and words – that they are unable to supply what really makes it a world, do not have to dwell on particular points of its mechanics during a screening. All the other films and products of the entertainment industry which they have seen have taught them what to expect; they react automatically. The might of industrial society is lodged in men's minds. The entertainments manufacturers know that their products will be consumed with alertness even when the customer is distraught, for each of them is a model of the huge economic machinery which has always sustained the masses, whether at work or at leisure – which is akin to work. From every sound film and every broadcast program the social effect can be inferred which is exclusive to none but is shared by all alike. The culture industry as a whole has molded men as a type unfailingly reproduced in every product. All the agents of this process, from the producer to the women's clubs, take good care that the simple reproduction of this mental state is not nuanced or extended in any way.

The art historians and guardians of culture who complain of the extinction in the West of a basic style-determining power are wrong. The stereotyped appropriation of everything, even the inchoate, for the purposes of mechanical reproduction surpasses the rigor and general currency of any "real style," in the sense in which cultural *cognoscenti* celebrate the organic pre-capitalist past. No Palestrina could be more of a purist in eliminating every unprepared and unresolved discord than the jazz arranger in suppressing any development which does not conform to the jargon. When jazzing up Mozart he changes him not only when he is too serious or too difficult but when he harmonizes the melody in a different way, perhaps more simply, than is customary now. No medieval builder can have scrutinized the subjects for church windows and sculptures more suspiciously than the studio hierarchy scrutinizes a work by Balzac or Hugo before finally approving it. No medieval theologian could have determined the degree of the torment to be suffered by the damned in accordance with the *ordo* of divine love more meticulously than the producers of shoddy epics calculate the torture to be undergone by the hero or the exact point to which the leading lady's hemline shall be raised. The explicit and implicit, exoteric and esoteric catalog of the forbidden and tolerated is so extensive that it not only defines the area of freedom but is all-powerful inside it. Everything down to the last detail is shaped accordingly. Like its counterpart, avant-garde art, the entertainment industry determines its own language, down to its very syntax and vocabulary, by the use of anathema. The constant pressure to produce new effects (which must conform to the old pattern) serves merely as another rule to increase the power of the conventions when any single effect threatens to slip through the net. Every detail is so firmly stamped with sameness that nothing can appear which is not marked at birth, or does not meet with approval at first sight. And the star performers, whether they produce or reproduce, use this jargon as freely and fluently and with as much gusto as if it were the very language which it silenced long ago. Such is the ideal of what is natural in this field of activity, and its influence becomes all the more powerful, the more technique is perfected and diminishes the tension between the finished product and everyday life. The paradox of this routine, which is essentially travesty, can be detected and is often predominant in everything that the culture industry turns out. A jazz musician who is playing a piece of serious music, one of Beethoven's simplest minuets, syncopates it involuntarily and will smile superciliously when asked to follow the normal divisions of the beat. This is the "nature" which, complicated by the ever-present and extravagant demands of the specific medium, constitutes the new style and is a "system of non-culture, to which one might even concede a certain "unity of style" if it really made any sense to speak of stylized barbarity."[1]

The universal imposition of this stylized mode can even go beyond what is quasi-officially sanctioned or forbidden; today a hit song is more readily forgiven for not observing the 32 beats or the compass of the ninth than for containing even the most clandestine melodic or harmonic detail which does not conform to the idiom. Whenever Orson Welles offends against the tricks of the trade, he is forgiven because his departures from the norm are regarded as calculated mutations which serve all the more strongly to confirm the validity of the system. The constraint of the technically-conditioned idiom which stars and directors have to produce as "nature" so that the people can appropriate it, extends to such fine nuances that they almost attain the subtlety of the devices of an avant-garde work as against those of truth. The rare capacity minutely to fulfill the obligations of the natural idiom in all branches of the culture industry becomes the criterion of efficiency. What and how they say it must be measurable by everyday language, as in logical positivism. The producers are experts. The idiom demands an astounding productive power, which it absorbs and squanders. In a diabolical way it has overreached the culturally conservative distinction between genuine and artificial style. A style might be called artificial which is imposed from without on the refractory impulses of a form. But in the culture industry every element of the subject matter has its origin in the same apparatus as that jargon whose stamp it bears. The quarrels in which the artistic experts become involved with sponsor and censor about a lie going beyond the bounds of credibility are evidence not so much of an inner aesthetic tension as of a divergence of interests. The reputation of the specialist, in which a last remnant of objective independence sometimes finds refuge, conflicts with the business politics of the Church, or the concern which is manufacturing the cultural commodity. But the thing itself has been essentially objectified and made viable before the established authorities began to argue about it. Even before Zanuck acquired her, Saint Bernadette was regarded by her latter-day hagiographer as brilliant propaganda for all interested parties. That is what became of the emotions of the character. Hence the style of the culture industry, which no longer has to test itself against any refractory material, is also the negation of style. The reconciliation of the general and particular, of the rule and the specific demands of the subject matter, the achievement of which alone gives essential, meaningful content to style, is futile because there has ceased to be the slightest tension between opposite poles: these concordant extremes are dismally identical; the general can replace the particular, and vice versa.

Nevertheless, this caricature of style does not amount to something beyond the genuine style of the past. In the culture industry the notion of genuine style is seen to be the aesthetic equivalent of domination. Style considered as mere aesthetic regularity is a romantic dream of the past. The unity of style not only of the Christian Middle Ages but of the Renaissance expresses in each case the different structure of social power, and not the obscure experience of the oppressed in which the general was enclosed. The great artists were never those who embodied a wholly flawless and perfect style, but those who used style as a way of hardening themselves against the chaotic expression of suffering, as a negative truth. The style of their works gave what was expressed that force without which life flows away unheard. Those very art forms which are known as classical, such as Mozart's music, contain objective trends which represent something different to the style which they incarnate. As late as Schönberg and Picasso, the great artists have retained a mistrust of style, and at crucial points have subordinated it to the logic of the matter. What Dadaists and Expressionists called the untruth of style as such triumphs today in the sung jargon of a crooner, in the carefully contrived elegance of a film star, and even in the admirable expertise of a photograph of a peasant's squalid hut. Style represents a promise in every work of art.

That which is expressed is subsumed through style into the dominant forms of generality, into the language of music, painting, or words, in the hope that it will be reconciled thus with the idea of true generality. This promise held out by the work of art that it will create truth by lending new shape to the conventional social forms is as necessary as it is hypocritical. It unconditionally posits the real forms of life as it is by suggesting that fulfillment lies in their aesthetic derivatives. To this extent the claim of art is always ideology too. However, only in this confrontation with tradition of which style is the record can art express suffering. That factor in a work of art which enables it to transcend reality certainly cannot be detached from style; but it does not consist of the harmony actually realized, of any doubtful unity of form and content, within and without, of individual and society; it is to be found in those features in which discrepancy appears: in the necessary failure of the passionate striving for identity. Instead of exposing itself to this failure in which the style of the great work of art has always achieved self-negation, the inferior work has always relied on its similarity with others – on a surrogate identity.

In the culture industry this imitation finally becomes absolute. Having ceased to be anything but style, it reveals the latter's secret: obedience to the social hierarchy. Today aesthetic barbarity completes what has threatened the creations of the spirit since they were gathered together as culture and neutralized. To speak of culture was always contrary to culture. Culture as a common denominator already contains in embryo that schematization and process of cataloging and classification which bring culture within the sphere of administration. And it is precisely the industrialized, the consequent, subsumption which entirely accords with this notion of culture. By subordinating in the same way and to the same end all areas of intellectual creation, by occupying men's senses from the time they leave the factory in the evening to the time they clock in again the next morning with matter that bears the impress of the labor process they themselves have to sustain throughout the day, this subsumption mockingly satisfies the concept of a unified culture which the philosophers of personality contrasted with mass culture.

And so the culture industry, the most rigid of all styles, proves to be the goal of liberalism, which is reproached for its lack of style. Not only do its categories and contents derive from liberalism – domesticated naturalism as well as operetta and revue – but the modern culture monopolies form the economic area in which, together with the corresponding entrepreneurial types, for the time being some part of its sphere of operation survives, despite the process of disintegration elsewhere. It is still possible to make one's way in entertainment, if one is not too obstinate about one's own concerns, and proves appropriately pliable. Anyone who resists can only survive by fitting in. Once his particular brand of deviation from the norm has been noted by the industry, he belongs to it as does the land-reformer to capitalism. Realistic dissidence is the trademark of anyone who has a new idea in business. In the public voice of modern society accusations are seldom audible; if they are, the perceptive can already detect signs that the dissident will soon be reconciled. The more immeasurable the gap between chorus and leaders, the more certainly there is room at the top for everybody who demonstrates his superiority by well-planned originality. Hence, in the culture industry, too, the liberal tendency to give full scope to its able men survives. To do this for the efficient today is still the function of the market, which is otherwise proficiently controlled; as for the market's freedom, in the high period of art as elsewhere, it was freedom for the stupid to starve. Significantly, the system of the culture industry comes from the more liberal industrial nations, and all its characteristic media, such as movies, radio, jazz, and magazines, flourish there. Its progress, to be sure, had its origin in the general laws of capital. Gaumont and Pathé, Ullstein and Hugenberg followed the international trend with some success; Europe's economic dependence on the United States after war and inflation was a contributory factor. The belief that the barbarity of the culture industry is a result of "cultural lag," of the fact that the American consciousness did not keep up with the growth of technology, is quite wrong. It was pre-Fascist Europe which did not keep up with the trend toward the culture monopoly. But it was this very lag which left intellect and creativity some degree of independence and enabled its last represent-atives to exist – however dismally. In Germany the failure of democratic control to permeate life had led to a paradoxical situation. Many things were exempt from the market mechanism which had invaded the Western countries. The German educa-tional system, universities, theaters with artistic standards, great orchestras, and museums enjoyed protection. The political powers, state and municipalities, which had inherited such institutions from absolutism, had left them with a measure of the freedom from the forces of power which dominates the market, just as princes and feudal lords had done up to the nineteenth century. This strengthened art in this late phase against the verdict of supply and demand, and increased its resistance far beyond the actual degree of protection. In the market itself the tribute of a quality for which no use had been found was turned into purchasing power; in this way, respectable literary and music publishers could help authors who yielded little more in the way of profit than the respect of the connoisseur. But what completely fettered the artist was the pressure (and the accompanying drastic threats), always to fit into business life as an aesthetic expert. Formerly, like Kant and Hume, they signed their letters "Your most humble and obedient servant," and undermined the foundations of throne and altar. Today they address heads of government by their first names, yet in every artistic activity they are subject to their illiterate masters. The analysis Tocqueville offered a century ago has in the meantime proved wholly accurate. Under the private culture monopoly it is a fact that "tyranny leaves the body free and directs its attack at the soul. The ruler no longer says: You must think as I do or die. He says: You are free not to think as I do; your life, your property, everything shall remain yours, but from this day on you are a stranger among us."[2] Not to conform means to be rendered powerless, economically and therefore spiritually – to be "self-employed." When the outsider is excluded from the concern, he can only too easily be accused of incompetence. Whereas today in material production the mechanism of supply and demand is disintegrating, in the superstructure it still operates as a check in the rulers' favor. The consumers are the workers and employees, the farmers and lower middle class. Capitalist production so confines them, body and soul, that they fall helpless victims to what is offered them. As naturally as the ruled always took the morality imposed upon them more seriously than did the rulers themselves, the deceived masses are today captivated by the myth of success even more than the successful are. Immovably, they insist on the very ideology which enslaves them. The misplaced love of the common people for the wrong which is done them is a greater force than the cunning of the authorities. It is stronger even than the rigorism of the Hays Office, just as in certain great times in history it has inflamed greater forces that were turned against it, namely, the terror of the tribunals. It calls for Mickey Rooney in preference to the tragic Garbo, for Donald Duck instead of Betty Boop. The industry submits to the vote which it has itself inspired. What is a loss for the firm which cannot fully exploit a contract with a declining star is a legitimate expense for the system as a whole. By craftily sanctioning the demand for rubbish it inaugurates total harmony. The connoisseur and the expert are despised for their pretentious claim to know better than the others, even though culture is democratic and distributes its privileges to all. In view of the ideological truce, the conformism of the buyers and the effrontery of the producers who supply them prevail. The result is a constant reproduction of the same thing.

A constant sameness governs the relationship to the past as well. What is new about the phase of mass culture compared with the late liberal stage is the exclusion of the new. The machine rotates on the same spot. While determining consumption it excludes the untried as a risk. The movie-makers distrust any manuscript which is not reassuringly backed by a bestseller. Yet for this very reason there is never-ending talk of ideas, novelty, and surprise, of what is taken for granted but has never existed. Tempo and dynamics serve this trend. Nothing remains as of old; everything has to run incessantly, to keep moving. For only the universal triumph of the rhythm of mechanical production and reproduction promises that nothing changes, and nothing unsuitable will appear. Any additions to the well-proven culture inventory are too much of a speculation. The ossified forms – such as the sketch, short story, problem film, or hit song – are the standardized average of late liberal taste, dictated with threats from above. The people at the top in the culture agencies, who work in harmony as only one manager can with another, whether he comes from the rag trade or from college, have long since reorganized and rationalized the objective spirit. One might think that an omnipresent authority had sifted the material and drawn up an official catalog of cultural commodities to provide a smooth supply of available mass-produced lines. The ideas are written in the cultural firmament where they had already been numbered by Plato – and were indeed numbers, incapable of increase and immutable.

Amusement and all the elements of the culture industry existed long before the latter came into existence. Now they are taken over from above and brought up to date. The culture industry can pride itself on having energetically executed the previously clumsy transposition of art into the sphere of consumption, on making this a principle, on divesting amusement of its obtrusive naïvetés and improving the type of commodities. The more absolute it became, the more ruthless it was in forcing every outsider either into bankruptcy or into a syndicate, and became more refined and elevated – until it ended up as a synthesis of Beethoven and the Casino de Paris. It enjoys a double victory: the truth it extinguishes without it can reproduce at will as a lie within. "Light" art as such, distraction, is not a decadent form. Anyone who complains that it is a betrayal of the ideal of pure expression is under an illusion about society. The purity of bourgeois art, which hypostasized itself as a world of freedom in contrast to what was happening in the material world, was from the beginning bought with the exclusion of the lower classes – with whose cause, the real universality, art keeps faith precisely by its freedom from the ends of the false universality. Serious art has been withheld from those for whom the hardship and oppression of life make a mockery of seriousness, and who must be glad if they can use time not spent at the production line just to keep going. Light art has been the shadow of autonomous art. It is the social bad conscience of serious art. The truth which the latter necessarily lacked because of its social premises gives the other the semblance of legitimacy. The division itself is the truth: it does at least express the negativity of the culture which the different spheres constitute. Least of all can the antithesis be reconciled by absorbing light into serious art, or vice versa. But that is what the culture industry attempts. The eccentricity of the circus, peepshow, and brothel is as embarrassing to it as that of Schönberg and Karl Kraus. And so the jazz musician Benny Goodman appears with the Budapest string quartet, more pedantic rhythmically than any philharmonic clarinettist, while the style of the Budapest players is as uniform and sugary as that of Guy Lombardo. But what is significant is not vulgarity, stupidity, and lack of polish. The culture industry did away with yesterday's rubbish by its own perfection, and by forbidding and domesticating the amateurish, although it constantly allows gross blunders without which the standard of the exalted style cannot be perceived. But what is new is that the irreconcilable elements of culture, art and distraction, are subordinated to one end and subsumed under one false formula: the totality of the culture industry. It consists of repetition. That its characteristic innovations are never anything more than improvements of mass reproduction is not external to the system. It is with good reason that the interest of innumerable consumers is directed to the technique, and not to the contents – which are stubbornly repeated, outworn, and by now half-discredited. The social power which the spectators worship shows itself more effectively in the omnipresence of the stereotype imposed by technical skill than in the stale ideologies for which the ephemeral contents stand in.

Nevertheless the culture industry remains the entertainment business. Its influence over the consumers is established by entertainment; that will ultimately be broken not by an outright decree, but by the hostility inherent in the principle of entertainment to what is greater than itself. Since all the trends of the culture industry are pro-foundly embedded in the public by the whole social process, they are encouraged by the survival of the market in this area. Demand has not yet been replaced by simple obedience. As is well known, the major reorganization of the film industry shortly before World War I, the material prerequisite of its expansion, was precisely its deliberate acceptance of the public's needs as recorded at the box-office – a procedure which was hardly thought necessary in the pioneering days of the screen. The same opinion is held today by the captains of the film industry, who take as their criterion the more or less phenomenal song hits but wisely never have recourse to the judg-ment of truth, the opposite criterion. Business is their ideology. It is quite correct that the power of the culture industry resides in its identification with a manufactured need, and not in simple contrast to it, even if this contrast were one of complete power and complete powerlessness. Amusement under late capitalism is the prolongation of work. It is sought after as an escape from the mechanized work process, and to recruit strength in order to be able to cope with it again. But at the same time mechanization has such power over a man's leisure and happiness, and so profoundly determines the manufacture of amusement goods, that his experiences are inevitably after-images of the work process itself. The ostensible content is merely a faded foreground; what sinks in is the automatic succession of standardized operations. What happens at work, in the factory, or in the office can only be escaped from by approximation to it in one's leisure time. All amusement suffers from this incurable malady. Pleasure hardens into boredom because, if it is to remain pleasure, it must not demand any effort and therefore moves rigorously in the worn grooves of association. No independent thinking must be expected from the audience: the product prescribes every reaction: not by its natural structure (which collapses under reflection), but by signals. Any logical connection calling for mental effort is painstakingly avoided. As far as possible, developments must follow from the immediately preceding situation and never from the idea of the whole. For the attentive movie-goer any individual scene will give him the whole thing. Even the set pattern itself still seems dangerous, offering some meaning – wretched as it might be – where only meaninglessness is acceptable. Often the plot is maliciously deprived of the development demanded by characters and matter according to the old pattern. Instead, the next step is what the script writer takes to be the most striking effect in the particular situation. Banal though elaborate surprise interrupts the story-line. The tendency mischievously to fall back on pure nonsense, which was a legitimate part of popular art, farce and clowning, right up to Chaplin and the Marx Brothers, is most obvious in the unpretentious kinds. This tendency has completely asserted itself in the text of the novelty song, in the thriller movie, and in cartoons, although in films starring Greer Garson and Bette Davis the unity of the socio-psychological case study provides something approximating a claim to a consistent plot. The idea itself, together with the objects of comedy and terror, is massacred and fragmented. Novelty songs have always existed on a contempt for meaning which, as predecessors and successors of psychoanalysis, they reduce to the monotony of sexual symbolism. Today detective and adventure films no longer give the audience the opportunity to experience the resolution. In the non-ironic varieties of the genre, it has also to rest content with the simple horror of situations which have almost ceased to be linked in any way.

Cartoons were once exponents of fantasy as opposed to rationalism. They ensured that justice was done to the creatures and objects they electrified, by giving the maimed specimens a second life. All they do today is to confirm the victory of technological reason over truth. A few years ago they had a consistent plot which only broke up in the final moments in a crazy chase, and thus resembled the old slapstick comedy. Now, however, time relations have shifted. In the very first sequence a motive is stated so that in the course of the action destruction can get to work on it: with the audience in pursuit, the protagonist becomes the worthless object of general violence. The quantity of organized amusement changes into the quality of organized cruelty. The self-elected censors of the film industry (with whom it enjoys a close relationship) watch over the unfolding of the crime, which is as drawn-out as a hunt. Fun replaces the pleasure which the sight of an embrace would allegedly afford, and postpones satisfaction till the day of the pogrom. In so far as cartoons do any more than accustom the senses to the new tempo, they hammer into every brain the old lesson that continuous friction, the breaking down of all individual resistance, is the condition of life in this society. Donald Duck in the cartoons and the unfortunate in real life get their thrashing so that the audience can learn to take their own punishment.

The enjoyment of the violence suffered by the movie character turns into violence against the spectator, and distraction into exertion. Nothing that the experts have devised as a stimulant must escape the weary eye; no stupidity is allowed in the face of all the trickery; one has to follow everything and even display the smart responses shown and recommended in the film. This raises the question whether the culture industry fulfills the function of diverting minds which it boasts about so loudly. If most of the radio stations and movie theaters were closed down, the consumers would probably not lose so very much. To walk from the street into the movie theater is no longer to enter a world of dream; as soon as the very existence of these institutions no longer made it obligatory to use them, there would be no great urge to do so. Such closures would not be reactionary machine wrecking. The disappointment would be felt not so much by the enthusiasts as by the slow-witted, who are the ones who suffer for everything anyhow. In spite of the films which are intended to complete her integration, the housewife finds in the darkness of the movie theater a place of refuge where she can sit for a few hours with nobody watching, just as she used to look out of the window when there were still homes and rest in the evening. The unemployed in the great cities find coolness in summer and warmth in winter in these temperature-controlled locations. Otherwise, despite its size, this bloated pleasure apparatus adds no dignity to man's lives. The idea of "fully exploiting" available technical resources and the facilities for aesthetic mass consumption is part of the economic system which refuses to exploit resources to abolish hunger.

The culture industry perpetually cheats its consumers of what it perpetually promises. The promissory note which, with its plots and staging, it draws on pleasure is endlessly prolonged; the promise, which is actually all the spectacle consists of, is illusory: all it actually confirms is that the real point will never be reached, that the diner must be satisfied with the menu. In front of the appetite stimulated by all those brilliant names and images there is finally set no more than a commendation of the depressing everyday world it sought to escape. Of course works of art were not sexual exhibitions either. However, by representing deprivation as negative, they retracted, as it were, the prostitution of the impulse and rescued by mediation what was denied. The secret of aesthetic sublimation is its representation of fulfillment as a broken promise. The culture industry does not sublimate; it represses. By repeatedly exposing the objects of desire, breasts in a clinging sweater or the naked torso of the athletic hero, it only stimulates the unsublimated forepleasure which habitual deprivation has long since reduced to a masochistic semblance. There is no erotic situation which, while insinuating and exciting, does not fail to indicate unmistakably that things can never go that far. The Hays Office merely confirms the ritual of Tantalus that the culture industry has established anyway. Works of art are ascetic and unashamed; the culture industry is pornographic and prudish. Love is downgraded to romance. And, after the descent, much is permitted; even license as a marketable speciality has its quota bearing the trade description "daring." The mass production of the sexual automatically achieves its repression. Because of his ubiquity, the film star with whom one is meant to fall in love is from the outset a copy of himself. Every tenor voice comes to sound like a Caruso record, and the "natural" faces of Texas girls are like the successful models by whom Hollywood has typecast them. The mechanical reproduction of beauty, which reactionary cultural fanaticism wholeheartedly serves in its methodical idolization of individuality, leaves no room for that unconscious idolatry which was once essential to beauty. The triumph over beauty is celebrated by humor – the *Schadenfreude* that every successful deprivation calls forth. There is laughter because there is nothing to laugh at. Laughter, whether conciliatory or terrible, always occurs when some fear passes. It indicates liberation either from physical danger or from the grip of logic. Conciliatory laughter is heard as the echo of an escape from power; the wrong kind overcomes fear by capitulating to the forces which are to be feared. It is the echo of power as something inescapable. Fun is a medicinal bath. The pleasure industry never fails to prescribe it. It makes laughter the instrument of the fraud practiced on happiness. Moments of happiness are without laughter; only operettas and films portray sex to the accompaniment of resounding laughter. But Baudelaire is as devoid of humour as Hölderlin. In the false society laughter is a disease which has attacked happiness and is drawing it into its worthless totality. To laugh at something is always to deride it, and the life which, according to Bergson, in laughter breaks through the barrier, is actually an invading barbaric life, self-assertion prepared to parade its liberation from any scruple when the social occasion arises. Such a laughing audience is a parody of humanity. Its members are monads, all dedicated to the pleasure of being ready for anything at the expense of everyone else. Their harmony is a caricature of solidarity. What is fiendish about this false laughter is that it is a compelling parody of the best, which is conciliatory. Delight is austere: *res severa verum gaudium*. The monastic theory that not asceticism but the sexual act denotes the renunciation of attainable bliss receives negative confirmation in the gravity of the lover who with foreboding commits his life to the fleeting moment. In the culture industry, jovial denial takes the place of the pain found in ecstasy and in asceticism. The supreme law is that they shall not satisfy their desires at any price; they must laugh and be content with laughter. In every product of the culture industry, the permanent denial imposed by civilization is once again unmistakably demonstrated and inflicted on its victims. To offer and to deprive them of something is one and the same. This is what happens in erotic films. Precisely because it must never take place, everything centers upon copulation. In films it is more strictly forbidden for an illegitimate relationship to be admitted without the parties being punished than for a millionaire's future son-in-law to be active in the labor movement. In contrast to the liberal era, industrialized as well as popular culture may wax indignant at capitalism, but it cannot renounce the threat of castration. This is fundamental. It outlasts the organized acceptance of the uniformed seen in the films which are produced to that end, and in reality. What is decisive today is no longer puritanism, although it still asserts itself in the form of women's organizations, but the necessity inherent in the system not to leave the customer alone, not for a moment to allow him any suspicion that resistance is possible. The principle dictates that he should be shown all his needs as capable of fulfillment, but that those needs should be so predetermined that he feels himself to be the eternal consumer, the object of the culture industry. Not only does it make him believe that the deception it practices is satisfaction, but it goes further and implies that, whatever the state of affairs, he must put up with what is offered. The escape from everyday drudgery which the whole culture industry promises may be compared to the daughter's abduction in the cartoon: the father is holding the ladder in the dark. The paradise offered by the culture industry is the same old drudgery. Both escape and elopement are predesigned to lead back to the starting point. Pleasure promotes the resignation which it ought to help to forget.

Amusement, if released from every restraint, would not only be the antithesis of art but its extreme role. The Mark Twain absurdity with which the American culture industry flirts at times might be a corrective of art. The more seriously the latter regards the incompatibility with life, the more it resembles the seriousness of life, its antithesis; the more effort it devotes to developing wholly from its own formal law, the more effort it demands from the intelligence to neutralize its burden. In some revue films, and especially in the grotesque and the funnies, the possibility of this negation does glimmer for a few moments. But of course it cannot happen. Pure amusement in its consequence, relaxed self-surrender to all kinds of associations and happy nonsense, is cut short by the amusement on the market: instead, it is interrupted by a surrogate overall meaning which the culture industry insists on giving to its products, and yet misuses as a mere pretext for bringing in the stars. Biographies and other simple stories patch the fragments of nonsense into an idiotic plot. We do not have the cap and bells of the jester but the bunch of keys of capitalist reason, which even screens the pleasure of achieving success. Every kiss in the revue film has to contribute to the career of the boxer, or some hit song expert or other whose rise to fame is being glorified. The deception is not that the culture industry supplies amusement but that it ruins the fun by allowing business considerations to involve it in the ideological clichés of a culture in the process of self-liquidation. Ethics and taste cut short unrestrained amusement as "naïve" – naïveté is thought to be as bad as intellectualism – and even restrict technical possibilities. The culture industry is corrupt; not because it is a sinful Babylon but because it is a cathedral dedicated to elevated pleasure. On all levels, from Hemingway to Emil Ludwig, from Mrs. Miniver to the Lone Ranger, from Toscanini to Guy Lombardo, there is untruth in the intellectual content taken ready-made from art and science. The culture industry does retain a trace of something better in those features which bring it close to the circus, in the self-justifying and nonsensical skill of riders, acrobats and clowns, in the "defense and justification of physical as against intellectual art."[3] But the refuges of a mindless artistry which represents what is human as opposed to the social mechanism are being relentlessly hunted down by a schematic reason which compels everything to prove its significance and effect. The consequence is that the nonsensical at the bottom disappears as utterly as the sense in works of art at the top.

The fusion of culture and entertainment that is taking place today leads not only to a depravation of culture, but inevitably to an intellectualization of amusement. This is evident from the fact that only the copy appears: in the movie theater, the photograph; on the radio, the recording. In the age of liberal expansion, amusement lived on the unshaken belief in the future: things would remain as they were and even improve. Today this belief is once more intellectualized; it becomes so faint that it loses sight of any goal and is little more than a magic-lantern show for those with their backs to reality. It consists of the meaningful emphases which, parallel to life itself, the screen play puts on the smart fellow, the engineer, the capable girl, ruthlessness disguised as character, interest in sport, and finally automobiles and cigarettes, even where the entertainment is not put down to the advertising account of the immediate producers but to that of the system as a whole. Amusement itself becomes an ideal, taking the place of the higher things of which it completely deprives the masses by repeating them in a manner even more stereotyped than the slogans paid for by advertising interests. Inwardness, the subjectively restricted form of truth, was always more at the mercy of the outwardly powerful than they imagined. The culture industry turns it into an open lie. It has now become mere twaddle which is acceptable in religious best-sellers, psychological films, and women's serials as an embarrassingly agreeable garnish, so that genuine personal emotion in real life can be all the more reliably controlled. In this sense amusement carries out that purgation of the emotions which Aristotle once attributed to tragedy and Mortimer Adler now allows to movies. The culture industry reveals the truth about catharsis as it did about style.

The stronger the positions of the culture industry become, the more summarily it can deal with consumers' needs, producing them, controlling them, disciplining them, and even withdrawing amusement: no limits are set to cultural progress of this kind. But the tendency is immanent in the principle of amusement itself, which is enlightened in a bourgeois sense. If the need for amusement was in large measure the creation of industry, which used the subject as a means of recommending the work to the masses – the oleograph by the dainty morsel it depicted, or the cake mix by a picture of a cake – amusement always reveals the influence of business, the sales talk, the quack's spiel. But the original affinity of business and amusement is shown in the latter's specific significance: to defend society. To be pleased means to say Yes. It is possible only by insulation from the totality of the social process, by desensitization and, from the first, by senselessly sacrificing the inescapable claim of every work, however inane, within its limits to reflect the whole. Pleasure always means not to think about anything, to forget suffering even where it is shown. Basically it is helplessness. It is flight; not, as is asserted, flight from a wretched reality, but from the last remaining thought of resistance. The liberation which amusement promises is freedom from thought and from negation. The effrontery of the rhetorical question, "What do people want?" lies in the fact that it is addressed – as if to reflective individuals – to those very people who are deliberately to be deprived of this individuality. Even when the public does – exceptionally – rebel against the pleasure industry, all it can muster is that feeble resistance which that very industry has inculcated in it. Nevertheless, it has become increasingly difficult to keep people in this condition. The rate at which they are reduced to stupidity must not fall behind the rate at which their intelligence is increasing. In this age of statistics the masses are too sharp to identify themselves with the millionaire on the screen, and too slow-witted to ignore the law of the largest number. Ideology conceals itself in the calculation of probabilities. Not everyone will be lucky one day – but the person who draws the winning ticket, or rather the one who is marked out to do so by a higher power – usually by the pleasure industry itself, which is represented as unceasingly in search of talent. Those discovered by talent scouts and then publicized on a vast scale by the studio are ideal types of the new dependent average. Of course, the starlet is meant to symbolize the typist in such a way that the splendid evening dress seems meant for the actress as distinct from the real girl. The girls in the audience not only feel that they could be on the screen, but realize the great gulf separating them from it. Only one girl can draw the lucky ticket, only one man can win the prize, and if, mathematically, all have the same chance, yet this is so infinitesimal for each one that he or she will do best to write it off and rejoice in the other's success, which might just as well have been his or hers, and somehow never is. Whenever the culture industry still issues an invitation naïvely to identify, it is immediately withdrawn. No one can escape from himself any more. Once a member of the audience could see his own wedding in the one shown in the film. Now the lucky actors on the screen are copies of the same category as every member of the public, but such equality only demonstrates the insurmountable separation of the human elements. The perfect similarity is the absolute difference. The identity of the category forbids that of the individual cases. Ironically, man as a member of a species has been made a reality by the culture industry. Now any person signifies only those attributes by which he can replace everybody else: he is interchangeable, a copy. As an individual he is completely expendable and utterly insignificant, and this is just what he finds out when time deprives him of this similarity. This changes the inner structure of the religion of success – otherwise strictly maintained. Increasing emphasis is laid not on the path *per aspera ad astra* (which presupposes hardship and effort), but on winning a prize. The element of blind chance in the routine decision about which song deserves to be a hit and which extra a heroine is stressed by the ideology. Movies emphasize chance. By stopping at nothing to ensure that all the characters are essentially alike, with the exception of the villain, and by excluding non-conforming faces (for example, those which, like Garbo's, do not look as if you could say "Hello sister!" to them), life is made easier for movie-goers at first. They are assured that they are all right as they are, that they could do just as well and that nothing beyond their powers will be asked of them. But at the same time they are given a hint that any effort would be useless because even bourgeois luck no longer has any connection with the calculable effect of their own work. They take the hint. Fundamentally they all recognize chance (by which one occasionally makes his fortune) as the other side of planning. Precisely because the forces of society are so deployed in the direction of rationality that anyone might become an engineer or manager, it has ceased entirely to be a rational matter who the one will be in whom society will invest training or confidence for such functions. Chance and planning become one and the same thing, because, given men's equality, individual success and failure – right up to the top – lose any economic meaning. Chance itself is planned, not because it affects any particular individual but precisely because it is believed to play a vital part. It serves the planners as an alibi, and makes it seem that the complex of transactions and measures into which life has been transformed leaves scope for spontaneous and direct relations between man. This freedom is symbolized in the various media of the culture industry by the arbitrary selection of average individuals. In a magazine's detailed accounts of the modestly magnificent pleasure-trips it has arranged for the lucky person, preferably a steno-typist (who has probably won the competition because of her contacts with local bigwigs), the powerlessness of all is reflected. They are mere matter – so much so that those in control can take someone up into their heaven and throw him out again: his rights and his work count for nothing. Industry is interested in people merely as customers and employees, and has in fact reduced mankind as a whole and each of its elements to this all-embracing formula. According to the ruling aspect at the time, ideology emphasizes plan or chance, technology or life, civilization or nature. As employees, men are reminded of the rational organization and urged to fit in like sensible people. As customers, the freedom of choice, the charm of novelty, is demonstrated to them on the screen or in the press by means of the human and personal anecdote. In either case they remain objects.

The less the culture industry has to promise, the less it can offer a meaningful explanation of life, and the emptier is the ideology it disseminates. Even the abstract ideals of the harmony and beneficence of society are too concrete in this age of universal publicity. We have even learned how to identify abstract concepts as sales propaganda. Language based entirely on truth simply arouses impatience to get on with the business deal it is probably advancing. The words that are not means appear senseless; the others seem to be fiction, untrue. Value judgments are taken either as advertising or as empty talk. Accordingly ideology has been made vague and non-committal, and thus neither clearer nor weaker. Its very vagueness, its almost scient-ific aversion from committing itself to anything which cannot be verified, acts as an instrument of domination. It becomes a vigorous and prearranged promulgation of the status quo. The culture industry tends to make itself the embodiment of author-itative pronouncements, and thus the irrefutable prophet of the prevailing order. It skilfully steers a winding course between the cliffs of demonstrable misinformation and manifest truth, faithfully reproducing the phenomenon whose opaqueness blocks any insight and installs the ubiquitous and intact phenomenon as ideal. Ideology is split into the photograph of stubborn life and the naked lie about its meaning – which is not expressed but suggested and yet drummed in. To demonstrate its divine nature, reality is always repeated in a purely cynical way. Such a photological proof is of course not stringent, but it is overpowering. Anyone who doubts the power of monotony is a fool. The culture industry refutes the objection made against it just as well as that against the world which it impartially duplicates. The only choice is either to join in or to be left behind: those provincials who have recourse to eternal beauty and the amateur stage in preference to the cinema and the radio are already – politically – at the point to which mass culture drives its supporters. It is sufficiently hardened to deride as ideology, if need be, the old wish-fulfillments, the father-ideal and absolute feeling. The new ideology has as its objects the world as such. It makes use of the worship of facts by no more than elevating a disagreeable existence into the world of facts in representing it meticulously. This transference makes existence itself a sub-stitute for meaning and right. Whatever the camera reproduces is beautiful. The disappointment of the prospect that one might be the typist who wins the world trip is matched by the disappointing appearance of the accurately photographed areas which the voyage might include. Not Italy is offered, but evidence that it exists. A film can even go so far as to show the Paris in which the American girl thinks she will still her desire as a hopelessly desolate place, thus driving her the more inexorably into the arms of the smart American boy she could have met at home anyhow. That this goes on, that, in its most recent phase, the system itself reproduces the life of those of whom it consists instead of immediately doing away with them, is even put down to its credit as giving it meaning and worth. Continuing and continuing to join in are given as justification for the blind persistence of the system and even for its immut-ability. What repeats itself is healthy, like the natural or industrial cycle. The same babies grin eternally out of the magazines; the jazz machine will pound away for ever. In spite of all the progress in reproduction techniques, in controls and the specialities, and in spite of all the restless industry, the bread which the culture industry offers man is the stone of the stereotype. It draws on the life cycle, on the well-founded amazement that mothers, in spite of everything, still go on bearing children and that the wheels still do not grind to a halt. This serves to confirm the immutability of circumstances. The ears of corn blowing in the wind at the end of Chaplin's *The Great Dictator* give the lie to the anti-Fascist plea for freedom. They are like the blond hair of the German girl whose camp life is photographed by the Nazi film company in the summer breeze. Nature is viewed by the mechanism of social domination as a healthy contrast to society, and is therefore denatured. Pictures showing green trees, a blue sky, and moving clouds make these aspects of nature into so many cryptograms for factory chimneys and service stations. On the other hand, wheels and machine components must seem expressive, having been degraded to the status of agents of the spirit of trees and clouds. Nature and technology are mobilized against all opposition; and we have a falsified memento of liberal society, in which people supposedly wallowed in erotic plush-lined bedrooms instead of taking open-air baths as in the case today, or experiencing breakdowns in prehistoric Benz models instead of shooting off with the speed of a rocket from A (where one is anyhow) to B (where everything is just the same). The triumph of the gigantic concern over the initiative of the entrepreneur is praised by the culture industry as the persistence of entrepreneurial initiative. The enemy who is already defeated, the thinking individual, is the enemy fought. The resurrection in Germany of the antibourgeois "Haus Sonnenstösser," and the pleasure felt when watching *Life with Father*, have one and the same meaning.

In one respect, admittedly, this hollow ideology is in deadly earnest: everyone is provided for. "No one must go hungry or thirsty; if anyone does, he's for the concentration camp!'' This joke from Hitler's Germany might shine forth as a maxim from above all the portals of the culture industry. With sly naïveté, it presupposes the most recent characteristic of society: that it can easily find out who its supporters are. Everybody is guaranteed formal freedom. No one is officially responsible for what he thinks. Instead everyone is enclosed at an early age in a system of churches, clubs, professional associations, and other such concerns, which constitute the most sensitive instrument of social control. Anyone who wants to avoid ruin must see that he is not found wanting when weighed in the scales of this apparatus. Otherwise he will lag behind in life, and finally perish. In every career, and especially in the liberal professions, expert knowledge is linked with prescribed standards of conduct; this can easily lead to the illusion that expert knowledge is the only thing that counts. In fact, it is part of the irrational planning of this society that it reproduces to a certain degree only the lives of its faithful members. The standard of life enjoyed corresponds very closely to the degree to which classes and individuals are essentially bound up with the system. The manager can be relied upon, as can the lesser employee Dagwood – as he is in the comic pages or in real life. Anyone who goes cold and hungry, even if his prospects were once good, is branded. He is an outsider; and, apart from certain capital crimes, the most mortal of sins is to be an outsider. In films he sometimes, and as an exception, becomes an original, the object of maliciously indulgent humor; but usually he is the villain, and is identified as such at first appearance, long before the action really gets going: hence avoiding any suspicion that society would turn on those of good will. Higher up the scale, in fact, a kind of welfare state is coming into being today. In order to keep their own positions, men in top posts maintain the economy in which a highly-developed technology has in principle made the masses redundant as producers. The workers, the real bread-winners, are fed (if we are to believe the ideology) by the managers of the economy, the fed. Hence the individual's position becomes precarious. Under liberalism the poor were thought to be lazy; now they are automatically objects of suspicion. Anybody who is not provided for outside should be in a concentration camp, or at any rate in the hell of the most degrading work and the slums. The culture industry, however, reflects positive and negative welfare for those under the administrators' control as direct human solidarity of men in a world of the efficient. No one is forgotten; everywhere there are neighbors and welfare workers, Dr. Gillespies and parlor philosophers whose hearts are in the right place and who, by their kind intervention as of man to man, cure individual cases of socially-perpetuated distress – always provided that there is no obstacle in the personal depravity of the unfortunate. The promotion of a friendly atmosphere as advised by management experts and adopted by every factory to increase output, brings even the last private impulse under social control precisely because it seems to relate men's circumstances directly to production, and to reprivatize them. Such spiritual charity casts a conciliatory shadow onto the products of the culture industry long before it emerges from the factory to invade society as a whole. Yet the great benefactors of mankind, whose scientific achievements have to be written up as acts of sympathy to give them an artificial human interest, are substitutes for the national leaders, who finally decree the abolition of sympathy and think they can prevent any recurrence when the last invalid has been exterminated.

By emphasizing the "heart of gold," society admits the suffering it has created: everyone knows that he is now helpless in the system, and ideology has to take this into account. Far from concealing suffering under the cloak of improvised fellowship, the culture industry takes pride in looking it in the face like a man, however great the strain on self-control. The pathos of composure justifies the world which makes it necessary. That is life – very hard, but just because of that so wonderful and so healthy. This lie does not shrink from tragedy. Mass culture deals with it, in the same way as centralized society does not abolish the suffering of its members but records and plans it. That it is why it borrows so persistently from art. This provides the tragic substance which pure amusement cannot itself supply, but which it needs if it is somehow to remain faithful to the principle of the exact reproduction of phenomena. Tragedy made into a carefully calculated and accepted aspect of the world is a blessing. It is a safeguard against the reproach that truth is not respected, whereas it is really being adopted with cynical regret. To the consumer who – culturally – has seen better days it offers a substitute for long-discarded profundities. It provides the regular movie-goer with the scraps of culture he must have for prestige. It comforts all with the thought that a tough, genuine human fate is still possible, and that it must at all costs be represented uncompromisingly. Life in all the aspects which ideology today sets out to duplicate shows up all the more gloriously, powerfully and magnificently, the more it is redolent of necessary suffering. It begins to resemble fate. Tragedy is reduced to the threat to destroy anyone who does not cooperate, whereas its paradoxical significance once lay in a hopeless resistance to mythic destiny. Tragic fate becomes just punishment, which is what bourgeois aesthetics always tried to turn it into. The morality of mass culture is the cheap form of yesterday's children's books. In a first-class production, for example, the villainous character appears as a hysterical woman who (with presumed clinical accuracy) tries to ruin the happiness of her opposite number, who is truer to reality, and herself suffers a quite untheatrical death. So much learning is of course found only at the top. Lower down less trouble is taken. Tragedy is made harmless without recourse to social psychology. Just as every Viennese operetta worthy of the name had to have its tragic finale in the second act, which left nothing for the third except to clear up misunderstandings, the culture industry assigns tragedy a fixed place in the routine. The well-known existence of the recipe is enough to allay any fear that there is no restraint on tragedy. The description of the dramatic formula by the housewife as "getting into trouble and out again" embraces the whole of mass culture from the idiotic women's serial to the top production. Even the worst ending which began with good intentions confirms the order of things and corrupts the tragic force, either because the woman whose love runs counter to the laws of the game plays with her death for a brief spell of happiness, or because the sad ending in the film all the more clearly stresses the indestructibility of actual life. The tragic film becomes an institution for moral improvement. The masses, demoralized by their life under the pressure of the system, and who show signs of civilization only in modes of behavior which have been forced on them and through which fury and recalcitrance show everywhere, are to be kept in order by the sight of an inexorable life and exemplary behavior. Culture has always played its part in taming revolutionary and barbaric instincts. Industrial culture adds its contribution. It shows the condition under which this merciless life can be lived at all. The individual who is thoroughly weary must use his weariness as energy for his surrender to the collective power which wears him out. In films, those permanently desperate situations which crush the spectator in ordinary life somehow become a promise that one can go on living. One has only to become aware of one's own nothingness, only to recognize defeat and one is one with it all. Society is full of desperate people and therefore a prey to rackets. In some of the most significant German novels of the pre-Fascist era such as Döblin's *Berlin Alexanderplatz* and Fallada's *Kleiner Mann, Was Nun,* this trend was as obvious as in the average film and in the devices of jazz. What all these things have in common is the self-derision of man. The possibility of becoming a subject in the economy, an entrepreneur or a proprietor, has been completely liquidated. Right down to the humblest shop, the independent enterprise, on the management and inheritance of which the bourgeois family and the position of its head had rested, became hopelessly dependent. Everybody became an employee; and in this civilization of employees the dignity of the father (questionable anyhow) vanishes. The attitude of the individual to the racket, business, profession or party, before or after admission, the Führer's gesticulations before the masses, or the suitor's before his sweetheart, assume specifically masochistic traits. The attitude into which everybody is forced in order to give repeated proof of his moral suitability for this society reminds one of the boys who, during tribal initiation, go round in a circle with a stereotyped smile on their faces while the priest strikes them. Life in the late capitalist era is a constant initiation rite. Everyone must show that he wholly identifies himself with the power which is belaboring him. This occurs in the principle of jazz syncopation, which simultaneously derides stumbling and makes it a rule. The eunuch-like voice of the crooner on the radio, the heiress's smooth suitor, who falls into the swimming pool in his dinner jacket, are models for those who must become whatever the system wants. Everyone can be like this omnipotent society; everyone can be happy, if only he will capitulate fully and sacrifice his claim to happiness. In his weakness society recognizes its strength, and gives him some of it. His defenselessness makes him reliable. Hence tragedy is discarded. Once the opposition of the individual to society was its substance. It glorified "the bravery and freedom of emotion before a powerful enemy, an exalted affliction, a dreadful problem."[4] Today tragedy has melted away into the nothingness of that false identity of society and individual, whose terror still shows for a moment in the empty semblance of the tragic. But the miracle of integration, the permanent act of grace by the authority who receives the defenseless person – once he has swallowed his rebelliousness – signifies Fascism. This can be seen in the humanitarianism which Döblin uses to let his Biberkopf find refuge, and again in socially-slanted films. The capacity to find refuge, to survive one's own ruin, by which tragedy is defeated, is found in the new generation; they can do any work because the work process does not let them become attached to any. This is reminiscent of the sad lack of conviction of the homecoming soldier with no interest in the war, or of the casual laborer who ends up by joining a paramilitary organization. This liquidation of tragedy confirms the abolition of the individual.

In the culture industry the individual is an illusion not merely because of the standardization of the means of production. He is tolerated only so long as his complete identification with the generality is unquestioned. Pseudo individuality is rife: from the standardized jazz improvization to the exceptional film star whose hair curls over her eye to demonstrate her originality. What is individual is no more than the generality's power to stamp the accidental detail so firmly that it is accepted as such. The defiant reserve or elegant appearance of the individual on show is mass-produced like Yale locks, whose only difference can be measured in fractions of millimeters. The peculiarity of the self is a monopoly commodity determined by society; it is falsely represented as natural. It is no more than the moustache, the French accent, the deep voice of the woman of the world, the Lubitsch touch: finger prints on identity cards which are otherwise exactly the same, and into which the lives and faces of every single person are transformed by the power of the generality. Pseudo individuality is the prerequisite for comprehending tragedy and removing its poison: only because individuals have ceased to be themselves and are now merely centers where the general tendencies meet, is it possible to receive them again, whole and entire, into the generality. In this way mass culture discloses the fictitious character of the "individual" in the bourgeois era, and is merely unjust in boasting on account of this dreary harmony of general and particular. The principle of individuality was always full of contradiction. Individuation has never really been achieved. Self-preservation in the shape of class has kept everyone at the stage of a mere species being. Every bourgeois characteristic, in spite of its deviation and indeed because of it, expressed the same thing: the harshness of the competitive society. The individual who supported society bore its disfiguring mark; seemingly free, he was actually the product of its economic and social apparatus. Power based itself on the prevailing conditions of power when it sought the approval of persons affected by it. As it progressed, bourgeois society did also develop the individual. Against the will of its leaders, technology has changed human beings from children into persons. However, every advance in individuation of this kind took place at the expense of the individuality in whose name it occurred, so that nothing was left but the resolve to pursue one's own particular purpose. The bourgeois whose existence is split into a business and a private life, whose private life is split into keeping up his public image and intimacy, whose intimacy is split into the surly partnership of marriage and the bitter comfort of being quite alone, at odds with himself and everybody else, is already virtually a Nazi, replete both with enthusiasm and abuse; or a modern city-dweller who can now only imagine friendship as a "social contact": that is, as being in social contact with others with whom he has no inward contact. The only reason why the culture industry can deal so successfully with individuality is that the latter has always reproduced the fragility of society. On the faces of private individuals and movie heroes put together according to the patterns on magazine covers vanishes a pretense in which no one now believes; the popularity of the hero models comes partly from a secret satisfaction that the effort to achieve individuation has at last been replaced by the effort to imitate, which is admittedly more breathless. It is idle to hope that this self-contradictory, disintegrating "person" will not last for genera-tions, that the system must collapse because of such a psychological split, or that the deceitful substitution of the stereotype for the individual will of itself become unbearable for mankind. Since Shakespeare's *Hamlet*, the unity of the personality has been seen through as a pretense. Synthetically produced physiognomies show that the people of today have already forgotten that there was ever a notion of what human life was. For centuries society has been preparing for Victor Mature and Mickey Rooney. By destroying they come to fulfill.

The idolization of the cheap involves making the average the heroic. The highest-paid stars resemble pictures advertising unspecified proprietary articles. Not without good purpose are they often selected from the host of commercial models. The prevailing taste takes its ideal from advertising, the beauty in consumption. Hence the Socratic saying that the beautiful is the useful has now been fulfilled – ironically. The cinema makes propaganda for the culture combine as a whole; on radio, goods for whose sake the cultural commodity exists are also recommended individually. For a few coins one can see the film which cost millions, for even less one can buy the chewing gum whose manufacture involved immense riches – a hoard increased still further by sales. *In absentia*, but by universal suffrage, the treasure of armies is revealed, but prostitution is not allowed inside the country. The best orchestras in the world – clearly not so – are brought into your living room free of charge. It is all a parody of the never-never land, just as the national society is a parody of the human society. You name it, we supply it. A man up from the country remarked at the old Berlin Metropol theater that it was astonishing what they could do for the money; his comment has long since been adopted by the culture industry and made the very substance of production. This is always coupled with the triumph that it is possible; but this, in large measure, is the very triumph. Putting on a show means showing everybody what there is, and what can be achieved. Even today it is still a fair, but incurably sick with culture. Just as the people who had been attracted by the fairground barkers overcame their disappointment in the booths with a brave smile, because they really knew in advance what would happen, so the movie-goer sticks knowingly to the institution. With the cheapness of mass-produced luxury goods and its complement, the universal swindle, a change in the character of the art commodity itself is coming about. What is new is not that it is a commodity, but that today it deliberately admits it is one; that art renounces its own autonomy and proudly takes its place among consumption goods constitutes the charm of novelty. Art as a separate sphere was always possible only in a bourgeois society. Even as a negation of that social purposiveness which is spreading through the market, its freedom remains essentially bound up with the premise of a commodity economy. Pure works of art which deny the commodity society by the very fact that they obey their own law were always wares all the same. In so far as, until the eighteenth century, the buyer's patronage shielded the artist from the market, they were dependent on the buyer and his objectives. The purposelessness of the great modern work of art depends on the anonymity of the market. Its demands pass through so many intermediaries that the artist is exempt from any definite requirements – though admittedly only to a certain degree, for throughout the whole history of the bourgeoisie his autonomy was only tolerated, and thus contained an element of untruth which ultimately led to the social liquidation of art. When mortally sick, Beethoven hurled away a novel by Sir Walter Scott with the cry: "Why, the fellow writes for money," and yet proved a most experienced and stubborn businessman in disposing of the last quartets, which were a most extreme renunciation of the market; he is the most outstanding example of the unity of those opposites, market and independence, in bourgeois art. Those who succumb to the ideology are precisely those who cover up the contradiction instead of taking it into the consciousness of their own production as Beethoven did: he went on to express in music his anger at losing a few pence, and derived the metaphysical *Es Muss Sein* (which attempts an aesthetic banishment of the pressure of the world by taking it into itself) from the housekeeper's demand for her monthly wages. The principle of idealistic aesthetics – purposefulness without a purpose – reverses the scheme of things to which bourgeois art conforms socially: purposelessness for the purposes declared by the market. At last, in the demand for entertainment and relaxation, purpose has absorbed the realm of purposelessness. But as the insistence that art should be disposable in terms of money becomes absolute, a shift in the internal structure of cultural commodities begins to show itself. The use which men in this antagonistic society promise themselves from the work of art is itself, to a great extent, that very existence of the useless which is abolished by complete inclusion under use. The work of art, by completely assimilating itself to need, deceitfully deprives men of precisely that liberation from the principle of utility which it should inaugurate. What might be called use value in the reception of cultural commodities is replaced by exchange value; in place of enjoyment there are gallery-visiting and factual knowledge: the prestige seeker replaces the connoisseur. The consumer becomes the ideology of the pleasure industry, whose institutions he cannot escape. One simply "has to" have seen *Mrs. Miniver*, just as one "has to" subscribe to *Life* and *Time*. Everything is looked at from only one aspect: that it can be used for something else, however vague the notion of this use may be. No object has an inherent value; it is valuable only to the extent that it can be exchanged. The use value of art, its mode of being, is treated as a fetish; and the fetish, the work's social rating (misinterpreted as its artistic status) becomes its use value – the only quality which is enjoyed. The commodity function of art disappears only to be wholly realized when art becomes a species of commodity instead, marketable and inter-changeable like an industrial product. But art as a type of product which existed to be sold and yet to be unsaleable is wholly and hypocritically converted into "unsale-ability" as soon as the transaction ceases to be the mere intention and becomes its sole principle. No tickets could be bought when Toscanini conducted over the radio; he was heard without charge, and every sound of the symphony was accompanied, as it were, by the sublime puff that the symphony was not interrupted by any advertising: "This concert is brought to you as a public service." The illusion was made possible by the profits of the united automobile and soap manufacturers, whose payments keep the radio stations going – and, of course, by the increased sales of the electrical industry, which manufactures the radio sets. Radio, the progressive latecomer of mass culture, draws all the consequences at present denied the film by its pseudo-market. The technical structure of the commercial radio system makes it immune from liberal deviations such as those the movie industrialists can still permit them-selves in their own sphere. It is a private enterprise which really does represent the

sovereign whole and is therefore some distance ahead of the other individual combines. Chesterfield is merely the nation's cigarette, but the radio is the voice of the
nation. In bringing cultural products wholly into the sphere of commodities, radio
does not try to dispose of its culture goods themselves as commodities straight to
the consumer. In America it collects no fees from the public, and so has acquired the
illusory form of disinterested, unbiased authority which suits Fascism admirably. The
radio becomes the universal mouthpiece of the Führer; his voice rises from street
loud-speakers to resemble the howling of sirens announcing panic – from which
modern propaganda can scarcely be distinguished anyway. The National Socialists
knew that the wireless gave shape to their cause just as the printing press did to the
Reformation. The metaphysical charisma of the Führer invented by the sociology of
religion has finally turned out to be no more than the omnipresence of his speeches
on the radio, which are a demoniacal parody of the omnipresence of the divine spirit.
The gigantic fact that the speech penetrates everywhere replaces its content, just as
the benefaction of the Toscanini broadcast takes the place of the symphony. No
listener can grasp its true meaning any longer, while the Führer's speech is lies anyway.
The inherent tendency of radio is to make the speaker's word, the false command-
ment, absolute. A recommendation becomes an order. The recommendation of the
same commodities under different proprietary names, the scientifically based praise of
the laxative in the announcer's smooth voice between the overture from *La Traviata*
and that from *Rienzi* is the only thing that no longer works, because of its silliness.
One day the edict of production, the actual advertisement (whose actuality is at
present concealed by the pretense of a choice) can turn into the open command of
the Führer. In a society of huge Fascist rackets which agree among themselves what
part of the social product should be allotted to the nation's needs, it would eventually
seem anachronistic to recommend the use of a particular soap powder. The Führer is
more up-to-date in unceremoniously giving direct orders for both the holocaust and
the supply of rubbish.

Even today the culture industry dresses works of art like political slogans and forces
them upon a resistant public at reduced prices; they are as accessible for public
enjoyment as a park. But the disappearance of their genuine commodity character
does not mean that they have been abolished in the life of a free society, but that the
last defense against their reduction to culture goods has fallen. The abolition of
educational privilege by the device of clearance sales does not open for the masses
the spheres from which they were formerly excluded, but, given existing social
conditions, contributes directly to the decay of education and the progress of barbaric
meaninglessness. Those who spent their money in the nineteenth or the early twentieth century to see a play or to go to a concert respected the performance as much as
the money they spent. The bourgeois who wanted to get something out of it tried
occasionally to establish some rapport with the work. Evidence for this is to be found
in the literary "introductions" to works, or in the commentaries on *Faust*. These were
the first steps toward the biographical coating and other practices to which a work of
art is subjected today. Even in the early, prosperous days of business, exchange-value
did carry use value as a mere appendix but had developed it as a prerequisite for its
own existence; this was socially helpful for works of art. Art exercised some restraint

on the bourgeois as long as it cost money. That is now a thing of the past. Now that it has lost every restraint and there is no need to pay any money, the proximity of art to those who are exposed to it completes the alienation and assimilates one to the other under the banner of triumphant objectivity. Criticism and respect disappear in the culture industry; the former becomes a mechanical expertise, the latter is succeeded by a shallow cult of leading personalities. Consumers now find nothing expensive. Nevertheless, they suspect that the less anything costs, the less it is being given them. The double mistrust of traditional culture as ideology is combined with mistrust of industrialized culture as a swindle. When thrown in free, the now debased works of art, together with the rubbish to which the medium assimilates them, are secretly rejected by the fortunate recipients, who are supposed to be satisfied by the mere fact that there is so much to be seen and heard. Everything can be obtained. The screenos and vaudevilles in the movie theater, the competitions for guessing music, the free books, rewards and gifts offered on certain radio programs, are not mere accidents but a continuation of the practice obtaining with culture products. The symphony becomes a reward for listening to the radio, and – if technology had its way – the film would be delivered to people's homes as happens with the radio. It is moving toward the commercial system. Television points the way to a development which might easily enough force the Warner Brothers into what would certainly be the unwelcome position of serious musicians and cultural conservatives. But the gift system has already taken hold among consumers. As culture is represented as a bonus with undoubted private and social advantages, they have to seize the chance. They rush in lest they miss something. Exactly what, is not clear, but in any case the only ones with a chance are the participants. Fascism, however, hopes to use the training the culture industry has given these recipients of gifts, in order to organize them into its own forced battalions.

Culture is a paradoxical commodity. So completely is it subject to the law of exchange that it is no longer exchanged; it is so blindly consumed in use that it can no longer be used. Therefore it amalgamates with advertising. The more meaningless the latter seems to be under a monopoly, the more omnipotent it becomes. The motives are markedly economic. One could certainly live without the culture industry, therefore it necessarily creates too much satiation and apathy. In itself, it has few resources itself to correct this. Advertising is its elixir of life. But as its product never fails to reduce to a mere promise the enjoyment which it promises as a commodity, it eventually co-incides with publicity, which it needs because it cannot be enjoyed. In a competitive society, advertising performed the social service of informing the buyer about the market; it made choice easier and helped the unknown but more efficient supplier to dispose of his goods. Far from costing time, it saved it. Today, when the free market is coming to an end, those who control the system are entrenching themselves in it. It strengthens the firm bond between the consumers and the big combines. Only those who can pay the exorbitant rates charged by the advertising agencies, chief of which are the radio networks themselves; that is, only those who are already in a position to do so, or are co-opted by the decision of the banks and industrial capital, can enter the pseudo-market as sellers. The costs of advertising, which finally flow back into the pockets of the combines, make it unnecessary to defeat unwelcome outsiders by laborious competition. They guarantee that power will remain in the same hands – not unlike those economic decisions by which the establishment and running of undertakings is controlled in a totalitarian state. Advertising today is a negative principle, a blocking device: everything that does not bear its stamp is economically suspect. Universal publicity is in no way necessary for people to get to know the kinds of goods – whose supply is restricted anyway. It helps sales only indirectly. For a particular firm, to phase out a current advertising practice constitutes a loss of prestige, and a breach of the discipline imposed by the influential clique on its members. In wartime, goods which are unobtainable are still advertised, merely to keep industrial power in view. Subsidizing ideological media is more important than the repetition of the name. Because the system obliges every product to use advertising, it has permeated the idiom – the "style" – of the culture industry. Its victory is so complete that it is no longer evident in the key positions: the huge buildings of the top men, floodlit stone advertisements, are free of advertising; at most they exhibit on the rooftops, in monumental brilliance and without any self-glorification, the firm's initials. But, in contrast, the nineteenth-century houses, whose architecture still shamefully indicates that they can be used as a consumption commodity and are intended to be lived in, are covered with posters and inscriptions from the ground right up to and beyond the roof: until they become no more than backgrounds for bills and sign-boards. Advertising becomes art and nothing else, just as Goebbels – with foresight – combines them: *l'art pour l'art*, advertising for its own sake, a pure representation of social power. In the most influential American magazines, *Life* and *Fortune*, a quick glance can now scarcely distinguish advertising from editorial picture and text. The latter features an enthusiastic and gratuitous account of the great man (with illustrations of his life and grooming habits) which will bring him new fans, while the advertisement pages use so many factual photographs and details that they represent the ideal of information which the editorial part has only begun to try to achieve. The assembly-line character of the culture industry, the synthetic, planned method of turning out its products (factory-like not only in the studio but, more or less, in the compilation of cheap biographies, pseudodocumentary novels, and hit songs) is very suited to advertising: the important individual points, by becoming detachable, interchangeable, and even technically alienated from any connected meaning, lend themselves to ends external to the work. The effect, the trick, the isolated repeatable device, have always been used to exhibit goods for advertising purposes, and today every monster close-up of a star is an advertisement for her name, and every hit song a plug for its tune. Advertising and the culture industry merge technically as well as economically. In both cases the same thing can be seen in innumerable places, and the mechanical repetition of the same culture product has come to be the same as that of the propaganda slogan. In both cases the insistent demand for effectiveness makes technology into psychotechnology, into a procedure for manipulating men. In both cases the standards are the striking yet familiar, the easy yet catchy, the skillful yet simple; the object is to overpower the customer, who is conceived as absent-minded or resistant.

By the language he speaks, he makes his own contribution to culture as publicity. The more completely language is lost in the announcement, the more words are debased as substantial vehicles of meaning and become signs devoid of quality; the more purely and transparently words communicate what is intended, the more impenetrable they become. The demythologization of language, taken as an element of the whole process of enlightenment, is a relapse into magic. Word and essential content were distinct yet inseparable from one another. Concepts like melancholy and history, even life, were recognized in the word, which separated them out and preserved them. Its form simultaneously constituted and reflected them. The absolute separation, which makes the moving accidental and its relation to the object arbitrary, puts an end to the superstitious fusion of word and thing. Anything in a determined literal sequence which goes beyond the correlation to the event is rejected as unclear and as verbal metaphysics. But the result is that the word, which can now be only a sign without any meaning, becomes so fixed to the thing that it is just a petrified formula. This affects language and object alike. Instead of making the object experiential, the purified word treats it as an abstract instance, and everything else (now excluded by the demand for ruthless clarity from expression – itself now banished) fades away in reality. A left-half at football, a black-shirt, a member of the Hitler Youth, and so on, are no more than names. If before its rationalization the word had given rise to lies as well as to longing, now, after its rationalization, it is a straitjacket for longing more even than for lies. The blindness and dumbness of the data to which positivism reduces the world pass over into language itself, which restricts itself to recording those data. Terms themselves become impenetrable; they obtain a striking force, a power of adhesion and repulsion which makes them like their extreme opposite, incantations. They come to be a kind of trick, because the name of the prima donna is cooked up in the studio on a statistical basis, or because a welfare state is anathematized by using taboo terms such as "bureaucrats" or "intellectuals," or because base practice uses the name of the country as a charm. In general, the name – to which magic most easily attaches – is undergoing a chemical change: a metamorphosis into capricious, manipulable designations, whose effect is admittedly now calculable, but which for that very reason is just as despotic as that of the archaic name. First names, those archaic remnants, have been brought up to date either by stylization as advertising trade-marks (film stars' surnames have become first names), or by collective standardization. In comparison, the bourgeois family name which, instead of being a trade-mark, once individualized its bearer by relating him to his own past history, seems antiquated. It arouses a strange embarrassment in Americans. In order to hide the awkward distance between individuals, they call one another "Bob" and "Harry," as interchangeable team members. This practice reduces relations between human beings to the good fellowship of the sporting community and is a defense against the true kind of relationship. Signification, which is the only function of a word admitted by semantics, reaches perfection in the sign. Whether folksongs were rightly or wrongly called upper-class culture in decay, their elements have only acquired their popular form through a long process of repeated transmission. The spread of popular songs, on the other hand, takes place at lightning speed. The American expression "fad," used for fashions which appear like epidemics – that is, inflamed by highly-concentrated economic forces – designated this phenomenon long before totalitarian advertising bosses enforced the general lines of culture. When the German Fascists decide one day to launch a word – say, "intolerable" – over the loudspeakers the next day the whole nation is saying "intolerable." By the same pattern, the nations against whom the weight of the German "blitzkrieg" was thrown took the word into their own jargon. The general repetition of names for measures to be taken by the authorities makes them, so to speak, familiar, just as the brand name on everybody's lips increased sales in the era of the free market. The blind and rapidly spreading repetition of words with special designations links advertising with the totalitarian watchword. The layer of experience which created the words for their speakers has been removed; in this swift appropriation language acquires the coldness which until now it had only on billboards and in the advertisement columns of newspapers. Innumerable people use words and expressions which they have either ceased to understand or employ only because they trigger off conditioned reflexes; in this sense, words are trade-marks which are finally all the more firmly linked to the things they denote, the less their linguistic sense is grasped: The minister for mass education talks incomprehendingly of "dynamic forces," and the hit songs unceasingly celebrate "reverie" and "rhapsody," yet base their popularity precisely on the magic of the unintelligible as creating the thrill of a more exalted life. Other stereotypes, such as memory, are still partly comprehended, but escape from the experience which might allow them content. They appear like enclaves in the spoken language. On the radio of Flesch and Hitler they may be recognized from the affected pronunciation of the announcer when he says to the nation, "Good night, everybody!" or "This is the Hitler Youth," and even intones "the Führer" in a way imitated by millions. In such clichés the last bond between sedimentary experience and language is severed which still had a reconciling effect in dialect in the nineteenth century. But in the prose of the journalist whose adaptable attitude led to his appointment as an all-German editor, the German words become petrified, alien terms. Every word shows how far it has been debased by the Fascist pseudofolk community. By now, of course, this kind of language is already universal, totalitarian. All the violence done to words is so vile that one can hardly bear to hear them any longer. The announcer does not need to speak pompously; he would indeed be impossible if his inflection were different from that of his particular audience. But, as against that, the language and gestures of the audience and spectators are colored more strongly than ever before by the culture industry, even in fine nuances which cannot yet be explained experimentally. Today the culture industry has taken over the civilizing inheritance of the zentrepreneurial and frontier democracy – whose appreciation of intellectual deviations was never very finely attuned. All are free to dance and enjoy themselves, just as they have been free, since the historical neutralization of religion, to join any of the innumerable sects. But freedom to choose an ideology – since ideology always reflects economic coercion – everywhere proves to be freedom to choose what is always the same. The way in which a girl accepts and keeps the obligatory date, the inflection on the telephone or in the most intimate situation, the choice of words in conversation, and the whole inner life as classified by the now somewhat devalued depth psychology, bear witness to man's attempt to make himself a proficient apparatus, similar (even in emotions) to the model served up by the culture industry. The most intimate reactions of human beings have been so thoroughly reified that the idea of anything specific to themselves now persists only as an utterly abstract notion: personality scarcely signifies anything more than shining white teeth and freedom from body odor and emotions. The triumph of advertising in the culture industry is that consumers feel compelled to buy and use its products even though they see through them.

Notes

1 Nietzsche, *Unzeitgemässe Betrachtungen, Werke*, vol. I (Leipzig, 1917), p. 187.
2 Alexis de Tocqueville, *De la Démocratie en Amérique*, vol. II (Paris, 1864), p. 151.
3 Frank Wedekind, *Gesammelte Werke*, vol. IX (Munich, 1921), p. 426.
4 Nietzsche, *Götzendämmerung, Werke*, vol. VIII, p. 136.

5

The Public Sphere:
An Encyclopedia Article*

Jürgen Habermas

The Concept. By "the public sphere" we mean first of all a realm of our social life in which something approaching public opinion can be formed. Access is guaranteed to all citizens. A portion of the public sphere comes into being in every conversation in which private individuals assemble to form a public body.[1] They then behave neither like business or professional people transacting private affairs, nor like members of a constitutional order subject to the legal constraints of a state bureaucracy. Citizens behave as a public body when they confer in an unrestricted fashion – that is, with the guarantee of freedom of assembly and association and the freedom to express and publish their opinions – about matters of general interest. In a large public body, this kind of communication requires specific means for transmitting information and influencing those who receive it. Today, newspapers and magazines, radio and television are the media of the public sphere. We speak of the political public sphere in contrast, for instance, to the literary one, when public discussion deals with objects connected to the activity of the state. Although state authority is, so to speak, the executor of the political public sphere, it is not a part of it.[2] To be sure, state authority is usually considered "public" authority, but it derives its task of caring for the well-being of all citizens primarily from this aspect of the public sphere. Only when the exercise of political control is effectively subordinated to the democratic demand that information be accessible to the public, does the political public sphere win an institutionalized influence over the government through the instrument of law-making bodies. The expression *public opinion* refers to the tasks of criticism and control which a public body of citizens informally – and, in periodic elections, formally as well – practices vis-à-vis the ruling structure organized in the form of a state. Regulations demanding that certain proceedings be public [*Publizitätsvorschriften*] – for example, those providing for open court hearings – are also related to this function of public opinion. The public sphere as a sphere which mediates between society and state, in which the public organizes itself as the bearer of public opinion,

* From Jürgen Habermas, *Critical Theory and Society: A Reader*, ed. Stephen Eric Bronner and Douglas M. Kellner, trans. by Sara Lennox and Frank Lennox (New York: Routledge, 1989), pp. 136–42.

accords with the principle of the public sphere[3] – that principle of public information which once had to be fought for against the arcane policies of monarchies and which since that time has made possible the democratic control of state activities.

It is no coincidence that these concepts of the public sphere and public opinion arose for the first time only in the eighteenth century. They acquire their specific meaning from a concrete historical situation. It was at that time that the distinction of "opinion" from "opinion publique" and "public opinion" came about. Though mere opinions (cultural assumptions, normative attitudes, collective prejudices and values) seem to persist unchanged in their natural form as a kind of sediment of history, public opinion can by definition come into existence only when a reasoning public is presupposed. Public discussions about the exercise of political power which are both critical in intent and institutionally guaranteed have not always existed – they grew out of a specific phase of bourgeois society and could enter into the order of the bourgeois constitutional state only as a result of a particular constellation of interests.

History. There is no indication that European society of the high Middle Ages possessed a public sphere as a unique realm distinct from the private sphere. Nevertheless, it was not coincidental that during that period symbols of sovereignty, for instance, the princely seal, were deemed "public." At that time there existed a public representation of power. The status of the feudal lord, at whatever level of the feudal pyramid, made it unnecessary to employ the categories "public" and "private." The holder of the position represented it publicly; he showed himself, presented himself as the embodiment of an ever-present "higher" power. The concept of this representation has been maintained up to the most recent constitutional history. Regardless of the degree to which it has loosened itself from the old base, the authority of political power today still demands a representation at the highest level by a head of state. Such elements, however, derive from a prebourgeois social structure. Representation in the sense of a bourgeois public sphere,[4] for instance, the representation of the nation or of particular mandates, has nothing to do with the medieval representative public sphere – a public sphere directly linked to the concrete existence of a ruler. As long as the prince and the estates of the realm still "are" the land, instead of merely functioning as deputies for it, they are able to "represent"; they represent their power "before" the people, instead of for the people.

The feudal authorities (Church, princes, and nobility), to which the representative public sphere was first linked, disintegrated during a long process of polarization. By the end of the eighteenth century they had broken apart into private elements on the one hand, and into public elements on the other. The position of the Church changed with the Reformation: the link to divine authority which the Church represented, that is, religion, became a private matter. So-called religious freedom came to insure what was historically the first area of private autonomy. The Church itself continued its existence as one public and legal body among others. The corresponding polarization within princely authority was visibly manifested in the separation of the public budget from the private household expenses of a ruler. The institutions of public authority, along with the bureaucracy and the military, and in part also with the legal institutions, asserted their independence from the privatized sphere of the princely court. Finally, the feudal estates were transformed as well: the nobility became the organs of public authority, parliament, and the legal institutions; while those occupied in trades and professions, insofar as they had already established urban corporations and territorial organizations, developed into a sphere of bourgeois society which would stand apart from the state as a genuine area of private autonomy.

The representative public sphere yielded to that new sphere of "public authority" which came into being with national and territorial states. Continuous state activity (permanent administration, standing army) now corresponded to the permanence of the relationships which with the stock exchange and the press had developed within the exchange of commodities and information. Public authority consolidated into a concrete opposition for those who were merely subject to it and who at first found only a negative definition of themselves within it. These were the "private individuals" who were excluded from public authority because they held no office. "Public" no longer referred to the "representative" court of a prince endowed with authority, but rather to an institution regulated according to competence, to an apparatus endowed with a monopoly on the legal exertion of authority. Private individuals subsumed in the state at whom public authority was directed now made up the public body.

Society, now a private realm occupying a position in opposition to the state, stood on the one hand as if in clear contrast to the state. On the other hand, that society had become a concern of public interest to the degree that the production of life in the wake of the developing market economy had grown beyond the bounds of private domestic authority. *The bourgeois public sphere* could be understood as the sphere of private individuals assembled into a public body, which almost immediately laid claim to the officially regulated "intellectual newspapers" for use against the public authority itself. In those newspapers, and in moralistic and critical journals, they debated that public authority on the general rules of social intercourse in their fundamentally privatized yet publicly relevant sphere of labor and commodity exchange.

The Liberal Model of the Public Sphere. The medium of this debate – public discussion – was unique and without historical precedent. Hitherto the estates had negotiated agreements with their princes, settling their claims to power from case to case. This development took a different course in England, where the parliament limited royal power, than it did on the Continent, where the monarchies mediatized the estates. The Third Estate then broke with this form of power arrangement, since it could no longer establish itself as a ruling group. A division of power by means of the delineation of the rights of the nobility was no longer possible within an exchange economy – private authority over capitalist property is, after all, unpolitical. Bourgeois individuals are private individuals. As such, they do not "rule." Their claims to power vis-à-vis public authority were thus directed not against the concentration of power, which was to be "shared." Instead, their ideas infiltrated the very principle on which the existing power is based. To the principle of existing power, the bourgeois public opposed the principle of supervision – that very principle which demands that proceedings be made public [*Publizität*]. The principle of supervision is thus a means of transforming the nature of power, not merely one basis of legitimation exchanged for another.

In the first modern constitutions, the catalogues of fundamental rights were a perfect image of the liberal model of the public sphere: they guaranteed the society as a sphere of private autonomy and the restriction of public authority to a few functions. Between these two spheres, the constitutions further insured the existence of a realm of private individuals assembled into a public body who as citizens transmit the needs of bourgeois society to the state, in order, ideally, to transform political into "rational" authority within the medium of this public sphere. The general interest, which was the measure of such rationality, was then guaranteed, according to the presuppositions of a society of free commodity exchange, when the activities of private individuals in the marketplace were freed from social compulsion and from political pressure in the public sphere.

At the same time, daily political newspapers assumed an important role. In the second half of the eighteenth century, literary journalism created serious competition for the earlier news sheets, which were mere compilations of notices. Karl Bücher characterized this great development as follows: "Newspapers changed from mere institutions for the publication of news into bearers and leaders of public opinion – weapons of party politics. This transformed the newspaper business. A new element emerged between the gathering and publication of news: the editorial staff. But for the newspaper publisher it meant that he changed from a vendor of recent news to a dealer in public opinion." The publishers insured the newspapers a commercial basis, yet without commercializing them as such. The press remained an institution of the public itself, effective in the manner of a mediator and intensifier of public discussion, no longer a mere organ for the spreading of news but not yet the medium of a consumer culture.

This type of journalism can be observed above all during periods of revolution, when newspapers of the smallest political groups and organizations spring up – for instance, in Paris in 1789. Even in the Paris of 1848 every half-way eminent politician organized his club, every other his journal: 450 clubs and over 200 journals were established there between February and May alone. Until the permanent legalization of a politically functional public sphere, the appearance of a political newspaper meant joining the struggle for freedom and public opinion, and thus for the public sphere as a principle. Only with the establishment of the bourgeois constitutional state was the intellectual press relieved of the pressure of its convictions. Since then it has been able to abandon its polemical position and take advantage of the earning possibilities of a commercial undertaking. In England, France, and the United States, the transformation from a journalism of conviction to one of commerce began in the 1830s at approximately the same time. In the transition from the literary journalism of private individuals to the public services of the mass media, the public sphere was transformed by the influx of private interests, which received special prominence in the mass media.

The Public Sphere in the Social Welfare State Mass Democracy. Although the liberal model of the public sphere is still instructive today with respect to the normative claim that information be accessible to the public,[5] it cannot be applied to the actual conditions of an industrially advanced mass democracy organized in the form of the social welfare state. In part, the liberal model had always included ideological components, but it is also in part true that the social preconditions, to which the ideological elements could at one time at least be linked, had been fundamentally transformed. The very forms in which the public sphere manifested itself, to which supporters of the liberal model could appeal for evidence, began to change with the Chartist movement in England and the February revolution in France. Because of the diffusion of press and propaganda, the public body expanded beyond the bounds of the bourgeoisie. The public body lost not only its social exclusivity; it lost in addition the coherence created by bourgeois social institutions and a relatively high standard of education. Conflicts hitherto restricted to the private sphere now intrude into the public sphere. Group needs which can expect no satisfaction from a self-regulating market now tend toward a regulation by the state. The public sphere, which must now mediate these demands, becomes a field for the competition of interests, competitions which assume the form of violent conflict. Laws which obviously have come about under the "pressure of the street" can scarcely still be understood as arising from the consensus of private individuals engaged in public discussion. They correspond in a more or less unconcealed manner to the compromise of conflicting private interests. Social organizations which deal with the state act in the political public sphere, whether through the agency of political parties or directly in connection with the public administration. With the interweaving of the public and private realms, not only do the political authorities assume certain functions in the sphere of commodity exchange and social labor, but, conversely, social powers now assume political functions. This leads to a kind of "refeudalization" of the public sphere. Large organizations strive for political compromises with the state and with one another, excluding the public sphere whenever possible. But at the same time the large organizations must assure themselves of at least plebiscitary support from the mass of the population through an apparent display of openness [*demonstrative Publizität*].[6]

The political public sphere of the social welfare state is characterized by a peculiar weakening of its critical functions. At one time the process of making proceedings public [*Publizität*] was intended to subject persons or affairs to public reason, and to make political decisions subject to appeal before the court of public opinion. But often enough today the process of making public simply serves the arcane policies of special interests; in the form of "publicity" it wins public prestige for people or affairs, thus making them worthy of acclamation in a climate of nonpublic opinion. The very words "public relations work" [*Öffentlichkeitsarbeit*] betray the fact that a public sphere must first be arduously constructed case by case, a public sphere which earlier grew out of the social structure. Even the central relationship of the public, the parties, and the parliament is affected by this change in function.

Yet this trend towards the weakening of the public sphere as a principle is opposed by the extension of fundamental rights in the social welfare state. The demand that information be accessible to the public is extended from organs of the state to all organizations dealing with the state. To the degree that this is realized, a public body of organized private individuals would take the place of the now-defunct public body of private individuals who relate individually to each other. Only these organized individuals could participate effectively in the process of public communication; only they could use the channels of the public sphere which exist within parties and associations and the process of making proceedings public [*Publizität*] which was established to facilitate the dealings of organizations with the state. Political compromises would have to be legitimized through this process of public communication. The idea of the public sphere, preserved in the social welfare state mass democracy, an idea which calls for a rationalization of power through the medium of public discussion among private individuals, threatens to disintegrate with the structural transformation of the public sphere itself. It could only be realized today, on an altered basis, as a rational reorganization of social and political power under the mutual control of rival organizations committed to the public sphere in their internal structure as well as in their relations with the state and each other.

Notes

1 Habermas's concept of the public sphere is not to be equated with that of "the public," i.e., of the individuals who assemble. His concept is directed instead at the institution, which to be sure only assumes concrete form through the participation of people. It cannot, however, be characterized simply as a crowd. (This and the following notes by Peter Hohendahl.)

2 The state and the public sphere do not overlap, as one might suppose from casual language use. Rather, they confront one another as opponents. Habermas designates that sphere as public which antiquity understood to be private, i.e., the sphere of nongovernmental opinion making.

3 The principle of the public sphere could still be distinguished from an institution which is demonstrable in social history. Habermas thus would mean a model of norms and modes of behavior by means of which the very functioning of public opinion can be guaranteed for the first time. These norms and modes of behavior include: a) general accessibility, b) elimination of all privileges, and c) discovery of general norms and rational legitimations.

4 The expression *represent* is used in a very specific sense in the following section, namely, to "present oneself." The important thing to understand is that the medieval public sphere, if it even deserves this designation, is tied to the *personal*. The feudal lord and estates create the public sphere by means of their very presence.

5 Here it should be understood that Habermas considers the principle behind the bourgeois public sphere, but not its historical form, as indispensable.

6 One must distinguish between Habermas's concept of "making proceedings public" [*Publizität*] and the "public sphere" [*Öffentlichkeit*]. The term *Publizität* describes the degree of public effect generated by a public act. Thus, a situation can arise in which the form of public opinion making is maintained, while the substance of the public sphere has long ago been undermined.

Part II

Social Life and Cultural Studies

Introduction to Part II

As we noted in our "Adventures in Media and Cultural Studies," a tradition of social science-based empirical research into mass communications and culture emerged in the United States during the 1940s and 1950s. The empirical methods of determining consumer demand, taste, opinions, and the effects of mass media were applied to a wide range of issues by Paul Lazarsfeld and a group of colleagues in the Bureau for Applied Social Research which Lazarsfeld founded at Columbia University. This project provided ground-breaking studies of the media and their effects, inaugurating debates that are still raging. In addition, communication departments were being established in the United States and elsewhere during the 1940s and 1950s which for the most part deployed empirical methods of communications research and made the study of mass communication a branch of academic inquiry.[1]

Opposed to what were seen as overly empiricist and conformist approaches to the study of communication and culture, more critical approaches emerged. Within the traditions of critical media and cultural criticism, there are many models of social approaches to culture and what has become known as cultural studies. In a sense, every essay in this reader can be seen as an example of a social-contextualizing approach, which sees culture as a form of social life, and thus as a type of cultural studies. This perspective situates cultural and media artifacts within the social relations of production and reception in which culture is produced, distributed, and consumed. It analyzes media and culture as part of society and relates text to context in order to properly analyze, interpret, or criticize meaning and effect.

In *Mythologies*, Roland Barthes critically dissects a wide range of contemporary forms of culture, producing a unique method of cultural interpretation and critique. The selection we have chosen, "Operation Margarine," embodies the fundamental rhetorical and ideological operations that Barthes dissects in the conclusion to *Mythologies*, part of which we also include. Margarine, on Barthes' account, is a highly artificial substance transfigured by advertising into a natural, beneficial, and acceptable substitution for butter. Analyzing ads which admit its deficiencies and then trumpet its benefits, Barthes claims that such operations provide an "inoculation" against criticism of its imperfections. A similar operation, he claims, is typical in discourses on topics such as the military, Church, or capitalism, in which their limitations are mentioned, to highlight their necessity and importance for the social order.

Likewise, mythologies disappear history, transforming contingent factors into natural essences, as if it were natural that an African soldier salute the French flag in Barthes' famous example that erases all of the evils of French colonization in an idealized image. Constructing an argument that anticipates postmodern emphasis on difference and otherness, Barthes points out how myths also erase what is different and dissimilar, assimilating otherness to nature, as when the image of the French soldier folds the African into the French empire, or margarine ads assimilate an artificial substance into the order of culinary appropriateness.

Myths, Barthes argues, also make use of the rhetorical figure of tautology, equating in the examples given above African blacks to France or margarine to natural substances such as butter. Myths may deploy in addition the figure of what Barthes calls "Neither–Norism," a liberal device that enjoins rejecting extremes to identify with common sense – which usually means conforming to existing attitudes and behavior. Translating quality into quantity sometimes takes the form of holding certain qualities (high art, religion, or the state) as impossible to grasp, as ineffable, and thus above criticism. Or it may take the form of reducing discussion of business or politics to quantity alone, as in lists of the most profitable corporations or most valuable stocks in business publications. Political discussions that focus on polls or ratings of candidates as opposed to more substantive and qualitative features also embody this operation. Such devices lend themselves to what Barthes calls "statements of fact," proverbial wisdom like "What's good for General Motors is good for America" or "God Save the Queen," in which a contingent and problematic institution is identified with the country itself.

Barthes thus constructed a method of analyzing rhetorical strategies of media culture, taking apart the mythologies that colonize social life, and helping to produce a critical consciousness on behalf of the reader. In *Understanding Media*, Marshall McLuhan taught his readers to take media seriously as important agents of change in the contemporary era. In the selections we have included, McLuhan sketches out his famous dictum "The Medium is the Message." As a salient example, McLuhan appeals to the electric light bulb: it was the medium of electricity that profoundly changed social life, making possible new activities, creating new cultural spaces, and overcoming the limitations of darkness. Likewise, McLuhan asserts, it is the formal effects of new media such as radio or television that are crucial: television, for instance, helps to construct privatized and passive cultural consumers, and thus is part of a colonization of leisure by media corporations. And while radio appeals to the ear, television, McLuhan suggests, is more synaesthetic, bringing into play a wide range of senses, and thus helps to produce a more sensual and tribal culture than the previous book culture.

Media for McLuhan are "translators" which provide access to a wide range of social experience. New media often transpose the old media in new forms, as television absorbed the formats of radio, translating radio genres or forms into a new medium. In our day, everything is becoming digitalized, translated into the language and form of the computer. McLuhan was a prophet of both the media and computer age, noting in the passage we have selected, "The Medium is the Message," how more and more forms of culture and consciousness are being rendered into "the form of information." Think of how individual personalities are translated into data in computer chat rooms, or e-mail discussions, and of how the computer is transforming more and more modes of culture from print material to music to visual media into its own digital form and technology. Reflecting on the growth and power of electronic and digital culture helps one grasp that McLuhan was a prophet of the computer age, as well as a provocative analyst of media culture.

McLuhan himself also became an apologist for the media and consumer society, advising corporations and governments (often ironically). By contrast, a group in Europe, called the "Situationist International," theorized the latest developments in the media and consumer society in the 1950s and 1960s and created oppositional practices to use the media against existing society. One of its key members, the French theorist and artist Guy Debord, described the contemporary scene as "the society of the spectacle." Debord and his comrades were themselves initially part of a French avant-garde artist milieu that was shaped by Dada, surrealism, lettrism, and modernist attempts to merge art and politics.[2] Influenced by Jean-Paul Sartre and his concept that human existence is always lived within a particular context and that individuals can create their own situations, Debord and his colleagues began devising strategies to construct new "situations" (see the 1957 Debord text in Knabb 1981: 17ff.). This project would merge art and everyday life in the spirit of the radical avant-garde, and would require a revolution of both art and life.

For Debord, the spectacle is a tool of pacification and depoliticization; it is a "permanent opium war" which stupefies social subjects and distracts them from the most urgent task of real life – recovering the full range of their human powers through creative practice. In Debord's formulation, the concept of the spectacle is integrally connected to the concept of separation, for in passively consuming spectacles, one is separated from actively producing one's life. Capitalist society estranges workers from the product of their labor, art from life, and spheres of production from consumption, thus inducing spectators to passively observe the products of social life. Debord and his group, the Situationist International, promoted an overcoming of all forms of separation against this passivity, in which individuals would directly produce their own life and modes of self-activity and collective practice.

Debord dissects a society saturated with spectacles which advertize its products, promote its politicians, and reproduce its social life. Consumers of the spectacle, Debord argues, are separated from the process of production of everyday life, lost in consumerist fantasies and media phantasmagoria – and, today, the new forms of cyberspace and computer technology. For those enamored of the spectacles of media and technology, "real life" is unreal, unglamorous, and boring, while the spectacles of, for example, shopping or watching sports events, are exciting, enthralling, and preferable to the perceived banality of the everyday world. Yet, Debord warns, the spectacle is entangling its devotees in the clutches of consumer capitalism, replicating consumption fetishism, and helping capital to commodify all domains of social and everyday life.

Walt Disney was perhaps the master of the spectacle during his day, and Ariel Dorfman and Armand Mattelart demystify the Disney spectacle. Reading Disney comic books in the specific conjuncture of intense cultural contestation in Chile during the early 1970s, they unveil the ideological messages and conservative subtext.

Both writers were political *émigrés* to Chile who were participating in the attempt to construct a socialist society when Salvador Allende was elected President – and eventually overthrown and murdered in 1973. In this highly charged political situation, Dorfman and Mattelart see Disney comic books as agents of American imperialism, attempting to inculcate values of capitalism, patriarchy, and social conformity into readers of seemingly harmless cultural artifacts.

Adopting a satiric and mocking tone in the introduction to their book that we include here, Dorfman and Mattelart make fun of those academics who would ignore the artifacts of media culture as beneath their dignity. They also poke fun at themselves as "subversive" critics of the highly popular Walt Disney comics. Yet the issues they are dealing with are very important and involve the early socialization of the child and the creation of its imagination and fantasy life. Mass culture, the authors contend, plays a key role in this domain in the contemporary era and is not always beneficent. Children's literature and media can, as we now are aware, cultivate violence, provide dubious role models, and teach problematic values and behavior.

Combining approaches of the humanities and social sciences (Dorfman has emerged as a major writer and cultural critic, and Mattelart is a world-famous communication researcher), the authors contextualize Disney comic books as effective purveyors of capitalist ideology and Disney's American middle-class values. Pointing out that there are no fathers in the Donald Duck comics, Disney himself, in the authors' view, emerges as a surrogate father, teaching proper (conservative) values through his figures, images, and stories. Relentlessly scrutinizing the world of Donald Duck, the authors detect conservative values and messages saturating the seemingly harmless and innocent "entertainment." Their work thus embodies a critique of ideology perspective that sees media culture as a crucial site of the cultural reproduction of the status quo.

In the article which we include in *KeyWorks*, Raymond Williams develops his own interpretation of "Base and Superstructure in Marxist Cultural Theory." Williams provides a clear and penetrating analysis of key concepts in Marxian theory including base and superstructure, determination, totality, hegemony, ideology, class, and practice. The selection provides a useful reprise of many of the key concepts introduced already by other theorists and adds some concepts to the critical arsenal. His discussion of the "Complexity of Hegemony" is especially interesting and points to his connections with British cultural studies.

Indeed, Williams is often interpreted as one of the precursors and key sources of British cultural studies that first emerged in the early 1960s and that has since become a global phenomenon.[3] Developing an expanded conception of culture that went beyond the literary conceptions dominant in the British academy, Williams conceptualized culture as "a whole way of life," that encompasses cultural artifacts, modes of sensibility, values, and practices (1958 and 1961). Arguing for the need to think together "culture and society," seeing the importance of media culture, and overcoming the division between "high" and "low" culture, Williams produced an impressive series of publications that deeply influenced the trajectory of British cultural studies. He polemicized against the concept of the masses which he claimed was condescending, elitist, and overly homogenizing, covering over real and important differences. This theme in turn came to run through the cultural populism which helped shape and distinguish British cultural studies.

The immediate precursors of British cultural studies created a critique of mass culture in some ways parallel to the work of the Frankfurt School, while more positively evaluating traditions of working-class culture and resistance. Richard Hoggart, Raymond Williams, and E. P. Thompson sought to affirm working-class culture against onslaughts of mass culture produced by the culture industries. Richard Hoggart's *The Uses of Literacy* (1957) contrasted the vitality of British working-class institutions and life with the artificiality of the products of the culture industry that were seen as a banal homogenization of British life and a colonization of its culture by heavily American-influenced institutions and capitalist ideology.

British cultural studies was also shaped by E. P. Thompson's studies of the English working-class culture and celebration of forms of resistance (1963). Like Williams and Hoggart, Thompson interpreted the vicissitudes of English culture as a response to industrialization and urbanization; all three affirmed cultural values that criticized the excesses and horrors of urban–industrial development and all saw culture as a potentially positive force, that could uplift and improve people. They were also strong democrats, seeing culture as an important force of democracy and were anti-elitist, opposing conservative traditions of cultural criticism in Britain. Williams and Hoggart were deeply involved in projects of working-class education and oriented toward socialist politics, seeing their form of cultural studies as an instrument of progressive social change. Their critiques of Americanism and mass culture paralleled to some extent the earlier critique of the Frankfurt School, yet valorized a working class that the Frankfurt School saw as defeated in Germany and much of Europe during the period of fascism and which they never saw as a strong resource for emancipatory social change.

The democratic and socialist humanism of Thompson, Williams, and Hoggart influenced the early Birmingham project that would continue their critique of modern culture and would seek forms of resistance to capitalist modernization. Resisting distinctions between high and low culture, Birmingham cultural studies valorized popular culture and active audiences, able to produce their own readings and meanings. Building on semiotic conceptions developed by Roland Barthes and Umberto Eco, Stuart Hall argued that a distinction must be made between the encoding of media texts by producers and the decoding by consumers in a study of "Encoding/ Decoding" which we include in our reader.[4] This distinction highlighted the ability of audiences to produce their own readings and meanings, to decode texts in aberrant or oppositional ways, as well as the "preferred" ways in tune with the dominant ideology.

In an article "On the Politics of Empirical Audience Research" which appears in *KeyWorks*, Ien Ang distinguishes the "new audience research" undertaken by British cultural studies and their followers from a more liberal-pluralist view of the active audience associated with "uses and gratifications" theory and mainstream communication research. While the latter adopts empiricist models to gain more accurate scientific knowledge to learn how audiences use and enjoy media such as television, the more critical cultural studies approach adopts "self-reflexive" and "interpretive" methods, critically reflecting on the presuppositions of audience research and the actual studies undertaken; it also employs a more explicitly interpretive methodology to make sense of the results of inquiry, aspiring to learn more about the contextual situation of audiences, their social relations, and how they both use and resist dominant cultures.

Hence, whereas empiricist approaches to the audience strive for pure knowledge, cultural studies aims at social critique and transformation, stressing the conflictual elements of audience reception and how audiences can oppose the dominant social order rather than simply being absorbed and integrated. Moreover, while uses and gratification theory reproduces a liberal-pluralist perspective, emphasizing consumer sovereignty, freedom of choice, and the individual creation of meaning, cultural studies adopts a more oppositionalist position, showing how audiences negotiate a complex relation to dominant institutions and forms of power. Consequently, although institutional power disappears or is ignored by empiricist approaches to the audience, cultural studies describes a complex interaction between audiences and dominant institutions and forces.

The British cultural studies' notion of the active audience has been criticized by political economists, as well as others who are skeptical about the unreserved celebration of audience agency and textual polysemy. Herbert Schiller (1989), for instance, sharply critiques the notion of "limited effects" and its contemporary corollary, "the active audience." The rhetoric of pluralism and diversity in the media pivots on the celebration of multiple channels and increasingly fragmented and individualized media offerings. Yet as Schiller points out, this impression of multiplicity diverts attention from the concentration of ownership behind the apparent diversity. Any potential for social transformation is impeded by, as he says, "a very considerable 'if' – if the instrumentation had different controllers" (p. 148). His analysis of the idea of an "active" audience is more pointed, as it engages questions of power between viewer and text as well as the complex relationships among media and other "cultural means that together provide the apparatus of domination and the conditions of dependency" (p. 151).

British cultural studies, however, insists that individuals use media culture to generate potentially oppositional readings, fashion identities, and create subcultures – see Jefferson (1976) and Hebdige (1979). In his book *Subculture: The Meaning of Style*, selections from which we are including in *KeyWorks*, Dick Hebdige analyzes the ways in which individuals and groups mobilize style and subcultures to produce their own often oppositional identities and groups. The introduction to his book draws on many of the figures that we have included in our collection – Gramsci, Barthes, Williams, British cultural studies, etc. Hebdige applies their positions in studies of various English subcultures, including mods, rockers, and punks. In the passage that we have chosen for inclusion, he discusses how subcultures break with the mainstream culture and provide alternative ways of life for their members.

Hebdige highlights the transgressive and potentially oppositional dimension of subcultures, but he also analyzes how subcultures can be incorporated back into mainstream cultures, or effectively marginalized. Subcultures can be commodified, as the sex, drugs, music, and fashion of the counterculture of the 1960s were successfully marketed after the initial shock of an oppositional culture was absorbed. Ideologically, subcultures can also be trivialized, in which differences with the mainstream are minimized and denied, or they can be exoticized, presented as marginal freaks – as the mainstream tried to accomplish with the more extreme yippies in the 1960s or punks of the 1970s.

British cultural studies was thus engaged in a sustained quest for new political subjects and movements when they discerned that the working class was integrated into existing capitalist societies. Their studies were highly political in nature and stressed the potentials for resistance in oppositional subcultures. The development of cultural studies and search for oppositional political forces were influenced by 1960s strife and political movements. The move toward feminism, often conflictual, was shaped by the women's movement, while the turn toward race as a significant factor of study was fuelled by the anti-racist struggles of the day. The focus in British cultural studies on education was related to political concern with the role of schooling in the continuing bourgeois hegemony despite the movements of the 1960s – as well as a return to a pedagogical concern that was at the origins of the work of the Birmingham group. The right turn in British politics with Thatcher's victory in 1979 led to concern with understanding the authoritarian populism of the new conservative hegemony.

Yet the Birmingham project also paved the way, as we suggest in a later section, for a postmodern populist turn in cultural studies, which responds to a later stage of capitalism. Emphasis on consumption, on audience creation of meaning, on difference and heterogeneity corresponds to the contemporary stage of global capitalism in which consumer sovereignty is celebrated, more differences are tolerated and marketed, and audiences are enjoined to embrace new products, technology, and to produce new identities. Hence, cultural studies today is extremely variegated on a global scale with a wealth of different perspectives, topics, and projects.

Notes

1   For Lazarsfeld's contributions to the history of mass communications, see Lazarsfeld (1983) and Merton (1980). On the role of Wilbur Schramm in the founding of communications departments in the United States and the discipline of academic communications study, see Schramm (1997). On Marxism, see Marx and Engels (1978). On the concept of ideology, see Thompson (1991).

2   On Debord and the Situationist International see Marcus (1989); Plant (1992), Wollen (1993), and the material in Substance 90 (1999).

3   For accounts of origins and genesis of British cultural studies, see Hall (1980); Johnson (1985/86); Fiske (1986); O'Conner (1989); Turner (1990); Agger (1992); McGuigan (1992); Kellner (1995); Dworkin (1997); and Grossberg (1997a, b). More polemical, alternative genealogies of cultural studies stress the broader historical antecedents, and include Davies (1995) who points to the origins of the problematic of British cultural studies in debates around the journals *University Review* and *New Left Review*. Steele (1997) wishes to go back and retrieve the roots of British cultural studies in an earlier adult education movement that he thinks provides important resources for cultural studies

today that have been covered over in the narratives of the progressive appropriations of theory that characterize most genealogies of cultural studies. He argues that the long and heroic march of the "theory express" of European Marxism and post-Marxism may have dumped "an extremely ripe mound of manure on the seedling of British cultural studies, only to bury some of their more fragile shoots" (1997: 205). And Ang and Stratton (1996) argue that identification of cultural studies with the British model perpetuates an imperialist ideology that identifies all-important cultural creation with the imperial power, relegating broader international developments in cultural studies to the margins. On earlier traditions of US cultural studies, see Ross (1989) and Aronowitz (1993). For readers which document the positions of British cultural studies, see the articles collected in Grossberg, Nelson, and Triechler (1992) and During (1993).

4   It might be pointed out that Walter Benjamin – loosely affiliated with the Frankfurt School, but not part of their inner circle – also took seriously media culture, saw its emancipatory potential, and posited the possibility of an active audience. Likewise T. W. Adorno and Leo Lowenthal focused attention on audience use and reception of artifacts of media culture, so there are precedents to the Birmingham focus on the audience and the reception and decoding of cultural texts. On Benjamin, see Buck-Morss (1989).

References

Agger, Ben (1992) *Cultural Studies*. London: Falmer Press.
Ang, Ien (1985) *Watching Dallas*. New York: Metheun.
——(1991) "On the Politics of Empirical Audience Research." In *Living Room Wars: Rethinking Media Audiences for a Postmodern World*, 35–52. New York and London: Routledge.
——(1991) *Desperately Seeking the Audience*. London and New York: Routledge.
Ang, Ien and J. Stratton (1996) "Asianing Australia: Notes Towards a Critical Transnational in Cultural Studies," *Cultural Studies* (10/1).
Aronowitz, Stanley (1993) *Roll Over Beethoven*. Hanover, N.H.: University Press of New England.
Barthes, Roland (1983) "Operation Margarine" and "Myth Today." In *Mythologies*, 41–2 and 150–9. Translated by Annette Lavers. New York: Hill and Wang.
Buck-Morss, Susan (1989) *The Dialectics of Seeing*. Cambridge, Mass.: MIT Press.
Davies, Ioan (1995) *Cultural Studies and After*. London and New York: Routledge.
Debord, Guy (1977) "The Consumption as Spectacle." In *Society of the Spectacle*, nos. 1–18 and 42. Detroit: Black & Red.
Dorfman, Ariel, and Armand Mattelart (1971) "Introduction: Instructions on How to Become a General in the Disneyland Club." In *How to Read Donald Duck*: 25–32. New York: International General.
During, Simon (Ed.) (1993) *The Cultural Studies Reader*. London and New York: Routledge.
Dworkin, Dennis (1997) *Cultural Marxism in Postwar Britain: History, the New Left, and the Origins of Cultural Studies*. Durham: Duke University Press.
Fiske, John (1986) "British Cultural Studies and Television." In *Channels of Discourse*, ed. R. C. Allen: 254–89. Chapel Hill: University of North Carolina Press.
——(1989) *Reading the Popular*. Boston, Mass.: Unwin Hyman.
——(1993) *Power Plays: Power Works*. New York and London: Verso.

Grossberg, Lawrence (1997a) *Bringing It All Back Home: Essays on Cultural Studies*. Durham, NC, and London: Duke University Press.

—— (1997b) *Dancing in Spite of Myself: Essays on Popular Culture*. Durham, N.C., and London: Duke University Press.

Grossberg, Lawrence, Nelson, Cary and Paula Treichler (1992) *Cultural Studies*. New York: Routledge.

Hall, Stuart (1980) "Encoding/Decoding." In *Culture, Media, Language*: 128–38, op. cit.

Hebdige, Dick (1979) *Subculture: The Meaning of Style*. New York and London: Routledge.

Hoggart, Richard (1957) *The Uses of Literacy*. New York: Oxford University Press.

Jefferson, Tony (Ed.) (1976) *Resistance through Rituals*. London: Hutchinson.

Johnson, Richard (1985/86) "What is Cultural Studies Anyway?" *Social Text*, 16: 38–80.

Kellner, Douglas (1995) *Media Culture: Cultural Studies, Identity, and Politics Between the Modern and the Postmodern*. London and New York: Routledge.

—— (1997) "Critical Theory and British Cultural Studies: The Missed Articulation," in *Cultural Methodologies*, edited by Jim McGuigan: 12–41. London: Sage.

Knabb, Ken (1981) *Situationist International Anthology*. Berkeley: Bureau of Public Secrets.

Lazarsfeld, Paul (1993) *On Social Research and its Language*, edited by Raymond Boudon. Chicago: University of Chicago Press.

Marcus, Greil (1989) *Lipstick Traces*. Cambridge, Mass.: Harvard University Press.

Marx, Karl and Engels, Friedrich (1978). *The Marx-Engels Reader*, ed. Robert Tucker. New York: Norton.

McGuigan, Jim (1992) *Cultural Populism*. London and New York: Routledge.

McLuhan, Marshall (1961) *The Gutenberg Galaxy*. New York: Signet.

—— (1964) *Understanding Media: The Extensions of Man*. New York: Signet.

Merton, Robert (1980) *Qualitative and Quantitive Social Research: Papers in Honor of Paul F. Lazarsfeld*. New York: Free Press.

O'Connor, Alan (1989) "The Problem of American Cultural Studies," *Critical Studies in Mass Communication* (December), 405–13.

Plant, Sadie (1992) *The Most Radical Gesture*. London and New York: Routledge.

Ross, Andrew (1989) *No Respect: Intellectuals and Popular Culture*. London and New York: Routledge.

Schiller, Herbert (1980) *Culture, Inc*. New York: Oxford University Press.

Schramm, Wilbur (1997) *The Beginnings of Communication Study in America: A Personal Memoir*. Altamira.

Steele, Tom (1997) *The Emergence of Cultural Studies 1945–65: Adult Education, Cultural Politics and the English Question*. London: Lawrence & Wishart.

Thompson, E. P. (1963) *The Making of the English Working Class*. New York: Pantheon.

Thompson, John (1991) *Ideology and Modern Culture*. Cambridge: Polity Press.

Turner, Graeme (1990) *British Cultural Studies: An Introduction*. New York: Unwin Hyman.

Williams, Raymond (1958) *Culture and Society*. New York: Columbia University Press.

—— (1961) *The Long Revolution*. London: Chatto & Windus.

—— (1962) *Communications*. London: Penguin.

—— (1980) *Problems in Materialism and Culture: Selected Essays*. London: Verso.

Wollen, Peter (1993) *Raiding the Icebox: Reflections on Twentieth Century Culture*. Bloomington, Ind.: Indiana University Press.

6

(i) Operation Margarine; (ii) Myth Today

Roland Barthes

(i) Operation Margarine*

To instil into the Established Order the complacent portrayal of its drawbacks has nowadays become a paradoxical but incontrovertible means of exalting it. Here is the pattern of this new-style demonstration: take the established value which you want to restore or develop, and first lavishly display its pettiness, the injustices which it produces, the vexations to which it gives rise, and plunge it into its natural imperfection; then, at the last moment, save it *in spite of*, or rather *by* the heavy curse of its blemishes. Some examples? There is no lack of them.

Take the army; show without disguise its chiefs as martinets, its discipline as narrow-minded and unfair, and into this stupid tyranny immerse an average human being, fallible but likeable, the archetype of the spectator. And then, at the last moment, turn over the magical hat, and pull out of it the image of an army, flags flying, triumphant, bewitching, to which, like Sganarelle's wife,[1] one cannot but be faithful although beaten (*From here to eternity*).

Take the Army again: lay down as a basic principle the scientific fanaticism of its engineers, and their blindness; show all that is destroyed by such a pitiless rigour: human beings, couples. And then bring out the flag, save the army in the name of progress, hitch the greatness of the former to the triumph of the latter (*Les Cyclones*, by Jules Roy).

Finally, the Church: speak with burning zeal about its self-righteousness, the narrow-mindedness of its bigots, indicate that all this can be murderous, hide none of the weaknesses of the faith. And then, *in extremis*, hint that the letter of the law, however unattractive, is a way to salvation for its very victims, and so justify moral austerity by the saintliness of those whom it crushes (*The Living Room*, by Graham Greene).

---

* From Roland Barthes, "Operation Margarine," *Mythologies*, trans. Annette Lavers (New York: Hill & Wang, 1983), pp. 41–2.

It is a kind of homeopathy: one cures doubts about the Church or the Army by the very ills of the Church and the Army. One inoculates the public with a contingent evil to prevent or cure an essential one. To rebel against the inhumanity of the Established Order and its values, according to this way of thinking, is an illness which is common, natural, forgivable; one must not collide with it head-on, but rather exorcize it like a possession: the patient is made to give a representation of his illness, he is made familiar with the very appearance of his revolt, and this revolt disappears all the more surely since, once at a distance and the object of a gaze, the Established Order is no longer anything but a Manichaean compound and therefore inevitable, one which wins on both counts, and is therefore beneficial. The immanent evil of enslavement is redeemed by the transcendent good of religion, fatherland, the Church, etc. A little 'confessed' evil saves one from acknowledging a lot of hidden evil.

One can trace in advertising a narrative pattern which clearly shows the working of this new vaccine. It is found in the publicity for *Astra* margarine. The episode always begins with a cry of indignation against margarine: 'A mousse? Made with margarine? Unthinkable!' 'Margarine? Your uncle will be furious!' And then one's eyes are opened, one's conscience becomes more pliable, and margarine is a delicious food, tasty, digestible, economical, useful in all circumstances. The moral at the end is well known: 'Here you are, rid of a prejudice which cost you dearly!' It is in the same way that the Established Order relieves you of your progressive prejudices. The Army, an absolute value? It is unthinkable: look at its vexations, its strictness, the always possible blindness of its chiefs. The Church, infallible? Alas, it is very doubtful: look at its bigots, its powerless priests, its murderous conformism. And then common sense makes its reckoning: what is this trifling dross of Order, compared to its advantages? It is well worth the price of an immunization. What does it matter, *after all*, if margarine is just fat, when it goes further than butter, and costs less? What does it matter, *after all*, if Order is a little brutal or a little blind, when it allows us to live cheaply? Here we are, in our turn, rid of a prejudice which cost us dearly, too dearly, which cost us too much in scruples, in revolt, in fights and in solitude.

(ii) Myth Today*

Since we cannot yet draw up the list of the dialectal forms of bourgeois myth, we can always sketch its rhetorical forms. One must understand here by *rhetoric* a set of fixed, regulated, insistent figures, according to which the varied forms of the mythical signifier arrange themselves. These figures are transparent inasmuch as they do not affect the plasticity of the signifier; but they are already sufficiently conceptualized to adapt to an historical representation of the world (just as classical rhetoric can account

---

* From Barthes, "Myth Today," *Mythologies*, trans. Annette Lavers (New York: Hill & Wang, 1983), pp. 150–9.

for a representation of the Aristotelian type). It is through their rhetoric that bourgeois myths outline the general prospect of this *pseudo-physis* which defines the dream
of the contemporary bourgeois world. Here are its principal figures:

1. *The inoculation.* I have already given examples of this very general figure,
which consists in admitting the accidental evil of a class-bound institution the better
to conceal its principal evil. One immunizes the contents of the collective imagination
by means of a small inoculation of acknowledged evil; one thus protects it against the
risk of a generalized subversion. This *liberal* treatment would not have been possible
only a hundred years ago. Then, the bourgeois Good did not compromise with
anything, it was quite stiff. It has become much more supple since: the bourgeoisie
no longer hesitates to acknowledge some localized subversions: the avant-garde, the
irrational in childhood, etc. It now lives in a balanced economy: as in any sound joint-
stock company, the smaller shares – in law but not in fact – compensate the big ones.

2. *The privation of history.* Myth deprives the object of which it speaks of all
History.[2] In it, history evaporates. It is a kind of ideal servant: it prepares all things,
brings them, lays them out, the master arrives, it silently disappears: all that is left for
one to do is to enjoy this beautiful object without wondering where it comes from.
Or even better: it can only come from eternity: since the beginning of time, it has
been made for bourgeois man, the Spain of the *Blue Guide* has been made for the
tourist, and 'primitives' have prepared their dances with a view to an exotic festivity.
We can see all the disturbing things which this felicitous figure removes from sight:
both determinism and freedom. Nothing is produced, nothing is chosen: all one has
to do is to possess these new objects from which all soiling trace of origin or choice
has been removed. This miraculous evaporation of history is another form of a
concept common to most bourgeois myths: the irresponsibility of man.

3. *Identification.* The petit-bourgeois is a man unable to imagine the Other.[3] If
he comes face to face with him, he blinds himself, ignores and denies him, or else
transforms him into himself. In the petit-bourgeois universe, all the experiences of
confrontation are reverberating, any otherness is reduced to sameness. The spectacle
or the tribunal, which are both places where the Other threatens to appear in full
view, become mirrors. This is because the Other is a scandal which threatens his
essence. Dominici cannot have access to social existence unless he is previously
reduced to the state of a small simulacrum of the President of the Assizes or the
Public Prosecutor: this is the price one must pay in order to condemn him justly, since
Justice is a weighing operation and since scales can only weigh like against like. There
are, in any petit-bourgeois consciousness, small simulacra of the hooligan, the parri-
cide, the homosexual, etc., which periodically the judiciary extracts from its brain,
puts in the dock, admonishes and condemns: one never tries anybody but analogues
who have gone astray: it is a question of direction, not of nature, for *that's how men
are*. Sometimes – rarely – the Other is revealed as irreducible: not because of a sudden
scruple, but because *common sense* rebels: a man does not have a white skin, but a
black one, another drinks pear juice, not *Pernod*. How can one assimilate the Negro,

the Russian? There is here a figure for emergencies: exoticism. The Other becomes a pure object, a spectacle, a clown. Relegated to the confines of humanity, he no longer threatens the security of the home. This figure is chiefly petit-bourgeois. For, even if he is unable to experience the Other in himself, the bourgeois can at least imagine the place where he fits in: this is what is known as liberalism, which is a sort of intellectual equilibrium based on recognized places. The petit-bourgeois class is not liberal (it produces Fascism, whereas the bourgeoisie uses it): it follows the same route as the bourgeoisie, but lags behind.

4. *Tautology.* Yes, I know, it's an ugly word. But so is the thing. Tautology is this verbal device which consists in defining like by like ('*Drama is drama*'). We can view it as one of those types of magical behaviour dealt with by Sartre in his *Outline of a Theory of the Emotions*: one takes refuge in tautology as one does in fear, or anger, or sadness, when one is at a loss for an explanation: the accidental failure of language is magically identified with what one decides is a natural resistance of the object. In tautology, there is a double murder: one kills rationality because it resists one; one kills language because it betrays one. Tautology is a faint at the right moment, a saving aphasia, it is a death, or perhaps a comedy, the indignant 'representation' of the *rights* of reality over and above language. Since it is magical, it can of course only take refuge behind the argument of authority: thus do parents at the end of their tether reply to the child who keeps on asking for explanations: '*because that's how it is*', or even better: '*just because, that's all*' – a magical act ashamed of itself, which verbally makes the gesture of rationality, but immediately abandons the latter, and believes itself to be even with causality because it has uttered the word which introduces it. Tautology testifies to a profound distrust of language, which is rejected because it has failed. Now any refusal of language is a death. Tautology creates a dead, a motionless world.

5. *Neither-Norism.* By this I mean this mythological figure which consists in stating two opposites and balancing the one by the other so as to reject them both. (I want *neither* this *nor* that.) It is on the whole a bourgeois figure, for it relates to a modern form of liberalism. We find again here the figure of the scales: reality is first reduced to analogues; then it is weighed; finally, equality having been ascertained, it is got rid of. Here also there is magical behaviour: both parties are dismissed because it is embarrassing to choose between them; one flees from an intolerable reality, reducing it to two opposites which balance each other only inasmuch as they are purely formal, relieved of all their specific weight. Neither-Norism can have degraded forms: in astrology, for example, ill-luck is always followed by equal good-luck; they are always predicted in a prudently compensatory perspective: a final equilibrium immobilizes values, life, destiny, etc.: one no longer needs to choose, but only to endorse.

6. *The quantification of quality.* This is a figure which is latent in all the preceding ones. By reducing any quality to quantity, myth economizes intelligence: it understands reality more cheaply. I have given several examples of this mechanism which bourgeois – and especially petit-bourgeois – mythology does not hesitate to

apply to aesthetic realities which it deems on the other hand to partake of an immaterial essence. Bourgeois theatre is a good example of this contradiction: on the one hand, theatre is presented as an essence which cannot be reduced to any language and reveals itself only to the heart, to intuition. From this quality, it receives an irritable dignity (it is forbidden as a crime of 'lese-essence' to speak about the theatre *scientifically*: or rather, any intellectual way of viewing the theatre is discredited as scientism or pedantic language). On the other hand, bourgeois dramatic art rests on a pure quantification of effects: a whole circuit of computable appearances establishes a quantitative equality between the cost of a ticket and the tears of an actor or the luxuriousness of a set: what is currently meant by the 'naturalness' of an actor, for instance, is above all a conspicuous quantity of effects.

7. *The statement of fact.* Myths tend towards proverbs. Bourgeois ideology invests in this figure interests which are bound to its very essence: universalism, the refusal of any explanation, an unalterable hierarchy of the world. But we must again distinguish the language-object from the metalanguage. Popular, ancestral proverbs still partake of an instrumental grasp of the world as object. A rural statement of fact, such as '*the weather is fine*' keeps a real link with the usefulness of fine weather. It is an implicitly technological statement; the word, here, in spite of its general, abstract form, paves the way for actions, it inserts itself into a fabricating order: the farmer does not speak *about* the weather, he 'acts it', he draws it into his labour. All our popular proverbs thus represent active speech which has gradually solidified into reflexive speech, but where reflection is curtailed, reduced to a statement of fact, and so to speak timid, prudent, and closely hugging experience. Popular proverbs foresee more than they assert, they remain the speech of a humanity which is making itself, not one which is. Bourgeois aphorisms, on the other hand, belong to metalanguage; they are a second-order language which bears on objects already prepared. Their classical form is the maxim. Here the statement is no longer directed towards a world to be made; it must overlay one which is already made, bury the traces of this production under a self-evident appearance of eternity: it is a counter-explanation, the decorous equivalent of a tautology, of this peremptory *because* which parents in need of knowledge hang above the heads of their children. The foundation of the bourgeois statement of fact is *common sense*, that is, truth when it stops on the arbitrary order of him who speaks it.

I have listed these rhetorical figures without any special order, and there may well be many others: some can become worn out, others can come into being. But it is obvious that those given here, such as they are, fall into two great categories, which are like the Zodiacal Signs of the bourgeois universe: the Essences and the Scales. Bourgeois ideology continuously transforms the products of history into essential types. Just as the cuttlefish squirts its ink in order to protect itself, it cannot rest until it has obscured the ceaseless making of the world, fixated this world into an object which can be for ever possessed, catalogued its riches, embalmed it, and injected into reality some purifying essence which will stop its transformation, its flight towards other forms of existence. And these riches, thus fixated and frozen, will at last become computable: bourgeois morality will essentially be a weighing operation, the essences will be placed in scales of which bourgeois man will remain the motionless beam. For the very end of myths is to immobilize the world: they must suggest and mimic a universal order which has fixated once and for all the hierarchy of possessions. Thus, every day and everywhere, man is stopped by myths, referred by them to this motionless prototype which lives in his place, stifles him in the manner of a huge internal parasite and assigns to his activity the narrow limits within which he is allowed to suffer without upsetting the world: bourgeois pseudo-physis is in the fullest sense a prohibition for man against inventing himself. Myths are nothing but this ceaseless, untiring solicitation, this insidious and inflexible demand that all men recognize themselves in this image, eternal yet bearing a date, which was built of them one day as if for all time. For the Nature, in which they are locked up under the pretext of being eternalized, is nothing but an Usage. And it is this Usage, however lofty, that they must take in hand and transform.

Necessity and Limits of Mythology

I must, as a conclusion, say a few words about the mythologist himself. This term is rather grand and self-assured. Yet one can predict for the mythologist, if there ever is one, a few difficulties, in feeling if not in method. True, he will have no trouble in feeling justified: whatever its mistakes, mythology is certain to participate in the making of the world. Holding as a principle that man in a bourgeois society is at every turn plunged into a false Nature, it attempts to find again under the assumed innocence of the most unsophisticated relationships, the profound alienation which this innocence is meant to make one accept. The unveiling which it carries out is therefore a political act: founded on a responsible idea of language, mythology thereby postulates the freedom of the latter. It is certain that in this sense mythology *harmonizes* with the world, not as it is, but as it wants to create itself (Brecht had for this an efficiently ambiguous word: *Einverstandnis*, at once an understanding of reality and a complicity with it).

This harmony justifies the mythologist but does not fulfil him: his status still remains basically one of being excluded. Justified by the political dimension, the mythologist is still at a distance from it. His speech is a metalanguage, it 'acts' nothing; at the most, it unveils – or does it? To whom? His task always remains ambiguous, hampered by its ethical origin. He can live revolutionary action only vicariously: hence the self-conscious character of his function, this something a little stiff and pains-taking, muddled and excessively simplified which brands any intellectual behaviour with an openly political foundation ('uncommitted' types of literature are infinitely more 'elegant'; they are in their place in metalanguage).

Also, the mythologist cuts himself off from all the myth-consumers, and this is no small matter. If this [is] applied to a particular section of the collectivity, well and good.[4] But when a myth reaches the entire community, it is from the latter that the mythologist must become estranged if he wants to liberate the myth. Any myth with some degree of generality is in fact ambiguous, because it represents the very humanity of those who, having nothing, have borrowed it. To decipher the Tour de France or the 'good French Wine' is to cut oneself off from those who are entertained or warmed up by them. The mythologist is condemned to live in a theoretical sociality; for him, to be in society is, at best, to be truthful: his utmost sociality dwells in his utmost morality. His connection with the world is of the order of sarcasm.

One must even go further: in a sense, the mythologist is excluded from this history in the name of which he professes to act. The havoc which he wreaks in the language of the community is absolute for him, it fills his assignment to the brim: he must live this assignment without any hope of going back or any assumption of payment. It is forbidden for him to imagine what the world will concretely be like, when the immediate object of his criticism has disappeared. Utopia is an impossible luxury for him: he greatly doubts that tomorrow's truths will be the exact reverse of today's lies. History never ensures the triumph pure and simple of something over its opposite: it unveils, while making itself, unimaginable solutions, unforeseeable synth-eses. The mythologist is not even in a Moses-like situation: he cannot see the Promised Land. For him, tomorrow's positivity is entirely hidden by today's nega-tivity. All the values of his undertaking appear to him as acts of destruction: the latter accurately cover the former, nothing protrudes. This subjective grasp of history in which the potent seed of the future *is nothing but* the most profound apocalypse of the present has been expressed by Saint-Just in a strange saying: '*What constitutes the Republic is the total destruction of what is opposed to it.*' This must not, I think, be understood in the trivial sense of: 'One has to clear the way before reconstructing.' The copula has an exhaustive meaning: there is for some men a subjective dark night of history where the future becomes an essence, the essential destruction of the past.

One last exclusion threatens the mythologist: he constantly runs the risk of causing the reality which he purports to protect, to disappear. Quite apart from all speech, the *D.S.19* is a technologically defined object: it is capable of a certain speed, it meets the wind in a certain way, etc. And this type of reality cannot be spoken of by the mythologist. The mechanic, the engineer, even the user, '*speak* the object'; but the mythologist is condemned to metalanguage. This exclusion already has a name: it is what is called ideologism. Zhdanovism has roundly condemned it (without proving, incidentally, that it was, *for the time being*, avoidable) in the early Lukàcs, in Marr's linguistics, in works like those of Bénichou or Goldmann, opposing to it the reticence of a reality inaccessible to ideology, such as that of language according to Stalin. It is true that ideologism resolves the contradiction of alienated reality by an amputation, not a synthesis (but as for Zhdanovism, it does not even resolve it): wine is objectively good, and *at the same time*, the goodness of wine is a myth: here is the aporia. The mythologist gets out of this as best he can: he deals with the goodness of wine, not with the wine itself, just as the historian deals with Pascal's ideology, not with the *Pensées* in themselves.[5]

It seems that this is a difficulty pertaining to our times: there is as yet only one possible choice, and this choice can bear only on two equally extreme methods: either to posit a reality which is entirely permeable to history, and ideologize; or, conversely, to posit a reality which is *ultimately* impenetrable, irreducible, and, in this case, poetize. In a word, I do not yet see a synthesis between ideology and poetry (by poetry I understand, in a very general way, the search for the inalienable meaning of things).

The fact that we cannot manage to achieve more than an unstable grasp of reality doubtless gives the measure of our present alienation: we constantly drift between the object and its demystification, powerless to render its wholeness. For if we penetrate the object, we liberate it but we destroy it; and if we acknowledge its full weight, we respect it, but we restore it to a state which is still mystified. It would seem that we are condemned for some time yet always to speak *excessively* about reality. This is probably because ideologism and its opposite are types of behaviour which are still magical, terrorized, blinded and fascinated by the split in the social world. And yet, this is what we must seek: a reconciliation between reality and men, between description and explanation, between object and knowledge.

Notes

1   In Molière's *Médecin malgré lui*.
2   Marx: '…we must pay attention to this history, since ideology boils down to either an erroneous conception of this history, *or to a complete abstraction from it*' (*The German Ideology*).
3   Marx: '…what makes them representative of the petit-bourgeois class, is that their minds, their consciousnesses, do not extend beyond the limits which this class has set to its activities' (*The Eighteenth Brumaire*). And Gorki: 'the petit-bourgeois is the man who has preferred himself to all else.'
4   It is not only from the public that one becomes estranged; it is sometimes also from the very object of the myth. In order to demystify Poetic Childhood, for instance, I have had, so to speak, *to lack confidence* in Minou Drouet the child. I have had to ignore, in her, under the enormous myth with which she is cumbered, something like a tender, open, possibility. It is never a good thing to speak *against* a little girl.
5   Even here, in these mythologies, I have used trickery: finding it painful constantly to work on the evaporation of reality, I have started to make it excessively dense, and to discover in it a surprising compactness which I savoured with delight, and I have given a few examples of 'substantial psycho-analysis' about some mythical objects.

7

The Medium is the Message*

Marshall McLuhan

In a culture like ours, long accustomed to splitting and dividing all things as a means of control, it is sometimes a bit of a shock to be reminded that, in operational and practical fact, the medium is the message. This is merely to say that the personal and social consequences of any medium – that is, of any extension of ourselves – result from the new scale that is introduced into our affairs by each extension of ourselves, or by any new technology. Thus, with automation, for example, the new patterns of human association tend to eliminate jobs, it is true. That is the negative result. Positively, automation creates roles for people, which is to say depth of involvement in their work and human association that our preceding mechanical technology had destroyed. Many people would be disposed to say that it was not the machine, but what one did with the machine, that was its meaning or message. In terms of the ways in which the machine altered our relations to one another and to ourselves, it mattered not in the least whether it turned out cornflakes or Cadillacs. The restructuring of human work and association was shaped by the technique of fragmentation that is the essence of machine technology. The essence of automation technology is the opposite. It is integral and decentralist in depth, just as the machine was fragmentary, centralist, and superficial in its patterning of human relationships.

The instance of the electric light may prove illuminating in this connection. The electric light is pure information. It is a medium without a message, as it were, unless it is used to spell out some verbal ad or name. This fact, characteristic of all media, means that the "content" of any medium is always another medium. The content of writing is speech, just as the written word is the content of print, and print is the content of the telegraph. If it is asked, "What is the content of speech?," it is necessary to say, "It is an actual process of thought, which is in itself nonverbal." An abstract painting represents direct manifestation of creative thought processes as they might appear in computer designs. What we are considering here, however, are the psychic and social consequences of the designs or

---

* From Marshall McLuhan, *Understanding Media: The Extensions of Man* (New York: Signet, 1964), pp. 23–35 and 63–7.

patterns as they amplify or accelerate existing processes. For the "message" of any medium or technology is the change of scale or pace or pattern that it introduces into human affairs. The railway did not introduce movement or transportation or wheel or road into human society, but it accelerated and enlarged the scale of previous human functions, creating totally new kinds of cities and new kinds of work and leisure. This happened whether the railway functioned in a tropical or a northern environment, and is quite independent of the freight or content of the railway medium. The airplane, on the other hand, by accelerating the rate of transportation, tends to dissolve the railway form of city, politics, and association, quite independently of what the airplane is used for.

Let us return to the electric light. Whether the light is being used for brain surgery or night baseball is a matter of indifference. It could be argued that these activities are in some way the "content" of the electric light, since they could not exist without the electric light. This fact merely underlines the point that "the medium is the message" because it is the medium that shapes and controls the scale and form of human association and action. The content or uses of such media are as diverse as they are ineffectual in shaping the form of human association. Indeed, it is only too typical that the "content" of any medium blinds us to the character of the medium. It is only today that industries have become aware of the various kinds of business in which they are engaged. When IBM discovered that it was not in the business of making office equipment or business machines, but that it was in the business of processing information, then it began to navigate with clear vision. The General Electric Company makes a considerable portion of its profits from electric light bulbs and lighting systems. It has not yet discovered that, quite as much as A.T.&T., it is in the business of moving information.

The electric light escapes attention as a communication medium just because it has no "content." And this makes it an invaluable instance of how people fail to study media at all. For it is not till the electric light is used to spell out some brand name that it is noticed as a medium. Then it is not the light but the "content" (or what is really another medium) that is noticed. The message of the electric light is like the message of electric power in industry, totally radical, pervasive, and decentralized. For electric light and power are separate from their uses, yet they eliminate time and space factors in human association exactly as do radio, telegraph, telephone, and TV, creating involvement in depth.

A fairly complete handbook for studying the extensions of man could be made up from selections from Shakespeare. Some might quibble about whether or not he was referring to TV in these familiar lines from *Romeo and Juliet*:

> But soft! what light through yonder window breaks?
> It speaks, and yet says nothing.

In *Othello*, which, as much as *King Lear*, is concerned with the torment of people transformed by illusions, there are these lines that bespeak Shakespeare's intuition of the transforming powers of new media:

> Is there not charms
> By which the property of youth and maidhood
> May be abus'd? Have you not read, Roderigo,
> Of some such thing?

In Shakespeare's *Troilus and Cressida*, which is almost completely devoted to both a psychic and social study of communication, Shakespeare states his awareness that true social and political navigation depend upon anticipating the consequences of innovation:

> The providence that's in a watchful state
> Knows almost every grain of Plutus' gold,
> Finds bottom in the uncomprehensive deeps,
> Keeps place with thought, and almost like the gods
> Does thoughts unveil in their dumb cradles.

The increasing awareness of the action of media, quite independently of their "content" or programming, was indicated in the annoyed and anonymous stanza:

> In modern thought, (if not in fact)
> Nothing is that doesn't act,
> So that is reckoned wisdom which
> Describes the scratch but not the itch.

The same kind of total, configurational awareness that reveals why the medium is socially the message has occurred in the most recent and radical medium theories. In his *Stress of Life*, Hans Selye tells of the dismay of a research colleague on hearing of Selye's theory:

> When he saw me thus launched on yet another enraptured description of what I had observed in animals treated with this or that impure, toxic material, he looked at me with desperately sad eyes and said in obvious despair: "But Selye, try to realize what you are doing before it is too late! You have now decided to spend your entire life studying the pharmacology of dirt!"   (Hans Selye, *The Stress of Life*)

As Selye deals with the total environmental situation in his "stress" theory of disease, so the latest approach to media study considers not only the "content" but the medium and the cultural matrix within which the particular medium operates. The older unawareness of the psychic and social effects of media can be illustrated from almost any of the conventional pronouncements.

In accepting an honorary degree from the University of Notre Dame a few years ago, General David Sarnoff made this statement: "We are too prone to make technological instruments the scapegoats for the sins of those who wield them. The products of modern science are not in themselves good or bad; it is the way they are used that determines their value." That is the voice of the current somnambulism. Suppose we were to say, "Apple pie is in itself neither good nor bad; it is the way it is used that determines its value." Or, "The small-pox virus is in itself neither good nor bad; it is the way it is used that determines its value." Again, "Firearms are in themselves neither good nor bad; it is the way they are used that determines their value." That is, if the slugs reach the right people firearms are good. If the TV tube fires the right ammunition at the right people it is good. I am not being perverse. There is simply nothing in the Sarnoff statement that will bear scrutiny, for it ignores the nature of the medium, of any and all media, in the true Narcissus style of one hypnotized by the amputation and extension of his own being in a new technical form. General Sarnoff went on to explain his attitude to the technology of print, saying that it was true that print caused much trash to circulate, but it had also disseminated the Bible and the thoughts of seers and philosophers. It has never occurred to General Sarnoff that any technology could do anything but *add* itself on to what we already are.

Such economists as Robert Theobald, W. W. Rostow, and John Kenneth Galbraith have been explaining for years how it is that "classical economics" cannot explain change or growth. And the paradox of mechanization is that although it is itself the cause of maximal growth and change, the principle of mechanization excludes the very possibility of growth or the understanding of change. For mechanization is achieved by fragmentation of any process and by putting the fragmented parts in a series. Yet, as David Hume showed in the eighteenth century, there is no principle of causality in a mere sequence. That one thing follows another accounts for nothing. Nothing follows from following, except change. So the greatest of all reversals occurred with electricity, that ended sequence by making things instant. With instant speed the causes of things began to emerge to awareness again, as they had not done with things in sequence and in concatenation accordingly. Instead of asking which came first, the chicken or the egg, it suddenly seemed that a chicken was an egg's idea for getting more eggs.

Just before an airplane breaks the sound barrier, sound waves become visible on the wings of the plane. The sudden visibility of sound just as sound ends is an apt instance of that great pattern of being that reveals new and opposite forms just as the earlier forms reach their peak performance. Mechanization was never so vividly fragmented or sequential as in the birth of the movies, the moment that translated us beyond mechanism into the world of growth and organic interrelation. The movie, by sheer speeding up the mechanical, carried us from the world of sequence and connections into the world of creative configuration and structure. The message of the movie medium is that of transition from lineal connections to configurations. It is the transition that produced the now quite correct observation: "If it works, it's obsolete." When electric speed further takes over from mechanical movie sequences, then the lines of force in structures and in media become loud and clear. We return to the inclusive form of the icon.

To a highly literate and mechanized culture the movie appeared as a world of triumphant illusions and dreams that money could buy. It was at this moment of the movie that cubism occurred, and it has been described by E. H. Gombrich (*Art and Illusion*) as "the most radical attempt to stamp out ambiguity and to enforce one reading of the picture – that of a man-made construction, a colored canvas." For cubism substitutes all facets of an object simultaneously for the "point of view" or facet of perspective illusion. Instead of the specialized illusion of the third dimension on canvas, cubism sets up an interplay of planes and contradiction or dramatic conflict of patterns, lights, textures that "drives home the message" by involvement. This is held by many to be an exercise in painting, not in illusion.

In other words, cubism, by giving the inside and outside, the top, bottom, back, and front and the rest, in two dimensions, drops the illusion of perspective in favor of instant sensory awareness of the whole. Cubism, by seizing on instant total awareness, suddenly announced that *the medium is the message*. Is it not evident that the moment that sequence yields to the simultaneous, one is in the world of the structure and of configuration? Is that not what has happened in physics as in painting, poetry, and in communication? Specialized segments of attention have shifted to total field, and we can now say, "The medium is the message" quite naturally. Before the electric speed and total field, it was not obvious that the medium is the message. The message, it seemed, was the "content," as people used to ask what a painting was *about*. Yet they never thought to ask what a melody was about, nor what a house or a dress was about. In such matters, people retained some sense of the whole pattern, of form and function as a unity. But in the electric age this integral idea of structure and configuration has become so prevalent that educational theory has taken up the matter. Instead of working with specialized "problems" in arithmetic, the structural approach now follows the linea of force in the field of number and has small children meditating about number theory and "sets."

Cardinal Newman said of Napoleon, "He understood the grammar of gunpowder." Napoleon had paid some attention to other media as well, especially the semaphore telegraph that gave him a great advantage over his enemies. He is on record for saying that "Three hostile newspapers are more to be feared than a thousand bayonets."

Alexis de Tocqueville was the first to master the grammar of print and typography. He was thus able to read off the message of coming change in France and America as if he were reading aloud from a text that had been handed to him. In fact, the nineteenth century in France and in America was just such an open book to de Tocqueville because he had learned the grammar of print. So he, also, knew when that grammar did not apply. He was asked why he did not write a book on England, since he knew and admired England. He replied:

> One would have to have an unusual degree of philosophical folly to believe oneself able to judge England in six months. A year always seemed to me too short a time in which to appreciate the United States properly, and it is much easier to acquire clear and precise notions about the American Union than about Great Britain. In America all laws derive in a sense from the same line of thought. The whole of society, so to speak, is founded upon a single fact; everything springs from a simple principle. One could compare America to a forest pierced by a multitude of straight roads all converging on the same point. One has only to find the center and everything is revealed at a glance. But in

England the paths run criss-cross, and it is only by travelling down each one of them that one can build up a picture of the whole.

De Tocqueville, in earlier work on the French Revolution, had explained how it was the printed word that, achieving cultural saturation in the eighteenth century, had homogenized the French nation. Frenchmen were the same kind of people from north to south. The typographic principles of uniformity, continuity, and lineality had overlaid the complexities of ancient feudal and oral society. The Revolution was carried out by the new literati and lawyers.

In England, however, such was the power of the ancient oral traditions of common law, backed by the medieval institution of Parliament, that no uniformity or continuity of the new visual print culture could take complete hold. The result was that the most important event in English history has never taken place; namely, the English Revolution on the lines of the French Revolution. The American Revolution had no medieval legal institutions to discard or to root out, apart from monarchy. And many have held that the American Presidency has become very much more personal and monarchical than any European monarch ever could be.

De Tocqueville's contrast between England and America is clearly based on the fact of typography and of print culture creating uniformity and continuity. England, he says, has rejected this principle and clung to the dynamic or oral common-law tradition. Hence the discontinuity and unpredictable quality of English culture. The grammar of print cannot help to construe the message of oral and nonwritten culture and institutions. The English aristocracy was properly classified as barbarian by Matthew Arnold because its power and status had nothing to do with literacy or with the cultural forms of typography. Said the Duke of Gloucester to Edward Gibbon upon the publication of his *Decline and Fall:* "Another damned fat book, eh, Mr. Gibbon? Scribble, scribble, scribble, eh, Mr. Gibbon?" De Tocqueville was a highly literate aristocrat who was quite able to be detached from the values and assumptions of typography. That is why he alone understood the grammar of typography. And it is only on those terms, standing aside from any structure or medium, that its principles and lines of force can be discerned. For any medium has the power of imposing its own assumption on the unwary. Prediction and control consist in avoiding this subliminal state of Narcissus trance. But the greatest aid to this end is simply in knowing that the spell can occur immediately upon contact, as in the first bars of a melody.

A Passage to India by E. M. Forster is a dramatic study of the inability of oral and intuitive oriental culture to meet with the rational, visual European patterns of experience. "Rational," of course, has for the West long meant "uniform and continuous and sequential." In other words, we have confused reason with literacy, and rationalism with a single technology. Thus in the electric age man seems to the conventional West to become irrational. In Forster's novel the moment of truth and dislocation from the typographic trance of the West comes in the Marabar Caves. Adela Quested's reasoning powers cannot cope with the total inclusive field of resonance that is India. After the Caves: "Life went on as usual, but had no consequences, that is to say, sounds did not echo nor thought develop. Everything seemed cut off at its root and therefore infected with illusion."

A Passage to India (the phrase is from Whitman, who saw America headed Eastward) is a parable of Western man in the electric age, and is only incidentally related to Europe or the Orient. The ultimate conflict between sight and sound, between written and oral kinds of perception and organization of existence is upon us. Since understanding stops action, as Nietzsche observed, we can moderate the fierceness of this conflict by understanding the media that extend us and raise these wars within and without us.

Detribalization by literacy and its traumatic effects on tribal man is the theme of a book by the psychiatrist J. C. Carothers, *The African Mind in Health and Disease* (World Health Organization, Geneva, 1953). Much of his material appeared in an article in *Psychiatry* magazine, November, 1959: "The Culture, Psychiatry, and the Written Word." Again, it is electric speed that has revealed the lines of force operating from Western technology in the remotest areas of bush, savannah, and desert. One example is the Bedouin with his battery radio on board the camel. Submerging natives with floods of concepts for which nothing has prepared them is the normal action of all of our technology. But with electric media Western man himself experiences exactly the same inundation as the remote native. We are no more prepared to encounter radio and TV in our literate milieu than the native of Ghana is able to cope with the literacy that takes him out of his collective tribal world and beaches him in individual isolation. We are as numb in our new electric world as the native involved in our literate and mechanical culture.

Electric speed mingles the cultures of prehistory with the dregs of industrial marketeers, the nonliterate with semiliterate and the postliterate. Mental break-down of varying degrees is the very common result of uprooting and inundation with new information and endless new patterns of information. Wyndham Lewis made this a theme of his group of novels called *The Human Age*. The first of these, *The Childermass*, is concerned precisely with accelerated media change as a kind of massacre of the innocents. In our own world as we become more aware of the effects of technology on psychic formation and manifestation, we are losing all confidence in our right to assign guilt. Ancient prehistoric societies regard violent crime as pathetic. The killer is regarded as we do a cancer victim. "How terrible it must be to feel like that," they say. J. M. Synge took up this idea very effectively in his *Playboy of the Western World*.

If the criminal appears as a nonconformist who is unable to meet the demand of technology that we behave in uniform and continuous patterns, literate man is quite inclined to see others who cannot conform as somewhat pathetic. Especially the child, the cripple, the woman, and the colored person appear in a world of visual and typographic technology as victims of injustice. On the other hand, in a culture that assigns roles instead of jobs to people – the dwarf, the skew, the child create their own spaces. They are not expected to fit into some uniform and repeatable niche that is not their size anyway. Consider the phrase "It's a man's world." As a quantitative observation endlessly repeated from within a homoge-nized culture, this phrase refers to the men in such a culture who have to be homogenized Dagwoods in order to belong at all. It is in our I.Q. testing that we have produced the greatest flood of misbegotten standards. Unaware of our typographic cultural bias, our testers assume that uniform and continuous habits are a sign of intelligence, thus eliminating the ear man and the tactile man.

C. P. Snow, reviewing a book of A. L. Rowse (*The New York Times Book Review*, December 24, 1961) on *Appeasement* and the road to Munich, describes the top level of British brains and experience in the 1930s. "Their I.Q.'s were much higher than usual among political bosses. Why were they such a disaster?" The view of Rowse, Snow approves: "They would not listen to warnings because they did not wish to hear." Being anti-Red made it impossible for them to read the message of Hitler. But their failure was as nothing compared to our present one. The American stake in literacy as a technology or uniformity applied to every level of education, government, industry, and social life is totally threatened by the electric technology. The threat of Stalin or Hitler was external. The electric technology is within the gates, and we are numb, deaf, blind, and mute about its encounter with the Gutenberg technology, on and through which the American way of life was formed. It is, however, no time to suggest strategies when the threat has not even been acknowledged to exist. I am in the position of Louis Pasteur telling doctors that their greatest enemy was quite invisible, and quite unrecognized by them. Our conventional response to all media, namely that it is how they are used that counts, is the numb stance of the technological idiot. For the "content" of a medium is like the juicy piece of meat carried by the burglar to distract the watchdog of the mind. The effect of the medium is made strong and intense just because it is given another medium as "content." The content of a movie is a novel or a play or an opera. The effect of the movie form is not related to its program content. The "content" of writing or print is speech, but the reader is almost entirely unaware either of print or of speech.

Arnold Toynbee is innocent of any understanding of media as they have shaped history, but he is full of examples that the student of media can use. At one moment he can seriously suggest that adult education, such as the Workers' Educational Association in Britain, is a useful counterforce to the popular press. Toynbee considers that although all of the oriental societies have in our time accepted the industrial technology and its political consequences: "On the cultural plane, however, there is no uniform corresponding tendency." (Somervell, I. 267) This is like the voice of the literate man, floundering in a milieu of ads, who boasts, "Personally, I pay no attention to ads." The spiritual and cultural reservations that the oriental peoples may have toward our technology will avail them not at all. The effects of technology do not occur at the level of opinions or concepts, but alter sense ratios or patterns of perception steadily and without any resistance. The serious artist is the only person able to encounter technology with impunity, just because he is an expert aware of the changes in sense perception.

The operation of the money medium in seventeenth-century Japan had effects not unlike the operation of typography in the West. The penetration of the money economy, wrote G. B. Sansom (in *Japan*, Cresset Press, London, 1931) "caused a slow but irresistible revolution, culminating in the breakdown of feudal government and the resumption of intercourse with foreign countries after more than two hundred years of seclusion." Money has reorganized the sense life of peoples just because it is an *extension* of our sense lives. This change does not depend upon approval or disapproval of those living in the society.

Arnold Toynbee made one approach to the transforming power of media in his concept of "etherialization," which he holds to be the principle of progressive simplification and efficency in any organization or technology. Typically, he is ignoring the *effect* of the challenge of these forms upon the response of our senses. He imagines that it is the response of our opinions that is relevant to the effect of media and technology in society, a "point of view" that is plainly the result of the typographic spell. For the man in a literate and homogenized society ceases to be sensitive to the diverse and discontinuous life of forms. He acquires the illusion of the third dimension and the "private point of view" as part of his Narcissus fixation, and is quite shut off from Blake's awareness or that of the Psalmist, that we become what we behold.

Today when we want to get our bearings in our own culture, and have need to stand aside from the bias and pressure exerted by any technical form of human expression, we have only to visit a society where that particular form has not been felt, or a historical period in which it was unknown. Professor Wilbur Schramm made such a tactical move in studying *Television in the Lives of Our Children*. He found areas where TV had not penetrated at all and ran some tests. Since he had made no study of the peculiar nature of the TV image, his tests were of "content" preferences, viewing time, and vocabulary counts. In a word, his approach to the problem was a literary one, albeit unconsciously so. Consequently, he had nothing to report. Had his methods been employed in 1500 A.D. to discover the effects of the printed book in the lives of children or adults, he could have found out nothing of the changes in human and social psychology resulting from typography. Print created individualism and nationalism in the sixteenth century. Program and "content" analysis offer no clues to the magic of these media or to their subliminal charge.

Leonard Doob, in his report *Communication in Africa*, tells of one African who took great pains to listen each evening to the BBC news, even though he could understand nothing of it. Just to be in the presence of those sounds at 7 p.m. each day was important for him. His attitude to speech was like ours to melody – the resonant intonation was meaning enough. In the seventeenth century our ancestors still shared this native's attitude to the forms of media, as is plain in the following sentiment of the Frenchman Bernard Lam expressed in *The Art of Speaking* (London, 1696):

> ' Tis an effect of the Wisdom of God, who created Man to be happy, that whatever is useful to his conversation (way of life) is agreeable to him ... because all victual that conduces to nourishment is relishable, whereas other things that cannot be assimilated and be turned into our substance are insipid. A Discourse cannot be pleasant to the Hearer that is not easie to the Speaker; nor can it be easily pronounced unless it be heard with delight.

Here is an equilibrium theory of human diet and expression such as even now we are only striving to work out again for media after centuries of fragmentation and specialism.

Pope Pius XII was deeply concerned that there be serious study of the media today. On February 17, 1950, he said:

> It is not an exaggeration to say that the future of modern society and the stability of its inner life depend in large part on the maintenance of an equilibrium between the strength of the techniques of communication and the capacity of the individual's own reaction.

Failure in this respect has for centuries been typical and total for mankind. Subliminal and docile acceptance of media impact has made them prisons without walls for their human users. As A. J. Liebling remarked in his book *The Press*, a man is not free if he cannot see where he is going, even if he has a gun to help him get there. For each of the media is also a powerful weapon with which to clobber other media and other groups. The result is that the present age has been one of multiple civil wars that are not limited to the world of art and entertainment. In *War and Human Progress*, Professor J. U. Nef declared: "The total wars of our time have been the result of a series of intellectual mistakes..."

If the formative power in the media are the media themselves, that raises a host of large matters that can only be mentioned here, although they deserve volumes. Namely, that technological media are staples or natural resources, exactly as are coal and cotton and oil. Anybody will concede that society whose economy is dependent upon one or two major staples like cotton, or grain, or lumber, or fish, or cattle is going to have some obvious social patterns of organization as a result. Stress on a few major staples creates extreme instability in the economy but great endurance in the population. The pathos and humor of the American South are embedded in such an economy of limited staples. For a society configured by reliance on a few commodities accepts them as a social bond quite as much as the metropolis does the press. Cotton and oil, like radio and TV, become "fixed charges" on the entire psychic life of the community. And this pervasive fact creates the unique cultural flavor of any society. It pays through the nose and all its other senses for each staple that shapes its life.

That our human senses, of which all media are extensions, are also fixed charges on our personal energies, and that they also configure the awareness and experience of each one of us, may be perceived in another connection mentioned by the psychologist C. G. Jung:

> Every Roman was surrounded by slaves. The slave and his psychology flooded ancient Italy, and every Roman became inwardly, and of course unwittingly, a slave. Because living constantly in the atmosphere of slaves, he became infected through the unconscious with their psychology. No one can shield himself from such an influence.
>
> (*Contributions to Analytical Psychology*, London, 1928)

8

The Commodity as Spectacle*

Guy Debord

1

In societies where modern conditions of production prevail, all of life presents itself as an immense accumulation of *spectacles*. Everything that was directly lived has moved away into a representation.

2

The images detached from every aspect of life fuse in a common stream in which the unity of this life can no longer be reestablished. Reality considered *partially* unfolds, in its own general unity, as a pseudo-world *apart*, an object of mere contemplation. The specialization of images of the world is completed in the world of the autonomous image, where the liar has lied to himself. The spectacle in general, as the concrete inversion of life, is the autonomous movement of the nonliving.

3

The spectacle presents itself simultaneously as all of society, as part of society, and as *instrument of unification*. As a part of society it is specifically the sector which concentrates all gazing and all consciousness. Due to the very fact that this sector is *separate*, it is the common ground of the deceived gaze and of false consciousness, and the unification it achieves is nothing but an official language of generalized separation.

4

The spectacle is not a collection of images, but a social relation among people, mediated by images.

---

* From Guy Debord, *Society of the Spectacle* (Detroit: Black and Red Books, 1977), nos. 1–18, 42.

5

The spectacle cannot be understood as an abuse of the world of vision, as a product of the techniques of mass dissemination of images. It is, rather, a *Weltanschauung* which has become actual, materially translated. It is a world vision which has become objectified.

6

The spectacle, grasped in its totality, is both the result and the project of the existing mode of production. It is not a supplement to the real world, an additional decoration. It is the heart of the unrealism of the real society. In all its specific forms, as information or propaganda, as advertisement or direct entertainment consumption, the spectacle is the present *model* of socially dominant life. It is the omnipresent affirmation of the choice *already made* in production and its corollary consumption. The spectacle's form and content are identically the total justification of the existing system's conditions and goals. The spectacle is also the *permanent presence* of this justification, since it occupies the main part of the time lived outside of modern production.

7

Separation is itself part of the unity of the world, of the global social praxis split up into reality and image. The social practice which the autonomous spectacle confronts is also the real totality which contains the spectacle. But the split within this totality mutilates it to the point of making the spectacle appear as its goal. The language of the spectacle consists of *signs* of the ruling production, which at the same time are the ultimate goal of this production.

8

One cannot abstractly contrast the spectacle to actual social activity: such a division is itself divided. The spectacle which inverts the real is in fact produced. Lived reality is materially invaded by the contemplation of the spectacle while simultaneously absorbing the spectacular order, giving it positive cohesiveness. Objective reality is present on both sides. Every notion fixed this way has no other basis than its passage into the opposite: reality rises up within the spectacle, and the spectacle is real. This reciprocal alienation is the essence and the support of the existing society.

9

In a world which *really is topsy-turvy*, the true is a moment of the false.

10

The concept of "spectacle" unifies and explains a great diversity of apparent phenomena. The diversity and the contrasts are appearances of a socially organized
appearance, the general truth of which must itself be recognized. Considered in its
own terms, the spectacle is *affirmation* of appearance and affirmation of all human
life, namely social life, as mere appearance. But the critique which reaches the truth of
the spectacle exposes it as the visible *negation* of life, as a negation of life which *has
become visible*.

11

To describe the spectacle, its formation, its functions and the forces which tend to
dissolve it, one must artificially distinguish certain inseparable elements. When *analyzing* the spectacle one speaks, to some extent, the language of the spectacular itself
in the sense that one moves through the methodological terrain of the very society
which expresses itself in the spectacle. But the spectacle is nothing other than the *sense*
of the total practice of a social-economic formation, its *use of time*. It is the historical
movement in which we are caught.

12

The spectacle presents itself as something enormously positive, indisputable and
inaccessible. It says nothing more than "that which appears is good, that which is
good appears." The attitude which it demands in principle is passive acceptance
which in fact it already obtained by its manner of appearing without reply, by its
monopoly of appearance.

13

The basically tautological character of the spectacle flows from the simple fact that its
means are simultaneously its ends. It is the sun which never sets over the empire of
modern passivity. It covers the entire surface of the world and bathes endlessly in its
own glory.

14

The society which rests on modern industry is not accidentally or superficially spectacular, it is fundamentally *spectaclist*. In the spectacle, which is the image of the ruling economy, the goal is nothing, development everything. The spectacle aims at nothing other than itself.

15

As the indispensable decoration of the objects produced today, as the general exposé of the rationality of the system, as the advanced economic sector which directly shapes a growing multitude of image-objects, the spectacle is the *main production* of present-day society.

16

The spectacle subjugates living men to itself to the extent that the economy has totally subjugated them. It is no more than the economy developing for itself. It is the true reflection of the production of things, and the false objectification of the producers.

17

The first phase of the domination of the economy over social life brought into the definition of all human realization the obvious degradation of *being* into *having*. The present phase of total occupation of social life by the accumulated results of the economy leads to a generalized sliding of *having* into *appearing*, from which all actual "having" must draw its immediate prestige and its ultimate function. At the same time all individual reality has become social reality directly dependent on social power and shaped by it. It is allowed to appear only to the extent that it *is not*.

18

Where the real world changes into simple images, the simple images become real beings and effective motivations of hypnotic behavior. The spectacle, as a tendency to *make one see* the world by means of various specialized mediations (it can no longer be grasped directly), naturally finds vision to be the privileged human sense which the sense of touch was for other epochs; the most abstract, the most mystifiable sense corresponds to the generalized abstraction of present-day society. But the spectacle is not identifiable with mere gazing, even combined with hearing. It is that which escapes the activity of men, that which escapes reconsideration and correction by their work. It is the opposite of dialogue. Wherever there is independent *representation*, the spectacle reconstitutes itself. . . .

42

The spectacle is the moment when the commodity has attained the *total occupation* of social life. Not only is the relation to the commodity visible but it is all one sees: the world one sees is its world. Modern economic production extends its dictatorship extensively and intensively. In the least industrialized places, its reign is already attested by a few star commodities and by the imperialist domination imposed by regions which are ahead in the development of productivity. In the advanced regions, social space is invaded by a continuous superimposition of geological layers of commodities. At this point in the "second industrial revolution," alienated consumption becomes for the masses a duty supplementary to alienated production. It is *all the sold labor* of a society which globally becomes the *total commodity* for which the cycle must be continued. For this to be done, the total commodity has to return as a fragment to the fragmented individual, absolutely separated from the productive forces operating as a whole. Thus it is here that the specialized science of domination must in turn specialize: it fragments itself into sociology, psychotechnics, cybernetics, semiology, etc., watching over the self-regulation of every level of the process.

9

Introduction: Instructions on How to Become a General in the Disneyland Club*

Ariel Dorfman and Armand Mattelart

My dog has become a famous lifeguard and my nephews will be brigadier-generals. To what greater honor can one aspire?

(Donald Duck, D 422)[1]

Baby frogs will be *big* frogs someday, which bring high prices on the market ... I'm going to fix some special *frog food* and speed up the growth of those little hoppers!

(Donald Duck, D 451, CS 5/60)

It would be wrong to assume that Walt Disney is merely a business man. We are all familiar with the massive merchandising of his characters in films, watches, umbrellas, records, soaps, rocking chairs, neckties, lamps, etc. There are Disney strips in five thousand newspapers, translated into more than thirty languages, spread over a hundred countries. According to the magazine's own publicity puffs, in Chile alone, Disney comics reach and delight each week over a million readers. The former Zig-Zag Company, now bizarrely converted into Pinsel Publishing Enterprise (Juvenile Publications Company Ltd.), supplies them to a major part of the Latin American continent. From their national base of operations, where there is so much screaming about the trampling underfoot (the suppression, intimidation, restriction, repression, curbing, etc.) of the liberty of the press, this consortium, controlled by financiers and "philanthropists" of the previous Christian Democrat regime (1964–70), has just permitted itself the luxury of converting several of its publications from biweeklies to weekly magazines.

Apart from his stock exchange rating, Disney has been exalted as the inviolable common cultural heritage of contemporary man; his characters have been

* From Ariel Dorfman and Armand Mattelart, *How to Read Donald Duck* (New York: International General, 1971), 27–32.

incorporated into every home, they hang on every wall, they decorate objects of every kind; they constitute a little less than a social environment inviting us all to join the great universal Disney family, which extends beyond all frontiers and ideologies, transcends differences between peoples and nations, and particularities of custom and language. Disney is the great supranational bridge across which all human beings may communicate with each other. And amidst so much sweetness and light, the registered trademark becomes invisible.

Disney is part – an immortal part, it would seem – of our common collective vision. It has been observed that in more than one country Mickey Mouse is more popular than the national hero of the day.

In Central America, AID (the U.S. Agency for International Development) – sponsored films promoting contraception feature the characters from "Magician of Fantasy." In Chile, after the earthquake of July 1971, the children of San Bernardo sent Disneyland comics and sweets to their stricken fellow children of San Antonio. And the year before, a Chilean women's magazine proposed giving Disney the Nobel Peace Prize.[2]

We need not be surprised, then, that any innuendo about the world of Disney should be interpreted as an affront to morality and civilization at large. Even to whisper anything against Walt is to undermine the happy and innocent palace of childhood, for which he is both guardian and guide.

No sooner had the first children's magazine been issued by the Chilean Popular Unity Government publishing house Quimantú, than the reactionary journals sprang to the defense of Disney:

> The voice of a newscaster struck deep into the microphone of a radio station in the capital. To the amazement of his listeners he announced that Walt Disney is to be banned in Chile. The government propaganda experts have come to the conclusion that Chilean children should not think, feel, love or suffer through animals.
>
> So, in place of Scrooge McDuck, Donald and nephews, instead of Goofy and Mickey Mouse, we children and grownups will have to get used to reading about our own society, which, to judge from the way it is painted by the writers and panegyrists of our age, is rough, bitter, cruel and hateful. It was Disney's magic to be able to stress the happy side of life, and there are always, in human society, characters who resemble those of Disney comics.
>
> Scrooge McDuck is the miserly millionaire of any country in the world, hoarding his money and suffering a heart attack every time someone tries to pinch a cent off him, but in spite of it all, capable of revealing human traits which redeem him in his nephews' eyes.
>
> Donald is the eternal enemy of work and lives dependent upon his powerful uncle. Goofy is the innocent and guileless common man, the eternal victim of his own clumsiness, which hurts no one and is always good for a laugh.
>
> Big Bad Wolf and Little Wolf are masterly means of teaching children pleasantly, not hatefully, the difference between good and evil. For Big Bad Wolf himself, when he gets a chance to gobble up the Three Little Pigs, suffers pangs of conscience and is unable to do his wicked deed.
>
> And finally, Mickey Mouse is Disney in a nutshell. What human being over the last forty years, at the mere presence of Mickey, has not felt his heart swell with emotion? Did

we not see him once as the "Sorcerer's Apprentice" in an unforgettable cartoon which was the delight of children and grownups, which preserved every single note of the masterly music of Prokoviev [a reference no doubt to the music of Paul Dukas]. And what of *Fantasia*, that prodigious feat of cinematic art, with musicians, orchestras, decorations, flowers, and every animate being moving to the baton of Leopold Stokowski? And one scene, of the utmost splendor and realism, even showed elephants executing the most elegant performance of "The Dance of the Dragonflies" [a reference no doubt to the "Dance of the hours"].

How can one assert that children do not learn from talking animals? Have they not been observed time and again engaging in tender dialogues with their pet dogs and cats, while the latter adapt to their masters and show with a purr or a twitch of the ears their understanding of the orders they are given? Are not fables full of valuable lessons in the way animals can teach us how to behave under the most difficult circumstances?

There is one, for instance, by Tomas de Iriarte which serves as a warning against the danger of imposing too stringent principles upon those who work for the public. The mass does not always blindly accept what is offered to them.[3]

This pronouncement parrots some of the ideas prevailing in the media about childhood and children's literature. Above all, there is the implication that politics cannot enter into areas of "pure entertainment," especially those designed for children of tender years. Children's games have their own rules and laws, they move, supposedly, in an autonomous and asocial sphere like the Disney characters, with a psychology peculiar to creatures at a "privileged" age. Inasmuch as the sweet and docile child can be sheltered effectively from the evils of existence, from the petty rancors, the hatreds, and the political or ideological contamination of his elders, any attempt to politicize the sacred domaine of childhood threatens to introduce perversity where there once reigned happiness, innocence and fantasy. Since animals are also exempt from the vicissitudes of history and politics, they are convenient symbols of a world beyond socio-economic realities, and the animal characters can represent ordinary human types, common to all classes, countries and epochs. Disney thus establishes a moral background which draws the child down the proper ethical and aesthetic path. It is cruel and unnecessary to tear it away from its magic garden, for it is ruled by the Laws of Mother Nature; children *are* just like that and the makers of comic books, in their infinite wisdom, understand their behavior and their biologically-determined need for harmony. Thus, to attack Disney is to reject the unquestioned stereotype of the child, sanctified as the law in the name of the immutable human condition.

There are *automagic*[4] antibodies in Disney. They tend to neutralize criticism because they are the same values already instilled into people, in the tastes, reflexes and attitudes which inform everyday experience at all levels. Disney manages to subject these values to the extremest degree of commercial exploitation. The potential assailer is thus condemned in advance by what is known as "public opinion," that is, the thinking of people who have already been conditioned by the Disney message and have based their social and family life upon it.

The publication of this book will of course provoke a rash of hostile comment against the authors. To facilitate our adversaries' task, and in order to lend uniformity to their criteria, we offer the following model, which has been drawn up with due consideration for the philosophy of the journals to which the gentlemen of the press are so attached:

Instructions on How to Expel Someone from the Disneyland Club

1. The authors of this book are to be defined as follows: indecent and immoral (while Disney's world is pure); hyper-complicated and hyper-sophisticated (while Walt is simple, open and sincere); members of a sinister elite (while Disney is the most popular man in the world); political agitators (while Disney is non-partisan, above politics); calculating and embittered (while Walt D. is spontaneous, emotional, loves to laugh and make laughter); subverters of youth and domestic peace (while W.D. teaches respect for parents, love of one's fellows and protection of the weak); unpatriotic and antagonistic to the national spirit (while Mr Disney, being international, represents the best and dearest of our native traditions); and finally, cultivators of "Marxism-fiction," a theory imported from abroad by "wicked for-eigners"[5] (while Unca Walt is against exploitation and promotes the classless society of the future).

2. Next, the authors of this book are to be accused of the very lowest of crimes: of daring to raise doubts about the child's imagination, that is, O horror!, to question the right of children to have a literature of their own, which interprets them so well, and is created on their behalf.

3. FINALLY, TO EXPEL SOMEONE FROM THE DISNEYLAND CLUB, ACCUSE HIM REPEATEDLY OF TRYING TO BRAINWASH CHILDREN WITH THE DOCTRINE OF COLORLESS SOCIAL REALISM, IMPOSED BY POLITICAL COMMISSARS.

There can be no doubt that children's literature is a genre like any other, mono-polized by specialized subsectors within the culture industry. Some dedicate them-selves to the adventure story, some to mystery, others to the erotic novel, etc. But at least the latter are directed towards an amorphous public, which buys at random. In the case of the children's genre, however, there is a virtually biologically captive, predetermined audience.

Children's comics are devised by adults, whose work is determined and justified by their idea of what a child is or should be. Often, they even cite "scientific" sources or ancient traditions ("it is popular wisdom, dating from time immemorial") in order to explain the nature of the public's needs. In reality, however, these adults are not about to tell stories which would jeopardize the future they are planning for their children.

So the comics show the child as a miniature adult, enjoying an idealized, gilded infancy which is really nothing but the adult projection of some magic era beyond the reach of the harsh discord of daily life. It is a plan for salvation which presupposes a primal stage within every existence, sheltered from contradictions and permitting imaginative escape. Juvenile literature, embodying purity, spontaneity, and natural virtue, while lacking in sex and violence, represents earthly paradise. It guarantees man's own redemption as an adult: as long as there are children, he will have the pretext and means for self-gratification with the spectacle of his own dreams. In his children's reading, man stages and performs over and over again the supposedly unproblematical scenes of his inner refuge. Regaling himself with his own legend, he falls into tautology; he admires himself in the mirror, thinking it to be a window. But the child playing down there in the garden is the purified adult looking back at himself.

So it is the adult who produces the comics, and the child who consumes them. The role of the apparent child actor, who reigns over this uncontaminated world, is at once that of audience and dummy for his father's ventriloquism. The father denies his progeny a voice of his own, and as in any authoritarian society, he establishes himself as the other's sole interpreter and spokesman. All the little fellow can do is to let his father represent him.

But wait a minute, gentlemen! Perhaps children really *are* like that?

Indeed, the adults set out to prove that this literature is essential to the child, satisfying his eager demands. But this is a closed circuit: children have been conditioned by the magazines and the culture which spawned them. They tend to reflect in their daily lives the characteristics they are supposed to possess, in order to win affection, acceptance, and rewards; in order to grow up properly and integrate into society. The Disney world is sustained by rewards and punishments; it hides an iron hand with the velvet glove. Considered, by definition, unfit to choose from the alternatives available to adults, the youngsters intuit "natural" behavior, happily accepting that their imagination be channelled into incontestable ethical and aesthetic ideals. Juvenile literature is justified by the children it has generated through a vicious circle.

Thus, adults create for themselves a childhood embodying their own angelical aspirations, which offer consolation, hope and a guarantee of a "better," but unchanging, future. This "new reality," this autonomous realm of magic, is artfully isolated from the reality of the everyday. Adult values are projected onto the child, as if childhood was a special domaine where these values could be protected uncritically. In Disney, the two strata – adult and child – are not to be considered as antagonistic; they fuse in a single embrace, and history becomes biology. The identity of parent and child inhibits the emergence of true generational conflicts. The pure child will replace the corrupt father, preserving the latter's values. The future (the child) reaffirms the present (the adult), which, in turn, transmits the past. The apparent independence which the father benevolently bestows upon this little territory of his creation, is the very means of assuring his supremacy.

But there is more: this lovely, simple, smooth, translucent, chaste and pacific region, which has been promoted as Salvation, is unconsciously infiltrated by a multiplicity of adult conflicts and contradictions. This transparent world is designed both to conceal and reveal latent traces of real and painful tensions. The parent suffers this split consciousness without being aware of his inner turmoil. Nostalgically, he appropriates the "natural disposition" of the child in order to conceal the guilt arising from his own fall from grace; it is the price of redemption for his own condition. By the standards of his angelic model, he must judge himself guilty; as much as he needs this land of enchantment and salvation, he could never imagine it with the necessary purity. He could never turn into his own child. But this salvation only offers him an imperfect escape; it can never be so pure as to block off all his real life problems.

In juvenile literature, the adult, corroded by the trivia of everyday life blindly defends his image of youth and innocence. Because of this, it is perhaps the best (and least expected) place to study the disguises and truths of contemporary man. For the adult, in protecting his dream-image of youth, hides the fear that to penetrate it would destroy his dreams and reveal the reality it conceals.

Thus, *the imagination of the child is conceived as the past and future utopia of the adult*. But set up as an inner realm of fantasy, this model of his Origin and his Ideal Future Society lends itself to the free assimilation of all his woes. It enables the adult to partake of his own demons, provided they have been coated in the syrup of paradise, and that they travel there with the passport of innocence.

Mass culture has granted to contemporary man, in his constant need to visualize the reality about him, the means of feeding on his own problems without having to encounter all the difficulties of form and content presented by the modern art and literature of the elite. Man is offered knowledge without commitment, a self-colonization of his own imagination. By dominating the child, the father dominates himself. The relationship is a sado-masochistic one, not unlike that established between Donald and his nephews. Similarly, readers find themselves caught between their desire and their reality, and in their attempt to escape to a purer realm, they only travel further back into their own traumas.

Mass culture has opened up a whole range of new issues. While it certainly has had a levelling effect and has exposed a wider audience to a broader range of themes, it has simultaneously generated a cultural elite which has cut itself off more and more from the masses. Contrary to the democratic potential of mass culture, this elite has plunged mass culture into a suffocating complexity of solutions, approaches and techniques, each of which is comprehensible only to a narrow circle of readers. The creation of children's culture is part of this specialization process.

Child fantasy, although created by adults, becomes the exclusive reserve of children. The self-exiled father, once having created this specialized imaginary world, then revels in it through the keyhole. The father must be absent, and without direct jurisdiction, just as the child is without direct obligations. Coercion melts away in the magic palace of sweet harmony and repose – the palace raised and administered at a distance by the father, whose physical absence is designed to avoid direct confrontation with his progeny. This absence is the prerequisite of his omnipresence, his total invasion. Physical presence would be superfluous, even counterproductive, since the whole magazine is already his projection. He shows up instead as a favorite uncle handing out free magazines. Juvenile literature is a father surrogate. The model of paternal authority is at every point immanent, the implicit basis of its structure and very existence. The natural creativity of the child, which no one in his right mind can deny, is channelled through the apparent absence of the father into an adult-authoritarian vision of the real world. Paternalism *in absentia* is the indispensable vehicle for the defense and invisible control of the ostensibly autonomous childhood model. The comics, like television, in all vertically structured societies, rely upon distance as a means of authoritarian reinforcement.

The authoritarian relationship between the real life parent and child is repeated and reinforced within the fantasy world itself, and is the basis for all relations in the entire world of the comics. Later, we shall show how the relationship of child-readers to the magazine they consume is generally based on and echoed in the way the characters experience their own fantasy world within the comic. Children will not only identify with Donald Duck because Donald's situation relates to their own life, but also because the way they read or the way they are exposed to it, imitates and prefigures the way Donald Duck lives out his own problems. Fiction reinforces, in a circular fashion, the manner in which the adult desires the comic be received and read.

Now that we have peeked into the parent–child relationship, let us be initiated into the Disney world, beginning with the great family of ducks and mice.

Notes

1 We use the following abbreviations: D = *Disneylandia* F = *Fantasias*, TR = *Tio Rico* (Scrooge McDuck), TB = *Tribilin* (Goofy). These magazines are published in Chile by Empresa Editorial Zig-Zag (now Pinsel), with an average of two to four large-and medium-sized stories per issue. We obtained all available back issues and purchased current issues during the months following March 1971. Our sample is thus inevitably somewhat random:

   Disneylandia: 185, 192, 210, 281, 292, 294, 297, 303, 329, 342, 347, 357, 364, 367, 370, 376, 377, 379, 381, 382, 383, 393, 400, 401, 421, 422, 423, 424, 431, 432, 433, 434, 436, 437, 439, 440, 441, 443, 444, 445, 446, 447, 448, 449, 451, 452, 453, 454, 455, 457.

   Tio Rico: 40, 48, 53, 57, 61, 96, 99, 106, 108, 109, 110, 111, 113, 115, 116, 117, 119, 120, 128.

   Fantasias: 57, 60, 68, 82, 140, 155, 160, 165, 168, 169, 170, 173, 174, 175, 176, 177, 178.

   Tribilin: 62, 65, 78, 87, 92, 93, 96, 99, 100, 101, 103, 104, 106, 107.

   (Translator's Note: Stories for which I have been able to locate the U.S. originals are coded thus: CS = (*Walt Disney's*) *Comics and Stories*; DA = *Duck Album*; DD = *Donald Duck*; GG = *Gyro Gearloose*; HDL = *Huey, Dewsy and Louie, Junior Woodchucks*; and US = *Uncle Scrooge*.

   The figures following represent the original date of issue; thus 7/67 means July 1967. Sometimes, however, when there is no monthly date, the issue number appears followed by the year.)

2 "At the time of his death (1966), a small, informal but worldwide group was promoting – with the covert assistance of his publicity department – his nomination for the Nobel Peace prize" (from Richard Schickel, *The Disney Version*, New York, 1968, p. 303). San Bernardo is a working-class suburb of greater Santiago; San Antonio a port in the central zone. (Trans.)

3 *La Segunda* (Santiago), July 20, 1971, p. 3. This daily belongs to the Mercurio group, which is controlled by Augustin Edwards, the major press and industrial monopolist in Chile. The writer of the article quoted worked as Public Relations officer for the American

copper companies Braden and Kennecott. (cf. A. Mattelart, "Estructura del poder informativo y dependencia" in "Los Medios de Communicación de Masas: La Ideologia de la Prensa Liberal en Chile" *Cuadernos de la Realidad Nacional* (CEREN, Santiago), 3, Marzo de 1970).

4   A word-play on the advertising slogan for a washing machine, which cleans "automagica-mente" (automatically and magically) – Trans.

5   Actual words of Little Wolf (D 210)

10

Base and Superstructure in Marxist Cultural Theory*

Raymond Williams

Any modern approach to a Marxist theory of culture must begin by considering the proposition of a determining base and a determined superstructure. From a strictly theoretical point of view this is not, in fact, where we might choose to begin. It would be in many ways preferable if we could begin from a proposition which originally was equally central, equally authentic: namely the proposition that social being determines consciousness. It is not that the two propositions necessarily deny each other or are in contradiction. But the proposition of base and superstructure, with its figurative element, with its suggestion of a fixed and definite spatial relationship, constitutes, at least in certain hands, a very specialized and at times unacceptable version of the other proposition. Yet in the transition from Marx to Marxism, and in the development of mainstream Marxism itself, the proposition of the determining base and the determined superstructure has been commonly held to be the key to Marxist cultural analysis.

It is important, as we try to analyse this proposition, to be aware that the term of relationship which is involved, that is to say 'determines', is of great linguistic and theoretical complexity. The language of determination and even more of determinism was inherited from idealist and especially theological accounts of the world and man. It is significant that it is in one of his familiar inversions, his contradictions of received propositions, that Marx uses the word which becomes, in English translation, 'determines' (the usual but not invariable German word is *bestimmen*). He is opposing an ideology that had been insistent on the power of certain forces outside man, or, in its secular version, on an abstract determining consciousness. Marx's own proposition explicitly denies this, and puts the origin of determination in men's own activities. Nevertheless, the particular history and continuity of the term serves to remind us that there are, within ordinary use – and this is true of most of the major European languages – quite different possible meanings and implications of the word 'determine'. There is, on the one hand, from its theological inheritance, the notion of an

* From Raymond Williams, *Problems in Materialism and Culture: Selected Essays* (London: Verso and NLB, 1980), pp. 31–49.

external cause which totally predicts or prefigures, indeed totally controls a sub-sequent activity. But there is also, from the experience of social practice, a notion of determination as setting limits, exerting pressures.[1]

Now there is clearly a difference between a process of setting limits and exerting pressures, whether by some external force or by the internal laws of a particular development, and that other process in which a subsequent content is essentially prefigured, predicted and controlled by a pre-existing external force. Yet it is fair to say, looking at many applications of Marxist cultural analysis, that it is the second sense, the notion of prefiguration, prediction or control, which has often explicitly or implicitly been used.

Superstructure: Qualifications and Amendments

The term of relationship is then the first thing that we have to examine in this proposition, but we have to do this by going on to look at the related terms themselves. 'Superstructure' (*Überbau*) has had most attention. In common usage, after Marx, it acquired a main sense of a unitary 'area' within which all cultural and ideological activities could be placed. But already in Marx himself, in the later correspondence of Engels, and at many points in the subsequent Marxist tradition, qualifications were made about the determined character of certain superstructural activities. The first kind of qualification had to do with delays in time, with complica-tions, and with certain indirect or relatively distant relationships. The simplest notion of a superstructure, which is still by no means entirely abandoned, had been the reflection, the imitation or the reproduction of the reality of the base in the super-structure in a more or less direct way. Positivist notions of reflection and reproduction of course directly supported this. But since in many real cultural activities this relationship cannot be found, or cannot be found without effort or even violence to the material or practice being studied, the notion was introduced of delays in time, the famous lags; of various technical complications; and of indirectness, in which certain kinds of activity in the cultural sphere – philosophy, for example – were situated at a greater distance from the primary economic activities. That was the first stage of qualification of the notion of superstructure: in effect, an operational qualification. The second stage was related but more fundamental, in that the process of the relationship itself was more substantially looked at. This was the kind of reconsideration which gave rise to the modern notion of 'mediation', in which something more than simple reflection or reproduction – indeed something radically different from either reflection or reproduction – actively occurs. In the later twentieth century there is the notion of 'homologous structures', where there may be no direct or easily apparent similarity, and certainly nothing like reflection or reproduction, between the superstructural process and the reality of the base, but in which there is an essential homology or correspondence of structures, which can be discovered by analysis. This is not the same notion as 'mediation', but it is the same kind of amendment in that the relationship between the base and the superstructure is not supposed to be direct, nor simply operationally subject to lags and complications and indirectnesses, but that of its nature it is not direct reproduction.

These qualifications and amendments are important. But it seems to me that what has not been looked at with equal care is the received notion of the 'base' (*Basis, Grundlage*). And indeed I would argue that the base is the more important concept to look at if we are to understand the realities of cultural process. In many uses of the proposition of base and superstructure, as a matter of verbal habit, 'the base' has come to be considered virtually as an object, or in less crude cases, it has been considered in essentially uniform and usually static ways. 'The base' is the real social existence of man. 'The base' is the real relations of production corresponding to a stage of development of the material productive forces. 'The base' is a mode of production at a particular stage of its development. We make and repeat propositions of this kind, but the usage is then very different from Marx's emphasis on productive activities, in particular structural relations, constituting the foundation of all other activities. For while a particular stage of the development of production can be discovered and made precise by analysis, it is never in practice either uniform or static. It is indeed one of the central propositions of Marx's sense of history that there are deep contradictions in the relationships of production and in the consequent social relationships. There is therefore the continual possibility of the dynamic variation of these forces. Moreover, when these forces are considered, as Marx always considers them, as the specific activities and relationships of real men, they mean something very much more active, more complicated and more contradictory than the developed metaphorical notion of 'the base' could possibly allow us to realize.

The Base and the Productive Forces

So we have to say that when we talk of 'the base', we are talking of a process and not a state. And we cannot ascribe to that process certain fixed properties for subsequent translation to the variable processes of the superstructure. Most people who have wanted to make the ordinary proposition more reasonable have concentrated on refining the notion of superstructure. But I would say that each term of the proposition has to be revalued in a particular direction. We have to revalue 'determination' towards the setting of limits and the exertion of pressure, and away from a predicted, prefigured and controlled content. We have to revalue 'superstructure' towards a related range of cultural practices, and away from a reflected, reproduced or specifically dependent content. And, crucially, we have to revalue 'the base' away from the notion of a fixed economic or technological abstraction, and towards the specific activities of men in real social and economic relationships, containing fundamental contradictions and variations and therefore always in a state of dynamic process.

It is worth observing one further implication behind the customary definitions. 'The base' has come to include, especially in certain twentieth-century developments, a strong and limiting sense of basic industry. The emphasis on heavy industry, even, has played a certain cultural role. And this raises a more general problem, for we find ourselves forced to look again at the ordinary notion of 'productive forces'. Clearly what we are examining in the base is primary productive forces. Yet some very crucial distinctions have to be made here. It is true that in his analysis of capitalist production Marx considered 'productive work' in a very particular and specialized sense corresponding to that mode of production. There is a difficult passage in the *Grundrisse* in which he argues that while the man who makes a piano is a productive worker, there is a real question whether the man who distributes the piano is also a productive worker; but he probably is, since he contributes to the realization of surplus value. Yet when it comes to the man who plays the piano, whether to himself or to others, there is no question: he is not a productive worker at all. So piano-maker is base, but pianist superstructure. As a way of considering cultural activity, and incidentally the economics of modern cultural activity, this is very clearly a dead-end. But for any theoretical clarification it is crucial to recognize that Marx was there engaged in an analysis of a particular kind of production, that is capitalist commodity production. Within his analysis of this mode, he had to give to the notion of 'productive labour' and 'productive forces' a specialized sense of primary work on materials in a form which produced commodities. But this has narrowed remarkably, and in a cultural context very damagingly, from his more central notion of *productive forces*, in which, to give just brief reminders, the most important thing a worker ever produces is himself, himself in the fact of that kind of labour, or the broader historical emphasis of men producing themselves, themselves and their history. Now when we talk of the base, and of primary productive forces, it matters very much whether we are referring, as in one degenerate form of this proposition became habitual, to primary production within the terms of capitalist economic relationships, or to the primary production of society itself, and of men themselves, the material production and reproduction of real life. If we have the broad sense of productive forces, we look at the whole question of the base differently, and we are then less tempted to dismiss as superstructural, and in that sense as merely secondary, certain vital productive social forces, which are in the broad sense, from the beginning, basic.

Uses of Totality

Yet, because of the difficulties of the ordinary proposition of base and superstructure, there was an alternative and very important development, an emphasis primarily associated with Lukács, on a social 'totality'. The totality of social practices was opposed to this layered notion of base and a consequent superstructure. This concept of a totality of practices is compatible with the notion of social being determining consciousness, but it does not necessarily interpret this process in terms of a base and a superstructure. Now the language of totality has become common, and it is indeed in many ways more acceptable than the notion of base and superstructure. But with one very important reservation. It is very easy for the notion of totality to empty of its essential content the original Marxist proposition. For if we come to say that society is composed of a large number of social practices which form a concrete social whole, and if we give to each practice a certain specific recognition, adding only that they interact, relate and combine in very complicated ways, we are at one level much more obviously talking about reality, but we are at another level withdrawing from the claim that there is any process of determination. And this I, for one, would be very unwilling to do. Indeed, the key question to ask about any notion of totality in cultural theory is this: whether the notion of totality includes the notion of intention.

If totality is simply concrete, if it is simply the recognition of a large variety of miscellaneous and contemporaneous practices, then it is essentially empty of any content that could be called Marxist. Intention, the notion of intention, restores the key question, or rather the key emphasis. For while it is true that any society is a complex whole of such practices, it is also true that any society has a specific organization, a specific structure, and that the principles of this organization and structure can be seen as directly related to certain social intentions, intentions by which we define the society, intentions which in all our experience have been the rule of a particular class. One of the unexpected consequences of the crudeness of the base/superstructure model has been the too easy acceptance of models which appear less crude – models of totality or of a complex whole – but which exclude the facts of social intention, the class character of a particular society and so on. And this reminds us of how much we lose if we abandon the superstructural emphasis altogether. Thus I have great difficulty in seeing processes of art and thought as superstructural in the sense of the formula as it is commonly used. But in many areas of social and political thought – certain kinds of ratifying theory, certain kinds of law, certain kinds of institution, which after all in Marx's original formulations were very much part of the superstructure – in all that kind of social apparatus, and in a decisive area of political and ideological activity and construction, if we fail to see a superstructural element we fail to recognize reality at all. These laws, constitutions, theories, ideologies, which are so often claimed as natural, or as having universal validity or significance, simply have to be seen as expressing and ratifying the domination of a particular class. Indeed the difficulty of revising the formula of base and superstructure has had much to do with the perception of many militants – who have to fight such institutions and notions as well as fighting economic battles – that if these institutions and their ideologies are not perceived as having that kind of dependent and ratifying relation-ship, if their claims to universal validity or legitimacy are not denied and fought, then the class character of the society can no longer be seen. And this has been the effect of some versions of totality as the description of cultural process. Indeed I think we can properly use the notion of totality only when we combine it with that other crucial Marxist concept of 'hegemony'.

The Complexity of Hegemony

It is Gramsci's great contribution to have emphasized hegemony, and also to have understood it at a depth which is, I think, rare. For hegemony supposes the existence of something which is truly total, which is not merely secondary or superstructural, like the weak sense of ideology, but which is lived at such a depth, which saturates the society to such an extent, and which, as Gramsci put it, even constitutes the substance and limit of common sense for most people under its sway, that it corresponds to the reality of social experience very much more clearly than any notions derived from the formula of base and superstructure. For if ideology were merely some abstract, imposed set of notions, if our social and political and cultural ideas and assumptions and habits were merely the result of specific manipulation, of a kind of overt training which might be simply ended or withdrawn, then the society would be very much easier to move and to change than in practice it has ever been or is. This notion of hegemony as deeply saturating the consciousness of a society seems to me to be fundamental. And hegemony has the advantage over general notions of totality, that it at the same time emphasizes the facts of domination.

Yet there are times when I hear discussions of hegemony and feel that it too, as a concept, is being dragged back to the relatively simple, uniform and static notion which 'superstructure' in ordinary use had become. Indeed I think that we have to give a very complex account of hegemony if we are talking about any real social formation. Above all we have to give an account which allows for its elements of real and constant change. We have to emphasize that hegemony is not singular; indeed that its own internal structures are highly complex, and have continually to be renewed, recreated and defended; and by the same token, that they can be continually challenged and in certain respects modified. That is why instead of speaking simply of 'the hegemony', 'a hegemony', I would propose a model which allows for this kind of variation and contradiction, its sets of alternatives and its processes of change.

For one thing that is evident in some of the best Marxist cultural analysis is that it is very much more at home in what one might call *epochal* questions than in what one has to call *historical* questions. That is to say, it is usually very much better at distinguishing the large features of different epochs of society, as commonly between feudal and bourgeois, than at distinguishing between different phases of bourgeois society, and different moments within these phases: that true historical process which demands a much greater precision and delicacy of analysis than the always striking epochal analysis which is concerned with main lineaments and features.

The theoretical model which I have been trying to work with is this. I would say first that in any society, in any particular period, there is a central system of practices, meanings and values, which we can properly call dominant and effective. This implies no presumption about its value. All I am saying is that it is central. Indeed I would call it a corporate system, but this might be confusing, since Gramsci uses 'corporate' to mean the subordinate as opposed to the general and dominant elements of hegemony. In any case what I have in mind is the central, effective and dominant system of meanings and values, which are not merely abstract but which are organized and lived. That is why hegemony is not to be understood at the level of mere opinion or mere manipulation. It is a whole body of practices and expectations; our assignments of energy, our ordinary understanding of the nature of man and of his world. It is a set of meanings and values which as they are experienced as practices appear as reciprocally confirming. It thus constitutes a sense of reality for most people in the society, a sense of absolute because experienced reality beyond which it is very difficult for most members of the society to move, in most areas of their lives. But this is not, except in the operation of a moment of abstract analysis, in any sense a static system. On the contrary we can only understand an effective and dominant culture if we understand the real social process on which it depends: I mean the process of incorporation. The modes of incorporation are of great social significance. The educational institutions are usually the main agencies of the transmission of an effective dominant culture, and this is now a major economic as well as a cultural activity; indeed it is both in the same moment. Moreover, at a philosophical level, at the true level of theory and at the level of the history of various practices, there is a process which I call the *selective tradition*: that which, within the terms of an effective dominant culture, is always passed off as '*the* tradition', '*the* significant past'. But always the selectivity is the point; the way in which from a whole possible area of past and present, certain meanings and practices are chosen for emphasis, certain other meanings and practices are neglected and excluded. Even more crucially, some of these meanings and practices are reinterpreted, diluted, or put into forms which support or at least do not contradict other elements within the effective dominant culture. The processes of education; the processes of a much wider social training within institutions like the family; the practical definitions and organization of work; the selective tradition at an intellectual and theoretical level: all these forces are involved in a continual making and remaking of an effective dominant culture, and on them, as experienced, as built into our living, its reality depends. If what we learn there were merely an imposed ideology, or if it were only the isolable meanings and practices of the ruling class, or of a section of the ruling class, which gets imposed on others, occupying merely the top of our minds, it would be – and one would be glad – a very much easier thing to overthrow.

It is not only the depths to which this process reaches, selecting and organizing and interpreting our experience. It is also that it is continually active and adjusting; it isn't just the past, the dry husks of ideology which we can more easily discard. And this can only be so, in a complex society, if it is something more substantial and more flexible than any abstract imposed ideology. Thus we have to recognize the alternative meanings and values, the alternative opinions and attitudes, even some alternative senses of the world, which can be accommodated and tolerated within a particular effective and dominant culture. This has been much under-emphasized in our notions of a superstructure, and even in some notions of hegemony. And the under-emphasis opens the way for retreat to an indifferent complexity. In the practice of politics, for example, there are certain truly incorporated modes of what are nevertheless, within those terms, real oppositions, that are felt and fought out. Their existence within the incorporation is recognizable by the fact that, whatever the degree of internal conflict or internal variation, they do not in practice go beyond the limits of the central effective and dominant definitions. This is true, for example, of the practice of parliamentary politics, though its internal oppositions are real. It is true about a whole range of practices and arguments, in any real society, which can by no means be reduced to an ideological cover, but which can nevertheless be properly analysed as in my sense corporate, if we find that, whatever the degree of internal controversy and variation, they do not in the end exceed the limits of the central corporate definitions.

But if we are to say this, we have to think again about the sources of that which is not corporate; of those practices, experiences, meanings, values which are not part of the effective dominant culture. We can express this in two ways. There is clearly something that we can call alternative to the effective dominant culture, and there is something else that we can call oppositional, in a true sense. The degree of existence of these alternative and oppositional forms is itself a matter of constant historical variation in real circumstances. In certain societies it is possible to find areas of social life in which quite real alternatives are at least left alone. (If they are made available, of course, they are part of the corporate organization.) The existence of the possibility of opposition, and of its articulation, its degree of openness, and so on, again depends on very precise social and political forces. The facts of alternative and oppositional forms of social life and culture, in relation to the effective and dominant culture, have then to be recognized as subject to historical variation, and as having sources which are very significant as a fact about the dominant culture itself.

Residual and Emergent Cultures

I have next to introduce a further distinction, between *residual* and *emergent* forms, both of alternative and of oppositional culture. By 'residual' I mean that some experiences, meanings and values, which cannot be verified or cannot be expressed in terms of the dominant culture, are nevertheless lived and practised on the basis of the residue – cultural as well as social – of some previous social formation. There is a real case of this in certain religious values, by contrast with the very evident incorp-oration of most religious meanings and values into the dominant system. The same is true, in a culture like Britain, of certain notions derived from a rural past, which have a very significant popularity. A residual culture is usually at some distance from the effective dominant culture, but one has to recognize that, in real cultural activities, it may get incorporated into it. This is because some part of it, some version of it – and especially if the residue is from some major area of the past – will in many cases have had to be incorporated if the effective dominant culture is to make sense in those areas. It is also because at certain points a dominant culture cannot allow too much of this kind of practice and experience outside itself, at least without risk. Thus the pressures are real, but certain genuinely residual meanings and practices in some important cases survive.

By 'emergent' I mean, first, that new meanings and values, new practices, new significances and experiences, are continually being created. But there is then a much earlier attempt to incorporate them, just because they are part – and yet not a defined part – of effective contemporary practice. Indeed it is significant in our own period how very early this attempt is, how alert the dominant culture now is to anything that can be seen as emergent. We have then to see, first, as it were a temporal relation between a dominant culture and on the one hand a residual and on the other hand an emergent culture. But we can only understand this if we can make distinctions, that usually require very precise analysis, between residual-incorporated and residual not incorporated. It is an important fact about any particular society, how far it reaches into the whole range of human practices and experiences in an attempt at incorpora-tion. It may be true of some earlier phases of bourgeois society, for example, that there were some areas of experience which it was willing to dispense with, which it was prepared to assign as the sphere of private or artistic life, and as being no particular business of society or the state. This went along with certain kinds of political tolerance, even if the reality of that tolerance was malign neglect. But I am sure it is true of the society that has come into existence since the last war, that progressively, because of developments in the social character of labour, in the social character of communications, and in the social character of decision, it extends much further than ever before in capitalist society into certain hitherto resigned areas of experience and practice and meaning. Thus the effective decision, as to whether a practice is alternative or oppositional, is often now made within a very much narrower scope. There is a simple theoretical distinction between alternative and oppositional, that is to say between someone who simply finds a different way to live and wishes to be left alone with it, and someone who finds a different way to live and wants to change the society in its light. This is usually the difference between individual and small-group solutions to social crisis and those solutions which properly belong to political and ultimately revolutionary practice. But it is often a very narrow line, in reality, between alternative and oppositional. A meaning or a practice may be tolerated as a deviation, and yet still be seen only as another particular way to live. But as the necessary area of effective dominance extends, the same meanings and practices can be seen by the dominant culture, not merely as disregarding or despising it, but as challenging it.

Now it is crucial to any Marxist theory of culture that it can give an adequate explanation of the sources of these practices and meanings. We can understand, from an ordinary historical approach, at least some of the sources of residual meanings and practices. These are the results of earlier social formations, in which certain real meanings and values were generated. In the subsequent default of a particular phase of a dominant culture, there is then a reaching back to those meanings and values which were created in real societies in the past, and which still seem to have some significance because they represent areas of human experience, aspiration and achievement, which the dominant culture under-values or opposes, or even cannot recognize. But our hardest task, theoretically, is to find a non-metaphysical and non-subjectivist explanation of emergent cultural practice. Moreover, part of our answer to this question bears on the process of persistence of residual practices.

Class and Human Practice

We have indeed one source to hand from the central body of Marxist theory. We have the formation of a new class, the coming to consciousness of a new class. This remains, without doubt, quite centrally important. Of course, in itself, this process of formation complicates any simple model of base and superstructure. It also complicates some of the ordinary versions of hegemony, although it was Gramsci's whole purpose to see and to create by organization that hegemony of a proletarian kind which would be capable of challenging the bourgeois hegemony. We have then one central source of new practice, in the emergence of a new class. But we have also to recognize certain other kinds of source, and in cultural practice some of these are very important. I would say that we can recognize them on the basis of this proposition: that no mode of production, and therefore no dominant society or order of society, and therefore no dominant culture, in reality exhausts the full range of human practice, human energy, human intention (this range is not the inventory of some original 'human nature' but, on the contrary, is that extraordinary range of variations, both practised and imagined, of which human beings are and have shown themselves to be capable). Indeed it seems to me that this emphasis is not merely a negative proposition, allowing us to account for certain things which happen outside the dominant mode. On the contrary, it is a fact about the modes of domination that they select from and consequently exclude the full range of actual and possible human practice. The difficulties of human practice outside or against the dominant mode are, of course, real. It depends very much whether it is in an area in which the dominant class and the dominant culture have an interest and a stake. If the interest and the stake are explicit, many new practices will be reached for, and if possible incorporated, or else extirpated with extraordinary vigour. But in certain areas, there will be in certain periods practices and meanings which are not reached for. There will be areas of practice and meaning which, almost by definition from its own limited character, or in its profound deformation, the dominant culture is unable in any real terms to recognize. This gives us a bearing on the observable difference between, for example, the practices of a capitalist state and a state like the contemporary Soviet Union in relation to writers. Since from the whole Marxist tradition literature was seen as an important activity, indeed a crucial activity, the Soviet state is very much sharper in investigating areas where different versions of practice, different meanings and values, are being attempted and expressed. In capitalist practice, if the thing is not making a profit, or if it is not being widely circulated, then it can for some time be overlooked, at least while it remains alternative. When it becomes oppositional in an explicit way, it does, of course, get approached or attacked.

I am saying then that in relation to the full range of human practice at any one time, the dominant mode is a conscious selection and organization. At least in its fully formed state it is conscious. But there are always sources of actual human practice which it neglects or excludes. And these can be different in quality from the developing and articulate interests of a rising class. They can include, for example, alternative perceptions of others, in immediate personal relationships, or new perceptions of material and media, in art and science, and within certain limits these new perceptions can be practised. The relations between the two kinds of source – the emerging class and either the dominatively excluded or the more generally new practices – are by no means necessarily contradictory. At times they can be very close, and on the relations between them much in political practice depends. But culturally and as a matter of theory the areas can be seen as distinct.

Now if we go back to the cultural question in its most usual form – what are the relations between art and society, or literature and society? – in the light of the preceding discussion, we have to say first that there are no relations between literature and society in that abstracted way. The literature is there from the beginning as a practice in the society. Indeed until it and all other practices are present, the society cannot be seen as fully formed. A society is not fully available for analysis until each of its practices is included. But if we make that emphasis we must make a corresponding emphasis: that we cannot separate literature and art from other kinds of social practice, in such a way as to make them subject to quite special and distinct laws. They may have quite specific features as practices, but they cannot be separated from the general social process. Indeed one way of emphasizing this is to say, to insist, that literature is not restricted to operating in any one of the sectors I have been seeking to describe in this model. It would be easy to say, it is a familiar rhetoric, that literature operates in the emergent cultural sector, that it represents the new feelings, the new meanings, the new values. We might persuade ourselves of this theoretically, by abstract argument, but when we read much literature, over the whole range, without the sleight-of-hand of calling Literature only that which we have already selected as embodying certain meanings and values at a certain scale of intensity, we are bound to recognize that the act of writing, the practices of discourse in writing and speech, the making of novels and poems and plays and theories, all this activity takes place in all areas of the culture.

Literature appears by no means only in the emergent sector, which is always, in fact, quite rare. A great deal of writing is of a residual kind, and this has been deeply true of much English literature in the last half-century. Some of its fundamental meanings and values have belonged to the cultural achievements of long-past stages of society. So widespread is this fact, and the habits of mind it supports, that in many minds 'literature' and 'the past' acquire a certain identity, and it is then said that there is now no literature: all that glory is over. Yet most writing, in any period, including our own, is a form of contribution to the effective dominant culture. Indeed many of the specific qualities of literature – its capacity to embody and enact and perform certain meanings and values, or to create in single particular ways what would be otherwise merely general truths – enable it to fulfil this effective function with great power. To literature, of course, we must add the visual arts and music, and in our own society the powerful arts of film and of broadcasting. But the general theoretical point should be clear. If we are looking for the relations between literature and society, we cannot either separate out this one practice from a formed body of other practices, nor when we have identified a particular practice can we give it a uniform, static and ahistorical relation to some abstract social formation. The arts of writing and the arts of creation and performance, over their whole range, are parts of the cultural process in all the different ways, the different sectors, that I have been seeking to describe. They contribute to the effective dominant culture and are a central articulation of it. They embody residual meanings and values, not all of which are incorporated, though many are. They express also and significantly some emergent practices and meanings, yet some of these may eventually be incorporated, as they reach people and begin to move them. Thus it was very evident in the sixties, in some of the emergent arts of performance, that the dominant culture reached out to transform, or seek to transform, them. In this process, of course, the dominant culture itself changes, not in its central formation, but in many of its articulated features. But then in a modern society it must always change in this way, if it is to remain dominant, if it is still to be felt as in real ways central in all our many activities and interests.

Critical Theory as Consumption

What then are the implications of this general analysis for the analysis of particular works of art? This is the question towards which most discussion of cultural theory seems to be directed: the discovery of a method, perhaps even a methodology, through which particular works of art can be understood and described. I would not myself agree that this is the central use of cultural theory, but let us for a moment consider it. What seems to me very striking is that nearly all forms of contemporary critical theory are theories of *consumption*. That is to say, they are concerned with understanding an object in such a way that it can profitably or correctly be consumed. The earliest stage of consumption theory was the theory of 'taste', where the link between the practice and the theory was direct in the metaphor. From taste there came the more elevated notion of 'sensibility', in which it was the consumption by sensibility of elevated or insightful works that was held to be the essential practice of reading, and critical activity was then a function of this sensibility. There were then more developed theories, in the 1920s with I. A. Richards, and later in New Criticism, in which the effects of consumption were studied directly. The language of the work of art as object then became more overt. 'What effect does this work ("the poem" as it was ordinarily described) have on me?' Or, 'what impact does it have on me?', as it was later to be put in a much wider area of communication studies. Naturally enough, the notion of the work of art as *object*, as *text*, as an isolated artefact, became central in all these later consumption theories. It was not only that the practices of *production* were then overlooked, though this fused with the notion that most important literature anyway was from the past. The real social conditions of production were in any case neglected because they were believed to be at best secondary. The true relationship was seen always as between the taste, the sensibility or the training of the reader and this isolated work, this object 'as in itself it really is', as most people came to put it. But the notion of the work of art as object had a further large theoretical effect. If you ask questions about the work of art seen as object, they may include questions about the components of its production. Now, as it happened, there was a use of the formula of base and superstructure which was precisely in line with this. The components of a work of art were the real activities of the base, and you could study the object to discover these components. Sometimes you even studied the components and then projected the object. But in any case the relationship that was looked for was one between an object and its components. But this was not only true of Marxist suppositions of a base and a superstructure. It was true also of various kinds of psychological theory, whether in the form of archetypes, or the images of the collective unconscious, or the myths and symbols which were seen as the *components* of particular works of art. Or again there was biography, or psychobiography and its like, where the components were in the man's life and the work of art was an object in which components of this kind were discovered. Even in some of the more rigorous forms of New Criticism and of structuralist criticism, this essential procedure of regarding the work as an object which has to be reduced to its components, even if later it may be reconstituted, came to persist.

Objects and Practices

Now I think the true crisis in cultural theory, in our own time, is between this view of the work of art as object and the alternative view of art as a practice. Of course it is at once argued that the work of art *is* an object: that various works have survived from the past, particular sculptures, particular paintings, particular buildings, and these are objects. This is of course true, but the same way of thinking is applied to works which have no such singular existence. There is no *Hamlet*, no *Brothers Karamazov*, no *Wuthering Heights*, in the sense that there is a particular great painting. There is no *Fifth Symphony*, there is no work in the whole area of music and dance and performance, which is an object in any way comparable to those works in the visual arts which have survived. And yet the habit of treating all such works as objects has persisted because this is a basic theoretical and practical presupposition. But in literature (especially in drama), in music and in a very wide area of the performing arts, what we permanently have are not objects but *notations*. These notations have then to be interpreted in an active way, according to the particular conventions. But indeed this is true over an even wider field. The relationship between the making of a work of art and its reception is always active, and subject to conventions, which in themselves are forms of (changing) social organization and relationship, and this is radically different from the production and consumption of an object. It is indeed an activity and a practice, and in its accessible forms, although it may in some arts have the character of a singular object, it is still only accessible through active perception and interpretation. This makes the case of notation, in arts like drama and literature and music, only a special case of a much wider truth. What this can show us here about the practice of analysis is that we have to break from the common procedure of isolating the object and then discovering its components. On the contrary we have to discover the nature of a practice and then its conditions.

Often these two procedures may in part resemble each other, but in many other cases they are of radically different kinds, and I would conclude with an observation on the way this distinction bears on the Marxist tradition of the relation between primary economic and social practices, and cultural practices. If we suppose that what is produced in cultural practice is a series of objects, we shall, as in most current forms of sociological-critical procedure, set about discovering their components. Within a Marxist emphasis these components will be from what we have been in the habit of calling the base. We then isolate certain features which we can so to say recognize *in component form*, or we ask what processes of transformation or mediation these components have gone through before they arrived in this accessible state.

But I am saying that we should look not for the components of a product but for the conditions of a practice. When we find ourselves looking at a particular work, or group of works, often realizing, as we do so, their essential community as well as their irreducible individuality, we should find ourselves attending first to the reality of their practice and the conditions of the practice as it was then executed. And from this I think we ask essentially different questions. Take for example the way in which an object – 'a text' – is related to a genre, in orthodox criticism. We identify it by certain leading features, we then assign it to a larger category, the genre, and then we may find the components of the genre in a particular social history (although in some variants of criticism not even that is done, and the genre is supposed to be some permanent category of the mind).

It is not that way of proceeding that is now required. The recognition of the relation of a collective mode and an individual project – and these are the only categories that we can initially presume – is a recognition of related practices. That is to say, the irreducibly individual projects that particular works are, may come in experience and in analysis to show resemblances which allow us to group them into collective modes. These are by no means always genres. They may exist as resemblances within and across genres. They may be the practice of a group in a period, rather than the practice of a phase in a genre. But as we discover the nature of a particular practice, and the nature of the relation between an individual project and a collective mode, we find that we are analysing, as two forms of the same process, both its active composition and its conditions of composition, and in either direction this is a complex of extending active relationships. This means, of course, that we have no built-in procedure of the kind which is indicated by the fixed character of an object. We have the principles of the relations of practices, within a discoverably intentional organization, and we have the available hypotheses of dominant, residual and emergent. But what we are actively seeking is the true practice which has been alienated to an object, and the true conditions of practice – whether as literary conventions or as social relationships – which have been alienated to components or to mere background.

As a general proposition this is only an emphasis, but it seems to me to suggest at once the point of break and the point of departure, in practical and theoretical work, within an active and self-renewing Marxist cultural tradition.

Note

1   For a further discussion of the range of meanings in 'determine' see *Keywords* (London, 1976) pp. 87–91.

11

Encoding/Decoding*

Stuart Hall

Traditionally, mass-communications research has conceptualized the process of communication in terms of a circulation circuit or loop. This model has been criticized for its linearity – sender/message/receiver – for its concentration on the level of message exchange and for the absence of a structured conception of the different moments as a complex structure of relations. But it is also possible (and useful) to think of this process in terms of a structure produced and sustained through the articulation of linked but distinctive moments – production, circulation, distribution/consumption, reproduction. This would be to think of the process as a 'complex structure in dominance', sustained through the articulation of connected practices, each of which, however, retains its distinctiveness and has its own specific modality, its own forms and conditions of existence. This second approach, homologous to that which forms the skeleton of commodity production offered in Marx's *Grundrisse* and in *Capital*, has the added advantage of bringing out more sharply how a continuous circuit – production–distribution–production – can be sustained through a 'passage of forms'.[1] It also highlights the specificity of the forms in which the product of the process 'appears' in each moment, and thus what distinguishes discursive 'production' from other types of production in our society and in modern media systems.

The 'object' of these practices is meanings and messages in the form of sign-vehicles of a specific kind organized, like any form of communication or language, through the operation of codes within the syntagmatic chain of a discourse. The apparatuses, relations and practices of production thus issue, at a certain moment (the moment of 'production/circulation') in the form of symbolic vehicles constituted within the rules of 'language'. It is in this discursive form that the circulation of the 'product' takes place. The process thus requires, at the production end, its material instruments – its 'means' – as well as its own sets of social (production) relations – the organization and combination of practices within media apparatuses. But it is in the *discursive* form that the circulation of the product takes place, as well as its distribution to different audiences. Once accomplished, the discourse must then be translated – transformed, again – into social practices if the circuit is to be both completed and

* From Stuart Hall, Dorothy Hobson, Andrew Lowe and Paul Willis (eds.), *Culture, Media, Language* (London: Hutchinson, 1980).

effective. If no 'meaning' is taken, there can be no 'consumption'. If the meaning is not articulated in practice, it has no effect. The value of this approach is that while each of the moments, in articulation, is necessary to the circuit as a whole, no one moment can fully guarantee the next moment with which it is articulated. Since each has its specific modality and conditions of existence, each can constitute its own break or interruption of the 'passage of forms' on whose continuity the flow of effective production (that is, 'reproduction') depends.

Thus while in no way wanting to limit research to 'following only those leads which emerge from content analysis',[2] we must recognize that the discursive form of the message has a privileged position in the communicative exchange (from the viewpoint of circulation), and that the moments of 'encoding' and 'decoding', though only 'relatively autonomous' in relation to the communicative process as a whole, are *determinate* moments. A 'raw' historical event cannot, *in that form*, be transmitted by, say, a television newscast. Events can only be signified within the aural-visual forms of the televisual discourse. In the moment when a historical event passes under the sign of discourse, it is subject to all the complex formal 'rules' by which language signifies. To put it paradoxically, the event must become a 'story' before it can become a *communicative event*. In that moment the formal sub-rules of discourse are 'in dominance', without, of course, subordinating out of existence the historical event so signified, the social relations in which the rules are set to work or the social and political consequences of the event having been signified in this way. The 'message form' is the necessary 'form of appearance' of the event in its passage from source to receiver. Thus the transposition into and out of the 'message form' (or the mode of symbolic exchange) is not a random 'moment', which we can take up or ignore at our convenience. The 'message form' is a determinate moment; though, at another level, it comprises the surface movements of the communications system only and requires, at another stage, to be integrated into the social relations of the communication process as a whole, of which it forms only a part.

From this general perspective, we may crudely characterize the television communicative process as follows. The institutional structures of broadcasting, with their practices and networks of production, their organized relations and technical infrastructures, are required to produce a programme. Using the analogy of *Capital*, this is the 'labour process' in the discursive mode. Production, here, constructs the message. In one sense, then, the circuit begins here. Of course, the production process is not without its 'discursive' aspect: it, too, is framed throughout by meanings and ideas: knowledge-in-use concerning the routines of production, historically defined technical skills, professional ideologies, institutional knowledge, definitions and assumptions, assumptions about the audience and so on frame the constitution of the programme through this production structure. Further, though the production structures of television originate the television discourse, they do not constitute a closed system. They draw topics, treatments, agendas, events, personnel, images of the audience, 'definitions of the situation' from other sources and other discursive formations within the wider socio-cultural and political structure of which they are a differentiated part. Philip Elliott has expressed this point succinctly, within a more traditional framework, in his discussion of the way in which the audience is both the 'source' and the 'receiver' of the television message. Thus – to borrow Marx's terms – circulation and reception are, indeed, 'moments' of the production process in television and are reincorporated, via a number of skewed and structured 'feed-backs', into the production process itself. The consumption or reception of the television message is thus also itself a 'moment' of the production process in its larger sense, though the latter is 'predominant' because it is the 'point of departure for the realization' of the message. Production and reception of the television message are not, therefore, identical, but they are related: they are differentiated moments within the totality formed by the social relations of the communicative process as a whole.

At a certain point, however, the broadcasting structures must yield encoded messages in the form of a meaningful discourse. The institution-societal relations of production must pass under the discursive rules of language for its product to be 'realized'. This initiates a further differentiated moment, in which the formal rules of discourse and language are in dominance. Before this message can have an 'effect' (however defined), satisfy a 'need' or be put to a 'use', it must first be appropriated as a meaningful discourse and be meaningfully decoded. It is this set of decoded mean-ings which 'have an effect', influence, entertain, instruct or persuade, with very complex perceptual, cognitive, emotional, ideological or behavioural consequences. In a 'determinate' moment the structure employs a code and yields a 'message': at another determinate moment the 'message', via its decodings, issues into the struc-ture of social practices (see figure 1). We are now fully aware that this re-entry into the practices of audience reception and 'use' cannot be understood in simple behavioural terms. The typical processes identified in positivistic research on isolated elements – effects, uses, 'gratifications' – are themselves framed by structures of understanding, as well as being produced by social and economic relations, which shape their 'realization' at the reception end of the chain and which permit the

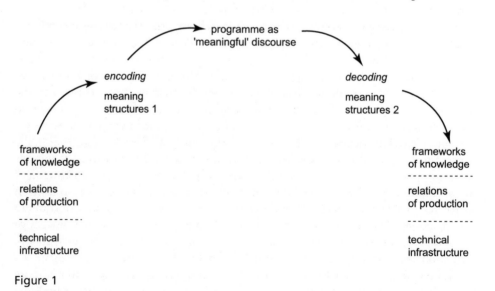

Figure 1

meanings signified in the discourse to be transposed into practice or consciousness (to acquire social use value or political effectivity).

Clearly, what we have labelled in figure 1 'meaning structures 1' and 'meaning structures 2' may not be the same. They do not constitute an 'immediate identity'. The codes of encoding and decoding may not be perfectly symmetrical. The degrees of symmetry – that is, the degrees of 'understanding' and 'misunderstanding' in the communicative exchange – depend on the degrees of symmetry/asymmetry (relations of equivalence) established between the positions of the 'personifications', encoder-producer and decoder-receiver. But this in turn depends on the degrees of identity/non-identity between the codes which perfectly or imperfectly transmit, interrupt or systematically distort what has been transmitted. The lack of fit between the codes has a great deal to do with the structural differences of relation and position between broadcasters and audiences, but it also has something to do with the asymmetry between the codes of 'source' and 'receiver' at the moment of transformation into and out of the discursive form. What are called 'distortions' or 'misunderstandings' arise precisely from the *lack of equivalence* between the two sides in the communicative exchange. Once again, this defines the 'relative autonomy', but 'determinateness', of the entry and exit of the message in its discursive moments.

The application of this rudimentary paradigm has already begun to transform our understanding of the older term, television 'content'. We are just beginning to see how it might also transform our understanding of audience reception, 'reading' and response as well. Beginnings and endings have been announced in communications research before, so we must be cautious. But there seems some ground for thinking that a new and exciting phase in so-called audience research, of a quite new kind, may be opening up. At either end of the communicative chain the use of the semiotic paradigm promises to dispel the lingering behaviourism which has dogged mass-media research for so long, especially in its approach to content. Though we know the television programme is not a behavioural input, like a tap on the knee cap, it seems to have been almost impossible for traditional researchers to conceptualize the communicative process without lapsing into one or other variant of low-flying behaviourism. We know, as Gerbner has remarked, that representations of violence on the TV screen 'are not violence but messages about violence':[3] but we have continued to research the question of violence, for example, as if we were unable to comprehend this epistemological distinction.

The televisual sign is a complex one. It is itself constituted by the combination of two types of discourse, visual and aural. Moreover, it is an iconic sign, in Peirce's terminology, because 'it possesses some of the properties of the thing represented'.[4] This is a point which has led to a great deal of confusion and has provided the site of intense controversy in the study of visual language. Since the visual discourse translates a three-dimensional world into two-dimensional planes, it cannot, of course, *be* the referent or concept it signifies. The dog in the film can bark but it cannot bite! Reality exists outside language, but it is constantly mediated by and through language: and what we can know and say has to be produced in and through discourse. Discursive 'knowledge' is the product not of the transparent representation of the 'real' in language but of the articulation of language on real relations and conditions.

Thus there is no intelligible discourse without the operation of a code. Iconic signs are therefore coded signs too – even if the codes here work differently from those of other signs. There is no degree zero in language. Naturalism and 'realism' – the apparent fidelity of the representation to the thing or concept represented – is the result, the effect, of a certain specific articulation of language on the 'real'. It is the result of a discursive practice.

Certain codes may, of course, be so widely distributed in a specific language community or culture, and be learned at so early an age, that they appear not to be constructed – the effect of an articulation between sign and referent – but to be 'naturally' given. Simple visual signs appear to have achieved a 'near-universality' in this sense: though evidence remains that even apparently 'natural' visual codes are culture-specific. However, this does not mean that no codes have intervened; rather, that the codes have been profoundly *naturalized*. The operation of naturalized codes reveals not the transparency and 'naturalness' of language but the depth, the habituation and the near-universality of the codes in use. They produce apparently 'natural' recognitions. This has the (ideological) effect of concealing the practices of coding which are present. But we must not be fooled by appearances. Actually, what naturalized codes demonstrate is the degree of habituation produced when there is a fundamental alignment and reciprocity – an achieved equivalence – between the encoding and decoding sides of an exchange of meanings. The functioning of the codes on the decoding side will frequently assume the status of naturalized perceptions. This leads us to think that the visual sign for 'cow' actually *is* (rather than *represents*) the animal, cow. But if we think of the visual representation of a cow in a manual on animal husbandry – and, even more, of the linguistic sign 'cow' – we can see that both, in different degrees, are *arbitrary* with respect to the concept of the animal they represent. The articulation of an arbitrary sign – whether visual or verbal – with the concept of a referent is the product not of nature but of convention, and the conventionalism of discourses requires the intervention, the support, of codes. Thus Eco has argued that iconic signs 'look like objects in the real world because they reproduce the conditions (that is, the codes) of perception in the viewer'.[5] These 'conditions of perception' are, however, the result of a highly coded, even if virtually unconscious, set of operations – decodings. This is as true of the photographic or televisual image as it is of any other sign. Iconic signs are, however, particularly vulnerable to being 'read' as natural because visual codes of perception are very widely distributed and because this type of sign is less arbitrary than a linguistic sign: the linguistic sign, 'cow' possesses *none* of the properties of the thing represented, whereas the visual sign appears to possess *some* of those properties.

This may help us to clarify a confusion in current linguistic theory and to define precisely how some key terms are being used in this article. Linguistic theory frequently employs the distinction 'denotation' and 'connotation'. The term 'denotation' is widely equated with the literal meaning of a sign: because this literal meaning is almost universally recognized, especially when visual discourse is being employed, 'denotation' has often been confused with a literal transcription of 'reality' in language – and thus with a 'natural sign', one produced without the intervention of a code. 'Connotation', on the other hand, is employed simply to refer to less fixed and therefore more conventionalized and changeable, associative meanings, which clearly vary from instance to instance and therefore must depend on the intervention of codes.

We do *not* use the distinction – denotation/connotation – in this way. From our point of view, the distinction is an *analytic* one only. It is useful, in analysis, to be able to apply a rough rule of thumb which distinguishes those aspects of a sign which appear to be taken, in any language community at any point in time, as its 'literal' meaning (denotation) from the more associative meanings for the sign which it is possible to generate (connotation). But analytic distinctions must not be confused with distinctions in the real world. There will be very few instances in which signs organized in a discourse signify *only* their 'literal' (that is, near-universally consensual-ized) meaning. In actual discourse most signs will combine both the denotative and the connotative *aspects* (as redefined above). It may, then, be asked why we retain the distinction at all. It is largely a matter of analytic value. It is because signs appear to acquire their full ideological value – appear to be open to articulation with wider ideological discourses and meanings – at the level of their 'associative' meanings (that is, at the connotative level) – for here 'meanings' are *not* apparently fixed in natural perception (that is, they are not fully naturalized), and their fluidity of meaning and association can be more fully exploited and transformed.[6] So it is at the connotative *level* of the sign that situational ideologies alter and transform signification. At this level we can see more clearly the active intervention of ideologies in and on discourse: here, the sign is open to new accentuations and, in Vološinov's terms, enters fully into the struggle over meanings – the class struggle in language.[7] This does not mean that the denotative or 'literal' meaning is outside ideology. Indeed, we could say that its ideological value is strongly *fixed* – because it has become so fully universal and 'natural'. The terms 'denotation' and 'connotation', then, are merely useful analytic tools for distinguishing, in particular contexts, between not the presence/absence of ideology in language but the different levels at which ideologies and discourses intersect.[8]

The level of connotation of the visual sign, of its contextual reference and position-ing in different discursive fields of meaning and association, is the point where *already coded* signs intersect with the deep semantic codes of a culture and take on additional, more active ideological dimensions. We might take an example from advertising discourse. Here, too, there is no 'purely denotative', and certainly no 'natural', representation. Every visual sign in advertising connotes a quality, situation, value or inference, which is present as an implication or implied meaning, depending on the connotational positioning. In Barthes's example, the sweater always signifies a 'warm garment' (denotation) and thus the activity/value of 'keeping warm'. But it is also possible, at its more connotative levels, to signify 'the coming of winter' or 'a cold day'. And, in the specialized sub-codes of fashion, sweater may also connote a fashionable style of *haute couture* or, alternatively, an informal style of dress. But set against the right visual background and positioned by the romantic sub-code, it may connote 'long autumn walk in the woods'.[9] Codes of this order clearly contract relations for the sign with the wider universe of ideologies in a society. These codes are the means by which power and ideology are made to signify in particular discourses. They refer signs to the 'maps of meaning' into which any culture is classi-fied; and those 'maps of social reality' have the whole range of social meanings, practices, and usages, power and interest 'written in' to them. The connotative levels of signifiers, Barthes remarked, 'have a close communication with culture, knowledge, history, and it is through them, so to speak, that the environmental world invades the linguistic and semantic system. They are, if you like, the fragments of ideology'.[10]

The so-called denotative *level* of the televisual sign is fixed by certain, very complex (but limited or 'closed') codes. But its connotative *level*, though also bounded, is more open, subject to more active *transformations*, which exploit its polysemic values. Any such already constituted sign is potentially transformable into more than one connotative configuration. Polysemy must not, however, be confused with pluralism. Connotative codes are *not* equal among themselves. Any society/culture tends, with varying degrees of closure, to impose its classifications of the social and cultural and political world. These constitute a *dominant cultural order*, though it is neither univocal nor uncontested. This question of the 'structure of discourses in dominance' is a crucial point. The different areas of social life appear to be mapped out into discursive domains, hierarchically organized into *dominant or preferred meanings*. New, problematic or troubling events, which breach our expectancies and run coun-ter to our 'common-sense constructs', to our 'taken-for-granted' knowledge of social structures, must be assigned to their discursive domains before they can be said to 'make sense'. The most common way of 'mapping' them is to assign the new to some domain or other of the existing 'maps of problematic social reality'. We say *dominant*, not 'determined', because it is always possible to order, classify, assign and decode an event within more than one 'mapping'. But we say 'dominant' because there exists a pattern of 'preferred readings'; and these both have the institutional/political/ideo-logical order imprinted in them and have themselves become institutionalized.[11] The domains of 'preferred meanings' have the whole social order embedded in them as a set of meanings, practices and beliefs: the everyday knowledge of social structures, of 'how things work for all practical purposes in this culture', the rank order of power and interest and the structure of legitimations, limits and sanctions. Thus to clarify a 'misunderstanding' at the connotative level, we must refer, *through* the codes, to the orders of social life, of economic and political power and of ideology. Further, since these mappings are 'structured in dominance' but not closed, the communicative process consists not in the unproblematic assignment of every visual item to its given position within a set of prearranged codes, but of *performative rules* – rules of competence and use, of logics-in-use – which seek actively to *enforce* or *pre-fer* one semantic domain over another and rule items into and out of their appropriate meaning-sets. Formal semiology has too often neglected this practice of *interpretative work*, though this constitutes, in fact, the real relations of broadcast practices in television.

In speaking of *dominant meanings*, then, we are not talking about a one-sided process which governs how all events will be signified. It consists of the 'work' required to enforce, win plausibility for and command as legitimate a *decoding* of the event within the limit of dominant definitions in which it has been connotatively signified. Terni has remarked:

By the word *reading* we mean not only the capacity to identify and decode a certain number of signs, but also the subjective capacity to put them into a creative relation between themselves and with other signs: a capacity which is, by itself, the condition for a complete awareness of one's total environment.[12]

Our quarrel here is with the notion of 'subjective capacity', as if the referent of a televisional discourse were an objective fact but the interpretative level were an individualized and private matter. Quite the opposite seems to be the case. The televisual practice takes 'objective' (that is, systemic) responsibility precisely for the relations which disparate signs contract with one another in any discursive instance, and thus continually rearranges, delimits and prescribes into what 'awareness of one's total environment' these items are arranged.

This brings us to the question of misunderstandings. Television producers who find their message 'failing to get across' are frequently concerned to straighten out the kinks in the communication chain, thus facilitating the 'effectiveness' of their communication. Much research which claims the objectivity of 'policy-oriented analysis' reproduces this administrative goal by attempting to discover how much of a message the audience recalls and to improve the extent of understanding. No doubt misunderstandings of a literal kind do exist. The viewer does not know the terms employed, cannot follow the complex logic of argument or exposition, is unfamiliar with the language, finds the concepts too alien or difficult or is foxed by the expository narrative. But more often broadcasters are concerned that the audience has failed to take the meaning as they – the broadcasters – intended. What they really mean to say is that viewers are not operating within the 'dominant' or 'preferred' code. Their ideal is 'perfectly transparent communication'. Instead, what they have to confront is 'systematically distorted communication'.[13]

In recent years discrepancies of this kind have usually been explained by reference to 'selective perception'. This is the door via which a residual pluralism evades the compulsions of a highly structured, asymmetrical and non-equivalent process. Of course, there will always be private, individual, variant readings. But 'selective perception' is almost never as selective, random or privatized as the concept suggests. The patterns exhibit, across individual variants, significant clusterings. Any new approach to audience studies will therefore have to begin with a critique of 'selective perception' theory.

It was argued earlier that since there is no necessary correspondence between encoding and decoding, the former can attempt to 'pre-fer' but cannot prescribe or guarantee the latter, which has its own conditions of existence. Unless they are wildly aberrant, encoding will have the effect of constructing some of the limits and parameters within which decodings will operate. If there were no limits, audiences could simply read whatever they liked into any message. No doubt some total misunderstandings of this kind do exist. But the vast range must contain *some* degree of reciprocity between encoding and decoding moments, otherwise we could not speak of an effective communicative exchange at all. Nevertheless, this 'correspondence' is not given but constructed. It is not 'natural' but the product of an articulation between two distinct moments. And the former cannot determine or guarantee, in a simple sense, which decoding codes will be employed. Otherwise communication would be a perfectly equivalent circuit, and every message would be an instance of 'perfectly transparent communication'. We must think, then, of the variant articulations in which encoding/decoding can be combined. To elaborate on this, we offer a hypothetical analysis of some possible decoding positions, in order to reinforce the point of 'no necessary correspondence'.[14]

We identify *three* hypothetical positions from which decodings of a televisual discourse may be constructed. These need to be empirically tested and refined. But the argument that decodings do not follow inevitably from encodings, that they are not identical, reinforces the argument of 'no necessary correspondence'. It also helps to deconstruct the common-sense meaning of 'misunderstanding' in terms of a theory of 'systematically distorted communication'.

The first hypothetical position is that of the *dominant-hegemonic position*. When the viewer takes the connoted meaning from, say, a television newscast or current affairs programme full and straight, and decodes the message in terms of the reference code in which it has been encoded, we might say that the viewer *is operating inside the dominant code*. This is the ideal-typical case of 'perfectly transparent communication' – or as close as we are likely to come to it 'for all practical purposes'. Within this we can distinguish the positions produced by the *professional code*. This is the position (produced by what we perhaps ought to identify as the operation of a 'metacode') which the professional broadcasters assume when encoding a message which has *already* been signified in a hegemonic manner. The professional code is 'relatively independent' of the dominant code, in that it applies criteria and transformational operations of its own, especially those of a technico-practical nature. The professional code, however, operates *within* the 'hegemony' of the dominant code. Indeed, it serves to reproduce the dominant definitions precisely by bracketing their hegemonic quality and operating instead with displaced professional codings which foreground such apparently neutral-technical questions as visual quality, news and presentational values, televisual quality, 'professionalism' and so on. The hegemonic interpretations of, say, the politics of Northern Ireland, or the Chilean *coup* or the Industrial Relations Bill are principally generated by political and military elites: the particular choice of presentational occasions and formats, the selection of personnel, the choice of images, the staging of debates are selected and combined through the operation of the professional code. How the broadcasting professionals are able *both* to operate with 'relatively autonomous' codes of their own *and* to act in such a way as to reproduce (not without contradiction) the hegemonic signification of events is a complex matter which cannot be further spelled out here. It must suffice to say that the professionals are linked with the defining elites not only by the institutional position of broadcasting itself as an 'ideological apparatus',[15] but also by the structure of *access* (that is, the systematic 'over-accessing' of selective elite personnel and their 'definition of the situation' in television). It may even be said that the professional codes serve to reproduce hegemonic definitions specifically by *not overtly* biasing their operations in a dominant direction: ideological reproduction therefore takes place here inadvertently, unconsciously, 'behind men's backs'.[16] Of course, conflicts, contradictions and even misunderstandings regularly arise between the dominant and the professional significations and their signifying agencies.

The second position we would identify is that of the *negotiated code* or position. Majority audiences probably understand quite adequately what has been dominantly defined and professionally signified. The dominant definitions, however, are hegemonic precisely because they represent definitions of situations and events which are 'in dominance', (*global*). Dominant definitions connect events, implicitly or explicitly, to grand totalizations, to the great syntagmatic views-of-the-world: they take 'large views' of issues: they relate events to the 'national interest' or to the level of geopolitics, even if they make these connections in truncated, inverted or mystified ways. The definition of a hegemonic viewpoint is (a) that it defines within its terms the mental horizon, the universe, of possible meanings, of a whole sector of relations in a society or culture; and (b) that it carries with it the stamp of legitimacy – it appears coterminous with what is 'natural', 'inevitable', 'taken for granted' about the social order. Decoding within the *negotiated version* contains a mixture of adaptive and oppositional elements: it acknowledges the legitimacy of the hegemonic definitions to make the grand significations (abstract), while, at a more restricted, situational (situated) level, it makes its own ground rules – it operates with exceptions to the rule. It accords the privileged position to the dominant definitions of events while reserving the right to make a more negotiated application to 'local conditions', to its own more *corporate* positions. This negotiated version of the dominant ideology is thus shot through with contradictions, though these are only on certain occasions brought to full visibility. Negotiated codes operate through what we might call particular or situated logics: and these logics are sustained by their differential and unequal relation to the discourses and logics of power. The simplest example of a negotiated code is that which governs the response of a worker to the notion of an Industrial Relations Bill limiting the right to strike or to arguments for a wages freeze. At the level of the 'national interest' economic debate the decoder may adopt the hegemonic definition, agreeing that 'we must all pay ourselves less in order to combat inflation'. This, however, may have little or no relation to his/her willingness to go on strike for better pay and conditions or to oppose the Industrial Relations Bill at the level of shop-floor or union organization. We suspect that the great majority of so-called 'misunderstandings' arise from the contradictions and disjunctures between hegemonic-dominant encodings and negotiated-corporate decodings. It is just these mismatches in the levels which most provoke defining elites and professionals to identify a 'failure in communications'.

Finally, it is possible for a viewer perfectly to understand both the literal and the connotative inflection given by a discourse but to decode the message in a *globally* contrary way. He/she detotalizes the message in the preferred code in order to retotalize the message within some alternative framework of reference. This is the case of the viewer who listens to a debate on the need to limit wages but 'reads' every mention of the 'national interest' as 'class interest'. He/she is operating with what we must call an *oppositional code*. One of the most significant political moments (they also coincide with crisis points within the broadcasting organizations themselves, for obvious reasons) is the point when events which are normally signified and decoded in a negotiated way begin to be given an oppositional reading. Here the 'politics of signification' – the struggle in discourse – is joined.

Notes

1   For an explication and commentary on the methodological implications of Marx's argument, see S. Hall, 'A reading of Marx's 1857 *Introduction to the Grundrisse*', in *WPCS*, 6 (1974).
2   J. D. Halloran, 'Understanding television', paper for the Council of Europe Colloquy on 'Understanding Television' (University of Leicester, 1973).
3   G. Gerbner et al., *Violence in TV Drama: A Study of Trends and Symbolic Functions* (The Annenberg School, University of Pennsylvania, 1970).
4   Charles Peirce, *Speculative Grammar*, in *Collected Papers* (Cambridge, Mass.: Harvard University Press, 1931–58).
5   Umberto Eco, 'Articulations of the cinematic code', in *Cinemantics*, no. 1.
6   See the argument in S. Hall, 'Determinations of news photographs', in *WPCS*, 3 (1972).
7   Vološinov, *Marxism and the Philosophy of Language* (London: The Seminar Press 1973).
8   For a similar clarification, see Marina Camargo Heck, 'Ideological dimensions of media messages', in Stuart Hall, Dorothy Hobson, Andrew Lowe and Paul Willis (eds), *Culture, Media, Language* (London: Hutchinsen, 1980), pp. 122–7.
9   Roland Barthes, 'Rhetoric of the image', in *WPCS*, 1 (1971).
10 Roland Barthes, *Elements of Semiology* (London: Jonathan Cape 1967).
11 For an extended critique of 'preferred reading', see Alan O'Shea, 'Preferred reading' (unpublished paper, CCCS, University of Birmingham).
12 P. Terni, 'Memorandum', Council of Europe Colloquy on 'Understanding Television' (University of Leicester, 1973).
13 The phrase is Habermas's, in 'Systematically distorted communications', in P. Dretzel (ed.), *Recent Sociology*, vol. 2 (London: Collier-Macmillan, 1970). It is used here, however, in a different way.
14 For a sociological formulation which is close, in some ways, to the positions outlined here but which does not parallel the argument about the theory of discourse, see Frank Parkin, *Class Inequality and Political Order* (London: MacGibon and Kee, 1971).
15 See Louis Althusser, 'Ideology and ideological state apparatuses', in *Lenin and Philosophy and Other Essays* (London: New Left Books, 1971).
16 For an expansion of this argument, see Stuart Hall, 'The external/internal dialectic in broadcasting', *4th Symposium on Broadcasting* (University of Manchester, 1972), and 'Broadcasting and the state: the independence/impartiality couplet', AMCR Symposium, University of Leicester, 1976 (CCCS unpublished paper).

12

On the Politics of Empirical
Audience Research*

Ien Ang

In his pioneering book *The 'Nationwide' Audience*, David Morley situates his research on which the book reports as follows:

> The relation of an audience to the ideological operations of television remains in principle an empirical question: the challenge is the attempt to develop appropriate methods of empirical investigation of that relation. (Morley 1980a: 162)

Although this sentence may initially be interpreted as a call for a methodological discussion about empirical research techniques, its wider meaning should be sought in the theoretical and political context of Morley's work. To me, the importance of *The 'Nationwide' Audience* does not so much reside in the fact that it offers an empirically validated, and thus 'scientific', account of 'the ideological operations of television', nor merely in its demonstration of some of the ways in which the television audience is 'active'. Other, more wide-ranging issues are at stake – issues related to the *politics* of research.

Since its publication in 1980, *The 'Nationwide' Audience* has played an important role in media studies. The book occupies a key strategic position in the study of media audiences – a field of study that went through a rapid development in the 1980s. It seems fair to say that this book forms a major moment in the growing popularity of an 'ethnographic' approach on media audiences – Morley himself has termed his project an 'ethnography of reading' (1981: 13). This type of qualitative empirical research, usually carried out in the form of in-depth interviews with a small number of people (and at times supplemented with some form of participant observation), is now recognized by many as one of the best ways to learn about the differentiated subtleties of people's engagements with television and other media.

This 'ethnographic' approach has gained popularity in both 'critical' media studies and 'mainstream' mass communications research (see, e.g., Hobson 1980 and 1982;

* From Ien Ang, *Living Room Wars: Rethinking Media Audiences for a Postmodern World* (London and New York: Routledge, 1991), pp. 35–52.

Lull 1980 and 1988; Radway 1984; Ang 1985; Jensen 1986; Lindlof 1987; Liebes and Katz 1990). A sort of methodological consensus has emerged, a common ground in which scholars from divergent epistemological backgrounds can thrive. On the one hand, qualitative methods of empirical research seem to be more acceptable than quantitative ones because they offer the possibility to avoid what C. Wright Mills (1970) has termed abstracted empiricism – a tendency often levelled at the latter by 'critical' scholars. On the other hand, some 'mainstream' audience researchers are now acknowledging the limitations on the kind of data that can be produced by large-scale, quantitative survey work, and believe that ethnographically oriented methods can overcome the shortcomings observed. Given this enthusiastic, rather new interest in qualitative research methods, I would like to reflect upon its general implications for our understanding of television audiences. What kind of knowledge does it produce? What can this manner of doing empirical research on audiences mean? In short, what are the politics of audience 'ethnography'?[1]

In exploring these questions, I want to clarify some of the issues that are at stake in developing a *critical* perspective in empirical audience studies. The term 'critical' as I would like to use it here refers first of all to a certain intellectual-political *orientation* towards academic practice: whatever its subject matter or methodology, essential to doing 'critical' research would be the adoption of a self-reflective perspective, one that is, first, conscious of the social and discursive nature of any research practice, and, second, takes seriously the Foucauldian reminder that the production of knowledge is always bound up in a network of power relations (Foucault 1979). By characterizing 'critical' research in this way, that is, as an orientation rather than as a fixed 'para-digm', I aim to relativize the more rigid ways in which 'critical' and 'mainstream' research have often been opposed to one another.

Formally speaking, positions can only be 'critical' or 'mainstream' in relation to other positions within a larger discursive field. The two terms thus do not primarily signify fixed contents of thought, but their status within a whole, often dispersed, field of statements, claims and knowledges, what Foucault calls a 'regime of truth'. The relations of force in that field can change over time: what was once 'critical' (or marginal) can become part of the 'mainstream'; what was once 'mainstream' (or dominant) can lose its power and be pushed aside to a marginal(ized) position. Furthermore, as Larry Grossberg (1987) has usefully remarked, the term 'critical' can bear uneasy arrogant connotations: after all, is there any scholar whose work is not 'critical' in some sense?

This does not mean, of course, that the distinction is totally devoid of any sub-stantive bearings. In media studies, for instance, the 'critical' tradition, whose begin-nings can be located in the work of the Frankfurt School, has generally derived its philosophical and political inspiration from European schools of thought such as Marxism and (post)structuralism. In terms of research problematics, 'critical' media researchers have mainly been concerned with the analysis of the ideological and/or economic role of the media in capitalist and patriarchal society. Furthermore, the epistemological underpinnings of this kind of work are generally characterized by a strident anti-positivist and anti-empiricist mentality.[2]

This distrust of positivist empiricism on the part of 'critical' theorists, however, does not necessarily imply an *inherent* incompatibility between 'critical' and empirical research, as is often contended by 'mainstream' scholars.[3] Indeed, if doing 'critical' research is more a matter of intellectual-political orientation than of academic paradigm building, then no fixed, universal yardstick, theoretical or methodological, for what constitutes 'critical' knowledge is possible. On the contrary, in my view what it means to be critical needs to be assessed and constantly reassessed in every concrete conjuncture, with respect to the concrete issues and directions that are at stake in any concrete research field. In other words, I am proposing an *open* and *contextual* definition of 'critical' research, one that does not allow itself to rest easily on pre-existent epistemological foundations but, on the contrary, is reassessed continuously according to the ways in which it contributes to our understanding of the world. In the following, I hope to clarify some of the implications of this perspective on doing 'critical' research for an evaluation of the current developments in audience studies as I indicated above.

More concretely, what I will discuss and try to elaborate in this chapter is what I take as the political and theoretical specificity of the *cultural studies* approach as a 'critical' perspective, from which David Morley, coming from the Birmingham Centre for Contemporary Cultural Studies, has developed his work (see Hall *et al.* 1980; Streeter 1984; Fiske 1987b). I will set this perspective on audience studies against some developments in and around the uses and gratifications approach, where an interest in 'ethnographic' methods has been growing recently. In doing this I will not be able to discuss the wide range of concrete studies that have been made in this area. Rather I will restrict myself, somewhat schematically and all too briefly, to the more programmatic statements and proposals pertaining to the identity and the future development of the field, and evaluate them in the light of what I see as important for a critical cultural studies approach. Furthermore, it is not my intention to construct an absolute antagonism between the two approaches. Rather, I would like to highlight some of the differences in preoccupation and perspective, in order to specify how ethnographic or ethnographically oriented studies of media audiences can contribute to a 'critical' approach in the sense I have outlined. Before doing this, I will first give a short sketch of the intellectual arena in which Morley intervened.

The Problem of the Disappearing Audience

The 'Nationwide' Audience appeared at a time when critical discourse about film and television in Britain was heavily preoccupied with what Morley (1980a: 161), following Steve Neale, calls an 'abstract text/subject relationship', formulated within a generally (post)structuralist and psychoanalytic theoretical framework. In this discourse, primarily developed in the journal *Screen*, film and television spectatorship is almost exclusively theorized from the perspective of the 'productivity of the text'. As a consequence, the role of the viewer was conceived in purely formalist terms: as a position inscribed in the text. Here, the subject-in-the-text tends to collapse with 'real' social subjects. In this model, there is no space for a dialogical relationship between texts and social subjects. Texts are assumed to be the only source of meaning; they construct subject positions which viewers are bound to take up if they are to make sense of the text. In other words, the reading of texts is conceived in '*Screen* theory' as entirely dictated by textual structures.

It is this model's textual determinism that fuelled Morley's dissatisfaction. Theoretically, it implied an ahistorical, asocial and generalist conception of film and TV spectatorship. Methodologically, the analysis of textual structures alone was considered to be sufficient to comprehend how viewers are implicated in the texts they encounter. Politically, this model left no room for manoeuvre for television viewers. They are implicitly conceived as 'prisoners' of the text. It was against this background that Morley decided to undertake an empirical investigation of how groups of viewers with different social positions read or interpret one particular text: an episode of the British TV magazine programme *Nationwide*. One of the most important motivations of Morley's intervention, then, was to overcome the textualism of *Screen* theory's discourse, in which the relation of text and subject is dealt with 'as an *a priori* question to be deduced from a theory of the ideal spectator 'inscribed' in the text' (Morley 1980a: 162). By looking at how one text could be decoded in different ways by different groups of social subjects, Morley's intention, in which he was successful, was to demonstrate that encounters between texts and viewers are far more complex than the textualist theory would suggest; they are overdetermined by the operation of a multiplicity of forces – certain historical and social structures, but also other texts – that simultaneously act upon the subjects concerned.[4] What *The 'Nationwide' Audience* explores is the notion that the moment of decoding should be considered as a relatively autonomous process in which a constant struggle over the meaning of the text is fought out. Textual meanings do not reside in the texts themselves: a certain text can come to mean different things depending on the interdiscursive context in which viewers interpret it.

The significance of Morley's turn towards empirical research of the television audience should be assessed against this critical background. It is first of all a procedure that is aimed at opening up a space in which watching television can begin to be understood as a complex cultural practice full of dialogical negotiations and contestations, rather than as a singular occurrence whose meaning can be determined once and for all in the abstract. Doing empirical research, then, is here used as a strategy to break out of a hermetically closed theoreticism in which an absolute certainty about the ideological effectivity of television is presumed. Thus, when Morley says that the relation of an audience to television 'remains an empirical question', what he is basically aiming at is to open up critical discourse on television audiences, and to sensitize it for the possibility of struggle in the practices of television use and consumption – a struggle whose outcome cannot be known in advance, for the simple reason that encounters between television and audiences are always historically specific and context-bound.

Academic Convergence?

The 'Nationwide' Audience has generally been received as an innovative departure within cultural studies, both theoretically and methodologically. If *Screen* theory can be diagnosed as one instance in which critical discourse on television suffered from 'the problem of the disappearing audience' (Fejes 1984), Morley's project represents an important acknowledgement within cultural studies that television viewing is a practice that involves the active production of meanings by viewers. But the book has not only made an impact in cultural studies circles. Curiously, but not surprisingly, it has also been welcomed by adherents of the uses and gratifications approach, one of the most influential 'mainstream' strands of audience research in mass communication scholarship. These scholars see books such as Morley's as an important step on the part of 'critical' scholars in their direction, that is, as a basic acceptance of, and possible contribution to, a refinement of their own basic axiomatic commitment to 'the active audience'. At the same time, some uses and gratifications researchers, for their part, have now incorporated some of the insights developed within the 'critical' perspective into their own paradigm. For example, they have adopted semiologically informed cultural studies concepts such as 'text' and 'reader' in their work. This move indicates an acknowledgement of the symbolic nature of negotiations between media texts and their readers which they, in their narrow functionalist interest in the multiple relationships between audience 'needs' and media 'uses', had previously all but ignored. As Jay Blumler, Michael Gurevitch and Elihu Katz admit:

> Gratifications researchers, in their paradigmatic personae, have lost sight of what the media are purveying, in part because of an over-commitment to the endless freedom of the audience to reinvent the text, in part because of a too rapid leap to mega-functions, such as surveillance or self-identity.   (Blumler *et al.* 1985: 272)

On top of this conceptual rapprochement, they have also expressed their delight in noticing a methodological 'concession' among 'critical' scholars: at last, so they exclaim, some 'critical' scholars have dropped their suspicion of doing empirical research. In a benevolent, rather fatherly tone, Blumler, Gurevitch and Katz, three senior ambassadors of the uses and gratifications approach, have thus proclaimed a gesture of 'reaching out' to the other 'camp' (1985: 275). Therefore the prospect is evoked of a merger of the two approaches, to the point that they may ultimately fuse into a happy common project in which the perceived hostility between the two 'camps' will have been unmasked as academic 'pseudo-conflicts'. As one leading gratifications researcher, Karl Erik Rosengren, optimistically predicts: 'To the extent that the same problematics are empirically studied by members of various schools, the present sharp differences of opinion will gradually diminish and be replaced by a growing convergence of perspectives' (1983: 203).[5]

However, to interpret these recent developments in audience studies in terms of such a convergence is to simplify and even misconceive what is at stake in the 'ethnographic turn' within cultural studies. For one thing, I would argue that cultural studies and uses and gratifications research only superficially share 'the same problematics', as Rosengren would have it. Also, what separates a 'critical' from a 'mainstream' perspective is more than merely some 'differences of opinion', sharp or otherwise. Rather, it concerns fundamental differences not only in epistemological but also in theoretical and political attitudes towards the aim and status of doing empirical work in the first place.

The academic idealization of joining forces in pursuit of a supposedly common goal as if it were a neutral, scientific project is a particularly depoliticizing strategy, because it tends to neutralize all antagonism and disagreement in favour of a forced consensus. If I am cautious and a little wary about this euphoria around the prospect of academic convergence, it is not my intention to impose a rigid and absolute, eternal dichotomy between 'critical' and 'mainstream' research. Nor would I want to assert that Morley's project is entirely 'critical' and the uses and gratifications approach completely 'mainstream'. As I have noted before, the relationship between 'critical' and 'mainstream' is not a fixed one; it does not concern two mutually exclusive, antagonistic sets of knowledge, as some observers would imply by talking in terms of 'schools', 'paradigms' or even 'camps'. In fact, many assumptions and ideas do not, in themselves, intrinsically belong to one or the other perspective. For example, the basic assumption that the audience is 'active' (rather than passive) and that watching television is a social (rather than an individual) practice is currently accepted in both perspectives. There is nothing spectacular about that.[6] What matters is how this idea of 'activeness' is articulated with a more general theory of social agency and power. Also, I would suggest that the idea that texts can generate multiple meanings because readers/viewers can 'negotiate' textual meanings is not in itself a sufficient condition for the declared convergence. For example, Tamar Liebes has suggested that 'the focus of the convergence is on the idea that the interaction between messages and receivers takes on the form of negotiation, and is not predetermined' (1986: 1). However, as I will try to show below, what makes all the difference is the way in which 'negotiation' is conceived. After all, 'not predetermined' does not mean 'undetermined'; on the contrary.

While uses and gratifications researchers generally operate within a liberal pluralist conception of society where individuals are seen as ideally free, that is, unhindered by external powers, in cultural studies, following Marxist/(post)structuralist assumptions, people are conceived as always-already implicated in, and necessarily constrained by, the web of relationships and structures which constitute them as social subjects. This doesn't mean that they are stripped of agency like preprogrammed automatons, but that that agency itself, or the 'negotiations' subjects undertake in constructing their lives, is *over*determined (i.e. neither predetermined nor undetermined) by the concrete conditions of existence they find themselves in. Following Hall (1986b: 46), 'determinacy' here is understood in terms of the setting of limits, the establishment of parameters, the defining of the space of operations, rather than in terms of the absolute predictability of particular outcomes. This is what Hall (1986c) calls a 'Marxism without guarantees', a non-determinist theory of determination, or, to put it simply, a recognition of the virtual truism that 'people make their own history but under conditions not of their own making'.

How complex structural and conjunctural determinations of viewership and audiencehood should be conceived remains therefore an important point of divergence between 'critical' and 'mainstream' studies. Finally, it is also noteworthy to point out that, while uses and gratifications researchers now seem to be 'rediscovering the text', researchers working within a cultural studies perspective seem to be moving away from the text. This is very clear in Morley's second book, *Family Television* (1986), on which I will comment later. In fact, it becomes more and more difficult to delineate what 'the television text' is in a media-saturated world.

In other words, in evaluating whether we can really speak of a paradigmatic convergence, it is not enough to establish superficially similar research questions, nor to take at face value a shared acknowledgement of the usefulness of certain methods of inquiry. Of course, such commonalities are interesting enough and it would be nonsense to categorically discard them. I do think it is important to avoid a dogmatism or antagonism-for-the-sake-of-it, and to try to learn from others wherever that is possible. But at the same time we should not lose sight of the fact that any call for a convergence itself is not an innocent gesture. It tends to be done from a certain point of view, and therefore necessarily involves a biased process in which certain issues and themes are highlighted and others suppressed. And it is my contention that an all too hasty declaration of convergence could lead to neglecting some of the most important distinctive features of cultural studies as a critical intellectual enterprise.

A difference in conceptualizing the object of study is a first issue that needs to be discussed here. As I have already suggested, in a cultural studies perspective 'audience activity' cannot and should not be studied nominalistically, decontextualized from the larger network of social relationships in which it occurs. The aim of cultural studies is not a matter of dissecting 'audience activity' in ever more refined variables and categories so that we can ultimately have a complete and generalizable formal 'map' of all dimensions of 'audience activity' (which seems to be the drive behind the uses and gratifications project; e.g. Levy and Windahl 1984, 1986). Rather, the aim, as I see it, is to arrive at a more historicized and contextualized insight into the ways in which 'audience activity' is articulated within and by a complex set of social, political, economic and cultural forces. In other words, what is at stake is not the understanding of 'audience activity' as such as an isolated and isolatable object of research, but the embeddedness of 'audience activity' in a complex network of ongoing cultural practices and relationships.

As a result, an audience researcher working within a cultural studies sensibility cannot restrict herself or himself to 'just' studying audiences and their activities (and, for that matter, relating those activities with other variables such as gratifications sought or obtained, dependencies, effects, and so on). She or he will also engage herself/himself with the structural and cultural *processes* through which the audiences she or he is studying are constituted and being constituted. Thus, one essential theoretical point of the cultural studies approach of the television audience is its foregrounding of the notion that the dynamics of watching television, no matter how heterogeneous and seemingly free, are always related to the operations of forms of social power. It is in this light that we should see Morley's decision to do research on viewers' decodings: it was first of all motivated by an interest in what he in the quote at the beginning of this chapter calls 'the ideological operations of television'.

It is important then to emphasize that the reference to 'the active audience' does not occupy the same theoretical status in the two approaches. From a cultural studies point of view, evidence that audiences are 'active' cannot simply be equated with the rather triumphant, liberal pluralist conclusion, often displayed by gratificationists, that media consumers are 'free' or even 'powerful' – a conclusion which allegedly undercuts the idea of 'media hegemony'. The question for cultural studies is not simply one of 'where the power lies in media systems' (Blumler *et al.* 1985: 260) – i.e. with the audience or with the media producers – but rather how relations of power are organized within the heterogeneous practices of media use and consumption. In other words, rather than constructing an opposition between 'the' media and 'the' audience, as if these were separate ontological entities, and, along with it, the application of a distributional theory of power – i.e. power conceived as a 'thing' that can be attributed to either side of the opposing entities – cultural studies is interested in understanding media consumption as a site of cultural struggle, in which a variety of forms of power are exercised, with different sorts of effects.[7] Thus if, as Morley's study has shown, viewers decode a text in different ways and sometimes even give oppositional meanings to it, this should be understood not as an example of 'audience freedom', but as a moment in that cultural struggle, an ongoing struggle over meaning and pleasure which is central to the fabric(ation) of everyday life.

I hope to have made it clear by now that in evaluating the possibility or even desirability of a paradigmatic convergence, it is important to look at how 'audience activity' is theorized or interpreted, and how research 'findings' are placed in a wider theoretical framework. So, if one type of 'audience activity' which has received much attention in both approaches has been the 'interpretive strategies' used by audiences to read media texts (conceptualized in terms of decoding structures, interpretive communities, patterns of involvement, and so on), how are we to make sense of those interpretive strategies? The task of the cultural studies researcher, I would suggest, is to develop *strategic interpretations* of them, different not only in form and content but also in scope and intent from those offered in more 'mainstream' accounts.[8] I will return to this central issue of interpretation below.

Beyond Methodology

A troubling aspect about the idea of (and desire for) convergence, then, is that it tends to be conceptualized as an exclusively 'scientific' enterprise. Echoing the tenets of positivism, its aim seems to be the gradual accumulation of scientifically confirmed 'findings'. It is propelled by the hope that by seeking a shared agreement on what is relevant to study and by developing shared methodological skills, the final scientific account of 'the audience' can eventually be achieved. In this framework, audience research is defined as a specialized niche within an academic discipline (e.g. 'mass communication'), in which it is assumed that 'the audience' is a proper object of study whose characteristics can be ever more accurately observed, described, categorized, systematized and explained until the whole picture is 'filled in'. In other words, this scientific project implicitly claims in principle (if not in practice) to be able to produce total knowledge, to reveal the full and objective 'truth' about 'the audience'.

The audience here is imagined as, and turned into, an object with researchable attributes and features (be it described in terms of preferences, uses, effects, decodings, interpretive strategies, or whatever) that can be definitively known – if only researchers of different breeding would stop quarrelling with each other and unite to work harmoniously together to accomplish the task.[9]

From such a point of view, the question of *methodology* becomes a central issue. After all, rigour of method has traditionally been seen as the guarantee *par excellence* for the 'scientific' status of knowledge. In positivist social science, the hypothetico-deductive testing of theory through empirical research, quantitative in form, is cherished as the cornerstone of the production of 'scientific' knowledge. Theory that is not empirically tested or that is too complex to be moulded into empirically testable hypotheses has to be dismissed as 'unscientific'. These assumptions, which are more or less central to the dominant version of the uses and gratifications approach as it was established in the 1970s, are now contested by a growing number of researchers who claim that reality cannot be grasped and explained through quantitative methods alone. Stronger still, they forcefully assert that to capture the multidimensionality and complexity of audience activity the use of qualitative methods – and thus a move towards the 'ethnographic' – is desperately called for (cf. Lull 1986; Jensen 1987; Lindlof and Meyer 1987).

From a 'scientific' point of view, it is this methodological challenge that forms the condition of possibility of the perceived convergence. However, although I think that the struggle for legitimization of qualitative research is a very important one, I do believe that it is not the central point for critical cultural studies. This is the case because, as the struggle is defined as a matter of methodology, its relevance is confined to the development of audience research as an *academic* enterprise. Of course, this development is in itself interesting given the decades-long hegemony of positivism and the quantifying attitude in audience research. Furthermore, the growing influence of alternative 'paradigms' such as ethnomethodology and symbolic interactionism should certainly be welcomed. The problem with many 'mainstream' claims about the usefulness of qualitative methods, however, is that they are put forward in the name of 'scientific progress', without questioning the epistemological distinction between Science and commonsense which lies at the heart of positivism. The aim still seems to be the isolation of a body of knowledge that can be recognized as 'scientific' (in its broadest meaning), the orientation being one towards the advancement of an academic discipline, and, concomitantly, the technical improvement of its instruments of analysis.

A cultural studies perspective on audience research cannot stop short at this level of debate. For a critical cultural studies, it is not questions of methodology, nor 'scientific progress' that prevail. On the contrary, we should relativize the academic commitment to increasing knowledge *per se*, and resist the temptation of what Stuart Hall (1986b: 56) has called the 'codification' of cultural studies into a stable realm of established theories and canonized methodologies. In this respect, the territorial conflict between 'mainstream' and 'critical' research, quantitative and qualitative methods, humanistic and social-scientific disciplines, and so on, should perhaps not bother us too much at all in the first place. As James Carey once remarked, '[p]erhaps all the talk about theory, method, and other such things prevents us from raising, or permits us to avoid raising, deeper and disquieting questions about the purposes of our scholarship' (1983: 5). And indeed: why are we so interested in knowing about audiences in the first place? In empirical audience research, especially, it is important to reflect upon the politics of the knowledge produced. After all, scrutinizing media audiences is not an innocent practice. It does not take place in a social and institutional vacuum. As we all know, historically, the hidden agenda of audience research, even when it presents itself as pure and objective, has all too often been its commercial or political usefulness. In other words, what we should reflect upon is the *political* interventions we make when studying audiences – political not only in the sense of some external societal goal, but, more importantly, in that we cannot afford to ignore the political dimensions of the process and practice of the production of knowledge itself. What does it mean to subject audiences to the researcher's gaze? How can we develop insights that do not reproduce the kind of objectified knowledge served up by, say, market research or empiricist effects research? How is it possible to do audience research which is 'on the side' of the audience?[10] These are nagging political questions which cannot be smoothed out by the comforting canons of epistemology, methodology and Science.

Of course it is not easy to pin down what such considerations would imply in concrete terms. But it could at least be said that we should try to avoid a stance in which 'the audience' is relegated to the status of exotic 'other' – merely interesting in so far as 'we', as researchers, can turn 'them' into 'objects' of study, and about whom 'we' have the privileged position of acquiring 'scientific' knowledge.[11] To begin with, I think, critical audience studies should not strive and pretend to tell 'the truth' about 'the audience'. Its ambitions should be much more modest. As Grossberg has suggested, 'the goal of [critical research] is to offer not a polished representation of the truth, but simply a little help in our efforts to better understand the world' (1987: 89). This modesty has less to do with some sort of false humility than with the basic acknowledgement that every research practice unavoidably takes place in a particular historical situation, and is therefore in principle of a partial nature. As Hammersley and Atkinson have provocatively put it, 'all social research takes the form of participant observation: it involves participating in the social world, in whatever role, and reflecting on the products of that participation' (1983: 16). The collection of data, either quantitative or qualitative in form, can never be separated from its interpretation; it is only through practices of interpretive theorizing that unruly social experiences and events related to media consumption become established as meaningful 'facts' about audiences. Understanding 'audience activity' is thus caught up in the discursive representation, not the transparent reflection, of diverse realities pertaining to people's engagements with media.

These considerations lead to another, more politicized conception of doing research. It is not the search for (objective, scientific) Truth in which the researcher is engaged, but the construction of *interpretations*, of certain ways of understanding the world, always historically located, subjective and relative. It is the decisive importance of this interpretive moment that I would like to highlight in exploring the possibilities of a critical audience studies.[12]

In positivism, the necessarily worldly nature of interpretation is repressed, relegated to the refuted realm of 'bias'. It is assumed to follow rather automatically – i.e. without the intervention of the subjective 'whims' of the researcher – from the controlled process of 'empirical testing of theory'. An apparent innocence of interpretation is then achieved, one that is seemingly grounded in 'objective social reality' itself. In fact, the very term 'interpretation' would seem to have definite negative connotations for positivists because of its connection with 'subjectivism'. And even within those social science approaches in which the interpretive act of the researcher – i.e. the moment of data analysis that comes after data collection – is taken more seriously, interpretation is more often than not problematized as a technical rather than a political matter, defined in terms of careful inference making rather than in terms of discursive constructions of reality.

It should be recognized, however, that because interpretations always inevitably involve the construction of certain representations of reality (and not others), they can never be 'neutral' and merely 'descriptive'. After all, the 'empirical', captured in either quantitative or qualitative form, does not yield self-evident meanings; it is only through the interpretive framework constructed by the researcher that understandings of the 'empirical' come about. No 'theory' brought to bear on the 'empirical' can ever be 'value-neutral'; it is always 'interested' in the strong sense of that word. Here, then, the thoroughly political nature of any research practice manifests itself. What is at stake is a *politics of interpretation*: '[T]o advance an interpretation is to insert it into a network of power relations' (Pratt 1986: 52).

Of course, this also implies a shift in the position of the researcher. She or he is no longer a bearer of the truth, but occupies a 'partial' position in two senses of the word. On the one hand, she or he is no longer the neutral observer, but is someone whose job it is to produce historically and culturally specific knowledges that are the result of equally specific discursive encounters between researcher and informants, in which the subjectivity of the researcher is not separated from the 'object' s/he is studying. The interpretations that are produced in the process can never claim to be definitive: on the contrary, they are necessarily incomplete (for they always involve simplification, selection and exclusion) and temporary. 'If neither history nor politics ever comes to an end, then theory (as well as research) is never completed and our accounts can never be closed or totalized' (Grossberg 1987: 89). On the other hand, and even more important, the position of the researcher is also more than that of the professional scholar: beyond being a capable interpreter she or he is also inherently a political and moral subject. As an intellectual s/he is responsible not only to the Academy, but to the social world s/he lives in as well, consciously or unconsciously so. It is at the interface of 'ethics' and 'scholarship' that the researcher's interpretations take on their distinctive political edge (cf. Rabinow 1986).

Of course, all this entails a different status for empirical research. Material obtained by ethnographic fieldwork or depth-interviews with audience members cannot simply be treated as direct slices of reality, as in naturalist conceptions of ethnography. Viewers' statements about their relation to television cannot be regarded as self-evident facts. Nor are they immediate, transparent reflections of those viewers' 'lived realities' that can speak for themselves. What is of critical importance, therefore, is the way in which those statements are made sense of, that is, interpreted. Here lies the ultimate political responsibility of the researcher. The comfortable assumption that it is the reliability and accuracy of the methodologies being used that will ascertain the validity of the outcomes of research, thereby reducing the researcher's responsibility to a technical matter, is rejected. In short, to return to Morley's opening statement, audience research is undertaken because the relation between television and viewers is an empirical *question*. But the empirical is not the privileged domain where the *answers* should be sought. Answers – partial ones, to be sure, that is, both provisional and committed – are to be constructed, in the form of interpretations.[13]

Towards Interpretive Ethnography

I would now like to return to Morley's work, and evaluate its place in the research field in the light of my reflections above. To be sure, Morley himself situates his work firmly within the academic context. And parallel to the recent calls for convergence and cross-fertilization of diverse perspectives, Morley seems to have dropped his original antagonistic posture. For example, while in *The 'Nationwide' Audience* he emphasizes that 'we need to break fundamentally with the 'uses and gratifications' approach' (1980a: 14),[14] in *Family Television*, he simply states that this new piece of research draws 'upon some of the insights' of this very approach (1986: 15). The latter book is also in a more general sense set in a less polemical tone than the first one: rather than taking up a dissident's stance against other theoretical perspectives, which is a central attribute of *The 'Nationwide' Audience, Family Television* is explicitly presented as a study that aims to combine the perspectives of separate traditions in order to overcome what Morley calls an 'unproductive form of segregation' (ibid.: 13). Furthermore, both books have been written in a markedly conventional style of academic social science, structured according to a narrative line which starts out with their contextualization within related academic research trends, followed by a methodological exposition and a description of the findings, and rounded off with a chapter containing an interpretation of the results and some more general conclusions. In both books Morley's voice is exclusively that of the earnest researcher; the writer's 'I', almost completely eliminated from the surface of the text, is apparently a disembodied subject solely driven by a disinterested wish to contribute to 'scientific progress'.[15]

Morley's academistic inclination tends to result in a lack of clarity about the critical import and political relevance of his analyses. For example, the relevance of *Family Television* as a project designed to investigate at the same time two different types of questions regarding television consumption – questions of television use, on the one hand, and questions of textual interpretation, on the other – is simply asserted by the statement that these are 'urgent questions about the television audience' (Morley 1986: 13). But why? What kind of urgency is being referred to here? Morley goes on to say that it is the analysis of the domestic viewing context as such which is his main interest, and that he wishes to identify the multiple meanings hidden behind the catch-all phrase 'watching television'. Indeed, central to *Family Television*'s discourse are, as Hall remarks in his introduction to the book, the notions of variability, diversity and difference:

> We are all, in our heads, several different audiences at once, and can be constituted as such by different programmes. We have the capacity to deploy different levels and modes of attention, to mobilise different competences in our viewing. At different times of the day, for different family members, different patterns of viewing have different 'saliences'. Here the monolithic conceptions of the viewer, the audience or of television itself have been displaced – one hopes forever – before the new emphasis on difference and variation.   (Hall 1986a: 10)

Yet when taken in an unqualified manner it is exactly this stress on difference that essentially connects Morley's project with the preoccupations of the gratificationists. After all, it is their self-declared distinctive mission to get to grips with 'the gamut of audience experience' (Blumler *et al.* 1985: 271). For them too, the idea of plurality and diversity is pre-eminently the guiding principle for research. A convergence of perspectives after all?

Despite all the agreements that are certainly there, however, a closer look at the ramifications of Morley's undertaking reveals other concerns than merely the characterization and categorizing of varieties within viewers' readings and uses of television. Ultimately, it is not difference as such that is of main interest in Morley's work. To be sure, differences are not just simple facts that emerge more or less spontaneously from the empirical interview material; it is a matter of interpretation what are established as *significant* differences – significant not in the formal, statistical sense of that word, but in a culturally meaningful, interpretive sense. In cultural studies, then, it is the meanings of differences that matter – something that can only be grasped, interpretively, by looking at their contexts, social and cultural bases, and impacts. Thus, rather than the classification of differences and varieties in all sorts of typologies, which is a major preoccupation of a lot of uses and gratifications work, cultural studies would be oriented towards more specific and conjunctural understandings of how and why varieties in experience occur – a venture, to be sure, that is a closer approach to the ethnographic spirit.

In *Family Television*, for example, Morley has chosen to foreground the pattern of differences in viewing habits that are articulated with gender. What Morley emphasizes is that men and women clearly relate in contrasting ways to television, not only as to programme preferences, but also in, for example, viewing styles. The wives interviewed by Morley tend to watch television less attentively, at the same time doing other things such as talking or doing some housework. The husbands, in contrast, state a clear preference for viewing attentively, in silence, without interruption, 'in order not to miss anything' (Morley 1986: chapter 6). These differences are substantiated and highlighted by Morley's research as empirical facts, but he is careful to avoid considering these as *essential* differences between men and women. As Charlotte Brunsdon has noted, it seems possible.

> to differentiate a male – fixed, controlling, uninterrupted gaze – and a female – distracted, obscured, already busy – manner of watching television. There is some empirical

truth in these characterizations, but to take this empirical truth for explanation leads to a
theoretical short-circuit.   (Brunsdon 1986: 105)

Indeed, in mainstream sociological accounts, gender would probably be treated as a
self-evident pregiven factor that can be used as 'independent variable' to explain these
differences. Male and female modes of watching television would then be constituted
as two separate, discrete types of experience, clearly defined, fixed, static 'objects' in
themselves as it were.[16] Such an empiricist account not only essentializes gender
differences, but also fails to offer an understanding of how and why differentiations
along gender lines take the very forms they do.

   In contrast to this, both Morley and Brunsdon start out to construct a tentative
interpretation which does not take the difference between male and female relations
to television as an empirical given. Neither do they take recourse to psychological
notions such as 'needs' or 'socialization' – as is often done in accounts of gender
differences, as well as in uses and gratifications research – to try to understand why
men and women tend to watch and talk about television in the disparate ways they do.
In their interpretive work Morley and Brunsdon emphasize the structure of domestic
power relations as constitutive for the differences concerned. The home generally has
different meanings for men and women living in nuclear family arrangements: for
husbands it is the site of leisure, for wives it is the site of work. Therefore, television as
a domestic cultural form tends to be invested with different meanings for men and
women. Television has for men become a central symbol for relaxation; women's
relation to television, on the other hand, is much more contradictory. Brunsdon has
this to say on Morley's research:

> The social relations between men and women appear to work in such a way that although
> the men feel ok about imposing their choice of viewing on the whole of the family, the
> women do not. The women have developed all sorts of strategies to cope with television
> viewing they don't particularly like. The men in most cases appear to feel it would be
> literally unmanning for them to sit quiet during the women's programmes. However, the
> women in general seem to find it almost impossible to switch into the silent communion
> with the television set that characterises so much male viewing.   (Brunsdon 1986: 104)

Women's distracted mode of watching television, then, does not have something to
do with some essential femininity, but is a result of a complex of cultural and social
arrangements which makes it difficult for them to do otherwise, even though they
often express a longing to be able to watch their favourite programmes without being
disturbed. Men, on the other hand, can watch television in a concentrated manner
because they control the conditions to do so. Their way of watching television,
Brunsdon concludes, 'seems not so much a masculine mode, but a mode of power'
(1986: 106).

   What clearly emerges here is the beginning of an interpretive framework in which
differences in television-viewing practices are not just seen as expressions of different
needs, uses or readings, but are connected with the way in which particular social
subjects are structurally positioned in relation to each other. In the context of the
nuclear family home, women's viewing patterns can only be understood in relation to

men's patterns; the two are in a sense constitutive of each other. Thus, if watching television is a social and even collective practice, it is not a harmonious practice.[17] Because subjects are positioned in different ways towards the set, they engage in a continuing struggle over programme choice and programme interpretation, styles of viewing and textual pleasure. What kind of viewer they become can be seen as the outcome of this struggle, an outcome, however, that is never definitive because it can always be contested and subverted. What we call 'viewing habits' are thus not a more or less static set of behaviours inhabited by an individual or group of individuals; rather they are the temporary result of a neverending, dynamic and conflictual process in which 'the fine-grained interrelationships between meaning, pleasure, use and choice' are shaped (Hall 1986a: 10).

Morley's empirical findings, then, acquire their relevance and critical value in the context of this emerging theoretical understanding. And of course it could only have been carried out from a specific interpretive point of view. Needless to say, the point of view taken up by Morley and Brunsdon is a feminist one, that is, a worldly intellectual position that is sensitive to the micro-politics of male/female relation-ships. Television consumption, so we begin to understand, contributes to the every-day construction of male and female subjectivities through the relations of power, contradiction and struggle that men and women enter into in their daily engagements with the TV sets in their homes. At this point, we can also see how Morley's research enables us to begin to conceive of 'the ideological operations of television' in a much more radical way than has hitherto been done. The relation between television and audiences is not just a matter of discrete 'negotiations' between texts and viewers. In a much more profound sense the process of television consumption – and the position-ing of television as such in the culture of modernity – has created new areas of constraints and possibilities for structuring social relationships, identities and desires. If television is an 'ideological apparatus', to use that oldfashioned-sounding term, then this is not so much because its texts transmit certain 'messages', but because it is a cultural form through which those constraints are negotiated and those possibilities take shape.

But, one might ask, do we need empirical research, or, more specifically, ethno-graphic audience research, to arrive at such theoretical understandings? Why examine audiences empirically at all? After all, some critical scholars still dismiss the idea of doing empirical audience research altogether, because, so they argue, it would neces-sarily implicate the researcher with the strategies and aims of the capitalist culture industry (e.g. Modleski 1986: xi–xii). Against this background, I would like to make one last comment on Morley's work here. Due to his academistic posture Morley has not deemed it necessary to reflect upon his own position as a researcher. We do not get to know how he found and got on with his interviewees, nor are we informed about the way in which the interviews themselves took place. One of the very few things we learn about this in *Family Television* is that he gave up interviewing the adults and the young children at the same time, reportedly 'because after an initial period of fascination the young children quite quickly got bored' (Morley 1986: 174)! But what about the adults? What were the reasons for their willingness to talk at such length to an outsider (or was David Morley not an outsider to them)? And how did the specific power relationship pervading the interview situation affect not only the families, but also the researcher himself? These are problems inherent to conducting ethnographic research that are difficult to unravel. But that does not mean that audience researchers should not confront them, and, eventually, draw the radical and no doubt uncomfortable conclusions that will emerge from that confrontation. We can think of Valerie Walkerdine's provocative and disturbing query:

> Much has been written about the activity of watching films in terms of scopophilia. But what of that other activity, [...] this activity of research, of trying so hard to understand what people see in films? Might we not call this the most perverse voyeurism? (Walkerdine 1986: 166)

It is, of course, important for us to recognize the inherent symbolic violence of any kind of research. However, we cannot renounce our inevitable complicity simply by not doing research at all, empirical or otherwise. Indeed, such a retreat would only lead to the dangerous illusion of our own exemption from the realities under scrutiny, including the realities of living with the media – as if it were possible to keep our hands clean in a fundamentally dirty world. It is precisely for this reason that I believe that, in the expanding field of audience studies, an ethnographic approach can and does have a distinct critical value. Ethnographic work, in the sense of drawing on what we can perceive and experience in everyday settings, acquires its critical edge when it functions as a reminder that reality is always more complicated and diversified than our theories can represent, and that there is no such thing as 'audience' whose characteristics can be set once and for all.[18] The critical promise of the ethnographic attitude resides in its potential to make and keep our interpretations sensitive to concrete specificities, to the unexpected, to history; it is a commitment to submit ourselves to the possibility of, in Paul Willis's words, 'being 'surprised', of reaching knowledge not prefigured in one's starting paradigm' (1980: 90). What matters is not the certainty of knowledge about audiences, but an ongoing critical and intellectual engagement with the multifarious ways in which we constitute ourselves through media consumption. Or, as in the words of Stuart Hall: 'I am not interested in Theory, I am interested in going on theorizing' (1986b: 60).

Notes

1   It should be noted that the term 'ethnography' is somewhat misplaced in this context. Within anthropology, ethnography refers to an in-depth field study of a culture and its inhabitants in their natural location, which would require the researcher to spend a fair amount of time in that location, allowing her/him to acquire a nuanced and comprehensive insight into the dynamics of the social relationships in the culture under study, and enabling her/him to produce a 'thick description' of it. Most qualitative studies of media audiences do not meet these requirements. In Morley's *Nationwide* study, for example, the informants were extracted from their natural viewing environment and interviewed in groups that were put together according to socio-economic criteria. In a looser sense, however, the

use of the term 'ethnographic' can be justified here in so far as the approach is aimed at getting a thorough insight into the 'lived experience' of media consumption.

2   It should be stressed, however, that the 'critical' tradition is not a monolithic whole: there is not one 'critical theory' with generally shared axioms, but many different, and often conflicting, 'critical perspectives', e.g. political economy and cultural studies.

3   Thus, the dichotomization of 'critical' and 'empirical' schools in communication studies, particularly in the United States, should be considered with some flexibility. See, e.g., the famous 'Ferment in the Field' issue of the *Journal of Communication* (1983).

4   The direct theoretical inspiration of Morley's research was the so-called encoding/decoding model as launched by Stuart Hall, which presented a theoretical intervention against '*Screen* theory'. See Hall (1980a, 1980b). Morley himself has elaborated on the 'interdiscursive' nature of encounters between text and subjects. See Morley (1980b).

5   See also Tamar Liebes (1986) and Kim Christian Schrøder (1987). Such an insistence upon convergence is not new among 'mainstream' communication researchers. For example, Jennifer Slack and Martin Allor have recalled how in the late 1930s Lazarsfeld hired Adorno in the expectation that the latter's critical theory could be used to 'revitalize' American empiricist research by supplying it with 'new research ideas'. The collaboration ended only one year later because it proved to be impossible to translate Adorno's critical analysis into the methods and goals of Lazarsfeld's project. Lazarsfeld has never given up the idea of a convergence, however (Slack and Allor 1983: 210).

6   Note, for instance, the striking similarities between the following two sentences, one from a uses and gratifications source, the other from a cultural studies one: 'There seems to be growing support for that branch of communications research which asserts that television viewing is an active and social process' (Katz and Liebes 1985: 187); 'Television viewing, the choices which shape it and the many social uses to which we put it, now turn out to be an irrevocably active and social process' (Hall 1986a: 8).

7   In stating this I do not want to suggest that cultural studies is a closed paradigm, nor that all cultural studies scholars share one – say, Foucauldian – conception of power. For example, the Birmingham version of cultural studies, with its distinctly Gramscian inflection, has been criticized by Lawrence Grossberg for its lack of a theory of pleasure. An alternative, postmodernist perspective on cultural studies is developed in Grossberg (1983).

8   Strategic interpretations, that is, interpretations that are 'political' in the sense that they are aware of the fact that interpretations are always concrete interventions into an already existing discursive field. They are therefore always partial in both senses of the word (i.e. partisan and incomplete), and involved in making sense of the world in specific, power-laden ways. See Mary Louise Pratt (1986).

9   Rosengren expresses this view in very clearcut terms, where he reduces the existence of disagreements between 'critical' and 'mainstream' researchers to 'psychological reasons' (1983: 191).

10   I have borrowed this formulation from Virginia Nightingale (1986: 21–2). Nightingale remarks that audience research has generally been 'on the side' of those with vested interests in influencing the organization of the mass-media in society, and that it is important to develop a research perspective that is 'on the side' of the audience. However, it is far from simple to work out exactly what such a perspective would mean. The notion of the 'active audience', for example, often put forward by uses and gratifications researchers not just as an object of empirical investigation but also as an article of faith, as an axiom to mark the distinctive identity of the 'paradigm', is not in itself a guarantee of a stance 'on the side of the audience'. In fact, the whole passive/active dichotomy in accounts of

audiences has now become so ideologized that it all too often serves as a mystification of the real commitments behind the research at stake.

11   Reflections on the predicaments and politics of research on and with living historical subjects have already played an important role in, for example, feminist studies and anthropology, particularly ethnography. At least two problems are highlighted in these reflections. First, there is the rather awkward but seldom discussed concrete relation between researcher and researched as concrete subjects occupying differential social positions, more and less invested with power; second, there is the problem of the discursive form in which the cultures of 'others' can be represented in non-objectifying (or, better, less objectifying) ways. See, e.g., Angela McRobbie (1982); James Clifford (1983); James Clifford and George Marcus (1986); Lila Abu-Lughold (1991). Researchers of media audiences have, as far as I know, generally been silent about these issues. However, for a thought-provoking engagement with the problem, see Valerie Walkerdine (1986).

12   See, for a more general overview of the interpretive or hermeneutic turn in the social sciences, Paul Rabinow and William M. Sullivan (1979). A more radical, Foucauldian conception of what they call 'interpretive analytics' is developed by Hubert Dreyfuss and Paul Rabinow (1982).

13   A concise and useful criticism of empiricist mass communication research is offered by Robert C. Allen (1985: chapter 2).

14   Morley's main objection to the uses and gratifications approach concerns 'its psychologistic problematic and its emphasis on individual differences of interpretation' (1983: 117). Elsewhere Morley even more emphatically expresses his distance from the uses and gratifications approach: 'Any superficial resemblance between this study of television audience and the 'uses and gratifications' perspective in media research is misleading' (ibid.).

15   Note that in positivist epistemology intersubjectivity is considered as one of the main criteria for scientific 'objectivity'. One of the myths by which the institution of Science establishes itself is that scientific discourse is a process without a subject. Hence the normative rule that the concrete historical subject of scientific practice, the researcher, should be interchangeable with any other so as to erase all marks of idiosyncratic subjectivity.

16   All sorts of cautious qualifications as to the generalizability of such 'findings', so routinely put forward in research reports so that the validity of the given typifications are said to be limited to certain demographic or subcultural categories (e.g. the urban working class), do not in principle affect this reification of experiential structures.

17   An image of the television audience as consisting of harmonious collectivities is suggested by Elihu Katz and Tamar Liebes, when they describe the process of decoding a television programme as an activity of 'mutual aid' (1985). While this idea is useful in that it highlights the social nature of processes of decoding, it represses the possibility of tension, conflict and antagonism between different decodings within the same group.

18   For epistemological deconstructions of the category of 'audience' as object of power/ knowledge, see Briankle G. Chang (1987); Martin Allor (1988); Ang (1991).

References

Abu-Lughold, L. (1991) 'Writing against culture', in R. G. Fox (ed.) *Recapturing Anthropology*, Sante Fe, NM: School of American Research Press.

Allen, R. C. (1985) *Speaking of Soap Operas*, Chapel Hill/London: University of North Carolina Press.

Allor, M. (1988) 'Relocating the site of the audience', *Critical Studies in Mass Communication*, 5(3): 217–33.

Ang, I. (1985) *Watching Dallas: Soap Opera and the Melodramatic Imagination*, London/New York: Methuen.

——(1991) *Desperately Seeking the Audience*, London/New York: Routledge.

Blumler, J. G., Gurevitch, M. and Katz, E. (1985) 'Reaching out: a future for gratifications research', in K. E. Rosengren, L. A. Wenner and P. Palmgreen (eds), *Media Gratifications Research: Current Perspectives*, Beverly Hills, CA: Sage.

Brunsdon, C. (1986) 'Women watching television', *MedieKultur*, 4.

Carey, J. (1983) 'Introduction', in M. S. Mander (ed.), *Communications in Transition*, New York: Praeger.

Chang, B. G. (1987) 'Deconstructing the audience: who are they and what do we know about them?', in M. L. McLaughlin (ed.), *Communication Yearbook*, 10, Beverly Hills CA: Sage.

Clifford, J. (1983) 'On ethnographic authority', *Representations*, 1 (Spring) 2: 118–46.

Clifford, J. and Marcus, G. E. (eds) (1986) *Writing Culture: The Poetics and Politics of Ethnography*, Berkeley/Los Angeles/London: University of California Press.

Dreyfuss, H. and Rabinow, P. (1982) *Michel Foucault: Beyond Structuralism and Hermeneutics*, Chicago: University of Chicago Press.

Fejes, F. (1984) 'Critical communications research and media effects: the problem of the disappearing audience', *Media, Culture and Society*, 6: 219–32.

Fiske, J. (1987) 'British cultural studies and television', in R. C. Allen (ed.), *Channels of Discourse*, Chapel Hill/London: University of North Carolina Press.

Foucault, M. (1979) *Discipline and Punishment*, trans. A. Sheridan, Harmondsworth: Penguin.

Grossberg, L. (1983) 'Cultural studies revisited and revised', in M. S. Mander (ed.), *Communications in Transition*, New York: Praeger.

——(1987) 'Critical theory and the politics of empirical research', in M. Gurevitch and M. R. Levy (eds), *Mass Communication Review Yearbook* 6, Newbury Park, CA: Sage.

Hall, S. (1980a) 'Encoding/decoding', in S. Hall, D. Hobson, A. Lowe and P. Willis (eds), *Culture, Media, Language*, London: Hutchinson.

——(1980b) 'Recent developments in theories of language and ideology: a critical note', in S. Hall, D. Hobson, A. Lowe and P. Willis (eds), *Culture, Media, Language*, London: Hutchinson.

——(1986a) 'Introduction', in D. Morley, *Family Television: Cultural Power and Domestic Leisure*, London: Comedia/Routledge.

——(1986b) 'On postmodernism and articulation: an interview with Stuart Hall', *Journal of Communication Inquiry*, 10(2): 45–60.

——(1986c) 'The problem of ideology – Marxism without Guarantees', *Journal of Communication Inquiry*, 10(2): 5–27.

Hall, S., Hobson, D., Lowe, A. and Willis, P. (eds) (1980) *Culture, Media, Language*, London: Hutchinson.

Hammersley, M. and Atkinson, P. (1983) *Ethnography: Principles in Practice*, London/New York: Tavistock.

Hobson, D. (1980) 'Housewives and the mass media', in S. Hall, D. Hobson, A. Lowe and P. Willis (eds), *Culture, Media, Language*, London: Hutchinson.

——(1982) *Crossroads: The Drama of a Soap Opera*, London: Methuen.

Jensen, K. B. (1986) *Making Sense of the News*, Århus: University of Århus Press.

——(1987) 'Qualitative audience research: towards an integrative approach to reception', *Critical Studies in Mass Communication*, 4: 21–36.

Katz, E. and Liebes, T. (1985) 'Mutual aid in the decoding of *Dallas*: preliminary notes from a cross-cultural study', in P. Drummond and R. Paterson (eds), *Television in Transition*, London: BFI.

Levy, M. R. and Windahl, S. (1984) 'Audience activity and gratifications: a conceptual clarification and exploration', *Communication Research*, 11: 51–78.

——(1986) 'The concept of audience activity', in K. E. Rosengren, L. Wenner and P. Palmgreen (eds), *Media Gratifications Research*, Beverly Hills: Sage.

Liebes, T. (1986) 'On the convergence of theories of mass communication and literature regarding the role of the reader', paper presented to the Sixth International Conference on Culture and Communication, October.

Liebes, T. and Katz, E. (1990) *The Export of Meaning: Cross-Cultural Readings of Dallas*, New York: Oxford University Press.

Lindlof, T. R. (ed.) (1987) *Natural Audiences*, Norwood, NJ: Ablex.

Lindlof, T. R. and Meyer, T. P. (1987) 'Mediated communication as ways of seeing, acting, and constructing culture: the tools and foundations of qualitative research', in T. R. Lindlof (ed.), *Natural Audiences*, Norwood, NJ: Ablex Publishing Company.

Lull, J. (1980) 'The social uses of television', *Human Communication Research*, 6(3): 198–209.

——(1986) 'The naturalistic study of media use and youth culture', in K. E. Rosengren, L. A. Wenner and P. Palmgreen (eds), *Media Gratifications Research: Current Perspectives*, Beverly Hills, CA: Sage.

——(ed.) (1988) *World Families Watch Television*, Newbury Park, CA: Sage.

McRobbie, A. (1982) 'The politics of feminist research: between talk, text and action', *Feminist Review*, 12 (October): 46–57.

Mills, C. W. (1970) *The Sociological Imagination*, Harmondsworth: Penguin.

——(1986) 'Introduction', in T. Modleski (ed.), *Studies in Entertainment: Critical Approaches to Mass Culture*, Bloomington/Indianapolis: Indiana University Press.

Morley, D. (1980a) *The 'Nationwide' Audience: Structure and Decoding*, London: BFI.

——(1980b) 'Texts, readers, subjects', in S. Hall, D. Hobson, A. Lowe and P. Willis (eds), *Culture, Media, Language*, London: Hutchinson.

——(1981) ' "The Nationwide Audience" – A Critical Postscript', *Screen Education*, 39 (Summer): 3–14.

——(1983) 'Cultural transformations: the politics of resistance', in H. Davies and P. Walton (eds), *Language, Image, Media*, Oxford: Basil Blackwell.

——(1986) *Family Television: Cultural Power and Domestic Leisure*, London: Comedia/Routledge.

Nightingale, V. (1986) 'What's happening to audience research?', *Media Information Australia*, 39 (February): 21–2.

Pratt, M. L. (1986) 'Interpretive strategies/strategic interpretations: on Anglo-American reader-response criticism', in J. Arac (ed.), *Postmodernism and Politics*, Minneapolis: University of Minnesota Press.

Rabinow, P. (1986) 'Representations are social facts: modernity and post-modernity in anthropology', in J. Clifford and G. E. Marcus (eds), *Writing Culture: The Poetics and Politics of Ethnography*, Berkeley/Los Angeles/London: University of California Press.

Rabinow, P. and Sullivan, W. M. (eds) (1979) *Interpretive Social Science*, Berkeley/Los Angeles/London: University of California Press.

Radway, J. (1984) *Reading the Romance: Women, Patriarchy, and Popular Literature*, Chapell Hill: University of North Carolina Press.

Rosengren, K. E. (1983) 'Communication research: one paradigm, or four?', *Journal of Communication*, 33: 185–207

Schrøder, K. C. (1987) 'Convergence of antagonistic traditions? the case of audience research', *European Journal of Communication*, 2(1): 7–31.

Slack, J. D. and Allor, M. (1983) 'The Political and Epistemological Constituents of Critical Communication Research', *Journal of Communication*, 33(3): 208–18

Streeter, T. (1984) 'An alternative approach to television research: developments in British cultural studies in Birmingham', in W. D. Rowland Jr and B. Watkins (eds), *Interpreting Television*, Beverly Hills, CA: Sage.

Walkerdine, V. (1986) 'Video replay: families, films and fantasy', in V. Burgin, J. Donald and C. Kaplan (eds), *Formations of Fantasy*, London/New York: Methuen.

13

(i) From Culture to Hegemony; (ii) Subculture: The Unnatural Break

Dick Hebdige

(i)　From Culture to Hegemony[*]

Culture

Culture: cultivation, tending, in Christian authors, worship; the action or practice of cultivating the soil; tillage, husbandry; the cultivation or rearing of certain animals (e.g. fish); the artificial development of microscopic organisms, organisms so produced; the cultivating or development (of the mind, faculties, manners), improvement or refinement by education and training; the condition of being trained or refined; the intellectual side of civilization; the prosecution or special attention or study of any subject or pursuit.

(*Oxford English Dictionary*)

Culture is a notoriously ambiguous concept as the above definition demonstrates. Refracted through centuries of usage, the word has acquired a number of quite different, often contradictory, meanings. Even as a scientific term, it refers both to a process (artificial development of microscopic organisms) and a product (organisms so produced). More specifically, since the end of the eighteenth century, it has been used by English intellectuals and literary figures to focus critical attention on a whole range of controversial issues. The 'quality of life', the effects in human terms of mechanization, the division of labour and the creation of a mass society have all been discussed within the larger confines of what Raymond Williams has called the 'Culture and Society' debate (Williams, 1961). It was through this tradition of

* From Dick Hebdige, *Subculture: The Meaning of Style* (London and New York: Routledge, 1979), pp. 5–19.

dissent and criticism that the dream of the 'organic society' – of society as an integrated, meaningful whole – was largely kept alive. The dream had two basic trajectories. One led back to the past and to the feudal ideal of a hierarchically ordered community. Here, culture assumed an almost sacred function. Its 'harmonious perfection' (Arnold, 1868) was posited against the Wasteland of contemporary life.

The other trajectory, less heavily supported, led towards the future, to a socialist Utopia where the distinction between labour and leisure was to be annulled. Two basic definitions of culture emerged from this tradition, though these were by no means necessarily congruent with the two trajectories outlined above. The first – the one which is probably most familiar to the reader – was essentially classical and conservative. It represented culture as a standard of aesthetic excellence: 'the best that has been thought and said in the world' (Arnold, 1868), and it derived from an appreciation of 'classic' aesthetic form (opera, ballet, drama, literature, art). The second, traced back by Williams to Herder and the eighteenth century (Williams, 1976), was rooted in anthropology. Here the term 'culture' referred to a

> particular way of life which expresses certain meanings and values not only in art and learning, but also in institutions and ordinary behaviour. The analysis of culture, from such a definition, is the clarification of the meanings and values implicit and explicit in a particular way of life, a particular culture. (Williams, 1965)

This definition obviously had a much broader range. It encompassed, in T. S. Eliot's words,

> all the characteristic activities and interests of a people. Derby Day, Henley Regatta, Cowes, the 12th of August, a cup final, the dog races, the pin table, the dart-board, Wensleydale cheese, boiled cabbage cut into sections, beetroot in vinegar, 19th Century Gothic churches, the music of Elgar.... (Eliot, 1948)

As Williams noted, such a definition could only be supported if a new theoretical initiative was taken. The theory of culture now involved the 'study of relationships between elements in a whole way of life' (Williams, 1965). The emphasis shifted from immutable to historical criteria, from fixity to transformation:

> an emphasis [which] from studying particular meanings and values seeks not so much to compare these, as a way of establishing a scale, but by studying their modes of change to discover certain general causes or 'trends' by which social and cultural developments as a whole can be better understood. (Williams, 1965)

Williams was, then, proposing an altogether broader formulation of the relationships between culture and society, one which through the analysis of 'particular meanings and values' sought to uncover the concealed fundamentals of history; the 'general causes' and broad social 'trends' which lie behind the manifest appearances of an 'everyday life'.

In the early years, when it was being established in the universities, Cultural Studies sat rather uncomfortably on the fence between these two conflicting definitions – culture as a standard of excellence, culture as a 'whole way of life' – unable to determine which represented the most fruitful line of enquiry. Richard Hoggart and Raymond Williams portrayed working-class culture sympathetically in wistful accounts of pre-scholarship boyhoods – Leeds for Hoggart (1958), a Welsh mining village for Williams (1960) – but their work displayed a strong bias towards literature and literacy[1] and an equally strong moral tone. Hoggart deplored the way in which the traditional working-class community – a community of tried and tested values despite the dour landscape in which it had been set – was being undermined and replaced by a 'Candy Floss World' of thrills and cheap fiction which was somehow bland *and* sleazy. Williams tentatively endorsed the new mass communications but was concerned to establish aesthetic and moral criteria for distinguishing the worthwhile products from the 'trash'; the jazz – 'a real musical form' – and the football – 'a wonderful game' – from the 'rape novel, the Sunday strip paper and the latest Tin Pan drool' (Williams, 1965). In 1966 Hoggart laid down the basic premises upon which Cultural Studies were based:

> First, without appreciating good literature, no one will really understand the nature of society, second, literary critical analysis can be applied to certain social phenomena other than 'academically respectable' literature (for example, the popular arts, mass communications) so as to illuminate their meanings for individuals and their societies.
>
> (Hoggart, 1966)

The implicit assumption that it still required a literary sensibility to 'read' society with the requisite subtlety, and that the two ideas of culture could be ultimately reconciled was also, paradoxically, to inform the early work of the French writer, Roland Barthes, though here it found validation in a method – semiotics – a way of reading signs (Hawkes, 1977).

Barthes: Myths and Signs

Using models derived from the work of the Swiss linguist Ferdinand de Saussure[2] Barthes sought to expose the *arbitrary* nature of cultural phenomena, to uncover the latent meanings of an everyday life which, to all intents and purposes, was 'perfectly natural'. Unlike Hoggart, Barthes was not concerned with distinguishing the good from the bad in modern mass culture, but rather with showing how *all* the apparently spontaneous forms and rituals of contemporary bourgeois societies are subject to a systematic distortion, liable at any moment to be dehistoricized, 'naturalized', converted into myth:

> The whole of France is steeped in this anonymous ideology: our press, our films, our theatre, our pulp literature, our rituals, our Justice, our diplomacy, our conversations, our remarks about the weather, a murder trial, a touching wedding, the cooking we

dream of, the garments we wear, everything in everyday life is dependent on the representation which the bourgeoisie *has and makes us have* of the relations between men and the world. (Barthes, 1972)

Like Eliot, Barthes' notion of culture extends beyond the library, the opera-house and the theatre to encompass the whole of everyday life. But this everyday life is for Barthes overlaid with a significance which is at once more insidious and more systematically organized. Starting from the premise that 'myth is a type of speech', Barthes set out in *Mythologies* to examine the normally hidden set of rules, codes and conventions through which meanings particular to specific social groups (i.e. those in power) are rendered universal and 'given' for the whole of society. He found in phenomena as disparate as a wrestling match, a writer on holiday, a tourist-guide book, the same artificial nature, the same ideological core. Each had been exposed to the same prevailing rhetoric (the rhetoric of common sense) and turned into myth, into a mere element in a 'second-order semiological system' (Barthes, 1972). (Barthes uses the example of a photograph in *Paris-Match* of a Negro soldier saluting the French flag, which has a first and second order connotation: (1) a gesture of loyalty, but also (2) 'France is a great empire, and all her sons, without colour discrimination, faithfully serve under her flag'.)

Barthes' application of a method rooted in linguistics to other systems of discourse outside language (fashion, film, food, etc.) opened up completely new possibilities for contemporary cultural studies. It was hoped that the invisible seam between language, experience and reality could be located and prised open through a semiotic analysis of this kind: that the gulf between the alienated intellectual and the 'real' world could be rendered meaningful and, miraculously, at the same time, be made to disappear. Moreover, under Barthes' direction, semiotics promised nothing less than the reconciliation of the two conflicting definitions of culture upon which Cultural Studies was so ambiguously posited – a marriage of moral conviction (in this case, Barthes' Marxist beliefs) and popular themes: the study of a society's total way of life.

This is not to say that semiotics was easily assimilable within the Cultural Studies project. Though Barthes shared the literary preoccupations of Hoggart and Williams, his work introduced a new Marxist 'problematic'[3] which was alien to the British tradition of concerned and largely untheorized 'social commentary'. As a result, the old debate seemed suddenly limited. In E. P. Thompson's words it appeared to reflect the parochial concerns of a group of 'gentlemen amateurs'. Thompson sought to replace Williams' definition of the theory of culture as 'a theory of relations between elements in a whole way of life' with his own more rigorously Marxist formulation: 'the study of relationships in a whole way of *conflict*'. A more analytical framework was required; a new vocabulary had to be learned. As part of this process of theorization, the word 'ideology' came to acquire a much wider range of meanings than had previously been the case. We have seen how Barthes found an 'anonymous ideology' penetrating every possible level of social life, inscribed in the most mundane of rituals, framing the most casual social encounters. But how can ideology be 'anonymous', and how can it assume such a broad significance? Before we attempt any reading of subcultural style, we must first define the term 'ideology' more precisely.

Ideology: A *Lived* Relation

In *The German Ideology*, Marx shows how the basis of the capitalist economic structure (surplus value, neatly defined by Godelier as 'Profit...is unpaid work' (Godelier, 1970)) is hidden from the consciousness of the agents of production. The failure to see through appearances to the real relations which underlie them does not occur as the direct result of some kind of masking operation consciously carried out by individuals, social groups or institutions. On the contrary, ideology by defini- tion thrives *beneath* consciousness. It is here, at the level of 'normal common sense', that ideological frames of reference are most firmly sedimented and most effective, because it is here that their ideological nature is most effectively concealed. As Stuart Hall puts it:

> It is precisely its 'spontaneous' quality, its transparency, its 'naturalness', its refusal to be made to examine the premises on which it is founded, its resistance to change or to correction, its effect of instant recognition, and the closed circle in which it moves which makes common sense, at one and the same time, 'spontaneous', ideological and *uncon- scious*. You cannot learn, through common sense, *how things are*: you can only discover *where they fit* into the existing scheme of things. In this way, its very taken-for-granted- ness is what establishes it as a medium in which its own premises and presuppositions are being rendered *invisible* by its apparent transparency.   (Hall, 1977)

Since ideology saturates everyday discourse in the form of common sense, it cannot be bracketed off from everyday life as a self-contained set of 'political opinions' or 'biased views'. Neither can it be reduced to the abstract dimensions of a 'world view' or used in the crude Marxist sense to designate 'false consciousness'. Instead, as Louis Althusser has pointed out:

> ...ideology has very little to do with 'consciousness'....It is profoundly *uncon- scious*.... Ideology is indeed a system of representation, but in the majority of cases these representations have nothing to do with 'consciousness': they are usually images and occasionally concepts, but it is above all as *structures* that they impose on the vast majority of men, not via their 'consciousness'. They are perceived-accepted-suffered cultural objects and they act functionally on men via a process that escapes them. (Althusser, 1969)

Although Althusser is here referring to structures like the family, cultural and political institutions, etc., we can illustrate the point quite simply by taking as our example a physical structure. Most modern institutes of education, despite the apparent neut- rality of the materials from which they are constructed (red brick, white tile, etc.) carry within themselves implicit ideological assumptions which are literally structured into the architecture itself. The categorization of knowledge into arts and sciences is reproduced in the faculty system which houses different disciplines in different buildings, and most colleges maintain the traditional divisions by devoting a separate floor to each subject. Moreover, the hierarchical relationship between teacher and taught is inscribed in the very lay-out of the lecture theatre where the seating arrangements – benches rising in tiers before a raised lectern – dictate the flow of information and serve to 'naturalize' professorial authority. Thus, a whole range of decisions about what is and what is not possible within education have been made, however unconsciously, before the content of individual courses is even decided.

These decisions help to set the limits not only on what is taught but on *how* it is taught. Here the buildings literally *reproduce* in concrete terms prevailing (ideological) notions about what education *is* and it is through this process that the educational structure, which can, of course, be altered, is placed beyond question and appears to us as a 'given' (i.e. as immutable). In this case, the frames of our thinking have been translated into actual bricks and mortar.

Social relations and processes are then appropriated by individuals only through the forms in which they are represented to those individuals. These forms are, as we have seen, by no means transparent. They are shrouded in a 'common sense' which simultaneously validates and mystifies them. It is precisely these 'perceived-accepted-suffered cultural objects' which semiotics sets out to 'interrogate' and decipher. All aspects of culture possess a semiotic value, and the most taken-for-granted phenomena can function as signs: as elements in communication systems governed by semantic rules and codes which are not themselves directly apprehended in experience. These signs are, then, as opaque as the social relations which produce them and which they re-present. In other words, there is an ideological dimension to every signification:

> A sign does not simply exist as part of reality – it reflects and refracts another reality. Therefore it may distort that reality or be true to it, or may perceive it from a special point of view, and so forth. Every sign is subject to the criteria of ideological evaluation .... The domain of ideology coincides with the domain of signs. They equate with one another. Whenever a sign is present, ideology is present too. Everything ideological possesses a semiotic value.   (Volosinov, 1973)

To uncover the ideological dimension of signs we must first try to disentangle the codes through which meaning is organized. 'Connotative' codes are particularly important. As Stuart Hall has argued, they ' ... cover the face of social life and render it classifiable, intelligible, meaningful' (Hall, 1977). He goes on to describe these codes as 'maps of meaning' which are of necessity the product of selection. They cut across a range of potential meanings, making certain meanings available and ruling others out of court. We tend to live inside these maps as surely as we live in the 'real' world: they 'think' us as much as we 'think' them, and this in itself is quite 'natural'. All human societies *reproduce* themselves in this way through a process of 'naturalization'. It is through this process – a kind of inevitable reflex of all social life – that *particular* sets of social relations, *particular* ways of organizing the world appear to us as if they were universal and timeless. This is what Althusser (1971a) means when he says that 'ideology has no history' and that ideology in this general sense will always be an 'essential element of every social formation' (Althusser and Balibar, 1968).

However, in highly complex societies like ours, which function through a finely graded system of divided (i.e. specialized) labour, the crucial question has to do with which specific ideologies, representing the interests of which specific groups and classes will prevail at any given moment, in any given situation. To deal with this question, we must first consider how power is distributed in our society. That is, we must ask which groups and classes have how much say in defining, ordering and classifying out the social world. For instance, if we pause to reflect for a moment, it should be obvious that access to the means by which ideas are disseminated in our society (i.e. principally the mass media) is *not* the same for all classes. Some groups have more say, more opportunity to make the rules, to organize meaning, while others are less favourably placed, have less power to produce and impose their definitions of the world on the world.

Thus, when we come to look beneath the level of 'ideology-in-general' at the way in which specific ideologies work, how some gain dominance and others remain marginal, we can see that in advanced Western democracies the ideological field is by no means neutral. To return to the 'connotative' codes to which Stuart Hall refers we can see that these 'maps of meaning' are charged with a potentially explosive significance because they are traced and re-traced along the lines laid down by the *dominant* discourses about reality, the *dominant* ideologies. They thus tend to represent, in however obscure and contradictory a fashion, the interests of the *dominant* groups in society.

To understand this point we should refer to Marx:

> The ideas of the ruling class are in every epoch the ruling ideas, i.e. the class which is the ruling *material* force of society is at the same time its ruling *intellectual* force. The class which has the means of material production at its disposal, has control at the same time over the means of mental production, so that generally speaking, the ideas of those who lack the means of mental production are subject to it. The ruling ideas are nothing more than the ideal expression of the dominant material relationships grasped as ideas; hence of the relationships which make the one class the ruling class, therefore the ideas of its dominance.   (Marx and Engels, 1970)

This is the basis of Antonio Gramsci's theory of *hegemony* which provides the most adequate account of how dominance is sustained in advanced capitalist societies.

Hegemony: The Moving Equilibrium

> Society cannot share a common communication system so long as it is split into warring classes.
>
>   (Brecht, *A Short Organum for the Theatre*)

The term hegemony refers to a situation in which a provisional alliance of certain social groups can exert 'total social authority' over other subordinate groups, not simply by coercion or by the direct imposition of ruling ideas, but by 'winning and shaping consent so that the power of the dominant classes appears both legitimate and natural' (Hall, 1977). Hegemony can only be maintained so long as the dominant classes 'succeed in framing all competing definitions within their range' (Hall, 1977), so that subordinate groups are, if not controlled; then at least contained within an ideological space which does not seem at all 'ideological': which appears instead to be permanent and 'natural', to lie outside history, to be beyond particular interests (see *Social Trends*, no. 6, 1975).

This is how, according to Barthes, 'mythology' performs its vital function of naturalization and normalization and it is in his book *Mythologies* that Barthes demonstrates most forcefully the full extension of these normalized forms and meanings. However, Gramsci adds the important proviso that hegemonic power, precisely *because* it requires the consent of the dominated majority, can never be permanently exercised by the same alliance of 'class fractions'. As has been pointed out, 'Hegemony... is not universal and 'given' to the continuing rule of a particular class. It has to be won, reproduced, sustained. Hegemony is, as Gramsci said, a 'moving equilibrium' containing relations of forces favourable or unfavourable to this or that tendency' (Hall *et al.*, 1976a).

In the same way, forms cannot be permanently normalized. They can always be deconstructed, demystified, by a 'mythologist' like Barthes. Moreover commodities can be symbolically 'repossessed' in everyday life, and endowed with implicitly oppositional meanings, by the very groups who originally produced them. The symbiosis in which ideology and social order, production and reproduction, are linked is then neither fixed nor guaranteed. It can be prised open. The consensus can be fractured, challenged, overruled, and resistance to the groups in dominance cannot always be lightly dismissed or automatically incorporated. Although, as Lefebvre has written, we live in a society where '...objects in practice become signs and signs objects and a second nature takes the place of the first – the initial layer of perceptible reality' (Lefebvre, 1971), there are, as he goes on to affirm, always 'objections and contradictions which hinder the closing of the circuit' between sign and object, production and reproduction.

We can now return to the meaning of youth subcultures, for the emergence of such groups has signalled in a spectacular fashion the breakdown of consensus in the post-war period. In the following chapters we shall see that it is precisely objections and contradictions of the kind which Lefebvre has described that find expression in subculture. However, the challenge to hegemony which subcultures represent is not issued directly by them. Rather it is expressed obliquely, in style. The objections are lodged, the contradictions displayed (and, as we shall see, 'magically resolved') at the profoundly superficial level of appearances: that is, at the level of signs. For the sign-community, the community of myth-consumers, is not a uniform body. As Volosinov has written, it is cut through by class:

> Class does not coincide with the sign community, i.e. with the totality of users of the same set of signs of ideological communication. Thus various different classes will use one and the same language. As a result, differently oriented accents intersect in every ideological sign. Sign becomes the arena of the class struggle. (Volosinov, 1973)

The struggle between different discourses, different definitions and meanings within ideology is therefore always, at the same time, a struggle within signification: a struggle for possession of the sign which extends to even the most mundane areas of everyday life. To turn once more to the examples used in the Introduction, to the safety pins and tubes of vaseline, we can see that such commodities are indeed open to a double inflection: to 'illegitimate' as well as 'legitimate' uses. These 'humble objects' can be magically appropriated; 'stolen' by subordinate groups and made to carry 'secret' meanings: meanings which express, in code, a form of resistance to the order which guarantees their continued subordination.

Style in subculture is, then, pregnant with significance. Its transformations go 'against nature', interrupting the process of 'normalization'. As such, they are gestures, movements towards a speech which offends the 'silent majority', which challenges the principle of unity and cohesion, which contradicts the myth of consensus. Our task becomes, like Barthes', to discern the hidden messages inscribed in code on the glossy surfaces of style, to trace them out as 'maps of meaning' which obscurely re-present the very contradictions they are designed to resolve or conceal.

Academics who adopt a semiotic approach are not alone in reading significance into the loaded surfaces of life. The existence of spectacular subcultures continually opens up those surfaces to other potentially subversive readings. Jean Genet, the archetype of the 'unnatural' deviant, again exemplifies the practice of resistance through style. He is as convinced in his own way as is Roland Barthes of the ideological character of cultural signs. He is equally oppressed by the seamless web of forms and meanings which encloses and yet excludes him. His reading is equally partial. He makes his own list and draws his own conclusions:

> I was astounded by so rigorous an edifice whose details were united against me. Nothing in the world is irrelevant: the stars on a general's sleeve, the stock-market quotations, the olive harvest, the style of the judiciary, the wheat exchange, the flower-beds, . . . Nothing. This order . . . had a meaning – my exile.   (Genet, 1967)

It is this alienation from the deceptive 'innocence' of appearances which gives the teds, the mods, the punks and no doubt future groups of as yet unimaginable 'deviants' the impetus to move from man's second 'false nature' (Barthes, 1972) to a genuinely expressive artifice; a truly subterranean style. As a symbolic violation of the social order, such a movement attracts and will continue to attract attention, to provoke censure and to act, as we shall see, as the fundamental bearer of significance in subculture.

No subculture has sought with more grim determination than the punks to detach itself from the taken-for-granted landscape of normalized forms, nor to bring down upon itself such vehement disapproval. We shall begin therefore with the moment of punk and we shall return to that moment throughout the course of this book. It is perhaps appropriate that the punks, who have made such large claims for illiteracy, who have pushed profanity to such startling extremes, should be used to test some of the methods for 'reading' signs evolved in the centuries-old debate on the sanctity of culture.

(ii) Subculture: The Unnatural Break*

I felt unclean for about 48 hours.

> (G.L.C. councillor after seeing a concert by the Sex Pistols,
> reported *New Musical Express*, 18 July 1977)

[Language is] of all social institutions, the least amenable to initiative. It blends with the life of society, and the latter, inert by nature, is a prime conservative force.

> (Saussure, 1974)

Subcultures represent 'noise' (as opposed to sound): interference in the orderly sequence which leads from real events and phenomena to their representation in the media. We should therefore not underestimate the signifying power of the spectacular subculture not only as a metaphor for potential anarchy 'out there' but as an actual mechanism of semantic disorder: a kind of temporary blockage in the system of representation. As John Mepham (1972) has written:

> Distinctions and identities may be so deeply embedded in our discourse and thought about the world whether this be because of their role in our practical lives, or because they are cognitively powerful and are an important aspect of the way in which we appear to make sense of our experience, that the theoretical challenge to them can be quite startling.

Any elision, truncation or convergence of prevailing linguistic and ideological categories can have profoundly disorienting effects. These deviations briefly expose the arbitrary nature of the codes which underlie and shape all forms of discourse. As Stuart Hall (1974) has written (here in the context of explicitly political deviance):

> New...developments which are both dramatic and 'meaningless' within the consensually validated norms, pose a challenge to the normative world. They render problematic not only how the...world is defined, but how it ought to be. They 'breach our expectancies'....

Notions concerning the sanctity of language are intimately bound up with ideas of social order. The limits of acceptable linguistic expression are prescribed by a number of apparently universal taboos. These taboos guarantee the continuing 'transparency' (the taken-for-grantedness) of meaning.

---

* From Dick Hebdige, *Subculture: The Meaning of Style* (New York and London: Routledge, 1979), pp. 90–9.

Predictably then, violations of the authorized codes through which the social world is organized and experienced have considerable power to provoke and disturb. They are generally condemned, in Mary Douglas' words (1967), as 'contrary to holiness' and Levi-Strauss has noted how, in certain primitive myths, the mispronunciation of words and the misuse of language are classified along with incest as horrendous aberrations capable of 'unleashing storm and tempest' (Levi-Strauss, 1969). Similarly, spectacular subcultures express forbidden contents (consciousness of class, consciousness of difference) in forbidden forms (transgressions of sartorial and behavioural codes, law breaking, etc.). They are profane articulations, and they are often and significantly defined as 'unnatural'. The terms used in the tabloid press to describe those youngsters who, in their conduct or clothing, proclaim subcultural membership ('freaks', 'animals . . . who find courage, like rats, in hunting in packs'[4]) would seem to suggest that the most primitive anxieties concerning the sacred distinction between nature and culture can be summoned up by the emergence of such a group. No doubt, the breaking of rules is confused with the 'absence of rules' which, according to Levi-Strauss (1969), 'seems to provide the surest criteria for distinguishing a natural from a cultural process'. Certainly, the official reaction to the punk subculture, particularly to the Sex Pistols' use of 'foul language' on television[5] and record[6], and to the vomiting and spitting incidents at Heathrow Airport[7] would seem to indicate that these basic taboos are no less deeply sedimented in contemporary British society.

Two Forms of Incorporation

> Has not this society, glutted with aestheticism, already integrated former romanticisms, surrealism, existentialism and even Marxism to a point? It has, indeed, through trade, in the form of commodities. That which yesterday was reviled today becomes cultural consumer-goods, consumption thus engulfs what was intended to give meaning and direction.   (Lefebvre, 1971)

We have seen how subcultures 'breach our expectancies', how they represent symbolic challenges to a symbolic order. But can subcultures always be effectively incorporated and if so, how? The emergence of a spectacular subculture is invariably accompanied by a wave of hysteria in the press. This hysteria is typically ambivalent: it fluctuates between dread and fascination, outrage and amusement. Shock and horror headlines dominate the front page (e.g. 'Rotten Razored', *Daily Mirror*, 28 June 1977) while, inside the editorials positively bristle with 'serious' commentary[8] and the centrespreads or supplements contain delirious accounts of the latest fads and rituals (see, for example, *Observer* colour supplements 30 January, 10 July 1977, 12 February 1978). Style in particular provokes a double response: it is alternately celebrated (in the fashion page) and ridiculed or reviled (in those articles which define subcultures as social problems).

In most cases, it is the subculture's stylistic innovations which first attract the media's attention. Subsequently deviant or 'anti-social' acts – vandalism, swearing, fighting, 'animal behaviour' – are 'discovered' by the police, the judiciary, the press; and these acts are used to 'explain' the subculture's original transgression of sartorial codes. In fact, either deviant behaviour or the identification of a distinctive uniform (or more typically a combination of the two) can provide the catalyst for a moral panic. In the case of the punks, the media's sighting of punk style virtually coincided with the discovery or invention of punk deviance. The *Daily Mirror* ran its first series of alarmist centrespreads on the subculture, concentrating on the bizarre clothing and jewellery during the week (29 Nov–3 Dec 1977) in which the Sex Pistols exploded into the public eye on the Thames *Today* programme. On the other hand, the mods, perhaps because of the muted character of their style, were not identified as a group until the Bank Holiday clashes of 1964, although the subculture was, by then, fully developed, at least in London. Whichever item opens the amplifying sequence, it invariably ends with the simultaneous diffusion and defusion of the subcultural style.

As the subculture begins to strike its own eminently marketable pose, as its vocabulary (both visual and verbal) becomes more and more familiar, so the referential context to which it can be most conveniently assigned is made increasingly apparent. Eventually, the mods, the punks, the glitter rockers can be incorporated, brought back into line, located on the preferred 'map of problematic social reality' (Geertz, 1964) at the point where boys in lipstick are 'just kids dressing up', where girls in rubber dresses are 'daughters just like yours' (see pp. 98–9; 158–9, n. 8). The media, as Stuart Hall (1977) has argued, not only record resistance, they 'situate it within the dominant framework of meanings' and those young people who choose to inhabit a spectacular youth culture are simultaneously *returned*, as they are represented on T.V. and in the newspapers, to the place where common sense would have them fit (as 'animals' certainly, but also 'in the family', 'out of work', 'up to date', etc.). It is through this continual process of recuperation that the fractured order is repaired and the subculture incorporated as a diverting spectacle within the dominant mythology from which it in part emanates: as 'folk devil', as Other, as Enemy. The process of recuperation takes two characteristic forms:

1. the conversion of subcultural signs (dress, music, etc.) into mass-produced objects (i.e. the commodity form);
2. the 'labelling' and re-definition of deviant behaviour by dominant groups – the police, the media, the judiciary (i.e. the ideological form).

The Commodity Form

The first has been comprehensively handled by both journalists and academics. The relationship between the spectacular subculture and the various industries which service and exploit it is notoriously ambiguous. After all, such a subculture is concerned first and foremost with consumption. It operates exclusively in the leisure sphere ('I wouldn't wear my punk outfit for work – there's a time and a place for everything' (see note 11)). It communicates through commodities even if the meanings attached to those commodities are purposefully distorted or overthrown. It is therefore difficult in this case to maintain any absolute distinction between commercial exploitation on the one hand and creativity/originality on the other, even though these categories are emphatically opposed in the value systems of most subcultures. Indeed, the creation and diffusion of new styles is inextricably bound up with the process of production, publicity and packaging which must inevitably lead to the defusion of the subculture's subversive power – both mod and punk innovations fed back directly into high fashion and mainstream fashion. Each new subculture establishes new trends, generates new looks and sounds which feed back into the appropriate industries. As John Clarke (1976b) has observed:

> The diffusion of youth styles from the subcultures to the fashion market is not simply a 'cultural process', but a real network or infrastructure of new kinds of commercial and economic institutions. The small-scale record shops, recording companies, the boutiques and one- or two-woman manufacturing companies – these versions of artisan capitalism, rather than more generalised and unspecific phenomena, situate the dialectic of commercial 'manipulation'.

However, it would be mistaken to insist on the absolute autonomy of 'cultural' and commercial processes. As Lefebvre (1971) puts it: 'Trade is . . . both a social and an intellectual phenomenon', and commodities arrive at the market-place already laden with significance. They are, in Marx's words (1970), 'social hieroglyphs'[9] and their meanings are inflected by conventional usage.

Thus, as soon as the original innovations which signify 'subculture' are translated into commodities and made generally available, they become 'frozen'. Once removed from their private contexts by the small entrepreneurs and big fashion interests who produce them on a mass scale, they become codified, made comprehensible, rendered at once public property and profitable merchandise. In this way, the two forms of incorporation (the semantic/ideological and the 'real'/commercial) can be said to converge on the commodity form. Youth cultural styles may begin by issuing symbolic challenges, but they must inevitably end by establishing new sets of conventions; by creating new commodities, new industries or rejuvenating old ones (think of the boost punk must have given haberdashery!). This occurs irrespective of the subculture's political orientation: the macrobiotic restaurants, craft shops and 'antique markets' of the hippie era were easily converted into punk boutiques and record shops. It also happens irrespective of the startling content of the style: punk clothing and insignia could be bought mail-order by the summer of 1977, and in September of that year *Cosmopolitan* ran a review of Zandra Rhodes' latest collection of couture follies which consisted entirely of variations on the punk theme. Models smouldered beneath mountains of safety pins and plastic (the pins were jewelled, the 'plastic' wet-look satin) and the accompanying article ended with an aphorism – 'To shock is chic' – which presaged the subculture's imminent demise.

The Ideological Form

The second form of incorporation – the ideological – has been most adequately treated by those sociologists who operate a transactional model of deviant behaviour. For example, Stan Cohen has described in detail how one particular moral panic (surrounding the mod–rocker conflict of the mid-60s) was launched and sustained.[10] Although this type of analysis can often provide an extremely sophisticated explanation of why spectacular subcultures consistently provoke such hysterical outbursts, it tends to overlook the subtler mechanisms through which potentially threatening phenomena are handled and contained. As the use of the term 'folk devil' suggests, rather too much weight tends to be given to the sensational excesses of the tabloid press at the expense of the ambiguous reactions which are, after all, more typical. As we have seen, the way in which subcultures are represented in the media makes them both more *and* less exotic than they actually are. They are seen to contain both dangerous aliens and boisterous kids, wild animals and wayward pets. Roland Barthes furnishes a key to this paradox in his description of 'identification' – one of the seven rhetorical figures which, according to Barthes, distinguish the meta-language of bourgeois mythology. He characterizes the petit-bourgeois as a person '...unable to imagine the Other...the Other is a scandal which threatens his existence' (Barthes, 1972).

Two basic strategies have been evolved for dealing with this threat. First, the Other can be trivialized, naturalized, domesticated. Here, the difference is simply denied ('Otherness is reduced to sameness'). Alternatively, the Other can be transformed into meaningless exotica, a 'pure object, a spectacle, a clown' (Barthes, 1972). In this case, the difference is consigned to a place beyond analysis. Spectacular subcultures are continually being defined in precisely these terms. Soccer hooligans, for example, are typically placed beyond 'the bounds of common decency' and are classified as 'animals'. ('These people aren't human beings', football club manager quoted on the *News at Ten*, Sunday, 12 March 1977.) (See Stuart Hall's treatment of the press coverage of football hooligans in *Football Hooliganism* (edited by Roger Ingham, 1978).) On the other hand, the punks tended to be resituated by the press in the family, perhaps because members of the subculture deliberately obscured their origins, refused the family and willingly played the part of folk devil, presenting themselves as pure objects, as villainous clowns. Certainly, like every other youth culture, punk was perceived as a threat to the family. Occasionally this threat was represented in literal terms. For example, the *Daily Mirror* (1 August 1977) carried a photograph of a child lying in the road after a punk–ted confrontation under the headline 'VICTIM OF THE PUNK ROCK PUNCH-UP: THE BOY WHO FELL FOUL OF THE MOB'. In this case, punk's threat to the family was made 'real' (that could be my child!) through the ideological framing of photographic evidence which is popularly regarded as unproblematic.

None the less, on other occasions, the opposite line was taken. For whatever reason, the inevitable glut of articles gleefully denouncing the latest punk outrage was counterbalanced by an equal number of items devoted to the small details of punk family life. For instance, the 15 October 1977 issue of *Woman's Own* carried an article entitled 'Punks and Mothers' which stressed the classless, fancy dress aspects of punk.[11] Photographs depicting punks with smiling mothers, reclining next to the family pool, playing with the family dog, were placed above a text which dwelt on the ordinariness of individual punks: 'It's not as rocky horror as it appears' . . . 'punk can be a family affair' . . . 'punks as it happens are non-political', and, most insidiously, albeit accurately, 'Johnny Rotten is as big a household name as Hughie Green'. Throughout the summer of 1977, the *People* and the *News of the World* ran items on punk babies, punk brothers, and punk–ted weddings. All these articles served to minimize the Otherness so stridently proclaimed in punk style, and defined the subculture in precisely those terms which it sought most vehemently to resist and deny.

Once again, we should avoid making any absolute distinction between the ideological and commercial 'manipulations' of subculture. The symbolic restoration of daughters to the family, of deviants to the fold, was undertaken at a time when the widespread 'capitulation' of punk musicians to market forces was being used throughout the media to illustrate the fact that punks were 'only human after all'. The music papers were filled with the familiar success stories describing the route from rags to rags and riches – of punk musicians flying to America, of bank clerks become magazine editors or record producers, of harassed seamstresses turned overnight into successful business women. Of course, these success stories had ambiguous implications. As with every other 'youth revolution' (e.g., the beat boom, the mod explosion and the Swinging Sixties) the relative success of a few individuals created an impression of energy, expansion and limitless upward mobility. This ultimately reinforced the image of the open society which the very presence of the punk subculture – with its rhetorical emphasis on unemployment, high-rise living and narrow options – had originally contradicted. As Barthes (1972) has written: 'myth can always, as a last resort, signify the resistance which is brought to bear against it' and it does so typically by imposing its own ideological terms, by substituting in this case 'the fairy tale of the artist's creativity'[12] for an art form 'within the compass of every consciousness',[13] a 'music' to be judged, dismissed or marketed for 'noise' – a logically consistent, self-constituted chaos. It does so finally by replacing a subculture engendered by history, a product of real historical contradictions, with a handful of brilliant nonconformists, satanic geniuses who, to use the words of Sir John Read, Chairman of EMI 'become in the fullness of time, wholly acceptable and can contribute greatly to the development of modern music'.[14]

Notes

1   Although Williams had posited a new, broader definition of culture, he intended this to complement rather than contradict earlier formulations:

> It seems to me that there is value in each of these kinds of definition. . . . the degree to which we depend, in our knowledge of many past societies and past stages of our

own, on the body of intellectual and imaginative work which has retained its major communicative power, makes the description of culture in these terms if not complete, then at least reasonable . . . there are elements in the 'ideal' definition which . . . seem to me valuable. (Williams, 1965)

2   In his *Course in General Linguistics* (1974), Saussure stressed the arbitrary nature of the linguistic sign. For Saussure, language is a system of mutually related values, in which arbitrary 'signifiers' (e.g., words) are linked to equally arbitrary 'signifieds' ('concepts . . . negatively defined by their relations with other terms in the system') to form signs. These signs together constitute a system. Each element is defined through its position within the relevant system – its relation to other elements – through the dialectics of identity and difference. Saussure postulated that other systems of significance (e.g., fashion, cookery) might be studied in a similar way, and that eventually linguistics would form part of a more general science of signs – a semiology.

3   The fashionable status of this word has in recent years contributed to its indiscriminate use. I intend here the very precise meaning established by Louis Althusser: 'the *problematic* of a word or concept consists of the theoretical or ideological framework within which that word or concept can be used to establish, determine and discuss a particular range of issues and a particular kind of problem' (Althusser and Balibar, 1968; see also Bennett, 1979).

4   This was part of a speech made by Dr George Simpson, a Margate magistrate, after the mod–rocker clashes of Whitsun 1964. For sociologists of deviance, this speech has become *the* classic example of rhetorical overkill and deserves quoting in full: 'These long-haired, mentally unstable, petty little hoodlums, these sawdust Caesars who can only find courage like rats, in hunting in packs' (quoted in Cohen, 1972).

5   On 1 December 1976 the Sex Pistols appeared on the Thames twilight programme *Today.* During the course of the interview with Bill Grundy they used the words 'sod', 'bastard' and 'fuck'. The papers carried stories of jammed switchboards, shocked parents, etc., and there were some unusual refinements. The *Daily Mirror* (2 December) contained a story about a lorry driver who had been so incensed by the Sex Pistols' performance that he had kicked in the screen of his colour television: 'I can swear as well as anyone, but I don't want this sort of muck coming into my home at teatime.'

6   The police brought an unsuccessful action for obscenity against the Sex Pistols after their first LP *Never Mind the Bollocks* was released in 1977.

7   On 4 January 1977 the Sex Pistols caused an incident at Heathrow Airport by spitting and vomiting in front of airline staff. The *Evening News* quoted a check-in desk girl as saying: 'The group are the most revolting people I have ever seen in my life. They were disgusting, sick and obscene.' Two days after this incident was reported in the newspapers, EMI terminated the group's contract.

8   The 1 August 1977 edition of the *Daily Mirror* contained just such an example of dubious editorial concern. Giving 'serious' consideration to the problem of ted–punk violence along the King's Road, the writer makes the obvious comparison with the seaside disturbances of the previous decade: '[The clashes] must not be allowed to grow into the pitched battles like the mods and rockers confrontations at several seaside towns a few years back.' Moral panics can be recycled; even the same events can be recalled in the same prophetic tones to mobilise the same sense of outrage.

9   The characters that stamp products as commodities, and whose establishment is a necessary preliminary to the circulation of commodities, have already acquired the stability of natural, self-understood forms of social life before man seeks to decipher, not their

historical character, for in his eyes they are immutable, but their meaning. (Marx and Engels, 1970).

10   The definitive study of a moral panic is Cohen's *Folk Devils and Moral Panics*. The mods and rockers were just two of the 'folk devils' – 'the gallery of types that society erects to show its members which roles should be avoided' – which periodically become the centre of a 'moral panic'.

> Societies appear to be subject, every now and then, to periods of moral panic. A condition, episode, person or group of persons emerges to become defined as a threat to societal values and interests; its nature is presented in a stylised and stereotypical fashion by the mass media; the moral barricades are manned by editors, bishops, politicians and other right-thinking people; socially accredited experts pronounce their diagnoses and solutions; ways of coping are evolved or (more often) resorted to; the condition then disappears, submerges or deteriorates and becomes more visible. (Cohen, 1972)

Official reactions to the punk subculture betrayed all the classic symptoms of a moral panic. Concerts were cancelled; clergymen, politicians and pundits unanimously denounced the degeneracy of youth. Among the choicer reactions, Marcus Lipton, the late MP for Lambeth North, declared: 'If pop music is going to be used to destroy our established institutions, then it ought to be destroyed first.' Bernard Brook-Partridge, MP for Havering-Romford, stormed, 'I think the Sex Pistols are absolutely bloody revolting. I think their whole attitude is calculated to incite people to misbehaviour.... It is a deliberate incitement to anti-social behaviour and conduct' (quoted in *New Musical Express*, 15 July 1977).

11   See also 'Punks have Mothers Too: They tell us a few home truths' in *Woman* (15 April 1978) and 'Punks and Mothers' in *Woman's Own* (15 October 1977). These articles draw editorial comment (a sign of recognition on the part of the staff of the need to reassure the challenged expectations of the reader?). The following anecdote appeared beneath a photograph showing two dancing teddy boys:

> The other day I overheard two elderly ladies, cringing as a gang of alarming looking punks passed them, say in tones of horror: 'Just imagine what their children will be like'. I'm sure a lot of people must have said exactly the same about the Teddy Boys, like the ones pictured ... and Mods and Rockers. That made me wonder what had happened to them when the phase passed. I reckon they put away their drape suits or scooters and settled down to respectable, quiet lives, bringing up the kids and desperately hoping they won't get involved in any of these terrible Punk goings-on.

12   'The fairy-tale of the artist's creativity is western culture's last superstition. One of Surrealism's first revolutionary acts was to attack this myth ...' (Max Ernst, 'What is Surrealism?' quoted in Lippard, 1970).

13   'Surrealism is within the compass of every consciousness' (surrealist tract quoted in Lippard, 1970). See also Paul Eluard (1933): 'We have passed the period of individual exercises'.

The solemn and extremely reverential exhibition of Surrealism, mounted at London's Hayward Gallery in 1978 ironically sought to establish the reputation of individual surrealists as artists and was designed to win public recognition of their 'genius'. It is fitting that punk should be absorbed into high fashion at the same time as the first major exhibition of Dada and surrealism in Britain was being launched.

14 On 7 December one month before EMI terminated its contract with the Sex Pistols, Sir John Read, the record company's Chairman, made the following statement at the annual general meeting:

> Throughout its history as a recording company, EMI has always sought to behave within contemporary limits of decency and good taste – taking into account not only the traditional rigid conventions of one section of society, but also the increasingly liberal attitudes of other (perhaps larger) sections...at any given time... What is decent or in good taste compared to the attitudes of, say, 20 or even 10 years ago?
>
>   It is against this present-day social background that EMI has to make value judgements about the content of records...Sex Pistols is a pop group devoted to a new form of music known as 'punk rock'. It was contracted for recording purposes by EMI...in October, 1976...In this context, it must be remembered that the recording industry has signed many pop groups, initially controversial, who have in the fullness of time become wholly acceptable and contributed greatly to the development of modern music...EMI should not set itself up as a public censor, but it does seek to encourage restraint.   (Quoted in Vermorel and Vermorel, 1978)

Despite the eventual loss of face (and some £40,000 paid out to the Pistols when the contract was terminated) EMI and the other record companies tended to shrug off the apparent contradictions involved in signing up groups who openly admitted to a lack of professionalism, musicianship, and commitment to the profit motive. During the Clash's famous performance of 'White Riot' at the Rainbow in 1977 when seats were ripped out and thrown at the stage, the last two rows of the theatre (left, of course, intact) were occupied almost exclusively by record executives and talent scouts: CBS paid for the damage without complaint. There could be no clearer demonstration of the fact that symbolic assaults leave real institutions intact. Nonetheless, the record companies did not have everything their own way. The Sex Pistols received five-figure sums in compensation from both A & M and EMI and when their LP (recorded at last by Virgin) finally did reach the shops, it contained a scathing attack on EMI delivered in Rotten's venomous nasal whine:

> You thought that we were faking
> That we were all just money-making
> You don't believe that we're for real
> Or you would lose your cheap appeal.
> Who?
> EMI – EMI
>
> Blind acceptance is a sign
> Of stupid fools who stand in line
> Like EMI – EMI
> ('EMI', Virgin, 1977)

References

Althusser, L. (1969), *For Marx*, Allen Lane.
—— (1971a), *Lenin and Philosophy and Other Essays*, New Left Books.
Althusser, L. and Balibar, E. (1968), *Reading Capital*, New Left Books.
Arnold, M. (1868), *Culture and Anarchy.*
Barthes, R. (1972), *Mythologies*, Paladin.
Bennett, T. (1979), *Formalism and Marxism*, Methuen.
Clarke, J. (1976a), 'The Skinheads and the Magical Recovery of Working Class Community', in S. Hall *et al.* (eds), *Resistance Through Rituals*, Hutchinson.
—— (1976b), 'Style', in S. Hall *et al.* (eds), *Resistance Through Rituals*, Hutchinson.
Cohen, S. (1972), *Folk Devils and Moral Panics*, MacGibbon & Kee.
Douglas, M. (1967), *Purity and Danger*, Penguin.
Eluard, P. (1933), *Food for Vision*, Editions Galliard.
Geertz, C. (1964), 'Ideology as a Cultural System', in D. E. Apter (ed.), *Ideology and Discontent*, Free Press.
—— (1967), *The Thief's Journal*, Penguin.
Godelier, M. (1970), 'Structure and Contradiction in 'Capital' ', in M. Lane (ed.), *Structuralism: A Reader*, Cape.
Hall, S. (1974), 'Deviancy, Politics and the Media', in P. Rock and M. McIntosh (eds), *Deviance and Social Control*, Tavistock.
—— (1977), 'Culture, the Media and the 'Ideological Effect' ', in J. Curran *et al.* (eds), *Mass Communication and Society*, Arnold.
Hall, S., Clarke, J., Jefferson, T. and Roberts, B. (eds) (1976a), *Resistance Through Rituals*, Hutchinson.
Hawkes, T. (1977), *Structuralism and Semiotics*, Methuen.
Hoggart, R. (1958), *The Uses of Literacy*, Penguin.
—— (1966), 'Literature and Society', *American Scholar*, Spring.
Ingham, R. (ed.) (1977), *Football Hooliganism*, Inter-action Imprint.
Lefebvre, H. (1971), *Everyday Life in the Modern World*, Allen Lane.
—— (1969), *The Elementary Structures of Kinship*, Eyre & Spottiswoode.
Lippard, L. (ed.) (1970), *Surrealists on Art*, Spectrum.
Marx, K. and Engels, F. (1970), *The German Ideology*, Lawrence & Wishart.
Mepham, J. (1972), 'The Structuralist Sciences and Philosophy', in D. Robey (ed.), *Structuralism: The Wolfson College Lectures 1972*, Cape, 1973.
Saussure, F. de (1974), *Course in General Linguistics*, Fontana.
Vermorel, F. and Vermorel, J. (1978), *The Sex Pistols*, Tandem.
Volosinov, V. N. (1973), *Marxism and the Philosophy of Language*, Seminar Press.
Williams, R. (1960), *Border Country*, Penguin.
—— (1961), *Culture and Society*, Penguin.
—— (1965), *The Long Revolution*, Penguin.
—— (1976), *Keywords*, Fontana.

Part III

Political Economy

Introduction to Part III

The essays selected in this section of the reader highlight some of the developments in the study of the political economy of the mass media – now a robust school of critical communication scholarship, but one that broke sharply with prevailing academic trends when it emerged in the 1960s. Scholars such as Harold Innis, Ben Bagdikian, Dallas Smythe, and Herbert Schiller in North America, and Nicholas Garnham, Peter Golding, Graham Murdock, and others in Britain, began to consider issues of the nature and effects of the system of production of media and information. The focus in US-based political economy of communication tends to emphasize the economic side of the equation with focus on ownership, corporatization, and consumption, whereas in Britain there has been a spotlighting of the political dimension, with emphasis on public service broadcasting, the importance of state-supported and regulated communications, and the politics of broadcasting.[1]

Even today, the place of political economy in critical cultural studies is a contested area. Advocates of British cultural studies have been emphatic in positioning their work in opposition to political economy approaches, emphasizing that cultural studies originated and developed through the critique of the Marxist base/superstructure model and its 'reductionist' economic determinism. Rather than affirm one side or another in this ongoing debate, we would suggest that the texts offered in *KeyWorks* can be used to overcome the divide rather than pitting one side against the other.

London-based communication scholar Nicholas Garnham attempted to counter charges of economic reductionism and determinism by offering a revision of the much-maligned base/superstructure model in an attempt to connect media and culture with developments within contemporary capitalism, and thus to rethink relations between economics and culture. In the 1986 essay included here, Garnham's revamped model moves away from what he calls 'the twin traps of economic reductionism and of the idealist autonomization of the ideological level.' Garnham proposes a more complex relational design that seeks to address the issues raised by cultural studies regarding ideology and autonomy, while retaining its engagement with classical Marxism. His most significant intervention is the idea that cultural artifacts are social and materialist phenomena articulated to specific historical moments in capitalist development and thus variable and shifting. Garnham's core point is that the production and dissemination of mass culture is rooted in the material dimension: the pressing need, he writes, is 'to distinguish between the media as processes of material production on the one hand, and as sites of ideological struggle on the other, and the relationship between those two levels or instances.' In his essay, Garnham offers a useful map of the terrain of the political economy of the mass media, areas of which are further explored in the other selections included here.[2]

Garnham's call for more concrete analysis of the economics of media production is illustrated by Canadian communications researcher Dallas Smythe's innovative 1981 reconceptualization of a political economy of the media which focuses on media consumption – but with a new critical twist. In Smythe's view, the audience of media in the act of consumption constitutes 'exchange value.' As Smythe points out, none of the literature on economics or political economy deals with 'the role of the markets for audiences, produced by the mass media, bought and used by advertisers.' Smythe revises the audience's role in the system as unpaid work in the service of the advertising industry. He was among the first to examine the connection between the apparently non-advertising content of the media with the paid advertisements, noting the symbiotic relationship between these two purportedly separate functions. Smythe's 'audience consumption' is very different from the 'active audience' of British cultural studies, and it is still a provocative challenge to the myths and claims of an uncritical celebration of audience empowerment.

In *Manufacturing Consent: The Political Economy of the Mass Media* (1988), Edward Herman and Noam Chomsky present a sharply critical analysis in their examination of the influence of market forces on media content, developing what they term a 'propaganda model' of the news that connects corporate and state power in a regulatory nexus. Exploding prevailing myths of US journalism that rest on ideas of pluralism and free agency in a democratic society, Herman and Chomsky demonstrate that the free-market economics model of media leads inevitably to normative and narrow reportorial frames. In the chapter included here, they detail the five 'filters' on which their propaganda model is based: media ownership and profit orientation; the influence of advertising; the role of experts; 'flak' as a means of disciplining the media; and the rhetorical strategy of anti-communism.

Herman and Chomsky's central point is that the media tend to 'marginalize dissent and allow the government and dominant private interests to get their messages across to the public' in ways that promote hegemonic constructions and suppress oppositional voices. Herman and Chomsky have together, individually, and with other collaborators, developed a large body of work critical of US foreign policy and the role of the media in promoting state and corporate interests.[3] Their work is highly controversial – it has been methodologically challenged, dismissed as derivative, and derided as a 'conspiracy theory.' We include a selection from *Manufacturing Consent* here in the belief that it can be viewed as a theoretical 'key' that opens up a radical critique of the media by integrating certain significant themes into a critical heuristic that encourages readers to analyze the frames and discourse within which political events are presented by mainstream media. Most notably, Herman and Chomsky remind us that in a nominal democracy with serious inequities of wealth of power, the media can function to 'manufacture consent' to policies that rarely represent the voices or interests of the majority of readers and citizens.

This idea is echoed in the work of Herbert Schiller, who also addresses an aspect of Nicholas Garnham's 'map' of political economy – 'the industrialization of culture.' In this perspective, culture is construed as an arm of the industrial–business sector, combined with the 'corporate takeover of public expression' whereby corporations come to control the media, education, public spaces, and cultural creation (1989). Schiller taught for some decades at the University of California at La Jolla, before his death in May 2000, and was a pioneer in analyzing the role of media and culture in the world economy, forging theoretical linkages of communication and information with political economy. His early work – starting with *Mass Communications and American Empire* (1969) – revealed the role of the media industries in the military–industrial complex and the interconnected power structures that shape the functioning and content of the mass media. The critical lens that Schiller applied to the examination of the role of popular culture in the spread of American corporate dominance illuminated the links between cultural and economic hegemonic processes.

We are including a 1991 text by Schiller that contains an early critique of the emerging concept of globalization. Recognizing that the collapse of the system of Soviet communism and triumph of the capitalist market system on a global scale represented a striking difference from the post-World War II geopolitical system, Schiller insists that the expansion of the capitalist market represents a metamorphosis and expansion of the system of economic domination and consumption. Arguing against the claim that the new global culture represents a field of diversity, heterogeneity, and difference, Schiller argues that US media cultural dominance continues apace and that corporate transnationalism and not an amorphous 'globalism' is the dominant economic force of the present moment.

The significance of Schiller's critique is that it does not allow the question of power to be elided. Moreover, he reminds us that people (especially in Asia, Latin America, and Africa) have vast unmet needs, yet these are consistently supplanted by the imperatives for profit of multinational US and European corporations. From this optic, the mass media are agents in an ongoing process of marginalization and displacement of people's genuine needs in favor of the consumption of global culture that narcotizes its audiences and induces conformity to the existing system.

Susan Willis brings the relationship between political economy and everyday life into sharp focus in her essay 'Unwrapping Use Value,' excerpted from her book *A Primer for Daily Life* (1993). A professor at Duke University, Willis examines mass culture and its implications for 'daily life,' a phrase borrowed from the writings of Henri Lefebvre and Michel de Certeau ('la vie quotidienne') and replete with notions of individual subversion and resistance. Willis argues that Marx's model of exchange value and use value (in which the difference between a consumption's exchange value and use value defines the economic relationships of capitalism) has been supplanted in the contemporary world by a fetishization of anticipated or hoped for use value. Packaging and advertising seize on this phenomenon of anticipation, rendering it into an almost sexual form of desire for commodities.

Willis's exploration of themes of political economy in consumer society recon-structs the concept of 'use value' from a wealth of theoretical perspectives. Her essay draws on the work of Lukács, Adorno, Benjamin, and Baudrillard, culminating with the idea that it is necessary to problematize the notion of 'use value' in order to fully grasp the formal logic of capitalism and its impact on daily life. She also uncovers the ways that advertising, packaging, and display mobilize desire, induce us to consume, and hide the poverty of everyday life, while revealing utopian possibilities by creating desires for genuine happiness and gratification.

The argument underpinning her position, and indeed that of the others in this section, is that there cannot be an engagement with cultural products without a consideration of the material realities of the context in which they are produced and consumed.[4] Political economy is thus a vital part of any useful critique of the media and mass culture, offering a space in which the material and the symbolic can converge. But more importantly, it brings us back to the essentially progressive nature of media criticism, the understanding that real lives and real human conditions are impacted by these systems of cultural production and distribution, and that improv-ing media and culture is a crucial part of social transformation.

A social and populist inflection to political economy is also found in the work of Mexican theorist Jésus Martín-Barbero, whose analysis 'The Processes: From Nation-alisms to Transnationals,' from his 1991 book *Communication, Culture and Hege-mony: From the Media to Mediations,* we include in our reader. Martín-Barbero stresses the active and processal mediations in which media are lived and experienced by the people, producing meanings, identities, and participation in national cultures. Focusing on a Latin American context, Martín-Barbero analyzes how the Mexican cinema, creole circus, radio theater, black music, and the popular press contributed to the development of national cultures and identities. In more recent time, Martín-Barbero notes that in an age of globalization, national and traditional cultures intersected with global culture, but had their distinctive mediations and forms. Concluding his study with an important discussion of 'the contradictions between technologies and uses,' he argues that all communication technology from loud-speakers to computers can be reconstructed and used to meet people's needs and to create distinctive cultural forms.

Political economy, then, involves a complex interaction between the economy, state, social movements, and popular participation in social and cultural processes. It encompasses analysis of production and consumption of media, goods, and services which incorporate individuals in a modern consumer and media society. Yet, political economies are historically specific, with differences between countries such as the United States and Britain in terms of ownership patterns of the media and such things as television consumer practices. Important differences also exist between the West-ern and non-Western countries in terms of how they appropriate the products of Western transnational media industries and create their own local cultural forms and meanings. Finally, globalization and new technologies are so dramatically altering the world economy that constant up-dating and rethinking of the political economy of communication is now more important than ever.

Notes

1   Of course, various practioners of the political economy of communication have mixed their
    focus on the economic and political sides of the field. For a useful overview of the current
    field of political economy of communication see Mosco (1996); on the history of broad-
    casting in America, see McChesney (1996, 1999); on the history of broadcasting in Britain,
    see Cristell (1997) and on British public-service broadcasting, see Scannell (1989) and
    O'Malley (1994).
2   Ironically, in some ways his vision of relating culture to an economic base in a nonreduc-
    tionist way echoes the themes in Stuart Hall's theory of articulation; although these
    theoreticians (and other scholars in the two schools of thought) locate themselves in
    opposition to one another, their positions in some areas reveal more parallels than the
    writers themselves might care to admit.
3   Chomsky has published by now a small library of books criticizing US media and foreign
    policy; see *The Chomsky Reader* (1987) for selections and the documentary film *Manufac-
    turing Consent* for an overview.
4   For recent work in feminist political economy, see the journal *Feminist Economics*.

References

Chomsky, Noam (1987) *The Chomsky Reader*, edited by James Peck. New York: Pantheon.

Cristell, Andrew (1997) *An Introductory History of British Broadcasting*. London: Routledge.

Garnham, Nicholas (1986) 'Contribution to a Political Economy of Mass Communication.' In
    Media, Culture & Society: A Critical Reader, 7–32. Edited by Richard Collins, James
    Curran, Nicholas Garnham, Paddy Scannell, Philip Schlesinger, and Colin Sparks. London:
    Sage.

Herman, Edward, and Noam Chomsky (1988) 'The Propaganda Model.' In *Manufacturing
    Consent: The Political Economy of the Mass Media*, 1–35. New York: Pantheon.

Martín-Barbero, Jésus (1991) 'The Processes: From Nationalisms to Transnationals.' In *Com-
    munication, Culture and Hegemony: From the Media to Mediations*, 150–86. Newbury Park,
    Cal.: Sage.

McChesney, Robert (1995) *Telecommunications, Mass Media and Democracy: The Battle for the
    Control of US Broadcasting, 1928–1935*. New York: Oxford University Press.

——(1999) *Rich Media, Poor Democracy*. Chicago: University of Illinois Press.

Mosco, Vincent (1996) *The Political Economy of Communication*. London: Sage.

O'Malley, Tom (1994) *Closedown? The BBC and Government Broadcasting Policy, 1979–1992*.
    London: Pluto Press.

Scannell, Paddy (1989) 'Public Service Broadcasting: The History of a Concept.' In Andrew
    Goodwin and Gary Whannel (Eds), *Understanding Television*. London: Routledge.

Schiller, Herbert I (1991) 'Not Yet the Post-Imperialist Era,' *Critical Studies in Mass Com-
    munication*, 8, 13–28.

Smythe, Dallas W. (1981) 'On the Audience Consumption and its Work.' In *Dependency Road:
    Communications, Capitalism, Consciousness and Canada*, 22–51. Norwood, NJ: Ablex.

Willis, Susan (1991) 'Unwrapping Use Value.' In *A Primer for Daily Life*, 1–22. New York and
    London: Routledge.

14

Contribution to a Political Economy of Mass-Communication*

Nicholas Garnham

Introduction

The major modern communication systems are now so evidently key institutions in advanced capitalist societies that they require the same kind of attention, at least initially, that is given to the institutions of industrial production and distribution. Studies of the ownership and control of the capitalist press, the capitalist cinema, and capitalist and state capitalist radio and television interlock, historically and theoretically, with wider analysis of capitalist society, capitalist economy and the neo-capitalist state. Further, many of the same institutions require analysis in the context of modern imperialism and neo-colonialism, to which they are crucially relevant.

Over and above their empirical results, these analyses force theoretical revision of the formula of base and superstructure and of the definition of productive forces, in a social area in which large scale capitalist economic activity and cultural production are now inseparable. Unless this theoretical revision is made, even the best work of the radical and anti-capitalist empiricists is in the end overlaid or absorbed by the specific theoretical structures of bourgeois cultural sociology.

(R. Williams, 1977: 136)

The purpose of this article is to support this call for a major revision within cultural theory, to explain why such a revision is necessary and to begin to explore some of its consequences.

The fact that Williams's own call for this theoretical revision is hidden, gnomically, in a book of literary theory, and has thus not received the attention it deserves within mass-media research, is itself symptomatic of the existing ideological resistances to such a revision, not only within 'bourgeois cultural theory', but also within what pass for Marxist alternatives. Indeed, I will go on to argue that in his effort to break with this all pervasive idealism, Williams, in formulating his own 'cultural materialism', has reacted by taking too materialist a stance.

* From *Media, Culture and Society: A Critical Reader*, eds. Richard Collins, James Curran, Nicholas Garnham, Paddy Scannell, Philip Schlesinger, and Colin Sparks (London: Sage, 1986), pp. 9–32.

What this article calls for, therefore, is the elaboration of a political economy of culture with a political economy of mass-communication taking its subsidiary place within that wider framework as the analysis of an important, but historically specific mode of the wider process of cultural production and reproduction. The need to elaborate such a political economy is intensely practical. It stems from actual changes in the structure of contemporary capitalism as they effect what has been dubbed 'The Culture Industry' and the relationship of that industry to the State. Symptoms of the urgent political problems raised by these changes can be observed throughout the developed, capitalist world. They can be seen in a whole range of Government Reports and interventions of which, in Britain, the most obvious recent examples are the Royal Commission on the Press, the Annan Committee Report and the subsequent White Paper on Broadcasting, the Prime Minister's Working Party on the Film Industry and its proposals for a British Film Authority. They can be seen underlying the present dispute at Times Newspapers, the debate over the allocation of the fourth TV channel and the present financial problems of the BBC. Parallels to these reports, problems and debates can be found in all the member countries of OECD. At an international level, recent debates in UNESCO and the continuing diplomatic activity surrounding the concept of a New World Information Order can only be properly understood in this context. In the face of such developments most current mass-media research and theorizing is demonstrably inadequate.

Before moving on to examine some of the theoretical problems raised by this shift in research emphasis, let me give just one concrete example of the kind of information to which it gives privileged attention and why. During the last few weeks in Britain we have witnessed the failure of the Government to provide the BBC with adequate finance, a matter of great and ill-understood strategic significance in the whole development of British broadcasting and a subject that will repay substantive analysis from the perspective I am here outlining in a future edition of this journal. We have also witnessed the reactivation of the debate on TV and Violence by the publication of Dr Belson's study, a matter of undoubted importance to anyone concerned with mass-media research in Britain. Nonetheless, in my view the most significant development of the period was hidden away on the financial pages, namely the take-over of British Relay Wireless by the Electronic Rental Group, making ERG the second largest TV rental group in the UK. The significance of this take-over is that it was financed by a £10 million loan from ERG's controlling share-holder Philips Electronic. Now Philips is one of the firms involved in the audio-visual sector of the culture industry, in terms of total sales the world's third largest after General Electric and ITT and in terms of the proportion of its business related to electronic audio-visual manufacture and production it is the world leader by some way. The next phase of development of the culture industry will involve the attempt to develop and exploit the domestic entertainment market, particularly through video. Control of a rental network will be one of the keys to success in the competitive struggle for this market for two reasons: firstly, as has been true for domestic TV receivers, because the necessary hardware can only be sold in sufficient quantity on credit, but secondly, and here we have a crucial distinction between the new developments and the rental of TV receivers, because there is no internationally agreed technical standard for video recorders and players (whether of cassettes or discs) with the result that the decision on the choice of hardware limits the consumer's subsequent choice of software. Now since, of all the world's major electronic companies, only Philips is already in a position to develop co-ordinated software production (through such subsidiaries as Polygram and Phonogram) control of tied rental outlets for their hardware would give them a vertically integrated international cultural monopoly of a scale and type not yet seen in this sector and with cultural consequences over the medium term (10 to 20 years) that make our petty domestic disputes over the allocation of the fourth channel pale into insignificance (see *Financial Times*, 19 December 1978).

A Necessary Return to Fundamentals

Before returning to further concrete examples of the problems a political economy of mass-communication tries to analyse, it is necessary, precisely because of the dominance of idealism within the analysis of culture and of the mass-media, to make an unavoidable theoretical digression in order to base subsequent discussion firmly within the necessary historical materialist perspective. In asking for a shift within mass-media research towards historical materialism, one is asserting an order of priorities which is both a hierarchy of concrete historical and material determinants in the real world as well as an order of research priorities. That is to say, we are faced with the problem of understanding an actual historical process which itself concretely exhibits structurally ordered determinants within which material production is ultimately determinant, which is what makes our theory materialist, while at the same time there are a limited number of researchers with limited material resources among which I include time, who must thus choose, from within the complex totality of the historical social process, to examine those aspects of the process which are likely to lead to the clearest understanding of the dynamics of that process and through that understanding to its human control. It is this question of choice which underlies Marx's own mode of abstraction. Thus, in opposition to that post-Althusserian/Lacanian current which has been dangerously dominant within recent British Marxist research in the area of mass-media, a current of which *Screen* is a representative example, one asserts, not that the problem of subjectivity for instance is of no interest, but that it is of less interest than that of class or capital accumulation. Moreover, one is not asserting that such a hierarchy of historical determinants of research concerns is universal, that there is A theory of mass-media, but that they correspond to the actual historically specific hierarchy of a particular social formation. Or as Marx himself put it,

> my analytical method ... does not start out from man, but from the analytically given social period.[1]

That is to say the economic is determinant under capitalism, because capitalism is a mode of social organization characterized by the domination of an abstract system of exchange relations. Further the particular relationship between the abstract and the concrete or between 'phenomenal forms' and 'real relations' or between ideas and matter, which is appropriate to historical materialism as a mode of analysis of capitalism, stems from the real relation between the abstract (exchange relations) and the concrete (individual lived experience, real labour etc.) within the social formation itself. In a social formation in which social relations were not abstracted into a relation of exchange a different theoretical relationship between the abstract and the concrete would hold.

Moreover, the abstract should not be opposed to the concrete, just as the phenomenal forms should not be opposed to the real relations. One is precisely a form of the other. That is to say, the exchange relation has a concrete material reality in the form of money, bills of exchange, credit cards, banks etc., but its mode of operation and with it the reproduction of the capitalist social formation depends upon its abstraction, the fact that it works 'behind men's backs' and thus 'can be determined with the precision of natural science'. It can only be determined with such precision so long as it is a supra-individual social process. This is both a methodological and historical postulate. That is to say, the necessary condition for a capitalist social formation is the existence of a more or less universal domination of social relations by the exchange relation, i.e. a market economy. Wherever such domination is challenged (and we do not and never have seen, in this sense, an 'ideal' capitalist social formation) by explicit political action, by human will and reason, the logic of capital is challenged. It is for this reason that the State is a necessarily contradictory form.

This leads us to the concept of ideology which so dominates our field of study and to the central problem within cultural theory, namely the base/superstructure relationship. The central postulate of historical materialism is that man as a biological organism must undertake a constant material exchange with nature and it is this exchange that is named labour. Within history the labour/nature relationship has become increasingly mediated through specific modes of production, thus making the links more difficult to analyse. Because of this difficulty the possibility of error and thus of ideology enters. But it remains a material fact that, ultimately, material production in this direct sense is determinate in that it is only the surplus produced by this labour that enables other forms of human activity to be pursued. Thus the superstructure remains dependent upon and determined by the base of material production in that very fundamental sense.

Clearly the greater the surplus to immediate physical reproductive needs the greater the autonomy of the superstructure and indeed the greater the possible variation and diversity within superstructural organization, always providing of course that the mode of material production is such as to guarantee the necessary surplus. In this important sense the superstructure/culture is and remains subordinate and secondary and the crucial questions are the relationship between, on the one hand, the mode of extraction and distribution of the material surplus, e.g. class relations and, on the other, the allocation of this material surplus within the superstructure, for instance, the problem of public expenditure among others. But while, historically, the superstructure has become more autonomous, there still remain direct, narrow material constraints upon individuals even within developed, industrial societies. Everyone has to eat and sleep and be maintained at a given body temperature in determinate temporal cycles. Thus, as Marx himself noted, every economy is an economy of time (Marx, 1973), which is why labour-time is so crucial an analytical concept. Cultural reproduction is still directly governed by these material determinants in the sense that the time and resources available to those who have to sell their labour power to capital, within labour-time constraints largely imposed by capital, remain limited and they still use the most significant proportion of their available time and material resources in order to ensure material, biological reproduction.

It is at this primary level both theoretically and actually that social being determines social consciousness. Thus economism, the concern for immediate physical survival and reproduction within the dominant relations of exchange is an immediate and rational response to the determinants of social being. What E. P. Thompson has recently dubbed 'lumped bourgeois intellectuals' (Thompson, 1978) too easily forget this, both because their material conditions of existence are often less immediately determinate and also because of a guilty conscience concerning the subjective relationship of exploitation in which they stand *vis-à-vis* productive material labour.

The Material, the Economic and the Ideological

No political economy of culture can avoid discussion of the base/superstructure relationship, but in so doing it needs to avoid the twin traps of economic reductionism and of the idealist autonomization of the ideological level. The central problem with the base/superstructure metaphor as with the related culture/society dichotomy is that being a metaphor of polarity, essentially binary in form, it is unable adequately to deal with the number of distinctions that are necessary, in this instance between the material, the economic and the ideological. These should be seen not as three levels, but as analytically distinct, but coterminous moments both of concrete social practices and of concrete analysis. Furthermore, any political economy needs to hold constantly to the historicity of the specific articulations between these moments. There is a sense in which the base/superstructure metaphor always does imply a notion of expressive totality, a totality in which either the superstructure is expressive of an economic base (under capitalism of a capitalist economic base) or, on the other hand, a tautological sense of expressive totality by which all phenomena of a social formation are expressive of that social formation. That is to say, the notion of expressive totality can be used either deterministically or relationally. For me at least it is clear that the analysis in *Capital* is of the latter type. That is to say what is being analysed is not, as Mandel (1975) has stressed, a social formation in equilibrium but in disequilibrium; an uncompleted at the time Marx wrote, and still incomplete, process of capitalist development, a development which was marked not by the total domination and determinacy of capitalist economic forms, an expressive totality in that sense, but on the contrary by a series of shifting relationships between the economic and other instances each interacting with the other in a process of uneven and contradictory development, so that the totality of the social formation at any historic moment was only expressive of the actual state of those shifting interrelationships.

Thus the pertinence or meaning of any analytical category, such as base and superstructure, expressing as it does a relationship, will shift as the historical reality it is used to explain shifts. Similarly, we could say that the purpose of a political economy of culture is to elucidate what Marx and Engels meant in the German Ideology by 'control of the means of mental production', while stressing that the meaning that they gave to the term was quite clearly historical and therefore shifting and was never meant to be frozen into some simple dichotomy as it has so often been in subsequent Marxist writing. Further the political economy of mass-media is the analysis of a specific historical phase of this general development linked to historically distinct modalities of cultural production and reproduction.

In his discussion of base and superstructure in *Marxism and Literature*, Williams points out that, although, in stressing the determinacy of the base against bourgeois idealism, one version of Marxist cultural theory has been accused, both by bourgeois and Marxist critics, of 'vulgar materialism', 'the truth is that it was never materialist enough'. And he continues:

> What any notion of a 'self-subsistent order' suppresses is the material character of the productive forces which produce such a version of production. Indeed it is often a way of suppressing full consciousness of the very nature of such a society. If 'production', in capitalist society, is the production of commodities for a market, then different but misleading terms are found for every other kind of production and productive force. What is most often suppressed is the direct material production of 'politics'. Yet any ruling class devotes a significant part of material production to establishing a political order. The social and political order which maintains a capitalist market, like the social and political struggle that created it, is necessarily a material production. From castles and palaces and churches to prisons and workhouses and schools; from weapons of war to a controlled press: any ruling class, in variable ways though always materially, produces a social and political order. These are never superstructural activities. They are the necessary material production within which an apparently self-subsistent mode of production can alone be carried on. The complexity of the process is especially remarkable in advanced capitalist societies, where it is wholly beside the point to isolate 'production' and 'industry' from the comparable material production of 'defence', 'law and order', 'welfare', 'entertainment' and 'public opinion'. In failing to grasp the material character of the production of a social and political order, this specialised (and bourgeois) materialism failed also, but even more conspicuously, to understand the material character of the production of a cultural order. The concept of the superstructure was then not a reduction but an evasion.   (Williams, 1977: 92–3)

Williams's stress here on the materiality of the cultural process is a necessary correction to both bourgeois idealism and its post-Althusserian Marxist variants. But this formulation also suffers from a misleading reductionism by failing to distinguish between the material and the economic. It is in fact a materialist rather than a historical materialist formulation. The absence of this necessary distinction is contained in the apparently insignificant but crucial phrase 'in variable ways though always materially', for it is precisely the specific articulations of these variable ways that characterize various stages of pre-capitalist and capitalist development, that characterize the shifting meaning of what Marx and Engels called 'control of the means of mental production', shifts which it is the central purpose of a political economy of mass-communication to map and analyse. Certainly a licensed press and a commercial, 'free' press are both material, but the economic differences between these two forms of 'political' control are precisely what differentiates a capitalist from a pre-capitalist form. Similarly, the difference between the economic structure of private and public education constitutes within the same materiality, the substance of 'political' struggle. While the materiality of politics, i.e. its maintenance out of the total social surplus of material production, is a general, universal phenomenon, the ways in which that surplus is extracted and distributed and the relation of that economic form to the political are historically distinct and specific, so that, at present, the matter of subsidies to political parties or to the Press becomes an object of 'political' struggle to change economic forms and by so doing to change 'political' structures.

Similarly, while Williams is correct to stress the materiality of all social practices it cannot be said, from an economic perspective, that it is wholly beside the point to isolate 'production' and 'industry' from the material production of 'defence', etc., when what is often in question when considering the relation between these various social practices is not their shared materiality, but on the contrary their significantly different economic articulation, for instance the variance between those practices carried on by private capital for profit, the publication of a newspaper for instance, and those practices carried on by the State outside direct commodity production, e.g. the BBC or the State education system. To collapse all this into a general category of 'material' production is precisely an 'evasion', both of the differing and developing economic articulations between various forms of material production and also of the amount of cultural production and reproduction that takes place within the industrial sphere as narrowly defined, in the organizations of the labour process with its industrial psychologists, its labour relations experts, its time and motion study experts, its production engineers and its personnel managers, in the structures of employer paternalism, in the organization of the market itself, etc. To take one example of such an articulation one might hypothesize that the relationship between the male predominance in newspaper readership compared with TV was not unconnected with the contrast between the culture of work as against the culture of home and has important political consequences.

This confusion between the material and the economic is common and it is worth dwelling briefly on the nature of the distinction. Insofar as historical materialism is materialist, it is based upon the postulates that Williams outlines. But insofar as it is historical, it is concerned to analyse the specific and shifting modes of this fundamental material relation, all of which are forms of that relation. In particular, it is postulated that any form of extended social relationship depends upon the extraction and distribution of material surplus and the means by which this is achieved is thus the central determining characteristic of any social formation. Such modes of social production and exchange are cultural, hence the very real problem of making a society/culture differentiation without narrowing the definition of culture to include only those elements of social interaction which involve a secondary level of abstraction, namely the representation of concrete, material relations in *symbolic* forms. Thus we must distinguish two types of form, a social form which is a series of material relations that, insofar as they operate unconsciously, can be abstractly analysed and determined with the precision of natural science, and a cultural form which, while it entails a material support, is not itself material and which has an essentially mediated relationship with the material reality it represents. Indeed, there is an essential divide between these distinct formal realms, the existence of which allows ideology to enter, because it allows denial and the lie, both of which depend upon a relationship which is not determinant. However, this autonomy is bought at the cost of a loss of real or material effectivity. Cultural forms only become effective when they are translated into social forms which do have material effectivity. Thus there is a constant dialectic at the cultural level between autonomy and effectivity and it is at the level of social effectivity that material production is ultimately determinant.

However, to return to the level of social forms, the economic is a specific historical form of the social relations of production and distribution. It is the form these relations take in a social formation within which commodity exchange is dominant. Thus, it is possible to argue that the economic is superstructural in relation to the material base or structure, that it could in fact be seen as the dominant level of the superstructure. For what Marx argues in *Capital* is that the real historical transition to capitalism involves a move from a system of social relations and domination based upon the direct physical control of landed property and people to one based upon the increasingly indirect control through commodity exchange and, in particular, through the exchange of the commodity of labour power, and that this real historical process is a real process of social abstraction which thus requires appropriate theoretical abstraction for its analysis. It is because the economic is the most abstract and fundamental form of the social relation within capitalism that it is primary both theoretically and actually, but as a historically specific representation of a predeterminate material relationship.

It is the real existence of this abstract economic level of extended commodity production that allows for the development of an increasing division of labour and thus for the development of the specific superstructural forms of capitalism. Thus the relative autonomy of the superstructure is a real and increasingly central characteristic of capitalism, but it is itself determined at the level of the economic and ultimately it is a form, at two levels of mediation, of a material relation which also remains determinant in and through the economic.

The Inadequacies of Existing Marxist Theory

From this perspective available historical materialist theories are inadequate to deal with the real practical challenges they face largely because they offer reductionist explanations which favour either a simple economic determinism or an ideological autonomy, thus failing to analyse and explain precisely that which makes the object of analysis centrally significant, namely the relationship between the economic and the ideological. Thus we are offered the following.

(a)   An unproblematic acceptance of the base/superstructure model drawn from a partial reading of the German Ideology which, unargued, simply states that the mass-media are ideological tools of ruling-class domination either through direct owner-ship or, as in the case of broadcasting, via ruling-class control of the State. Such a position neglects both the specific effects of subordinating cultural production and reproduction to the general logic of capitalist commodity production and the specifi-cities of the varying and shifting relationships between economic, ideological and political levels within actual concrete historical moments. Miliband in *Marxism and Politics* expresses a classic version of this theory:

> Whatever else the immense output of the mass media is intended to achieve, it is *also* intended to help prevent the development of class-consciousness in the working class and to reduce as much as possible any hankering it might have for a radical alternative to capitalism. The ways in which this is attempted are endlessly different; and the degree of success achieved varies considerably from country to country and from one period to another – there are other influences at work. But the fact remains that 'the class which has the means of material production at its disposal' does have, 'control at the same time of the means of mental production': and that it does seek to use them for the weakening of opposition to the established order. Nor is the point much affected by the fact that the state in almost all capitalist countries 'owns' the radio and television – its purpose is identical.   (Miliband, 1977: 50)

It should be noted here that for all its philosophical sophistication the Althusserian position on ISA represents little if any advance on this position, as indeed Simon Clarke (1977) has correctly noted with respect to the Milliband/Poulantzas con-troversy.

(b)   Secondly, and in partial reaction against this classic Marxist explanation of the role of the mass-media, we are offered an elaboration of the relative autonomy of the superstructure and within the superstructure of the ideological and political levels. All such theories in their effort to reject economism or, as Althusser puts it, 'the idea of a 'pure and simple' non-overdetermined contradiction', to a greater or lesser extent have also removed economic determinacy, i.e. as Althusser again puts it, in such theories 'the lonely hour of the 'last instance' never comes' (Althusser, 1969: 113). This general position has rightly developed the insights of the Frankfurt School into the importance of the superstructure and of mediation, while damagingly neglecting a crucial component of the Frankfurt School's original position, namely the fact that under monopoly capitalism the superstructure becomes precisely indus-trialized; it is invaded by the base and the base/superstructure distinction breaks down but via a collapse into the base rather than, as is the tendency with the post-Althusserian position, via the transformation of the base into another autonomous superstructural discourse.

> In our age the objective social tendency is incarnate in the hidden subjective purpose of company directors, the foremost among whom are in the most powerful sectors of industry – steel, petroleum, electricity and chemicals. Culture monopolies are weak

and dependant in comparison. They cannot afford to neglect their appeasement of the real holders of power if their sphere of activity in mass-society is not to undergo a series of purges.   (Adorno and Horkheimer, 1977: 351)

The truth of this original insight is demonstrated monthly as firms in the cultural sector are absorbed into large industrial conglomerates and brought under the sway of their business logic. Indeed, the real weakness of the Frankfurt School's original position was not their failure to realize the importance of the base or the economic, but insufficiently to take account of the economically contradictory nature of the process they observed and thus to see the industrialization of culture as unproblematic and irresistible. Those who have come after, while rightly criticizing the Frankfurt School for its absence of concrete class analysis, an absence stemming precisely from their insufficiently nuanced analysis of the economic level, in developing their theories of the effectivity of the superstructure have, ironically, massively compounded the original error.

The most distinguished exponent of the post-Althusserian position in Britain, Stuart Hall, in his essay 'Culture, the Media and the Ideological Effect' (Curran *et al.*, 1977), recognizes that there is a decisive relationship between the growth of the mass-media and 'everything that we now understand as characterizing 'monopoly capitalism'', but at the same time refuses an analysis of this decisive relationship claiming that 'these aspects of the growth and expansion of the media historically have to be left to one side by the exclusive attention given here to media as 'ideological apparatuses'.' Murdoch and Golding (1979) rightly criticize Hall and claim that 'on the contrary the ways in which the mass-media function as 'ideological apparatuses' can only be adequately understood when they are systematically related to their position as large scale commercial enterprises in a capitalist economic system and if these relations are examined historically'. Hall's failure to do this leads him to explain the ideological effect in terms of pre-existent and ideologically predetermined communicators or encoders choosing from a pre-existent and ideologically predetermined set of codes so that there is a systematic tendency of the media to reproduce the ideological field of society in such a way as to reproduce also its structure of domination. That is to say he offers the description of an ideological process, but not an explanation of why or how it takes place, except in tautological terms.

Moreover, he is led by his mode of analysis, as again Murdoch and Golding rightly point out, to favour a specific and atypical instance of media practice, namely public service broadcasting and indeed within that, an atypical form, namely informational broadcasting. While stressing that the production of the ideological effect requires work and struggle, his mode of analysis does not allow him to deal, for instance, with an important and developing moment in that struggle within the Press caused by a contradiction between the crucial underpinning idea of a 'free press' and the economic pressures towards monopoly or the relationship precisely between the ideological effect of broadcasting and the fact that it is perceived by its audience to be under State control as opposed to the biased privately owned press.

(c) A further elaboration of the post-Althusserian position, popular within film studies leads in its elaboration of a theory of autonomous discourses effectively to an evacuation of the field of historical materialism, whatever its materialistic rhetoric, placing its determinacy in the last instance on the unconscious as theorized within an essentially idealist, indeed Platonist, problematic. Such idiocies need detain us no further.[2]

(d) Finally, Dallas Smythe, identifying the excessive stress on the autonomy of the ideological level within Western Marxism as its 'Blind-spot', rightly redirects our attention away from the mass-media as ideological apparatuses and back to their economic function within capitalism. But in so doing, he proposes an extreme reductionist theory. For Smythe, any political economy of mass-media must be based upon an analysis of its commodity form and for him the commodity form specific to the mass-media is the Audience, that is to say, for Smythe, the crucial function of the mass-media is not to sell packages of ideology to consumers, but audiences to advertisers. Now it is undoubtedly important to focus attention upon the ways in which the mass-media manufacture and sell audiences as one moment in the complex circuit of capital that structures the operation of the mass-media economically. Moreover, to stress this moment as the crucial one and to concentrate on the mass-media's directly functional role for capital as advertising vehicles is undoubtedly a more plausible reflection of reality in the North American context than it would be in Europe. However, Smythe's theory misunderstands the function of the commodity form as an abstraction within Marxist economic theory and thus neglects the relationship between specific forms of the commodity, in this case the audience, and the commodity form in general. As a result, his theory lacks any sense of contradiction, failing to account for the function of those cultural commodities directly exchanged, failing to account for the role of the State, failing sufficiently to elaborate the function for capital of advertising itself and, perhaps most crucially of all, failing to relate the process of audience production by the mass-media to determinants of class and to class-struggle.[3]

The Ideological Level

What problems is it, then, that a political economy of mass-communication attempts to analyse? The research perspective, whose theoretical and historical basis I have briefly outlined, attempts to shift attention away from the conception of the mass-media as ISAs and sees them first as economic entities with both a direct economic role as creators of surplus value through commodity production and exchange and an indirect role, through advertising, in the creation of surplus value within other sectors of commodity production. Indeed, a political economy of mass-communication in part chooses its object of study precisely because it offers a challenge to the Althusser/Poulantzas theorization of the social formation as structured into the relatively autonomous levels of the economic, the ideological and the political. For the major institutions of mass-communication, the press and broadcasting, although, as will be analysed later, displaying notable differences of articulation, both at the same time display the close inter-weaving within concrete institutions and within their specific commodity forms of the economic, the ideological and the political. When we buy a newspaper we participate simultaneously in an economic exchange, in subjection to or reaction against an ideological formation and often in a quite specific act of political identification or at least involvement. We also know from historical analysis of the development of the press that the nature of the political involvement is quite specifically economically conditioned. Similarly, TV news is economically determined within commodity production in general, performs an ideological function and explicitly operates within politics, in terms of balance, etc.

While accepting that the mass media can be and are politically and ideologically over-determined within many specific conjunctures, a political economy, as I understand it, rests upon ultimate determination by the economic (a level that itself always remains problematic and to be defined in the process of analysis).

Indeed, one of the key features of the mass media within monopoly capitalism has been the exercise of political, and ideological domination through the economic.[4] What concerns us in fact is firstly to stress, from the analytical perspective, the validity of the base/superstructure model while at the same time pointing to and analysing the ways in which the development of monopoly capitalism has industrialized the superstructure. Indeed Marx's own central insight into the capitalist mode of production stressed its generalizing, abstracting drive; the pressure to reduce everything to the equivalence of exchange value.

Before going on to examine the economic level and its specific articulations within the cultural sphere, let us look at the relationship between the material conditions of production (not, as we have seen, to be confused with the economic far less the capitalist modes of such production, which are specific forms) on the one hand and ideological forms on the other. That is to say how do we relate Williams's correct stress, within the limits indicated, upon the materiality of cultural production, to Marx's famous distinction 'between the material transformations of the economic conditions of production, which can be determined with the precision of natural science, and the legal, political, aesthetic or philosophic – in short, ideological – forms in which men become conscious of this conflict and fight it out' (Marx, 1859).

What the quotation from Marx underlines is the importance of the distinction between the two levels, a distinction focused upon the difference between the *unconscious* forces governing material production 'beyond our will', etc. and the conscious form of ideology. If we follow the Althusserians and make ideology an unconscious process this crucial distinction is lost.

As far as the mass-media specifically are concerned this distinction points to the need to distinguish between the media as processes of material production (whether capitalist or not is precisely a question for analysis) on the one hand, and as sites of ideological struggle on the other and the relationship between those two levels or instances.

There are here two distinctions to be made. I think we can liken ideological practice to what Marx called the 'real labour process'.

Looking at the process of production from its real side, i.e. as a process which creates new use-values by performing useful labour with existing use-values, we find it to be a *real labour process*. As such its element, its conceptually specific components, are those of the labour process itself, of any labour process, irrespective of the mode of production or the stage of economic development in which they find themselves. (Marx, 1976)

That is to say the processes of consciousness and of representation, for instance, language, are real processes by which human beings socially appropriate their environment (nature) which pre-exist and continue to exist within specifically capitalist modes of ideological production and indeed upon which these capitalist modes rest.

The materiality of such ideological production *qua* ideology rests upon the fact that consciousness is a human transformation of 'real' experience, it is in that sense 'practical knowledge'. Clearly therefore, the relationship of any particular instance of ideological production to the totality of social experience will depend upon an analysis of the experiential position of the human consciousness in question, e.g. the conventional and simple definition of class consciousness as based upon the direct experience of a given position within the capital/labour relationship. Of course in any complex society such direct experience becomes highly mediated both diachronically and synchronically. But its translation into forms of representation is nonetheless a process of consciousness which is different from and in its forms has no necessary correspondence with, the economic processes to which it relates or of which it is a representation. Indeed as a representation it is precisely by definition distinct from those processes which it represents.

Moreover ideological forms can never be simply collapsed into a system of exchange values, i.e. the specifically capitalist mode of production, precisely because ideological forms, forms of consciousness, are concerned with difference, with distinction; they are by definition heterogeneous (as Marx himself remarked when discussing the limited possibilities for the subsumption of ideological production under capitalism, 'I want the doctor and not his errand boy'). Whereas exchange value is precisely the realm of equivalence.[5]

Material and Mental Production

In order to study the connection between intellectual and material production it is above all essential to conceive the latter in its determined historical form and not as a general category. For example, there corresponds to the capitalist mode of production a type of intellectual production quite different from that which corresponded to the mediaeval mode of production. Unless material production itself is understood in its specific historical form, it is impossible to grasp the characteristics of the intellectual production which corresponds to it or the reciprocal action between the two.

(Marx, 1963: 96–7)

We need to lay stress on and distinguish two distinct but related moments in a historical materialist analysis of intellectual production.

(a) Culture as a superstructural phenomenon in relation to non-cultural modes of material production, i.e. on the one hand, the dominant or hegemonic cultural production paid for out of capitalist *revenue* and, on the other, a subordinate working class or oppositional culture paid for out of wages. Cultural production in this sense and its articulations with the sphere of material production involves one specific interpretation of the meaning in The German Ideology of 'control of the means of mental production', i.e. through the direct payment of ideologists and the necessary maintenance of the physical instruments of their ideological production. It is within that analytical perspective that we need to analyse the historical development of the 'historically specific needs' of the working class and their sustenance of 'organic intellectuals' and of specific instruments of cultural production such as trade-unions.

(b) Culture as part of material production itself, directly subordinate to or at least in a closely determined articulation with the laws of development of capital. This is both a latter historical phase, part of developing monopoly capitalism, the phenomenon dubbed 'the industrialization of culture', but it also lives alongside the other moment and in specific instances we need to analyse the interrelationship between these two distinct modes of intellectual production within intellectual production (Culture in its narrow sense) in general.

What, in general, has been lost in Marxist studies of the mass media is the precise historical elaboration of what Marx and Engels meant in The German Ideology by 'control of the means of mental production'.

In general it is clear, I think, in The German Ideology that, reflecting the contemporary stage of capitalist development, Marx and Engels were concerned with the payment of ideologists, of intellectuals, out of capitalist revenue. It is this perspective that Raymond Williams picks up in the passage already cited. That is to say they rightly saw that superstructural activities require a cohort of mental workers who were not directly economically or materially productive and thus whose price of reproduction must be borne by the sphere of material production. Since under capitalism it was capitalists who were extracting this surplus, it was they who could redistribute this surplus into superstructural activities of their choosing and by so doing exert direct economic pressures on the ideologists who were their hired servants.

> The creation of surplus labour on the one side corresponds to the creation of minus labour, relative idleness (or non-productive labour at best) on the other. This goes without saying as regards capital itself; but holds then also for the classes with which it shares; hence of paupers, flunkeys, lick-spittles, etc. living from the surplus product, in short, the whole train of retainers; the part of the *servant* class which lives not from capital but from revenue. (Marx, 1973: 401)

This direct relationship remains important and should not be forgotten. That is to say the working class also developed, out of its wages, a subordinate or counter culture with its own 'organic intellectuals' such as paid trade-union officials, co-operative organizers, journalists, etc., but the surplus available for this purpose was exiguous both really and comparatively, so that this direct ideological power was decisively weighted in favour of capital and remains so. Compare a small organization like Counter Information Services with the public relations and research investment of a major company. Look at the way in which large companies manipulate the legal system by their ability to sustain expensive, long drawn out actions (e.g. the Thalidomide case). Look at the way media research itself has been and is significantly influenced by the flow of funds from vested commercial interests.

There now exists of course, as the division of labour has developed further, a more mediated version of this employment of ideologists out of revenue, namely, as Bourdieu has analysed, the creation of a subordinate fraction of the capitalist class who possess cultural capital (Bourdieu and Passeron, 1977). Just as younger sons of the aristocracy went into Church and army, so now a section of the capitalist class occupies key positions in the cultural sector. The class origins of ideological workers remains an important but neglected aspect of media analysis. This does not of course mean that such people necessarily reproduce ruling class ideology (see Engels and William Morris for obvious counter-examples). It does mean that there is a structural tendency so to do.

Neglect of this aspect of direct economic control of ideologists is reflected in current discussion of the ideological role of the media where there is much sophisticated discussion of professionalization, of heirarchies of discourse, of hegemonic and subordinate codes, etc. discussions which often serve to mask a reality which is ever present to those actually working in the media, namely the possibility of losing one's job. This economic reality is of course often internalized by both employee and employer in the form of the ideologies of professionalism or managerialism but it remains nonetheless potent for that, indeed is the underpinning which professionalism requires. Once again, this was a fact that Adorno and Horkheimer did not make the mistake of forgetting:

> Under the private culture monopoly it is a fact that 'tyranny leaves the body free and directs its attack at the soul'. The ruler no longer says, 'You must think as I do, or die'. He says, 'You are free not to think as I do, your life, your property, everything shall remain yours, but from this day on you are a stranger among us'. Not to conform means to be rendered powerless, economically and therefore, spiritually – to be 'self-employed'. When the outsider is excluded from the concern, he can only too easily be accused of incompetence. Whereas today in material production the mechanism of supply and demand is disintegrating in the superstructure it still operates as a check in the ruler's favour.[6]

The second moment, upon which of course increasingly in the actual historical development the former moment has come to depend, is the actual control by capital within the process of commodity production of the means of cultural production. This moment was clearly under-developed at the time when The German Ideology was written but, while not entirely superceding the other moment as I have indicated, it is this moment that has become crucial for an analysis of cultural reproduction under monopoly capitalism.[7] Within the sphere of cultural production the development of specifically economic, industrial forms was in part possible precisely because of the effect of the other moment, i.e. working class powers of cultural resistance were weakened. A good example of this is R. Williams' suggestion that the popular success of ITV and of the general invasion of American commercialized cultural forms was a reaction on the part of the working class to the liberating overthrow of a particular hegemonic cultural formation represented by the BBC. It is in particular on the implications of this second moment that I wish to concentrate, i.e. the effects of the imposition of capital logic upon cultural production.

As I have indicated there has been a tendency to see such an imposition as ideologically non-contradictory. One must stress at the outset that this is not so. Because capital controls the means of cultural production in the sense that the production and exchange of cultural commodities become the dominant forms of cultural relationship, it does not follow that these cultural commodities will necessarily support, either in their explicit content or in their mode of cultural appropriation, the dominant ideology. Indeed as Terry Lovell has recently stressed and as, once again, Adorno and Horkheimer made clear, the cultural commodity possesses an inherent contradiction, a contradiction which, as with the other contradictions within the capitalist mode of production, may be profoundly subversive.[8] Whether it is or not depends upon a concrete analysis of a specific conjuncture. Before turning to the general implications of the proposition that one definition of the control of the means of mental production is the take-over of large areas of cultural production and reproduction by capitalist commodity production, what the proposition leads one to question is that stress on intentionality which we find in theories such as that of Milliband. It is quite clear in Marx's analysis of *Capital* that he wished to distinguish firmly between the logic of capital and the intention of individual capitalists, even at the economic, let alone the ideological, level:

> The fact that baking, shoemaking, etc. are only just being put on a capitalist basis in England is entirely due to the circumstances that English capital cherished feudal preconceptions of 'respectability'. It was 'respectable' to sell Negroes into slavery, but it was not respectable to make sausages, shoes or bread.   (Marx, 1976: 1014, footnote)

It is perhaps worth noting in passing that this characteristic of British capital still operates with respect to the media, which still carry a certain bohemian, mountebank and marginal reputation. Hence the characteristics of the particular capitals who started ITV for instance or who developed the British film industry in the 1930s or the role of colonial capital via Beaverbrook and Murdoch in the British Press. Such attitudes still affect the Tory party in its ambivalent relation to commercial broadcasting.

> The function fulfilled by the capitalist is no more than the function of capital – viz. the valorization of value by absorbing living labour – executed *consciously* and *willingly*. The capitalist functions only as personified capital, capital as a person, just as the worker is no more than *labour* personified.   (Marx, 1976: 989)

What this quotation points to is the importance of not viewing capitalists, for analytical purposes, as unified subjects. That is to say a given person or group can only be described as capitalist in those moments when s/he or they are acting in conscious and willed accord with the logic of capital accumulation. Thus there may well be many such conscious, willed actions, never mind unconscious actions, that are contradictory to the logic of capital, of course always within determinate limits. There may be therefore a clear divergence between the functions of capital within the material process of mental production and the conscious, willed intentions of the capitalist or of their ideologues. We cannot predict *a priori* which at any time will be predominant, e.g. how long a Harmsworth, a Beaverbrook or a Thomson will keep a loss-making newspaper going for reasons of social prestige or political power, although clearly the outer limits of such possibilities of deviation by the individual capitalist will be determined by the norms of capital's logic.

There is then, and this cannot be sufficiently stressed, no necessary coincidence between the effects of the capitalist process proper and the ideological needs of the dominant class. On the contrary the entire thesis of capital points to the opposite conclusion.

This, for instance, affects assumptions concerning the relationship between capital and the State. To take one example, the proportion of the budget of the COI that has to be devoted to paid access to the media, i.e. the use of paid advertising for Government propaganda or information, has risen in the last decade from 20 per cent to 50 per cent. Such evidence can be interpreted in two ways. Either there is an observable conflict between the ideological needs of the State and the accumulation process within the media sector (leaving aside the question of whether the State is in fact the representative of capital or of the dominant class and therefore whether such a conflict would represent a contradiction between the economic and ideological needs of that class in general or whether it represents a contradiction between the ideological needs of capital in general versus the economic needs of a class fraction who control the media sector). Alternatively, this evidence can be interpreted to show the increasing sway of capitalist logic over the political and ideological level, i.e. forcing it to work increasingly through direct exchange relations within the economic.

This question of intentionality within ideological production is, of course, central to the media debate, within both the bourgeois and Marxist problematic. That is to say one argument runs, for instance the Frankfurt School tradition, that the mass media are important because monopoly capitalism has moved from direct coercion of the working class, for instance within the labour process, to ideological coercion as its preferred method of domination and the mass-media or ISA's are crucial in this process.

But do we in fact require this shift onto the terrain of ideology in order to explain the absence of direct coercion. Marx himself on the contrary saw the avoidance of such coercion as central to the economic mechanism of capitalism. That is to say the abstraction of exchange value, the wage-form, etc. were in themselves quite powerful enough to explain the dominance of capital and indeed that this non-coercive dominance was both historically necessary and progressive. Bourdieu has developed this general proposition.[9]

Thus at the level of material production, of the life process in the realm of the social – for that is what the process of production is – we find the *same* situation that we find in *religion* at the ideological level, namely the inversion of subject into object and vice-versa. Viewed *historically* this inversion is the indispensable transition without which wealth as such, i.e. the relentless productive forces of social labour, which alone can form the material base of a free human society, could not possibly be created by force at the expense of the majority.   (Marx, 1976: 990)

Mental Production and Capitalist Commodity Production

Let us now turn back to look at mental production, of which the mass media are an example, as processes of capitalist production and at the implications for our modes of social communication of the subsumption by capital of the real forms of ideological production.

This needs to be looked at historically, i.e. unlike the capital logic or capital derivation school we must not see capitalism as a mode of production which arrives *sui generis* and then sprouts a social formation like dragon's teeth. It is rather a specific form which grew within a pre-existing social formation and is involved in a process of expansion and conquest of non-capitalist sectors, a process which is incomplete and contradictory. This process of expansion involves both the subsumption of other areas of material production and pre-capitalist forms of economic organisation and also of non-economic activity under the sway of the economic in its capitalist form.

When examining mass communication within predominantly capitalist social formations we must not make the mistake of assuming that they are therefore necessarily capitalist, i.e. we cannot make the easy elision Miliband makes between those sectors controlled by private capital and those controlled by the State. Nor can we assume that all non-State sectors are in fact capitalist. Indeed the relationship between pre-capitalist and capitalist forms within the media sector is a significant feature both economically and ideologically, i.e. the relationship between notions of creative freedom, freedom of the Press, the Fourth Channel debate, community communication, etc. This relationship significantly determines the forms of the struggle within the media over the labour process.

Thus artisanal modes of labour organization ranging from individual craft production, i.e. the authorship of a book, to the small group, i.e. the independent film company or record producer, remain common and important within the cultural sphere. Such residues have been the focus for struggle against the logic of capital and have produced a powerful anti-economic cultural ideology (see the whole culture/society tradition). Nonetheless in certain instances such artisanal organization may be functional for capital so long as capital controls the means of mass reproduction of the authorial product and of the means of mass distribution, because it ensures the necessary production of a range of heterogeneous cultural artefacts from which capital can choose for further exploitation without capital having to bear the risks and overheads for this production which are born directly by labour. Indeed, the ideology of creative freedom can be used by capital to keep their labour force divided and weak and with no control over the strategic moments of the total labour process.

Thus, for instance, while the Open Broadcasting Authority will be fought for by cultural workers under the banner of creative freedom and against the apparent interests of capital in the form of ITV, such a structure of small-scale freelance production, if it were to be realized, would be more functional for capital in general than an extension of the present structure, because it would open British broadcasting more fully both to advertising and to the pressures of the international market.[10]

Nor must we make the mistake of assuming an easy equation between private ownership and capitalism.

> Where capital still appears only in its elementary forms such as commodities . . . or money, the capitalist manifests himself in the already familiar character of the owner of money or commodities. But such a person is no more a capitalist in himself than money or commodities are capital in themselves. They become translated into capital only in certain specific circumstances and their owners likewise become capitalist only when these circumstances obtain. (Marx, 1976: 976)

What then are these circumstances? The central characteristic of capital is growth or accumulation.

> In itself the sum of money may only be defined as capital if it is employed, spent, with the aim of increasing it, if it is spent expressly in order to increase it. In the case of the sum of value or money this phenomenon is its destiny, its inner law, its tendency, while to the capitalist, i.e. the owner of the sum of money, in whose hands it shall acquire its function, it appears as intention, purpose. (Marx, 1976: 976)

Thus to examine the specifically capitalist mode of media production we need to see the ways in which capital uses the real process of media production in order to increase its value, in order to grow, and the barriers which are placed in the way of this process either by the inherent contradictions of the process itself or by external forces.

At a minimum in order to accumulate capital must bring living labour into the production process by exchanging in the sphere of circulation through the wage bargain. It must combine this living labour in a determinate manner with objectified labour as means of production (raw materials and instruments) in the production of a commodity in the exchange of which surplus value will be realized.

In a fully constituted capitalist mode based upon relative surplus value and competition between capitals this process of growth requires ever increased productivity and ever widening markets.

Historically the sphere of mental production or non-material production presented and continues to present important barriers to this process and the forms and dynamics of the mass media can in part be understood as resulting from a continuous attempt to surmount those barriers and from the concretely various successes and failures of this attempt.

We thus start from the historical materialist assumption that the development of capitalism or the capitalist mode of production is:

(a)   a contradictory process;
(b)   not yet complete.

The contradictory nature of the process is in part intrinsic, i.e. the conflict between capital and labour, the conflict between capital accumulation and the socialization of the forces and relations of production, the conflict between the drive to accumulate through the extraction of relative surplus value and labour power as the creator of surplus value, a contradiction expressed in the tendency of the rate of profit to fall.

In part the contradictions are extrinsic, that is to say related precisely to the relationship between developing capitalism and the non-capitalist areas of the social formation. The necessary expansion of the valorization process is not a process of automatic expansion; it comes up against social and political barriers; it needs to conquer physical barriers, e.g. communication and transport; it requires the necessary accumulation of capital, etc.

We see these contradictions in the field of mass-media:

(a)   in resistances both actual and ideological to the industrialization of the artisanal modes of cultural production;
(b)   in the conflicts between national and international capitals, sometimes mediated through the State and sometimes direct, e.g. the split in the Tory party over the original introduction of commercial broadcasting – or the developing struggle over national versus supra-national control of European satellite broadcasting – or the existence of quotas on the importation of foreign film and TV material;
(c)   growing Third World demand for a New World Information Order.

The problem with cultural and informational goods is that, because their use value is almost limitless, i.e. cannot be destroyed or consumed by use, it is extremely difficult to attach an exchange value to them. They are in fact, in general, classic public goods. What we are considering is what Marx called 'non-material production'. Marx discusses such production in the context of a discussion of the distinction between productive and non-productive labour (whether such a distinction can be maintained and, if so, its analytical significance, is a matter of general importance within the field of the political economy of culture which we cannot pursue further here). In brief, Marx clearly foresaw difficulties in subsuming non-material production under capitalism. He identified two possible forms of such production:

> (1) It results in commodities which exist separately from the producer, i.e. they can circulate in the interval between production and consumption as commodities, e.g. books, paintings and all products of art as distinct from the artistic achievement of the practising artist. Here capitalist production is possible only within very narrow limits. Apart from such cases as, say, sculptors who employ assistants, these people (where they are not independent) mainly work for merchants capital, e.g. booksellers, a pattern that is only transitional in itself and can only lead to a capitalist mode of production in the formal sense. Nor is the position altered by the fact that exploitation is at its greatest precisely in these transitional forms.

(2) The product is not separable from the act of producing. Here too the capitalist mode of production occurs only on a limited scale and in the nature of the case it can only operate in certain areas (I want the doctor not his errand boy). For example, in teaching institutions the teacher can be no more than wage-labour for the entrepreneur of the learning factory. Such peripheral phenomena can be ignored when considering capitalist production as a whole.   (Marx, 1976: 1047–1048)

This passage would be worth lengthy analysis. At this stage I would only like to point to the following.

(a)   The relevance of example (1) for the debate between Marcuse and Benjamin concerning the role of the aura of a work of art and the effect on that aura of the attempt to subject culture production to at least the forces of capitalist production.[11]
(b)   The need to look, with reference to the observation concerning the degree of exploitation in this field, at the evidence of the persistent low pay of cultural workers and the extent to which even the most advanced sectors of capitalist cultural production depend upon drawing relative surplus value from sectors which still operate a pre-capitalist artisanal mode of economic organization.[12]
(c)   The above relates to the need to examine the relationship between Marx's belief that capitalist production of cultural goods was possible only within very narrow limits, the phenomenon of Baumol's disease (Baumol and Bouran, 1976) and the ever increasing pressure on the State to intervene in the cultural sector.
(d)   Similar considerations are raised by Marx's second example where the product is not separable from the act of producing, thus raising strict limits to productivity and thus raising relative costs.

The economic contradictions that arise from the nature of cultural commodities takes different forms within different sectors of the media and at different historical moments.

Five main ways have been adopted in an attempt to circumvent the problem.

(a)   Copyright. This is in effect an attempt to commoditize information via the uniqueness of authorship or by turning the author into a commodity. But this only works if you either then make the commodity scarce, i.e. stress its uniqueness. We see this in the economics of the art market. Or if you control supply, i.e. control access to the means of reproduction such as printing presses and film laboratories. However, if such control is used to over-price it will encourage the development of pirating alternatives. This is now a major problem internationally for the cultural industries in records, books, films and even TV programmes.
(b)   Control of access to consumption through a box-office mechanism at the point of sale and/or through economic control of the channels of distribution, i.e. newspapers and cinema. The problem here is that such control is resistant to economies of scale and as the theatre found when faced by the cinema and the cinema when faced by broadcasting, is highly susceptible to competition from

more efficient technologies of reproduction and distribution. However, as broadcasting demonstrates, the massive economies of scale produced by these more efficient means of distribution by destroying the box office, i.e. by making access open, create major problems of creating the necessary moment of exchange.

(c) Built-in obsolescence through the manipulation of time. This was the great achievement of the newspaper which, by creating rapidly decaying information, created thereby a constant need to re-consume. But this manipulation of time has its limits since consumption time is physically limited. (The central import-ance of time within the economics of the mass-media is a subject to which I intend to give substantive treatment in a subsequent article.)

(d) The creation, packaging and sale, not of cultural and informational goods to direct consumers, but of audiences to advertisers (Smythe, 1977).

(e) State patronage. The inherent tendency towards the socialization of cultural and informational goods has always given the State an important role in this field from the days of direct patronage of cultural workers by King, Aristocracy and Church via the early subsidy of newspapers by governments and political parties, through public libraries and public education, to the key contemporary example of broadcasting.

In brief therefore, the specific nature of the commodity form within cultural produc-tion leads to a constant problem of realization and thus to a two-way pressure either towards advertising finance or towards State finance. We find these pressures quite clearly at the moment in the growing controversy over sponsorship in sport and the arts.[13]

The questions these pressures raise is in what ways (a) advertising and (b) State intervention in this sphere is functional or dysfunctional for capitalism in general on the one hand and on the other the effect of such pressures upon cultural production itself.

The Modes of Extraction and Distribution of the Cultural Surplus

Since all cultural forms are material in the sense that they take time which will only be available after the needs of physical reproduction are satisfied, the material require-ments of the cultural process must be extracted as surplus from direct material production. As we have seen this can be done by paying for cultural production directly out of revenue. But as Marx remarked of capitalism in general, it has found it more efficient as a means of control to extract surpluses directly by means of economic processes. Thus the developments of the capitalist mode of production and its associated division of mental and manual labour have led to the development of the extraction of the necessary surplus for the maintenance of cultural production and reproduction directly via the commodity and exchange form. But this process will only take place to the extent that:

(a)   there is surplus capital searching for opportunities for valorization;
(b)   the anticipated rate of profit in the chosen sphere of cultural production is at least as high as that available elsewhere.

Where these conditions do not exist cultural processes will have to continue to be undertaken by the direct transfer of resources, i.e. by the expenditure of surplus. This may take place under the following conditions.

(a)   By capitalists as individuals or groups funding such activities, e.g. the classic model of arts patronage. Such a form may be sustained within the contemporary capitalist social formation by means of tax concessions. It may be channelled through charitable foundations, etc.

Such funding leads to direct ideological control, legitimated as the cultural extension of private property, namely personal taste. This sphere can give rise to significant political battles, e.g. the wealth tax/national heritage debate.

But examples within the media field are the direct subsidy of newspapers by political parties or by politically ambitious individuals, e.g. Beaverbrook, Goldsmith and possibly now Broakes and Matthews, the new owners of the *Express* Group and Morgan-Grampian.

(b)   Via the State. Here electronic communication is the key case. The exact mix in the field of both telephonic and broadcast communication between the State and capital needs examination state by state. As any superficial examination will show, key differences between Western Europe and the United States give the lie to any simple capital logic explanation of how the particular economic and institutional forms, within which electronic communication has developed, have arisen.

The explanation of such differences and the present conjunctural relations between national capitals and the State, between states and between international capital and states in this area would have to take account of the following.

(1)   The structures of national capitals.
(2)   The existing State structure, i.e. federal structure of US and Germany as opposed to centralized structure of Britain and even more, France.
(3)   The strategic requirements of the State, e.g. the State-inspired creation of RCA as the first step in a long history of the US government's explicit geo-political involvement in communication, the clearest case of which is satellites, such a policy requiring intervention to restructure national capitals.
(4)   The balance of forces between sections of capital and the relations of that balance of force to the State's assessment of both economic and strategic requirements, e.g. the foundation of the BBC in which we see an interaction between the needs of the nascent British electronic industry, which the State wished to foster both for strategic and economic reasons, but which was only interested in the sales of hardware and was able to shift the expense and ideological problems of programme production onto the State, because the

State needed also to take account both of the economically and politically powerful British press, which was opposed to competition for advertising and of a culturally conservative and elitist ruling class fraction.[14]

To sum up, historically the development of the material process known as the superstructure depended upon the availability of a surplus in the sphere of direct material production, i.e. the sphere of the extraction, shaping and consumption of nature. Historically the shape of that superstructure is determined by the social relations of production, because it is these social relations that determine the distribution of that surplus. For example, Athenian democracy as a form of political practice depends directly materially upon the slave economy that supported it by making time available for political activity to a non-productive class. Such directly material considerations remain important, i.e. in a planned economy like the Soviet Union direct choices have to be made between for instance producing more shoes or the paper for more newspapers. Such considerations may be acute in the planning of media systems in Third World countries and indeed it is the influencing of such decisions in the interest not of the indigenous economy or social formation but of a foreign high surplus economy that is one of the matters at issue in the media imperialism debate. It is a less obvious form of the starvation caused in some countries by the development of industrialized agriculture serving a world market. Under developing capitalism the means of cultural production may be provided either in commodity form as part of the accumulation process, e.g. records or as part of the realization process of other sectors of the capitalist economy, e.g. advertising or directly out of capitalist revenue, e.g. arts patronage or the Thompson family and *The Times* or through the State.

Each of the above means of surplus distribution to the cultural sphere will differentially affect the ways in which the dominant class controls the means of cultural production. Different contradictions will come into play, contradictions which need to be specifically analysed in each conjunctural case. Not only are these contradictions intrinsic to each subsidiary mode of cultural production but there are also contradictions which arise because of conflicts between them, e.g. between broadcasting whether state or private and the press, a conflict in its turn differentially mediated through competition for readers/viewers and through competition for advertising.

The Industrialization of Culture

While drawing different conclusions as to the significance of the phenomenon both bourgeois and Marxist economists agree that the current phase of capitalist development is characterized by the following.

(a)   Unprecedented capital concentration in all the key traditional manufacturing sectors accompanied in general by a rising surplus.

(b)   A resulting problem of valorization which drives surplus capital in search of other areas of investment.

(c)   An associated development of the so-called service sector characterized by the industrialization of sectors which were either more primitively organized or, as in the sphere of domestic labour, altogether outside the market.

These tendencies are now rapidly affecting the whole cultural, mass-media sector. This has been extensively documented by A. Mattelart in his recent 'Multi-nationales et systeme de communication' and, for France, by A. Huet *et al.* in their 'Capitalisme et industries culturelles'. So all I wish to do here, is point out certain key aspects and examples of this tendency.

This absorption of the sphere of reproduction into full-scale commodity production is characterized by the following.

(a)   Increased international competition and the resulting take-over of domestic, national publishing companies, advertising agencies, private broadcasting stations etc. by multinational companies. See, for instance, the example of Philips given at the start of this piece. This competition also leads to increasing penetration by international media products, particularly Anglo-Saxon.[15]

(b)   A sharpening struggle within cultural production over the labour process in an attempt by capital to increase productivity in a sector which is notoriously resistant to such increases. This struggle has been most marked recently in the newspaper industry with the present dispute at Times Newspapers being the most notorious and current example in Britain.

(c)   Increasingly persistent attempts to open up new markets in order to absorb excess capital. The most obvious example of this is the increasing pressure throughout Western Europe to privatize public broadcasting. See, for instance, the case of Italy, but the current crisis in the financing of the BBC and Annan's proposals for an advertising financed O.B.A. must be seen in this light.

(d)   Attempts to open up new markets for both cultural hard-ware and soft-ware by introducing new communication technologies, such as cable TV, satellites, Teletext, etc. Because of the huge infrastructural investments involved and the comparatively low rate of return on such investments these moves involve close alliances between capital and the State in an attempt to get the tax-payer to carry the cost of the distribution system, while private capital takes the profits from the sale of hardware and from the subsequent development of a consumer durable market in such items as teletext decoders and of a software market, e.g. Pay TV. The full development of this push into new technologies has undoubtedly been slowed down significantly by the current recession in the Western economies, but the long-term implications for national cultures, for class cultures and for freedom of expression of all these trends, not only in the Third World where the problem is dramatized as media imperialism, but in the capitalist heartlands, are profoundly significant.

Thus I return to where I started by reiterating that the development of political economy in the cultural sphere is not a mere matter of theoretical interest but of urgent practical political priority. So long as Marxist analysis concentrates on the ideological content of the mass media it will be difficult to develop coherent political strategies for resisting the underlying dynamics of development in the cultural sphere in general which rest firmly and increasingly upon the logic of generalized commodity production. In order to understand the structure of our culture, its production, consumption and reproduction and of the role of the mass media in that process, we increasingly need to confront some of the central questions of political economy in general, the problem of productive and non-productive labour, the relation between the private and public sectors and the role of the State in capitalist accumulation, the role of advertising within late capitalism, etc.

As long ago as 1960, Asa Briggs wrote in his Fisher Memorial Lecture:

> The provision of entertainment has never been a subject of great interest either to economists or to economic historians – at least in their working hours. Yet in 20th century conditions it is proper to talk of a highly organized entertainment industry, to distinguish within it between production and distribution, to examine forces making for competition, integration, concentration and control and to relate such study to the statistics of national income and output, the development of advertising, international economic relations and – not least – to the central economic concept of the market which, in the 20th century, is as much concerned with leisure as it is with work.   (Briggs, 1960)

Nearly two decades later that research gap remains and there has been little coherent effort to understand the process known as 'the industrialization of culture', a process by which, as Briggs put it, 'Massive market interests have come to dominate an area of life which, until recently, was dominated by individuals themselves' (Briggs, 1960).

Notes

1 See Marx, 'Notes on Adolph Wagner' in Marx (1975). Quoted in Corrigan and Singer (1978). Here Corrigan and Singer present an extended version of this methodological argument. See also Sayer (forthcoming).

2 We intend to publish a detailed critique of this position in a forthcoming issue. In the meantime, see Thompson (1978), Williams (1977) and Corrigan and Singer (1978). [Editorial note to original.]

3 See Smythe (1977), Murdoch (1978), Smythe (1978) and Levant (1978).

4 See J. Curran, 'Capitalism and Control of the Press 1800–1979', in Curran et al. (1977).

5 For a detailed discussion of this problem see Baudrillard (1972, 1975).

6 Adorno and Horkheimer, 'The Dialectic of Enlightenment', in Curran et al. (1977: 133, 358–9).

7 But note Marx's own comments in the Grundrisse, p. 532: 'The highest development of capital exists when the general conditions of the process of social production are not paid out of *deduction from the social revenue*, the state's taxes – where revenue and not capital appears as the labour fund, and where the worker, although he is a free wage worker like any other, nevertheless stands economically in a different relation – but rather out of *capital as capital*. This shows the degree to which capital has subjugated all conditions of social production to itself, on the one side; and, on the other side, hence, the extent to which

social reproduction wealth has been *capitalised* and all needs are satisfied through the exchange form' (Marx's italics).

8   See T. Lovell (1979) and Adorno and Horkheimer: 'Nevertheless the culture industry remains the entertainment business. Its influence over the consumer is established by entertainment; that will ultimately be broken not by an outright decree, but by the hostility inherent in the principle of entertainment to what is greater than itself' (in Curran *et al.*, 1977: 361).

9   See Bourdieu (1971: 183–197): 'It is in the degree of objectification of the accumulated social capital that one finds the basis of all pertinent differences between the modes of domination ... Objectification guarantees the permanence and cumulativity of material and symbolic acquisition which can thus subsist without agents having to recreate them continously and in their entirety by deliberate action; but, because the profits of their institutions are the object of differential appropriation, objectification also and inseparably ensures the reproduction of the structure of distribution of the capital which, in its various forms, is the precondition for such appropriation, and in so doing, reproduces the structure of the relation of dominance and dependence' (p. 184).

10   For a fuller elaboration of the modes of labour organization within capitalist cultural industries, see Huet *et al.* (1978).

11   See Benjamin (1977) for the positive view and Marcuse (1972) for the negative view.

12   See Huet *et al.* (1978) for theoretical elaboration and Krust (1977) for data. See also discussion in Owen, Beebe and Manning (1974), which shows, from a neo-classical perspective that the so-called economic efficiency of US TV depends upon high un-employment in Hollywood.

13   See, for instance, P. Harland (1978) and recent correspondence in *The Times* concerning the Arts Council's expression of disapproval of its grant recipients giving too large a billing to commercial sponsors at the expense of itself.

14   For a discussion of the relationship between the French State and private capital in the development of the electronic audio-visual field in general, see Flichy (1978) and Huet *et al.* (1978).

15   It should be noted that from this point of view the UK is in a privileged position since it is second only to the USA as a media exporter.

References

Adorno, T. and Horkheimer, M. (1977). The culture industry (abridged), in J. Curran *et al.*, (eds), *Mass Communication and Society*, Edward Arnold, London.

Althusser, L. (1969). *Contradiction and Over-determination*, Allen Lane, London.

Baudrillard, J. (1972). *Pour une Critique de l'Economic Politique du Signe*, Gallimard, Paris.

Baudrillard, J. (1975). *The Mirror of Production*, Tela Press, St. Louis.

Baumol, W. J. and Bouran, W. G. (1976). On the performing arts: the anatomy of their economic problems, in M. Blang, (ed.), *The Economics of the Arts*, Martin Robertson, London.

Benjamin, W. (1977). The work of art in the age of mechanical reproduction, in Curran *et al.*, op. cit.

Bottomore, T. and Rubel, M. (1963). Theories of surplus value, in *K. Marx on Sociology and Social Philosophy*, pp. 96, 97, Pelican.

Bourdieu, P. (1971). *Outline of a Theory of Practice*, CUP.

Bourdieu, P. and Passeron, J. L. (1977). *Reproduction*, Sage, London.

Briggs, A. (1960). Fisher Memorial Lecture, University of Adelaide.

Clarke, S. (1977). Marxism, sociology and Poulantzas's theory of the state, *Capital and Class*, no. 2, Summer.

Corrigan, P. and Singer, D. (1978). Hindess and Hirst: a critical review, *Socialist Register*, Merlin, London.

Curran, J. *et al.*, (eds) (1977). *Mass-Communication and Society*, Edward Arnold, London.

Financial Times (1978). Electronic Rentals ups its ratings, 19 December.

Flichy, P. (1978). *Contribution à une Étude du Industries de l'Audiovisual*, Institut National de l'Audiovisual.

Harland, P. (1978). Enter the money men, stage right, *Sunday Times*, 11 June.

Huet, A. *et al.* (1978). *Capitalisme et Industries Culturelles*, University of Grenoble Press.

Krust, M. (1977). *Droit au Travail et Problems d'Emploi du Travailleur Culturels du Spectacle et de l'Interpretation Musicale dans la Communante Economique Europeenne*, CCE.

Levant, P. (1978). The audience commodity: on the blindspot debate, *Canadian Journal of Political and Social Theory*.

Lovell, T. (1979). *Realism, Ideology and Film*, British Film Institute, London (forthcoming).

Mandel, E. (1975). *Late Capitalism*, ch. 1, NLB, London.

Marcuse, H. (1972). Art as a form of reality, *New Left Review* 74.

Marx, K. (1859). Preface to a contribution to a critique of political economy, in Marx, K. and Engels, F., (eds), *Selected Works*, vol. 1, p. 364, Lawrence and Wishart, London (1962).

Marx, K. (1973). *Grundrisse*, Pelican, London.

Marx, K. (1975). Notes on Adolph Wagner, in T. Carver, (ed.), *Texts on Method*, p. 201, Blackwell, Oxford.

Marx, K. (1976). Results of the immediate process of production, in *Capital*, vol. 1, Pelican.

Milliband, R. R. (1977). *Marxism and Politics*, p. 50, OUP.

Murdoch, G. (1978). Blindspots about Western Marxism: a reply to Dallas Smythe, *Canadian Journal of Political and Social Theory*, vol. 2, no. 2.

Murdoch, G. and Golding, P. (1979). Ideology and the mass media: the question of determination, in M. Barrett *et al.* (eds) *Ideology and Cultural Production*, Croom-Helm, London.

Owen, B., Beebe, J. and Manning, W. (1974). *TV Economics*, D. C. Heath, London.

Sayer, D. (1979). *Marx's Method*, Harvester Press, forthcoming.

Smythe, D. (1977). Communication: blindspot of Western Marxism, *Canadian Journal of Political and Social Theory*, vol. 1, no. 3.

Smythe, D. (1978). Rejoinder to Graham Murdoch, *Canadian Journal of Political and Social Theory*, vol. 2, no. 2.

Thompson, E. P. (1978). *The Poverty of Theory*, Merlin, London.

Williams, R. (1977). *Marxism and Literature*, OUP, London.

15

On the Audience Commodity and its Work*

Dallas W. Smythe

> Obviously communications and their equipment, and labor and its equipment are inseparable except in the mind. Both complexes are useful and marketable, therefore commodities, whatever the theoretical assumptions may be.
>
> (M. M. Knight, letter to author, 23 January 1978)

To suggest that the mass media audience is a commodity and that audiences "work" is to raise many questions which unsettle established ways of thinking. As most audience "work" centers in the home, all the other functions of the family become involved in considering the implications of the proposition. Marital relations, child care and development, leisure time activities, consumer expenditure, decision making – all these functions are somehow involved with audience work. Beyond these, for possible consideration, are the relations of family life and of audience work to alcoholism, drug and tranquilizer addiction, crime and violence – all of which in one way or another focus on the family. In raising these issues in the context of the North American capitalist core, I cannot answer many of the significant questions which are generated. Indeed, so complex and unanalyzed are the issues I shall be discussing that it may be as much as can be done on this occasion to try to pose the "right" questions. Traditional behavioral research (and its popular handmaiden, market research) is simply tangential, self-interested, and irrelevant to the complex dialectical processes of contradictions which are working before our eyes. In order to analyze our largely commoditized society, we must beware thinking of people and commodities as disconnected things and see them as relationships in a social process.

What is the principal product of the mass media? To answer this central question one needs tools – theories. There may be two modes of theory: subjective, idealist concepts, or objective and realistic concepts. Until now, all theory relevant to our

* From Dallas W. Smythe, *Dependency Road: Communications, Capitalism, Consciousness and Canada* (Norwood, N.J.: Ablex, 1981), 22–51.

principal question has been subjective and idealist. My argument is that this is so and that an objective and realistic theory is needed. Before entering into explanation of such a realistic theory, it is necessary to state why theory concerning the mass media and their principal product has been subjective and idealist. It is easy to see why conventional, bourgeois theory about communication is idealist. The entire literature – bourgeois and Marxist alike – about mass communications has defined the principal product of the mass media as "messages," "information," "images," "meaning," "entertainment," "education," "orientation," "manipulation," etc. *All* these concepts are subjective mental entities; all deal with superficial appearances, divorced from real life processes. The concepts of entertainment, education, orientation, and manipulation do not even refer to any aspects of mass media content but to its *effects, or purpose.*

Of course, this is not to say that abstract, subjective processes are not real. Much of the work that audience power does for advertisers takes place in the heads of audience members. My argument, however, is that there is a material base of work which people must do under monopoly capitalism. Food, clothing, etc., must be bought, and it is this aspect of audience work which "pays off" for the advertiser. At the same time, with inadequate income to meet the demands on the family budget, sacrifices must be made in order that the values of family life may be achieved. Parents postpone some expenditures on their own needs in order that the children or grandma may receive dental care. There is a dialectical tension between the work for advertisers and the effort necessary to put into practice the values which people believe are necessary to make a home, a community, and a nation of which they can be proud. Practical consciousness (awareness of what it means to live – to put it briefly) is objectively and realistically powerfully affected by the outcome of this dialectical contradictory process. (See chapter 11 [Smythe, 1981].)

Naturally, the general literature about economics has, for the past century, had opportunity to recognize and analyze the significance of the mass media, advertising, audiences, and Consciousness Industry. None of it deals with the role of the markets for audiences, produced by the mass media, bought and used by advertisers. It is not surprising that this is true of neoclassical marginal utility economists whose interest concerns imaginary competitive models which correspond to nothing significant in the real world of oligopolistic reality. Those in the Keynesian tradition do notice advertising but only in subjective psychological terms as aimed at "control of the buyer's consciousness" (Chamberlin, 1931, pp. 113–34). But having noticed it they then disregard it. Some bourgeois economists, increasingly since the 1960s, have shown interest in developing theories of taste and buying behavior, joining in management's interest in market research or in efforts to enforce antimonopoly laws. Without exception, they ignore the role of demand management by monopoly capitalism and the role of the mass media in producing the marketing agent (the audience) for it. Instead they treat advertising expenditures in relation to firm profitability in purely statistical terms as if nothing real was being purchased or used.[1] Among institutional economists, J. K. Galbraith alone has pursued the matter of demand management by giant corporations by means of advertising but stops short at the brink of discovering the audience market:

The present disposition of conventional economic theory to write off annual outlays of tens of billions of dollars of advertising and similar sales costs by the industrial system as without purpose or consequence is, to say the least, drastic. No other legal economic activity is subject to similar rejection. The discovery that sales and advertising expenditures have an organic role in the system will not, accordingly, seem wholly implausible.   (Galbraith, 1967, p. 205)

Unfortunately he does not explore that "organic role," nor describe and analyze the relation of mass media, audiences, and advertisers to each other (Smythe, 1980).

How does it happen that Marxists have not pursued a materialist, realistic theory of communications? Marxists from Marx down to about 1920, and including Lenin, could hardly be expected to recognize and deal with the demand-management function of advertising and mass communication on behalf of monopoly capitalism because it was hardly evident until after World War I. In the period of newspaper and magazine development before the 1880s, the press was mostly supported by money and influence from political parties – not advertisers. The press which politicians subsidized thus seemed to influence audiences toward the point of view of the subsidizer through the editorial content (everything but the relatively insignificant advertisements). Because the only market substantially involved in the sale of newspapers and magazines was that in which people bought them, it was easy for them to fall into a psychological, subjective answer to the question, what does the press produce. It produced newspapers and magazines and sold them; no organized market for the production and sale of audiences then existed. So for Marxists the press was lumped together with educational and other high culture institutions of the state as part of its "superstructure," while productive *work* took place at the base – the "infrastructure" – where people were paid for working. After 1920, Marxists continued to assume that the principal product of the mass media is influence.

Gramsci, the Frankfurt School (Adorno, Horkheimer, Lowenthal, Marcuse, Habermas), Raymond Williams, Poulantzas, Althusser, and Marxists concerned particularly with the problems of countries peripheral to the capitalist core (e.g., Samir Amin, Clive Y. Thomas) – none addresses the Consciousness Industry from the standpoint of its historical-materialist role in making monopoly capitalism function through demand management (advertising, marketing, and mass media).[2] Baran and Sweezy in *Monopoly Capital* (1966) do indeed emphasize the importance of demand management by monopoly capitalism but they unfortunately stop short of analyzing realistically *how* it takes place, contenting themselves with a manipulative assumption about the mass media and advertising. The same blind spot afflicts communications scholars who take a more or less Marxist view of communications (Nordenstreng, Enzensberger, Hamelink, Schiller, Murdock, Golding, and me until recently). Because they do not take account of how the mass media under monopoly capitalism produce audiences to market commodities, candidates, and issues to themselves, theory and practice regarding the production of ideology continues on a subjective, unrealistic, and essentially ahistorical basis. *Why* they continue to suffer this blind spot it is not my present task to determine.[3]

The answer given in chapter 1 [Smythe, 1981] to the question, what is the principal function which the commercial mass media perform for the capitalist system was essentially to set an agenda for the production of consciousness with two mutually reinforcing objectives: (1) to mass market the mass-produced consumer goods and services generated by monopoly capitalism by using audience power to accomplish this end; (2) to mass market legitimacy of the state and its strategic and tactical policies and actions, such as election of government officers, military thrusts against states which show signs of moving toward socialism (Vietnam, Korea, Cuba, Chile, Dominican Republic, etc.), and policies against youthful dissent ("Middle America"). The answer to the question, what is the principal product of the commercial mass media in monopoly capitalism was simple: audience power. *This* is the concrete product which is used to accomplish the economic and political tasks which are the reason for the existence of the commercial mass media. Let us consider this strange commodity, audience power.

Because audience power is produced, sold, purchased and consumed, it commands a price and is a commodity. Like other "labor power" it involves "work." So at the outset let us consider what we mean by *work*. By common usage under capitalism, *work* may be defined as whatever one does for which one receives pay (wages, salaries, etc.). (Let us defer for the moment the fact that audience members do not get paid for the use of their audience power.) As such it has come to be regarded generally as doing something which you would prefer not to do, something unpleasant, alienating, and frustrating. It also is thought of as something linked with a job, a factory, an office, or a store. It was not always this way. At its base, work is doing something creative, something distinctively human – for the capacity to work is one of the things which distinguishes human beings from other animals. "By changing the world they live in through labor, human beings *at the same time* alter their own nature, for the lives of people *are influenced both by what they* produce and how they produce" (Rinehart, 1975; emphasis added).

It seems that with other animals (e.g., beavers, ants, bees) work skills are programmed through the genes, whereas with human beings, they are learned after birth – i.e., are social products. This fact conceals a secret which explains both the unlimited creativity of which human beings are capable in their work and their alienation in the processes of work under capitalism. The secret is that for human beings, work involves both thinking and the application or testing of ideas in practice. The link between thinking and practice (or theory and practice) – that *thinking may be joined to, or separated from, practice* – is basic to the power struggle between capital and labor. (Parenthetically, it is the grasp of this fact which gives the thought of Mao Zedong and the Chinese people the basis of their amazing accomplishments.) (Mao Zedong, 1968) The revolutionary success of capitalism as a system rests on the division of labor and its command of capital to multiply the "productivity" of work using ever more sophisticated machines, at the human cost of effectively denying the creative process by fragmenting workers' practice and divorcing it from the interaction of thought and practice. This is the practical effect of "scientific management" (see Smythe, 1981).

Let us pose and answer some questions which should serve to identify and describe the audience commodity more precisely:

What do advertisers buy with their advertising expenditures? As hardnosed business-men they are not paying for advertising for nothing, nor from altruism. What they buy are the services of audiences with predictable specifications which will pay atten-tion in predictable numbers and at particular times to particular means of commun-ication (television, radio, newspapers, magazines, billboards, and third-class mail) in particular market areas.[4] As collectivities these audiences are commodities. As com-modities they are dealt with in markets by producers and buyers (the latter being advertisers). Such markets establish prices in the familiar mode of monopoly capital-ism. Both these markets and the audience commodities traded in are specialized. The audience commodities bear specifications known in the business as "the demo-graphics." The specifications for the audience commodities include age, sex, income level, family composition, urban or rural location, ethnic character, ownership of home, automobile, credit card status, social class, and, in the case of hobby and fan magazines, a dedication to photography, model electric trains, sports cars, philately, do-it-yourself crafts, foreign travel, kinky sex, etc.

Are audiences homogeneous? By no means, although all of them have the common features of being produced by mass media and priced and sold in oligopolistic markets to advertisers for whom they perform services which earn their keep, i.e., keep advertisers advertising because the expenditure is productive from the advertisers' standpoint. Audiences produced for sale to advertisers fall into two groups: those produced in connection with marketing consumers' goods and those for producers' goods. The latter are typically produced by trade or business media (magazines, newspapers, or direct mail). The buyers of producers' goods are typically institutions (government, in the case of the "military sales effort," or private corporations) which presumably buy on specifications of objective qualities. Moreover, such advertising is a relatively small part of the total; hence, the following analysis disregards this category of audience. The second and strategically most important class of audiences is produced for advertisers marketing consumers' goods. Again, these audiences fall into two classes: The first of these are for producers of what Julian L. Simon (1970, p. 71) calls *homogenous package goods* (HPG) which have certain common features:

(1) Slight or no objective physical difference between the brands, (2) Low unit cost, (3) Short time period between repeated purchases, (4) Large total dollar volume for each product industry, (5) Except for liquor, heavy use of television as an advertising medium, and (6) Large proportions of sales spent for advertising.

In the HPG category are soft drinks, gum, candy, soaps, cleaners, waxes, etc., tobacco products, beer, wine, liquor, gasoline, patent drugs, perfumes, cosmetics, deodorants, razor blades, etc., as well as fast foods and restaurants. The second subclass of audiences for consumers' goods is that for durable consumer goods. Here are automobiles, snowmobiles, clothes, boats, shoes, hobby equipment (e.g., cameras, sports equipment, household tools), household appliances, etc. Although objective qualitative characteristics are ascertainable, annual style changes dominate them. It is the consumer goods advertisers whose audiences are produced by the mass media to generate the "demand" which can increase GNP.

How are advertisers assured that they are getting what they pay for when they buy audience power? After all, the skeptic asks, how does the advertiser know that I am in his audience? And even if I am in the room when the television set is on, why does he think that I am paying attention to the commercials (I may time my visits to the refrigerator or toilet to coincide with the appearance of the commercials)? The answer is simple. The advertiser is assured that he/she gets the audience power that is paid for in just the same way that an insurance company profits by insuring your life. You may drop dead the day after taking out the policy, or you may pay premiums for 50 years. The insurance company "gambles" on the probability of your living a certain number of years. Probability, working with large numbers, removes the risk from the gamble. Similarly with advertising, the assurance lies in the law of large numbers and the experience with audience probabilities which yields the basis for prediction on which the price of audience power is based. So it matters not if some audience members withdraw their attention; that is expected and discounted in advance by the advertiser.

As to the statistical basis of the experience and prediction of audience size: that is the specialized business of a subindustry sector of the Consciousness Industry which checks to determine audience size. The behavior of the members of the audience under the impact of advertising and the other content of the mass media is the object of market research by a large number of independent market research agencies as well as by similar staffs in advertising agencies, in the corporations which advertise, and in media enterprises. The raw data for their demographic and psychographic research are gathered by intensive interview studies and extrapolated to estimates of total audiences, using reports from A. C. Neilsen and a host of competitors who specialize in rapid assessment of the delivered audience commodity. Scientific sampling yields results as reliable for audiences as it does for grain, sugar, and other basic commodities which also can be "graded" only on the basis of probability and experience.

What institutions produce the commodity which advertisers buy with their advertising expenditures? There seem to be two levels to the answer to this question. The first, immediate levels is the media enterprises and the family which is the nexus of audiences. Media enterprises include those which operate commercial television and radio stations (and networks of such stations), newspapers, magazines and which produce billboard and third-class mail advertising. The second, deeper level is that of the factor supply services for the media. Feeding these media enterprises with what might be thought of as the producers' goods which support the commercial media "side" of the production process are all the advertising agencies, talent agencies, package program producers, specialist firms in producing commercial announcements, film producers, the wire services (AP, UPI, Reuters, Canadian Press, etc.), "syndicators" of news columns, writers' agents, book publishers, motion picture producers and distributors.

But powerful institutions feed the audience production process from the family or audience side as well. Here the role of the educational institutions, especially at the primary and secondary levels, is important. Preparation of children for their role in audiences in those institutions is both explicit in classroom experience which "educates" children as to how media and business function (e.g., classes in business

English or other vocational skills related to salesmanship, advertising, etc.) and implicit in the submissiveness to authority which the schools impart. Obviously, underlying both the media side and the audience side of the process of producing audiences is the electronics-photography industry complex which conceives, produces, and markets both the "software" (package programs, wire service copy, for example) and the hardware (high-speed presses, porto-pak television cameras, home receivers for television, radio, etc.).

How are prices for audience power determined? Monopoly and oligopoly characterize the supply of audiences produced by the newspaper industry. Single newspaper ownership is practically universal in American and Canadian urban areas, and the only effective ceiling on audience prices demanded by newspaper publishers is the opportunity cost to the advertiser of using alternative media (direct mail, billboards, radio and television). Cross-ownership of radio and television stations by newspaper publishers is so common as to inhibit intermedia competition in the sale of audience power. Moreover oligopolistic price setting is supported by long-established trade associations for each of the media. Prices are differentiated according to types of demand for audience power. Basic to newspaper pricing is the separation of "national" from "retail" advertisers, with the former being charged substantially higher rates than the latter. A separate price schedule governs sales to "classified" advertisers. Within the retail category, different prices are commonly charged for different classes of advertisers, e.g., on "business pages" – main financial pages, notices of dividents, corporate meetings, etc. – or listings of restaurants, amusements, books, resorts, etc. Quantity reductions are commonly granted for larger spaces; frequency discounts, for multiple exposures over time. The levels of rates are set on the basis of ability to pay (Simon, 1970, pp. 146–7). Magazine prices for audiences are classified as "national" for magazines producing nationwide audiences, and "local," for magazines with more limited geographic scope.

The markets for radio and television audiences, except for the relatively small proportion served only by single stations, display more competition for the advertisers' expenditures than do those of newspapers. For television audiences, the competition between networks is intense. Audiences for television (and radio before radio networks atrophied after television was innovated) command different prices according to whether they are priced as a network package or the product of a single station. They were originally priced differently if they were sold as produced by a "sponsored program," or as spot announcements *between* programs. By the 1970s, few "sponsored" programs were broadcast (mostly soap operas and one-time "specials" in prime time); the great bulk of audience time on both television and radio is now sold via spot announcements – mostly those sold by networks, but some directly by stations through "station representatives" to advertisers.

Erik Barnouw (1978, pp. 69–70) describes the television market for audience power in terms analogous to markets for spot and future transactions in commodities like wheat or copper:

> A central point was that a sale designated a particular *program* – not merely a time period. The advertiser had taken the position that he must have program settings suitable to his

messages and purposes, and the networks had accepted this as reasonable. From this flowed many consequences.

One was the disappearance of fixed prices. The rate card became virtually obsolete. A slot in a program that had, at the moment, a top Nielsen or Arbitron rating could be sold for a higher price than a slot in a program with a lower rating. Thus the business gravitated toward endless bargaining. Prices fluctuated as on a stock market.

A sharp rise in ratings brought a rise in asking price. When NBC decided in 1970 to schedule a series around the comedian Flip Wilson – then a relatively unknown quantity – network time salesmen began by selling 30-second slots for about $35,000 each. As the program won unexpected success and climbing ratings, the asking price went to $40,000, $45,000, $50,000 and beyond. On a single broadcast, one slot might have been sold at the lowest, earliest price; others at later prices. On some series, ratings and prices went down instead of up.

The buying and selling was generally done in clusters or packages. In view of the staggering number of spots involved, this seemed inevitable. For the sponsor it was also a way to hedge his bets. Unexpected failures could be balanced by unexpected successes. There was a safety in this "scatter" buying.

In the bargaining process, a sponsor might indicate through his advertising agency that he was ready to invest $1,400,000 in time purchases for Mouthwash X; the network was asked to provide a suggested list of available slots. Some would be rejected as unsuitable, others accepted. Eventually there would be agreement on a spectrum of spots, and on a package price. A specific dollar value would be assigned to each spot; this was essential because a program cancellation would require the network to make a refund, or provide a comparable spot. The spots in a package might have wildly diverse price tags, reflecting their ratings and other bargaining factors. They might include 30-second slots in a football bowl game at $90,000 each; in a popular mystery series at $55,000 each; in an evening news series at $18,000 each; in a documentary prime time special at $14,000 each; and in an early morning show at $4,000 each.

A documentary special, even in prime time, was likely to go at a "bargain price" unless some sensational element was involved. A special could not have a track record, so its ratings could only be guessed at. And most sponsors were in any case reluctant to consider a slot in what might prove controversial; some flatly refused to take the risk.

To see that audience power is literally a commodity, consider the following packages of audience power available in the Vancouver, British Columbia, area for local television advertisers in May 1978:

For One 30-Second Spot on Bulk Basis
(Dollar cost per 1,000 persons)

	M*A*S*H (prime time)	Hockey Night in Canada (prime time)	Batman (Saturday AM)
Total viewers	2.32	1.99	0.96
Adults, total	3.00	2.29	—
Men	5.84	3.45	—
Women	5.13	5.98	7.35
Teenagers	25.39	42.44	3.85
Children	50.78	50.78	1.89

If the demographic and psychographic characteristics of women in these audiences in this market fitted the demand-management needs of an advertiser, M*A*S*H would be a better buy than either of the other programs. Similarly, if the advertiser's marketing strategy was aimed at children, the best buy of the three would be the Batman program on Saturday morning.

These audience power markets establish prices in the familiar oligopolistic mode of monopoly capitalism. And an advertiser's power in the audience market has been a significant factor in building monopoly corporate empires. A sympathetic expert on advertising, Julian Simon (1970, pp. 222–3) says:

> At the corporate level, advertising sometimes has led to increased concentration by diversification because of multiproduct volume discounts on advertising time and space. For example, the FTC record revealed that Procter & Gamble could buy television time for 5 percent less than could the Clorox Company and this was an admitted motivation in Procter & Gamble's purchase.... Blake and Blum (1965) have compiled their relevant data on these volume discounts and provide compelling analysis to show that they must have been an important reason for firms that advertise heavily to seek mergers and reduce the cost of advertising.
>
> This effect is illustrated by a recent trade-paper story: "The proposed Cadbury-Schweppes merger, which sees economies in advertising and overseas expansion as its chief benefits, will create (if the Board of Trade permits) the United Kingdom's fourth largest food group, with estimated sales of $600,000,000. Savings would come from the group buying of television time, which accounts for at least 75 per cent of the companies' joint budget in that medium. In 1968, the two companies put out $13,650,000 for advertising, the second largest in the country...." (*Advertising Age*, March 3, 1969, p. 26)

Simon also points out that the better the advertiser's ability to measure the productivity of his purchased audience power, the more sensitive the advertiser will be to rate changes. And he uses as example, the case of mail order advertisers who buy magazine audience power:

> Mail order advertisers have an almost perfect measure of the effect of their advertising, and they receive sharp discounts below the rates paid by general advertisers. (Simon, 1970, p. 146)

Who pays how much for the production of audience power? On the surface it seems as if the exchange of audience power for commercial media content is equal or perhaps is even tilted in favour of the audience. You audience members contribute your unpaid work time and in exchange you receive the program material and the explicit advertisements. What better way to spend those "leisure hours" anyway? Especially if, as audience research suggests, television audience behavior since the mid-1960s increasingly tends to treat television as aural-visual wallpaper: the set is left on and audience members either attend to it or drift between the television room and adjacent (or remote) rooms, "glimpsing" the television set in passing and monitoring it auditorily all the while (Lyle, 1972, p. 23). Is there inconsistency between the concept of audience power as a commodity and such disrespectful behavior? Of course not. Is the tendency of workers on the production line to skimp or sabotage their work processes inconsistent with the fact that they have sold their labor power to the boss?

If we would understand the full audience contribution to producing their own audience power in a capitalist system, we must start by asking what value the system places on that audience power. And we shall find (in the next two chapters) that it is of vital importance to the system which could not survive without it. But, and the contradiction is significant, the system gets it "dirt-cheap."

Regarding television and radio broadcasting, advertisers spent in Canada in 1976 about $417 million on television and $279 million on radio.[5] For the 6,684,000 Canadian households with television sets in 1976 (and they were 97 percent of all households), advertisers spent $62 per household. Assuming a 23-hour week for television viewing per household (a very conservative figure), advertisers paid 5.2 cents an hour for the audience power of the average television household in 1976. Similarly, the 6,918,000 Canadian households with radio (100 percent saturation) cost the advertisers an average of $40 per household per annum. Assuming 18 hours per week of radio listening per household, this equaled 4.2 cents per household per hour of radio listening. Even without sophisticated productivity analysis of these costs, it is evident that the productivity of audience power need not be very high for all the individuals in the audience in order for it to be profitable for advertisers to recoup the costs – to them – of putting audience power to work.

From the standpoint of the audience, however, it bears much heavier costs than the advertisers. For what? For the privilege of working without pay as audience members, marketing consumer goods and services to themselves. And these heavier costs ignore the hidden costs they incur through commodity purchases. Table 15.1 compares the direct cost to audiences in Canada and the United States of commercial television and radio programming. It shows that, in 1976, Canadian audience members paid $2.188 billion as the direct cost of owning and operating their television receivers, whereas advertisers spent a mere $417 million. In other words, for every dollar spent by advertisers to buy media-produced television audiences, Canadian householders spent five. And whereas the depreciated investment in property, plant, and equipment of the combined over-the-air and cable television industry and the over-the-air radio broadcast industry in Canada was $645 million in 1976, the audience's depreciated investment in television and radio receivers was $3.905 billion. (Because CBC does not report investment in television and radio property separately, it is necessary to combine them.) In other words, for every dollar invested by the television-cable and radio broadcast industry in plant and equipment, Canadian householders had invested more than six dollars in their television and radio receivers.

In the United States, audience members paid $21.949 billion to own and operate their television receivers in 1976; advertisers spent $6.721 billion to buy the television audiences – a ratio of three dollars spent by the audience to one by the advertisers. A similar ratio of three to one existed between costs for radio receivers ($2.330 billion) and advertiser expenditures to buy radio audiences ($8.040 billion). Curiously, although these ratios for operating costs were lower in the United States than in Canada, the ratios for depreciated investment by audiences were higher. Thus

Table 15.1 Comparative cost of television and radio in Canada and the United States, 1976

	Canada		USA	
	TV	Radio	TV	Radio
Audience Costs, Direct:				
Basic Data:				
Number of receivers (000)[a]	9,895	23,400	121,000	402,000
Average purchase price (est. $)	600	80	540	72
Average useful life (est. years)	7	7	7	7
Average remaining useful life (est. years)	3.5	3.5	3.5	3.5
Interest rate on investment (est. %)	10	10	8	8
Average cost of power (est. $)	15	4	15	4
Average cost of repairs (est. $)	70	3	60	3
Annual Costs per Set ($):				
Depreciation (1/7 of price)	86	11	77	10
Interest (on 1/2 of price)	30	4	22	3
Power	15	4	15	4
Repairs	70	3	60	3
Total	201	22	174	20
Total Audience Cost (total cost per set times number of receivers/million $ per year)	1,989	515	21,054	8,040
Add cable costs for cabled households (million $ per year)[b]	199	—	895	—
Total Audience Cost (million $)	2,188	515	21,949	8,040
Advertiser Costs (million $ per year)[c]	417	279	6,721	2,330
Audience and Industry Investment:				
Depreciated audience investment (1/2 original cost, million $)	2,969	936	32,670	14,472
Depreciated investment in broadcast property, plant and equipment (million $):				
Over-air industry (except CBC)[d]	101	56	850	504
Over-air industry (including CBC)[d]		409	—	—
Cable industry	236	—	?	—
Total Cable and Over-Air (Canada)		645		
Profitability of Industry:				
Net profit before taxes (million $):				
Over-air industry[d]	60	36	1,546	158
Cable (Canada)[b]	36	—	—	—
Rate of return (%)				
Over-air industry	59	65	182	31
Cable (Canada)	15	—	—	—

[a] UNESCO *Statistical Yearbook*, 1977, pp. 996, 1016.
[b] Statistics Canada, *Cable Television*, Cat. 56, 205, 1976; United States Bureau of the Census, *Statistical*

Abstract, 1978. Aspen Institute, *The Mass Media*, 1978, p. 215.
[c] For Canada, see footnote 5 (in text); for United States, Aspen Institute, *The Mass Media*, 1978, p. 203.
[d] For Canada, Statistics Canada, *Television and Radio Broadcasting*, Cat. 56, 204, 1976; for United States, Federal Communications Commission, *Annual Report*, 1976, pp. 130, 141; Aspen Institute.

for television, audience investment was $32.670 billion, but over-the-air television depreciated investment was $850 million – a ratio of 33 to 1. And for radio broadcasting, audience investment was $14.472 billion as against $504 million by the radio broadcast networks and stations – a ratio of 33 to 1.

If one examines the basic data on audience receiver costs in Table 15.1 closely, it is evident that I have had to make rough estimates for all of them. The estimates appear to be conservative. At any event, the gross imbalance between audience costs and investment on the one hand, and expenditures by advertisers and investment by television and radio broadcast industries is obvious. Even if the real costs of depreciation, interest, power, repairs were a third less than my estimates suggest, television audiences in Canada and the United States would still be paying twice as much as advertisers.

What seems surprising from this analysis is that this preponderant investment and expense by audience members is virtually unnoticed by them and by scholars working in the mass media field. By what magicians term *misdirection*, attention is so focused on the exotic performances and lives of media stars and the showbiz glamor of program production and network and station operations that the real situation is mystified out of existence, as far as popular consciousness is concerned.

Who pays how much for the production of audience power other than via television-radio? For newspapers and magazines, advertisers pay the great bulk of the cost – typically from 70 to 90 percent. Audience subscription and newsstand purchase payments cover approximately only the delivery cost of the newspapers and magazines. "Community" and "shopping" newspapers which have no subscription price are paid for entirely by advertisers. Direct mail advertising materials are at the expense of advertisers, subsidized by heavy drains on revenues from first class mail and general tax revenues through below-cost postal rates. A similar postal subsidy for magazines and newspapers has shifted substantial portions of the costs of magazines and newspapers to the postal service in Canada and the United States since the last quarter of the nineteenth century.

What is the nature of the content of the commercial mass media under monopoly capitalism? In chapter 1 [Smythe, 1981], we considered the many ways in which there is unity between the apparently advertising and the apparently nonadvertising content of the commercial mass media. Both types have the same features. But it would be a serious error to ignore the importance of the formal difference between the "advertising" and the "program" or "editorial" content. The fiction that the advertising supports or makes possible the news, entertainment, or "educational" content has been a public relations mainstay of the commercial mass media. The professional *esprit de corps* of journalists hinges on it. And the textbooks, courses of instruction, teachers, and researchers in the mass media accept this fiction as defining the boundaries of their concerns. Either they deal with editorial content (in the case of newspapers and magazines) or program content, or they are hived off into textbooks, research, etc., about advertising. The only connection commonly made between advertising and the nonadvertising content of the media is to raise and dispel the suspicion that advertisers commonly tell the editorial departments of newspapers and magazines or the program producers of television and radio what *not* to say in the nonadvertising portions. (Of course, they seldom do this; it is not necessary because the editorial policy of the media selects people for employment and predetermines the limits of what is "acceptable" noneditorial content.)

As a necessary consequence of the prevalence of this fiction, audience members and social scientists have come to regard the nonadvertising content as the sufficient attraction which warrants audiences spending time attending to the whole media product. So A. J. Liebling's (1961) point that the nonadvertising content is the "free lunch" does have a solid basis in public consciousness, a basis cynically reinforced by the newspapers' practice of referring to the space between the advertisements as the *holes* which must be filled with appropriately sized chunks of "news." The appropriateness of the analogy is manifest. As with the *hors d'oeuvres* or potato chips and peanuts given to the customers of the pub, bar, or cocktail lounge, the function of the free lunch is to whet the appetite. In this case, to whet the prospective audience members' appetites and thus (1) attract and keep them attending to the program, newspaper, or magazine; (2) cultivate a mood conducive to favorable reaction to the advertisers' explicit and implicit messages.

In the policy of the mass media, the characteristics of the free lunch must always be subordinated to those of the formal advertisements, because the purpose of the mass media is to produce audiences to sell to the advertisers. Therefore a program which is more arousing than the adjacent advertisements will not survive; it could survive the preliminary screening only because of faulty judgment on part of the media management and advertisers. The cost per unit of time or space of producing an explicit advertisement is many times the cost per unit of time or space of producing the free lunch (in a ratio of 8 or 10 to 1 in television) which is a rough index of the relative attention paid to the arousal qualities of the two.

There is, of course, a market for the free lunch, and this market spans not only the totally advertiser-dependent media (television and radio) but also the cinema, magazines, newspapers, and book industries. A particular commodity in the free lunch market (*Roots*, for example) will appear in more than one of these media, sometimes simultaneously (as with the book and film *China Syndrome*), often successively, in each case appropriately edited to fit the media's needs.

Qualification is necessary regarding the free lunch. On the one hand, in the case of newspapers and magazines, many readers buy the publication *because* they want the advertisements. This is especially true with classified advertisements and display advertising of products and prices by local merchants in newspapers. It is also true of most "hobby" magazines where the product information in advertisements may be as much an inducement as the free lunch to prospective readers. On the other hand, cable television, coupled with commercial television broadcasting, results in audience members paying directly for *both* the free lunch *and* the advertisements, as inescapably they will for pay-television – if and when that becomes widespread and able to preempt mass appeal free lunch programs, such as championship sports events.

By emphasizing the economic role of the free lunch in media content, I by no means wish to minimize its importance in its own right. As a social institution with the agenda-setting role which it has, the mass media free lunch puts into words and images the view of events in the local community, the region, the country, and the world which journalists produce and media entrepreneurs publish. That the mass media in Canada and the United States on occasion expose and attack corruption and otherwise critically examine the working of the present social system is undeniable. We need not expand on that here because the literature on the mass media amply celebrates these efforts. But as is demonstrated in chapter 11 [Smythe, 1981], the overwhelming tendency of the free lunch is to reaffirm the status quo and retard change.

Nor should one minimize the propaganda value of the free lunch. Its production by Consciousness Industry is a process of interpreting and homogenizing the entire cultural heritage in current commoditized terms. (A sign over a Hollywood publicity agent's desk reads, "You never lose money by underestimating the level of popular taste.") As and when bourgeois literature, drama, art, and music, and traditional folk cultural materials (e.g., Calypso music) provide profitable opportunities, it all becomes raw material for commercial media free lunch and advertising content. The ideological basis of it all is possessive individualism with the corollaries described in Chapter 1. Beginnings are being made in the exploration of the concrete reality of how the process works (Dorfman and Mattelart, 1975; Schiller, 1969, 1973, 1976; Kellner, 1979; Gitlin, 1979). The range and subtlety of the propaganda is evidenced by the following testimony before a United States congressional subcommittee, "On Winning the Cold War," by Dr. Joseph Klapper. Although it is an evaluation of a form of propaganda addressed to foreigners, it is equally applicable to domestic media content:

> Now, of course the broadcasting of popular music is not likely to have an immediate effect on the audience's political attitude, but this kind of communication nevertheless provides a sort of entryway of Western ideas and Western concepts, even though these concepts may not be explicitly and completely stated at any one particular moment in the communication. In addition, and simply because the communication does fill a need which the audience enjoys having filled, it probably serves to build up a certain credibility and respect for the source of that communication. . . . And this building of source credibility is one of the numerous possible preparatory steps toward the eventual clinching moment of persuasion.   (U.S. Congress, House, 1967, pp. 64–5)

The free lunch thus provides material which, taken jointly with the explicit advertising, gives the audience material to work on.

What is the nature of the service performed for the advertiser by the members of the purchased audience? In economic terms, the audience commodity is a nondurable producer's good which is bought and used in the marketing of the advertiser's product. The work which audience members perform for the advertiser to whom they have been sold is learning to buy goods and to spend their income accordingly. Sometimes, it is to buy any of the class of goods (e.g., an aircraft manufacturer is selling air transport in general, or the dairy industry, all brands of milk) but most often it is a particular "brand" of consumer goods. In short, they work to create the demand for advertised goods which is the purpose of the monopoly-capitalist advertisers. Audience members may resist, but the advertiser's expectations are realized sufficiently that the results perpetuate the system of demand management.

People in audiences, we should remember, have had a rich history of education for their work as audience members. As children, teenagers, and adults they have observed old and new models of particular brands of products on the street, in homes of friends, at school, at the job front, etc. Much time will have been spent in discussing the "good" and "bad" features of brands of commodities in hundreds of contexts. A constant process of direct experience with commodities goes on and blends into all aspects of people's lives all the time. Advertisers get this huge volume of audience work (creation of consumer consciousness) as a bonus even before a specific media free-lunch-advertising program appears on the tube face and initiates a new episode in audience work (See Smythe, 1981).

While people do their work as audience members they are simultaneously reproducing their own labor power. In this respect, we may avoid the trap of a manipulation-explanation by noting that if such labor power is, in fact, loyally attached to the monopoly-capitalist system, this would be welcome to the advertisers whose existence depends on the maintenance of that system. But in reproducing their labor power, workers respond to other realistic conditions which may on occasion surprise and disappoint the advertisers.

The nature of audience work may best be approached through successive approximations. At a superficial level it looks like this: "Customers do not buy things. They buy tools to solve problems," according to Professor T. N. Levitt (1976, p. 73) of Harvard Business School. The nature of the work done by audience power thus seems to be to use the advertising free lunch combination of sensory stimuli to determine whether s/he (1) has the "problem" the advertiser is posing (e.g., loneliness, sleeplessness, prospective economic insecurity for loved ones after the breadwinner's death, etc.), (2) is aware that there is a class of commodities which, if purchased and used will "solve" that problem (e.g., shampoo, nonprescription sleeping drugs, life insurance) and that people like him/her use this class of commodity for this purpose, (3) ought to add brand ZX of that class of commodities to the mental or physical shopping list for the next trip to the store. This is the advertisers' rational basis. For audience members, however, their work is not so rational.

There is an *ever-increasing* number of decisions forced on audience members by new commodities and their related advertising. In addition to the many thousands of different items stocked by a typical supermarket at any one time, more than a thousand new consumer commodities appear each year. Literally millions of possible comparative choices face the audience member who goes shopping. As a long line of books stretching back to the 1920s has argued (for example, Chase and Schlink, 1927), the consumer is totally unable to *know* either the craftsman's sense of quality or the "scientific" basis of quality as built into consumers goods by modern mass production techniques. Imagine yourself entering a toilet-goods section of a modern department store in which every product was in a similar glass container and the containers bore only the chemical description of the contents and the price. Unless you were a very experienced chemist specializing in cosmetics and other toiletries (and even then you would have to do a lot of thinking), how could you know which was a "best buy," or even what the product was intended to do: be a shampoo, deodorant, skin-care cream, or what? Lacking the product brand name, the shape and symbolic decoration of the package, you would be helpless.[6]

It must be assumed that when most people go shopping, even for H.P.G., there is real necessity moving them. The refrigerator needs restocking. Soap is needed for washing, and so on. And that they are increasingly aware of the squeeze of increasing cost of living versus inadequate income. The recent appearance of "no-name brand" commodities is a response of monopoly capitalism to consumer resistance to the usual brand pricing practice. In the 1950s there was a flurry of "discount stores" where "standard" brand merchandise (acquired from bankrupt stores, from usual sources, or from thieves) was sold at substantial discounts. This was a tactical response of the system to consumer resistance. And with the artificial prosperity of the Vietnam war period these stores disappeared. It is probable that "no-name brand" merchandise is a similar, temporary tactical concession. In any event, "no-name brands" amount in fact to new "house brands" with, for the present, reduced prices.

Your work, as audience member, has to do with how your life's problems interact with the advertising-free-lunch experience. But how? How, in light of that experience do you decide whether you really have the "problem" to which the advertiser has sought to sensitize you? And if the answer to this question be affirmative, how do you decide that the class of commodities which have been produced to cope with that problem will really serve their advertised purpose? And if the answer to that question be affirmative, how do you decide whether to buy brand A, B, or n? *The process contains a monstrous contradiction. It is totally rational from the advertisers' perspective and totally irrational from the audience members'*.

Faced with the necessity to make some decisions as to what classes and what brands of commodities to put on the shopping list (if only to preserve a shred of self-respect as one capable of making one's own decisions), it seems that Staffen B. Linder (1970, p. 59) may be correct in saying that the most important way by which consumers can cope with commodities and advertising is to limit the time spent per purchase in thinking about what to buy:

> Reduced time for reflection previous to a decision would apparently entail a growing irrationality. However, since it is extremely rational to consider less and less per decision there exists a rationale of irrationality.

"Impulse purchasing" has increasingly become the practice of Consciousness Industry, as market researchers have studied the effect of store layout, shelf-level display, and commodity package design and artwork on customers pushing their basket-carts through supermarket aisles. Studies of eye-blink rates indicate that a semihypnotic condition of the customer results in impulse purchases for which no rationale can be remembered when the customer returns home. "Consumers" produced and delivered by Consciousness Industry are in the position of trying to cope with a giant con game. They know that they do not really have all the problems which advertisers press them to solve by buying their products. Placed in a time- and income-spending bind, the impossibility of making rational shopping decisions forces consumers to "take a chance." The lottery is perhaps the best model for explaining what happens at the moment of truth when the customer reaches for the package from the shelf. And it is perhaps significant that lotteries, so long excluded from socially sanctioned practice, have recently become legal and generally used in North America. For consumers accustomed to taking a chance on a $9.99 item on the supermarket shelf, the option of a statistically sheer random "chance" to win a million dollars can be very attractive and compelling. Yet the rationale of irrationality (Linder's) is unsatisfactory as an explanation of audience work. It may serve as a first approximation to an explanation. But we must dig deeper into the process of which audience work is a part.

How can audience power be "work" when it takes place in "free" or "leisure" time? What becomes of the labor theory of value if audiences are working? Is it not true that what people do when not working at the job front (where they are paid money for their work) is their free or leisure time *by definition?* Is it not true that "you can do as you please" in this "free" time? Have not "modern" household appliances relieved women of household work?

At the outset it is important to note that the idea of such free or leisure time is a hand-me-down from the upper classes in bourgeois society. It derives from the upper-class notion of leisure for the enjoyment of "official culture" (see chapter 9 [Smythe, 1981]). At the height of imperialist power toward the end of the nineteenth century, it took the form of emulating the *conspicuous* consumption of the rich and powerful, as Veblen so bitingly revealed in *The Theory of the Leisure Class* (1899). As transformed by monopoly capitalism, it meant the imitation of *expensive* consumption, for, as Veblen also pointed out, the policy of monopoly capitalism was to be "a competition in publicity and scarcity" (Smythe, 1981). David Riesman (1950) and Stuart Ewen (1976) focused on the illusory semblance of reality in such "leisure" and "free time."

It is necessary to state clearly that just as people are rarely totally controlled by Consciousness Industry, so marketed commodities rarely have absolutely no use value. Repeatedly, in different ways I emphasize that most people embody a dialectical tension: they feel it necessary to cooperate with the monopoly-capitalist system in a variety of ways and for a variety of reasons; yet at the same time, as human beings they resist such cooperation in a variety of ways, for a variety of reasons. An analogous internal dialectical tension seems to exist *within* most commodities under capitalism. The gas-guzzling, overpowered, dangerous private automobile *also* transports you from home to work and back again; when suitably "hotted up," it may even lure into a lasting relationship a commoditized person of the opposite sex, just as the advertisements promise. The relative strength of the repressive and emancipatory ingredients in a commodity obviously differs greatly as between different commodities, e.g., an adulterated drug as against ordinary packaged milk. As we shall see in chapter 10 [Smythe, 1981], this dialectical conflict within commodities exists within producer goods as well as consumer goods, which is the reason that the term *technology,* with its assumed neutral quality, is dangerously misleading. For most people in the core area today, leisure or free time, like technology, are propaganda devices which obscure and confuse the real contradictions between the respects in which people cooperate with and resist the monopoly-capitalist system and its commodities.

Except for those people who have been so rich that they did not have to work, all people have always had to work – one way or another – when not at the job in order to prepare themselves to work *tomorrow*. *Before* the mass production of consumer goods – roughly before 1875 – in capitalist core countries, people's work to prepare themselves to work tomorrow (e.g., to reproduce their labor power) was done under conditions of cottage industry. For example they baked their own bread using flour which they might have ground themselves and yeast which they cultured for themselves. But with the mass production of consumer goods, their work to reproduce their labor power depends on buying and using consumer goods *in end-product form*. They have become dependent on factory-baked bread. And if sophisticated durable goods, e.g., vacuum cleaners, have relieved them of the necessity to sweep with brooms, it has required them to spend time buying filters and other equipment and arranging for maintenance of such equipment by "service men." And the endless proliferation of new commodities which clamor for their place in household consumption (e.g., electric can openers, electric carving knives, power lawn mowers, etc.) demands so much of so-called free time to buy, use, and maintain them that the idea of "free time" has become ridiculous. Consider what has happened to the time available to workers and the way it is used in the past century.

In 1850, under conditions of cottage industry, i.e., unbranded consumer goods, the average work week of employed men was about 70 hours per week in the United States.[7] The average worker could devote about 42 hours per week to such cottage industry types of reproduction of his labor power. By 1960, the time spent on the job was about 39.5 hours per week – an apparent reduction in time spent on the job of about 30 hours per week (to which should be added 2.5 hours as a generous estimate of the weekly equivalent of paid vacations).

Advertisers and home economists regularly argued that the apparent reduction in "work" hours created new leisure time for workers and housewives between 1910 and 1940, as Stuart Ewen's *Captains of Consciousness* (1976) demonstrated. Consumer durable goods like washing machines, vacuum cleaners, etc., were said to *free* housekeepers from work. Some time was indeed freed from drudgery in this way, but the illusion that most people had large blocks of free time was a myth created by Consciousness Industry. Upon close inspection, as we shall argue, leisure time for most people is work time. As Marylee Stephenson (1977, p. 32) puts it: "over 90 per cent of 51 per cent of the adult population is engaged in . . . wageless labor (known as housework) for their entire adult life. . . ."

In fact, the meaning of the almost 30 hours per week by which the *job* work week shrank between 1850 and 1960 was transformed doubly by monopoly capitalism. One transformation removed huge chunks of people's time from their discretion by metropolitan sprawl and by the nature of unpaid work which workers were obligated to perform. For example, recently travel time to and from the job has been estimated at 8.5 hours per week; "moonlighting" employment at a minimum of one hour per week; repair work around the home at another five hours per week; and men's work on household chores and shopping at another 2.3 hours per week. As I write this the postman drops through the slot a piece of direct mail advertising for a *Do-It-Yourself* manual. It tells me that owning this manual:

...is like having the experts at your side...but without having to pay for them! You can save the expense of countless calls for cabinetmaker, carpenter, decorator, electrician, heating expert, locksmith, mason, painter, paper-hanger, plasterer, plumber, roofer, rug cleaner, tile layer.

And it lists more than 50 "projects you can build for your home or garden" with the manual.

A total of 16.8 hours per week of the roughly 32 hours of time suposedly "freed" as a result of "modernization" is thus anything but free. A further 7 hours of the 32 hours of "freed" time disappears when a correction for part-time female employment is made in the reported hours per week in 1960.[8]

A second transformation involved the pressure placed by the system on the remaining hours of the week. If sleeping is estimated at 8 hours a day, the remainder of the 168 hours in the week after subtracting sleeping time and the unfree work time identified earlier was 42 hours in 1850 and 49 hours in 1960. The apparent increase in "free" time has thus shrunk to 7 hours per week (instead of about 30 hours). We lack systematic information about the use of this increased free time for both dates. We do know that certain types of activities were common to both dates: personal care, making love, visiting with relatives and friends, preparing and eating meals, attending union, church, and other associative institutions, including saloons. We also know that in 1960 (but not in 1850) there was a vast array of *branded* consumer goods and services pressed on workers through advertising, retail establishment displays, and peer group influence. Attendance at spectator sports and participation in such activities as little leagues, bowling, camping, and "pleasure driving" of the automobile or snowmobile – all promoted for the sake of equipment and energy sales by the Consciousness Industry – now takes time that was devoted to noncommercial activities in 1850. In-house time must now be devoted to deciding whether to buy and to use (by whom, where, under what conditions, and why) an endless proliferation of goods for personal care, household furnishings, clothing, music reproduction equipment, etc. And thus far we have not mentioned mass media *use*, although it should be noted that workers are guided in all income and time expenditures by the mass media – through the blend of explicit advertising and advertising implicit in the program content.

Let us now introduce mass media use as it relates to the seven hours of "free" time thus far identified (ignoring the pressures on the audience to use its time and income referred to in the preceding paragraph). How much time do most people spend as part of the audience product of the mass media – their time which is sold by the media to advertisers? David Blank, economist for the Columbia Broadcasting System, found in 1970 that the average person watched television for 3.3 hours per day (23 hours per week) on an annual basis, listened to radio for 2.5 hours per day (18 hours per week), and read newspapers and magazines for 1 hour per day (7 hours per week) (Blank, 1970). Recent years show similar magnitudes. If we look at the audience product in terms of families rather than individuals, we find that in 1973 advertisers in the United States purchased television audiences for an average of a little more than 43 hours per home per week.[9] By industry usage, this lumps together specialized audience commodities sold independently as "housewives," "children," and "families." In the prime time evening hours (7:00 PM to 11:00 PM), the television audience commodity consisted of a daily average of 83.8 million people, with an average of two persons viewing per home. Women were a significantly higher proportion of this prime time audience than men (42 percent as against 32 percent; children were 16 percent; teenagers 10 percent).

Let us sum up these figures. Television, radio, and newspapers plus magazines take up 48 hours per week, for the average American! And they have only seven hours more free time than in 1850! Obviously some doubling up takes place. So let us estimate that half of the radio listening takes place while traveling to or from work; perhaps another quarter while doing the personal care chores at the beginning and end of the day. As for television, perhaps a fourth of it (on average) is glimpsed while preparing meals, eating, washing dishes, or doing other household tasks or repair/ construction work. Estimate half of newspaper and magazine reading as taking place while traveling between home and job, while eating, etc. Our reduced exclusive audience time with the four commercial media is now down to 22 hours per week. Obviously more doubling takes place between audience time and other activities, and the reader is invited to make more precise estimates based on (perhaps) some empirical research. On television broadcasts of commercial sports events in the United States one sees some spectators *in the stadia* who are simultaneously watching the live event and portable television sets (for the "instant replay" in stadia not blessed with huge overhead television screens for that purpose), or listening to the radio (for the sportscaster's instant comments on the play just completed).

Perhaps the only conclusion to be drawn at this time on this point is that there is no free time devoid of audience activity which is not preempted by other activities which are market-related (including sleep which is necessary if you are to be fit to meet your market tests on the morrow). In *any* society, sleep and other nonwork activities are necessary to restore and maintain life and labor power. Work itself is not intrinsically oppressive. It is the inclusion in so-called leisure time of commodity-producing work under monopoly capitalism which creates the contradiction between oppressive liberating activity in time for which people are not paid.

The bitter reality for most Canadians and Americans is that the commodity rat race – as they call it – makes a mockery of free time and leisure, both during their years at the job and after retirement.

What time is *not* work time in the mature capitalist core area? For the great majority of the population – all except those who are so rich that they can afford to have their shopping done by servants – 24 hours a day is work time. Modern machinery requires maintenance when idle between shifts. The human body requires rest, time for reflection, time for the cultivation of the arts (see chapter 9 [Smythe, 1981]), time for the subtleties of raising children, time for community activities, etc. But the pressures for audience-oriented work exerted by Consciousness Industry are relentless. George Allen, famous American football coach, tells his players, "Nobody should work all the time. Leisure time is the five or six hours you sleep at night. You can combine two good things at once, sleep and leisure" (quoted in Terkel, 1974, p. 389).

How does the view that all the time of most of the people in the capitalist core countries is work time relate to Karl Marx's theory of labor power? As Bill Livant puts it, the power of the concept of surplus value "... rests wholly on the way Marx solved the great value problems of classical political economy, by *splitting the notion of labour in two*, into labour in productive use and labour power (the capacity to labor)."[10]

Labor in productive use in the production of commodities-in-general was Marx's concern in the three volumes of *Capital* (except for vol. 1, chap. 6) and scattered passages in the *Grundrisse*. It is clear from those exceptions that Marx assumed that labor power is produced by the laborer and by his or her immediate family, i.e., under the conditions of handicraft production prevailing when he wrote. In a word, labor power was "home made" (in the absence of dominant brand name commodities, mass advertising, and the mass media which monopoly capitalism had not yet invented). In Marx's period and in his analysis, the principal aspect of capitalist production was the alienation of workers from the means of producing commodities-in-general. Today and for some time past, the principal aspect of capitalist production has been the alienation of workers from the means of producing and reproducing themselves.

The prevailing Western Marxist view today still holds the incorrect assumption that the laborer is an *independent* commodity producer of labor power *which is his to sell*. But

> What often escapes attention is that just because the labourer sells it (his or her labour power) does not mean that he or she produces it. We are misled by fixating on the true fact that a human must eat and sleep into thinking that therefore the seller of labour power must also be the producer. Again the error of two combines into one (Livant, 1975b).

> Livant goes on to say that a Marxist view: ... sees leisure time correctly as time of production, reproduction and repair of labour power. This production, reproduction and repair are activities. They are things people must do. As such they require labour power. To be sure, this latter labour power you do not have to sell directly to capital. But you do have to use it to produce labour power in the form you do have to sell.

(Chapters 3 and 4 [Smythe, 1981] discuss just how the contradictions within capitalism produced monopoly capitalism, Consciousness Industry, and the mass media.)

Under capitalism your labor power becomes a personal possession. It seems that you can do what you want with it. If you work at a job where you are paid, you sell it. Away from the job, it seems that your work is something you do not sell. But there is common misunderstanding at this point. At the job you are not paid for all the labor time you do sell (otherwise interest, profits, and management salaries could not be paid). And away from the job, your labor time *is* sold (through the audience commodity), although you do not sell it. What is produced at the job where you get paid are commodities used for consumption or for further production. And what is produced by you away from the job is your labor power for tomorrow and for the next generation: ability to work and to live (Livant, 1975a).

The point to be pursued here is that the ruling groups cultivated "high" or bourgeois culture (in the fine arts) both for their own enjoyment and as an invaluable ideological feature of monopoly capitalism (itself dealt with in chapter 9 [Smythe, 1981]). Liberal notions about "leisure" to which a substantial amount of effort by bourgeois sociologists has been devoted (see, for example, Kaplin, 1960, 1975) perpetuate the mystification of leisure, treating it "apolitically." In fact, the system used labor unions, religious organizations, and community arts organizations (musical, painting, sculpture, literary, poetic, etc.), to turn the "high culture" from Greece on down into a means of attaching workers loyally to the system. A considerable literature about "popular culture" and "mass culture" deals with this relationship, which is also dealt with in chapter 9 [Smythe, 1981] (see, for example, Garnham, 1977). The unrelenting pressures of Consciousness Industry, however, reveal the yawning gap between high culture notions of leisure, which are the stuff of establishment propaganda regarding "national identity," and the vulgar, atomized, and capitalized exploitation of leisure as a cover for an ever-expanding range of commodity markets.

Audiences for the commercial mass media are a strange type of institution. They are more a statistical abstraction than are, for example, the audience of the live or motion picture theater because they have no possibility of simultaneously and totally interacting internally to create an audience mood or affect. Yet we know that they are far from merely being statistical abstractions. Orson Welles' "Invasion from Mars" radio broadcast precipitated mass hysteria (Cantril et al., 1940). And the record industry depends on radio stations to produce "hit parades" which mobilize fans of popular music stars to buy records on a mass scale. We are far from having a full understanding of the audience commodity, but there is no doubt that it is a qualitatively new major social institution, a collectivity, and a commodity. As Bill Livant (1979a, p. 103) says:

> Virtually everyone is organized into the complex tapestry of these audiences, whose underlying properties we are just beginning to understand. For one thing, the production, destruction, division and recombination of audiences is a vast and turbulent motion. For another, the Audience Commodity is a multipurpose capacity. It is the other side of the labour power that Marx discovered in the production of commodities-in-general, and it is as Protean in its capacities.
>
> The *first* great form of the organization of this commodity [is] the Audience Commodity as a Market. This form emerged first historically and with the greatest clarity in the United States. . . . This form is the first, *but not the last*.

We can already observe that the audience commodity has changed the social form for political party electoral behavior in the capitalist world. Murdock (1978, p. 117) refers to the changing form of social conflict in Europe:

> The expansion of consumerism was accompanied by a dampening down of industrial conflict and class struggle. The contradiction between capital and labor receded from the centre of attention and its place was taken by conflicts grounded in age, in gender, in nationality, in race, and above all in the yawning gap between the developed and underdeveloped worlds, between the colonizers and the colonized.

The rationalization by Consciousness Industry of the process of conducting elections through mass media "pseudo events" and advertising is, through the telltale demographics, evidence of the audience commodity, having been produced for the election market and paid for by the parties, at work in ways quite familiar in the North American scene. Richeri (1978) has linked the rapid transformation of the Italian political constituency system to the rapid introduction of the production of audiences by commercial television and radio stations in recent years. An analogous transformation of the electoral process took place in the United States and Canada between the mid-1930s and 1960s as political campaigning/advertising via radio broadcasting, public opinion polling, and interlocking ownership interests in radio (and later television) stations between politicians and newspaper publishers were substituted for nineteenth-century modes of mobilizing people for elections. Richard Nixon's flat statement in 1957 that political candidates must now be merchandised like any other consumer product recognized the reality. Europe, lagged by a decade or so, has now experienced the same transformation more quickly.

The work of the audience commodity poses severe problems for Marxist theory derived from Europe and based upon the analysis of competitive capitalism, nineteenth-century style. The *base* or *infrastructure* in that theory was defined as the job front where pay was received for productive work. There were two main reasons for this: (1) The factory system of nineteenth-century capitalism embodied mass production of (almost all unbranded) commodities with all the improved efficiency traceable to the Industrial Revolution. (2) The tradition in economic theory begun by the Physiocrats and running through Marx that production was closely allied to natural resources and especially agriculture. The superstructure in that theory was where the ruling class in the state inculcated ideology by its press, its educational and religious institutions, and its monopoly of force (police and military).

The clear dichotomy between base and superstructure was no longer possible under monopoly capitalism, with Consciousness Industry buying audiences comprising virtually the whole population to aid it in managing demand for its commodity output. For the audiences are engaged in production which is an essential to the capitalist system as was the production at the job front in the early nineteenth century. Perhaps the audience market even takes priority away from the job front because the former "beckons" the latter into action very directly through the mode of operation of giant integrated corporations. The superstructure (in nineteenth-century terms) is thus decisively engaged in production. And increasingly, as welfare programs of employers have engaged people at the job front in all manner of popular cultural activities and vocational training, it seems as if the old "infrastructure" has taken on in part the ideological training functions previously associated with the old "superstructure." (See chapters 3 and 4 [Smythe, 1981].) It is not clear now how Marxists will resolve the anomalies in their theory as it applies to core area monopoly capitalism, especially because current Marxist theorists do not recognize that the audience commodity even exists.

It appears, as will be argued further in chapters 11 and 12 [Smythe, 1981], that in seeming to perfect its system for managing demand through producing and consuming audiences in order to market its products, monopoly capital has produced its principal antagonist in the core area: people commodified in audience markets who are consciously seeking noncommodified group relations. A symptom may be apparent in a downward trend in television viewing in 1977 and 1979 in the United States after 30 years of rising viewing.[11]

It has long been noticed that all traditional social institutions (family, church, labor union, political party, etc.) have been stripped of much of their traditional purpose by the impact of mass-produced communications. The mysticism attached to technique (and "technology") has incorrectly assumed that the medium basically defines the audience. But as a historical analysis of the rise of the mass media will show, the opposite has been true: the availability and actions of the audience is the basic feature in the definition of the media, singly and collectively. By placing the contradiction between advertisers/media on the one hand and audiences on the other on the level of social relations we are on solid ground and can repudiate the mysticism of the technological trap by which audiences are tied to hardware, software, and technique (as in Innis, McLuhan, and others).

In order to dig deeper into the process of which audience work is a part, it is necessary to consider how we got this way. In other words, we must review some history of monopoly capitalism. This will be the burden of chapters 3 and 4 [Smythe, 1981].

Notes

1 This literature is reviewed in Simon (1970); Schmalensee (1972); also, Pollak (1978); Pessemier (1978); and Marschak (1978).
2 Raymond Williams comes closer than many Marxists to a realistic treatment of communications and may be singled out for comment. In his *Marxism and Literature* (1978) he sees the full range of "cultural industry," including entertainment, as "necessary material production." He does not include advertising in cultural industry and is vague as to what, if any, activities besides official "culture" are included in it. He criticizes the base–superstructure dichotomy in twentieth-century Marxism and shows that it derived from Plekhanov, not Marx. Williams' *Television: Technology and Cultural Form* (1975) is disappointing. Broadcasting was called into existence by "a new way of life." The innovation of broadcasting is similarly mystified. It is traced to "no more than a set of particular social decisions, in particular circumstances, which were then so widely if imperfectly ratified than it is now difficult to see them as decisions rather than as (retrospectively) inevitable results" (p. 23). By whom, why, in what circumstances, the decisions were made he doesn't say. "Ideological control" was vaguely a purpose, again with no indication of how or who was involved. He never defines "technology" and uses the term as politically neutral. He sees broadcasting in technical terms, worldwide in scope, and advertising as " . . . a feature not of broadcasting itself but of its uses in a specific society [unnamed]" (p. 68). He does a fair critical analysis of McLuhan, not noticing that he himself had given us a line from McLuhan (" . . . the means of communication preceded their content," p. 25). In reality, of course, it was the prospective audience which beckoned both the means and the content into existence. In neither book does he recognize the media as producing audiences for sale to advertisers or that advertisers use the audience power to complete the marketing of their consumer

goods production. In neither does he recognize demand management by TNCs in monopoly capitalism – terms strangely lacking from his books.

3   I first addressed this criticism to Marxist theories in "Communications: Blindspot of Western Marxism" (1977). Also see Murdock, Graham, "Blindspots about Western Marxism: A Reply to Dallas Smythe" (1978) and my "Rejoinder to Graham Murdock" (Smythe, 1978), and Livant (1979a).

4   One of my critics argues that a better term for what advertisers buy would be *attention*. At our present naive stage concerning the matter, it does *seem* as if attention is indeed what is bought. But where people are paid for working on the job, should one say that what the employer buys is "labor power" or "the manual dexterity and attention necessary for tending machines?" Where I refer to audiences as being produced, purchased, and used, let it be understood that I mean "audience power," however it may turn out upon further realistic analysis to be exercised.

5   These estimates are made by applying to Canadian time sales by television and radio the same ratio which such time sales bear to total advertising expenditures on television and radio in the United States. In the United States in 1976, 77 percent of advertising expenditures on television went for network and station time ($5.198 billion), and 22 percent for production of program and advertising content; in radio 87 percent ($2.019 billion) went to network and station time and 13 percent to program and advertising content. In Canada the official statistics are nonsensical. Statistics Canada reported total advertising expenditures on television of $341.8 million; time sales of networks and stations to advertisers were given as $322.6 million. For radio, $111.1 million advertising expenditures were reported; time sales of networks and stations to advertisers (which represent only part of advertising expenditures) were given as $241.8 million. I have assumed that Canadian practice followed the United States model.

6   I am indebted to William Leiss for this hypothetical and chastening idea. See his *The Limits to Satisfaction* (1976, p. 81).

7   The following analysis of time use is based on de Grazia (1964).

8   Part-time workers (probably more female than male) amounted in 1960 to 19 percent of the employed labor force in the United States and they worked an average of 19 hours weekly. If we exclude such workers in order to get a figure comparable to the 70 hours in 1850, we consider the weekly hours worked by the average American male who worked at least 35 hours per week. We then find that they averaged 46.4 hours (as against 39.5 hours for all workers). For the sake of brevity, I omit the counterpart calculation of "free time" for women jobholders. No sexist implications are intended.

9   *Broadcasting Yearbook*, 1974, p. 69.

10 Livant (1975c); Bill Livant, University of Regina, has helped to develop the analysis of the audience commodity and I acknowledge this emphatically.

11 *Time*, 12 March 1979, p. 57.

References

Baran, P. T., and Sweezy, P. (1966) *Monopoly Capital*. New York: Monthly Review.

Barnouw, Erik (1978) *The Sponsor*. New York: Oxford University Press.

Blank, David M. (1970) "Pleasurable Pursuits – The Changing Structure of Leisure Time Spectator Activities," National Association of Business Economists, Annual Meeting, September (unpublished paper).

Cantril, Hadley, Gaudet, Hazel, and Herzog, Herta (1940) *Invasion from Mars*. Princeton: Princeton University Press.

Chamberlin, E. H. (1931) *The Theory of Monopolistic Competition*. Cambridge: Harvard University Press.

Chase, Stuart, and Schlink, F. J. (1927) *Your Money's Worth: A Study in the Waste of the Consumer's Dollar*. New York: Macmillan.

de Grazia, Sebastian (1964) *Of Time, Work and Leisure*. New York: Anchor.

Dorfman, Ariel, and Mattelart, Armand (1975) *How to Read Donald Duck: Imperialist Ideology in the Disney Comic*. New York: International General.

Ewen, Stuart (1976) *Captains of Consciousness*. New York: McGraw-Hill.

Galbraith, J. K. (1967) *The New Industrial State*. Boston: Houghton Mifflin.

Garnham, Nicholas (1977) "Towards a Political Economy of Culture," *NUQ*, Summer, pp. 341–57.

Citlin, Todd (1979) "Prime Time Ideology: The Hegemonic Process in Television Entertainment," *Social Problems*, vol. 26, no. 3, pp. 257–66.

Kaplin, Max (1960) *Leisure in America: A Social Inquiry*. New York: Wiley.

—— (1975) *Leisure: Theory and Policy*. New York: Wiley.

Kellner, Douglas (1979) "TV, Ideology and Emancipatory Popular Culture," *Socialist Review*, vol. 9, no. 3, May–June, pp. 13–53.

Leiss, William (1976) *The Limits to Satisfaction: An Essay on the Problems of Needs and Commodities*. Toronto: University of Toronto Press.

Levitt, T. N. (1976) "The Industrialization of Service," *Harvard Business Review*, September–October, pp. 63–74.

Liebling, A. J. (1961) *The Press*. New York: Ballantine.

Linder, Staffen B. (1970) *The Harried Leisure Class*. New York: Columbia University Press.

Livant, Bill (1975a) "The Communication Commodity," University of Regina, 25 December (unpublished paper).

—— (1975b) "More on the Production of Damaged Labour Power," 1 April (unpublished paper).

—— (1975c) "Notes on the Development of the Production of Labour Power" (unpublished paper).

Lyle, Jack (1972) "Television in Daily Life: Patterns of Use," in Rubenstein, E. A., Comstock, G. H., and Murray, J. P. (eds.), *Television and Social Behaviour*, vol. IV, pp. 1–32. Rockville, Md., National Institute of Mental Health.

Mao Zedong (1968) *Four Essays on Philosophy*. Beijing: Foreign Language Press.

Marschak, T. A. (1978) "On the Study of Taste-Changing Policies," *American Economic Review*, vol. 68, no. 2, pp. 386–391.

Murdock, Graham (1978) "Blindspots about Western Marxism: A Reply to Dallas Smythe," *Canadian Journal of Political and Social Theory*, vol. 2, no. 2, pp. 109–119.

Pessemier, Edgar A. (1978) "Stochastic Properties of Changing Preferences," *American Economic Review*, vol. 68, no. 2, pp. 380–5.

Pollak, Robert A. (1978) "Endogenous Taste in Demand and Welfare Analysis," *American Economic Review*, vol. 68, no. 2, pp. 374–9.

Richeri, Giuseppe (1978) "Italy: A Democratization of the Media," paper at Congress of International Association for Mass Communication Research, Warsaw, Poland.

Riesman, David (1950) *The Lonely Crowd*. New Haven: Yale University Press, 1950.

Rinchart, James W. (1975) *The Tyranny of Work*. Don Mills, Ontario: General Publishing.

Schiller, Herbert I. (1969) *Mass Communications and American Empire*. New York: A. M. Kelley.

—— (1973) *The Mind Managers*. Boston: Beacon Press.

Schiller, Herbert, I., and Phillips, J. D. (1976) *Superstate*. Urbana: University of Illinois Press.

Schmalensee, R. (1972) *The Economics of Advertising*. Amsterdam: North Holland.

Simon, Julian L. (1970) *Issues in the Economics of Advertising*. Urbana: University of Illinois Press.

Smythe, Dallas W. (1977) "Communications: Blindspot of Western Marxism," *Canadian Journal of Political and Social Theory*, vol. 1, no. 3, pp. 1–28.

——(1978) "Rejoinder to Graham Murdock," *Canadian Journal of Political and Social Theory*, vol. 2, no. 2, pp. 120–7.

——(1980) "Communications: Blindspot of Economics," in Melody, W. (ed.), *Culture, Communication and Dependency: The Tradition of H. A. Innis*. Norwood, N.J.: Ablex.

——(1981) *Dependency Road: Communications, Capitalism, Consciousness Canada*. Norwood, N.J.: Ablex).

Stephenson, Marylee (1977) "Never Done, Never Noticed: Women's Work in Canada," *This Magazine*, vol. 11, no. 6, pp. 31–3.

Terkel, Louis (1974) *Working*. New York: Pantheon.

US Congress (1967) House of Representatives. Subcommittee on International Organizations and Movements. Committee on Foreign Affairs, Report no. 5, *Winning the Cold War: The United States Ideological Offensive*. 90th Congress, 1st Session, House of Representatives.

Veblen, Thorstein (1927 [1899]) *The Theory of the Leisure Class*. New York: Macmillan.

Williams, Raymond (1975) *Television: Technology and Cultural Form*. New York: Schocken Books.

——(1978) *Marxism and Literature*. Oxford: Oxford University Press.

16

A Propaganda Model*

Edward Herman and Noam Chomsky

The mass media serve as a system for communicating messages and symbols to the general populace. It is their function to amuse, entertain, and inform, and to inculcate individuals with the values, beliefs, and codes of behavior that will integrate them into the institutional structures of the larger society. In a world of concentrated wealth and major conflicts of class interest, to fulfil this role requires systematic propaganda.[1]

In countries where the levers of power are in the hands of a state bureaucracy, the monopolistic control over the media, often supplemented by official censorship, makes it clear that the media serve the ends of a dominant elite. It is much more difficult to see a propaganda system at work where the media are private and formal censorship is absent. This is especially true where the media actively compete, periodically attack and expose corporate and governmental malfeasance, and aggressively portray themselves as spokesmen for free speech and the general community interest. What is not evident (and remains undiscussed in the media) is the limited nature of such critiques, as well as the huge inequality in command of resources, and its effect both on access to a private media system and on its behavior and performance.

A propaganda model focuses on this inequality of wealth and power and its multilevel effects on mass-media interests and choices. It traces the routes by which money and power are able to filter out the news fit to print, marginalize dissent, and allow the government and dominant private interests to get their messages across to the public. The essential ingredients of our propaganda model, or set of news "filters," fall under the following headings: (1) the size, concentrated ownership, owner wealth, and profit orientation of the dominant mass-media firms; (2) advertising as the primary income source of the mass media; (3) the reliance of the media on information provided by government, business, and "experts" funded and approved by these primary sources and agents of power; (4) "flak" as a means of disciplining the media; and (5) "anticommunism" as a national religion and control mechanism. These elements interact with and reinforce one another. The raw material of news must pass through successive filters, leaving only the cleansed residue fit to print.

* From Edward Herman and Noam Chomsky, *Manufacturing Consent: The Political Economy of the Mass Media* (New York: Pantheon, 1988), pp. 1–35.

They fix the premises of discourse and interpretation, and the definition of what is newsworthy in the first place, and they explain the basis and operations of what amount to propaganda campaigns.

The elite domination of the media and marginalization of dissidents that results from the operation of these filters occurs so naturally that media news people, frequently operating with complete integrity and goodwill, are able to convince themselves that they choose and interpret the news "objectively" and on the basis of professional news values. Within the limits of the filter constraints they often are objective; the constraints are so powerful, and are built into the system in such a fundamental way, that alternative bases of news choices are hardly imaginable. In assessing the newsworthiness of the U.S. government's urgent claims of a shipment of MIGs to Nicaragua on November 5, 1984, the media do not stop to ponder the bias that is inherent in the priority assigned to government-supplied raw material, or the possibility that the government might be manipulating the news,[2] imposing its own agenda, and deliberately diverting attention from other material.[3] It requires a macro, alongside a micro- (story-by-story), view of media operations, to see the pattern of manipulation and systematic bias.

Let us turn now to a more detailed examination of the main constituents of the propaganda model, which will be applied and tested in the chapters that follow.

Size, Ownership, and Profit Orientation of the Mass Media: The First Filter

In their analysis of the evolution of the media in Great Britain, James Curran and Jean Seaton describe how, in the first half of the nineteenth century, a radical press emerged that reached a national working-class audience. This alternative press was effective in reinforcing class consciousness: it unified the workers because it fostered an alternative value system and framework for looking at the world, and because it "promoted a greater collective confidence by repeatedly emphasizing the potential power of working people to effect social change through the force of "combination" and organized action."[4] This was deemed a major threat by the ruling elites. One MP asserted that the working-class newspapers "inflame passions and awaken their selfishness, contrasting their current condition with what they contend to be their future condition – a condition incompatible with human nature, and those immutable laws which Providence has established for the regulation of civil society."[5] The result was an attempt to squelch the working-class media by libel laws and prosecutions, by requiring an expensive security bond as a condition for publication, and by imposing various taxes designed to drive out radical media by raising their costs. These coercive efforts were not effective, and by mid-century they had been abandoned in favor of the liberal view that the market would enforce responsibility.

Curran and Seaton show that the market *did* successfully accomplish what state intervention failed to do. Following the repeal of the punitive taxes on newspapers between 1853 and 1869, a new daily local press came into existence, but not one new local working-class daily was established through the rest of the nineteenth century. Curran and Seaton note that

> Indeed, the eclipse of the national radical press was so total that when the Labour Party developed out of the working-class movement in the first decade of the twentieth century, it did not obtain the exclusive backing of a single national daily or Sunday paper.[6]

One important reason for this was the rise in scale of newspaper enterprise and the associated increase in capital costs from the mid-nineteenth century onward, which was based on technological improvements along with the owners' increased stress on reaching large audiences. The expansion of the free market was accompanied by an "industrialization of the press." The total cost of establishing a national weekly on a profitable basis in 1837 was under a thousand pounds, with a break-even circulation of 6,200 copies. By 1867, the estimated start-up cost of a new London daily was 50,000 pounds. The *Sunday Express*, launched in 1918, spent over two million pounds before it broke even with a circulation of over 250,000.[7]

Similar processes were at work in the United States, where the start-up cost of a new paper in New York City in 1851 was $69,000; the public sale of the *St. Louis Democrat* in 1872 yielded $456,000; and city newspapers were selling at from $6 to $18 million in the 1920s.[8] The cost of machinery alone, of even very small newspapers, has for many decades run into the hundreds of thousands of dollars; in 1945 it could be said that "Even small-newspaper publishing is big business . . . [and] is no longer a trade one takes up lightly even if he has substantial cash – or takes up at all if he doesn't."[9]

Thus the first filter – the limitation on ownership of media with any substantial outreach by the requisite large size of investment – was applicable a century or more ago, and it has become increasingly effective over time.[10] In 1986 there were some 1,500 daily newspapers, 11,000 magazines, 9,000 radio and 1,500 TV stations, 2,400 book publishers, and seven movie studios in the United States – over 25,000 media entities in all. But a large proportion of those among this set who were news dispensers were very small and local, dependent on the large national companies and wire services for all but local news. Many more were subject to common ownership, sometimes extending through virtually the entire set of media variants.[11]

Ben Bagdikian stresses the fact that despite the large media numbers, the twenty-nine largest media systems account for over half of the output of newspapers, and most of the sales and audiences in magazines, broadcasting, books, and movies. He contends that these "constitute a new Private Ministry of Information and Culture" that can set the national agenda.[12]

Actually, while suggesting a media autonomy from corporate and government power that we believe to be incompatible with structural facts (as we describe below), Bagdikian also may be understating the degree of effective concentration in news manufacture. It has long been noted that the media are tiered, with the top tier – as measured by prestige, resources, and outreach – comprising somewhere between ten and twenty-four systems.[13] It is this top tier, along with the government and wire services, that defines the news agenda and supplies much of the national and international news to the lower tiers of the media, and thus for the general public.[14] Centralization within the top tier was substantially increased by the post-World War II rise of television and the national networking of this important medium. Pre-television news markets were local, even if heavily dependent on the higher tiers and a narrow set of sources for national and international news; the networks provide national and international news from three national sources, and television is now the principal source of news for the public.[15] The maturing of cable, however, has resulted in a fragmentation of television audiences and a slow erosion of the market share and power of the networks.

Table 16.1 provides some basic financial data for the twenty-four media giants (or their controlling parent companies) that make up the top tier of media companies in the United States.[16] This compilation includes: (1) the three television networks: ABC (through its parent, Capital Cities), CBS, and NBC (through its ultimate parent, General Electric [GE]); (2) the leading newspaper empires: *New York Times, Washington Post, Los Angeles Times* (Times-Mirror), *Wall Street Journal* (Dow Jones), Knight-Ridder, Gannett, Hearst, Scripps-Howard, Newhouse (Advance Publications), and the Tribune Company; (3) the major news and general-interest magazines: *Time, Newsweek* (subsumed under *Washington Post*), *Reader's Digest, TV Guide* (Triangle), and *U.S. News & World Report*; (4) a major book publisher (McGraw-Hill); and (5) other cable-TV systems of large and growing importance: those of Murdoch, Turner, Cox, General Corp., Taft, Storer,[17] and Group W (Westinghouse). Many of these systems are prominent in more than one field and are only arbitrarily placed in a particular category (Time, Inc., is very important in cable as well as magazines; McGraw-Hill is a major publisher of magazines; the Tribune Company has become a large force in television as well as newspapers; Hearst is important in magazines as well as newspapers; and Murdoch has significant newspaper interests as well as television and movie holdings).

These twenty-four companies are large, profit-seeking corporations, owned and controlled by quite wealthy people. It can be seen in Table 16.1 that all but one of the top companies for whom data are available have assets in excess of $1 billion, and the median size (middle item by size) is $2.6 billion. It can also be seen in the table that approximately three-quarters of these media giants had after-tax profits in excess of $100 million, with the median at $183 million.

Many of the large media companies are fully integrated into the market, and for the others, too, the pressures of stockholders, directors, and bankers to focus on the bottom line are powerful. These pressures have intensified in recent years as media stocks have become market favorites, and actual or prospective owners of newspapers and television properties have found it possible to capitalize increased audience size and advertising revenues into multiplied values of the media franchises – and great wealth.[18] This has encouraged the entry of speculators and increased the pressure and temptation to focus more intensively on profitability. Family owners have been increasingly divided between those wanting to take advantage of the new opportunities and those desiring a continuation of family control, and their splits have often precipitated crises leading finally to the sale of the family interest.[19]

Table 16.1 Financial data for twenty-four large media corporations (or their parent firms), December 1986

Company	Total assets ($ millions)	Profits before taxes ($ millions)	Profits after taxes ($ millions)	Total revenue ($ millions)
Advance Publications (Newhouse)[a]	2,500	NA	NA	2,200
Capital Cities/ABC	5,191	688	448	4,124
CBS	3,370	470	370	4,754
Cox Communications[b]	1,111	170	87	743
Dow Jones & Co.	1,236	331	183	1,135
Gannett	3,365	540	276	2,801
General Electric (NBC)	34,591	3,689	2,492	36,725
Hearst[c]	4,040	NA	215	2,100
			(1983)	(1983)
Knight-Ridder	1,947	267	140	1,911
McGraw-Hill	1,463	296	154	1,577
News Corp. (Murdoch)[d]	8,460	377	170	3,822
New York Times	1,405	256	132	1,565
Reader's Digest[e]	NA	75–110	NA	1,400
		(1985)		(1985)
Scripps-Howard[f]	NA	NA	NA	1,062
Storer[g]	1,242	68	(−17)	537
Taft	1,257	(−11)	(−53)	500
Time, Inc.	4,230	626	376	3,762
Times-Mirror	2,929	680	408	2,948
Triangle[h]	NA	NA	NA	730
Tribune Co.	2,589	523	293	2,030
Turner Broadcasting	1,904	(−185)	(−187)	570
U.S. News & World Report[i]	200+	NA	NA	140
Washington Post	1,145	205	100	1,215
Westinghouse	8,482	801	670	10,731

NA = not available

[a] The asset total is taken from *Forbes* magazine's wealth total for the Newhouse family for 1985; the total revenue is for media sales only, as reported in *Advertising Age*, June 29, 1987.

[b] Cox Communications was publicly owned until 1985, when it was merged into another Cox family company, Cox Enterprises. The data presented here are for year-end 1984, the last year of public ownership and disclosure of substantial financial information.

[c] Data compiled in William Barrett, "Citizens Rich," *Forbes*, Dec. 14, 1987.

[d] These data are in Australian dollars and are for June 30, 1986; at that date the Australian dollar was worth 68/100 of a U.S. dollar.

[e] Data for 1985, as presented in the *New York Times*, Feb. 9, 1986.

[f] Total revenue for media sales only, as reported in *Advertising Age*, June 29, 1987.

[g] Storer came under the control of the Wall Street firm Kohlberg Kravis Roberts & Co. in 1985; the data here are for December 1984, the last period of Storer autonomy and publicly available information.

[h] Total revenue for media sales only; from *Advertising Age*, June 29, 1987.

[i] Total assets as of 1984–85, based on "Mort Zuckerman, Media's New Mogul," *Fortune*, Oct. 14, 1985; total revenue from *Advertising Age*, June 29, 1987.

This trend toward greater integration of the media into the market system has been accelerated by the loosening of rules limiting media concentration, cross-ownership, and control by non-media companies.[20] There has also been an abandonment of restrictions – previously quite feeble anyway – on radio–TV commercials, entertainment-mayhem programming, and "fairness doctrine" threats, opening the door to the unrestrained commercial use of the airwaves.[21]

The greater profitability of the media in a deregulated environment has also led to an increase in takeovers and takeover threats, with even giants like CBS and Time, Inc., directly attacked or threatened. This has forced the managements of the media giants to incur greater debt and to focus ever more aggressively and unequivocally on profitability, in order to placate owners and reduce the attractiveness of their properties to outsiders.[22] They have lost some of their limited autonomy to bankers, institutional investors, and large individual investors whom they have had to solicit as potential "white knights."[23]

While the stock of the great majority of large media firms is traded on the securities markets, approximately two-thirds of these companies are either closely held or still controlled by members of the originating family who retain large blocks of stock. This situation is changing as family ownership becomes diffused among larger numbers of heirs and the market opportunities for selling media properties continue to improve, but the persistence of family control is evident in the data shown in Table 16.2. Also evident in the table is the enormous wealth possessed by the controlling families of the top media firms. For seven of the twenty-four, the market value of the media properties owned by the controlling families in the mid-1980s exceeded a billion dollars, and the median value was close to half a billion dollars.[24] These control groups obviously have a special stake in the status quo by virtue of their wealth and their strategic position in one of the great institutions of society. And they exercise the power of this strategic position, if only by establishing the general aims of the company and choosing its top management.[25]

The control groups of the media giants are also brought into close relationships with the mainstream of the corporate community through boards of directors and social links. In the cases of NBC and the Group W television and cable systems, their respective parents, GE and Westinghouse, are themselves mainstream corporate giants, with boards of directors that are dominated by corporate and banking executives. Many of the other large media firms have boards made up predominantly of insiders, a general characteristic of relatively small and owner-dominated companies. The larger the firm and the more widely distributed the stock, the larger the number and proportion of outside directors. The composition of the outside directors of the media giants is very similar to that of large non-media corporations. Table 16.3 shows that active corporate executives and bankers together account for a little over half the total of the outside directors of ten media giants; and the lawyers and corporate-banker retirees (who account for nine of the thirteen under "Retired") push the corporate total to about two-thirds of the outside-director aggregate. These 95 outside directors had directorships in an additional 36 banks and 255 other companies (aside from the media company and their own firm of primary affiliation).[26]

Table 16.2 Wealth of the control groups of twenty-four large media corporations (or their parent companies), February 1986

Company	Controlling family or group	Percentage of voting stock by control group (%)	Value of controlling stock interest ($ millions)
Advance Publications	Newhouse family	Closely held	2,200[F]
Capital Cities	Officers and directors (ODs)	20.7 (Warren Buffett, 17.8)	711[P]
CBS	ODs	20.6[a]	551[P]
Cox Communications	Cox family	36	1,900[F]
Dow Jones & Co.	Bancroft-Cox families	54	1,500[P]
Gannett	ODs	1.9	95[P]
General Electric	ODs	Under 1	171[P]
Hearst	Hearst family	33	1,500[F]
Knight-Ridder	Knight and Ridder families	18	447[P]
McGraw-Hill	McGraw family	c.20	450[F]
News Corp.	Murdoch family	49	300[F]
New York Times	Sulzberger family	80	450[F]
Reader's Digest	Wallace estate managed by trustees; no personal beneficiaries	NA	NA
Scripps-Howard	Scripps heirs	NA	1,400[F]
Storer	ODs	8.4	143[P]
Taft	ODs	4.8	37[P]
Time, Inc.	ODs	10.7 (Luce 4.6, Temple 3.2)	406[P]
Times-Mirror	Chandlers	35	1,200[P]
Triangle	Annenbergs	Closely held	1,600[F]
Tribune Co.	McCormick heirs	16.6	273[P]
Turner Broadcasting	Turner	80	222[P]
U.S. News & World Report	Zuckerman	Closely held	176[b]
Washington Post	Graham family	50+	350[F]
Westinghouse	ODs	Under 1	42[P]

[a] These holdings include William Paley's 8.1 percent and a 12.2 percent holding of Laurence Tisch through an investment by Loews. Later in the year, Loews increased its investment to 24.9 percent, and Laurence Tisch soon thereafter became acting chief executive officer.

[b] This is the price paid by Zuckerman when he bought *U.S. News* in 1984. See Gwen Kinkead, "Mort Zuckerman, Media's New Mogul," *Fortune*, Oct. 14, 1985, p. 196.

Sources: P means taken from proxy statements and computed from stock values as of February 1986; F. means taken from *Forbes* magazine's annual estimate of wealth holdings of the very rich.

Table 16.3 Affiliations of the outside directors of ten large media companies (or their parents) in 1986[a]

Primary affiliation	Number	Percent
Corporate executive	39	41.1
Lawyer	8	8.4
Retired (former corporate executive or banker)	13 (9)	13.7 (9.5)
Banker	8	8.4
Consultant	4	4.2
Nonprofit organization	15	15.8
Other	8	8.4
Total	95	100.0

Other relationships		
Other directorships (bank directorships)	255 (36)	
Former government officials	15	
Member of Council on Foreign Relations	20	

[a] Dow Jones & Co.; Washington Post; New York Times; Time, Inc.; CBS; Times-Mirror; Capital Cities; General Electric; Gannett; and Knight-Ridder.

In addition to these board linkages, the large media companies all do business with commercial and investment bankers, obtaining lines of credit and loans, and receiving advice and service in selling stock and bond issues and in dealing with acquisition opportunities and takeover threats. Banks and other institutional investors are also large owners of media stock. In the early 1980s, such institutions held 44 percent of the stock of publicly owned newspapers and 35 percent of the stock of publicly owned broadcasting companies.[27] These investors are also frequently among the largest stockholders of individual companies. For example, in 1980–81, the Capital Group, an investment company system, held 7.1 percent of the stock of ABC, 6.6 percent of Knight-Ridder, 6 percent of Time, Inc., and 2.8 percent of Westinghouse.[28] These holdings, individually and collectively, do not convey control, but these large investors can make themselves heard, and their actions can affect the welfare of the companies and their managers.[29] If the managers fail to pursue actions that favor shareholder returns, institutional investors will be inclined to sell the stock (depressing its price), or to listen sympathetically to outsiders contemplating takeovers. These investors are a force helping press media companies toward strictly market (profitability) objectives.

So is the diversification and geographic spread of the great media companies. Many of them have diversified out of particular media fields into others that seemed like growth areas. Many older newspaper-based media companies, fearful of the power of television and its effects on advertising revenue, moved as rapidly as they could into broadcasting and cable TV. Time, Inc., also, made a major diversification move into cable TV, which now accounts for more than half its profits. Only a small minority of the twenty-four largest media giants remain in a single media sector.[30]

The large media companies have also diversified beyond the media field, and non-media companies have established a strong presence in the mass media. The most important cases of the latter are GE, owning RCA, which owns the NBC network, and Westinghouse, which owns major television-broadcasting stations, a cable network, and a radio-station network. GE and Westinghouse are both huge, diversified multinational companies heavily involved in the controversial areas of weapons production and nuclear power. It may be recalled that from 1965 to 1967, an attempt by International Telephone and Telegraph (ITT) to acquire ABC was frustrated following a huge outcry that focused on the dangers of allowing a great multinational corporation with extensive foreign investments and business activities to control a major media outlet.[31] The fear was that ITT control "could compromise the independence of ABC's news coverage of political events in countries where ITT has interests."[32] The soundness of the decision disallowing the acquisition seemed to have been vindicated by the later revelations of ITT's political bribery and involvement in attempts to overthrow the government of Chile. RCA and Westinghouse, however, had been permitted to control media companies long before the ITT case, although some of the objections applicable to ITT would seem to apply to them as well. GE is a more powerful company than ITT, with an extensive international reach, deeply involved in the nuclear power business, and far more important than ITT in the arms industry. It is a highly centralized and quite secretive organization, but one with a vast stake in "political" decisions.[33] GE has contributed to the funding of the American Enterprise Institute, a right-wing think tank that supports intellectuals who will get the business message across. With the acquisition of ABC, GE should be in a far better position to assure that sound views are given proper attention.[34] The lack of outcry over its takeover of RCA and NBC resulted in part from the fact that RCA control over NBC had already breached the gate of separateness, but it also reflected the more pro-business and *laissez-faire* environment of the Reagan era.

The non-media interests of most of the media giants are not large and, excluding the GE and Westinghouse systems, they account for only a small fraction of their total revenue. Their multinational outreach, however, is more significant. The television networks, television syndicators, major news magazines, and motion-picture studios all do extensive business abroad, and they derive a substantial fraction of their revenues from foreign sales and the operation of foreign affiliates. *Reader's Digest* is printed in seventeen languages and is available in over 160 countries. The Murdoch empire was originally based in Australia, and the controlling parent company is still an Australian corporation; its expansion in the United States is funded by profits from Australian and British affiliates.[35]

Another structural relationship of importance is the media companies' dependence on and ties with government. The radio-TV companies and networks all require government licenses and franchises and are thus potentially subject to government control or harassment. This technical legal dependency has been used as a club to discipline the media, and media policies that stray too often from an establishment orientation could activate this threat.[36] The media protect themselves from this contingency by lobbying and other political expenditures, the cultivation of political relationships, and care in policy. The political ties of the media have been impressive.

Table 16.3 shows that fifteen of ninety-five outside directors of ten of the media giants are former government officials, and Peter Dreier gives a similar proportion in his study of large newspapers.[37] In television, the revolving-door flow of personnel between regulators and the regulated firms was massive during the years when the oligopolistic structure of the media and networks was being established.[38]

The great media also depend on the government for more general policy support. All business firms are interested in business taxes, interest rates, labor policies, and enforcement and nonenforcement of the antitrust laws. GE and Westinghouse depend on the government to subsidize their nuclear power and military research and development, and to create a favorable climate for their overseas sales. The *Reader's Digest*, *Time*, *Newsweek*, and movie- and television-syndication sellers also depend on diplomatic support for their rights to penetrate foreign cultures with U.S. commercial and value messages and interpretations of current affairs. The media giants, advertising agencies, and great multinational corporations have a joint and close interest in a favorable climate of investment in the Third World, and their interconnections and relationships with the government in these policies are symbiotic.[39]

In sum, the dominant media firms are quite large businesses; they are controlled by very wealthy people or by managers who are subject to sharp constraints by owners and other market-profit-oriented forces;[40] and they are closely interlocked, and have important common interests, with other major corporations, banks, and government. This is the first powerful filter that will affect news choices.

The Advertising License to do Business: The Second Filter

In arguing for the benefits of the free market as a means of controlling dissident opinion in the mid-nineteenth century, the Liberal chancellor of the British exchequer, Sir George Lewis, noted that the market would promote those papers "enjoying the preference of the advertising public."[41] Advertising did, in fact, serve as a powerful mechanism weakening the working-class press. Curran and Seaton give the growth of advertising a status comparable with the increase in capital costs as a factor allowing the market to accomplish what state taxes and harassment failed to do, noting that these "advertisers thus acquired a de facto licensing authority since, without their support, newspapers ceased to be economically viable."[42]

Before advertising became prominent, the price of a newspaper had to cover the costs of doing business. With the growth of advertising, papers that attracted ads could afford a copy price well below production costs. This put papers lacking in advertising at a serious disadvantage: their prices would tend to be higher, curtailing sales, and they would have less surplus to invest in improving the salability of the paper (features, attractive format, promotion, etc.). For this reason, an advertising-based system will tend to drive out of existence or into marginality the media companies and types that depend on revenue from sales alone. With advertising, the free market does not yield a neutral system in which final buyer choice decides. The *advertisers'* choices influence media prosperity and survival.[43] The ad-based media receive an advertising subsidy that gives them a price-marketing-quality edge, which allows them to encroach on and further weaken their ad-free (or ad-disadvantaged) rivals.[44] Even if ad-based media cater to an affluent ("upscale") audience, they easily pick up a large part of the "down-scale" audience, and their rivals lose market share and are eventually driven out or marginalized.

In fact, advertising has played a potent role in increasing concentration even among rivals that focus with equal energy on seeking advertising revenue. A market share and advertising edge on the part of one paper or television station will give it additional revenue to compete more effectively – promote more aggressively, buy more salable features and programs – and the disadvantaged rival must add expenses it cannot afford to try to stem the cumulative process of dwindling market (and revenue) share. The crunch is often fatal, and it helps explain the death of many large-circulation papers and magazines and the attrition in the number of newspapers.[45]

From the time of the introduction of press advertising, therefore, working-class and radical papers have been at a serious disadvantage. Their readers have tended to be of modest means, a factor that has always affected advertiser interest. One advertising executive stated in 1856 that some journals are poor vehicles because "their readers are not purchasers, and any money thrown upon them is so much thrown away."[46] The same force took a heavy toll of the post-World War II social-democratic press in Great Britain, with the *Daily Herald, News Chronicle*, and *Sunday Citizen* failing or absorbed into establishment systems between 1960 and 1967, despite a collective average daily readership of 9.3 million. As James Curran points out, with 4.7 million readers in its last year, "the *Daily Herald* actually had almost double the readership of *The Times*, the *Financial Times* and the *Guardian* combined." What is more, surveys showed that its readers "thought more highly of their paper than the regular readers of any other popular newspaper," and "they also read more in their paper than the readers of other popular papers despite being overwhelmingly working class...."[47] The death of the *Herald*, as well as of the *News Chronicle* and *Sunday Citizen*, was in large measure a result of progressive strangulation by lack of advertising support. The *Herald*, with 8.1 percent of national daily circulation, got 3.5 percent of net advertising revenue; the *Sunday Citizen* got one-tenth of the net advertising revenue of the *Sunday Times* and one-seventh that of the *Observer* (on a per-thousand-copies basis). Curran argues persuasively that the loss of these three papers was an important contribution to the declining fortunes of the Labour party, in the case of the *Herald* specifically removing a mass-circulation institution that provided "an alternative framework of analysis and understanding that contested the dominant systems of representation in both broadcasting and the mainstream press."[48] A mass movement without any major media support, and subject to a great deal of active press hostility, suffers a serious disability, and struggles against grave odds.

The successful media today are fully attuned to the crucial importance of audience "quality": CBS proudly tells its shareholders that while it "continuously seeks to maximize audience delivery," it has developed a new "sales tool" with which it approaches advertisers: "Client Audience Profile, or CAP, will help advertisers optimize the effectiveness of their network television schedules by evaluating audience segments in proportion to usage levels of advertisers' products and services."[49] In short, the mass media are interested in attracting audiences with buying power, not audiences per se; it is affluent audiences that spark advertiser interest today, as in the nineteenth century. The idea that the drive for large audiences makes the mass media "democratic" thus suffers from the initial weakness that its political analogue is a voting system weighted by income!

The power of advertisers over television programming stems from the simple fact that they buy and pay for the programs – they are the "patrons" who provide the media subsidy. As such, the media compete for their patronage, developing special-ized staff to solicit advertisers and necessarily having to explain how their programs serve advertisers' needs. The choices of these patrons greatly affect the welfare of the media, and the patrons become what William Evan calls "normative reference organ-izations,"[50] whose requirements and demands the media must accommodate if they are to succeed.[51]

For a television network, an audience gain or loss of one percentage point in the Nielsen ratings translates into a change in advertising revenue of from $80 to $100 million a year, with some variation depending on measures of audience "quality." The stakes in audience size and affluence are thus extremely large, and in a market system there is a strong tendency for such considerations to affect policy profoundly.

This is partly a matter of institutional pressures to focus on the bottom line, partly a matter of the continuous interaction of the media organization with patrons who supply the revenue dollars. As Grant Tinker, then head of NBC-TV, observed, television "is an advertising-supported medium, and to the extent that support falls out, programming will change."[52]

Working-class and radical media also suffer from the political discrimination of advertisers. Political discrimination is structured into advertising allocations by the stress on people with money to buy. But many firms will always refuse to patronize ideological enemies and those whom they perceive as damaging their interests, and cases of overt discrimination add to the force of the voting system weighted by income. Public-television station WNET lost its corporate funding from Gulf + Western in 1985 after the station showed the documentary "Hungry for Profit," which contains material critical of multinational corporate activities in the Third World. Even before the program was shown, in anticipation of negative corporate reaction, station officials "did all we could to get the program sanitized" (according to one station source).[53] The chief executive of Gulf + Western complained to the station that the program was "virulently anti-business if not anti-American," and that the station's carrying the program was not the behavior "of a friend" of the corpora-tion. The London *Economist* says that "Most people believe that WNET would not make the same mistake again."[54]

In addition to discrimination against unfriendly media institutions, advertisers also choose selectively among programs on the basis of their own principles. With rare exceptions these are culturally and politically conservative.[55] Large corporate advert-isers on television will rarely sponsor programs that engage in serious criticisms of corporate activities, such as the problem of environmental degradation, the workings of the military-industrial complex, or corporate support of and benefits from Third World tyrannies. Erik Barnouw recounts the history of a proposed documentary series on environmental problems by NBC at a time of great interest in these issues. Barnouw notes that although at that time a great many large companies were spending money on commercials and other publicity regarding environmental problems, the documentary series failed for want of sponsors. The problem was one of excessive objectivity in the series, which included suggestions of corporate or systemic failure, whereas the corporate message "was one of reassurance."[56]

Television networks learn over time that such programs will not sell and would have to be carried at a financial sacrifice, and that, in addition, they may offend powerful advertisers.[57] With the rise in the price of advertising spots, the forgone revenue increases; and with increasing market pressure for financial performance and the diminishing constraints from regulation, an advertising-based media system will gradually increase advertising time and marginalize or eliminate altogether programming that has significant public-affairs content.[58]

Advertisers will want, more generally, to avoid programs with serious complexities and disturbing controversies that interfere with the "buying mood." They seek programs that will lightly entertain and thus fit in with the spirit of the primary purpose of program purchases – the dissemination of a selling message. Thus over time, instead of programs like "The Selling of the Pentagon," it is a natural evolution of a market seeking sponsor dollars to offer programs such as "A Bird's-Eye View of Scotland," "Barry Goldwater's Arizona," "An Essay on Hotels," and "Mr. Rooney Goes to Dinner" – a CBS program on "how Americans eat when they dine out, where they go and why."[59] There are exceptional cases of companies willing to sponsor serious programs, sometimes a result of recent embarrassments that call for a public-relations offset.[60] But even in these cases the companies will usually not want to sponsor close examination of sensitive and divisive issues – they prefer programs on Greek antiquities, the ballet, and items of cultural and national history and nostalgia. Barnouw points out an interesting contrast: commercial-television drama "deals almost wholly with the here and now, as processed via advertising budgets," but on public television, culture "has come to mean "other cultures." ... American civilization, here and now, is excluded from consideration."[61]

Television stations and networks are also concerned to maintain audience "flow" levels, i.e., to keep people watching from program to program, in order to sustain advertising ratings and revenue. Airing program interludes of documentary-cultural matter that cause station switching is costly, and over time a "free" (i.e., ad-based) commercial system will tend to excise it. Such documentary-cultural-critical materials will be driven out of secondary media vehicles as well, as these companies strive to qualify for advertiser interest, although there will always be some cultural-political programming trying to come into being or surviving on the periphery of the mainstream media.

Sourcing Mass-media News: The Third Filter

The mass media are drawn into a symbiotic relationship with powerful sources of information by economic necessity and reciprocity of interest. The media need a steady, reliable flow of the raw material of news. They have daily news demands and imperative news schedules that they must meet. They cannot afford to have reporters and cameras at all places where important stories may break. Economics dictates that they concentrate their resources where significant news often occurs, where important rumors and leaks abound, and where regular press conferences are held. The White House, the Pentagon, and the State Department, in Washington, D.C., are central nodes of such news activity. On a local basis, city hall and the police department are the subject of regular news "beats" for reporters. Business corporations and trade groups are also regular and credible purveyors of stories deemed newsworthy. These bureaucracies turn out a large volume of material that meets the demands of news organizations for reliable, scheduled flows. Mark Fishman calls this "the principle of bureaucratic affinity: only other bureaucracies can satisfy the input needs of a news bureaucracy."[62]

Government and corporate sources also have the great merit of being recognizable and credible by their status and prestige. This is important to the mass media. As Fishman notes,

> Newsworkers are predisposed to treat bureaucratic accounts as factual because news personnel participate in upholding a normative order of authorized knowers in the society. Reporters operate with the attitude that officials ought to know what it is their job to know.... In particular, a newsworker will recognize an official's claim to knowledge not merely as a claim, but as a credible, competent piece of knowledge. This amounts to a moral division of labor: officials have and give the facts; reporters merely get them.[63]

Another reason for the heavy weight given to official sources is that the mass media claim to be "objective" dispensers of the news. Partly to maintain the image of objectivity, but also to protect themselves from criticisms of bias and the threat of libel suits, they need material that can be portrayed as presumptively accurate.[64] This is also partly a matter of cost: taking information from sources that may be presumed credible reduces investigative expense, whereas material from sources that are not prima facie credible, or that will elicit criticism and threats, requires careful checking and costly research.

The magnitude of the public-information operations of large government and corporate bureaucracies that constitute the primary news sources is vast and ensures special access to the media. The Pentagon, for example, has a public-information service that involves many thousands of employees, spending hundreds of millions of dollars every year and dwarfing not only the public-information resources of any dissenting individual or group but the *aggregate* of such groups. In 1979 and 1980, during a brief interlude of relative openness (since closed down), the U.S. Air Force revealed that its public-information outreach included the following:

140 newspapers, 690,000 copies per week
Airman magazine, monthly circulation 125,000
34 radio and 17 TV stations, primarily overseas

45,000 headquarters and unit news releases
615,000 hometown news releases
6,600 interviews with news media
3,200 news conferences
500 news media orientation flights
50 meetings with editorial boards
11,000 speeches[65]

This excludes vast areas of the air force's public-information effort. Writing back in 1970, Senator J. W. Fulbright had found that the air force public-relations effort in 1968 involved 1,305 full-time employees, exclusive of additional thousands that "have public functions collateral to other duties."[66] The air force at that time offered a weekly film-clip service for TV and a taped features program for use three times a week, sent to 1,139 radio stations; it also produced 148 motion pictures, of which 24 were released for public consumption.[67] There is no reason to believe that the air force public-relations effort has diminished since the 1960s.[68]

Note that this is just the air force. There are three other branches with massive programs, and there is a separate, overall public-information program under an assistant secretary of defense for public affairs in the Pentagon. In 1971, an *Armed Forces Journal* survey revealed that the Pentagon was publishing a total of 371 magazines at an annual cost of some $57 million, an operation sixteen times larger than the nation's biggest publisher. In an update in 1982, the *Air Force Journal International* indicated that the Pentagon was publishing 1,203 periodicals.[69] To put this into perspective, we may note the scope of public-information operations of the American Friends Service Committee (AFSC) and the National Council of the Churches of Christ (NCC), two of the largest of the nonprofit organizations that offer a consistently challenging voice to the views of the Pentagon. The AFSC's main office information-services budget in 1984–85 was under $500,000, with eleven staff people.[70] Its institution-wide press releases run at about two hundred per year, its press conferences thirty a year, and it produces about one film and two or three slide shows a year. It does not offer film clips, photos, or taped radio programs to the media. The NCC Office of Information has an annual budget of some $350,000, issues about a hundred news releases per year, and holds four press conferences annually.[71] The ratio of air force news releases and press conferences to those of the AFSC and NCC taken together are 150 to 1 (or 2,200 to 1 if we count hometown news releases of the air force), and 94 to 1 respectively. Aggregating the other services would increase the differential by a large factor.

Only the corporate sector has the resources to produce public information and propaganda on the scale of the Pentagon and other government bodies. The AFSC and NCC cannot duplicate the Mobil Oil company's multimillion-dollar purchase of newspaper space and other corporate investments to get its viewpoint across.[72] The number of individual corporations with budgets for public information and lobbying in excess of those of the AFSC and NCC runs into the hundreds, perhaps even the thousands. A corporate *collective* like the U.S. Chamber of Commerce had a 1983 budget for research, communications, and political activities of $65 million.[73] By

1980, the chamber was publishing a business magazine (*Nation's Business*) with a circulation of 1.3 million and a weekly newspaper with 740,000 subscribers, and it was producing a weekly panel show distributed to 400 radio stations, as well as its own weekly panel-discussion programs carried by 128 commercial television stations.[74]

Besides the U.S. Chamber, there are thousands of state and local chambers of commerce and trade associations also engaged in public-relations and lobbying activities. The corporate and trade-association lobbying network community is "a network of well over 150,000 professionals,"[75] and its resources are related to corporate income, profits, and the protective value of public-relations and lobbying outlays. Corporate profits before taxes in 1985 were $295.5 billion. When the corporate community gets agitated about the political environment, as it did in the 1970s, it obviously has the wherewithal to meet the perceived threat. Corporate and trade-association image and issues advertising increased from $305 million in 1975 to $650 million in 1980.[76] So did direct-mail campaigns through dividend and other mail stuffers, the distribution of educational films, booklets and pamphlets, and outlays on initiatives and referendums, lobbying, and political and think-tank contributions. Aggregate corporate and trade-association political advertising and grass-roots outlays were estimated to have reached the billion-dollar-a-year level by 1978, and to have grown to $1.6 billion by 1984.[77]

To consolidate their preeminent position as sources, government and business-news promoters go to great pains to make things easy for news organizations. They provide the media organizations with facilities in which to gather; they give journalists advance copies of speeches and forthcoming reports; they schedule press conferences at hours well-geared to news deadlines;[78] they write press releases in usable language; and they carefully organize their press conferences and "photo opportunity" sessions.[79] It is the job of news officers "to meet the journalist's scheduled needs with material that their beat agency has generated at its own pace."[80]

In effect, the large bureaucracies of the powerful *subsidize* the mass media, and gain special access by their contribution to reducing the media's costs of acquiring the raw materials of, and producing, news. The large entities that provide this subsidy become "routine" news sources and have privileged access to the gates. Non-routine sources must struggle for access, and may be ignored by the arbitrary decision of the gatekeepers. It should also be noted that in the case of the largesse of the Pentagon and the State Department's Office of Public Diplomacy,[81] the subsidy is at the taxpayers' expense, so that, in effect, the citizenry pays to be propagandized in the interest of powerful groups such as military contractors and other sponsors of state terrorism.

Because of their services, continuous contact on the beat, and mutual dependency, the powerful can use personal relationships, threats, and rewards to further influence and coerce the media. The media may feel obligated to carry extremely dubious stories and mute criticism in order not to offend their sources and disturb a close relationship.[82] It is very difficult to call authorities on whom one depends for daily news liars, even if they tell whoppers. Critical sources may be avoided not only because of their lesser availability and higher cost of establishing credibility, but also because the primary sources may be offended and may even threaten the media using them.

Powerful sources may also use their prestige and importance to the media as a lever to deny critics access to the media: the Defense Department, for example, refused to participate in National Public Radio discussions of defense issues if experts from the Center for Defense Information were on the program; Elliott Abrams refused to appear on a program on human rights in Central America at the Kennedy School of Government, at Harvard University, unless the former ambassador, Robert White, was excluded as a participant;[83] Claire Sterling refused to participate in television-network shows on the Bulgarian Connection where her critics would appear.[84] In the last two of these cases, the authorities and brand-name experts were successful in monopolizing access by coercive threats.

Perhaps more important, powerful sources regularly take advantage of media routines and dependency to "manage" the media, to manipulate them into following a special agenda and framework (as we will show in detail in the chapters that follow).[85] Part of this management process consists of inundating the media with stories, which serve sometimes to foist a particular line and frame on the media (e.g., Nicaragua as illicitly supplying arms to the Salvadoran rebels), and at other times to help chase unwanted stories off the front page or out of the media altogether (the alleged delivery of MIGs to Nicaragua during the week of the 1984 Nicaraguan election). This strategy can be traced back at least as far as the Committee on Public Information, established to coordinate propaganda during World War I, which "discovered in 1917–18 that one of the best means of controlling news was flooding news channels with "facts," or what amounted to official information."[86]

The relation between power and sourcing extends beyond official and corporate provision of day-to-day news to shaping the supply of "experts." The dominance of official sources is weakened by the existence of highly respectable unofficial sources that give dissident views with great authority. This problem is alleviated by "co-opting the experts"[87] – i.e., putting them on the payroll as consultants, funding their research, and organizing think tanks that will hire them directly and help disseminate their messages. In this way bias may be structured, and the supply of experts may be skewed in the direction desired by the government and "the market."[88] As Henry Kissinger has pointed out, in this "age of the expert," the "constituency" of the expert is "those who have a vested interest in commonly held opinions; elaborating and defining its consensus at a high level has, after all, made him an expert."[89] It is therefore appropriate that this restructuring has taken place to allow the commonly held opinions (meaning those that are functional for elite interests) to continue to prevail.

This process of creating the needed body of experts has been carried out on a deliberate basis and a massive scale. Back in 1972, Judge Lewis Powell (later elevated to the Supreme Court) wrote a memo to the U.S. Chamber of Commerce urging business "to buy the top academic reputations in the country to add credibility to corporate studies and give business a stronger voice on the campuses."[90] One buys them, and assures that – in the words of Dr. Edwin Feulner, of the Heritage Foundation – the public-policy area "is awash with in-depth academic studies" that have the proper conclusions. Using the analogy of Procter & Gamble selling tooth-paste, Feulner explained that "They sell it and resell it every day by keeping the product fresh in the consumer's mind." By the sales effort, including the dissemina-tion of the correct ideas to "thousands of newspapers," it is possible to keep debate "within its proper perspective."[91]

In accordance with this formula, during the 1970s and early 1980s a string of institutions was created and old ones were activated to the end of propagandizing the corporate viewpoint. Many hundreds of intellectuals were brought to these institu-tions, where their work was funded and their outputs were disseminated to the media by a sophisticated propaganda effort.[92] The corporate funding and clear ideological purpose in the overall effort had no discernible effect on the credibility of the intellectuals so mobilized; on the contrary, the funding and pushing of their ideas catapaulted them into the press.

As an illustration of how the funded experts preempt space in the media, Table 16.4 describes the "experts" on terrorism and defense issues who appeared on the "McNeil – Lehrer News Hour" in the course of a year in the mid-1980s. We can see that, excluding journalists, a majority of the participants (54 percent) were present or former government officials, and that the next highest category (15.7 percent) was drawn from conservative think tanks. The largest number of appearances in the latter category was supplied by the Georgetown Center for Strategic and International Studies (CSIS), an organization funded by conservative foundations and corpora-tions, and providing a revolving door between the State Department and CIA and a nominally private organization.[93] On such issues as terrorism and the Bulgarian Connection, the CSIS has occupied space in the media that otherwise might have been filled by independent voices.[94]

The mass media themselves also provide "experts" who regularly echo the official view. John Barron and Claire Sterling are household names as authorities on the KGB

Table 16.4 Experts on terrorism and defense on the "McNeil-Lehrer News Hour," January 14, 1985, to January 27, 1986[a]

Category of expert	No.	%	No. excluding journalists	% Excluding journalists
Government official	24	20	24	27
Former government official	24	20	24	27
Conservative think tank	14	11.7	14	15.7
Academic	12	10	12	13.5
Journalist	31	25.8	—	—
Consultant	3	2.5	3	3.4
Foreign government official	5	4.2	5	5.6
Other	7	5.8	7	7.8
Totals	120	100	89	100

[a] This is a compilation of all appearances on the news hour concerning the Bulgarian Connection (3), the shooting down of the Korean airliner KAL 007 (5), and terrorism, defense, and arms control (33), from January 14, 1985, through January 27, 1986.

and terrorism because the *Reader's Digest* has funded, published, and publicized their work; the Soviet defector Arkady Shevchenko became an expert on Soviet arms and intelligence because *Time*, ABC-TV, and the *New York Times* chose to feature him (despite his badly tarnished credentials).[95] By giving these purveyors of the preferred view a great deal of exposure, the media confer status and make them the obvious candidates for opinion and analysis.

Another class of experts whose prominence is largely a function of serviceability to power is former radicals who have come to "see the light." The motives that cause these individuals to switch gods, from Stalin (or Mao) to Reagan and free enterprise, is varied, but for the establishment media the reason for the change is simply that the ex-radicals have finally seen the error of their ways. In a country whose citizenry values acknowledgement of sin and repentance, the turncoats are an important class of repentant sinners. It is interesting to observe how the former sinners, whose previous work was of little interest or an object of ridicule to the mass media, are suddenly elevated to prominence and become authentic experts. We may recall how, during the McCarthy era, defectors and ex-Communists vied with one another in tales of the imminence of a Soviet invasion and other lurid stories.[96] They found that news coverage was a function of their trimming their accounts to the prevailing demand. The steady flow of ex-radicals from marginality to media attention shows that we are witnessing a durable method of providing experts who will say what the establishment wants said.[97]

Flak and the Enforcers: The Fourth Filter

"Flak" refers to negative response to a media statement or program. It may take the form of letters, telegrams, phone calls, petitions, lawsuits, speeches and bills before Congress, and other modes of complaint, threat, and punitive action. It may be organized centrally or locally, or it may consist of the entirely independent actions of individuals.

If flak is produced on a large scale, or by individuals or groups with substantial resources, it can be both uncomfortable and costly to the media. Positions have to be defended within the organization and without, sometimes before legislatures and possibly even in courts. Advertisers may withdraw patronage. Television advertising is mainly of consumer goods that are readily subject to organized boycott. During the McCarthy years, many advertisers and radio and television stations were effectively coerced into quiescence and blacklisting of employees by the threats of determined Red hunters to boycott products. Advertisers are still concerned to avoid offending constituencies that might produce flak, and their demand for suitable programming is a continuing feature of the media environment.[98] If certain kinds of fact, position, or program are thought likely to elicit flak, this prospect can be a deterrent.

The ability to produce flak, and especially flak that is costly and threatening, is related to power. Serious flak has increased in close parallel with business's growing resentment of media criticism and the corporate offensive of the 1970s and 1980s. Flak from the powerful can be either direct or indirect. The direct would include letters or phone calls from the White House to Dan Rather or William Paley, or from the FCC to the television networks asking for documents used in putting together a program, or from irate officials of ad agencies or corporate sponsors to media officials asking for reply time or threatening retaliation.[99] The powerful can also work on the media indirectly by complaining to their own constituencies (stockholders, employees) about the media, by generating institutional advertising that does the same, and by funding right-wing monitoring or think-tank operations designed to attack the media. They may also fund political campaigns and help put into power conservative politicians who will more directly serve the interests of private power in curbing any deviationism in the media.

Along with its other political investments of the 1970s and 1980s, the corporate community sponsored the growth of institutions such as the American Legal Foundation, the Capital Legal Foundation, the Media Institute, the Center for Media and Public Affairs, and Accuracy in Media (AIM). These may be regarded as institutions organized for the specific purpose of producing flak. Another and older flak-producing machine with a broader design is Freedom House. The American Legal Foundation, organized in 1980, has specialized in Fairness Doctrine complaints and libel suits to aid "media victims." The Capital Legal Foundation, incorporated in 1977, was the Scaife vehicle for Westmoreland's $120-million libel suit against CBS.[100]

The Media Institute, organized in 1972 and funded by corporate-wealthy patrons, sponsors monitoring projects, conferences, and studies of the media. It has focused less heavily on media failings in foreign policy, concentrating more on media portrayals of economic issues and the business community, but its range of interests is broad. The main theme of its sponsored studies and conferences has been the failure of the media to portray business accurately and to give adequate weight to the business point of view,[101] but it underwrites works such as John Corry's exposé of the alleged left-wing bias of the mass media.[102] The chairman of the board of trustees of the institute in 1985 was Steven V. Seekins, the top public-relations officer of the American Medical Association; chairman of the National Advisory Council was Herbert Schmertz, of the Mobil Oil Corporation.

The Center for Media and Public Affairs, run by Linda and Robert Lichter, came into existence in the mid-1980s as a "non-profit, non-partisan" research institute, with warm accolades from Patrick Buchanan, Faith Whittlesey, and Ronald Reagan himself, who recognized the need for an objective and fair press. Their *Media Monitor* and research studies continue their earlier efforts to demonstrate the liberal bias and anti-business propensities of the mass media.[103]

AIM was formed in 1969, and it grew spectacularly in the 1970s. Its annual income rose from $5,000 in 1971 to $1.5 million in the early 1980s, with funding mainly from large corporations and the wealthy heirs and foundations of the corporate system. At least eight separate oil companies were contributors to AIM in the early 1980s, but the wide representation in sponsors from the corporate community is impressive.[104] The function of AIM is to harass the media and put pressure on them to follow the corporate agenda and a hard-line, right-wing foreign policy. It presses the media to join more enthusiastically in Red-scare bandwagons, and attacks them for alleged deficiencies whenever they fail to toe the line on foreign policy. It conditions the media to expect trouble (and cost increases) for violating right-wing standards of bias.[105]

Freedom House, which dates back to the early 1940s, has had interlocks with AIM, the World Anticommunist League, Resistance International, and U.S. government bodies such as Radio Free Europe and the CIA, and has long served as a virtual propaganda arm of the government and international right wing. It sent election monitors to the Rhodesian elections staged by Ian Smith in 1979 and found them "fair," whereas the 1980 elections won by Mugabe under British supervision it found dubious. Its election monitors also found the Salvadoran elections of 1982 admirable.[106] It has expended substantial resources in criticizing the media for insufficient sympathy with U.S. foreign-policy ventures and excessively harsh criticism of U.S. client states. Its most notable publication of this genre was Peter Braestrup's *Big Story*, which contended that the media's negative portrayal of the Tet offensive helped lose the war. The work is a travesty of scholarship, but more interesting is its premise: that the mass media not only should support any national venture abroad, but should do so with enthusiasm, such enterprises being by definition noble (see the extensive review of the Freedom House study in chapter 5 and appendix 3 [Herman and Chomsky 1988]). In 1982, when the Reagan administration was having trouble containing media reporting of the systematic killing of civilians by the Salvadoran army, Freedom House came through with a denunciation of the "imbalance" in media reporting from El Salvador.[107]

Although the flak machines steadily attack the mass media, the media treat them well. They receive respectful attention, and their propagandistic role and links to a larger corporate program are rarely mentioned or analyzed. AIM head, Reed Irvine's diatribes are frequently published, and right-wing network flaks who regularly assail the "liberal media," such as Michael Ledeen,[108] are given Op-Ed column space, sympathetic reviewers, and a regular place on talk shows as experts. This reflects the power of the sponsors, including the well-entrenched position of the right wing in the mass media themselves.[109]

The producers of flak add to one another's strength and reinforce the command of political authority in its news-management activities. The government is a major producer of flak, regularly assailing, threatening, and "correcting" the media, trying to contain any deviations from the established line. News management itself is designed to produce flak. In the Reagan years, Mr. Reagan was put on television to exude charm to millions, many of whom berated the media when they dared to criticize the "Great Communicator."[110]

Anticommunism as a Control Mechanism

A final filter is the ideology of anticommunism. Communism as the ultimate evil has always been the specter haunting property owners, as it threatens the very root of their class position and superior status. The Soviet, Chinese, and Cuban revolutions were traumas to Western elites, and the ongoing conflicts and the well-publicized abuses of Communist states have contributed to elevating opposition to communism to a first principle of Western ideology and politics. This ideology helps mobilize the populace against an enemy, and because the concept is fuzzy it can be used against anybody advocating policies that threaten property interests or support accommodation with Communist states and radicalism. It therefore helps fragment the left and labor movements and serves as a political-control mechanism. If the triumph of communism is the worst imaginable result, the support of fascism abroad is justified as a lesser evil. Opposition to social democrats who are too soft on Communists and "play into their hands" is rationalized in similar terms.

Liberals at home, often accused of being pro-Communist or insufficiently anti-Communist, are kept continuously on the defensive in a cultural milieu in which anticommunism is the dominant religion. If they allow communism, or something that can be labeled communism, to triumph in the provinces while they are in office, the political costs are heavy. Most of them have fully internalized the religion anyway, but they are all under great pressure to demonstrate their anti-Communist credentials. This causes them to behave very much like reactionaries. Their occasional support of social democrats often breaks down where the latter are insufficiently harsh on their own indigenous radicals or on popular groups that are organizing among generally marginalized sectors. In his brief tenure in the Dominican Republic, Juan Bosch attacked corruption in the armed forces and government, began a land-reform program, undertook a major project for mass education of the populace, and maintained a remarkably open government and system of effective civil liberties. These policies threatened powerful internal vested interests, and the United States resented his independence and the extension of civil liberties to Communists and radicals. This was carrying democracy and pluralism too far. Kennedy was "extremely disappointed" in Bosch's rule, and the State Department "quickly soured on the first democratically elected Dominican President in over thirty years." Bosch's overthrow by the military after nine months in office had at least the tacit support of the United States.[111] Two years later, by contrast, the Johnson administration invaded the Dominican Republic to make sure that Bosch did not resume power.

The Kennedy liberals were enthusiastic about the military coup and displacement of a populist government in Brazil in 1964.[112] A major spurt in the growth of neo-Fascist national-security states took place under Kennedy and Johnson. In the cases of the U.S. subversion of Guatemala, 1947–54, and the military attacks on Nicaragua, 1981–87, allegations of Communist links and a Communist threat caused many liberals to support counterrevolutionary intervention, while others lapsed into silence, paralyzed by the fear of being tarred with charges of infidelity to the national religion.

It should be noted that when anti-Communist fervor is aroused, the demand for serious evidence in support of claims of "communist" abuses is suspended, and charlatans can thrive as evidential sources. Defectors, informers, and assorted other opportunists move to center stage as "experts," and they remain there even after exposure as highly unreliable, if not downright liars.[113] Pascal Delwit and Jean-Michel Dewaele point out that in France, too, the ideologues of anticommunism "can do and say anything."[114] Analyzing the new status of Annie Kriegel and Pierre Daix, two former passionate Stalinists now possessed of a large and uncritical audience in France,[115] Delwit and Dewaele note:

> If we analyse their writings, we find all the classic reactions of people who have been disappointed in love. But no one dreams of criticising them for their past, even though it has marked them forever. They may well have been converted, but they have not changed....no one notices the constants, even though they are glaringly obvious. Their best sellers prove, thanks to the support of the most indulgent and slothful critics anyone could hope for, that the public can be fooled. No one denounces or even notices the arrogance of both yesterday's eulogies and today's diatribes; no one cares that there is never any proof and that invective is used in place of analysis. Their inverted hyper-Stalinism – which takes the usual form of total manicheanism – is whitewashed simply because it is directed against Communism. The hysteria has not changed, but it gets a better welcome in its present guise.[116]

The anti-Communist control mechanism reaches through the system to exercise a profound influence on the mass media. In normal times as well as in periods of Red scares, issues tend to be framed in terms of a dichotomized world of Communist and anti-Communist powers, with gains and losses allocated to contesting sides, and rooting for "our side" considered an entirely legitimate news practice. It is the mass media that identify, create, and push into the limelight a Joe McCarthy, Arkady Shevchenko, and Claire Sterling and Robert Leiken, or an Annie Kriegel and Pierre Daix. The ideology and religion of anticommunism is a potent filter.

Dichotomization and Propaganda Campaigns

The five filters narrow the range of news that passes through the gates, and even more sharply limit what can become "big news," subject to sustained news campaigns. By definition, news from primary establishment sources meets one major filter requirement and is readily accommodated by the mass media. Messages from and about dissidents and weak, unorganized individuals and groups, domestic and foreign, are at an initial disadvantage in sourcing costs and credibility, and they often do not comport with the ideology or interests of the gatekeepers and other powerful parties that influence the filtering process.[117]

Thus, for example, the torture of political prisoners and the attack on trade unions in Turkey will be pressed on the media only by human-rights activists and groups that have little political leverage. The U.S. government supported the Turkish martial-law government from its inception in 1980, and the U.S. business community has been warm toward regimes that profess fervent anticommunism, encourage foreign investment, repress unions, and loyally support U.S. foreign policy (a set of virtues that are frequently closely linked). Media that chose to feature Turkish violence against their own citizenry would have had to go to extra expense to find and check out information sources; they would elicit flak from government, business, and organized rightwing flak machines, and they might be looked upon with disfavor by the corporate community (including advertisers) for indulging in such a quixotic interest and crusade. They would tend to stand alone in focusing on victims that from the standpoint of dominant American interests were *unworthy*.[118]

In marked contrast, protest over political prisoners and the violation of the rights of trade unions in Poland was seen by the Reagan administration and business elites in 1981 as a noble cause, and, not coincidentally, as an opportunity to score political points. Many media leaders and syndicated columnists felt the same way. Thus information and strong opinions on human-rights violations in Poland could be obtained from official sources in Washington, and reliance on Polish dissidents would not elicit flak from the U.S. government or the flak machines. These victims would be generally acknowledged by the managers of the filters to be *worthy*. The mass media never explain *why* Andrei Sakharov is worthy and José Luis Massera, in Uruguay, is unworthy – the attention and general dichotomization occur "naturally" as a result of the working of the filters, but the result is the same as if a commissar had instructed the media: "Concentrate on the victims of enemy powers and forget about the victims of friends."[119]

Reports of the abuses of worthy victims not only pass through the filters; they may also become the basis of sustained propaganda campaigns. If the government or corporate community and the media feel that a story is useful as well as dramatic, they focus on it intensively and use it to enlighten the public. This was true, for example, of the shooting down by the Soviets of the Korean airliner KAL 007 in early September 1983, which permitted an extended campaign of denigration of an official enemy and greatly advanced Reagan administration arms plans. As Bernard Gwertzman noted complacently in the *New York Times* of August 31, 1984, U.S. officials "assert that worldwide criticism of the Soviet handling of the crisis has strengthened the United States in its relations with Moscow." In sharp contrast, the shooting down by Israel of a Libyan civilian airliner in February 1973 led to no outcry in the West, no denunciations for "cold-blooded murder,"[120] and no boycott. This difference in treatment was explained by the *New York Times* precisely on the grounds of utility: "No useful purpose is served by an acrimonious debate over the assignment of blame for the downing of a Libyan airliner in the Sinai peninsula last week."[121] There was a very "useful purpose" served by focusing on the Soviet act, and a massive propaganda campaign ensued.[122]

Propaganda campaigns in general have been closely attuned to elite interests. The Red scare of 1919–20 served well to abort the union-organizing drive that followed World War I in the steel and other industries. The Truman-McCarthy Red scare helped inaugurate the Cold War and the permanent war economy, and it also served to weaken the progressive coalition of the New Deal years. The chronic focus on the plight of Soviet dissidents, on enemy killings in Cambodia, and on the Bulgarian Connection helped weaken the Vietnam syndrome, justify a huge arms buildup and a more aggressive foreign policy, and divert attention from the upward redistribution of income that was the heart of Reagan's domestic economic program.[123] The recent propaganda-disinformation attacks on Nicaragua have been needed to avert eyes from the savagery of the war in El Salvador and to justify the escalating U.S. investment in counterrevolution in Central America.

Conversely, propaganda campaigns will *not* be mobilized where victimization, even though massive, sustained, and dramatic, fails to meet the test of utility to elite interests. Thus, while the focus on Cambodia in the Pol Pot era (and thereafter) was exceedingly serviceable, as Cambodia had fallen to the Communists and useful lessons could be drawn by attention to their victims, the numerous victims of the U.S. bombing *before* the Communist takeover were scrupulously ignored by the U.S. elite press. After Pol Pot's ouster by the Vietnamese, the United States quietly shifted support to this "worse than Hitler" villain, with little notice in the press, which adjusted once again to the national political agenda.[124] Attention to the Indonesian massacres of 1965–66, or the victims of the Indonesian invasion of East Timor from 1975 onward, would also be distinctly unhelpful as bases of media campaigns, because Indonesia is a U.S. ally and client that maintains an open door to Western investment, and because, in the case of East Timor, the United States bears major responsibility for the slaughter. The same is true of the victims of state terror in Chile and Guatemala, U.S. clients whose basic institutional structures, including the state terror system, were put in place and maintained by, or with crucial assistance from, U.S. power, and who remain U.S. client states. Propaganda campaigns on behalf of these victims would conflict with government-business-military interests and, in our model, would not be able to pass through the filtering system.[125]

Propaganda campaigns may be instituted either by the government or by one or more of the top media firms. The campaigns to discredit the government of Nicaragua, to support the Salvadoran elections as an exercise in legitimizing democracy, and to use the Soviet shooting down of the Korean airliner KAL 007 as a means of mobilizing public support for the arms buildup, were instituted and propelled by the government. The campaigns to publicize the crimes of Pol Pot and the alleged KGB plot to assassinate the pope were initiated by the *Reader's Digest*, with strong follow-up support from NBC-TV, the *New York Times*, and other major media companies.[126] Some propaganda campaigns are jointly initiated by government and media; all of them require the collaboration of the mass media. The secret of the unidirectionality of the politics of media propaganda campaigns is the multiple filter system discussed above: the mass media will allow any stories that are hurtful to large interests to peter out quickly, if they surface at all.[127]

For stories that are *useful*, the process will get under way with a series of government leaks, press conferences, white papers, etc., or with one or more of the mass media starting the ball rolling with such articles as Barron and Paul's "Murder of a Gentle Land" (Cambodia), or Claire Sterling's "The Plot to Kill the Pope," both in the *Reader's Digest*. If the other major media like the story, they will follow it up with their own versions, and the matter quickly becomes newsworthy by familiarity. If the articles are written in an assured and convincing style, are subject to no criticisms or alternative interpretations in the mass media, and command support by authority figures, the propaganda themes quickly become established as true even without real evidence. This tends to close out dissenting views even more comprehensively, as they would now conflict with an already established popular belief. This in turn opens up further opportunities for still more inflated claims, as these can be made without fear of serious repercussions. Similar wild assertions made in contradiction of official views would elicit powerful flak, so that such an inflation process would be controlled by the government and the market. No such protections exist with system-supportive claims; there, flak will tend to press the media to greater hysteria in the face of enemy evil. The media not only suspend critical judgment and investigative zeal, they compete to find ways of putting the newly established truth in a supportive light. Themes and facts – even careful and well-documented analyses – that are incompatible with the now institutionalized theme are suppressed or ignored. If the theme collapses of its own burden of fabrications, the mass media will quietly fold their tents and move on to another topic.[128]

Using a propaganda model, we would not only anticipate definitions of worth based on utility, and dichotomous attention based on the same criterion, we would also expect the news stories about worthy and unworthy victims (or enemy and friendly states) to differ in *quality*. That is, we would expect official sources of the United States and its client regimes to be used heavily – and uncritically – in connection with one's own abuses and those of friendly governments, while refugees and other dissident sources will be used in dealing with enemies.[129] We would anticipate the uncritical acceptance of certain premises in dealing with self and friends – such as that one's own state and leaders seek peace and democracy, oppose terrorism, and tell the truth – premises which will not be applied in treating enemy states. We would expect different criteria of evaluation to be employed, so that what is villainy in enemy states will be presented as an incidental background fact in the case of oneself and friends.[130] What is on the agenda in treating one case will be off the agenda in discussing the other.[131] We would also expect great investigatory zeal in the search for enemy villainy and the responsibility of high officials for abuses in enemy states, but diminished enterprise in examining such matters in connection with one's own and friendly states.

The quality of coverage should also be displayed more directly and crudely in placement, headlining, word usage, and other modes of mobilizing interest and outrage. In the opinion columns, we would anticipate sharp restraints on the range of opinion allowed expression. Our hypothesis is that worthy victims will be featured prominently and dramatically, that they will be humanized, and that their victimization will receive the detail and context in story construction that will generate reader interest and sympathetic emotion. In contrast, unworthy victims will merit only slight detail, minimal humanization, and little context that will excite and enrage.

Meanwhile, because of the power of establishment sources, the flak machines, and anti-Communist ideology, we would anticipate outcries that the worthy victims are being sorely neglected, that the unworthy are treated with excessive and uncritical generosity,[132] that the media's liberal, adversarial (if not subversive) hostility to government explains our difficulties in mustering support for the latest national venture in counterrevolutionary intervention.

In sum, a propaganda approach to media coverage suggests a systematic and highly political dichotomization in news coverage based on serviceability to important domestic power interests. This should be observable in dichotomized choices of story and in the volume and quality of coverage. In the chapters that follow we will see that such dichotomization in the mass media is massive and systematic: not only are choices for publicity and suppression comprehensible in terms of system advantage, but the modes of handling favored and inconvenient materials (placement, tone, context, fullness of treatment) differ in ways that serve political ends.

Notes

1   See note 4 of the Preface [to Herman and Chomsky's *Manufacturing Consent*].
2   Media representatives claim that what the government says is "newsworthy" in its own right. If, however, the government's assertions are transmitted without context or evaluation, and without regard to the government's possible manipulative intent, the media have set themselves up to be "managed." Their objectivity is "nominal," not substantive.

    In early October 1986, memos were leaked to the press indicating that the Reagan administration had carried out a deliberate campaign of disinformation to influence events in Libya. The mass media, which had passed along this material without question, expressed a great deal of righteous indignation that they had been misled. To compound the absurdity, five years earlier the press had reported a CIA-run "disinformation program designed to embarrass Qaddafi and his government," along with terrorist operations to overthrow Qaddafi and perhaps assassinate him (*Newsweek*, Aug. 3, 1981; P. Edward Haley, *Qaddafi and the United States since 1969* [New York: Praeger, 1984], p. 272). But no lessons were learned. In fact, the mass media are gulled on an almost daily basis, but rarely have to suffer the indignity of government *documents* revealing their gullibility. With regard to Libya, the media have fallen into line for each propaganda ploy, from the 1981 "hit squads" through the Berlin discothèque bombing, swallowing each implausible claim, failing to admit error in retrospect, and apparently unable to learn from successive entrapment – which suggests willing error. See Noam Chomsky, *Pirates & Emperors* (New York: Claremont, 1986), chapter 3. As we show throughout the present book, a series of lies by the government, successively exposed, never seems to arouse skepticism in the media regarding the next government claim.
3   For a description of the government's strategy of deflecting attention away from the Nicaraguan election by the fabricated MIG story, and the media's service in this government program, see chapter 3 [of Herman and Chomsky's *Manufacturing Consent*], under "The MIG Crisis Staged during the Nicaraguan Election Week."
4   James Curran and Jean Seaton, *Power without Responsibility: The Press and Broadcasting in Britain*, 2d ed. (London: Methuen, 1985), p. 24.
5   Quoted in ibid., p. 23.
6   Ibid., p. 34.
7   Ibid., pp. 38–9.
8   Alfred McClung Lee, *The Daily Newspaper in America* (New York: Macmillan, 1937), pp. 166, 173.
9   Earl Vance, "Freedom of the Press for Whom," *Virginia Quarterly Review* (Summer 1945), quoted in *Survival of a Free, Competitive Press: The Small Newspaper: Democracy's Grass Roots*, Report of the Chairman, Senate Small Business Committee, 80th Cong., 1st session, 1947, p. 54.
10 Note that we are speaking of media with substantial outreach – mass media. It has always been possible to start small-circulation journals and to produce mimeographed or photocopied newsletters sent around to a tiny audience. But even small journals in the United States today typically survive only by virtue of contributions from wealthy financial angels.

11   In 1987, the Times–Mirror Company, for example, owned newspapers in Los Angeles, Baltimore, Denver, and Hartford, Connecticut, had book publishing and magazine subsidiaries, and owned cable systems and seven television stations.

12   Ben Bagdikian, *The Media Monopoly,* 2nd ed. (Boston, Mass.: Beacon Press, 1987), p. xvi.

13   David L. Paletz and Robert M. Entman, *Media, Power, Politics* (New York: Free Press, 1981), p. 7; Stephen Hess, *The Government/Press Connection: Press Officers and Their Offices* (Washington: Brookings, 1984), pp. 99–100.

14   The four major Western wire services – Associated Press, United Press International, Reuters, and Agence-France-Presse – account for some 80 percent of the international news circulating in the world today. AP is owned by member newspapers; UPI is privately owned; Reuters was owned mainly by the British media until it went public in 1984, but control was retained by the original owners by giving lesser voting rights to the new stockholders; Agence-France-Presse is heavily subsidized by the French government. As is pointed out by Jonathan Fenby, the wire services "exist to serve markets," and their prime concern, accordingly, "is with the rich media markets of the United States, Western Europe, and Japan, and increasingly with the business community. . . ." They compete fiercely, but AP and UPI "are really U.S. enterprises that operate on an international scale. . . . Without their domestic base, the AP and UPI could not operate as international agencies. With it, they must be American organizations, subject to American pressures and requirements" (*The International News Services* [New York: Schocken, 1986], pp. 7, 9, 73–74). See also Anthony Smith, *The Geopolitics of Information: How Western Culture Dominates the World* (New York: Oxford University Press, 1980), chapter 3.

15   The fourteenth annual Roper survey, "Public Attitudes toward Television and Other Media in a Time of Change" (May 1985), indicates that in 1984, 64 percent of the sample mentioned television as the place "where you usually get most of your news about what's going on in the world today" (p. 3). It has often been noted that the television networks themselves depend heavily on the prestige newspapers, wire services, and government for their choices of news. Their autonomy as newsmakers can be easily exaggerated.

16   The members of the very top tier qualify by audience outreach, importance as setters of news standards, and asset and profit totals. The last half dozen or so in our twenty-four involve a certain amount of arbitrariness of choice, although audience size is still our primary criterion. McGraw-Hill is included because of its joint strength in trade books and magazines of political content and outreach.

17   As noted earlier, Storer came under the temporary control of the securities firm Kohlberg Kravis Roberts & Co. in 1985. As its ultimate fate was unclear at the time of writing, and as financial data were no longer available after 1984, we have kept Storer on the table and list it here, despite its uncertain status.

18   John Kluge, having taken the Metromedia system private in a leveraged buyout in 1984 worth $1.1 billion, sold off various parts of this system in 1985–86 for $5.5 billion, at a personal profit of some $3 billion (Gary Hector, "Are Shareholders Cheated by LBOs?" *Fortune,* Jan. 17, 1987, p. 100). Station KDLA-TV, in Los Angeles, which had been bought by a management-outsider group in a leveraged buyout in 1983 for $245 million, was sold to the Tribune Company for $510 million two years later (Richard Stevenson, "Tribune in TV Deal for $510 Million," *New York Times,* May 7, 1985). See also "The Media Magnates: Why Huge Fortunes Roll Off the Presses," *Fortune,* October 12, 1987.

19   A split among the heirs of James E. Scripps eventually resulted in the sale of the *Detroit Evening News.* According to one news article, "Daniel Marentette, a Scripps family member and a self described "angry shareholder," says family members want a better

return on their money. "We get better yields investing in a New York checking account," says Mr. Marentette, who sells race horses" (Damon Darlin, "Takeover Rumors Hit Detroit News Parent," *Wall Street Journal*, July 18, 1985). The Bingham family division on these matters led to the sale of the *Louisville Courier-Journal*; the New Haven papers of the Jackson family were sold after years of squabbling, and "the sale price [of the New Haven papers], $185 million, has only served to publicize the potential value of family holdings of family newspapers elsewhere" (Geraldine Fabrikant, "Newspaper Properties, Hotter than Ever," *New York Times*, Aug. 17, 1986).

20 The Reagan administration strengthened the control of existing holders of television-station licenses by increasing their term from three to five years, and its FCC made renewals essentially automatic. The FCC also greatly facilitated speculation and trading in television properties by a rule change reducing the required holding period before sale of a newly acquired property from three years to one year.

The Reagan era FCC and Department of Justice also refused to challenge mergers and takeover bids that would significantly increase the concentration of power (GE–RCA) or media concentration (Capital Cities–ABC). Furthermore, beginning April 2, 1985, media owners could own as many as twelve television stations, as long as their total audience didn't exceed 25 percent of the nation's television households; and they could also hold twelve AM and twelve FM stations, as the 1953 "7-7-7 rule" was replaced with a "12-12-12 rule." See Herbert H. Howard, "Group and Cross-Media Ownership of Television Stations: 1985" (Washington: National Association of Broadcasters, 1985).

21 This was justified by Reagan-era FCC chairman Mark Fowler on the grounds that market options are opening up and that the public should be free to choose. Criticized by Fred Friendly for doing away with the law's public-interest standard, Fowler replied that Friendly "distrusts the ability of the viewing public to make decisions on its own through the marketplace mechanism. I do not" (Jeanne Saddler, "Clear Channel: Broadcast Takeovers Meet Less FCC Static, and Critics Are Upset," *Wall Street Journal*, June 11, 1985). Among other problems, Fowler ignores the fact that true freedom of choice involves the ability to select options that may not be offered by an oligopoly selling audiences to advertisers.

22 CBS increased its debt by about $1 billion in 1985 to finance the purchase of 21 percent of its own stock, in order to fend off a takeover attempt by Ted Turner. The *Wall Street Journal* noted that "With debt now standing at 60 per cent of capital, it needs to keep advertising revenue up to repay borrowings and interest" (Peter Barnes, "CBS Profit Hinges on Better TV Ratings," June 6, 1986). With the slowed-up growth of advertising revenues, CBS embarked on an employment cutback of as many as six hundred broadcast division employees, the most extensive for CBS since the loss of cigarette advertising in 1971 (Peter Barnes, "CBS Will Cut up to 600 Posts in Broadcasting," *Wall Street Journal*, July 1, 1986). In June 1986, Time, Inc., embarked on a program to buy back as much as 10 million shares, or 16 percent of its common stock, at an expected cost of some $900 million, again to reduce the threat of a hostile takeover (Laura Landro, "Time Will Buy as Much as 16 per cent of Its Common," *Wall Street Journal*, June 20, 1986).

23 In response to the Jesse Helms and Turner threats to CBS, Laurence Tisch, of Loews Corporation, was encouraged to increase his holdings in CBS stock, already at 11.7 percent. In August 1986, the Loews interest was raised to 24.9 percent, and Tisch obtained a position of virtual control. In combination with William Paley, who owned 8.1 percent of the shares, the chief executive officer of CBS was removed and Tisch took

over that role himself, on a temporary basis (Peter Barnes, "Loews Increases Its Stake in CBS to Almost 25 per cent," *Wall Street Journal*, Aug. 12, 1986).

24 The number would be eight if we included the estate of Lila Wallace, who died in 1984, leaving the controlling stock interest in *Reader's Digest* to the care of trustees.

25 As we noted in the preface, the neoconservatives speak regularly of "liberal" domination of the media, assuming or pretending that the underlings call the shots, not the people who own or control the media. These data, showing the wealth position of media owners, are understandably something they prefer to ignore. Sometimes, however, the neoconservatives go "populist," and – while financed by Mobil Oil Corporation and Richard Mellon Scaife – pretend to be speaking for the "masses" in opposition to a monied elite dominating the media. For further discussion, see Edward S. Herman's review of *The Spirit of Democratic Capitalism*, "Michael Novak's Promised Land: Unfettered Corporate Capitalism," *Monthly Review* (October 1983).

26 Similar results are found in Peter Dreier, "The Position of the Press in the U.S. Power Structure," *Social Problems* (February 1982), pp. 298–310.

27 Benjamin Compaine et al., *Anatomy of the Communications Industry: Who Owns the Media?* (White Plains, N.Y.: Knowledge Industry Publications, 1982), p. 463.

28 Ibid., pp. 458–60.

29 See Edward S. Herman, *Corporate Control, Corporate Power* (New York: Cambridge University Press, 1981), pp. 26–54.

30 For the interests of fifteen major newspaper companies in other media fields, and a checklist of other fields entered by leading firms in a variety of media industries, see Compaine, *Anatomy of the Communications Industry*, tables 2.19 and 8.1, pp. 11 and 452–53.

31 The merger had been sanctioned by the FCC but was stymied by intervention of the Department of Justice. See "A broken engagement for ITT and ABC," *Business Week*, January 6, 1967.

32 Ibid.

33 On the enormous and effective lobbying operations of GE, see Thomas B. Edsall, "Bringing Good Things to GE: Firm's Political Savvy Scores in Washington," *Washington Post*, April 13, 1985.

34 The widely quoted joke by A. J. Liebling – that if you don't like what your newspaper says you are perfectly free to start or buy one of your own – stressed the impotence of the individual. In a favorable political climate such as that provided by the Reagan administration, however, a giant corporation not liking media performance *can* buy its own, as exemplified by GE.

35 Allan Sloan, "Understanding Murdoch – The Numbers Aren't What Really Matters," *Forbes*, March 10, 1986, pp. 114ff.

36 On the Nixon–Agnew campaign to bully the media by publicity attacks and threats, see Marilyn Lashner, *The Chilling Effect in TV News* (New York: Praeger, 1984). Lashner concluded that the Nixon White House's attempt to quiet the media "succeeded handily, at least as far as television is concerned" (p. 167). See also Fred Powledge, *The Engineering of Restraint: The Nixon Administration and the Press* (Washington: Public Affairs Press, 1971), and William E. Porter, *Assault on the Media: The Nixon Years* (Ann Arbor: University of Michigan Press, 1976).

37 Of the 290 directors in his sample of large newspapers, 36 had high-level positions – past or present – in the federal government (Dreier, "The Position of the Press," p. 303).

38   One study showed that out of sixty-five FCC commissioners and high-level staff personnel
     who left the FCC between 1945 and 1970, twelve had come out of the private-commun-
     ications sector before their FCC service, and thirty-four went into private-firm service
     after leaving the commission (Roger Noll et al., *Economic Aspects of Television Regulation*
     [Washington: Brookings, 1973], p. 123).

39   "The symbolic growth of American television and global enterprise has made them so
     interrelated that they cannot be thought of as separate. They are essentially the same
     phenomenon. Preceded far and wide by military advisers, lobbyists, equipment salesmen,
     advertising specialists, merchandising experts, and telefilm salesmen as advance agents, the
     enterprise penetrates much of the non-socialist world. Television is simply its most visible
     portion" (Erik Barnouw, *The Sponsor* [New York: Oxford University Press, 1978], p. 158).
     For a broader picture, see Herbert I. Schiller, *Communication and Cultural Domination*
     (White Plains, N.Y.: International Arts and Sciences Press, 1976), especially chapters 3–4.

40   Is it not possible that if the populace "demands" program content greatly disliked by the
     owners, competition and the quest for profits will cause them to offer such programming?
     There is some truth in this, and it, along with the limited autonomy of media personnel,
     may help explain the "surprises" that crop up occasionally in the mass media. One limit to
     the force of public demand, however, is that the millions of customers have no means of
     registering their demand for products that are not offered to them. A further problem is
     that the owners' class interests are reinforced by a variety of other filters that we discuss
     below.

41   Quoted in Curran and Seaton, *Power without Responsibility*, p. 31.

42   Ibid., p. 41.

43   "Producers presenting patrons [advertisers] with the greatest opportunities to make a
     profit through their publics will receive support while those that cannot compete on this
     score will not survive" (Joseph Turow, *Media Industries: The Production of News and
     Entertainment* [New York: Longman, 1984], p. 52).

44   Noncommercial television is also at a huge disadvantage for the same reason, and will
     require a public subsidy to be able to compete. Because public television does not have the
     built-in constraints of ownership by the wealthy, and the need to appease advertisers, it
     poses a threat to a narrow elite control of mass communications. This is why conservatives
     struggle to keep public television on a short leash, with annual funding decisions, and
     funding at a low level (see Barnouw, *The Sponsor*, pp. 179–82). Another option pursued in
     the Carter–Reagan era has been to force it into the commercial nexus by sharp defunding.

45   Bagdikian, *Media Monopoly*, pp. 118–26. " "The dominant paper ultimately thrives,"
     Gannett Chairman Allen H. Neuharth says. "The weaker paper ultimately dies" " (Joseph
     B. White, "Knight-Ridder's No-Lose Plan Backfires," *Wall Street Journal*, Jan. 4, 1988).

46   Quoted in Curran and Seaton, *Power without Responsibility*, p. 43.

47   "Advertising and the Press," in James Curran (ed.), *The British Press: A Manifesto*
     (London: Macmillan, 1978), pp. 252–55.

48   Ibid., p. 254.

49   *1984 CBS Annual Report*, p. 13. This is a further refinement in the measurement of
     "efficiency" in "delivering an audience." In the magazine business, the standard measure
     is CPM, or "costs per thousand," to an advertiser to reach buyers through a full-page,
     black-and-white ad. Recent developments, like CBS's CAP, have been in the direction of
     identifying the special characteristics of the audience delivered. In selling itself to adver-
     tisers, the *Soap Opera Digest* says: "But you probably want to know about our first
     milestone: today *Soap Opera Digest* delivers more women in the 18–49 category at the

lowest CPM than any other women's magazine" (quoted in Turow, *Media Industries*, p. 55).

50   William Evan, *Organization Theory* (New York: Wiley, 1976), p. 123.

51   Turow asserts that "The continual interaction of producers and primary patrons plays a dominant part in setting the general boundary conditions for day-to-day production activity" (*Media Industries*, p. 51).

52   Quoted in Todd Gitlin, *Inside Prime Time* (New York: Pantheon, 1983), p. 253.

53   Pat Aufderheide, "What Makes Public TV Public?" *The Progressive* (January 1988).

54   "Castor oil or Camelot?" December 5, 1987. For further information on such interventions, see Harry Hammitt, "Advertising Pressures on Media," Freedom of Information Center Report no. 367 (School of Journalism, University of Missouri at Columbia, February 1977). See also James Aronson, *Deadline for the Media* (New York: Bobbs-Merrill, 1972), pp. 261–3.

55   According to Procter & Gamble's instructions to their ad agency, "There will be no material on any of our programs which could in any way further the concept of business as cold, ruthless, and lacking in all sentiment or spiritual motivation." The manager of corporate communications for General Electric has said: "We insist on a program environment that reinforces our corporate messages" (quoted in Bagdikian, *Media Monopoly*, p. 160). We may recall that GE now owns NBC-TV.

56   Barnouw, *The Sponsor*, p. 135.

57   Advertisers may also be offended by attacks on themselves or their products. On the tendency of the media to avoid criticism of advertised products even when very important to consumer welfare [e.g., the effects of smoking], see Bagdikian, *Media Monopoly*, pp. 168–73.

58   This is hard to prove statistically, given the poor data made available by the FCC over the years. The long-term trend in advertising time/programming time is dramatically revealed by the fact that in 1929 the National Association of Broadcasting adopted as a standard of commercial practice on radio the following: "Commercial announcements . . . shall not be broadcast between 7 and 11 P.M." William Paley testified before the Senate Commerce Committee in 1930 that only 22 percent of CBS's time was allocated to commercially sponsored programs, with the other 78 percent sustaining; and he noted that advertising took up only "seven-tenths of 1 percent of all our time" (quoted in *Public Service Responsibility of Broadcast Licenses*, FCC [Washington: GPO, March 7, 1946], p. 42). Frank Wolf states in reference to public-affairs programming: "That such programs were even shown at all on commercial television may have been the result of FCC regulation" (*Television Programming for News and Public Affairs* [New York: Praeger, 1972], p. 138; see also pp. 99–139).

59   Barnouw, *The Sponsor*, p. 134.

60   For Alcoa's post-antitrust-suit sponsorship of Edward R. Murrow, and ITT's post-early-1970s-scandals sponsorship of "The Big Blue Marble," see Barnouw, *The Sponsor*, ibid., pp. 51–2, 84–6. Barnouw shows that network news coverage of ITT was sharply constrained during the period of ITT program sponsorship.

61   Barnouw, *The Sponsor*, p. 150.

62   Mark Fishman, *Manufacturing the News* (Austin: University of Texas Press, 1980), p. 143.

63   Ibid., pp. 144–5.

64   Gaye Tuchman, "Objectivity as Strategic Ritual: An Examination of Newsmen's Notions of Objectivity," *American Journal of Sociology*, 77, no. 2 (1972), pp. 662–64.

65   United States Air Force, "Fact Sheet: The United States Air Force Information Program"
     (March 1979); "News Releases: 600,000 in a Year," *Air Force Times*, April 28, 1980.

66   J. W. Fulbright, *The Pentagon Propaganda Machine* (New York: H. Liveright, 1970),
     p. 88.

67   Ibid., p. 90.

68   An Associated Press report on "Newspapers Mustered as Air Force Defends BiB,"
     published in the *Washington Post*, April 3, 1987, indicates that the U.S. Air Force had
     277 newspapers in 1987, as compared with 140 in 1979.

69   "DOD Kills 205 Periodicals; Still Publishes 1,203 Others," *Armed Forces Journal Inter-
     national* (August 1982), p. 16.

70   Its nine regional offices also had some public-information operations, but personnel and
     funding are not readily allocable to this function. They are smaller than the central office
     aggregate.
         The AFSC aggregate public-information budget is about the same size as the contract
     given by the State Department to International Business Communications (IBC) for
     lobbying on behalf of the contras ($419,000). This was only one of twenty-five contracts
     investigated by the GAO that "the Latin American Public Diplomacy office awarded to
     individuals for research and papers on Central America, said a GAO official involved in the
     investigation" (Rita Beamish, "Pro-contra Contracts are Probed," *Philadelphia Inquirer*,
     July 22, 1987, p. 4A).

71   The NCC's news services are concentrated in the Office of Information, but it has some
     dispersed staff in communications functions elsewhere in the organization that produce a
     few newsletters, magazines, and some videotapes and filmstrips.

72   In 1980, Mobil Oil had a public-relations budget of $21 million and a public-relations
     staff of seventy-three. Between 1976 and 1981 it produced at least a dozen televised
     special reports on such issues as gasoline prices, with a hired television journalist inter-
     viewing Mobil executives and other experts, that are shown frequently on television, often
     without indication of Mobil sponsorship. See A. Kent MacDougall, *Ninety Seconds To Tell
     It All* (Homewood, Ill.: Dow Jones–Irwin, 1981), pp. 117–20.

73   John S. Saloma III, *Ominous Politics: The New Conservative Labyrinth* (New York: Hill &
     Wang, 1984), p. 79.

74   MacDougall, *Ninety Seconds*, pp. 116–17.

75   Thomas B. Edsall, *The New Politics of Inequality* (New York: Norton, 1984), p. 110.

76   Peggy Dardenne, "Corporate Advertising," *Public Relations Journal* (November 1982),
     p. 36.

77   S. Prakash Sethi, *Handbook of Advocacy Advertising: Strategies and Applications* (Cam-
     bridge, Mass.: Ballinger, 1987), p. 22. See also Edsall, *New Politics*, chapter 3, "The
     Politicization of the Business Community"; and Saloma, *Ominous Politics*, chapter 6,
     "The Corporations: Making Our Voices Heard."

78   The April 14, 1986, U.S. bombing of Libya was the first military action timed to preempt
     attention on 7 P.M. prime-time television news. See Chomsky, *Pirates & Emperors*,
     p. 147.

79   For the masterful way the Reagan administration used these to manipulate the press, see
     "Standups," *The New Yorker*, December 2, 1985, pp. 81ff.

80   Fishman, *Manufacturing the News*, p. 153.

81   See note 70.

82   On January 16, 1986, the American Friends Service Committee issued a news release,
     based on extended Freedom of Information Act inquiries, which showed that there had

been 381 navy nuclear-weapons accidents and "incidents" in the period 1965–77, a figure far higher than that previously claimed. The mass media did not cover this hot story directly but through the filter of the navy's reply, which downplayed the significance of the new findings and eliminated or relegated to the background the AFSC's full range of facts and interpretation of the meaning of what they had uncovered. A typical heading: "Navy Lists Nuclear Mishaps: None of 630 Imperilled Public, Service Says," *Washington Post*, January 16, 1986.

83 The Harvard professor in charge of the program, Harvey Mansfield, stated that the invitation to White had been a mistake anyway, as he "is a representative of the far left," whereas the forum was intended to involve a debate "between liberals and conservatives" (*Harvard Crimson*, May 14, 1986).

84 See Edward S. Herman and Frank Brodhead, *The Rise and Fall of the Bulgarian Connection* (New York: Sheridan Square Publications, 1986), pp. 123–4.

85 Mark Hertsgaard, "How Reagan Seduced Us: Inside the President's Propaganda Factory," *Village Voice*, September 18, 1984; see also "Standups," cited in note 79 above.

86 Stephen L. Vaughn, *Holding Fast the Inner Lines* (Chapel Hill: University of North Carolina Press, 1980), p. 194.

87 Bruce Owen and Ronald Braeutigam, *The Regulation Game: Strategic Use of the Administrative Process* (Cambridge, Mass.: Ballinger, 1978), p. 7.

88 See Edward S. Herman, "The Institutionalization of Bias in Economics," *Media, Culture and Society* (July 1982), pp. 275–91.

89 Henry Kissinger, *American Foreign Policy* (New York: Norton, 1969), p. 28.

90 Quoted in Alex Carey, "Managing Public Opinion: The Corporate Offensive" (University of New South Wales, 1986, mimeographed), p. 32.

91 Ibid., pp. 46–7, quoting Feulner papers given in 1978 and 1985.

92 For a good discussion of many of these organizations and their purpose, funding, networking, and outreach programs, see Saloma, *Ominous Politics*, chapters 4, 6, and 9.

93 See Herman and Broadhead, *Bulgarian Connection*, p. 259; Fred Landis, "Georgetown's Ivory Tower for Old Spooks," *Inquiry*, September 30, 1979, pp. 7–9.

94 The CSIS's expert on terrorism, Robert Kupperman, was probably the most widely used participant on radio and television talk shows on terrorism in the last several years.

95 On Sterling's qualifications as an expert, see Herman and Broadhead, *Bulgarian Connection*, pp. 125–46; on Shevchenko, see Edward J. Epstein, "The Invention of Arkady Shevchenko, Supermole: The Spy Who Came in to be Sold," *New Republic*, July 15–22, 1985.

96 See David Caute, *The Great Fear: The Anti-Communist Purge under Truman and Eisenhower* (New York: Simon & Schuster, 1978), pp. 114–38, who stresses the importance of the *lying* informer. This McCarthyite pathology was replicated in Robert Leiken's 1982 book on "Soviet hegemonism" – the standard Maoist phrase – which conjures up a Soviet strategy of taking over the Western hemisphere by means of Cuba and the Sandinistas, and guerrilla movements elsewhere (Leiken, *Soviet Strategy in Latin America* [New York: Praeger, 1982]).

97 Then and now, former dissidents are portrayed as especially valuable experts for the seeming authenticity they can bring to the mistakes of their former associates. The fact that their claims are often fraudulent is not a problem because the mass media refuse to point this out. Thus Jean Lacouture lent credence to his criticisms of the Khmer Rouge by claiming to have been a former sympathizer – not only a falsehood, as he was pro-Sihanouk, but an absurdity, as nothing had been known about the the Khmer Rouge.

David Horowitz added to his value as a born-again patriot by claiming that along with protesters against the Vietnam War generally, he came "to acquire a new appreciation for foreign tyrants like Kim Il Sung of North Korea" (Peter Collier and David Horowitz, "Confessions of Two New-Left Radicals: Why We Voted for Reagan," *Washington Post National Weekly Edition*, April 8, 1985). Robert Leiken became more potent as a critic of the Sandinistas as an alleged former peace-movement activist and early supporter of the Sandinistas. Each of these claims was a fabrication, but this fact went unmentioned in the mass media. On Leiken's claims, and the "special force" his anti-Sandinista writings gained by his alleged conversion from "fan of the Sandinistas," see Michael Massing, "Contra Aides," *Mother Jones* (October 1987). While dismissing this pretense, Massing credits Leiken's claim that he "was active in the antiwar movement," but that is highly misleading. Activists in the Boston area, where he claims to have been an antiwar organizer, recall no participation by Leiken until about 1970 – at which time McGeorge Bundy could also have been described as an activist leader.

98 See above, note 55.

99 See "The Business Campaign Against "Trial by TV,""" *Business Week*, June 22, 1980, pp. 77–79; William H. Miller, "Fighting TV Hatchet Jobs," *Industry Week*, January 12, 1981, pp. 61–64.

100 See Walter Schneir and Miriam Schneir, "Beyond Westmoreland: The Right's Attack on the Press," *The Nation*, March 30, 1985.

101 An ad widely distributed by United Technologies Corporation, titled "Crooks and Clowns on TV," is based on the Media Institute's study entitled *Crooks, Conmen and Clowns: Businessmen in TV Entertainment*, which contends that businessmen are treated badly in television entertainment programs.

102 John Corry, *TV News and the Dominant Culture* (Washington: Media Institute), 1986.

103 See S. Robert Lichter, Stanley Rothman, and Linda Lichter, *The Media Elite* (Bethesda, MD: Adler & Adler, 1986). For a good discussion of the Lichters' new center, see Alexander Cockburn, "Ashes and Diamonds," In *These Times*, July 8–21, 1987.

104 Louis Wolf, "Accuracy in Media Rewrites News and History," *Covert Action Information Bulletin* (Spring 1984), pp. 26–29.

105 AIM's impact is hard to gauge, but it must be recognized as only a part of a larger corporate right-wing campaign of attack. It has common funding sources with such components of the conservative labyrinth as AEI, Hoover, the Institute for Contemporary Studies, and others (see Saloma, *Ominous Politics*, esp. chapters 2, 3, and 6), and has its own special role to play. AIM's head, Reed Irvine, is a frequent participant in television talk shows, and his letters to the editor and commentary are regularly published in the mass media. The media feel obligated to provide careful responses to his detailed attacks on their news and documentaries, and the Corporation for Public Broadcasting even helped fund his group's reply to the PBS series on Vietnam. His ability to get the publisher of the *New York Times* to meet with him personally once a year – a first objective of any lobbyist – is impressive testimony to influence. On his contribution to the departure of Raymond Bonner from the *Times*, see Wolf, "Accuracy in Media Rewrites News and History," pp. 32–3.

106 For an analysis of the bias of the Freedom House observers, see Edward S. Herman and Frank Brodhead, *Demonstration Elections: U.S.-Staged Elections in the Dominican Republic, Vietnam, and El Salvador* (Boston: South End Press, 1984), appendix I, "Freedom House Observers in Zimbabwe Rhodesia and El Salvador."

107   R. Bruce McColm, "El Salvador: Peaceful Revolution or Armed Struggle?" *Perspectives on Freedom* I (New York: Freedom House, 1982); James Nelson Goodsell, "Freedom House Labels US Reports on Salvador Biased," *Christian Science Monitor*, February 3, 1982.

108   For a discussion of Ledeen's views on the media, see Herman and Brodhead, *Bulgarian Connection*, pp. 166–70.

109   Among the contributors to AIM have been the Reader's Digest Association and the DeWitt Wallace Fund, Walter Annenberg, Sir James Goldsmith (owner of the French *L'Express*), and E. W. Scripps II, board chairman of a newspaper-television-radio system.

110   George Skelton, White House correspondent for the *Los Angeles Times*, noted that in reference to Reagan's errors of fact, "You write the stories once, twice, and you get a lot of mail saying, "You're picking on the guy, you guys in the press make mistakes too." And editors respond to that, so after a while the stories don't run anymore. We're intimidated" (quoted in Hertsgaard, "How Reagan Seduced Us").

111   Piero Gleijeses, *The Dominican Crisis* (Baltimore: Johns Hopkins University Press, 1978), pp. 95–9.

112   Jan K. Black, *United States Penetration of Brazil* (Philadelphia: University of Pennsylvania Press, 1977), pp. 39–56.

113   See above, pp. 24–5; below, pp. 157–61.

114   "The Stalinists of Anti-Communism," in Ralph Miliband, John Saville, and Marcel Liebman, *Socialist Register, 1984: The Uses of Anticommunism* (London: Merlin Press, 1984), p. 337.

115   Daix, in 1949, referred to the Stalin concentration camps as "one of the Soviet Union's most glorious achievements," displaying "the complete suppression of man's exploitation of man" (quoted in Miliband et al., *Socialist Register*, p. 337). Kriegel, formerly a hard-line Communist party functionary, was the author of a 1982 book explaining that the KGB organized the Sabra–Shatila massacres, employing German terrorists associated with the PLO and with the tacit cooperation of the CIA, in order to defame Israel as part of the Soviet program of international terrorism. For more on this profound study, and its influence, see Noam Chomsky, *Fateful Triangle* (Boston: South End Press, 1983), pp. 291–2, 374–5.

116   *Socialist Register*, p. 345.

117   Where dissidents are prepared to denounce official enemies, of course, they can pass through the mass-media filtering system, in the manner of the ex-Communist experts described in "Anticommunism as a Control Mechanism" (p. 29).

118   See chapter 2 [of Herman and Chomsky's *Manufacturing Consent*]: "Worthy and Unworthy Victims." Of interest in the Turkish case is the Western press's refusal to publicize the Turkish government's attacks on the press, including the U.S. press's own reporters in that country. UPI's reporter Ismet Ismet, beaten up by the Turkish police and imprisoned under trumped-up charges, was warned by UPI not to publicize the charges against him, and UPI eventually fired him for criticizing their badly compromised handling of his case. See Chris Christiansen, "Keeping in with the Generals," *New Statesman*, January 4, 1985.

119   We believe that the same dichotomization applies in the domestic sphere. For example, both British and American analysts have noted the periodic intense focus on – and indignation over – "welfare chiselers" by the mass media, and the parallel de-emphasis of and benign attitudes toward the far more important fraud and tax abuses of business and the affluent. There is also a deep-seated reluctance on the part of the mass media to

examine the structural causes of inequality and poverty. Peter Golding and Sue Middleton, after an extensive discussion of the long-standing "criminalization of poverty" and incessant attacks on welfare scroungers in Britain, point out that tax evasion, by contrast, is "acceptable, even laudable," in the press, that the tax evader "is not merely a victim but a hero." They note, also, that "The supreme achievement of welfare capitalism" has been to render the causes and condition of poverty almost invisible (*Images of Welfare: Press and Public Attitudes to Poverty* [Oxford: Martin Robertson, 1982], pp. 66–7, 98–100, 186, 193).

In a chapter entitled "The Deserving Rich," A. J. Liebling pointed out that in the United States as well, "The crusade against the destitute is the favorite crusade of the newspaper publisher," and that "There is no concept more generally cherished by publishers than that of the Undeserving Poor" (*The Press* [New York: Ballantine, 1964], pp. 78–9). Liebling went into great detail on various efforts of the media to keep welfare expenses and taxes down "by saying that they [the poor] have concealed assets, or bad character, or both" (p. 79). These strategies not only divert, they also help split the employed working class from the unemployed and marginalized, and make these all exceedingly uncomfortable about participating in a degraded system of scrounging. See Peter Golding and Sue Middleton, "Attitudes to Claimants: A Culture of Contempt," in *Images of Welfare*, pp. 169ff. President Reagan's fabricated anecdotes about welfare chiselers, and his complete silence on the large-scale chiseling of his corporate sponsors, have fitted into a long tradition of cynical and heartless greed.

120   For a full discussion of this dichotomized treatment, see Edward S. Herman, "Gatekeeper versus Propaganda Models: A Critical American Perspective," in Peter Golding, Graham Murdock and Philip Schlesinger (eds.), *Communicating Politics* (New York: Holmes & Meier, 1986), pp. 182–94.

121   Editorial, March 1, 1973. The Soviets apparently didn't know that they were shooting down a civilian plane, but this was covered up by U.S. officials, and the false allegation of a knowing destruction of a civilian aircraft provided the basis for extremely harsh criticism of the Soviets for barbaric behavior. The Israelis openly admitted knowing that they were shooting down a civilian plane, but this point was of no interest in the West in this particular case.

122   The *New York Times Index*, for example, has seven full pages of citations to the KAL 007 incident for September 1983 alone.

123   Patriotic orgies, such as the 1984 Olympic Games in Los Angeles, the space-shuttle flights, and "Liberty Weekend," perform a similar function in "bringing us all together." See Elayne Rapping, *The Looking Glass World of Nonfiction TV* (Boston: South End Press, 1987), chapter 5, "National Rituals."

124   See below [see chapter 6 of Herman and Chomsky's *Manufacturing Consent*].

125   On issues where the elite is seriously divided, there will be dissenting voices allowed in the mass media, and the inflation of claims and suspension of critical judgment will be subject to some constraint. See the discussion of this point in the preface, and examples in the case studies that follow.

126   The role of the government in these cases cannot be entirely discounted, given the close ties of the *Reader's Digest* to the CIA and the fact that Paul Henze, one of the primary sources and movers in the Bulgarian Connection campaign, was a longtime CIA official. On the CIA–*Reader's Digest* connection, see Epstein, "The Invention of Arkady Shevchenko," pp. 40–1. On Henze, see below, chapter 4. On the strong likelihood that an influential *Reader's Digest* best seller on Cambodia was in part a CIA disinformation

effort, see below [see chapter 6 of Herman and Chomsky's *Manufacturing Consent*] and sources cited.

127   We provide many illustrations of these points in the chapters that follow. Watergate and, more recently, the late-Reagan-era exposures of Iran-Contragate, which are put forward as counterexamples, are discussed below.

128   These points apply clearly to the case of the alleged Bulgarian Connection in the plot to assassinate the pope. See below.

129   We have noted elsewhere that the *New York Times* regularly relied upon Indonesian officials in "presenting the facts" about East Timor, which was being invaded by Indonesia, and ignored refugees, church sources, etc. In contrast, refugees, not state officials, were the prime source in the *Times*'s reporting on postwar events in Vietnam and Cambodia (*The Washington Connection and Third World Fascism* [Boston: South End Press, 1979], pp. 151–2, 169–76, 184–7). On attempts to evade the obvious implications, see chapter 6 [of Herman and Chomsky's *manufacturing Consent*], under "The Pol Pot Era" (pp. 284–5).

130   Thus when the CIA directs Nicaraguan contras to attack such "soft targets" as farming cooperatives, with explicit State Department approval, the media commentators, including doves, either applaud or offer philosophical disquisitions on whether such targets are legitimate, given that they are defended by lightly armed militia. Terrorist attacks on Israeli kibbutzim, also defended by armed settlers, are regarded somewhat differently. For details, see Noam Chomsky, *The Culture of Terrorism* (Boston: South End Press, 1988).

131   The variable use of agendas and frameworks can be seen with great clarity in the treatment of Third World elections supported and opposed by the United States.

132   Classic in their audacity are Michael Ledeen's assertions that: (1) Qaddafi's word is given more credence in the mass media than that of the U.S. government; and (2) "Relatively minor human rights transgressions in a friendly country (especially if ruled by an authoritarian government of the Right) are given far more attention and more intense criticism than far graver sins of countries hostile to us." (*Grave New World* [New York: Oxford University Press, 1985], p. 131; Qaddafi's superior credence is described on pp. 132–33). See chapter 2 [of Herman and Chomsky's *Manufacturing Consent*], for documentation on the reality of mass-media treatment of abuses by clients and enemy states.

17

Not Yet the Post-Imperialist Era*

Herbert I. Schiller

Apart from the persistent explanatory and semantic efforts in recent years to minimize or discredit the idea of cultural domination (Ang, 1985; Liebes & Katz, 1990), changing conditions make it desirable to reassess the original thesis.

Two governing circumstances strongly influenced the early elaboration of the theory of cultural dominance in the mid-1960s. The first was the then-existing world balance of forces.

Twenty-five years ago, the international order could be divided into three major groups. The most powerful of these was the so-called First World, including essentially those countries that were grounded in private propertied relations and whose production was undertaken by capitalist enterprise. The Second World comprised those nations that were organized along state ownership of property lines and that called themselves socialist. The last category (in every sense) was the Third World, containing those countries that had just emerged from the collapsed European colonial empires. In the case of Latin America, these nations continued to suffer economic exploitation although they had been nominally independent for over a century. In most of the Third World states, national liberation movements still existed, and the social structures had not yet been completely captured by new, privileged elites.

In this general map, the United States was by far the most powerful individual state in the First World and in the other two categories as well. Although the Soviet Union, after the Second World, claimed superpower status on the basis of possessing nuclear weapons, its economic and technological position was decidedly subordinate.

The other determining feature of this period in the cultural realm was the rapid development of television and its capability for transmitting compelling imagery and messages to vast audiences.

These geopolitical and technological conditions provided the social landscape for the era's cultural domination perspective. The essential assumptions undergirding it were (and are) few and relatively straightforward: Media-cultural imperialism is a

* Herbert I. Schiller, "Not Yet the Post-Imperialist Era," *Critical Studies in Mass Communication* (1991), vol. 8, pp. 13–28. Copyright of the National Communications Association, 1991, reproduced by permission of the publisher.

subset of the *general* system of imperialism. It is not freestanding; the media-cultural component in a developed, corporate economy supports the economic objectives of the decisive industrial-financial sectors (i.e., the creation and extension of the consumer society); the cultural and economic spheres are indivisible. Cultural, no less than automobile, production has its political economy. Consequently, what is regarded as cultural output also is ideological and profit-serving to the system at large. Finally, in its latest mode of operation, in the late twentieth century, the corporate economy is increasingly dependent on the media-cultural sector.

The thesis assumed that the state socialist (Second) World was, if not immune to Western cultural-informational pressure, at least to some degree insulated from it and would, under certain circumstances, support limits on its advance. The Third World, in contrast, was seen as an extremely vulnerable and deliberate target of American cultural exports. At the same time, it also was viewed as a potentially organizable force – not yet frozen in class relationships – that might give leadership to a comprehensive restructuring of the world information system. The movement for a new international information order was one vehicle for such a mobilization.

The charge that American-produced cultural commodities – television programs in particular – were overwhelming a good part of the world hardly needed documentation. But the data were there (Nordenstreng & Varis, 1974).

Changes in the International Geopolitical Arena

Twenty-five years later, some of this map has changed. Most importantly, the Second World (the socialist "camp") has all but disappeared. With the (temporary?) exceptions of China, Albania, North Korea, Vietnam, and Cuba, there is no longer a state socialist sphere in the global arena.

The Eastern European states, along with the Soviet Union, are in varying stages of capitalist restoration. Rather than providing an oppositional pole to the First World, they are now eager adherents to that world, as well as its supplicants. They offer national space to the marketing and ideological message flows of their former adversaries.

In a material sense, the strength and influence of the First World, especially that of its most powerful members, are less restrained than they were in the preceding period. This is observable not only with regard to the erstwhile socialist bloc but even more so with respect to the people and nations of Africa, Asia, and Latin America.

Actually, the condition of the Third World vis-à-vis the North (Western Europe, Japan, and the United States) is one of near-desperation. Now under the control of elites that accept and benefit from the workings of the world market economy, the African, Asian, and Latin American nations are deeply in debt and stalled for the most part in efforts for improvement. Most of the Third World nations seem more helpless than ever to resist the demands of their creditors and overseers. Despite some variability in this condition and occasional balking by a recalcitrant ruling group, the general situation reveals practically an abandonment of the challenging economic and cultural positions this group advanced not so long ago.

The role of television in the global arena of cultural domination has not diminished in the 1990s. Reinforced by new delivery systems – communication satellites and cable networks – the image flow is heavier than ever. Its source of origin also has not changed that much in the last quarter of a century. There is, however, one significant difference. Today, television is but one element, however influential, in an all-encompassing cultural package.

The corporate media-cultural industries have expanded remarkably in recent decades and now occupy most of the global social space. For this reason alone, cultural domination today cannot be measured by a simple index of exposure to American television programming. The cultural submersion now includes the English language itself, shopping in American-styled malls, going to theme parks (of which Disney is the foremost but not exclusive example), listening to the music of internationally publicized performers, following news agency reports or watching the Cable News Network in scores of foreign locales, reading translations of com- mercial best sellers, and eating in franchised fast-food restaurants around the world. Cultural domination means also adopting broadcasting systems that depend on advertising and accepting deregulatory practices that transform the public mails, the telephone system, and cable television into private profit centers (Engelhardt, 1990).

Alongside this all-service-supplying cultural-media environment, the relative eco- nomic and political power of the United States continues to diminish. This suggests that American cultural domination is not guaranteed in perpetuity. Yet irrefutably that domination has been preeminent for the last four decades and remains so to this date, though subsumed increasingly under transnational corporate capital and control. The cultural primacy that the ruling national power in the world economy historically exercised may now be changing.

The commanding position of American media products in the post-World War II era, the expertise derived from more than a century of successful marketing activity, and the now near-universal adoption of English as the international lingua franca still confer extraordinary influence on U.S.-produced cultural commodities. How long this influence can be sustained while American systemic power declines is an open question. But in any case, American *national* power no longer is an exclusive deter- minant of cultural domination.

The domination that exists today, though still bearing a marked American imprint, is better understood as *transnational corporate cultural domination*. Philips of the Netherlands, Lever Brothers of Britain, Daimler-Benz of Germany, Samson of Korea, and Sony of Japan, along with some few thousand other companies, are now the major players in the international market. The media, public relations, advertising, polling, cultural sponsorship, and consultants these industrial giants use and support hardly are distinguishable from the same services at the disposal of American-owned corporations. Still, a good fraction of these informational-cultural activities continue to be supplied by American enterprises.

These developments leave most of the peoples and nations in the world more vulnerable than ever to domination – cultural, military, and economic. Former oppositional forces have collapsed.

Unsurprisingly, at this moment, there seems a barely contained euphoria in Washington and other centers where capital rules. George Bush, speaking at the United Nations General Assembly in New York in October 1990, proclaimed "a new era of peace and competition and freedom." He saw "a world of open borders, open trade and, most importantly, open minds" (Transcript of President's address to U.N. General Assembly, 1990, p. A-6).

How aptly expressed are the current objectives of the for-the-moment unrestrained global corporate order – open borders, which can be transgressed; open trade, which enables the most powerful to prevail; open minds, which are at the mercy of the swelling global flows of the cultural industries. At least for now, the celebratory mood seems justified. Still, the currently triumphant corporate juggernaut is not on an open freeway with no stop lights and road checks. Possible sources of slowdown will be considered later.

Cheerful Surveyors of the Current Scene

Not all view the developments described above with skepticism or dismay. Indeed, some see the phenomena that now characterize daily life in a very large, and growing, part of the world as evidence that cultural domination no longer exists, or that what appears as domination actually fosters resistance to itself.

The idea of cultural diversity, for example, enjoys great popularity among many cultural observers. The central assumption – that many diverse cultural tendencies and movements operate, with no one element dominating – is the familiar pluralist argument, now applied to the cultural field. A more recent construct is the notion of "globalization." In this proposition, the world is moving, however haltingly, toward a genuinely global civilization. There is also the very widely accepted hypothesis of an "active audience," one in which viewers, readers, and listeners make their own meaning from the messages that come their way, often to the point of creating resistance to hegemonic meanings. Most comprehensive of all is the postmodern perspective. Whatever else this approach offers, it insists that systemic explanations of social phenomena are futile and wrong-headed. Mike Featherstone, editor of *Global Culture*, writes:

> Postmodernism is both a symptom and a powerful cultural image of the swing away from the conceptualization of global culture less in terms of alleged homogenizing processes (e.g. theories which present cultural imperialism, Americanization, and mass consumer culture as a proto-universal culture riding on the back of Western economic and political domination) and more in terms of the diversity, variety and richness of popular and local discourses, codes and practices which resist and play-back systemicity and order. (Featherstone, 1990, p. 2)

Each of these presently prevailing ideas asserts that:

1. Imperialism no longer exists. (A variant is that U.S. imperialism, in particular, is a
    spent force.)
2. A new global community is now emerging – global civil society, so to speak – that
    is independent of the interstate system. It is busily constructing alternative
    linkages and networks that provide space for new cultural environments.
3. Finally, it is of little consequence if cultural outputs from one source occupy a
    preponderant share of an audience's attention, because individuals reshape the
    material to their own tastes and needs. In this schema, the individual receptor
    takes precedence over the cultural producer.

How do these propositions stand up when examined against the actual context of
observable conditions?

Imperialism's Vital Signs are Unimpaired

Is imperialism dead? Is the United States a declining imperialist power? These are two
separate though connected questions.

Imperialism, understood as a system of exploitative control of people and
resources, is alive and well. At the same time, opposition and resistance to imperialism
are far more intense now than at the end of the nineteenth century. The existence of
125 new nations testifies to the fact that many relations of domination have been
broken. But powerful means of control still exist. Most of the African, Asian, and
Latin American nations continue to experience economic, financial, and even military
domination.

Although the term "imperialism" rarely appears in Western media, the word seems
to befit the deployment of more than 400,000 U.S. troops in Saudi Arabia. It is also a
signal that people's efforts to arrange their affairs without regard for the interests of
current controllers (of oil, real estate, or good geographical bases) will be met with
overpowering force. Moreover, the Middle East situation reveals another aspect of
contemporary imperialist strategy: the ability to mobilize international organizations
– now that the Soviet presence has been integrated into the West – for imperialist
aims. President Bush explained it this way: "Not since 1945 have we seen the real
possibility of using the United Nations as it was designed, as a center for international
collective security" (Transcript of President's address to U.N. General Assembly,
1990, p. A-6).

A good part of the world's population lives in desperation, often below the
subsistence level. A recent dispatch from Mexico City starkly described the appalling
conditions in the capital city of the country directly south of the United States
(Guillermoprieto, 1990). Hundreds of millions of people on all continents are
similarly affected.

When efforts are made – as they continuously are – to radically change these awful
conditions, invariably there is foreign intervention to maintain the arrangements that
offer advantage to one or another global governor and their local surrogates, the so-
called national elites. In recent years, Central and South America serve as models of

this process. Chile, Guatemala, El Salvador, the Dominican Republic, Nicaragua, and Cuba have felt the force of U.S. intervention – economic, military, ideological – when they have tried to create new living conditions. Similar treatment has been meted out across Africa – e.g., Angola, Mozambique, Zaire – and Asia as well – e.g., Vietnam, Afghanistan.

The U.S. military deployment in Saudi Arabia is only the most recent instance of imperialism. This action takes place amidst growing contradictions, however. The relative position of the United States in the world economy seems to be declining, yet it embarks on a costly and potentially disastrous adventure to maintain control of an economically and strategically valuable region and a source of colossal profit-ability.

One explanation, one most pleasing to officialdom, is that American power is still dominant. It is expressed best by Joseph Nye, a former top-level State Department official and currently a professor of international relations at Harvard University:

> Obviously, we have strengths and weaknesses.... But the mistake many analysts were making was to take a single anecdote illustrating American weakness, such as a decline in auto sales or the fact that the Germans concluded a deal with Gorbachev, and extra-polating from that to some very broad general conclusions that we were going down the tubes. We still have a lot more strengths than weaknesses.   (Nye, 1990, p. 1)

Interestingly, Nye finds some of these strengths in what he calls "soft power." "Soft power – the ability to co-opt rather than command – rests on intangible resources: culture, ideology, the ability to use international institutions to determine the frame-work of debate" (p. A-33). Soft power, as Nye defines it, is essentially the control of communications and definitional power. This is cultural imperialism with a semantic twist.

Nye may be overly sanguine about the capabilities of "soft power" to do the job, but he is not totally off the mark, especially with respect to "hard power." *Fortune*'s 1990 list of "The Global 500," the 500 biggest industrial corporations in the world reveals that "The U.S. leads all countries, with 167 companies on the list. That's more than Japan, West Germany, and Canada combined.... Americans are No. 1 in 14 of the 25 industries on the Global 500." Still, the magazine notes, "Impressive as these figures are, U.S. dominance is slowly giving way. In 1980, 23 U.S. companies made the top 50, compared with only 5 Japanese. Now there are 17 American and 10 Japanese."

But other factors must be considered in evaluating the present strength or weakness of the American global imperial position. One momentous development is the break-up of Communist Eastern Europe and the accelerating restoration of capitalist forms and practices there and in the Soviet Union. Removed thereby is an oppositional pole that served to severely limit, though not fully check, the exercise of American power in the postwar years. One (possibly too extravagant) reading of this situation is that "Washington may enjoy a greater freedom of action in foreign affairs than at any time since the end of World War II" (Toth, 1990, p. A–6).

Certainly, the Saudi Arabian intervention would have been inconceivable a few years ago. In any case, whatever the extent of the expanded range of American power, for the poorer people and countries in the world, the new situation is a disaster (Ramirez, 1990). The unrestrained use of what is called "low intensity warfare," against desperate people, now moves closer to realization as American military power no longer has to be concerned with Soviet counterforce (Klare, 1990). Whether it can disregard the financial cost of such undertakings is another matter.

Domination is further strengthened by the enfeeblement of the Non-Aligned Movement of the nations of Africa, Asia, and Latin America, established in Belgrade in 1961. Its present weakness can be attributed, in large part, to the enormous growth of transnational corporate power in the last twenty years, the collapse of the nonmarket sector of the world, and its own internal class stratification. Today, the ruling strata in the periphery have nowhere to turn except to the reservoirs of corporate capital. And they are doing just that.

Once assertive and insisting on national sovereignty, governments on all continents – Brazil, India, Mexico – headed by their dominant classes are enlisting the support of Western banks and the flow of Western–Japanese capital. One-time stalwarts of independence have demonstrated their new accommodationist outlook by engaging in sweeping denationalizations and privatizations.

Some still believe that these vast regions soon will be the vanguard of a new revolutionary upsurge (Amin, 1990). Perhaps, if the time frame is long enough, this will prove true. But in the meantime, their integration into the world market economy moves ahead. As part of their integration, the people are exposed to the drumbeat of corporate consumerism, no matter how limited the ordinary individual's spending power. The consumerist virus is an inseparable element in the rising global volume of marketing messages. This virus will impair the ability of leaders, still unborn, to act for the national community's social benefit.

A new hope for overcoming the deepening economic and social disparities around the world is seen in what is called the trend to globalization. This development, according to Featherstone (1990), one of its proponents, "emphasizes the autonomy of the globalization process, which should be seen not as the outcome of inter-state processes, but to operate in *relative* independence of conventionally designated societal and social-cultural processes." Contributing to this movement are "the increase in the number of international agencies and institutions, the increasing global forms of communication, the acceptance of unified global time, the development of standard notions of citizenship, rights and conception of humankind" (p. 6). It is emphasized that "the focus on the globe is to suggest that a new level of conceptualization is necessary." This new conceptualization can be comprehended in what it wants to dispose of: the center-periphery model of analysis and the very notion of intense social conflict. "From the vantage point of the late twentieth century it seems that the era of revolution is now finally over" (p. 4).

In short, globalization is defined to exclude domination, cultural control (soft or hard), and social revolution. The growth of the global institutions enumerated above is supposed to make these relationships and processes irrelevant, if not obsolete.

Globalism or Corporate Transnationalism?

It is indisputable that extranational cultural and political relationships have expanded spectacularly in recent decades. But what has been the engine of this growth? Is it a multifaceted outpouring of impulses toward a still-distant but slowly emerging world order? Do the forms and structures, however embryonic, indicate a looming era of universality?

It would be comforting to believe this. It would also be profoundly delusionary. The genuine character of the globalization drive can be appreciated by examining the fate of United Nations structures in the last fifteen years and the apparent reversal of their prospects since the Iraq–Kuwait imbroglio.

Until the fall of 1990, the experiences of the World Health Organization (WHO), the Food and Agriculture Organization (FAO), and, especially, the United Nations Educational, Scientific and Cultural Organization (UNESCO) – the entity established to encourage education, science, and culture on a world scale – tell a uniform story. Each of these organizations, as well as the United Nations itself, has been harshly attacked by the U.S. government and the American media. Each has been financially disabled for pursuing goals unacceptable to powerful American interests, i.e., the media, right-wing anti-abortion and anti-environmental groups, and the military-industrial complex. In mid-1990, the United States owed $750 million to the U.N. overall, exclusive of unpaid dues to WHO and FAO (*The New York Times*, September 13, 1990, p. A-10).

Such massive withholding of funds has crippled major health, agricultural, and educational programs worldwide. UNESCO has been a special target of Washington's anger because it served as a forum – nothing more – to express the complaints of 125 nations against the prevailing international information order. The United States withdrew from UNESCO in 1984 and has remained outside that organization since (Preston, Herman & Schiller, 1989).

Now, however, a new era seems to be opening up. It was inaugurated with U.N. support (thus far) for the U.S.-initiated embargo of Iraq and the American military deployment in Saudi Arabia. A newfound appreciation of the international organization has emerged in Washington and across the American media.

Does this suggest a better-late-than-never response to global organization and international cooperation? More realistically, what the new spirit reveals is the current U.S.–U.S.S.R. accommodation, achieved on the collapse of the Soviet economy and consequent Soviet eagerness to acquiesce in whatever initiatives its former adversary may propose – embargoes, aid termination to Angola and Cuba, unification of Germany and its adherence to NATO.

Equally important in this era of seemingly widespread international agreement is the indebtedness and paralyzing weakness of the Third World and its resultant inability to express any serious opposition to current developments. This species of "internationalism", based on either the weakness or the opportunism of most of the participants, can hardly be viewed as a movement toward global equilibrium and social peace.

The actual sources of what is being called globalization are not to be found in a newly achieved harmony of interests in the international arena. To the contrary, the infrastructure of what is hopefully seen as the first scaffolding of universalism is supplied by the transnational corporate business order, actively engaged on all continents, in all forms of economic and cultural organization, production, and distribution. Many of the actual international structures that monitor these activities are staffed and managed or advised by personnel on leave from the major (mostly American) companies in the system (D. Schiller, 1985).

This worldwide system now enlists American, Japanese, German, Korean, Brazilian, English, and other nationally based but globally engaged corporations. These private giant economic enterprises pursue – sometimes competitively, sometimes cooperatively – historical capitalist objectives of profit making and capital accumulation in continuously changing market and geopolitical conditions.

The actual practices of individual companies vary from one national setting to another, and there is no general coordination of the system at large. (This does not mean that there is an absence of uncoordinated ensemble action. Capital flight, for example, demonstrates how many groups and companies, acting independently when there is a perceived threat to their interests, can cripple the economy from which the capital flows). Still, with different specific interests and objectives, and often rival aims, harmonization of the global business system is out of the question. Yet the *generalized interest* of some thousands of super-companies is not that different. In their quest for both markets and consumers, they adopt fairly similar practices and institutional processes – technological, economic, political, and cultural. They are at one in maintaining the existing global hierarchy of power, though individual positions in that hierarchy constantly change. They utilize the communication and telecommunication systems, locally and globally, to direct their complex and geographically dispersed operations. They have pressed for and obtained privatization of communication facilities in one national locale after another, enabling them to have the greatest possible flexibility of decision making and allowing them a maximum of social unaccountability. They fill the media circuits with their marketing messages. Their combined efforts in the places they exercise the greatest influence have produced the consumer society, of which the United States stands as model.

Although the super-companies are owned for the most part by national groups of investors and are based in specific national settings, national concerns are not necessarily primary in the calculations and decisions of these enterprises. As the chief executive of Fiat, Italy's largest industrial corporation, pointed out: "Reasoning in nationalist terms does not make sense anymore" (Greenhouse, 1990, p. C-11). This seems to be the case for at least some of the transnational corporate companies.

How this works itself out in the world-at-large is still unclear, and not all transnationals behave identically. Still, the question of national sovereignty has become quite murky in the intersection of national interest and the profit-driven activities of these economic colossuses.

Insofar as the visible slippage of the U.S. economy in the global hierarchy of advantage is concerned, American companies' constant search for low-cost sites of production has contributed considerably to this condition. Yet there is one sector in which American dominance remains, if not intact, at least very considerable: the media-cultural arena.

U.S. Media-Cultural Dominance

American films, TV programs, music, news, entertainment, theme parks, and shopping malls set the standard for worldwide export and imitation. How long this dominance can endure alongside a receding economic primacy is uncertain. Already, many U.S. media enterprises have been acquired by Japanese (film and TV), German (publishing and music distribution), British (advertising), and other competing groups. Yet even when this occurs, the new owners, at least for the time being, usually are intent on keeping American creative and managerial media people in executive positions.

American cultural domination remains forceful in a rapidly changing international power scene. It is also undergoing transformation. This occurs by acquisition and, more importantly, by its practices being adopted by the rest of the transnational corporate system. What is emerging, therefore, is a world where alongside the American output of cultural product are the practically identical items marketed by competing national and transnational groups.

For some time, critics of media-imperialism theory have offered, as evidence of the doctrine's fatal flaw, the emergence of new centers of media production. Brazil, in particular, is hailed as a strikingly successful example of this development. Its achievement in television production and export is supposed to demolish the notion of a single center of cultural domination (Rogers & Antola, 1985; Straubhaar, 1989; Tracy, 1988).

In reality, according to the work of Brazilian researcher Omar Souki Oliveira (1990), Brazilian TV now broadcasts a minimum of U.S. programming. The biggest audiences watch and prefer Brazilian shows, which are widely exported abroad. Globo, the main Brazilian private TV network, currently exports shows to 128 countries. "Its productions outnumber those of any other station [sic] in the world." Oliveira writes that one American researcher (Straubhaar, 1989) has concluded that Brazilian television programs have been "Brazilianized almost beyond (American) recognition." Other U.S. researchers (Rogers & Antola, 1985) see Brazil's exports as "reverse media imperialism." A third observer (Tracy, 1988) writes that "in Brazil one sees a television devoted to national culture."

In Oliveira's reading of the same evidence, Brazilian programming is "the creolization of U.S. cultural products. It is the spiced up Third World copy of Western values, norms, patterns of behavior and models of social relations." He states that "the over whelming majority of Brazilian soaps have the same purpose as their U.S. counterparts, i.e., to sell products" – and, it should be emphasized, to sell goods made by the same transnational corporations who advertise in Brazil as well as in the United States. The "local" sponsors are Coca-Cola, Volkswagen, General Motors, Levi's, etc.

"In most Brazilian soaps," Oliveira finds, "the American lifestyle portrayed by Hollywood production reappears with a "brazilianized face." Now we don't see wealthy Anglos any more, but rich white Brazilians enjoying standards of living that would make any middle class American envious." Oliveira concludes: "Glamorous as they [TV series] are – even outshining Hollywood – their role within Brazilian society isn't different from that of U.S. imports. Unfortunately, the refinements applied to the genre were not to enhance diversity, but domination."

Domination is precisely what cultural imperialism is all about. With that domination comes the definitional power, Nye's "soft power," that sets the boundaries for national discourse.

Meanwhile, despite the developments already noted, the global preeminence of American cultural product is being not only maintained but extended to new locales. U.S. media incursions into Eastern Europe and the Soviet Union are assuming the dimension of a full-scale takeover, albeit shared with German and British media conglomerates.

American-owned and -styled theme parks, with their comprehensive ideological assumptions literally built into the landscape and architecture, are being staked out across Europe and Japan. "Euro-Disneyland will open its first park at Marne la Vallee in 1992, with a second possible in 1996. Anheuser-Busch [the second-largest theme park owner after Disney] has launched a theme park development in Spain, and other U.S. corporations are exploring projects elsewhere in Europe" (Sloan, 1990, p. D-3).

It must be emphasized that the corporate takeover of (popular) culture for marketing and ideological control is not a patented American practice, limited exclusively to U.S. companies. It is, however, carried to its fullest development in the United States. Cultural-recreational activity is now the very active site for spreading the transnational corporate message, especially in professional sports, where American practice again provides the basic model.

In the United States, practically no sports activity remains outside the interest and sponsorship of the big national advertisers. The irresistible lure of big sponsorship money has become the lubricant for a sport's national development. Accordingly, sports events and games have become multi-billion-dollar businesses, underwritten by the major corporations who stake out huge TV audiences. The hunt for sports events that can be made available to advertisers now includes university and, in increasing instances, high-school games. Assuming the mantle of moral concern, *The New York Times* editorialized: "College athletic departments have abandoned any pretense of representing cap and gown and now they roam the country in naked pursuit of hundreds of millions of television dollars" (Bright lights, big college money, 1990, p. A-22).

Unsurprisingly, the practice has become internationalized. A report from Italy describes the frenzied pursuit, by the largest Italian corporations, to own soccer and basketball franchises. "A growing trend in Italy...[is] the wholesale takeover of a sport by the captains of industry in search of new terrain from which to promote a corporate product or image" (Agnew, 1990, p. 14). The new patrons of Italian sports include the agro-chemicals giant Montedison, which also owns the widely read Rome daily *Il Mesaggero*; the Agnelli family, owners of the giant Fiat company, who also own the successful Juventus soccer club; and Silvio Berlusconi, the Italian TV and film mogul, who owns the AC Milan soccer club and other teams.

Recent developments in East Germany illustrate the extent to which sports have become a venue of corporate image promotion and an aggressive marketing instrument. *Business Week* ("Look Out" Wimbleton [sic], 1990) reports that

> the women's Grand Prix tennis tournament scheduled for the final week of September [1990] is moving from Mahwah, New Jersey to Leipzig, East Germany.... the tournament [is] the first successful effort to lure big corporate sponsors into a major tourney behind the old Iron Curtain.... a number of heavyweight sponsors ... include Volkswagen, Isostar, Sudmilch, Kraft-General Foods and American Airlines.

Major sports are now transmitted by satellite to global audiences. The commercial messages accompanying the broadcast, ringing the stadia, and often worn on the uniforms of the athletes constitute a concerted assault of corporate marketing values on global consciousness.

The Total Cultural Package and the "Active Audience"

The envelopment of professional and amateur sports for transnational corporate marketing objectives and ideological pacification is a good point at which to return to another one of the arguments contradicting the cultural imperialist concept. This is the belief in the existence of an "active audience," a view supported by a good number of Anglo-U.S. communications researchers.

According to this view, the audience is supposed to make its own meaning of the messages and images that the media disseminate, thereby playing a relatively autonomous role that is often interpreted as resistance to these messages and meanings (see Budd, Entman, & Steinman, 1990; H. Schiller, 1989). Active-audience theorizing has been largely preoccupied with the analysis of individual cultural products – a program or a TV series, a movie, or a genre of fiction. The theory follows closely in the tradition of "effects" research, though not necessarily coming to the same conclusions.

Leaving specific studies aside, it can be argued that one overarching condition invalidates, or at least severely circumscribes, the very idea of an active audience, to say nothing of one resisting a flow of messages. This is the current state – impossible to miss – of Western cultural enterprise. How can one propose to extract *one* TV show, film, book, or even a group, from the now nearly seamless media-cultural environment, and examine it (them) for specific effects? This is not to say there are no *generalized* effects – but these are not what the reception theorists seem to be concerned with.

Cultural/media production today has long left the cottage industry stage. Huge conglomerates like Time-Warner, with nearly $20 billion in assets, sit astride publishing, TV production, film making, and music recording, as well as book publishing and public classroom education. Theme park construction and ownership, shopping malls, and urban architectural design also are the domain of the same or related interests.

In this totalizing cultural space, who is able to specify the individual source of an idea, value, perspective, or reaction? A person's response, for example, to the TV series *Dallas* may be the outcome of half-forgotten images from a dozen peripheral encounters in the cultural supermarket. Who is to say what are the specific sites from which individual behavior and emotions now derive?

In 1990, even actual war locales become the setting for the marketing message. *Business Week* ("Publicity?" 1990) announces: "Welcome to the New World Order, Marketing Dept. Where companies are using history-making events as occasions to promote their products." The magazine explains: "With U.S. troops digging in their heels in Saudi Arabia, companies all around the country are vying to supply them with everything from nonalcoholic beer to video cassettes. . . . if a soldier is going to be photographed sipping a cold drink or playing poker, most marketers agree that he or she might as well be using their product." In this new world of pervasive corporate message making, the dispatch of over 450,000 troops provides an opportunity to cultivate this or that taste for consumption, along with a powerful patriotic backdrop for the company and the product. How does the audience engage this spectacle of democracy and consumption?

There is much to be said for the idea that people don't mindlessly absorb everything that passes before their eyes. Yet much of the current work on audience reception comes uncomfortably close to being apologetics for present-day structures of cultural control.

Meaningful Resistance to the Cultural Industries

There is good reason to be skeptical about the resistance of an audience, active or not, to its menu of media offerings. Yet this does not mean that the cultural conglomerates and the social system they embody are without an opposition. It is a resistance, however, that differs enormously from the kind of opposition that is supposed to occur in reinterpreting the message of a TV sitcom.

Some may believe in the end of history and others may insist that the era of revolution is finally over and that social (class) conflict is obsolete. The daily newspaper headlines tell a different story (though of course they don't explain it). What *is* apparent is that aroused people, if not their leaderships, all around the world are protesting their existing living conditions.

In the United States itself, still the most influential single unit of the world market economy, numerous oppositional elements force at least minimal acknowledgment, and some limited accommodation, from the governing crowd. For example, the congressional fight over the national budget in the fall of 1990 was essentially a class conflict, however obscured this was in its media coverage. To be sure, the class most directly affected – the working people – was largely absent from the deliberations. But the main question at issue was which class would be compelled to shoulder the burden of America's deepening crisis. This debate, and others underway, reveal the fragile condition of the dominating power in the country.

Between 1980 and 1990, the wealthiest 1 percent saw their incomes rise by 75 percent, while the income of the bottom 20 percent actually declined. The richest $2\frac{1}{2}$ million Americans' combined income nearly equaled that of the 100 million Americans at the bottom of the pyramid (Meisler, 1990).

It is the still growing disparities between the advantaged and the disadvantaged countries, as well as the widening gap *inside* the advantaged and disadvantaged societies, that constitute the fault line of the still seemingly secure world market economy. To this may be added the ecological disaster in the making, which is the inevitable accompaniment of the market forces that are roaring triumphantly across the continents.

A routine headline in the Western media reads: "Indonesia: The Hottest Spot in Asia." Elaborating, *Business Week* ("Indonesia: The Hottest Spot," 1990) rhapsodizes: "With a 7 per cent growth rate, a population of 182 million – the world's fifth largest – and a wealth of natural resources, Indonesia is poised to be the region's new success story." As the twentieth century winds down, success presumably is achieved by adopting the long-standing Western industrialization model, profligate with resource use and wastage, and exploiting the work force to satisfy foreign capital's search for the maximum return.

Indonesia, with an average wage of $1.25 *a day*, is an irresistible site. The chairman of the American Chamber of Commerce in Indonesia explains: "Indonesia will have a cheap labor supply well into the 21st century.... Nobody else in Asia except China can offer that." Not unexpectedly, "The income gap between affluent business people and the millions of impoverished who eke out a living in the villages and Jakarta's teeming slums is widening" (p. 45).

The Indonesian "success story," and others like it, are hardly confirmation for the end-of-social-conflict perspective. Much more convincing is the expectation that the next century will be the truly revolutionary era, accomplishing what the twentieth began but could not finish. In any case, communication theory, tied to the assumptions of political or cultural pluralism, harmonization of interests between the privileged and the deprived, resistance to domination residing in individualized interpretation of TV or film shows, or, overall, the long-term viability of capitalist institutions, is and will be unable to explain the looming social turbulence.

Certainly, there are no grounds for complacency about the prospects of the First and Third Worlds (the latter now including the once-Second World states) in the years ahead. Yet Western communication researchers seem intent on holding on to these assumptions. James Curran, surveying the English and continental research scene over the last fifteen years, concludes that

> a major change has taken place. The most important and significant overall shift has been the steady advance of pluralist themes within the radical tradition, in particular, the repudiation of the totalizing, explanatory framework of Marxism, the reconceptualization of the audience as creative and active and the shift from the political to a popular aesthetic.... A sea change has occurred in the field, and this will reshape – for better or worse – the development of media and cultural studies in Europe.
>
> (1990, pp. 157–8)

The same tendencies are well advanced, if not dominant, in the United States, though they have not totally swept the field as they seem to have done in England. There is still more than a little life left in those who look at the material side of the economy in general and the cultural industries in particular. Expressing this perspective is David Harvey, in his comprehensive approach to *The Condition of Postmodernity* (1989). Reviewing the same years that Curran surveyed, from the 1970s on, and relying on many of the same basic sources (though not as focused on the field of communication research), Harvey also finds that "there has been a sea-change in cultural as well as in political-economic practices since around 1972" (p. vii). He concludes that these changes, and the rise of postmodernist cultural forms, "when set against the basic rules of capitalist accumulation, appear more as shifts in surface appearance rather than as signs of the emergence of some entirely new post-capitalist or even post-industrial society" (p. vii).

Yet these "shifts in surface appearance" have contributed greatly to the capability of the corporate business system to maintain, and expand, its global reach. For this reason, the acknowledgement of and the struggle against cultural imperialism are more necessary than ever if the general system of domination is to be overcome.

References

Agnew, P. (1990, September 4). "Italy's sport madness has a very business like basis." *International Herald Tribune*, p. 14.

Amin, S. (1990). "The future of socialism." *Monthly Review, 42*(3), 10–29.

Ang, I. (1985). *Watching "Dallas": Soap Opera and the Melodramatic Imagination*. London: Methuen.

"Bright lights, big college money." (1990, September 13). *The New York Times*, p. A-22.

Budd, M., Entman, R. M., & Steinman, C. (1990). "The affirmative character of U.S. cultural studies." *Critical Studies in Mass Communication, 7*, 169–184.

Curran, J. (1990). "The new revisionism in mass communication research." *European Journal of Communication, 5*, 135–164.

Engelhardt, T. (1990). "Bottom line dreams and the end of culture." *The Progressive, 54*(10), 30–35.

Featherstone, M. (Ed.). (1990). *Global Culture*. London: Sage.

"The global 500, the world's biggest industrial corporations." (1990, July 30). *Fortune*, p. 265.

Greenhouse, S. (1990, October 5). "Alliance is formed by Fiat and French company." *The New York Times*. p. C-11.

Guillermoprieto, A. (1990, September 17). "Letter from Mexico City." *The New Yorker*, 93–104.

Harvey, D. (1989). *The Condition of Postmodernity*. Oxford: Basil Blackwell.

"Indonesia:" The hottest spot in Asia. (1990, August 27). *Business Week*, pp. 44–45.

Klare, M. T. (1990). "Policing the gulf – and the world." *The Nation, 251*(12), 1, 416, 418, 420.

Liebes, T., & Katz, E. (1990). *The Export of Meaning: Cross-cultural Readings of "Dallas."* New York: Oxford University Press.

"Look out Wimbleton [sic], here comes Leipzig." (1990, September 24). *Business Week*, p. 54.

Meisler, S. (1990, July 24). "Rich-poor gap held widest in 40 years." *Los Angeles Times*, p. A-11.

Nordenstreng, K., & Varis, T. (1974). "Television traffic – A one-way street." *Reports and Papers on Mass Communication*, No. 70. Paris: UNESCO.

Nye, J. S., Jr. (1990, October 3). "No, the U.S. isn't in decline." *The New York Times*, p. A-33.

Oliveira, O. S. (1990, October 8–10). *Brazilian Soaps Outshine Hollywood: Is cultural Imperialism Fading Out?* Paper presented at the meetings of the Deutsche Gesellschaft für Semiotik, Internationaler Kongress, Universität Passau.

Preston, W., Jr., Herman, E., & Schiller, H. (1989). *Hope & Folly: The United States and Unesco, 1945–1985*. Minneapolis: University of Minnesota Press.

"Publicity? Why it never even occurred to us." (1990, September 24). *Business Week*, p. 46.

Ramirez, A. (1990, September 14). "2 American makers agree to sell Soviets 34 billion cigarettes." *The New York Times*, p. A-14.

Rogers, E., & Antola, L. (1985). "*Telenovelas:* A Latin American success story." *Journal of Communication*, 35(4), 24–35.

Schiller, D. (1985). "The emerging global grid: Planning for what?" *Media, Culture and Society*, 7, 105–125.

Schiller, H. I. (1989). *Culture, Inc.: The Corporate Takeover of Public Expression*. New York: Oxford University Press.

Sloan, A. K. (1990, August 22). "Europe is ripe for theme parks." *Los Angeles Times*, p. D-3.

Straubhaar, J. (1989, May 25–29). *Change in Assymetrical Interdependence in Culture: The Brazilianization of Television in Brazil*. Paper presented at the International Communication Association, San Francisco.

Toth, R. C. (1990, September 12). "With Moscow crippled, U.S. emerges as top power." *Los Angeles Times*, p. D-3.

Tracy, M. (1988, March). "Popular culture and the economics of global television." *Intermedia*, 19–25.

Transcript of President's address to U.N. General Assembly. (1990, October 2). *The New York Times*, p. A-6.

18

Unwrapping Use Value*

Susan Willis

Everything is packaged. Late twentieth-century commodity production has generated a companion production of commodity packaging that is so much a part of the commodity form itself as to be one of the most unremarked features of daily life. Only when we have to drag all those 30 gallon black plastic trash bags out to the curb or haul them to the town dump are we likely to grasp the enormity of packaging. Otherwise, it goes unnoticed even in drug stores and discount department stores where fully 80 per cent of the merchandise is packaged. Whether items are individually boxed or mounted for display on strips of cardboard backing, most packaging today includes a plastic see-through window or bubble. Packaging catches the consumer's eye, even though as a phenomenon of daily life, it is all but invisible. The package is a device for hailing the consumer and cueing his or her attention, by the use of color and design, to a particular brand-name commodity. The plastic cover replicates the display case or store window and suggests that each and every item is worthy of display.

Packaging also enables the standardization of weights and measures. For today's consumer, the "net weight" label is the only guarantee that a box of laundry detergent indeed weighs 4 lb or that the peanut butter in a particular jar really does amount to 1 lb 2 oz. The standardization of weights and measures represents a rationalization of sales similar to the Taylorization of production. In the workplace, Taylorization increased efficiency and productivity because in breaking production down into rationalized units, it offered the owners of the means of production greater control over the production process and a more systematic exploitation of the workforce. Taylorization has its end in the consumption of rationalized commodity units. Many of the basic foodstuff items that fill our kitchen cupboards today, such as crackers, cereal, flour, and pickles, were originally sold in bulk. Richard Ohmann describes the moment when Quaker Oats were first available as a packaged commodity, and develops the relationship between early instances of mass commodity packaging in the late nineteenth century and the expansion of the professional class, the first class in this country to function *en masse* as consumers (Ohmann, 1988). By comparison with commodities previously sold in bulk, mass-produced and packaged

---

* From Susan Willis, *A Primer for Daily Life* (New York and London: Routledge, 1991) pp. 1–22.

commodities, like Quaker Oats in the original 2lb package, were advertised as a more efficient means to buy and store basic household necessities. While it is true that increased urbanization from the 1890s on meant that more and more families did not have storage space for bulk merchandise, the underlying effect of mass commodity packaging is to break sales down into standardized units, thus enabling commodity producers to have greater control over consumption and a more systematic means of exploiting the consumer through advertising. Prior to the 1890s, there was no advertising for what would later become Quaker Oats, because, if such advertising had existed, it could only have promoted oats in general. The point of advertising is the designation of the commodity (and, by extension, the consumer) as a discrete unit.

The immensely popular advertising campaign devised for marketing California raisins suggests a new conceptualization of the commodity in keeping with post-modern capitalism. Where raisins from California were once marketed according to specific brand-name identities such as "Sun Maid," they are now promoted as the "California Raisins" and embodied in a band of wrinkly faced black "dudes" with skinny arms and legs, who chant "I Heard it Through the Grapevine" while soaking up the California sun. "California Raisins" do not represent a return to the pre-brand-name generic commodity, but rather the hyper-commodity whose connection to rock music and black culture heroes precipitates a vast array of spin-off products, from grotesque dolls to beach towels emblazoned with the "Raisins." If brand-name marketing represents the Taylorization of consumers, mass-marketing spin-off advertising is the postmodern form. Rather than fragmenting the broad mass of consumers into discrete and manageable units, postmodern advertising assumes a consuming subject capable of being interpolated from a number of angles at once. We will consume the "California Raisins" even if we never eat dried fruit.

Another significant function of packaging is to promote the notion of product purity. When Henry P. Crowell first packaged oats, he marketed them as "pure" by comparison with oats sold in bins and exposed to the air as well as the hands and coughs of salespersons. In late twentieth-century consumer culture, hygiene has complex ideological associations, most of which derive from the notion of progress which makes a primary distinction between the developed societies of the First World and the underdeveloped societies of the Third World. Purity is synonymous with the modern First World supermarket, where items are discretely shelved; bruised fruit, greying meat, and milk past its freshness date are removed; and where everything is enveloped in air-conditioning – yet another form of packaging whose frigid, artificial air exudes the very notion of purity. After all, germs cannot survive freezing temper-atures; and in the First World, purity means being germ-free, even if the elimination of microbes requires heavy doses of pesticides, chemical preservatives, fumigation, radiation, and other artificial stratagems. To the First World imagination, the open-air markets of the Third World are a riot of impurities. The aromas of ripe fruits, meats, and cheeses cannot be conceptualized without the consequent horror of bacteria. Foods brimming over in baskets or loosely arranged on counters, in bins, or on the pavement suggest an indiscrete mingling of merchandise – and worse yet, people. In the First World, the package is the fetishized sign of the desire for purity, which, in the fullest sense, is also a desire for security. The ultimate outrage in commodity capitalism is product adulteration. Haunting the desire for purity are the tales told of food-service workers who, when angry or bored, spit, even urinate, into the not yet frozen or sealed TV dinners. Similarly, the consumer's desire for security meets its most chilling nightmare in the case of the deranged product tamperer, for whom the security seal on a bottle of Tylenol is a challenge to cyanide.

These functions of packaging and their ideological implications demonstrate that the throwaways of commodity consumption may well offer the most fruitful way into the culture as a whole. While the foregoing themes may well be complex and interesting, none, however, really scrutinizes packaging as a dimension of the commodity form itself. Such an analysis would look at packaging as a metaphor for the formal economic contradiction of the commodity. In *Capital*, Marx initiated his analysis of the entire system of capitalist economic relationships with an account of the commodity form. This is the nexus of capitalism as well as the means of understanding contradiction. Where Marx began with the commodity, I would begin to understand the commodity as it is metaphorically reiterated in its packaging.

Of all the attributes of mass-produced commodity packaging today, the most important is the use of plastic. The plastic cover acts as a barrier between the consumer and the product, while at the same time it offers up a naked view of the commodity to the consumer's gaze. Sometimes the plastic covering is moulded to fit the contours of the commodity and acts like a transparent skin between the consumer's hand and the object. Shaped and naked, but veiled and withheld, the display of commodities is sexualized. Plastic packaging defines a game of câche – câche where sexual desire triggers both masculine and feminine fantasies. Strip-tease or veiled phallus – packaging conflates a want for a particular object with a sexualized form of desire.

Packaging prolongs the process of coming into possession of the commodity. A buyer selects a particular item, pays for it, but does not fully possess it until he or she pulls open its plastic case or cardboard box. Possession delivers a commodity's use value into the hands of the consumer. Packaging acts to separate the consumer from the realization of use value and heightens his or her anticipation of having and using a particular commodity. Packaging may stimulate associations with gift-wrapped Christmas and birthday presents. However, plastic commodity packaging reveals what gift-wrapping hides. The anticipation we associate with the gift-wrapped present is for the unknown object. In anticipating a plastic-wrapped commodity, we imagine the experience of its use since its identity is already revealed. In all our experiences of consumption, we are little different from the child who convinces his mother to buy the latest Ghostbuster action figure. From the moment he picks the packaged toy off the shelf, to the moment he passes through the checkout, he will trace the contours of the package with his hands, attempt to scrutinize the toy's detail with his eyes, and lose himself in imagining how it will finally feel to push the lever that makes the Ghostbuster's hair stand on end and eyes pop out with fright at the delightfully cold and gelatinous slime – also included in the package, but not yet available to the touch.

Tania Modleski, in her analysis of soap operas (Modleski, 1982) makes a point about the genre's form that provides a clue to the deciphering of commodity packaging. Modleski identifies "waiting" as the most salient formal feature of soap operas. As we all know, nothing ever really happens nor is any problem ever fully resolved in a soap. The characters who open a particular episode may drop out of sight for a day or two, a character might announce a dramatic or scandalous event, but its culmination and consequences may drag on for weeks. Viewers learn to hold plots and people in suspension, waiting from daily episode to daily episode in unbelieving anticipation of dénouement. As Modleski puts it: "soap operas are important to their viewers in part because they never end ... The narrative, by placing ever more complex obstacles between desire and fulfillment, makes anticipation an end in itself" (Modleski, 1982: 88). Modleski astutely compares waiting as a formal feature of soap operas with the lived experience of the housewife. Alone at home, her husband at work, some or all of her children at school, the housewife performs all the daily chores necessary to maintain house and family in an all-encompassing ambience of waiting:

> Soap operas invest exquisite pleasure in the central condition of a woman's life: waiting – whether for her phone to ring, for the baby to take its nap, or for the family to be reunited shortly after the day's final soap opera has left its family still struggling against dissolution.   (Modleski, 1982: 88)

Modleski concludes that the appeal of soap operas resides in the way they make waiting enjoyable. The soap opera turns waiting into an aesthetic. This, then, lifts the housewife viewer out of her real and frustrating experience of waiting, and allows her to apprehend waiting as pleasure.

I would extend Modleski's observations to the way we as consumers relate to the use value of commodities. Mass commodity packaging makes the anticipation of use value into an aesthetic in the same way that the soap opera transforms waiting from an experience into a form. Moreover, commodity packaging defines the anticipation of use value as the commodity's most gratifying characteristic. No commodity ever lives up to its buyer's expectations or desires. This is because in commodity capitalism, use value cannot be fully realized, but rather haunts its fetishized manifestations in the objects we consume. This is true regardless of our economic level of consumption. The shoddy purchase that does not fulfill its advertised promise promotes the pleasurable anticipation of the next (hopefully less shoddy) purchase. Similarly, the high-class piece of merchandise, for instance the sumptuous and expensive new fashion, that in itself seems to live up to all our expectations, also activates anticipation for the next purchase when we take our designer fashion home and hang it next to our now worn and boring collection of clothes. In defining the anticipation of use value as the site of pleasure in the commodity form, capitalism puts the consumer (whether woman, man, child, or adult) in a position analogous to Modleski's house-wife. Waiting can only be rendered aesthetically pleasing to someone who is socially isolated and powerless. The housewife who comes to appreciate waiting as pleasure hardly has access to another, more active and affirming mode of getting through the day. Similarly, the consumer learns to associate pleasure with the anticipation of use value simply because commodity culture does not offer use value itself as appreciable or accessible.

Commodity capitalism fully develops the anticipation of use value while use value itself seems to serve no other purpose but to create the basis for its anticipation. Such a separation between anticipation and use value underlies Wolfgang Haug's *Critique of Commodity Aesthetics* (1986). Haug focuses on advertising in order to develop a definition of commodity fetishism in the context of late capitalism. He draws on Marx's definition of commodity fetishism, but translates the Marxian contradiction between exchange value and use value into the terms of the market economy where the primary contradiction is between buyer and seller. Where Marx saw the commodity form as the embodiment of human labor in the abstract and this as the basis for its creation of exchange value, Haug sees the commodity's use value pressed into the service of sales. The buyer "values the commodity as a means for survival," whereas the seller "sees such necessities as a means for valorization" (Haug, 1986: 15). Haug concludes that commodities have a "double reality." First, they have a use value; "second, and more importantly, the *appearance* of use value" (Haug, 1986: 16). For Haug, the appearance of use value is essentially "detached" (Haug, 1986: 17) from the object itself. This is the aspect of the commodity form that advertising seizes upon and renders sensually perceptible in its words and images. The aspect of the commodity form that Haug defines as appearance would seem to correspond with the category of anticipation. Both suggest that the fetishization of the commodity is for the consumer the fetishization of use. Marx recognized this when he commented: "whenever, by an exchange we equate as values our different products, by that very act, we also equate, as human labour, the different kinds of labour expended upon them. We are not aware of this, nevertheless we do it" (Tucker, 1978: 322). The abstraction of labour which is the real basis of the fetish quality of commodities, is not something we as consumers can directly grasp, rather it enters our daily life experience as the inability to apprehend fully or even imagine non-fetishized use values.

Haug's account of commodity aesthetics, particularly the way he sees human sensuality wholly inscribed in the appearance of use value, where it is abstracted and turned into market value, bears a strong resemblance to the way in which earlier Marxist intellectuals developed the notion of reification. The landmark text on reification is included in Georg Lukács' *History and Class Consciousness*. Lukács begins with Marx's notion that "in the commodity the social character of men's labour appears to them as an objective character stamped upon the product of that labour" (Lukács, 1971: 86), and develops the point that commodity fetishism is both an objective and a subjective phenomenon (Lukács, 1971: 87). Objectively, there is a world of commodities and a market economy, whose laws we might apprehend, but which nevertheless seems to obey "invisible forces that generate their own power" (Lukács, 1971: 87). Subjectively, people in commodity capitalism experience the estrangement of their activities as these, too, become commodities. Crucial to Lukács' definition of reification is the notion that once labor power comes into being as the abstraction of human activity, it extends its influence to human qualities and personality as well. Such objectification, coupled with the highly fragmented and rationalized process of capitalist production, produces "the atomization of the individual" (Lukács, 1971: 91) in consciousness as well as labor. Reification defines the translation of commodity fetishism into human experiential terms.

The transformation of the commodity relation into a thing of "ghostly objectivity" cannot therefore content itself with the reduction of all objects for the gratification of human needs to commodities. It stamps its imprint upon the whole consciousness of man; his qualities and abilities are no longer an organic part of his personality, they are things which he can "own" or "dispose of" like the various objects of the external world. And there is no natural form in which human relations can be cast, no way in which man can bring his physical and psychic "qualities" into play without their being subjected increasingly to this reifying process. (Lukács, 1971: 100)

Common to both Lukács' and Haug's analyses of the commodity form is the notion that under capitalism human qualities and the sensual dimension of experience are objectified and abstracted – or "detached" – from people and their activities so that they become commodities in their own right, "reified" or "aestheticized." The problem is, then, how to reverse – or break through – the process so as to recover and affirm all the human qualities that the commodity form negates by abstraction. The most challenging thinking along these lines is Theodor Adorno's *Negative Dialectics* (1973). Like Lukács, Adorno sees consciousness – our mode of conceptualizing self and world – inexorably shaped by capitalism. Adorno too draws directly on Marx's theory of the commodity, particularly the phenomenon of equivalence. In order for exchange to take place, commodities, which would otherwise be distinct because of their vastly different properties, must achieve equivalence. As previously remarked, it is the abstraction of labor into labor power that produces equivalence. As Marx put it, "the equalization of the most different kinds of labour can be the result only of an abstraction from their inequalities, or of reducing them to their common denominator, viz. the expenditure of human labour-power as human labour in the abstract" (Tucker, 1978: 322). Where Marx uses the term "equivalence," Adorno, whose argument is more properly philosophical, develops the notion of "identity" (Adorno, 1973: 146). The whole of *Negative Dialectics* is aimed at "breaking through the appearance of total identity," in order to smash the "coercion" (Adorno, 1973: 146) of identification as a form that has its roots in economics and dominates all human endeavor and thought.

> The [exchange] principle, the reduction of human labour to the abstract universal concept of average working hours, is fundamentally akin to the principle of identification. [Economic exchange] is the social model of the principle, and without the principle there would be no [exchange]; it is through [exchange] that nonidentical individuals and performances become commensurable and identical. The spread of the principle imposes on the whole world an obligation to become identical, to become total. (Adorno, 1973: 146)

Adorno sees the possibility of negative dialectics in the fact that capitalism as a system and as a form of consciousness is both total and not total. The abstraction of human labor that permits equivalence both denies and requires the existence of multiple and qualitatively different labors. This is capitalism's contradiction. According to Adorno, contradiction "indicates the untruth of identity" (Adorno, 1973: 5) – not because it affirms some wholly other position outside of capitalism, but because it is "nonidentity under the aspect of identity" (Adorno, 1973: 5). *Negative Dialectics* holds tremendous possibilities for rethinking and reclaiming daily-life social practice under capitalism, because unlike the concept of reification, it apprehends fetishism as a tension between the abstracting forces of domination and their utopian antitheses. But how are we to apprehend contradiction? Adorno equates the possibility of contradiction in capitalism as an economic system with the possibility of realizing contradiction in thought. As he sees it, the translation of things into their conceptions leaves something out: a "remainder" which functions as the concept's contradiction. The project of translating negative dialectics into daily life would, then, require ferreting out all the remainders – the resistant, and perhaps quirky, material of practice and relationships that cannot be assimilated in the process of coming to equivalence.

Negative Dialectics is written as an unrelenting exposé – of the overwhelming tendency toward identity and its manifestations in philosophical thought. In the more mundane world of daily life, negative dialectics opposes the homogenization of mass culture, where standardization is marketed as a sign of quality, and the great range of qualitatively different social and cultural forms is transformed into the design details of commodities. What is most interesting about Adorno's writing is that while the notion of identity and all its ramifications are wholly revealed, the category of "nonidentity" is never fully described, or analyzed. Adorno implies that to do so would dissolve the contradictory character of "nonidentity." The closest Adorno comes to specifying "nonidentity" in philosophical terms occurs in his introductory remarks, when he states that "what defies subsumption under identity [is] the "use value" in Marxist terminology" (Adorno, 1973: 11).

This brings the discussion back to the initial problem of whether or not use value can be recognized and appreciated in commodity capitalism – or if, as Haug and Lukács affirm, the consumer is by definition embraced by abstraction and knows use value only as an "appearance" or "reification."

Contrary to this line of reasoning, there is another wholly different approach to Marxist popular culture criticism that abandons the possibility of redeeming concrete use values, and turns instead to the area of appearance as the only social reality in capitalism and, therefore, the only possible site for the transformation of social life. In this approach, appearance comes to mean something more than it does for Haug, as it takes on the complex proportions of the imaginary. Where Haug defined the appearance of use value as a wholly fetishized and manipulated concept, the imaginary is seen as a highly conflictual zone that brings together social and psychic life, needs and desires, and where the forces that seek to dominate, control, and recuperate social life are contested by desire, meaning-making, and a full array of practices that connote cultural resistance. This definition of the function of the imaginary in popular culture originates in Walter Benjamin's landmark essay "The work of art in the age of mechanical reproduction." This may well be the single most important essay in the development of Marxist popular culture criticism. It assesses the influence of mechanical reproduction in a bold and liberatory way. Yet many students today fail to grasp the revolutionary thrust of the essay, and apprehend it instead as a nostalgic complaint for the loss of "aura," the concept Benjamin uses to describe all the unique magical qualities of great traditional art. How is it possible to construct two very different readings: the one revolutionary, the other nostalgic? It may well be that Benjamin intended his reader to have to deal with nostalgia. After all, we are all products of the class history that privatized art, privileged its meanings, and thus endowed it with "aura." Furthermore, we have not attained the socialist transformation of society that would allow us fully to understand the democratizing potential of mechanical repro-duction. To this end, Benjamin uses phrases that inevitably elicit regret. He describes "aura" as "withering" (Benjamin, 1969: 221) and tells us that mechanical reproduc-tion "depreciates" art. Even his use of "authenticity" (Benjamin, 1969: 220) to designate original works of art is apt to stir up a longing for something concrete – even if it is bought at the price of private ownership.

> The technique of reproduction detaches the reproduced object from the domain of tradition. By making many reproductions it substitutes a plurality of copies for a unique existence. And in permitting the reproduction to meet the beholder or listener in his own particular situation, it reactivates the object reproduced. These two processes lead to a tremendous *shattering* of tradition which is the obverse of the contemporary crisis [facism] and the renewal of mankind. Both processes are intimately connected with the contemporary mass movements. Their most powerful agent is the film. Its social sig-nificance, particularly in its most positive form, is inconceivable without its destructive, cathartic aspect, that is, the *liquidation* of the traditional value of the cultural herit-age. (Benjamin, 1969: 221)

Here Benjamin defines two points that have become fundamental to much recent work in Marxian popular culture criticism: (1) mechanical reproduction destroys traditional forms and their meanings; and (2) in "meet[ing] the beholder or listener in his own particular situation," the reproduction enables people actively to make their own cultural meanings. The elimination of "aura" is thus the basis for a radically optimistic definition of mass culture. Contemporary interpretors of Benjamin include Dick Hebdige, whose work on British youth subcultural groups demonstrates how such groups "shatter" traditional definitions of race and class and use music and dress to make new social meanings (Hebdige, 1979). Another contemporary exponent of Benjamin is John Fiske, who develops countercultural readings of shopping malls and supermarkets based on the notion of making meanings. Fiske sees all activities that run counter to the demands of production and consumption ("hanging-out in shopping malls") as instances where we as individuals control and define use. Fiske's point is that supermarket foods may be fetishized commodities, but when we take them home and work them into a meal – be it ordinary or special – we make daily-life cultural meanings (Fiske, 1989). The critic who best sums up this approach to mass culture, and who explicitly links his work to that of Benjamin, is Simon Frith, whose book on rock music, *Sound Effects*, portrays culture as a struggle over meanings. Paraphrasing Benjamin, Frith points out that once "the artistic authority of cultural goods had been broken, their significance had become a matter of dispute: the ideological meaning of mass culture was decided in the process of consumption, and the grasping of particular works by particular audiences was a political rather than a psychological event" (Frith, 1981: 57).

Some problems arise when Benjamin's observations on the mechanical reproduction of art are brought forward into the present. Benjamin's essay responds to a moment in the history of cultural production when film was still fairly new and the notion of a non-reproducible art had not as yet been eclipsed by the wholesale mass production of culture. By comparison with our own moment in history when the desire for music is met by radio, record, tape, or CD, and drama can mean up to two or three rental videos a night, Benjamin, in his *Moscow Diary* (1986), recounts a world where the theater was a regular component of the day's activities and where shopping for a child's gift meant purchasing a handcrafted toy. Do we as a culture have any sense of what a non-reproducible audio or visual work of art might be? When Benjamin says that film has the power to smash traditional art forms and their inscribed meanings, he documents a world that better remembers traditional forms and their traditional meanings.

By comparison, late twentieth-century capitalist culture is cluttered with an ever-expanding array of already reproduced works of art. In such a world, the struggle over meanings often defines cultural commodities in conflicting ways. A 1988 TV advertisement for the Las Vegas narcotics squad portrayed the "narks" in the dress and language of the youth gangs who are "traditionally" cast as dopers and dealers. The "narks" were shown to have a battering-ram equipped vehicle whose special audio system blasts rap music, also traditionally associated with street gangs, while it batters down people's doors. Today, subcultural groups are indeed making meanings and smashing traditions, but so, too, are the forces of containment. Once meanings become detached from their inscription in traditionally defined class art, they, like the cultural objects themselves, can be used – defined and redefined in almost any way to serve almost any class interest. The critic engrossed in mass culture as a struggle over meanings runs the risk of being captured in a system of ricocheting – sometimes revolutionary and sometimes recuperated meanings. Such a view of society and such an approach to culture may not be in a position fully to grasp contradiction. While it articulates the liberatory potential of cultural practice, it may stop short with a reading of culture that cannot escape its own description of resistance and recuperation. This is because the concept of making and struggling over meanings is not primarily based on an understanding of the commodity form. It assumes the commodity as an unavoidable fact of mass culture, but does not question the consequences of fetishism on the meanings made.

The Marxian account of commodity fetishism does not represent a negation of use value. Rather, it demonstrates that use value is dialectically referred to in our fetishized objects of consumption, just as all of mass culture is haunted by the desire for non-alienated social relations. This mass culture cannot fulfill, even while its utopian possibility sustains daily life. The essays in this book are aimed at revealing some of the ways we do indeed recover use value in daily-life social practice, use value that largely goes unrecognized because, living in a world that tends toward homogenization, we are ill-equipped to think dialectically and have very few models that exemplify contradiction of the sort Adorno defines. Nevertheless, the entire system of capitalism is predicated on the production of use values, just as it is motivated by exchange value. In Adorno's terms, "the utopia [promised by the realization of use value] extends to the sworn enemies of its realization" (Adorno, 1973: 11). Use value exists in all of its negations. It is undeniable, even while it is denied realization. The great problem that occurs when we contemplate how use value might be made visible is that once we make it accessible to critical discourse we risk transforming it into another reified object for consumption. Adorno's reluctance to flesh out the category of non-identity may well stem from his recognition that to do so he would either risk "relinquishing the otherness in dialectics" (Adorno, 1973: 375) or he would end up positing something so transcendent as to become solid and "arrest dialectics" (Adorno, 1973: 375) entirely.

Nevertheless, contemporary mass culture yearns for the recovery of use value. Nowhere is such yearning more explicit than in the historical theme park. Some, like Mystic Seaport in Connecticut or Calico Ghost Town in California, are more commercially oriented than others, such as Sturbridge Village in Massachusetts. All occupy authentic historical sites that have been refurbished and opened to the public as private or state-run tourist attractions. Historical theme parks have aspects of the theater, the museum, and the amusement park without wholly replicating any of these. They put the late twentieth-century visitor into the re-created daily-life context of a 100-year-old town, a 200-year-old village, or a 300-year-old fort. Tourists wearing T-shirts and shorts, carrying cameras and pushing baby strollers, share a cobble-stone or packed-earth road with the park's costume-clad employee hosts, whose dress meticulously replicates all the social strata of the park's historical referent. In the historical theme park, "You are there," you are "in" history in a far more real and tangible way than was ever possible in the early 1960s TV dramatization that took this phrase for its title.

The visitor to a historical theme park is free to wander in and out of the site's various buildings with no more than a map or a schedule of events as a programmatic guide. Throughout the park – in its schoolhouse, forge, or ship's store – the material culture is rarely displayed as it would be in a museum; rather, it is performed. At Mystic Seaport, there are coopers, smiths, caulkers – all of them plying their trades. While making their wares, the tradespeople explain the process and the use of their goods to the tourists. In this, the costumed role-players necessarily betray the authenticity of the historical experience as their pedagogical function requires them to explain rather than theatrically enact what might have been daily-life conversations.

The growing number and popularity of historical theme parks today testifies to a strong curiosity about and attraction to societies where the production and exchange of useful objects was the tangible basis for the way people defined themselves in community with others. In such a society, the objects of daily life were the bearers of a particular tradesman's care and craft. The same could be said of the implements and skills that defined women's domestic labor. The historical theme park allows the visitor fully to imagine what it might have been like to live in a culture where use values more directly shaped lives and relationships than they appear to do in late twentieth-century capitalism. This does not occur in a traditional museum, where the visitor might find all the same objects that exist in a particular historical theme park. Objects in a museum do not suggest use values even though they may readily be perceived as useful. Everything from Native American bone needles to colonial spinning wheels is defined, by the very nature of the museum, as an artifact: an object severed from its historical context, whose only current purpose is to be collected, studied, preserved, and displayed. The artifact underscores the visitor's role as spectator rather than participant; someone wholly isolated from the social and historical context that produced the object and able to apprehend it only as a curiosity.

I would argue that this is not the case when, during the process of putting in a garden or rummaging through an abandoned shed, we turn up a horseshoe or some other piece of long disused farm machinery. The discovery of a historical object during the course of our own daily-life activities, defines us as something more than spectators. We might be tempted to compare our world and the sort of activities we perform with the imagined world of the object when it was in use. The question is whether such musing inevitably slides into nostalgia. Many of us will find Adorno's flat declaration that "The right to nostalgia cannot be validated" (Adorno, 1982: 109) much easier to affirm than it is to achieve. Nevertheless, those instances when we actively come upon the past are better able to produce critical rupture with the present than is possible when the past is merely displayed for us. The horseshoe that we turn up, that abrupts into the normalcy of digging in a garden, is very different from a horseshoe mounted on a wall and perceived as a decorative object. While every encounter with the past runs the risk of recuperation, those moments when we use the past to engage with the present have the power to escape nostalgia.

A trip to a historical theme park is never a wholly nostalgic experience. This is because the visitor is not only a spectator, but a participant in communication with the role-players and in the recreation of the world of the past. The historical theme park may be likened to a stage play where the audience joins the actors on the stage. Indeed, this is how Walt Disney first defined the relationship between the visitors to Disneyland and the costumed role-playing employees who do everything to maintain his "magic kingdom," from sweeping the streets to selling the tickets and parading about disguised as Mickey or Pluto. The extensive portfolio handed out to employees at the original Disneyland in California dispenses with the notion of work and employees by renaming all jobs according to the language of theater and film. Most workers are designated as players; managerial people are stage managers and set directors. The recent opening of the Disney–MGM Studios Theme Park in Florida climaxes the transformation of labor into a commodity by incorporating the visitor consumer more fully into the spectacle of production. Here, the visitors are costumed and made up in order to join the paid employee role-players in the recreation of TV dramas such as *I Love Lucy*. The Disney people call it "interactive entertainment." What is interesting is the way this theme park problematizes the function and relationship of actor and audience; and with it, worker (producer) and consumer. But the impulse to think through these relationships creatively is foreclosed by the way the amusement park is not conceived as a site of production, but is felt instead to be a commodity itself. The labor of the paid employees and the unpaid labor of the consumers is wholly devoted to producing and maintaining the park as a simulacrum of Hollywood in the 1940s, complete with palm trees, the Brown Derby Restaurant, and Chinese Theater.

What sets the historical theme park apart from Disneyland, even if the former includes rides on bygone buggies, boats, or railroads, is that the production of amusement is secondary to the production of the historical setting. In the historical theme park, work is a performance whose theatricality is obscured by the totality of the world being created. The only historical discrepancy is that the objects produced in the historical theme park will never be sold or used as they were originally intended. The candles may be hand-dipped to historical specification, but they will be sold in the park's gift shop as Christmas presents for people who light their homes by other means.

Even if the image of historical totality disintegrates at the point of sales and use, the performance of work in historical theme parks may at times appear to transcend theatricality. A friend, Alexander Wilson, when researching a book on the construction of landscape in capitalism, told of a visit to Old Fort William in Thunder Bay, Canada. It was mid-December; a light snow was falling. Besides himself there was only one other visitor to the park. Nevertheless, there were some twenty costumed employees busily tarring canoes, repairing traps – doing all the things that the original residents of the fort did during the winter months to ensure production during the spring, summer, and fall. With only two paying visitors and twenty paid employees, the distinction between amusement park, theater, and the real production of eighteenth-century daily life is significantly blurred. In order for the historical theme park successfully to create history as "aura" – that is, embued with time and place, as Benjamin defined it – it has to produce its use values all year round. A historical theme park that only functioned seasonally would not escape theatricality and amusement.

We need not go so far as Thunder Bay, or even Sturbridge Village, to witness the fully theatrical production of use value. Today's neighborhood supermarket is in many respects a mundane version of the historical theme park. Indeed, the supermarket is something of a postmodern museum of the third world, whose displays of exotic fruits and vegetables, such as breadfruit, cactus apples, passion fruit, star fruit, and horn melons often include museum-like inscriptions, such as this one from a San Diego supermarket: "Cherimoya, prized by the Incas, now grown in Santa Barbara." Where the supermarket most closely replicates the historical theme park is in its presentation of labor. The current practice in many supermarkets is to put a theatrical form of production on display, while the real work that goes into maintaining the store and serving the customers is either hidden from view or made to appear trival because of deskilling. The work of pricing the merchandise, stocking the shelves, cleaning the store, and preparing the meat and produce for sale is accomplished by a largely invisible workforce, whose members labor behind the scene in a backroom warehouse, or at night after the store is closed. The work of managing, which includes decisions over purchases and personnel, is conducted by a number of upper-level employees whose photos sometimes decorate the store's service counter, but who are seldom seen by shoppers. The work of checking, which in a bygone era would have anchored the customer's apprehension of work in the supermarket, has today been greatly undermined by the installation of computerized scanners that weigh and price the commodities and often speak to the customer. The supermarket checker has been deskilled to the point of becoming a human robotoid extension of the checkout system.

As if to compensate for the marginalization and in some cases the erasure, of productive labor, the supermarket offers an array of theatrical labors, whose importance has more to do with the spectacle they create than the actual services they render. Most supermarkets today offer in-store bakeries, deli-counters, florist shops, and gourmet food sections. These are staffed by a corps of store personnel whose uniforms are more theatrical than practical. Often, the employees' pert hats and aprons mimic the colors and patterns of the store's interior decor, making the supermarket something of a stage for sales and the costumed employees the actors enacting service. If we take the supermarket as the place where we most commonly come into contact with the fetishized commodities of daily life, then all the strategies developed by the supermarket to render service personal, to make it visible, redound in a theatricality whose effect is to create the appearance of use value in the commodities we buy. This is most clearly the case when one of the costumed employees stands mid-aisle, blocking shopping cart traffic, and commences to operate one of the store's speciality machines. These include coffee grinders, orange and grapefruit juicers, peanut-butter mills, and pineapple corers. The employee who husks and cores pineapples to produce those Dole-like rings does so with a single thrust of a chrome-plated lever. The performance brings the image of work and a wholesome product into the shopping area.

This is an instance where labor is truly rendered as performance; and hence, a commodity – customers consume the spectacle of work whether or not they actually buy the pineapples. Such spectacle stands in the place of any reference to the hundreds of laborers who cultivated, harvested, packed, shipped, and marketed the pineapple. Their erasure from the commodity form is the basis of its fetishism. The impossibility of retrieving their labor in the supermarket setting condemns the attempt to create use values to spectacle.

There is one perspective on use value that I have not as yet brought into this discussion. It is by far the most radical, the most utopian, and the most difficult to imagine how it might be translated into daily-life social practice. I am referring to Jean Baudrillard's critique of political economy, and with it Marxian theory, which he sees as replicating the mode and logic of capitalism. According to Baudrillard, the construction of value under capitalism, which derives from the relationship of exchange value to use value, is homologous to the system of signification defined by Saussure, where meaning is born of the relationship of signifier to signified. This defines a more fundamental unity between consciousness and capitalism than obtains in Lukács' theory of reification. For Baudrillard, the logic of capitalism is the logic of meaning.

In such a system, there is no possibility of a redemptive notion of use value. Rather, it (like the concrete and the referent) is implicit in the structure of capitalist economics. For Baudrillard, use value cannot in any way oppose exchange value, undermine it, or offer an alternative to it; rather, use value ensures exchange value and underwrites its centrality. Hence, according to Baudrillard, any critique of consumer society that posits use value as its point of critical distantiation or its transcendent "other" (as my own efforts aim to do) is inevitably inscribed in the logic of capitalism. As Baudrillard flatly puts it, use value does not exist, except, perhaps, as capitalism's "alibi" (Baudrillard, 1988: 71).

> In fact the use value of labor power does not exist any more than the use value of products or the autonomy of signified and referent. The same fiction reigns in the three orders of production, consumption, and signification. Exchange value is what makes the use value of products appear as its anthropological horizon. The exchange value of labor power is what makes its use value, the concrete origin and end of the act of labor, appear as its "generic" alibi. This is the logic of signifiers which produces the "evidence" of the "reality" of the signified and the referent. In every way, exchange value makes concrete production, concrete consumption, and concrete signification appear only in distorted, abstract forms. But it foments the concrete as its ideological ectoplasm, its phantasm of origin and transcendence ["*dépassement*"]. In this sense need, use value, and the referent "do not exist." They are only concepts produced and projected into a generic dimension by the development of the very system of exchange value.   (Baudrillard, 1975; 30)

Baudrillard challenges us to think outside of value altogether. How might we begin to imagine a society devoted to the elimination of value? Baudrillard appeals to the work of the anthropologist, Marcel Mauss, whose elaboration of the gift ("*le don*") in primitive society offers an alternative to societies based, like our own, on accumulation rather than dispersal. Central to Mauss' description and to Baudrillard's analysis is the annual potlatch ceremony practiced by the Kwakiutl Indians where accumulated wealth and possessions were not just redistributed, but wholly used up. Baudrillard sees the potlatch as the basis for reciprocal social relations, based on a form of exchange that destroys value. Baudrillard's term for such a social dynamic is "symbolic exchange," which he alludes to as the anti-form of capitalism, whose cursory and subtle manifestations might be glimpsed at unexpected moments even in consumer society. Baudrillard cites play, the spontaneous gift, destruction as pure loss, and symbolic reciprocity as examples of symbolic acts (Baudrillard, 1988: 93). As social forms, these are hardly fully realized in our daily lives. Many readers come away from Baudrillard's illusive descriptions of the symbolic dissatisfied at not finding more fully fleshed out images of alternative practices. Indeed, all of Baudrillard's examples of symbolic exchange present themselves as somewhat inaccessible to discursive elaboration. As Baudrillard allows us to imagine it, the symbolic might erupt out of the economic fabric of capitalism as it does when workers initiate a wildcat strike; or it might trick us, like a *trompe-l'œil*, seduce us unawares, causing received cultural meanings to disintegrate. The oblique references to the symbolic that emerge in Baudrillard's writing bear a striking resemblance to the way Adorno presents the negative dialectic. We can not imagine what the negative dialectic would really look like as a social reality, nor can we grasp what our daily lives might be like if we fully participated in symbolic exchange. This is because capitalism is a totality. Both the negative dialectic and symbolic exchange are "elsewheres" (Baudrillard, 1988: 71) that cannot possibly be fully realized or apprehended in capitalism. Then, too, any attempt to render the symbolic concrete risks reification and the cancellation of its alterity.

What is clear is that today's so-called aberrant forms of consumption, which we might be tempted to interpret as negations of value, are, instead, affirmations of value. For instance, imagine a society whose dominant social form is anorexia. Would a society that absolutely denies all forms of consumption abolish value? According to Baudrillard's account of use value as the alibi of exchange value, the renunciation of consumption in a highly commodified society such as our own merely affirms the fact of consumption, as well as the power of temptation and revulsion associated with commodities. Unlike the potlatch, an anoretic society would not destroy accumulated value, rather it stands as firm testament to the dead weight of *value*. Unlike the community of Kwakiutl, whose social relationships are the expression of reciprocity, a society of anoretics exemplifies the extreme isolation of the individual, whose only, and overwhelmingly obsessive, relationship is to the rejected world of commodities.

What about a bulimic society? Would a society that consumes "to the max" finally use everything up and therefore eliminate value? By comparison to Baudrillard's definition of the potlatch where a community's wealth is used up in order to prevent accumulation, the cycle of bulimic engorgement, evacuation, engorgement merely demonstrates that the supply of commodities is never-ending and cannot ever be used up. In consumer society, bulimia is the antithesis and the negation of potlatch. Where potlatch disperses desire and enables gratification, bulimia is burdened by desire and the impossibility of ever attaining satisfaction. Bulimia does not destroy value, rather it flattens the distinction between exchange value and use value, by rendering all value equal to consumption.

As social forms, anorexia and bulimia are not "other" to capitalism. They may be labelled "consumption disorders" but they express the formal logic of capitalism. A radical theory of use value would resist the desire to render it concrete, and therefore readily imaginable and easily instituted. A facile notion of use value as a whole term conditions the impulse to imagine that either a bulimic or an anoretic society represents an anti-capitalist definition of use. Gayatri Spivak warns against similarly simplistic conceptualizations of use value when she states that students who claim they "read literature for pleasure rather than interpretation" or academics who take pride in their hands-on word processor production techniques are merely fulfilling romantic notions about use value as having something to do with handicrafts and barter (Spivak, 1987: 162). Spivak argues for a "discontinuous" theory (Spivak, 1987) of use value in keeping with Adorno's notion of the negative dialectics, and I would say Baudrillard's sense of symbolic exchange. Spivak sees use value as a "classic example of a deconstructive lever" (Spivak, 1987: 162). This means that it has the potential to undermine and transform the logic of capitalism, because, according to Spivak, it "is both outside and inside the system of value-determination. It is outside because it cannot be measured by the labor theory of value" (Spivak, 1987: 162) and because we can conceive of things being use values without their being accessible to economic exchange. However, use value is inside the system of value because there would be no possibility of exchange value without it. This makes use value an unstable category. It is never whole, or concrete. In it, "there is something left untranslated (not included in the system of value determination), which is its contradiction." This is what Spivak means when she defines use value as "discontinuous" and therefore capable of putting "the entire textual chain of value into question" (Spivak, 1987: 162).

I challenge the reader to resist reading prescriptive models of use value into the following essays.

Background Sources and Further Reading

The dialectics of use value

In *Capital*, volume I, parts I and II, Karl Marx defines the commodity form, commodity fetishism, use value, exchange value, labor power, and the creation of surplus value. These concepts are essential to all considerations of value in capitalist society. Other examples of dialectical criticism that bear on the question of value include the following.

Adorno, Theodor (1973) *Negative Dialectics*. London: Routledge and Kegan Paul.
Baudrillard, Jean (1975) *The Mirror of Production*. St Louis: Telos Press.
Baudrillard, Jean (1981) *For a Critique of the Political Economy of the Sign*. St Louis: Telos Press.
Goux, Jean-Joseph (1990) *Symbolic Economies: After Marx and Freud*. Ithaca: Cornell University Press.
Spivak, Gayatri (1987) *In Other Worlds*. London: Methuen.

Commodity fetishism

Studies in advertising lead the way in defining commodity fetishism in late twentieth-century capitalism.

Haug, Wolfgang (1986) *Critique of Commodity Aesthetics*. Minneapolis: University of Minnesota Press.
Leiss, William, Kline, Stephen, and Jhally, Sut (1988) *Social Communication in Advertising*. London: Routledge, Chapman and Hall.
Leiss, William, Kline, Stephen, and Jhally, Sut (1985) "Magic in the marketplace: an empirical test for commodity fetishism," *Canadian Journal of Political and Social Theory*, 9 (3).
Marchand, Roland (1985) *Advertising the American Dream*. Berkeley: University of California Press.
Williamson, Judith (1978) *Decoding Advertisement*. London: Marion Boyars.

References

Adorno, Theodor (1973) *Negative Dialectics*. London: Routledge and Kegan Paul.

——(1982) *Prisms*. Cambridge Mass.: MIT Press.

Baudrillard, Jean (1970) *La Societé de Consommation*. Paris: Denoel.

——(1975) *The Mirror of Production*. St Louis: Telos Press.

——(1981) *Simulacres et Simulations*. Paris: Editions Galilee.

——(1988) *Selected Writings*, Stanford. Cal.: *Stanford University Press*.

Benjamin, Walter (1969) *Illuminations*. New York: Schocken.

——(1986) *Moscow Diary.* Cambridge, Mass.: Harvard University Press.

Fiske, John (1989) *Understanding Popular Culture*. Boston, Mass.: Unwin Hyman.

Frith, Simon (1981) *Sound Effects*. New York: Pantheon.

Haug, Wolfgang (1986) *Critique of Commodity Aesthetics*. Minneapolis: University of Minnesota Press.

Hebdige, Dick (1979) *Subculture: The Meaning of Style*. London: Routledge, Chapman & Hall.

Lukács, Georg (1962) *The Historical Novel*. Boston, Mass.: Beacon Press.

——(1971) *History and Class Consciousness*. Cambridge, Mass.: MIT Press.

Modleski, Tania (1982) *Loving with a Vengeance*. New York: Methuen.

Ohmann, Richard (1988) "History and literary history: the case of mass culture," *Poetics Today*, 9: 357–75.

Spivak, Gayatri (1987) *In Other Worlds*. London: Methuen.

Tucker, Robert C. (ed.) (1978) *The Marx–Engels Reader*, New York: W. W. Norton.

19

The Processes: From Nationalisms to Transnationals*

Jésus Martín-Barbero

A Difference that is More than Underdevelopment

Any reference to a 'Latin America' beyond the original unity imposed by the Spanish conquest and domination lies necessarily in the other 'visible unification' that J. L. Romero speaks of in his study of the region's incorporation into the processes of industrial modernization and international trade. Dispersion and fragmentation were the main forces at work in Latin America from the time of the struggles for independence to the reorganization of imperialism in the twentieth century. Because of internal conflicts and the stratagems of division encouraged by the new centres of empire, the fragile national formations were in a state of almost continual break-up. If it is true that the different Latin American nationalisms took different routes and rates of development, starting in the 1930s, this diversity of patterns, as a whole, began to undergo a profound transformation.

After the 1930s the possibility of 'becoming a nation' in the *modern* sense of this term hinged on establishing a national market, something that, in turn, depended on adjusting to the needs and requirements of the international market. The fact that Latin America's access to modernization was through political-economic dependency revealed its processes of 'unequal development', the basic inequality on which capitalist development rests. This dependency also revealed the contradictions of its 'simultaneous discontinuities' in which Latin America lives and carries out its modernization (Lechner, 1981: 12). These discontinuities occur at three levels: firstly, the processes of becoming a state and a nation are often out of phase with each other so that some states become nations much later and some nations delay a long time in becoming a state; secondly, the 'deviant' way in which the popular classes enter the political system and become part of the process of forming the nation state – more as the result of the general crisis of the system, setting the popular classes in confrontation with the state, than as a product of the autonomous

* From Jésus Martín-Barbero, *Communication, Culture and Hegemony: From the Media to Mediations*, translated by Elizabeth Fox and Robert A. White (Newbury Park: Sage, 1991), pp. 150–86.

development of their own organizations; and, thirdly, the fact that the mass media play not just an ideological but a *political* role in the incorporation of the masses into the nation.

Before examining each of these levels in further detail, it is important to clarify the concept of discontinuity, that is, the nature of a 'modernity which is not contemporary', in order to free the concept from misunderstandings that frequently limit its usefulness. The 'non-contemporary' of which we speak must be clearly separated from the notion of constitutive backwardness, that is, the backwardness which is made the explanation of cultural differences. There are two versions of this conception of discontinuity as backwardness. One suggests that the originality of the Latin American countries and of Latin America as a whole has been constituted by factors which lie outside the logic of capitalist development. Another thinks of modernization as the recovery of lost time and therefore identifies development with the definitive leaving behind of what Latin America once was in order to become, at last, modern.

The conception of discontinuity which we propose implies a quite different line of thinking which allows us to break with both an ahistorical and culturalist model and with the paradigm of accumulative rationality with its pretensions of unifying and subsuming all cultural histories in one linear timeline. Our perspective enables us, firstly, to think of historical differences and backwardness not as lost time but as a backwardness which is *produced by historical circumstances* – children who are dying every day because of malnutrition or dysentery, the millions of illiterate people, the caloric deficit in the nutrition of the great majority, the low level of life expectancy, etc. Secondly, we are able to take into consideration cultural differences which are not related to backwardness: the multiplicity of cultural histories of the native Americans, the Afro-Americans, people of European descent and, above all, the cultural history which emerges from the *mestizaje* of all these races and their histories.

Only in the tensions of discontinuities are we able to conceive of a modernity which is not reduced to imitation and of cultural differences which are not identified with backwardness. This was the aim of Bolivar's struggle: to apply the political doctrines of his time to the 'grammar of racial, geographical, and cultural diversity' of the Latin American countries; to adjust liberal ideals to the requirements of a new society where liberalism in the name of equality usually meant the rule of the mighty (Bolivar, 1972). Bolivar did not propose a type of nation based on the model of the European nation, but a type of state, which, in abolishing absolute power, would still be strong enough to defend the weak against the wealthy classes.

Martí continued Bolivar's line of thought and his struggle, arguing that the main obstacle in the construction of the Latin American nations is the lack of understanding 'of the disorganized mix of elements from which the new nations were so hurriedly formed' (Martí, 1971). Mariátegui also resolutely insisted that the task of these nations was not to catch up with Europe but to rediscover the value of and the meaning of the Latin American myth. Latin America 'must let loose its fantasies, liberate its storytelling capacities from old chains in order to discover its reality' (Mariátegui, 1978).

The Discontinuity between the State and the Nation

Beginning in the 1920s, most Latin American countries launched a process of reorganizing their economies and transforming their political institutions. Industrialization was carried out on the basis of import substitution, the formation of an internal market, and bringing manpower into an employed sector. Various forms of supportive intervention of the state and the state's investment in the transportation and communication infrastructure were crucial in this. Thus, even though the take off of industrialization responded to the general conditions of the international market, there were significant differences depending on the model and maturity of the 'national project' formulated by the bourgeoisie of each country in the second half of the nineteenth century.

There is much debate as to whether we can speak of a 'national bourgeoisie' existing in Latin America in the last century, and there is also a debate about their contradictory role in the formation of the nation states. But, as Malcolm Deas stated, 'How could there have been a national politics and a national economy without the articulation of class interests at a national level' (Deas, 1983: 150). Certainly, the national bourgeoisie have had different degrees of power and capacity for strategic influence in countries as different, for example, as Brazil and Ecuador. These differences, however, were not at the level of the Darwinist, evolutionary conceptions that oriented modernization and national development but, rather, in the size of the countries which provided greater scope for action. All countries, however, shared similar experiences of urban growth and erosion of the traditional society. The explosive urbanization of Latin America was the result of population growth and migration from the countryside, augmented, in some countries such as Argentina, by the waves of immigration. These processes produced mass societies with classes and social groups in conflict with the dominant, normative sector of society.

Whether or not the hegemonic groups that appeared were, strictly speaking, a 'national bourgeoisie', certainly there were in the various countries new bourgeoisie sectors which controlled both the worlds of business enterprise and politics, and these sectors were responsible for the growing interdependence of these two worlds (Romero, 1976: 268). What stimulated this interweaving of business and politics was not just the new economic take off, but the assumption by these bourgeoisie sectors in Latin America that modernization implied the unavoidable necessity of incorporating their countries into the way of life of the 'modern countries'. They believed that only one model of transformation could bring their countries out of the morass of backwardness: the path toward a Europeanized urban society. Therefore, the social philosophers and men of science thought it was quite legitimate, indeed, inevitable, to marginalize and exploit the 'passive masses' and any other social group that constituted a delay or obstacle. Otherwise the very existence of the nation was in danger.

The new bourgeoisie profited from the old national project of the creoles, changing the meaning of this project even as they sought to carry it to completion.[1] It was through a process of elaborating and moving ahead this national project that the creole classes took on attributes of national scope and became national themselves. 'This continuing, prolonged enterprise of the creole class to construct the state and the nation came to be known as the national project' (Palacios, 1983: 16). The project failed in the nineteenth century, but the new project of constructing a modern nation was built upon the foundations of the old project and took on the same structure of internal power relations.

A new nationalism emerged, based on the idea of national culture which would be the synthesis of different cultural realities and a political unity bringing together cultural, ethnic and regional differences. The nation absorbed the people, 'transforming the multiplicity of the diverse cultures into a single aspiration, namely the feeling of nationhood'. Thus, the diversity legitimated the irreplaceable unity of the nation. To work for the nation means, above all, to work for unification, overcoming the fragmentation that generated the regional and federal wars of the nineteenth century. Unification through roads, railways, telegraph networks, telephones and radio broadcasting made possible communication between regions, but above all between the regions and the centre, the capital.

There were two schools of thought in this effort, although they shared many elements. One school identified national progress with the advance of the governing social class and with efforts toward rapid industrialization. Another, present in those countries with the sociocultural formation that Darcy Ribeiro has called 'peoples of witness' (Ribeiro, 1971), attempted to fuse the new sense of nationhood with the conception which existed before and which comes from below. The goal of the first school of thought was to industrialize in order to join the ranks of civilized nations; in the second there was tension between the compulsive desire to industrialize and the awareness of their uniqueness as a nation. This tension gave rise to the debate in Peru at the end of the 1920s that brought into open confrontation the project of 'the national problem' argued by Haya de la Torre and the project of 'the indigenous problem' put forward by José Carlos Mariátegui.[2]

In Latin America as a whole, the idea of modernization which oriented the processes of change and which provided the nationalisms with a concrete agenda of action was more a movement of economic and cultural *adaptation* than a reinforcement of independence. E. Squeff, referring to Brazilian nationalism, affirms, 'We were able to achieve our modernization only by translating our raw materials into an expression that would gain recognition abroad' (Squeff and Wisnik, 1983: 55). Thus, the dynamics of cultural policies began to take shape around economic policies. This, however, did not mean the development of an internal market, but rather the introduction into national institutions of a dynamic of conformity to demands which came from outside. Latin American countries wanted to be nations in order to at last define their identities, but the achievement of that identity implied the translation of these identities into the modernizing discourse of the hegemonic countries, for only in terms of that discourse could the efforts and achievements of nationhood be evaluated and validated. The logic of developmentist ideology could not be otherwise for the fundamental orientations were already contained in the modernizing nationalisms of the 1930s – the prior and indispensable stage of later development.

The political structure required for the modernizing project emerged out of the centralizing and initiating role of the state. It was impossible to conceive of national unity without strengthening the 'centre', that is, organizing the administration of the country around a central point of decision making. In some countries this centralization would have as its plan of action and justification the establishment of the basic mechanisms of a still non-existent state administration with the organization of systems of national accounts, taxation, and public records.[3] In other countries, where a public administration already existed, centralism meant not simply unification but introducing a homogenizing uniformity of rhythms of life, gestures and ways of speaking. The heterogeneous traditions from which the Latin American countries are composed became merely external ritual functions. Where there have been significant, unavoidable regional cultural differences, this local originality and uniqueness was projected upon the whole nation. Where the differences were not sufficiently great to constitute a national tradition, these were transformed into folklore and offered to foreigners as a curiosity. However, neither the national absorption of the differences nor the transformation into folklore were simply functional strategies of the centralizing policies. For a time, at least, as the prominence of the Indian nativist genre of novels indicates, these cultural differences were used as a means of manifesting 'the consciousness of a new country', a form of affirming a national identity still in the process of formation.

Another pivotal point of nationalism in the 1930s is the protagonist role of the state. Although this will be treated in greater detail later when we analyse populism as a way of incorporating the masses into the nation, it is important to point out its significance. In some countries, such as Mexico, the initiative of the state was so strong that it made the state the 'hegemonic agent par excellence' (S. Zermeño, in Lechner, 1981: 75). Contributing to this state hegemony in Mexico was the continually erupting 'plebeian volcano', the country's civil and external wars, and the constant erosion of the power of the upper classes, requiring a strong state. All this tended to demand of the state an interventionism that translated into a paradox of overpoliticization and desocialization.

In Chile the strengthening of the protagonistic role of the state, at the expense of the institutions and class organizations of civil society, eventually made politics an autonomous process and led to an instrumentalist conception of democracy.[4] And it could not have been otherwise in Chile since the path to industralization was considered to be the exclusive work of the state.

> In Latin America, the 'spirit of enterprise' that defines certain basic characteristics of the industrial bourgeoisie in developed capitalist countries was a characteristic of the state, especially in these decisive periods. Instead of the social class for which history clamored with small success, it was the government of the populist *caudillos* that embodied the nation and gave the masses political and economic access to the benefits of industrialization. (Galeano, 1973: 230)

And something similar happened in the cultural sphere. Coming back to the case of Mexico, for Vasconcelos the Revolution, rather than being the moment when the masses marched onto the stage of history, was the opportunity to civilize the masses under the direction of the state, the great educator. His conception was portrayed in the murals 'Exalting the armies of Zapata and the international proletariat, but on the walls of government buildings'.[5] The muralists added peasant armies and the international proletariat to the humanist and culturalist project of Vasconcelos, but 'the state dictated the rules of nationhood and monopolized the historical sentiments and the national heritage of art and culture' (Monsiváis, 1981: 38).

Paradoxically, the growth of the Mexican state was a 'conquest by the people', a popular revolution against the creole castes, private corporations and foreign threats. In this paradox lies the strength of the national culture in Mexico, a strength that continued even when the state abandoned its patronage in great part and passed this role to the culture industry. Even then, nationhood is not only what the state has identified and brought into existence but the way in which the masses have experienced once again the social legitimacy of their aspirations. If no other Latin American country has as strong a sense of nationalism as Mexico, the reasons for this must be sought in the fact that other countries have not had the kind of revolution which conferred on the Mexican state a popular representativeness that is not just formal. The absence of a revolution in other Latin American countries, even those with a strong state, explains why the national culture continues to be so disconnected from the real culture and why the concern of the state for cultural identity continues to sound like empty rhetoric.

Massification, Social Movements and Populism

If the 1930s were important years in Latin America for the economic processes of industrialization and modernization, politically they were even more important for the 'irruption' of the masses in the cities. Just at the time that the cities begin to fill with people due to both the demographic increase and the rural exodus, there was a crisis of hegemony produced by the absence of a class which could assume the direction of society. This brought the state in many countries to seek its *national* legitimacy in the masses. The maintenance of power was impossible without assuming in some way the vindication of the demands of the urban masses. Populism became the form of a state which sought to strengthen its legitimacy by taking upon itself the popular aspirations. This was not a strategy from a position of power, but rather an organization of power which expressed concretely the contract between the masses and the state. The ambiguousness of this contract resulted both from the vacuum of power which the state was supposed to fill – with the paternalistic authoritarianism which this produces – and from the political reformism which the masses demanded. If we wish, however, to avoid the extremes of attributing to populism an effectiveness which it never had or on the other hand perceiving the masses as in a state of passive manipulation, which is also false, it is important to clarify the implications of the social presence of the masses and the process of massification which came into existence.

Migration and the new sources and types of work nurtured the hybridization of the popular classes, a new form of becoming present in the city. 'There was a kind of explosion among the people, and it was impossible to measure exactly how much was due to their larger numbers and how much was the result of the decision of many to make themselves known and their presence felt'.[6] The crisis of the 1930s unleashed an offensive of the country against the city and a recomposition of social groups. There was a quantitative and qualititative change in the popular classes as a result of the appearance of a *mass* which could no longer be defined within the traditional social structure and that 'dismantled the traditional forms of participation and representation' (Falleto et al., 1982: 109). The presence of that mass would soon affect the whole of urban society, its way of life and thinking, and, eventually, the physiognomy of the city itself.

With the formation of the urban masses, not only was there a quantitative growth of the popular classes, but the appearance of a new mode of existence of the popular: 'The disarticulation of the popular world, (constituting it) as the space of the Other, the space of the forces negating the mode of capitalist production' (Sunkel, 1985: 16). The insertion of the popular classes in the conditions of existence of a 'mass society' pushed the popular movement toward a new strategy of alliances. The new social experience fashioned a new vision, a new conception of action less openly confrontational. 'It was the vision of a society which could be reformed little by little, a society which could come to be more just' (Gutiérrez and Romero, 1981: 8).

For a time, the masses were marginal. Compared with the mainstream of society, the mass was heterogeneous and *mestizo*. The people coming from the country had to learn to cope with a host of strange ways. It was necessary to learn how to catch a bus, how to find one's way through the streets, how to apply for identification papers. The old society responded to the immigrants with a disdain that covered over not just repugnance but fear. More than an assault, the appearance of the masses meant that it was now impossible to continue maintaining the rigid hierarchical organization of differences that constituted the society. For this reason, the aggressiveness of the masses seemed non-violent yet equally dangerous; it was not the uprising of a social class but the freeing of an uncontrollable energy. The 'proletariat formed a massive flood' (Romero, 1982: 54) which did not find its political expression in the traditional parties and organizations of the working class but whose manifestations of violence revealed the force of which it was capable.

The presence of the masses in the city slowly acquired more specific characteristics. The sheer numbers meant a shortage of housing, a transportation problem, a new way of living in the city, a different pattern of walking the streets, a distinct way of behaving. On the peripheries of the city there sprang up the *barrios* created by invasions, and in the centre there was a visible breakdown of the organization of urban planning. The city began to lose its centre. In the face of the formless spreading out of the city that the invasions on the periphery implied – the *favelas*, the *villas miseria*, the *callampas* – the rich responded by moving out to still another periphery. But the mass continued invading everywhere. For in the midst of the ignorance of the masses regarding the norms of the city and the way that their mere presence was challenging the order of this environment, there was a secret desire to get possession of the good life that the city represented. The masses wanted work, health, education and entertainment. But they could not claim their right to these goods without massifying everything. The revolution of expectations drove home the meaning of the paradox – subversion lies embedded in integration. Massification meant simultaneously the integration of the popular classes in society and the acceptance by society of the masses' right to everything, a right to the goods and services which, until then, were the privilege of a few. This society could not accept the newcomers without a profound transformation. This transformation, however, did not follow the patterns nor the directions that revolutionaries expected, and therefore the revolutionaries thought that no transformation had occurred.

Massification affected everyone, but not all perceived and experienced it in the same way. The upper classes quickly learned to separate the demands of the masses – with their measure of political threat but also the potential for stimulating economic growth – from the massive supply of material and cultural goods 'without differentiating style'. For this latter, the upper classes felt only disdain. Massification was especially painful for the middle classes, the petit bourgeoisie, who, as much as they desired, could not distance themselves from the masses. Massification 'threatened their dream of interiority that was their characteristic, their jealously guarded individuality and their condition as differentiated persons' (Romero, 1976: 374).

For the popular classes, however, although they were more defenceless in the face of the new conditions, massification implied more gain than loss. Not only did they find better conditions for physical survival, but also the possibility of cultural access and ascent. The new mass culture began not only as a culture directed to the popular classes but a culture in which the masses found synthesized in the music and in the narratives of radio and film some of the basic forms of their own way of perceiving, experiencing and expressing their world.

We are indebted to José Luis Romero not only for one of the most original terms for mass culture, 'alluvial folklore', but also for the first sociological and phenomenological characterization of this culture in Latin America (1982: 67ff). Like Benjamin, Romero views mass culture from the perspective of experiences that provide access to forms of expression rather than as simply manipulation. Romero, following the path of Arguedas, has been interested in the analysis of the culture of *mestizaje*, the process of cultural hybridization and the re-elaboration of various cultural sources in a new synthesis. It is an approach that destroys the myth of cultural purity and has no repugnance in using modern instruments in the rendition of traditional indigenous music or in broadcasting such music over the radio. It is a study of the transition from the folkloric to the popular (Arguedas, 1977: 124–5).

Mass culture is the hybrid of foreign and national, of popular informality and bourgeois concern with upward mobility. It is the hybrid of two classic types: those who try to look rich without the means to do so, 'who imitate the eternal forms that characterize those "better" than they are', and the opposite, those crushed by the hopelessness of the slums on the edges of the cities and in the underworld. Mass culture is essentially an urban culture which compensates its open materialism – the supreme values are economic success and social ascent – with a superabundance of the sentimental and the passionate.

From the perspective of the 'official policies' of both the left and the right, the masses and mass culture are looked upon with suspicion. The right takes a defensive position, seeing in the masses a threat to their established social privileges and to the sacredness of the cultural borders that separate them from those without taste. The left sees in the masses a dead weight, a proletariat without class consciousness or vocation for social struggle. The mass is a cultural fact that does not fit into their social conceptions. It is a challenge and an obstacle to their essentially Enlightenment frame of reference. Only for the populists does the presence of the urban mass seem to offer a significant new political reality. The populists 'drafted the principles of a new ideology that channelled the explosive tendencies of the masses within norms that ensured the preservation of the basic social structures' (Romero, 1976: 381).

Between 1930 and 1960, populism was the political strategy that characterized, with varying degrees of intensity, the social struggle in virtually all Latin American societies. 'It was the first strategy that attempted to resolve the crisis of the state which began in the 1930s in much of the region' (Lechner, 1981: 304). Among the first of the great populist leaders was Getulio Vargas, who orchestrated the process that led to the destruction of the 'oligarchic state' and the organization of the 'New State'. Beginning in 1930 the socio-economic conditions of mass society – the rapid industrial growth and the inability of the oligarchy to control it, the liberal-democratic aspirations of the urban middle classes, and the pressures from below of the immigrants pouring into the cities from the rural areas – created the setting for a political pact between the masses and the state that was the root of populism (Weffort, 1978). The state, assuming the role of referee between conflicting class interests, set aside the aspirations of the popular masses, and, through a dictatorship in the name of the people, exercised a direct manipulation of the masses and their economic ambitions. Only in 1945 were democratic tendencies finally able to introduce intermediaries between the state and the masses.

In 1934, Lázaro Cárdenas assumed the presidency of Mexico and proposed a programme of government which took up once again the objectives of the Revolution and attempted to give back to the masses their role as protagonists in the national political process. Supported by the achievements of the Revolution already legislated and legitimated, Cárdenas set forth for the first time a model of economic development based on a 'third way' which made the capitalist class responsible for the increase in production and the popular classes the movers of social progress. The role of the state was to reconcile these two sets of interests. Evidence of Cárdenas' socially advanced conception of populism was his defence of the workers' right to strike and refusal of the capitalists' right to close their factories (Cordova, 1974). At the same time, the state, committed to an expensive programme of public works, assumed the burden of the high-risk industries, leaving the most lucrative activities for the private sector.

In Argentina, the outcries of the masses freed Perón from prison in Argentina in 1945 and elected him president in 1946, initiating the classic paradigm of populist government in Latin America. But it was also the regime that generated the most intense debate. Like the earlier populist leaders, Perón proposed a policy of economic development directed by the state, the only institution that could reconcile conflicting interests. By 1946, however, social conflicts had grown to such an extent that it became necessary to transform the nexus between the state and the masses into an 'organic' relationship, and in this originated both the strength and the ambiguous role of the labour unions. Perón's populism also contained a larger measure of the symbolic force of the *caudillo* – and of a charismatic wife, Evita – than occurred with any other leader of these years. The mythic symbolism of Perón resided not just in his dramatic 'gestures' but in the discourse he created and his capacity to re-semanticize the disparate themes of various social movements, thereby drawing their symbols into the official language. O. Landi has studied this cultural process basic to all Latin American populisms – an appeal to the working class masses, proposing 'a new system of acknowledgement of the characteristics of the workers, giving a name to the worker in another form' (Landi, 1983: 30; see also de Ipola, 1982).

For a long period, social analysis cancelled the theme of populism from the subjects of current debate, and an overly simplistic Marxism identified populism as, in practice, the same as fascism. The 1980s, however, opened up the topic again, and suggested that the Marxist conceptions be reexamined. Here, we can only briefly point to three examples of this new line of thought. In the text of Ernest Laclau (1977), which has gained acceptance in the region as one of the most balanced in the Marxist renewal, a new understanding of the role of populism is central. In the 1980 seminar organized by the communication research institute, Desco, in Lima on the theme, 'Democracy and Popular Movements', with some of the most representative social science researchers of Latin America present, populism was one of the key issues of the discussions (Moulian et al., 1981). The same year, 'Populism and Communication' was the theme of the annual meeting of the Brazilian Association of Communication Researchers (Marquez de Melo, 1981).

What is important in this renewal of interest in populism is a profound change of historical perspective. The political processes from 1930 to 1960 now appear to have been greatly oversimplified by the dependency theory that considered the state to be merely a conduit for the interests of the hegemonic countries. This made it difficult to conceive of the 'national problem' in terms of class relationships. Another evidence of how current events have a 'contaminating' influence on developments of social theory is the interest in the energetic presence of popular movements. This change of perspective has been particularly well documented by J. C. Portantiero who sees the need to accept within social theory what can be called 'The Latin American deviation'. This is the view that the popular classes have become social actors, not by the classic route, but through the political crisis that accompanied the processes of industrialization in the 1930s, placing the popular classes in direct relation with the state and making them part of the political process before they became constituted as a social class and protagonists of the social transformations (Portantiero, 1981: 217–40).

This suggestion that the Latin American process was different has had two important consequences for the established schemas of social theory. The first is the development of a politicized labour movement that defines itself and its actions in relation to the state rather than in relation to industry because its fate is determined largely by government economic policy. That this is a deviation from the classical schema becomes even more clear when we note the insistence on defining the relationship between the 'social process' and the 'political process' not in terms of unions and political parties but as a relation of the labour movement with the movement toward nationhood. A second difference is to attribute to populism 'an experience of social class which nationalizes the masses and gives them citizenship' (Portantiero, 1981: 234). This implies that even though populism as a state project might be a thing of the past, its influence as a 'phase in which the popular sectors are established as a political force' persists.

Historical memory sometimes tricks the analyst, showing that the relation between the subordinated classes and the people is not always clear. There is a space of conflict that does not coincide entirely with the relationships of class and production. It is a different and specific form of contradiction situated at the level of social formations that put the people in conflict with those in power (Laclau, 1977). This is a 'popular democratic' struggle which is characterized precisely by the historical continuity of popular traditions in contrast with the discontinuity which characterizes the structures of class.

The peculiarities of the way in which the Latin American masses have made themselves present as actors on the social scene are related, in the final analysis, with the double form of appeal which motivated the masses from the moment of the urban explosion: an appeal to a sense of class which is perceived only by a small minority and the popular-nationalistic appeal which affects the great majority. But, could this mass mobilization have been merely a manipulation of the people by the state with the aid of the mass media? Today we know that this was not the case. Populism's appeal to the 'popular classes' did contain elements of manipulation – higher salaries, the right to organize, etc. – but, when projected through the mass media, this appeal was transformed into a discourse constituting the worker as a citizen in a national social formation. Here, with all its ambiguity, lay the effectiveness of the appeal to popular traditions and the construction of a national culture. Here also we find the specific role of the mass media, especially film and radio, that constructed their discourse on the continuous link of the imagination of the masses from the old narrative memory, with its vivid *mise-en-scène* and popular iconography, to the proposal of new images charged with nationalistic sensibility.

The Mass Media in the Formation of National Cultures

If we are to understand the discontinuities between the state and the nation and the twisted, tortured path by which the masses burst into and became part of Latin American politics we must accept a profound change of perspective regarding the history of the mass media. For, although the social and political demands of the underclasses made themselves heard through the national-popular movements, it was through the discourse of the mass society that the national-popular became a recognizable identity for the great majority of people. With some exceptions, historians of the mass media have studied only the economic structure and the ideological content of the mass media; few have given close attention to the mediations through which the media have acquired a concrete institutional form and become a reflection of the culture. Studies have oscillated between attributing to the media the dynamics of profound historical changes in Latin America or reducing the media to mere passive instruments in the hands of powerful class interests acting with almost absolute autonomy.

If the cultural and political mediations have not been recognized in the history of the mass media, it is without doubt due to the fact that much of the general history leaves out culture or reduces it to high culture in its manifestations of art and literature. In the same way, the political history of Latin America consists of the great moments and important figures and almost never the events and political culture of the popular classes. It was left to an English historian to ask the following kind of questions about Colombian history: 'What was the popular impact of independence? What do we know about the political practices of the illiterate? What do we know about informal communication in politics or how local ideas about national politics are formed?' (see Deas, 1983: 151ff).

To introduce the analysis of the cultural sphere does not mean, however, that we add a new and separate theme, but that we focus on those aspects of the social process that articulate the *meaning* of the economic and the political. This would mean writing the history of the mass media from the perspective of cultural processes as articulators of the communication practices – hegemonic and subaltern – of social movements. Some studies have begun to work from this perspective, and their findings provide a starting point for understanding the mediations from which, for example, information technologies become the media of communication.

The focus on mediations and social movements has shown the necessity of distinguishing two quite different stages in the introduction of media institutions and the constitution of mass culture in Latin America. In the first stage, which stretches from the 1930s to the end of the 1950s, the efficacy and social significance of the mass media do not lie primarily in the industrial organization and the ideological content, but rather in the way the popular masses have appropriated the mass media and the way the masses have recognized their identity in the mass media. Of course, economics and ideology influence how the media functioned, but to discover the meaning and ideology of economic structure we must go deeper to the conflict which in that historical moment gave structure and dynamism to the social movements, namely, the conflict between the masses and the state and the resolution of this conflict in the nationalist populisms and populist nationalisms.

During this first stage, the decisive role of the mass media was their ability to convey the challenge and the appeal of populism, which transformed the mass into the people and the people into the nation.

This appeal came from the state, but it was effective only to the extent that the masses perceived in it some of their basic demands and forms of expression. The function of the *caudillos* and the mass media was to re-semanticize the masses' demands and expressions. This occurred not only in those countries that experienced the 'dramatization' of populism, but also in other countries which, under forms, names and rhythms other than populism, experienced the crisis of hegemony, the birth of nationality and the beginnings of modernity. Film in many countries and radio in virtually all countries gave the people of the different regions and provinces their first taste of nation.[7]

This function of the media is acknowledged, although unfortunately only in the conclusions, by a recent history of radio in Colombia.

> Before the appearance and growth of radio, the country was a patchwork of regions, each separate and isolated. Before 1940, Colombia could very well call itself a country of countries rather than a nation. Hyperbole aside, radio allowed the country to experience an invisible national unity, a cultural identity shared simultaneously by the people of the coast, Antioquia, Pasto, Santander and Bogota.   (Pareja, 1984: 177)

This observation puts us on the trail of another dimension of the formation of mass culture: transforming the political 'idea' of nationhood into the daily experience and feeling of nationhood.

The second stage in the constitution of mass culture in Latin America began after 1960. When the model of import substitution 'reached the limits of its coexistence with the archaic sectors of society' and populism could no longer be sustained without radicalizing the first social reforms, the myth and strategies of *development* with its technocratic solutions and encouragement of a consumer society began to replace the worn out populist policies (Intercom, 1981: 21). At this point, the political function of the media was removed and the economic function took over. The state continued to maintain the rhetoric that the air waves were a public, social service – as rhetorical as the social function of property – but, in fact, the state handed over the management of education and culture to the private sector. Ideology became the backbone of a mass discourse whose function was to make the poor dream the same dreams as the rich. As Galeano has said, 'The system spoke a surrealist language'. Not only was the wealth of the land transformed into the poverty of mankind, but scarcity and mankind's basic aspirations were converted into consumerism. The logic of this transformation would not become fully apparent until some years later when the economic crisis of the 1980s revealed the worldwide crisis of capitalism. The crisis could be solved only by making the model and decisions of production transnational and by standardizing, or, at least, pretending to standardize world culture. But by then mass culture would be riddled with new tensions that had their origins in the different national representations of popular culture, the multiplicity of cultural matrices and the new conflicts and resistances mobilized by transnationalization.

A cinema in the image of the people

Let us begin our analysis of the role of media in the period from 1930 to the late 1950s with that media experience which is the clearest and most easily identifiable expression of Latin American nationalism and mass, popular culture: the cinema of Mexico. According to Edgar Morin, until 1950, film was the backbone of mass culture (1977); and Mexican film performed this function in a special way for the mass culture of Latin America. Film was the centre of gravity of the new culture because

> the Mexican and the Latin American public in general did not experience cinema as a specific artistic or industrial phenomenon. The fundamental reason for the success of

film was structural and touched the centre of life. In films this public saw the possibility of experimenting, of adopting new habits and of seeing codes of daily life reiterated and dramatized by the voices they would like to have or hear. They did not go to the movies to dream; they went to learn. Watching the styles and fashions of the actors, the public learned to recognize and transform itself, finding solace, comfort and, secretly, exalta-tion.   (Monsiváis, 1976b: 446)[8]

Note carefully this quote because it synthesizes so well our argument. A first interesting aspect is how the great majority of the public perceived and experienced these films. This experience, more than the talent of the actors or the commercial strategies of the entrepreneurs, was responsible for the success of films. Going to the movies was not a purely psychological event, but the point of encounter between the collective lived experience generated by the Revolution and the mediation which, even though it deformed this experience, gave it social legitimacy. Freud has made clear that there is no access to language without passing through the shaping structures of symbolism, and Gramsci has explained that there is no social legitimation without re-semantization through the hegemonic code. Cinema was the living, social mediation that constituted the new cultural experience, and cinema became the first language of the popular urban culture. Beyond the reactionary subject matter and the rigidity of its forms, film connected with the yearnings of the masses to make themselves socially visible. Film became part of the movement to give 'national identity' an image and a voice. People went to the movies more to see themselves in a sequence of images that gave them gestures, faces, manners of speaking and walking, landscapes and colours than to identify with the plots.

In the process of permitting people to see themselves, film formed them into a national body; not in the sense of giving them a nationality but in the way they experienced being a single nation. Along with all of its mystifications and chauvinistic attitudes, film provided an identity for the urban masses which diminished the impact of cultural conflicts and enabled them for the first time to conceive of the country in their own image. Monsiváis sums up the ambiguity and force of this national image in five verbs: people *recognize* themselves in film with a recognition that is not passive but that *transforms* them; for a people coming from the Revolution, this meant to *pacify* and *resign* oneself, but also to secretly *move upwards*. In other words, it was an experience not only of consolation but of revenge.

Three mechanisms were at work in the new experience of nationalism that film provided. The first was theatrical – film as the dramatic staging and legitimation of peculiarly Mexican models of gestures, linguistic expressions and feeling. It was film which taught the people how to be Mexican in the national sense. The second mechanism was degradation. That is, in order for the people to recognize themselves, it was necessary to place nationhood within their reach. From then on, the national image is one of 'being irresponsible, being filled with filial affection for one's mother, to be an idler, the drunk, the sentimental slob . . . the programmed humiliation of women, the religious fanaticism, the obsessive respect for private property' (Monsiváis, 1976a: 86). The third mechanism was modernization. Often the mixture of images contradicted the traditional plots and brought up to date old myths, introduced customs and new models of moral behaviour and gave public access to the new rebelliousness and forms of speaking. 'Without an explicit message, film could not have entered where it did. Without the visible subversion, it could not have found the acceptance it did among a public that was at once so eager and so repressed. Film was the apparent guardian of the traditions it subverted' (Monsiváis, 1983: 29). Examples of this are the coherent incoherence which intertwines the bodily expressions of Cantinflas with his labyrinthine verbal locutions or the eroticism of prostitutes cutting across a message defending monogamy.

The keys to film's seduction, however, were the melodrama and the stars. The melodrama was the dramatic backbone of all the plots, bringing together social impotency and heroic aspirations, appealing to the popular world from a 'familiar understanding of reality'. The melodrama made it possible for film to weave together national epics and intimate drama, display eroticism under the pretext of condemning incest, and dissolve tragedy in a pool of tears, depoliticizing the social contradictions of daily life. The stars – María Félix, Dolores del Río, Pedro Armendariz, Jorge Negrete, Ninón Sevilla – provided the faces, bodies, voices and tones of expression for a people eager to see and hear themselves. Above and beyond the make-up and the commercial star industry, the movie stars who were truly stars for the people gathered their force from a secret pact that bonded their faces with the desires and obsessions of their publics.

Mexican film had three stages of development. Between 1920 and 1940 movies rewrote the popular legends. Pancho Villa was passed through the traditional models and myths of banditry which made cruelty a form of generosity. The Revolution appeared more as a backdrop than a storyline – the heroic death of the rebel, the assault on the rich hacienda, the march of the soldiers – appear again and again as the scene of the film action. The struggle against injustice was transformed from a fight for an ideal into a fight motivated by loyalty to the leader. This melodramatic transformation stripped the Revolution of its political meaning, but did not become reactionary until the second stage, after the 1930s, when the *ranchero* appeared, making *machismo* the expression of a nationalism that by now had become folklore. This was a *machismo* that was no longer a way that the people could understand and confront death but a compensatory mechanism for social inferiority. *Machismo* becomes the 'excess that redeemed the original sin of poverty...a plaintive cry for recognition' (Monsiváis, 1977: 31–2).

After the 1940s, Mexican films began to diversify their subject matter. We find now the urban comedy in which the neighbourhood replaced the countryside as the place where the old values found refuge and where the personal relations cut off by the city could be re-created. Other films about the lives of show girls and prostitutes depicted the 'adventures' and eroticism that challenged the traditional family. Both types of films were a bridge between a rural past and an urban present, films in which the city was essentially a place of confusion where memories were lost. In some ways the people projected on to and re-created memories in films that simultaneously degraded and elevated them, capitalizing on their weaknesses and their search for new signs of identity.

From the creole circus to radio theatre

In Latin America the Argentinians became the masters of radio drama. Mario Vargas Llosa describes this so vividly in his novel about radio and the people working in it in the years when radio was first launched in Latin America. Why Argentina? Perhaps it is due to the fact of the pioneering forms of radio there, as recent studies show. Another factor may have been the early commercial organization of radio with the creation of networks and the extremely rapid popular access to radio – from 1,000 receivers in 1922 to a million and a half in 1936. In 1928 there were already weekly magazines devoted to the world of radio (see Rivera, 1981; Terrero, 1981; Ford et al., 1985).

But the early development of a technical infrastructure in Argentina tells only half of the story. It attributes to the medium alone something that must be traced back to a sociocultural process and 'connects' radio with the country's long tradition of popular cultural expressions. In Argentina, the 'literary' country of Latin America *par excellence*, the disdain of writers for radio lasted many years and marked the 'distance between a media filled with possibilities and a cultural structure riddled with surprising paradoxes' (Rivera, 1980c: 383). Radio became the domain of the popular, the realm of the oral. The world of minstrels and travelling circuses helped to build a bridge between gaucho novels, wandering comedians and the radio. From the beginning, radio in Argentina was filled with popular music, readings of poetry, football matches, and, starting in 1931, radio was above all drama. Argentine radio did not receive any 'cultural recognition' until much later. In 1947, Peronism placed radio on the same level as other literary forms, awarding radio prizes and giving the medium other forms of recognition through the National Commission of Culture (Rivera, 1980c: 587).

The true importance of radio theatre in Argentina was its bridging role between the cultural traditions of the people and mass culture. Patricia Terrero views the function of Argentine radio theatre in terms of its continuity, examining 'its proximity to certain expressions of the national, popular imagination and its relationship to mythification, popular beliefs, and the formation of the social and cultural identity of the popular sectors' (1983: 5). Terrero's analysis looks beyond the radio medium itself to the experiences of listeners and the strategies of reception. It means taking into consideration the presence of the audiences in the studios where the radio dramas were transmitted, the provincial road tours of theatre groups presenting summaries of the broadcast dramas, listeners' letters, etc. This approach to analysis of radio brings to the fore once again the relation of the forms of listening to radio and the way people collectively listened to reading which, for so long, was customary in the popular culture. Fernando Ortiz makes this relationship explicit in his study of the evolution from collective reading to radio listening in the tobacco factories (Ortiz, 1947).

The spill-over of the study of the media into the surrounding cultural context brings into relief the importance of the 'creole circus', that unusual kind of circus that combines circus rings and the stage, acrobats and dramatic plays under the same tent (Seibel, 1984; Franco, 1981). When we examined the melodrama of the 1800s, it became clear that the roots of the modern popular spectacle of melodrama were in the circus and the travelling road shows. We find that, in Argentina, it was in the circus that a tradition of popular theatre was formed, gathering the memories of the minstrels and gaucho myths in the 'histories' of *Juan Moreira, Juan Cuello, Hormiga Negra, Santos Vega* and *Martín Fierro*. The creole circus was the first to build a bridge between the narrative tradition of the serial and the road show. The pantomime of *Juan Moreira* in the Podestá Circus (1884) adapted the serials of Eduardo Gutiérrez, published between 1879 and 1880, to the stage. The mixture of circus comedy and popular drama gave birth to a radio theatre with the same actors and the same relationship with the public. 'Without asking anyone's permission, the popular theatre was born in the circus of the Podestá, grew up in the tours of the creole circus tents, and came of age in the theatre companies of the radio dramas' (Seibel, 1982: 12). This gave the Argentine radio theatre its particular characteristics and justified its name. In other countries without this tradition it was called the *radionovela*. The serial novel that became the theatre of the creole circus, later, in radio, continued to have strong ties with the theatre, not only because of radio's transmission of the play before a public in the studio, but because the theatre companies of the radio dramas travelled throughout the provinces, allowing the people to 'see what they heard'. The radio theatres' success owed less to the medium, radio, than to the mediation already established with a cultural tradition.

If the creole circus was the place of osmosis, the gaucho serials were the place of 'origin' of the popular mythology that eventually found its way into radio. Of all the serials, those by Gutiérrez had the most prestige, shocking literary critics by bringing together the urban and rural worlds, popular and mass cultures, but providing for the people the key to their access to national sentiments. The characters of the serials stepped out of the verses of the troubadours that had circulated in printed sheets, booklets and magazines, but they also stepped out of police files. The serials presented a new dramatic universe, 'a frontier world' that, in its own way, registered the changes and the crises brought by the modernization of Argentina beginning at the end of the nineteenth century. 'Eduardo Gutiérrez basically worked with a popular audience that began to form with the modernization of Argentine society' (Rivera, 1982: 9). He established a fundamental complicity with his audience, countering the heroes who broke with 'a reinterpretation in the mass of readers and spectators that made possible the acknowledgement of the crisis and the discord it brought to society and their own lives' (Rivera, 1980b: 222).

The Argentine radio theatre had several stages of development.[9] In the first stage, dialogue was minimal, and presentations were built around songs, ballads and country music. In a second stage, beginning after 1935, the radio theatre found its own form. The theatrical companies came together, music was used dramatically and as a function of the plot, and the plots used themes from the gaucho tradition or from history. Gaucho literature was represented mainly in the works of González Pulido who collected the legends, verses and stories in a mythology of the outlaw, with their models of social protest and demands. The historical themes, the work of Héctor Pedro Blomberg, were based on archetypal characters among which the *Amores célebres de América Latina*, portraying the lives of the heroines of the independence movement, were especially popular with the public. The production of the radio theatre diversified after the mid-1940s in a way similar to what occurred with Mexican films. Although the gaucho legends continued to be important, two new themes entered the repertoires: detective stories and children's stories, most of which were adaptations. 'Love stories' appeared with enormous popular success. Most of these were produced in Argentina, but they already contain some of the characteristic stereotypes that would be used in the melodramas of the culture industry. An important aspect of this subgenre is that many of the producers were women. Studies carried out with women on the significance of radio theatre for its audience have revealed to what extent the interpretation by the public activates the keys to meaning which connect radio theatre with expressions of culture and elements of popular life. Before becoming Peronism, Argentine populism was a way of plugging mass culture into a wide family of existing expressions of popular culture. How significant it is that Evita became much more than just an actress through her role in a radio theatre company!

The urban legitimation of black music

'To firmly stabilize a music expression from a popular background as a means of getting control of a language that reconciles a nation horizontally across geography and vertically across classes'.[10] With this phrase Mario de Andrade described the role of music in the nationalizing project of Brazil in the 1930s. Perhaps in no other country of Latin America did music express so strongly the secret link between the integrating 'ethos' and the 'pathos' in the universe of feeling as it did in Brazil. This link made music especially appropriate for populist uses. What happened in Brazil with black music, especially its aberrant, off-course path to social and cultural legitimation, reveals the inability of both intellectual and populist currents of thought to comprehend the web of contradictions and seductions forming the relationship between popular and mass, the urban beginnings of populism.

The path that led Brazilian music from the samba chorus – with this ritual space: the *terreiro de candomblé* – to the radio and to records, passes through a multiplicity of manifestations that can be organized in terms of two historical moments: the social incorporation of the productive physical 'gestural style' of the black people and the cultural legitimation of the musical rhythm that this gesture contained. National populism accompanied and in some ways made possible the passage from one stage to the next. Populism, however, was overwhelmed by a process that was too big for its political framework, that defied both the authoritarian pedantry of the Enlightenment tradition and purist idealism of Romanticism.

At the historical point when political independence was attempting to gather strength by radically changing the economy, slave labour began to be less productive and less of an economic advantage than free labour. The opening up of the national market to the whole population broke down the traditional isolation of the plantation, revealing the productivity of the physical gestural style of the blacks at the social and national level. The conclusion was reached that if black people produce as much as the immigrant, then let us encourage their productivity by giving them what they are worth. The physical gesture of the blacks, however, was not just an external manifestation. The social incorporation of the black gestural style set in motion a process at another level. 'To the extent that the blacks survived exclusively by physical labour, it was in the "gesture", in the physical manifestation of their humanity, that they imposed their culture' (Squeff and Wisnik, 1983: 43).

A link, unknown to whites, emerged between the gestures of physical work and the rhythm of the dance, the symbiosis of work and rhythm that was the survival strategy of the slave. Black people, using an almost hypnotic cadence, were able to survive backbreaking work; fatigue and effort became less painful when trapped in a frenetic rhythm. It was an intoxication without alcohol but heavy with fantasy and dreams. This does not attempt to reduce all meaning of the dance to work, but tries to reveal in the 'indecency' of black gestures and movements not just an 'unabashed' relationship with sex but a process of work that is at the heart of the dance, in its rhythm. The dialectic of this double indecency is what truly scandalized 'society'. It did not, however, prevent this society from accepting the profitable productivity of blacks, but this acceptance was kept on the economic level. For an acceptance of blacks at a cultural level, a political crisis would be necessary.

In this analysis of the relationship between populism and the creation of mass culture, it is important to note that the national crises of Latin America in these years, especially in Brazil, were not simply a result of the worldwide economic depression of 1929. It was also a crisis of internal hegemony that placed the masses in conflict with the state. The state attempted to resolve this crisis by taking upon itself the title of defender of the popular classes and, at the same time, the motor of the modernization of the country. But this strategy led the state into a series of contradictions: the state attempted to achieve the independence of the nation by imitating the nations it now depended on; and the state tried to respond to democratic demands with authoritarian policies. The same contradictions that tore populism apart at the political level revealed themselves even more forcefully in the cultural expressions. The development of music reveals with striking clarity these cultural contradictions.

The nationalistic project in musical expression operated at an internal and external level. Internally, a quarantine was placed around 'good' popular music – folk music from the rural areas – to separate and protect it from the 'bad' popular music, that is, the commercialized and foreign-influenced music made in the cities. The strategy looking to the external image of the country determined that only the music resulting from the synthesis of the best of Brazilian folk and the best of classical European music could be offered to the civilized world, a music that, while it clearly reflected national characteristics, could be listened to without seeming strange or unusual. The music of Villa-Lobos would be considered a splendid achievement of this project.

Nevertheless, this internal–external strategy turned out to be part of an ambiguous process and a cultural policy full of contradictions. 'In an attempt to benefit the whole nation, the policy stirred up the aspirations of popular culture while at the same time it tried to control these aspirations' (Squeff and Wisnik, 1983: 173). In the end, this limited legitimation of popular music proved to be equally disconcerting to two quite opposed vanguards of cultural nationalism. For those in the elitist, more rationalistic Enlightenment tradition, it was a degrading remnant of the illiterate, superstitious and indolent masses. For the purists of the Romantic tradition, it awakened political aspirations, caused strikes and incited dirty tastes. The appeal of a unifying national sentiment was not able to cover over all of these tensions and social wounds that were brought into the open.

Nevertheless, populist nationalism was an essential stage of development because in this process 'the state sought legitimation in the image of the popular masses and the popular masses sought citizenship in the official recognition of the state' (Squeff and Wisnik, 1983: 175). This mutual need made possible the emergence of a culture that was both urban and popular. By this time, however, the process was no longer led by the state but by the dynamics of the market for records, radio and the leaders of foreign tastes.

In order to become urban, black music had to cross two ideological barriers. The first of these barriers was the populist concept of culture which insisted that the only authentically popular culture was that which could be traced back in its essence and roots, not to the actual historically verified origins, but to an idealized origin in a rural, peasant context.[11] Because of this illusion, populism could never resolve the contradiction between its romantic notion of the people and the reality of the urban masses – rootless, politicized, bitterly resentful, with degraded tastes, cosmopolitan – characteristics and aspirations which populism was somehow supposed to assume as its own. A second quite contrary ideological barrier for black music was the intellectual tradition of the Enlightenment which identified culture with fine arts, an art which emphasized its distance and distinction, careful social limits and discipline to dramatize its difference from the new, undisciplined and unclassifiable musical manifestations of the city. Popular music could become art only when it was elevated, distanced from its immediate environment and put into the form, for example, of a sonata. The incorporation of popular culture is always dangerous for an 'intelligentsia' who feel the permanent threat of confusion, the abolition of forms and rules defining the distances. For these reasons, it was the 'dirty' culture industry and the dangerous artistic vanguard that ended up incorporating the black rhythms in the culture of the city and legitimating urban popular culture as culture – a new culture 'which was created by polymorphous appropriation and the establishment of a musical market where popular music in transformation lived side-by-side with elements of international music and the influences of urban daily life' (Squeff and Wisnik, 1983: 148).

The black physical gesture, tearing itself loose from the myth of origins, became the base of the new culture. It was a culture which no longer merely supplied the roots the city dweller lacks, the same lack revealed in the urban use of folkcrafts 'in which the nostalgic feelings of the past are evoked in order to provide greater depth to domestic intimacy stereotyped by industrially produced household appliances' (García Canclini, 1982: 156). The black physical gesture became the heart of popular, mass culture, that is, a field of contradictory affirmations of work and leisure, sex, religion and politics. The passage which started from the *candomblé* and, following a winding path, twisted and overlaid with other meanings, finally brought music to the record and the radio. It was a journey marked by the conflicts, subterfuges and strategies that have always filled the path to social recognition followed by the downtrodden. It was like the form of fighting which the Brazilian blacks call *capoeira*, the fusion of combat and play, combat and dance, charged with *mandinga*, with seduction and malice capable of 'throwing the enemy off his chosen path' (Muñiz Sodré, 1983: 205). It was another kind of logic that would find its highest point of recognition, dislocation, and parody in the carnival (Da Matta, 1981). Black music had to achieve its citizenship, 'sideways', so to speak, and 'the contradictions contained in this voyage were considerable, but the voyage generalized and consummated one of the most important Brazilian cultural events, the modern, urban development of black music' (Squeff and Wisnik, 1983: 161).

The birth of the popular mass press

The media which we have examined so far – film, radio and especially music – were born 'popular' precisely because they were accessible to illiterate and uneducated publics. The press, however, also played a role in granting citizenship to the urban masses. This occurred after the changes which dislodged the press from the circle of the literate and learned and tore it loose from the matrix of the dominant culture.

Of all the media the press has the most written history, not only because it is the oldest, but because it is where those who write about history receive cultural acknowledgement. The history of the press looks mainly at the 'serious press'. When it examines the sensationalist press, it does so almost exclusively in economic terms: the growth of circulation and advertising. According to this type of journalism history, it is impossible to speak of politics, much less of culture, when one is dealing with newspapers that are nothing more than a business and scandal-mongering, exploiting the ignorance and low passions of the masses. In contrast to this concept that denies the sensationalist press any political meaning, another type of historical analysis has begun to introduce questions from the sociology of culture and political science. In Europe, this line of research, represented by Raymond Williams and Theodore Zeldin, has acquired a certain importance.[12] In Latin America, Guillermo Sunkel has carried out a pioneering study on the mass popular media in Chile. The subtitle of his recent book reveals the new approach: *A Study of the Relationship between Popular Culture, Mass Culture and Political Culture* (Sunkel, 1985).

Sunkel begins his study with a historical event – the bringing together, beginning in the 1930s, of the life and struggle of the people with the conditions of existence of mass society. This has been accompanied by a profound theoretical reconceptualization of the people in the political culture of the Marxist left. We will leave the analysis of this theoretical and methodological proposal until later and turn now to the map of mediations that shaped the development of the popular mass press in Chile.

A process of political change beginning in the 1920s culminated in 1938 with the formation of the Popular Front and the participation of the parties of the left in the government. During these years the Chilean press changed radically. The workers' press became the left-wing newspapers, and the sensationalist daily papers appeared.

The first change was basically a shift in the workers' papers from a purely local setting to an interest in national topics or a presentation of local topics in a national language. This implied at least a potential new group of followers for the left-wing discourse: the mass public. The form of discourse of these newspapers, however, remained within the constraining matrix of the rationalistic Enlightenment, performing a function of popular educational formation and political propaganda. The objectives continued to be the education of the populace – raising their political consciousness – and to represent the interests of the masses in relation to the state. But that representation was limited to those issues that the Marxist left considered political or potentially political. Their concept of politics – and therefore of popular representation – did not include other actors than the working class and employers. Such a political press was concerned only with the conflicts that emerged out of the relationships of production – the clash between labour and capital – and only with the factory and labour union. It was a heroic vision that ignored daily life, personal subjectivity and sexuality as well as the cultural practices of the people such as their story telling, their religious customs and the fund of knowledge of the people. All this was ignored or, worse still, stigmatized as sources of alienation and obstacles in political struggle.

Thus, the transformation of the left-wing press was largely the adoption of national-level themes and language as well as a concentration in a smaller number of papers. Of the more than one hundred labour newspapers which existed at one time or another between 1900 and 1920 – with their diversity of ideological positions along socialist, anarchist or radical lines – in 1929 only five continued to be published regularly. The official paper of the Communist Party, *El Siglo*, appeared in 1940, culminating a process beginning with the newspaper, *Frente Unico*, which circulated between 1934 and 1936, and *Frente Popular*, from 1936 to 1940.

In the United States and Europe the appearance of the sensationalist press is normally 'explained' as a function of the development of printing technology and the competition between the big newspapers. In Latin America, when the sensationalist press is studied, it is to provide a clear example of the penetration of North American models that, by putting profits ahead of any other criteria, have corrupted the region's tradition of serious journalism. Sunkel looks at the history of the sensationalist press from another angle, and he finds within Chile itself the antecedent press discourses and forms that evolved into the Chilean sensationalist press.

Chile, like many other Latin American countries since the second half of the nineteenth century, has had a great many popular publications which, like the *gacetas* in Argentina (Rivera, 1980a) or the literature of the *cordel* in Brazil (Luyten, 1981), mixed together news, poetry, and popular narratives. In Chile, these were called *liras populares*, and after the First World War they began to gain in news value what lost in the quality of their poetry. Thus, they began to 'assume the functions of journalism at a historical moment when the experiences of popular culture were on the threshold of mass culture' (Sunkel, 1985: 80). In this prototype of popular journalism, written mainly for oral distribution, that is, to be read, declaimed or sung in public places such as the markets, the railway station or in the street, we find the beginnings of the sensationalist press. Already they have the large headlines calling attention to the main story, the prominent graphics illustrating the story, the melodramatization of a discourse gripped by violence and the macabre, and the exaggerated fascination with the stars of sports and entertainment.

From the 1920s, Chile had newspapers that began to adopt and develop the forms of the *liras populares*. In 1922, *Los Tiempos*, already in tabloid form, introduced a new style of journalism. Some years earlier, *Crítica* in Argentina had revolutionized journalism, breaking the solemnity and pomposity of the 'serious press' and introducing new elements that explicitly employed manners of popular expression: the graphic reconstruction of the scene of the crime; a short verse commenting on the episode that appeared with the story; a street scene or description of local customs; and a phrase taken from the vocabulary of the thieves (Rivera, 1980c). The Chilean newspaper, *Los Tiempos*, was also characterized by its lively style and use of scandal and humour in reporting the news. *Las Noticias Gráficas* appeared in 1944, presenting itself as 'the paper of the people' and printing the demands of people from the popular classes that were normally not represented or were ignored in the traditional political discourse: the interests of women, the retired people, the world of the jails and the reformatories, the problems of alcoholism and prostitution. This type of press put more emphasis on the police chronicles and took a more irreverent and scandalous tone, with a frequent use of local slang from popular ways of speaking. The new journalism found its best expression in *Clarin*, founded in 1954, where commercial criteria were always tied to and determined by political and cultural criteria. In *Clarin* it was clear that the change in journalistic language was not only a question of attracting the public but of searching out and incorporating other languages circulating at the margins of society. It is in this light that one must interpret the caricature of the forms of speech of different social groups and the transposition of the discourse of crime to political discussion.

The issue of sensationalism calls attention to traces in the discourse of the press of another cultural matrix, much more symbolic and dramatic, which have their origins in the practices and moulds of popular culture. This matrix does not operate on the basis of concepts and generalizations but expresses itself in images and concrete situations. Rejected by the world of official education and serious politics, it survives in the world of the culture industry, and from this base it continues to exercise a powerful appeal to the popular. It is, of course, much easier and less dangerous to continue to reduce sensationalism to a 'bourgeois tool' of manipulation and alienation. It took courage to affirm that 'behind the notion of sensationalism as the commercial exploitation of crime, pornography and vulgar language lies a purist vision of the popular world' (Sunkel, 1985: 115). Only by taking this risk, however, was it possible to discover the *cultural* connection between the melodramatic aesthetic and the forms of survival and revenge in the matrix pervading popular cultures. The melodramatic aesthetic dared to violate the rationalistic division between serious and frivolous themes, to treat political events as dramatic events, and break with 'objectivity' by observing the situation from the perspective that appeals to the subjectivity of the readers.

Developmentalism and Transnationalization

The first Latin American version of modernity had at its centre the idea of the *Nation* – to become a modern nation. The second version, beginning in the 1960s, was associated with development, a new understanding of the idea of progress. Development was taken as an objective step forward that could be quantified both in terms of economic growth and in its 'natural' consequence, political democratization. The flow of democratization from economic growth was considered natural because an increase in production would increase consumption, redistribute goods and thereby strengthen democracy. In this way, democracy was a 'spin-off of modernization' (Faletto, 1982: 119); it depended on economic growth, the fruit of a reform of society in which the state was conceived 'no longer as the incarnation of the personalized vote for a social contract but as a neutral technical body carrying out the directives of development' (Lechner, 1981: 306).

During the 1960s, the majority of the Latin American countries experienced a rapid growth and diversification of industry and an expansion of internal markets. But this was accompanied by the rise of almost insoluble contradictions. For the left, these contradictions simply made visible the incompatibility between capitalist accumulation and social change. For the right, the contradictions demonstrated the incompatibility of economic development with democracy. Brazil, the first to experience a right-wing coup, followed by Chile's election of a socialist government, raised misgivings about the 'naturalness' of development. Within a few years, the takeover by military regimes in a majority of Latin American countries showed clearly that the interests of capital were the only truly quantifiable objective of development. Developmentalism also illustrated something even more fundamental to the model: 'the failure of the political principle of generalized modernization' (Mendes et al., 1977: 139). Clear testimony to this failure were the spread of government by force in the 1970s, the oppressive growth of foreign debt in the 1980s, and, above all, the new meaning of transnationalization that 'jumped' from an economic model to the internationalization of a political model in response to the crisis of hegemony. 'What allows us to speak of a transnational phase is its political nature. The rupture of the dike of national borders in the face of capitalist concentration radically changed the nature and function of the state by diminishing its ability to play a role in the economy and the historical development of a country' (Roncagliolo, 1982: 27).

What is the role of the mass media in the new phase of Latin American modernization? What changes have occurred in the role media plays in the creation of a mass society and in relation to the masses themselves? To answer these questions it is necessary to differentiate between what happened during the years of euphoria, the years of the 'miracles of development' in the early 1960s (and in some countries up to the mid-1970s), and what happened in the 1980s when the world crisis heightened the contradiction between the national character of the political structure and the transnational character of the economic structure.

A new meaning of massification

In contrast to what happened during the period of the populisms, when the 'mass' meant the ambiguous political weight of the masses in the city and their explosive charge of social realism, in the years of developmentalism, mass came to connote exclusively the means for homogenization and control of the masses. Massification was felt even where there were no masses. The media, which formerly were mediators between the state and the masses, between the rural and the urban, between tradition and modernity, increasingly tended to become only a simulation or even the instrument of deactivation of these relationships. Although the media continued to 'mediate', and although simulation was already at the root of their social role, something was beginning to change. It was not an abstract change in the sense that the media became the message. It was a change in the same direction as development, the schizophrenic growth of a society whose reality did not coincide with its demands. Only with such changes in meaning could communication be measured in the quantitative circulation of newspapers and the number of radio and television receivers. Indeed, measurement became the cornerstone of development. The experts of the Organization of American States could proclaim, 'Without communication there is no development'. Now the radio dial became saturated with stations in cities with no running water, and slums sprouted TV aerials. Indeed, the TV aerials were symptomatic of changes that had occurred in the concept of mass.

Marching hand in hand with the diffusion of innovations as the 'motor' of development were two key dimensions of the new field of communications: the hegemonic role of television and the functional diversification of radio.

Television implied not only an escalation of the economic investment and complexity of industrial organization of the media, but also a qualitative refinement of the ideological influences. In the model of democratizing development in its most complete form, television achieves its central role in so far as there is unification of consumer demand, the only way to expand the hegemony of the market without subsidiaries resenting the expansion. If we are able to consume the same things that developed peoples consume, then, clearly, we have finally achieved development.[13] Looking beyond the percentages of programming imported from the United States and even the imitations of US programme formats, what most influenced Latin America was the importation of the North American *model* of television. This does not mean simply the privatization of the networks. There are some countries, such as Colombia, where television belongs to and is administered by the state in a way that is quite compatible with the dominant model. Rather, the heart of the model lies in the tendency to constitute, through television, a single public,[14] and to reabsorb the sociocultural differences of a country to the point that one can confuse a higher degree of communicability with a higher degree of economic profitability. Within a few years after the introduction of television the audience rating systems became standardized among the world's television systems, and something the model already logically implied became explicit: the tendency for television to constitute a discourse that, in order to speak to the largest number of people, had to reduce the differences to the minimum. This required of the audiences the least possible effort in decodification and posed the least possible conflict with the sociocultural prejudices of the majority.

The press, even after it became a mass medium, always reflected cultural and political differences. This was not only its need for 'social distinction', but corresponded to the press's liberal model that attempted to give expression to the diversity of liberal society. Radio also, for the quite different reasons of its closeness to popular culture, placed an emphasis on social and cultural diversity from the very beginning. Television, on the other hand, tends to absorb differences as much as possible. I use the word 'absorb' because this best describes the way television attempts to deny differences: showing such differences with all implicit conflict stripped away. No other medium has the potential for providing access to such a wide variety of human experiences, countries, cultures and situations. But no other medium has channelled cultural perceptions to such a degree that, instead of encouraging a collapse of nationalistic ethnocentrism, reinforces it. As the spectacle of daily life is channelled into television,[15] the hegemonic model of television reconstructs reality with a paradoxical control of differences. Television's mechanisms of proximity and familiarization, by capitalizing on surface similarities, end up convincing viewers that if they get close enough to a reproduction of reality, the 'farthest away' in time and space is in fact no different from us. On the other hand, the mechanisms of distancing and making something exotic convert what is different into something totally and radically strange, without any relation to us and without any meaning in our world. Both sets of mechanisms make it impossible for differences to challenge the viewer and question or undermine the myth of development sustaining the world view that there is only one model of society compatible with progress and, therefore, with the future.

Radio experienced a transformation in the 1960s as a result of the complex changes imposed by developmentalism and the crisis of the radio medium set in motion by the domination of television. Radio reacted to the competition from television by exploiting the stamp of popular culture which it bears, that is, its special way of 'capturing' the popular world, 'the way radio works with its following and its system of appeals' (Alfaro, 1985b: 53). Its closeness to popular culture is also implied in its technical characteristics: all you have to do is listen; its limitation to voice and music allowing it to develop a particular form of colloquial expression; and its non-exclusive form of use making it compatible with simultaneous activities and time frames (Gutiérrez and Munizaga, 1983: 15ff). These technical–discursive factors allowed radio to 'mediate with the popular' in a way no other medium could. They renewed radio as a privileged link between modernizing, informative–instrumental rationality and the expressive–symbolic mentality of the popular world. The modernization project becomes in radio an *educational project*, encouraging both the technical adaptation of the practices of the peasants to the requirements and objectives of development and an ideological readjustment – overcoming the religious superstitions hampering technological progress and the benefits of consumerism.[16]

On the other hand, radio responded to the hegemony of television by 'diversifying' and attracting more varied publics. Diversification was compatible with the demands of the market, but it spoke of something else: 'The homogenization of the consumer made it necessary to categorize the receiver producing a classification that transformed previous social identities into a society where the category of citizen broadened to include spectator, fan, youth, women, etc.' (Gutiérrez and Munizaga, 1983: 20). At first, the segmentation of publics corresponded to a diversification of programming types or specific programmes within a radio station. Later, it became a specialization of stations for groups of publics or listeners appealing to different cultural sectors or generations. The crisis of identity of the traditional political parties and the absence of an effective appeal to the popular world by the political left, made it easy for the mass media and especially radio to form new social identities that responded more to an economic model than to a renovation of politics. The transnationalization of mass culture in the 1980s was supported internally by this political vacuum and by the integrating diversification of radio counterbalancing the unifying tendencies of television.

The contradictions between technologies and uses

Since the end of the 1980s the 'new technologies' have been the protagonists of Latin American communications. Seen from the perspective of the technology-producing countries, the new communication technologies – satellites, cable, videotext, teletext, etc. – represent a new stage in the continuous process of the acceleration of modernity that now takes a qualitative leap from the industrial revolution to the electronic revolution. No country can afford, culturally or economically, not to be part of this leap ahead. The new technologies raise many questions in Latin America, questions that are not resolved by the old dilemma: a 'yes' or a 'no' to technology is a 'yes' or 'no' to development itself. For the questions shift the focus from the technologies themselves to the model of production which they imply and to the modes of access, acquisition and use of these technologies. The shift is from technology in the abstract to the processes of imposition, deformation and dependence the technologies imply, to domination but also to resistance, recycling and redesign. The appearance of new technologies in Latin America is part of the old schizophrenia between modernization and the likelihood of actually realizing the social and cultural appropriation of the tools with which to modernize. 'Adapt to the information technologies, or die', is the slogan of a capitalism in crisis and in dire need of expanding consumption of new information technologies.

Marks of schizophrenia are apparent at many levels, from the most mundane to decisions involving enormous investments and changes in national policies. There is a 'semantic hole' in the argument which pushes the daily consumption of technologies without any reference to the context in which they are produced, a hole most people end up filling with the language of magic or religion. Another sign of schizophrenic thinking about new technologies are decisions by governments or political parties to throw out of shape the existing policies of national investment and informatization with no reasonable consideration for the economic and social costs they imply. A recent study by Mattelart and Schmucler (1983) showed that the levels of technological expansion in the field of communications are very different in each country but the levels of fascination and seduction by the technologies are very similar. One finds an omnipresent compulsive need for microcomputers, VCRs, video games and videotext not only in the capital cities but in the provincial towns.

The new communication technologies in Latin America raise two questions from the perspective of culture. Firstly, as a result of the rationality they materialize and of the way they operate, these technologies produce a crisis in the 'fiction of identity' on which national cultures rest in these countries. Secondly, sophisticated technologies carry to the extreme the simulation of rationality – or, in Baudrillard's terms, the 'sham' of rationality – and make visible that remnant of Latin American society which cannot be pushed into the simulation of rationality, that which, because of its cultural otherness, resists the generalized homogenization. This remnant is not something strange or mysterious; it is the conflictive and dynamic presence in Latin America of the popular cultures.

The questions which the new technologies raise regarding cultural identities operate at quite different levels that need to be clearly distinguished. One is the challenge to the attempts to seek refuge in the past, the old idealist temptation to postulate an identity whose meaning is in the remote origins, far back in history and out of sight, outside the historical dynamics of the present. Another challenge is the meaning new technologies acquire as the summit of human development (Muñiz Sodré, 1983: 32). This reactivation of evolutionist logic reduces, radically and without exception, all that lies outside a certain linear conception of history to the status of 'backwardness', making what remains of identity in the other cultures merely a 'reflective' identity, that is, an identity which has no value except to reflect the differences with hegemonic culture. This is a negative identity, defining what we are not, emphasizing our deficiencies. And the implied message is that what we 'lack', what we most need today is the technology produced by the industrialized countries, the technology that ultimately is going to allow us to make the definitive leap to modernity.

This is a fabulous paradox, if it were not so bloody. In the name of an electronic memory our countries are being asked to renounce the right to have and develop their own memory. In the dilemma of choice between underdevelopment and modernization, cultural memory does not count and has no place. It cannot be operationalized in terms of information and therefore it cannot be used. In contrast to instrumental memory, 'cultural memory' does not work with pure information or as a process of linear accumulation. It is articulated through experience and events. Instead of simply accumulating, it filters and weighs. It is not a memory we can *use*, but the memory of which we are made. Cultural memory has nothing to do with nostalgia; its function in the community is not to talk of the past but to give continuity to the ongoing construction of collective identity. The logic of cultural memory, however, operating for example in the popular narrative where the quality of communication is far from proportional to the quantity of information, resists analysis by the categories of informatics.

Equally tragic is the pillaging of this cultural memory, the narrative tradition of East and West, to give some 'substance' to the fetishistic form of representation of the new technologies. The new technologies are made 'stars' by science fiction movies and television series (Gubern, 1982). As we enter into the playful mood of the most popular genres – the epics, the adventures, the tales of terror – we are shown a future that distorts and dissolves the present. Technology is made to appear spectacular and innocent at the same time. From the robot who is always so pleasant and good natured, or at least working with 'the good guys', we pass to the embellishment of war machines as beautiful as they are deadly. In the films with brilliant special effects and visual beauty or, in their cheapened version, in the thousand cartoons for television, the 'image of the new technologies' educates the popular classes of Latin America in a way that is most convenient for the producers of the technologies, a fascination with the new fetishism.

A central chapter in the research on new technologies is their effect on culture. Starting with the concept of 'effect', however, the relation between technology and culture brings us back to the old conception of media: one side has all the action and the other side is merely a passive receiver. The use of this concept is aggravated by the continuation of the idea of a single cultural identity at the base of all identity. Technologies are the many, culture is only one. In Latin America, at least, exactly the opposite is true. Technology, with its 'logo-tecnica' is one of the strongest and most profound sources of standardization, while the differences, the cultural plural- ism, unmask this standardization by bringing to light the 'discontinuities' making up the cultural reality of the region. One of the novelties of the new communication technologies is the coordination between the tempo of production by the rich countries and the tempo of consumption by the poor. For the first time, we are not buying second-hand machinery! It is, however, a false coordination of tempos. It cloaks a lack of coordination between objects and practices, technologies and users, making it impossible to understand the historical meaning of the appropriation of technology.

This lack of contemporaneity occurs at the national level in the clash of tempos and the crisis which the technological transnationalization accelerates or sets in motion, for example, in the lack of cultural articulation in the national projects. It also occurs in popular culture, which, confronted by new technologies, feels forced to take refuge in concepts and practices rooted in nostalgia and a simplistic transparency of meaning. The view of technologies from the perspective of cultural differences has nothing to do with a yearning or restlessness in the face of technological complexity or the abstraction of the mass media. Nor does it have anything to do with a voluntarist overconfidence in the ultimate triumph of the good. Technologies are not transpar- ent tools that can be used in any manner. They are the materialization of the rationality of a culture and of a 'global model of organization of power' (Mattelart and Schmucler, 1983).

The redesign of technology, however, is possible, if not as a strategy, at least as a tactic in the definition given by de Certeau: a manner of fighting of the person who cannot fight on his own grounds and is obliged to fight on the grounds of his adversary (de Certeau, 1984). The key lies in taking the original imported technology as energy, as a potential to develop on the basis of the requirements of the national culture. This does not ignore the fact that at times the only way to actively take control of what is imposed on us is the tactic of the anti-design, a design which is a parody and involves technology in a game which denies it as a value in itself. In any event when the machinery itself cannot be redesigned, at least its function can.

In a poor slum of Lima, a group of women attempted to better organize the market place. In the market area, they found a tape recorder and some loudspeakers which were being used only occasionally by the administrator. With the help of a group from a communication centre, the women began to use the tape recorder to interview people of the neighbourhood as to what they thought about the market and to provide music and celebrations on festival days and other holidays. And so they continued until they were criticized by a person of higher status, a nun, who ridiculed the way they talked and condemned their audacity to speak over the loudspeakers 'without knowing how to talk properly'. This caused a crisis and for some weeks the women did not want to have anything more to do with the loudspeakers. But then some of the women went to the communication centre to announce dejectedly, 'We discovered that the nun was right. We don't know how to talk and in this society those who don't know how to talk do not have the least possibility of defending themselves or doing anything. But we also have understood that with the help of this little machine – the recorder – we can learn how to speak.' And from that day the women of the market decided to tell stories about their own lives. They no longer used the recorder just to listen to others but began to use it to learn how to speak (Alfaro, 1983).

Notes

1   Regarding the 'origins' of that project, using Guatemala as an example, see *La patria del criollo* (Costa Rica, 1972).
2   For an analysis of this debate from a current perspective in Peru, see Cornejo et al. (1981).
3   Colombia appears to be a typical case of this. See Uribe Celis (1984).
4   This is the conclusion reached by M. A. Garretón in his analysis of the crisis of 1973. See 'Prospecto nacional, una perspectiva socio-política', in Garretón et al. (1983).
5   See Monsiváis (1981: 35): Regarding the education project of Vasconcelos, see also Taboada (1982).
6   In these pages, the basic ideas are taken from Romero (1976: 318).
7   The media built on the groundwork laid by the education system in the provision of this daily experience of nationhood. A key text that provides a general framework for this process and some specific national case studies is Braslavsky and Tedesco (1982).
8   Monsiváis (1976b: 446). This analysis is based on the work of Monsiváis.
9   Here we are following studies cited by Terrero.
10 Squeff and Wisnik (1983: 148). In addition to this text, which seems basic, our analysis is based on the collective article 'Questao popular' (Chaui et al., 1980).
11 This is the biological–telluric paradigm mentioned by N. García Canclini (1984).
12 These two authors are discussed in Part I of this book [see Martín-Barbero, *Communication, Culture and Hegemony*].
13 Beltrán and Fox (1980) provide data and measures of some of these changes.
14 Muñiz Sodré (1981) is one of the best sources regarding this.
15 The relationship between entertainment and daily life has been examined in detail in Part II [see Martín-Barbero, *Communication, Culture and Hegemony*].

16 A model of this modernizing education project was Radio Sutatenza with its network of training centres. See Pareja (1984).

References

Alfaro, R. M. (1983) 'Del periódico al altoparlante', *Materiales para la Communicación Popular*, 1 (Lima).

—— (1985) 'Modelos radiales y proceso de popularización de la radio', *Contratexto*, 1 (Lima)

Arguedas, J. M. (1977) *Formación de una Cultura Nacional Indoamericana*. Mexico: Siglo XXI.

Beltrán, L. R. and Fox, E. (1980) *Communicación Dominada: Estados Unidos en los Medios de América Latina*. Mexico: Nueva Imagen.

Bolivar, Simon (1972) 'Carta de Jamaica', in *Escritos Políticos* (Madrid).

Braslavsky, C. and Tedesco, J. C. (1982) 'Tendencias históricas de la educación popular como expresiones de los proyectos políticos de los estados latino-americanos'. Investigaciones Educativas (Mexico).

Chaui, M. et al. (1980) 'Questao popular', *Arte em Revista*, 3 (São Paulo).

Cordova, A. (1974) *La Política de Masas del Cardenismo* (Mexico).

Cornejo, A. et al. (1981) *Problema Nacional: Cultura y Clases Sociales*. Lima: Desco.

Da Matta, R. (1981) *Carnavais, Malandros e Heróis*. Rio de Janeiro: Zahar.

Deas, M. (1983) 'La presencia de la política nacional en la vida provinciana, pueblerina y rural de Colombia'. In Palacios, M. (ed.), *La Unidad Nacional en América Latina: del Regionalismo a la Nacionalidad*. Mexico: El Colegio de México.

de Certeau, M. (1984) *The Practice of Everyday Life*. Berkeley and London: University of California Press.

de Ipola, E. (1982) *Ideología y Discurso Populista*. Mexico: Folios.

Faletto, E. (1982) 'Estilos alternativos de desarrollo y opciones políticas', in Faletto, E. et al., *América Latina: Desarrollo y Perspectivas Democráticas*. Costa Rica: Flacso.

Faletto, E. et al. (1982) *América Latina: Desarrollo y Perspectivas Democráticas*. Costa Rica: Flacso.

Ford, A., Rivera, J. B. and Romano, E. (1985) *Medios de Comunicación y Cultura Popular*. Buenos Aires.

Franco, L. (1981) *El Circo Criollo*. Buenos Aires: CE de América Latina.

Galeano, E. (1973) *Open Veins in Latin America: Five Centuries of the Pillage of a Continent*. New York: New York Monthly Review Press.

García Canclini, N. (1982) *Las Culturas Populares en el Capitalismo*. Mexico: Nueva Imagen.

—— (1984) 'Las políticas culturales en América Latina', *Materiales para la Communicación Popular*, 1. Lima.

Garretón, M. A. et al. (1983) *La Cuestión Nacional: Perspectiva Democrática*. Santiago: ILET.

Gubern, R. (1982) 'Fascinación tecnológica o apocalípsis de sociedad industrial', *Papeles de Comunicación*, 1 (Madrid).

Gutiérrez, L. H. and Romero, L. A. (1981) 'Buenos Aires 1920–1945: Una propuesta para el estudio de la cultura de los sectores populares', mimeo (Buenos Aires).

Gutiérrez, P. and Munizaga, G. (1983) *Radio y Cultura Popular de Masas*. Santiago: Ceneca.

Intercom (1981) 'Documento básico', in Márquez de Melo, J. (ed.), *Populismo e Comunicaçao*. São Paulo: Cortez.

Laclau, E. (1977) *Politics and Ideology in Marxist Theory: Capitalism, Fascism, Populism*. London: New Left Books.

Landi, O. (1983) *Crisis y Lenguajes Políticos*. Buenos Aires: Cedes.

Lechner, N. (ed.) (1981) *Estado y Política en América Latina*. Mexico: Siglo XXI.

Luyten, J. M. (1981) *A Literatura de Cordel em São Paulo*. São Paulo.

Mariátegui, J. C. (1978) *Signos y Obras*. Lima: Amauta.

Márquez de Melo, J. (ed.) (1981) *Populismo e Comunicaçao*. São Paulo: Cortez.

Martí, J. (1971) *Nuestra América*. Havana.

Mattelart, A. and Schmucler, H. (1983) *América Latina en la Encrucijada Telemática*. Barcelona: Paidós.

Mendes, C. et al. (1977) *El Mito del Desarrollo*. Barcelona: Kairos.

Monsiváis, C. (1976a) 'Cultura urbana y creación intelectual', *Casa de las Américas*, 116 (Havana).

—— (1976b) 'Notas sobre la cultura mexicana en el siglo XX', in *Historia General de México*, vol. IV. Mexico: El Colegio de México.

—— (1977) *Amor Perdido*. Mexico: Era.

—— (1981) 'Notas sobre el estado, la cultura nacional y las culturas populares en México', *Cuadernos Políticos*, 30 (Mexico).

—— (1983) 'La cultura popular en el ámbito urbano. El caso de México', mimeo (Mexico).

Morin, E. (1977) *O Espirito do Tempo, 2: Necrose*. Rio de Janeiro: Forense Universitária.

Moulian, T. et al. (1982) *Autoritarismo y Alternativas Populares en América Latina*. Costa Rica: Flasco.

Muñiz Sodré (1981) *O Monopolisa da Fala. Funçao e Linguagem da Televisao no Brasil*. Petrópolis: Vozes.

—— *A Verdade Seduzida. Por um Conceito de Cultura no Brasil*. Rio de Janeiro: Codecri.

Ortiz, F. (1947) *Cuban Counterpoint: Tobacco and Sugar*. New York: Knopf.

Palacios, M. (ed.) (1983) *La Unidad Nacional en América Latina: del Regionalismo a la Nacionalidad*. Mexico: El Colegio de México.

Pareja, R. (1984) *Historia de la Radio en Colombia*. Bogotá: SC de CS.

Portantiero, J. C. (1981) 'Lo nacional-popular y la alternativa democrática en América Latina', in *América Latina 80: Democracia y Movimiento Popular*. Lima: Desco.

Ribeiro, D. (1971) *The Americas and Civilization*. London: Allen & Unwin.

Rivera, J. B. (1980a) *El Escritor y la Industria Cultural*. Buenos Aires: CE de AL.

—— (1980b) *El Folletín: Eduardo Gutiérrez*. Buenos Aires: CE de AL.

—— J. B. (1980c) *La Forja del Escritor Profesional*. Buenos Aires: CE de AL.

—— J. B. (1981) *El Auge de la Industria Cultural (1930–1955)*. Buenos Aires: Centro Editor de América Latina.

—— (1982) *El Folletín*. Buenos Aires: CE de AL.

Romero, J. L. (1976) *Latinoamérica: Las Ciudades y las Ideas*. Mexico: Siglo XXI.

—— (1982) *Las Ideologías de la Cultura Nacional*. Buenos Aires: CEDAL.

Romero Tobar, L. (1976) *La Novela Popular Española del Siglo XIX*. Barcelona: Ariel.

Roncagliolo, R. (1982) *Comunicación Transnacional: Conflicto Político y Cultural*. Lima: DESCO/Ilet.

Seibel, B. (1982) *Los Cómicos Ambulantes*. Buenos Aires: CE de AL.

—— (1984) *El Teatro 'Bárbaro' del Interior*. Buenos Aires: De la Pluma.

Squeff, E. and Wisnik, J. M. (1983) *O Nacional e o Popular na Cultura Brasileira: Música*. São Paulo: Brasiliense.

Sunkel, G. (1985) *Razón y Pasión en la Prensa Popular*. Santiago: ILET.

Taboada, E. (1982) 'Educación y lucha ideológicas en el México post-revolucionario: 1920–1940', *Cuadernos de Investigaciones Educativas*, 6, Mexico.

Terrero, P. (1981) *El Radioteatro*. Buenos Aires: CE de AL.

—— 'Radioteatro y teleteatro', mimeo (Buenos Aires).

Uribe Celis, L. (1984) *Los Años Veinte en Colombia: Ideologia y Cultura*. Bogotá: Aurora.

Weffort, F. (1978) *O Populismo na Política Brasileira*. Rio de Janeiro.

Part IV

The Politics of Representation

Introduction to Part IV

The groundbreaking work of critical media theorists such as the Frankfurt School, the British Cultural Studies group, and the French structuralists and poststructuralists revealed that culture is a social construct, intrinsically linked to the vicissitudes of the social and historically specific milieu in which it is conceived. Media and cultural studies unavoidably had to engage the politics of representation, which drew upon feminist approaches and multicultural theories to fully analyze the functions of gender, class, race, ethnicity, nationality, sexual preference and so on – social dimensions that are vital to the constitution of cultural texts and their effects, as well as being fundamentally constitutive of audiences who appropriate and use texts. British cultural studies, for instance, adopted a feminist dimension, paid greater attention to race, ethnicity and nationality, and concentrated on sexuality, as assorted discourses of race, gender, sex, nationality and so on circulated in response to social struggles and movements (see Gilroy 1991; McRobbie, 1994). An increasingly complex, culturally hybrid and diasporic world calls for sophisticated understandings of the interplay of representations, politics, and the forms of media, and the readings in this section were groundbreaking in offering new perspectives on these problematics.

Laura Mulvey's essay "Visual Pleasure and Narrative Cinema" has now achieved the status of a "classic" in critical media studies. Contested, challenged, and reworked over the years since its first appearance in *Screen* in 1975, its significance lies in the original theoretical framework it offered for considering the relationship between the viewer – or the viewing subject – and the cinematic text. Using psychoanalytic conceptions of the subject, Mulvey's analysis explores the ways in which cinematic techniques interpellate the viewer as subject and articulate the spectator's "look" at the screen with the intra-diegetic "looks" of a film. Mulvey provides a feminist inflection, as the viewer's gaze is construed in her analysis as male. Mulvey contends that the cinematic apparatus legitimates and perpetuates a patriarchal order in which the object of the look is female and the subject of the look is male. At the time of its publication, Mulvey's article offered a radical tool for analyzing the representation of sexual difference and desire in cinema. In the more than twenty years since it first appeared, critics have questioned the binarism of its argument and the fixity of its constructions of gender; a spate of scholarship has emerged as a result of questions and challenges raised by this piece – see Dyer (1982); Doane (1983); Willemen

(1994), for example – thus signaling its position as a Keywork work in media and cultural studies.

Sexuality and representation are also the focus of Larry Gross's groundbreaking article, "Out of the Mainstream: Sexual Minorities and the Mass Media." Gross's essay was an early venture into considerations of sexual orientation and the mass media; gay and lesbian studies is today a rich and prolific academic discipline, but when Gross first wrote this piece in 1989, little work had directly addressed the role of the media in portraying sexual difference. This essay, while dated, is included here because it raised issues previously ignored pertaining to sexuality and the media. In more recent work, Gross has developed and more rigorously theorized the issues of representation and sexuality (Gross, 1999); the early version which we include was a "key" that unlocked certain core aspects of gay/lesbian media studies.

In particular, Gross writes that "the mass media provide the chief common ground among the different groups that make up a heterogeneous national community." This "common ground" leads to rhetorical and ideological convergence and homogeneity, he argues, rather than representations of diversity or challenges to power. Gross looks at the media as an institutionalized apparatus with the authority to define and frame sexuality. Particularly in the case of representations of gay and lesbian people, the media work to "symbolically annihilate" their lives. "The stereotypic depiction of lesbians and gay men as abnormal, and the suppression of positive or even 'unexceptional' portrayals, serve to maintain and police the boundaries of the moral order," he writes. He argues for alternative representations – a call that has to a certain degree been heard and answered by emerging gay and lesbian media producers coming to prominence in the contemporary era.

Indeed, gay and lesbian figures have been present in many films and even current television series in America, including *Ellen*, in which the major character came out as a lesbian, and *Will and Grace*, that features a gay male. Yet mainstream representations of gays and lesbians remain controversial and often continue to promote stereotypes and derogatory caricatures. One has to turn to the independent film and video movement, or alternative cultural forms, to find more positive and empowering representations of sexual diversity and otherness.

Relations of looking, sexuality and desire are further taken up by bell hooks in her essay "Eating the Other: Desire and Resistance," drawn from *Black Looks: Race and Representation* (1992). hooks was among the first African-American feminist scholars to call attention to the interlockings of race, class, gender and additional markers of identity in the constitution of subjectivity – early in her career she challenged feminists to recognize and confront the ways in which race and class inscribe women's (and men's) experiences. A hallmark of hooks's work is its admixture of astute theoretical analysis with everyday language and sensibilities. Her goal is to make social and cultural criticism accessible to people beyond the halls of academe, and to combine intellectual energy with activism. In the essay selected, hooks explores cultural constructions of the "Other" as an object of desire, tying such positioning to consumerism and commodification as well as to issues of racial domination and subordination. Cautioning against the seductiveness of celebrating "Otherness," hooks uses various media cultural artifacts – clothing catalogs, films, rap music – to debate issues of cultural appropriation versus cultural appreciation, and to uncover the personal and political crosscurrents at work in mass media representation.

Herman Gray scrutinizes the related trajectory of black representation on network television in an analysis that takes into account the structures and conventions of the medium as well as the socio-political conditions of textual production. Gray's examination of race and representation highlights the articulations between contemporary/recent representations of blacks and earlier depictions. He argues that "our contemporary moment continues to be shaped discursively by representations of race and ethnicity that began in the formative years of television." Current cultural production is still in dialogue with these earliest moments, he writes, and he is aware of the regressive as well as the progressive aspects of this engagement. Importantly, Gray identifies certain turning points in television's representation of blackness, situating these "signal moments" within the cultural and political contexts in which they were generated. His analysis brings us to a confrontation with the possibilities of mass cultural texts engaging the politics of difference in a complex and meaningful way.

Chandra Mohanty raises issues of nation, identity and power in her often-cited essay "Under Western Eyes: Feminist Scholarship and Colonial Discourses" (1991). While this essay does not specifically address media culture, it offers a critique that must be taken into consideration in any discussion of the politics of representation. Mohanty challenges the appropriation and coding of "Third World women" in Western feminist scholarship, reminding us that the Third World is more complex, diverse and multiform than dominant constructions allow. Even the supposedly oppositional discourses of feminism often end up being reductive and ahistorical in terms of what Mohanty calls "Third World difference." Mohanty, like hooks, poses an important challenge to the notion that the category of "woman" can be considered without acknowledging class, ethnic, and racial locations. Her objection is to "the elision . . . between 'women' as a discursively constructed group and 'women' as material subjects of their own history." In arguing for historically and culturally grounded understandings of women's multiple experiences, Mohanty presents important theoretical and methodological issues that impel us to challenge hegemonies and asymmetries of power in critical cultural studies as well as in mainstream scholarship.

Mohanty's work reminds us that social and political changes have implications far beyond a single nation's borders. Just as Mulvey, hooks, and Gray recognize the multilayered, intertextual and heterogeneous character of racial and gendered representation in the United States, Néstor García Canclini grapples with the theoretical consequences of the decentering of the nation-state and the impact of postmodern, postnational and global cultures on Latin American cultural production. In traditional media studies, Latin America's "Third World" status of economic dependency on America led to theories of "cultural imperialism" wherein the USA was perceived to have a hegemonic and monolithically destructive impact on the indigenous cultural production of its neighbors to the south. Yet more recent work by Latin American scholars identifies transnationalism as a force calling for fresh research perspectives. New technologies and new markets have impacts that are not simply oppressive, they argue, but rather make way for local and regional cultural production that has progressive potential.

In his 1995 book *Hybrid Cultures: Strategies for Entering and Leaving Modernity*, García Canclini describes the far-reaching implosions of modern and traditional culture in Latin America, and the way that postmodern global culture is complexifying the situation. In his essay "Hybrid Cultures, Oblique Powers," while still taking into account the exercise of power between "First" and "Third" world nations, García Canclini argues that the mass media have not erased traditional Latin American forms of cultural expression; rather, he claims, they have contributed to a cultural reconfiguration that has displaced established modes of thinking about culture. This transformation, however, is tied to other social shifts, including the expansion of metropolitan areas, the decrease in collective public action, and the unfinished projects of political change in many Latin American countries. The mass media constitute a new kind of public sphere as they simulate the integration of a disintegrated society. Contrasting media culture with traditional symbols of modernity – monuments and museums – García Canclini focuses on the central question of how the new, dense networks of economic and ideological crossings, and the deterritorializations and hybridities born of them, reconfigure power relations.

Focus on the politics of representation thus calls attention to the fact that culture is produced within relationships of domination and subordination and tends to reproduce or resist existing structures of power. Such a perspective also provides tools for cultural studies whereby the critic can denounce aspects of cultural texts that reproduce class, gender, racial and diverse forms of domination and positively valorize aspects that subvert existing dominations, or depict forms of resistance and movements against them.

References

Doane, Mary Ann (1982) "Film and the masquerade: Theorizing the female spectator," *Screen*, 23 (3/4): 74–87.

Dyer, Richard (1982) "Don't Look Now: The Male Pin-up," *Screen*, 23 (3/4): 61–73.

García-Canclini, Néstor (1995) "Hybrid Cultures, Oblique Powers." In *Hybrid Cultures: Strategies for Entering and Leaving Modernity*, 207–49, 258–63. Translated by Christopher L. Chiappari and Silvia L. Lopez. Minneapolis: University of Minnesota Press.

Gilroy, Paul (1991) *There Ain't No Black in the Union Jack*. Chicago: University of Chicago Press.

Gray, Herman (1995) "The Politics of Representation in Network Television." In *Watching Race: Television and the Struggle for "Blackness"*, 70–92. Minneapolis: University of Minnesota Press.

Gross, Larry (1989) "Out of the Mainstream: Sexual Minorities and the Mass Media." In *Remote Control: Television, Audiences and Cultural Power*, ed. Ellen Seiter, 130–49. New York: Routledge.

Gross, Larry, and Woods, James D. (1999) "Introduction: Being Gay in American Media and Society." In *The Columbia Reader on Lesbians and Gay Men in Media, Society, and Politics*, 3–22. New York: Columbia University Press.

hooks, bell (1992) "Eating the Other: Desire and Resistance." In *Black Looks: Race and Representation*, 21–39. Boston, Mass.: South End Press.

McRobbie, Angela (1994) *Postmodernism and Popular Culture*. New York and London: Routledge.

Mohanty, Chandra Talpade (1991) "Under Western Eyes: Feminist Scholarship and Colonial Discourse." In C. T. Mohanty, A. Russo, and L. Torres (Eds.), *Third World Women and the Politics of Feminism*, 51–80. Bloomington: Indiana University Press.

Mulvey, Laura (1992 [1975]) "Visual Pleasure and Narrative Cinema." In *The Sexual Subject: A Screen Reader in Sexuality*, 22–34. New York and London: Routledge.

Willemen, Paul (1994) "The Fourth Look." In *Looks and Frictions: Essays in Cultural Studies and Film Theory*, pp. 99–110. Bloomington: Indiana University Press.

20

Visual Pleasure and Narrative Cinema*

Laura Mulvey

Introduction

A political use of psychoanalysis

This paper intends to use psychoanalysis to discover where and how the fascination of film is reinforced by pre-existing patterns of fascination already at work within the individual subject and the social formations that have moulded him. It takes as starting point the way film reflects, reveals and even plays on the straight, socially established interpretation of sexual difference which controls images, erotic ways of looking and spectacle. It is helpful to understand what the cinema has been, how its magic has worked in the past, while attempting a theory and a practice which will challenge this cinema of the past. Psychoanalytic theory is thus appropriated here as a political weapon, demonstrating the way the unconscious of patriarchal society has structured film form.

The paradox of phallocentrism in all its manifestations is that it depends on the image of the castrated woman to give order and meaning to its world. An idea of woman stands as linchpin to the system: it is her lack that produces the phallus as a symbolic presence, it is her desire to make good the lack that the phallus signifies. Recent writing in *Screen* about psychoanalysis and the cinema has not sufficiently brought out the importance of the representation of the female form in a symbolic order in which, in the last resort, it speaks castration and nothing else. To summarize briefly: the function of woman in forming the patriarchal unconscious is twofold, she first symbolizes the castration threat by her real absence of a penis and second thereby raises her child into the Symbolic. Once this has been achieved, her meaning in the process is at an end, it does not last into the world of law and language except as a memory which oscillates between memory of maternal plenitude and memory of lack. Both are posited on nature (or on anatomy in Freud's famous

* From Laura Mulvey, *The Sexual Subject: A Screen Reader in Sexuality* (New York: Routledge, 1992), pp. 22–34.

phrase). Woman's desire is subjected to her image as bearer of the bleeding wound, she can exist only in relation to castration and cannot transcend it. She turns her child into the signifier of her own desire to possess a penis (the condition, she imagines, of entry into the Symbolic). Either she must gracefully give way to the word, the Name of the Father and the Law, or else struggle to keep her child down with her in the half-light of the Imaginary. Woman then stands in patriarchal culture as signifier for the male other, bound by a symbolic order in which man can live out his phantasies and obsessions through linguistic command by imposing them on the silent image of woman still tied to her place as bearer of meaning, not maker of meaning.

There is an obvious interest in this analysis for feminists, a beauty in its exact rendering of the frustration experienced under the phallocentric order. It gets us nearer to the roots of our oppression, it brings an articulation of the problem closer, it faces us with the ultimate challenge: how to fight the unconscious structured like a language (formed critically at the moment of arrival of language) while still caught within the language of the patriarchy. There is no way in which we can produce an alternative out of the blue, but we can begin to make a break by examining patriarchy with the tools it provides, of which psychoanalysis is not the only but an important one. We are still separated by a great gap from important issues for the female unconscious which are scarcely relevant to phallocentric theory: the sexing of the female infant and her relationship to the Symbolic, the sexually mature woman as non-mother, maternity outside the signification of the phallus, the vagina.... But, at this point, psychoanalytic theory as it now stands can at least advance our understanding of the status quo, of the patriarchal order in which we are caught.

Destruction of pleasure as a radical weapon

As an advanced representation system, the cinema poses questions of the ways the unconscious (formed by the dominant order) structures ways of seeing and pleasure in looking. Cinema has changed over the last few decades. It is no longer the monolithic system based on large capital investment exemplified at its best by Hollywood in the 1930s, 1940s and 1950s. Technological advances (16mm, etc.) have changed the economic conditions of cinematic production, which can now be artisanal as well as capitalist. Thus it has been possible for an alternative cinema to develop. However self-conscious and ironic Hollywood managed to be, it always restricted itself to a formal *mise-en-scène* reflecting the dominant ideological concept of the cinema. The alternative cinema provides a space for a cinema to be born which is radical in both a political and an aesthetic sense and challenges the basic assumptions of the mainstream film. This is not to reject the latter moralistically, but to highlight the ways in which its formal preoccupations reflect the psychical obsessions of the society which produced it, and, further, to stress that the alternative cinema must start specifically by reacting against these obsessions and assumptions. A politically and aesthetically avant-garde cinema is now possible, but it can still only exist as a counterpoint.

The magic of the Hollywood style at its best (and of all the cinema which fell within its sphere of influence) arose, not exclusively, but in one important aspect, from its skilled and satisfying manipulation of visual pleasure. Unchallenged, mainstream film coded the erotic into the language of the dominant patriarchal order. In the highly developed Hollywood cinema it was only through these codes that the alienated subject, torn in his imaginary memory by a sense of loss, by the terror of potential lack in phantasy, came near to finding a glimpse of satisfaction: through its formal beauty and its play on his own formative obsessions. This article will discuss the interweaving of that erotic pleasure in film, its meaning, and in particular the central place of the image of woman. It is said that analysing pleasure, or beauty, destroys it. That is the intention of this article. The satisfaction and reinforcement of the ego that represent the high point of film history hitherto must be attacked. Not in favour of a reconstructed new pleasure, which cannot exist in the abstract, nor of intellectualized unpleasure, but to make way for a total negation of the ease and plenitude of the narrative fiction film. The alternative is the thrill that comes from leaving the past behind without rejecting it, transcending outworn or oppressive forms, or daring to break with normal pleasurable expectations in order to conceive a new language of desire.

Pleasure in Looking/Fascination with the Human Form

A

The cinema offers a number of possible pleasures. One is scopophilia. There are circumstances in which looking itself is a source of pleasure, just as, in the reverse formation, there is pleasure in being looked at. Originally, in his 'Three Essays on the Theory of Sexuality', Freud isolated scopophilia as one of the component instincts of sexuality which exist as drives quite independently of the erotogenic zones. At this point he associated scopophilia with taking other people as objects, subjecting them to a controlling and curious gaze. His particular examples centre around the voyeuristic activities of children, their desire to see and make sure of the private and the forbidden (curiosity about other people's genital and bodily functions, about the presence or absence of the penis and, retrospectively, about the primal scene). In this analysis scopophilia is essentially active. (Later, in 'Instincts and their Vicissitudes', Freud developed his theory of scopophilia further, attaching it initially to pre-genital auto-eroticism, after which the pleasure of the look is transferred to others by analogy. There is a close working here of the relationship between the active instinct and its further development in a narcissistic form.) Although the instinct is modified by other factors, in particular the constitution of the ego, it continues to exist as the erotic basis for pleasure in looking at another person as object. At the extreme, it can become fixated into a perversion, producing obsessive voyeurs and Peeping Toms, whose only sexual satisfaction can come from watching, in an active controlling sense, an objectified other.

At first glance, the cinema would seem to be remote from the undercover world of the surreptitious observation of an unknowing and unwilling victim. What is seen of the screen is so manifestly shown. But the mass of mainstream film, and the conventions within which it has consciously evolved, portray a hermetically sealed world which unwinds magically, indifferent to the presence of the audience, producing for them a sense of separation and playing on their voyeuristic phantasy. Moreover, the extreme contrast between the darkness in the auditorium (which also isolates the spectators from one another) and the brilliance of the shifting patterns of light and shade on the screen helps to promote the illusion of voyeuristic separation. Although the film is really being shown, is there to be seen, conditions of screening and narrative conventions give the spectator an illusion of looking in on a private world. Among other things, the position of the spectators in the cinema is blatantly one of repression of their exhibitionism and projection of the repressed desire on to the performer.

B

The cinema satisfies a primordial wish for pleasurable looking, but it also goes further, developing scopophilia in its narcissistic aspect. The conventions of mainstream film focus attention on the human form. Scale, space, stories are all anthropomorphic. Here, curiosity and the wish to look intermingle with a fascination with likeness and recognition: the human face, the human body, the relationship between the human form and its surroundings, the visible presence of the person in the world. Jacques Lacan has described how the moment when a child recognizes its own image in the mirror is crucial for the constitution of the ego. Several aspects of this analysis are relevant here. The mirror phase occurs at a time when the child's physical ambitions outstrip his motor capacity, with the result that his recognition of himself is joyous in that he imagines his mirror image to be more complete, more perfect than he experiences his own body. Recognition is thus overlaid with misrecognition: the image recognized is conceived as the reflected body of the self, but its misrecognition as superior projects this body outside itself as an ideal ego, the alienated subject, which, re-introjected as an ego ideal, gives rise to the future generation of identification with others. This mirror moment predates language for the child.

Important for this article is the fact that it is an image that constitutes the matrix of the imaginary, of recognition/misrecognition and identification, and hence of the first articulation of the 'I', of subjectivity. This is a moment when an older fascination with looking (at the mother's face, for an obvious example) collides with the initial inklings of self-awareness. Hence it is the birth of the long love affair/despair between image and self-image which has found such intensity of expression in film and such joyous recognition in the cinema audience. Quite apart from the extraneous similarities between screen and mirror (the framing of the human form in its surroundings, for instance), the cinema has structures of fascination strong enough to allow temporary loss of ego while simultaneously reinforcing the ego. The sense of forgetting the world as the ego has subsequently come to perceive it (I forgot who I am and where I was) is nostalgically reminiscent of that pre-subjective moment of image recognition. At the same time the cinema has distinguished itself in the production of ego ideals as expressed in particular in the star system, the stars centring both screen presence and screen story as they act out a complex process of likeness and difference (the glamorous impersonates the ordinary).

C

Subsections A and B above have set out two contradictory aspects of the pleasurable structures of looking in the conventional cinematic situation. The first, scopophilic, arises from pleasure in using another person as an object of sexual stimulation through sight. The second, developed through narcissism and the constitution of the ego, comes from identification with the image seen. Thus, in film terms, one implies a separation of the erotic identity of the subject from the object on the screen (active scopophilia), the other demands identification of the ego with the object on the screen through the spectator's fascination with and recognition of his like. The first is a function of the sexual instincts, the second of ego libido. This dichotomy was crucial for Freud. Although he saw the two as interacting and overlaying each other, the tension between instinctual drives and self-preservation continues to be a dramatic polarization in terms of pleasure. Both are formative structures, mechanisms not meaning. In themselves they have no signification, they have to be attached to an idealization. Both pursue aims in indifference to perceptual reality, creating the imagized, eroticized concept of the world that forms the perception of the subject and makes a mockery of empirical objectivity.

During its history, the cinema seems to have evolved a particular illusion of reality in which this contradiction between libido and ego has found a beautifully complementary phantasy world. In *reality* the phantasy world of the screen is subject to the law which produces it. Sexual instincts and identification processes have a meaning within the symbolic order which articulates desire. Desire, born with language, allows the possibility of transcending the instinctual and the imaginary, but its point of reference continually returns to the traumatic moment of its birth: the castration complex. Hence the look, pleasurable in form, can be threatening in content, and it is woman as representation/image that crystallizes this paradox.

Woman as Image, Man as Bearer of the Look

A

In a world ordered by sexual imbalance, pleasure in looking has been split between active/male and passive/female. The determining male gaze projects its phantasy on to the female figure which is styled accordingly. In their traditional exhibitionist role women are simultaneously looked at and displayed, with their appearance coded for strong visual and erotic impact so that they can be said to connote *to-be-looked-at-ness*. Woman displayed as sexual object is the leitmotif of erotic spectacle: from pin-ups to striptease, from Ziegfeld to Busby Berkeley, she holds the look, plays to and signifies male desire. Mainstream film neatly combined spectacle and narrative. (Note, however, how in the musical song-and-dance numbers break the flow of the diegesis.) The presence of woman is an indispensable element of spectacle in normal narrative film, yet her visual presence tends to work against the development of a story line, to freeze the flow of action in moments of erotic contemplation. This alien presence then has to be integrated into cohesion with the narrative. As Budd Boetticher has put it:

> What counts is what the heroine provokes, or rather what she represents. She is the one, or rather the love or fear she inspires in the hero, or else the concern he feels for her, who makes him act the way he does. In herself the woman has not the slightest importance.

(A recent tendency in narrative film has been to dispense with this problem altogether; hence the development of what Molly Haskell has called the 'buddy movie', in which the active homosexual eroticism of the central male figures can carry the story without distraction.) Traditionally, the woman displayed has functioned on two levels: as erotic object for the characters within the screen story, and as erotic object for the spectator within the auditorium, with a shifting tension between the looks on either side of the screen. For instance, the device of the showgirl allows the two looks to be unified technically without any apparent break in the diegesis. A woman performs within the narrative: the gaze of the spectator and that of the male characters in the film are neatly combined without breaking narrative verisimilitude. For a moment the sexual impact of the performing woman takes the film into a no man's land outside its own time and space. Thus Marilyn Monroe's first appearance in *The River of No Return* and Lauren Bacall's songs in *To Have or Have Not*. Similarly, conventional close-ups of legs (Dietrich, for instance) or a face (Garbo) integrate into the narrative a different mode of eroticism. One part of a fragmented body destroys the Renaissance space, the illusion of depth demanded by the narrative, it gives flatness, the quality of a cutout or icon rather than verisimilitude to the screen.

B

An active/passive heterosexual division of labour has similarly controlled narrative structure. According to the principles of the ruling ideology and the psychical structures that back it up, the male figure cannot bear the burden of sexual objectification. Man is reluctant to gaze at his exhibitionist like. Hence the split between spectacle and narrative supports the man's role as the active one of forwarding the story, making things happen. The man controls the film phantasy and also emerges as the representative of power in a further sense: as the bearer of the look of the spectator, transferring it behind the screen to neutralize the extra-diegetic tendencies represented by woman as spectacle. This is made possible through the processes set in motion by structuring the film around a main controlling figure with whom the spectator can identify. As the spectator identifies with the main male[1] protagonist, he projects his look on to that of his like, his screen surrogate, so that the power of the male protagonist as he controls events coincides with the active power of the erotic look, both giving a satisfying sense of omnipotence. A male movie star's glamorous characteristics are thus not those of the erotic object of the gaze, but those of the more perfect, more complete, more powerful ideal ego conceived in the original moment of recognition in front of the mirror. The character in the story can make things happen and control events better than the subject/spectator, just as the image in the mirror was more in control of motor co-ordination. In contrast to woman as icon, the active male figure (the ego ideal of the identification process) demands a three-dimensional space corresponding to that of the mirror-recognition in which the alienated subject internalized his own representation of this imaginary existence. He is a figure in a landscape. Here the function of film is to reproduce as accurately as possible the so-called natural conditions of human perception. Camera technology (as exemplified by deep focus in particular) and camera movements (determined by the action of the protagonist), combined with invisible editing (demanded by realism) all tend to blur the limits of screen space. The male protagonist is free to command the stage, a stage of spatial illusion in which he articulates the look and creates the action.

C1

Subsections A and B immediately above have set out a tension between a mode of representation of woman in film and conventions surrounding the diegesis. Each is associated with a look: that of the spectator in direct scopophilic contact with the female form displayed for his enjoyment (connoting male phantasy) and that of the spectator fascinated with the image of his like set in an illusion of natural space, and through him gaining control and possession of the woman within the diegesis. (This tension and the shift from one pole to the other can structure a single text. Thus both in *Only Angels Have Wings* and in *To Have and Have Not*, the film opens with the woman as object of the combined gaze of spectator and all the male protagonists in the film. She is isolated, glamorous, on display, sexualized. But as the narrative progresses she falls in love with the main male protagonist and becomes his property, losing her outward glamorous characteristics, her generalized sexuality, her showgirl connotations; her eroticism is subjected to the male star alone. By means of identification with him, through participation in his power, the spectator can indirectly possess her too.)

But in psychoanalytic terms, the female figure poses a deeper problem. She also connotes something that the look continually circles around but disavows: her lack of a penis, implying a threat of castration and hence unpleasure. Ultimately, the meaning of woman is sexual difference, the absence of the penis as visually ascertainable, the material evidence on which is based the castration complex essential for the organization of entrance to the Symbolic order and the Law of the Father. Thus the woman as icon, displayed for the gaze and enjoyment of men, the active controllers of the look, always threatens to evoke the anxiety it originally signified. The male unconscious has two avenues of escape from this castration anxiety: preoccupation with the re-enactment of the original trauma (investigating the woman, demystifying her mystery), counterbalanced by the devaluation, punishment or saving of the guilty object (an avenue typified by the concerns of the *film noir*); or else complete disavowal of castration by the substitution of a fetish object or turning the represented figure itself into a fetish so that it becomes reassuring rather than dangerous (hence overvaluation, the cult of the female star). This second avenue, fetishistic scopophilia, builds up the physical beauty of the object, transforming it into something satisfying in itself. The first avenue, voyeurism, on the contrary, has associations with sadism: pleasure lies in ascertaining guilt (immediately associated with castration), asserting control and subjecting the guilty person through punishment or forgiveness. This sadistic side fits in well with narrative. Sadism demands a story, depends on making something happen, forcing a change in another person, a battle of will and strength, victory/defeat, all occurring in a linear time with a beginning and an end. Fetishistic scopophilia, on the other hand, can exist outside linear time as the erotic instinct is focused on the look alone. These contradictions and ambiguities can be illustrated more simply by using works by Hitchcock and Sternberg, both of whom take the look almost as the content or subject matter of many of their films. Hitchcock is the more complex, as he uses both mechanisms. Sternberg's work, on the other hand, provides many pure examples of fetishistic scopophilia.

C2

It is well known that Sternberg once said he would welcome his films being projected upside down so that story and character involvement would not interfere with the spectator's undiluted appreciation of the screen image. This statement is revealing but ingenuous. Ingenuous in that his films do demand that the figure of the woman (Dietrich, in the cycle of films with her, as the ultimate example) should be identifiable. But revealing in that it emphasizes the fact that for him the pictorial space enclosed by the frame is paramount rather than narrative or identification processes. While Hitchcock goes into the investigative side of voyeurism, Sternberg produces the ultimate fetish, taking it to the point where the powerful look of the male protagonist (characteristic of traditional narrative film) is broken in favour of the image in direct erotic rapport with the spectator. The beauty of the woman as object and the screen space coalesce; she is no longer the bearer of guilt but a perfect product, whose body, stylized and fragmented by close-ups, is the content of the film and the direct recipient of the spectator's look. Sternberg plays down the illusion of screen depth; his screen tends to be one-dimensional, as light and shade, lace, steam, foliage, net, streamers, etc. reduce the visual field. There is little or no mediation of the look through the eyes of the main male protagonist. On the contrary, shadowy presences like La Bessière in *Morocco* act as surrogates for the director, detached as they are from audience identification. Despite Sternberg's insistence that his stories are irrelevant, it is significant that they are concerned with situation, not suspense, and cyclical rather than linear time, while plot complications revolve around misunderstanding rather than conflict. The most important absence is that of the controlling male gaze within the screen scene. The high point of emotional drama in the most typical Dietrich films, her supreme moments of erotic meaning, take place in the absence of the man she loves in the fiction. There are other witnesses, other spectators watching her on the screen, their gaze is one with, not standing in for, that of the audience. At the end of *Morocco*, Tom Brown has already disappeared into the desert when Amy Jolly kicks off her gold sandals and walks after him. At the end of *Dishonoured*, Kranau is indifferent to the fate of Magda. In both cases, the erotic impact, sanctified by death, is displayed as a spectacle for the audience. The male hero misunderstands and, above all, does not see.

In Hitchcock, by contrast, the male hero does see precisely what the audience sees. However, in the films I shall discuss here, he takes fascination with an image through scopophilic eroticism as the subject of the film. Moreover, in these cases the hero portrays the contradictions and tensions experienced by the spectator. In *Vertigo* in particular, but also in *Marnie* and *Rear Window*, the look is central to the plot, oscillating between voyeurism and fetishistic fascination. As a twist, a further manipulation of the normal viewing process which in some sense reveals it, Hitchcock uses the process of identification normally associated with ideological correctness and the recognition of established morality and shows up its perverted side. Hitchcock has never concealed his interest in voyeurism, cinematic and non-cinematic. His heroes are exemplary of the symbolic order and the law – a policeman (*Vertigo*), a dominant male possessing money and power (*Marnie*) – but their erotic drives lead them into compromised situations. The power to subject another person to the will sadistically or to the gaze voyeuristically is turned on to the woman as the object of both. Power is backed by a certainty of legal right and the established guilt of the woman (evoking castration, psychoanalytically speaking). True perversion is barely concealed under a shallow mask of ideological correctness – the man is on the right side of the law, the woman on the wrong. Hitchcock's skilful use of identification processes and liberal use of subjective camera from the point-of-view of the male protagonist draw the spectators deeply into his position, making them share his uneasy gaze. The audience is absorbed into a voyeuristic situation within the screen scene and diegesis which parodies his own in the cinema. In his analysis of *Rear Window*, Douchet takes the film as a metaphor for the cinema. Jeffries is the audience, the events in the apartment block opposite correspond to the screen. As he watches, an erotic dimension is added to his look, a central image to the drama. His girlfriend Lisa had been of little sexual interest to him, more or less a drag, so long as she remained on the spectator side. When she crosses the barrier between his room and the block opposite, their relationship is reborn erotically. He does not merely watch her through his lens, as a distant meaningful image, he also sees her as a guilty intruder exposed by a dangerous man threatening her with punishment, and thus finally saves her. Lisa's exhibitionism has already been established by her obsessive interest in dress and style, in being a passive image of visual perfection; Jeffries's voyeurism and activity have also been established through his work as a photo-journalist, a maker of stories and captor of images. However, his enforced inactivity, binding him to his seat as a spectator, puts him squarely in the phantasy position of the cinema audience.

In *Vertigo*, subjective camera predominates. Apart from one flashback from Judy's point-of-view, the narrative is woven around what Scottie sees or fails to see. The audience follows the growth of his erotic obsession and subsequent despair precisely from his point-of-view. Scottie's voyeurism is blatant: he falls in love with a woman he follows and spies on without speaking to. Its sadistic side is equally blatant: he has chosen (and freely chosen, for he had been a successful lawyer) to be a policeman, with all the attendant possibilities of pursuit and investigation. As a result, he follows, watches and falls in love with a perfect image of female beauty and mystery. Once he actually confronts her, his erotic drive is to break her down and force her to tell by persistent cross-questioning. Then, in the second part of the film, he re-enacts his obsessive involvement with the image he loved to watch secretly. He reconstructs Judy as Madeleine, forces her to conform in every detail to the actual physical appearance of his fetish. Her exhibitionism, her masochism, make her an ideal passive counterpart to Scottie's active sadistic voyeurism. She knows her part is to perform, and only by playing it through and then replaying it can she keep Scottie's erotic interest. But in the repetition he does break her down and succeeds in exposing her guilt. His curiosity wins through and she is punished. In *Vertigo*, erotic involvement with the look is disorientating: the spectator's fascination is turned against him as the narrative carries him through and entwines him with the processes that he is himself exercising. The Hitchcock hero here is firmly placed within the symbolic order, in narrative terms. He has all the attributes of the patriarchal superego. Hence the spectator, lulled into a false sense of security by the apparent legality of his surrogate, sees through his look and finds himself exposed as complicit, caught in the moral ambiguity of looking. Far from being simply an aside on the perversion of the police, *Vertigo* focuses on the implications of the active/looking, passive/looked-at split in terms of sexual difference and the power of the male Symbolic encapsulated in the hero. Marnie, too, performs for Mark Rutland's gaze and masquerades as the perfect to-be-looked-at image. He, too, is on the side of the law until, drawn in by obsession with her guilt, her secret, he longs to see her in the act of committing a crime, make her confess and thus save her. So he, too, becomes complicit as he acts out the implications of his power. He controls money and words, he can have his cake and eat it.

Summary

The psychoanalytic background that has been discussed in this article is relevant to the pleasure and unpleasure offered by traditional narrative film. The scopophilic instinct (pleasure in looking at another person as an erotic object), and, in contra-distinction, ego libido (forming identification processes) act as formations, mechanisms, which this cinema has played on. The image of woman as (passive) raw material for the (active) gaze of man takes the argument a step further into the structure of representation, adding a further layer demanded by the ideology of the patriarchal order as it is worked out in its favourite cinematic form – illusionistic narrative film. The argument returns again to the psychoanalytic background in that woman as representation signifies castration, inducing voyeuristic or fetishistic mechanisms to circumvent her threat. None of these interacting layers is intrinsic to film, but it is only in the film form that they can reach a perfect and beautiful contradiction, thanks to the possibility in the cinema of shifting the emphasis of the look. It is the place of the look that defines cinema, the possibility of varying it and exposing it. This is what makes cinema quite different in its voyeuristic potential from, say, striptease, theatre, shows, etc. Going far beyond highlighting a woman's to-be-looked-at-ness, cinema builds the way she is to be looked at into the spectacle itself. Playing on the tension between film as controlling the dimension of time (editing, narrative) and film as controlling the dimension of space (changes in distance, editing), cinematic codes create a gaze, a world and an object, thereby producing an illusion cut to the measure of desire. It is these cinematic codes and their relationship to formative external structures that must be broken down before mainstream film and the pleasure it provides can be challenged.

To begin with (as an ending), the voyeuristic-scopophilic look that is a crucial part of traditional filmic pleasure can itself be broken down. There are three different looks associated with cinema: that of the camera as it records the profilmic event, that of the audience as it watches the final product, and that of the characters at each other within the screen illusion. The conventions of narrative film deny the first two and subordinate them to the third, the conscious aim being always to eliminate intrusive camera presence and prevent a distancing awareness in the audience. Without these two absences (the material existence of the recording process, the critical reading of the spectator), fictional drama cannot achieve reality, obviousness and truth. Nevertheless, as this article has argued, the structure of looking in narrative fiction film contains a contradiction in its own premises: the female image as a castration threat constantly endangers the unity of the diegesis and bursts through the world of illusion as an intrusive, static, one-dimensional fetish. Thus the two looks materially present in time and space are obsessively subordinated to the neurotic needs of the male ego. The camera becomes the mechanism for producing an illusion of Renaissance space, flowing movements compatible with the human eye, an ideology of representation that revolves around the perception of the subject; the camera's look is disavowed in order to create a convincing world in which the spectator's surrogate can perform with verisimilitude. Simultaneously, the look of the audience is denied an intrinsic force: as soon as fetishistic representation of the female image threatens to break the spell of illusion, and the erotic image on the screen appears directly (without mediation) to the spectator, the fact of fetishization, concealing as it does castration fear, freezes the look, fixates the spectator and prevents him from achieving any distance from the image in front of him.

This complex interaction of looks is specific to film. The first blow against the monolithic accumulation of traditional film conventions (already undertaken by radical filmmakers) is to free the look of the camera into its materiality in time and space and the look of the audience into dialectics, passionate detachment. There is no doubt that this destroys the satisfaction, pleasure and privilege of the 'invisible guest', and highlights how film has depended on voyeuristic active/passive mechanisms. Women, whose image has continually been stolen and used for this end, cannot view the decline of the traditional film form with anything much more than sentimental regret.

Note

1   There are films with a woman as the main protagonist, of course. To analyse this phenom-
    enon seriously here would take me too far afield. Pam Cook and Claire Johnston's study of
    The Revolt of Mamie Stover in Phil Hardy (ed.), *Raoul Walsh*, Edinburgh, Edinburgh Film
    Festival (1974), shows in a striking case how the strength of this female protagonist is more
    apparent than real.

21

Out of the Mainstream: Sexual Minorities and the Mass Media*

Larry Gross

In a society dominated by centralized sources of information and imagery, in which economic imperatives and pervasive values promote the search for large, common-denominator audiences, what is the fate of those groups who for one or another reason find themselves outside the mainstream? Briefly, and it is hardly a novel observation, such groups share a common fate of relative invisibility and demeaning stereotypes. But there are differences as well as similarities in the ways various minorities (racial, ethnic, sexual, religious, political) are treated by the mass media. And, given important differences in their life situations, members of such groups experience varying consequences of their mediated images.

In this chapter I will discuss the general question of minority perspectives applied to the study of mass media content and effects, and I will elaborate in greater detail the situation of sexual minorities (lesbian women and gay men) as members of the mass media audience.

Sexual minorities differ in important ways from the "traditional" racial and ethnic minorities; they are, in an interesting sense, akin to political minorities (so-called radicals and "fringe" groups). In both cases their members typically are self-identified at some point in their lives, usually in adolescence or later, and they are not necessarily easily identifiable by others. These two groups also constitute by their very existence a presumed threat to the "natural" (sexual and/or political) order of things, and thus they are inherently problematic and controversial for the mass media. These char-acteristics can be seen to affect the way members of such groups are depicted in the media (when they do appear), and also suggest ways to think about the effects of such depictions on the images held by society at large and by members of these minority groups.

Before turning to the discussion of minority audience perspectives, it would be helpful to characterize briefly the role of the mass media, television in particular, in our society.

* From Larry Gross, *Remote Control: Television, Audiences and Cultural Power*, ed. Ellen Seiter et al. (New York: Routledge, 1989), pp. 130–49.

The System is the Message

First, the economic, political, and social integration of modern industrial society allows few communities or individuals to maintain an independent integrity. We are parts of a Leviathan, like it or not, and its nervous system is telecommunications. Our knowledge of the "wide world" is what this nervous system transmits to us. The mass media provide the chief common ground among the different groups that make up a heterogeneous national community. Never before have all classes and groups (as well as ages) shared so much of the same culture and the same perspectives while having so little to do with their creation.

Second, representation in the mediated "reality" of our mass culture is in itself power; certainly it is the case that non-representation maintains the powerless status of groups that do not possess significant material or political power bases. That is, while the holders of real power – the ruling class – do not require (or seek) mediated visibility, those who are at the bottom of the various power hierarchies will be kept in their places in part through their relative invisibility. This is a form of what Gerbner and I have termed symbolic annihilation.[1] Not all interests or points of view are equal; judgments are made constantly about exclusions and inclusions and these judgments broaden or narrow (mostly narrow) the spectrum of views presented.

Third, when groups or perspectives do attain visibility, the manner of that representation will itself reflect the biases and interests of those elites who define the public agenda. And these elites are (mostly) white, (mostly) middle-aged, (mostly) male, (mostly) middle and upper-middle class, and entirely heterosexual (at least in public).

Fourth, we should not take too seriously the presumed differences between the various categories of media messages – particularly in the case of television. News, drama, quiz shows, sports, and commercials share underlying similarities of theme, emphasis, and value. Even the most widely accepted distinctions (i.e. news vs. fiction programs vs. commercials) are easily blurred. Decisions about which events are newsworthy and about how to present them are heavily influenced by considerations of dramatic form and content (e.g. conflict and resolution) that are drawn from fictional archetypes; and the polished mini-dramas of many commercials reveal a sophisticated mastery of fictional conventions, just as dramatic programs promote a style of consumption and living that is quite in tune with their neighboring commercial messages. More important, the blending of stylistic conventions allows for greater efficacy and mutual support in packaging and diffusing common values.

Fifth, the dominant conventions of our mass media are those of "realism" and psychologically grounded naturalism. Despite a limited degree of reflexivity which occasionally crops up, mainstream film and television are nearly always presented as transparent mediators of reality which can and do show us how people and places look, how institutions operate; in short, the way it is. These depictions of the way things are, and why, are personified through dramatic plots and characterizations which take us behind the scenes to the otherwise inaccessible backstages of individual motivation, organizational performance, and subcultural life.

Normal adult viewers, to be sure, are aware of the fictiveness of media drama: no one calls the police when a character on television is shot. But we may still wonder how often and to what extent viewers suspend their disbelief in the persuasive realism of the fictional worlds of television and film drama. Even the most sophisticated among us can find many components of our "knowledge" of the real world which derive wholly or in part from fictional representations. And, in a society which spans a continent, in a cosmopolitan culture which spans much of the globe, television and film provide the broadest common background of assumptions about what things are, how they work (or should work), and why.

Finally, the contributions of the mass media are likely to be most powerful in cultivating images of groups and phenomena about which there is little first-hand opportunity for learning; particularly when such images are not contradicted by other established beliefs and ideologies. By definition, portrayals of minority groups and "deviants" will be relatively distant from the real lives of a large majority of viewers.

Television as the Mainstream

The average American adult spends several hours each day in this television world, children spend even more of their lives immersed in its "fictional reality." As I have already suggested, the mass media, and television foremost among them, have become the primary sources of the common information and images that create and maintain a world view and a value system. In a word, the mass media have become central agents of enculturation. In the Cultural Indicators Project we have used the concept of "cultivation" to describe the influence of television on viewers' conceptions of social reality.[2]

On issue after issue we find that assumptions, beliefs, and values of heavy viewers of television differ systematically from those of light viewers in the same demographic groups. Sometimes these differences appear as overall, main effects, whereby those who watch more television are more likely – in all groups – to give what we call "television answers" to our questions. But in many cases the patterns are more complex. We have found that television viewing, not surprisingly, serves as a stable factor differentially integrated into and interacting with different groups' life situations and world views. In our recent work we have isolated a consistent pattern which we have termed "mainstreaming."[3]

The mainstream can be thought of as a relative commonality of outlooks and values that television tends to cultivate in viewers. By mainstreaming we mean the sharing of that commonality among heavy viewers in those demographic groups whose light viewers hold divergent positions. In other words, differences deriving from other factors and social forces – differences that may appear in the responses of light viewers in various groups – may be diminished or even absent when the heavy viewers in these same groups are compared. Overall, television viewing appears to signal a convergence of outlooks rather than absolute, across-the-board increments in all groups.

Choices or echoes?

The mainstream which we have identified as the embodiment of a dominant ideology, cultivated through the repetition of stable patterns across the illusory boundaries of media and genre, and absorbed by otherwise diverse segments of the population, nevertheless has to contend with the possibility of oppositional perspectives and interpretations. What options and opportunities are available to those groups whose concerns, values and even very existence are belittled, subverted, and denied by the mainstream? Can the power of the mass media's central tendencies be resisted? Can one avoid being swept into the mainstream? The answers to such questions depend in large part on which group or segment we are discussing; while many minorities are similarly ignored or distorted by the mass media, not all have the same options for resistance and the development of alternative channels.

In general the opportunities for organized opposition are greatest when there is a visible and even organized group which can provide solidarity and institutional means for creating and disseminating alternative messages. There are numerous examples of groupings that have sprung up, as it were, along the right bank of the mainstream. Most organized and visible among these are the Christian fundamentalist syndicated television programs. These programs provide their (generally older and less educated) viewers with an array of programs, from news to talk shows to soap operas to church services and sermons, all reflecting perspectives and values that they quite correctly feel are not represented in mainstream, prime-time television or in the movies.[4] As one of Hoover's conservative, religious respondents put it, in discussing network television:

> I think a good deal of it is written by very liberal, immoral people ... Some of the comedies, the weekly things that go on every week, they make extramarital affairs, and sex before marriage an everyday thing like everybody should accept it ... and they present it in a comic situation, a situation that looks like it could be fun and a good deal of these weekly shows I don't like go for that.[5]

The religious sponsoring and producing organizations are not merely engaged in meeting their audiences' previously unmet needs for a symbolic environment in which they feel at home; they are also attempting to translate the (usually exaggerated) numbers of their audiences and their (constantly solicited) financial contributions into a power base from which they can exert pressure to alter the channel of the mainstream and bring it even closer to where they now reside, up on the right bank.

At the moment, and for the foreseeable future in the United States, at least, there is no comparable settlement on the left bank of the mainstream. There are many reasons why the organized left has been unable to match the right's success in harnessing the available resources of media technology. It is not hard to see that some minority perspectives are in fact supportive of the dominant ideology, however much the media's need for massive audiences might sacrifice or offend their interests, while other minority values are truly incompatible with the basic power relationships embodied in that mainstream.

Minority positions and interests which present radical challenges to the established order will not only be ignored, they will be discredited. Those who benefit from the status quo present their position as the moderate center, balanced between equal and opposing "extremes" – thus the American news media's cult of "objectivity," achieved through a "balance" which reflects an invisible, taken-for-granted ideology. As a CBS spokesman explained it, when dismissing attempts by Jesse Helms and Ted Turner to take over the network:

> Anyone . . . who buys a media company for ideological reasons must be prepared to pay dearly for that conviction. The right-wingers and the left-wingers in this country are vociferous but small in number compared to the ordinary citizen, who, when it comes down to it, is a centrist.[6]

The fatal flaw in the credo of centrism and moderation is that how one defines the "responsible" extremes will determine where the center will fall. In the United States the mass media-legitimated spectrum runs a lot further right than it does left, which puts the "objectively balanced" mainstream clearly to the right of center. Jesse Helms can be elected and re-elected to the Senate and can embark on a public campaign to take over CBS; his opposite number on the left, whoever that might be, couldn't conceivably claim or receive that degree of visibility, power, and legitimacy.

Yet, in the final analysis, neither flank can avoid serving in one way or another to buttress the ramparts of the status quo, and to keep the truly oppositional from being taken seriously. American presidential politics recently featured a matched pair of Christian candidates, but neither the minister of the left, Jesse Jackson, nor the minister of the right, Pat Robertson, could hope to do more than exert some small pressure on their respective branches of the Property Party, whose two official divisions – the Democrats and the Republicans – offer an illusion of choice within the political mainstream.

Homosexuals and Television: Fear and Loathing

Close to the heart of our cultural and political system is the pattern of roles associated with sexual identity: our conceptions of masculinity and femininity, of the "normal" and "natural" attributes and responsibilities of men and women. And, as with other pillars of our moral order, these definitions of what is normal and natural serve to support the existing social power hierarchy.

The maintenance of the "normal" gender role system requires that children be socialized – and adults retained – within a set of images and expectations which limit and channel their conceptions of what is possible and proper for men and for women. The gender system is supported by the mass media treatment of sexual minorities. Mostly, they are ignored or denied – symbolically annihilated; when they do appear they do so in order to play a supportive role for the natural order and are thus narrowly and negatively stereotyped. Sexual minorities are not, of course, unique in this regard.[7] However, lesbians and gay men are unusually vulnerable to mass media power; even more so than blacks, national minorities, and women. Of all social groups (except perhaps communists), we are probably the least permitted to speak for ourselves in the mass media. We are also the only group (again, except for communists and, currently, Arab "terrorists") whose enemies are generally uninhibited by the consensus of "good taste" which protects most minorities from the more public displays of bigotry.

The reason for this vulnerability lies in large part in our initial isolation and invisibility. The process of identity formation for lesbian women and gay men requires the strength and determination to swim against the stream. A baby is born and immediately classified as male or female, white or black, and is treated as such from that moment, for better or worse. That baby is also defined as heterosexual and treated as such. It is made clear throughout the process of socialization – a process in which the mass media play a major role – that one will grow up, marry, have children and live in nuclear familial bliss, sanctified by religion and licensed by the state. Women are surrounded by other women, people of color by other people of color, etc., and can observe the variety of choices and fates that befall those who are like them. Mass media stereotypes selectively feature and reinforce some of the available roles and images for women, national minorities, people of color, etc.; but they operate under constraints imposed by the audiences' immediate environment.

Lesbians and gay men, conversely, are a self-identifying minority. We are assumed (with few exceptions, and these – the "obviously" effeminate man or masculine woman – may not even be homosexual) to be straight, and are treated as such, until we begin to recognize that we are not what we have been told we are, that we are different. But how are we to understand, define, and deal with that difference? Here we generally have little to go on beyond very limited direct experience with those individuals who are close enough to the accepted stereotypes to be labeled publicly as queers, faggots, dykes, etc. And we have the mass media.

The mass media play a major role in this process of social definition, and rarely a positive one. In the absence of adequate information in their immediate environment, most people, gay or straight, have little choice other than to accept the narrow and negative stereotypes they encounter as being representative of gay people. The mass media have rarely presented portrayals which counter or extend the prevalent images. On the contrary, they take advantage of them. Typically, media characterizations use popular stereotypes as a code which they know will be readily understood by the audience, thus further reinforcing the presumption of verisimilitude while remaining "officially" innocent of dealing with a sensitive subject.

But there is more to it than stereotyping. For the most part gay people have been simply invisible in the media. The few exceptions were almost invariably either victims – of violence or ridicule – or villains. As Vito Russo noted recently, "it is not insignificant that out of 32 films with major homosexual characters from 1961 through 1976, 13 feature gays who commit suicide and 18 have the homosexual murdered by another character."[8] Even this minimal and slanted presence, however, seems to be so threatening to the "industry" that gay characterizations and plot elements always come accompanied by pressbook qualifications and backpedaling. In his survey of the treatment of gay people in American film,[9] Russo presents a sample of the predictable distancing that gay themes evoke from directors ("*The Children's Hour* is not about lesbianism, it's about the power of lies to destroy people's lives," William Wyler, 1962; "*Sunday, Bloody Sunday* is not about the sexuality of these people, it's about human loneliness," John Schlesinger, 1972; "*Windows* is not about homosexuality, it's about insanity," Gordon Willis, 1979), and actors ("*The Sergeant* is not about homosexuality, it's about loneliness," Rex Harrison, 1971). It is easy to imagine how comforting these explanations must have been to lesbian and gay audience members looking for some reflection of their lives in the media. But it is not only the audiences who appear to require protective distancing from gay characters and themes. We are frequently treated to showbiz gossip intended to convey the heterosexual bona fides of any actor cast in a gay role, as when the actor playing the swish drag queen Albin in the stage version of *La Cage aux folles* told several interviewers that he had consulted with his wife and children before accepting the role.

The gay liberation movement emerged in the late 1960s in the United States, spurred by the examples of the black and feminist movements. Consequently, media attention to gay people and gay issues increased in the early 1970s, much of it positive (at least in comparison with previous and continuing heterosexist depictions and discussions), culminating (in the sense of greater media attention – in the pre-AIDS era) in 1973, with the decision by the American Psychiatric Association to delete homosexuality from its "official" list of mental diseases. By the middle 1970s, however, a backlash against the successes of the gay movement began to be felt around the country, most visibly in Anita Bryant's successful campaign to repeal a gay rights ordinance in Dade County, Florida, in 1977. Since then the gay movement and its enemies, mostly among the "new right," have been constant antagonists (right-wing fund-raisers acknowledge that anti-homosexual material is their best bet to get money from supporters), and television has often figured in the struggle. But, although the right wing has attacked the networks for what they consider to be overly favorable attention to homosexuals, in fact gay people are usually portrayed and used in news and dramatic media in ways that serve to reinforce rather than challenge the prevailing images.

Kathleen Montgomery observed the efforts of the organized gay movement to improve the ways network programmers handle gay characters and themes. In particular she describes the writing and production of a made-for-television network movie that had a gay-related theme, and involved consultation with representatives of gay organizations. And the result?

> Throughout the process all the decisions affecting the portrayal of gay life were influenced by the constraints which commercial television as a mass medium imposes upon the creation of its content. The fundamental goal of garnering the largest possible audience necessitated that (a) the program be placed in a familiar and successful television genre – the crime-drama; (b) the story focus upon the heterosexual male lead character and his reactions to the gay characters rather than upon the homosexual characters themselves; and (c) the film avoid any overt display of affection which might be offensive to certain segments of the audience. These requirements served as a filter

through which the issue of homosexuality was processed, resulting in a televised picture of gay life designed to be acceptable to the gay community and still palatable to a mass audience.[10]

Acceptability to the gay community, in this case, means that the movie was not an attack on our character and a denial of our basic humanity; it could not be mistaken for an expression of our values or perspectives. But of course they were not aiming at us, either; they were merely trying to avoid arguing with us afterwards. In Vito Russo's words, "mainstream films about homosexuals are not for homosexuals. They address themselves exclusively to the majority."[11] However, there will inevitably be a great many lesbians and gay men in the audience.

The rules of the mass media game have a double impact on gay people: not only do they mostly show us as weak and silly, or evil and corrupt, but they exclude and deny the existence of normal, unexceptional as well as exceptional lesbians and gay men. Hardly ever shown in the media are just plain gay folks, used in roles which do not center on their deviance as a threat to the moral order which must be countered through ridicule or physical violence. Television drama in particular reflects the deliberate use of clichéed casting strategies which preclude such daring innovations.

The sterotypic depiction of lesbians and gay men as abnormal, and the suppression of positive or even "unexceptional" portrayals, serve to maintain and police the boundaries of the moral order. It encourages the majority to stay on their gender-defined reservation, and tries to keep the minority quietly hidden out of sight. For the visible presence of healthy, non-stereotypic lesbians and gay men does pose a serious threat: it undermines the unquestioned normalcy of the status quo, and it opens up the possibility of making choices to people who might never otherwise have considered or understood that such choices could be made.

The situation has only been worsened by the AIDS epidemic. By 1983 nearly all mass media attention to gay men was in the context of AIDS-related stories, and because this coverage seems to have exhausted the media's limited interest in gay people, lesbians became even less visible than before (if possible). AIDS reinvigorated the two major mass media "roles" for gay people: victim and villain. Already treated as an important medical topic, AIDS moved up to the status of "front page" news after Rock Hudson emerged as the most famous person with the disease. At present AIDS stories appear daily in print and broadcast news – often with little or no new or important content – and the public image of gay men has been inescapably linked with the specter of plague. Television dramatists have presented the plight of (white, middle-class) gay men with AIDS, but their particular concern is the agony of the families/friends who have to face the awful truth: their son (brother, boyfriend, husband, etc.) is, gasp, gay! But, even with AIDS, not too gay, mind you. In the major network made-for-television movie on AIDS, NBC's *An Early Frost*, a young, rich, white, handsome lawyer is forced out of the closet by AIDS. "We know he is gay because he tells his disbelieving parents so, but his lack of a gay sensibility, politics and sense of community make him one of those homosexuals heterosexuals love."[12]

An Early Frost is thus another example of the pattern discerned by Montgomery: although this time the familiar and successful genre is family- not crime-drama, the focus is still on the heterosexual characters and their reactions. As William Henry notes in a recent overview of television's treatment of gays (or lack of same) during the past fifteen years,

> when TV does deal with gays it typically takes the point of view of straights struggling to understand. The central action is the progress of acceptance – not self-acceptance by the homosexual, but grief-stricken resignation to fate by his straight loved ones, who serve as surrogates for the audience. Homosexuality thus becomes not a fact of life, but a moral issue on which everyone in earshot is expected to voice some vehement opinion. Just as black characters were long expected to talk almost exclusively about being black, and handicapped characters (when seen at all) were expected to talk chiefly about their disabilities, so homosexual characters have been defined almost entirely by their "problem."[13]

Being defined by their "problem," it is no surprise therefore that gay characters have mostly been confined to television's favorite problem-of-the-week genre, the made-for-television movie, with a very occasional one-shot appearance of a gay character on a dramatic series (examples include episodes of *Lou Grant, Medical Center* and *St. Elsewhere*). Continuing gay characters tend to be so subtle as to be readily misunderstood by the innocent (as in the case of Sidney in *Love, Sidney*, whose homosexuality seemed to consist entirely of crying at the movies and having a photo of his dead lover on the mantelpiece), or confused about their sexuality and never seen in an ongoing romantic relationship (as in the case of the off-again-on-again Steven Carrington in *Dynasty*, whose lovers have an unfortunate tendency to get killed).

Despite their greater freedom from the competition for massive mainstream audiences – perhaps because of their need to compete for the primary audience of teens and young adults – commercial films are no more welcoming to gay characters than television. In fact, as Vito Russo shows in the revised edition of his 1981 study, *The Celluloid Closet* (1987), recent films are awash with gay villains and victims once more:

> The use of the word faggot has become almost mandatory. Outright slurs that would never be tolerated in reference to any other group of people are commonly used onscreen against homosexuals. . . . Anti-gay dialogue is most often given to the very characters with whom the audience is supposed to identify.[14]

Films offer their makers a degree of license which isn't available to television producers – an opportunity to use language and depictions of sexuality that go far beyond the limits imposed on television – but as far as gay people are concerned, this mostly serves as a hunting license.

Colonization: The Straight Gay

There are several categories of response to the mainstream media's treatment of minorities; among them are internalization, subversion, secession, and resistance.

To begin with, as we have already noted, we are all colonized by the majority culture. Those of us who belong to a minority group may nevertheless have absorbed the values of the dominant culture, even if these exclude or diminish us. We are all aware of the privileging of male-identified attributes in our patriarchal culture, and the dominance of the male perspective in the construction of mass-mediated realities. Similarly, the US media offer a white-angled view of the world which is shared with people of color everywhere. In a study of Venezuelan children in which they were asked to describe their heroes, the hero was North American in 86 per cent of the cases and Venezuelan in only 8 per cent; English-speaking in 82 per cent and Spanish-speaking in 15 per cent; white heroes outnumbered black heroes 11 to 1; and heroes were wealthy in 72 per cent of the cases.[15]

Sexual minorities are among the most susceptible to internalizing the dominant culture's values because the process of labelling generally occurs in isolation and because:

> We learn to loathe homosexuality before it becomes necessary to acknowledge our own . . . . Never having been offered *positive* attitudes to homosexuality, we inevitably adopt *negative* ones, and it is from these that all our values flow.[16]

Internalization and colonization can also result in the adoption of assimilationist strategies which promise upward (or centerward) mobility, although at the cost of cutting off one's "roots." Gay people by and large know how to "pass"; after all, it's what they have been doing most of their lives. But the security attained is fragile and often illusory, and certainly will not provide support in resisting the inferiorizing pressures of the straight culture they attempt to blend into. And all too often, there really isn't any resistance anyway, as the process of internalization has achieved the desired goal. The Zionist polemicist Ahad Ha-Am drew on a biblical analogy to describe this phenomenon, in his essay on Moses: "Pharaoh is gone, but his work remains; the master has ceased to be master, but the slaves have not ceased to be slaves."[17]

The supposedly liberal and tolerant domain of the media does not necessarily permit homosexuals (or other minorities) to overcome the burdens of self-oppression:

> When it comes to keeping minorities in their place, the entertainment industry continues to divide and conquer. For all the organizing that women have done, for instance, in their attempts to break down the barriers, well-placed women executives say they've received very little mutual support from their equally well-placed peers. The old-boy network rules, and the individual women, gays, blacks, or hispanics who attain some degree of success usually have to camouflage themselves in the trappings of their masters.[18]

Similarly, gay writer Merle Miller recalled that, "as editor of a city newspaper, he indulged in "queer-baiting" to conceal his own homosexuality."[19] Openly gay actor Michael Kearns speaks of "a gay agent who makes it a habit to tell "fag jokes" at the close of interviews with new actors. If an actor laughs, he's signed up; if he doesn't, he isn't."[20] Working backstage, it would seem, does not exempt one from falling under the spell of the hegemonic values cultivated and reflected by the media. However, as Raymond Williams has suggested, hegemony "is never either total or exclusive. At any time, forms of alternative or directly oppositional politics and culture exist as significant elements in the society."[21]

Resistance and Opposition

The most obvious form of resistance, but possibly the most difficult, would be simply to ignore the mass media, and refuse to be insulted or injured by their derogation and denial of one's identity and integrity as a member of a minority group. Unfortunately, although some of us can personally secede from the mass-mediated mainstream, or sample from it with great care and selectivity, we cannot thereby counter its effect on our fellow citizens. We cannot even prevent our fellow minority-group members from attending to messages which we feel are hostile to their interests (this is, of course, a familiar dilemma for parents who feel that commercial television is not in the best interests of their children). Given the generally high levels of television viewing at the lower rungs of the socio-economic ladder, it can be expected that large segments of the population consume media fare that serves to maintain their subordinate status. In the United States, black households are disproportionately heavy television consumers: "Black households, which represented about 9 percent of all television households surveyed, accounted for about 14 percent of all household viewing. According to the United States Census Bureau, blacks constituted 12 percent of the population last year."[22]

We might expect self-identified ideological minorities to be better able to resist the siren's song of the mass media; and we have noted that the religious right has developed alternative channels to provide their adherents with a source of value-congruent media fare. We've also noted the absence of equivalent programming on the left bank of the mainstream. Leftists, it seems, are faced with fewer choices, and they experience the ambivalence of being aware of the central role the media play in consensualizing a dominant ideology and yet not wanting (or being able) to pull completely out of the mainstream themselves. In an ongoing study of American leftists' relationships to the mass media, Eugene Michaud has encountered many expressions of such hostility and ambivalence, despite which the respondents interviewed continue to watch television:

> "Frankly, I detest TV. It's the source of many family disputes. I really find TV obnoxious and really intrusive on whatever you're trying to do.... For most people, I think TV is a way of relaxing – it's a distraction... life is hard – so it's very easy to watch TV." (Male, 36)
>
> "I have a lot of trouble with the TV news. I get upset and I want to run away. Or I get obnoxious and start sneering at it, and my wife gets upset because she's trying to listen.... I realize that there's this vast treasure trove of ideas and images from TV which most people are plugged into." (Male, 44)

"I hate watching the TV news and having someone give me the straight administration line....The way I watch TV is if I don't have anything else to do and I'm bored." (Female, 32)

"We watch network news sometimes, but I feel like it's junkfood news. I find it very frustrating. They never analyse anything. . . . It's also so easy to turn on TV, and there's all this visual stuff. It's so effortless." (Female, 32)

"I do watch *Nightline*, but it pisses me off to no end...the way they manipulate things to put forth a certain point-of-view. It's total set-up." (Male, 32)[23]

Observers of the current television scene will not be surprised to learn that there are one or two shows that do manage to appeal to Michaud's leftist respondents. Most frequently praised is *Hill Street Blues*, although it's generally judged to have declined after its first few seasons. Its spin-off, *St. Elsewhere*, receives similar reviews. The decline is often interpreted in ideological terms:

"I used to watch *Hill Street Blues* regularly, but I mostly don't bother any more...it used to try to demonstrate the ambiguity people felt towards each other and towards their work. Now, it's just the traditional good guys against the bad guys. I think it's a reflection of the Reagan era." (Female, 34)

The ratings smash hit *Cosby Show* is popular among some leftists, despite its upscale values, because it features a black family and because "there's a lot of love, which is appealing, and it does capture the real dynamics of family life in a funny way" (Male, 30).

Lesbian women and gay men do not constitute an ideological minority in the same way that American leftists do (although those gay people who are part of the "movement" certainly tend to be left-identified), and they are less likely to condemn the mass media in the way the left does. However, few lesbian women and gay men could remain unaware of how they are treated in the media – when their existence is even acknowledged – and their relationship to the media is likely to be colored by this awareness. Just as racial and ethnic minority groups pay close attention to programs which feature their members, so too gay people will tune in regularly to any program which promises an openly or explicitly lesbian or gay character (or even a favorite performer assumed to be gay). The images and messages they will encounter will not, as we have already noted, provide them with much comfort or support. More typically, they will again be marginalized, trivialized, and insulted.

While working on this paper I went to see the latest film written and directed by Woody Allen, *Radio Days*, and was irritated, though not surprised, by the inclusion of a gay character whose only function is to evoke a laugh at his own expense, and to further underline the hopelessness of a woman who would fall in love with him. My irritation was caused not only by Woody Allen's gratuitous insult – I've come to expect these from him – but also by the hilarity it produced among the audience. The experience of having one's status as "fair game" emphasized in this graphic fashion while sitting in a movie theater is familiar to gay people, just as it is to people of color and to women. Even when a gay characterization is intended to be sympathetic (as in the wildly successful *La Cage aux folles*), the gay members of the audience may wince at the falsity of the image, and find themselves laughing at different times from the straight audience. There can be a perverse pleasure in this perception – Elizabeth Ellsworth describes lesbian feminist reviewers of *Personal Best* (a film written and directed by a straight man, which includes a lesbian relationship as a central theme, despite the usual pressbook obfuscation) who "expressed pleasure in watching the dominant media "get it wrong" in watching it attempt, but fail, to colonize "real" lesbian space."[24]

It can be argued that the best stance for gay people to adopt *vis-à-vis* the mass media would be to repay them with the same indifference and contempt they reveal toward us. Unfortunately, while this might be a gratifying and appropriate individual solution, it is not realistic as a general strategy. One may be able to reduce one's own irritation by ignoring the media, but their insidious impact is not so easily avoided. What cannot be avoided, however, can be better understood, and studies of lesbian and gay audiences and their responses should be included in the emerging research agenda.

Subversion

A second oppositional strategy is the subversion and appropriation of mainstream media, as well as the occasionally successful infiltration. The classic gay (male) strategy of subversion is camp – an ironic stance toward the straight world rooted in a gay sensibility:

> a creative energy reflecting a consciousness that is different from the mainstream; a heightened awareness of certain human complications of feeling that spring from the fact of social oppression; in short, a perception of the world which is coloured, shaped, directed and defined by the fact of one's gayness.[25]

This characterization would, of course, also fit many other minorities who experience oppression, but the gay sensibility differs in that we encounter and develop it at a later stage in our lives; it is nobody's native tongue. Moreover, while sharing much with other minority perspectives, camp is notably marked by irony and a theatrical perspective on the world which can be traced to the particular realities of gay experience:

> The stigma of gayness is unique insofar as it is not immediately apparent either to ourselves or to others. Upon discovery of our gayness, however, we are confronted with the possibility of avoiding the negative sanctions attached to our supposed failing by concealing information (i.e. signs which other people take for gay) from the rest of the world. This crucial fact of our existence is called *passing for straight*, a phenomenon generally defined in the metaphor of theatre, that is, playing a role: pretending to be something one is not; or, to shift the motive somewhat, to camouflage our gayness by withholding facts about ourselves which might lead others to the correct conclusion about our sexual orientation.[26]

Camp offers a subversive response to mainstream culture, and provides both in-group solidarity and an opportunity to express distance from and disdain for the roles most gay people play most of the time. Exchanged in private settings, camp is a mechanism of oppositional solidarity which repairs the damage inflicted by the majority and prepares us for further onslaughts. As a restricted code used in public settings, camp can be a way to identify and communicate with other "club members" under the unknowing eyes of the straight world – in itself an act of subversive solidarity (as well as self-protection). Camp can also be a form of public defiance, and a risky expression of a difference which dares to show its face.

Camp is also the quintessentially gay strategy for undermining the hegemonic power of media images.[27] The sting can be taken out of oppressive characterizations and the hot air balloons of official morality can be burst with the ironic prick of camp humor. Most importantly, by self-consciously taking up a position outside the mainstream, if only in order to look back at it, camp cultivates a sense of detachment from the dominant ideology.

> The sense of being different . . . made me feel myself as "outside" the mainstream in fundamental ways – and this does give you a kind of knowledge of the mainstream you cannot have if you are immersed in it. I do not necessarily mean a truer perspective, so much as an awareness of the mainstream as a mainstream, and not just the way everything and everybody inevitably are; in other words, it denaturalizes normality. This knowledge is the foundation of camp.[28]

Camp can also be seen in the appropriation of mainstream figures and products when they are adopted as "cult" objects by marginal groups. Camp cult favorites are often women film stars who can be seen as standing up to the pressures of a male-dominated movie industry and despite all travails remaining in command of their careers (Bette Davis, Joan Crawford, Mae West), or at least struggling back from defeat (Judy Garland[29]).

Cult movies like *The Rocky Horror Picture Show* provide occasions for meeting others with the same perspective, and turning a media product into the pretext for communal interaction. In a study of patrons waiting to see *Rocky Horror* outside a Rochester, NY, movie theater, it was learned that, excluding the first-timers, the mean number of times respondents had seen the movie was eleven.[30] The audience members are there to participate in a ritual and a social event which create and reinforce a solidarity of non-mainstream identification. The *Rocky Horror* cult has served all over the United States as an opportunity for lesbian and gay teenagers to meet and support each other in the coming-out process.

In Our Own Voice

The most effective form of resistance to the hegemonic force of the dominant media is to speak for oneself. At one level this means attempting to be included in the category of recognized positions and groupings acknowledged by the mass media.

Achieving this degree of legitimation is not a negligible accomplishment, and it is not to be despised or rejected as an important minority goal. The success of various minorities in exerting pressure on the media can be seen in the care with which images of these groups are balanced and presented. In fact, the television networks have taken to complaining about the difficulties they face in finding acceptable villains.

> "In their desire to avoid stereotyping, I think broadcast standards and practices some-times goes to an absurd extreme," said Bruce J. Sallan, ABC's vice president in charge of motion pictures on television. "There are almost no ethnic villains on television. We can't do a Mafia picture at ABC, because broadcast standards won't let us deal with Italians involved in organized crime."[31]

A recent ABC-TV film, *The Children of Times Square*, was allowed to have a black villain after he was balanced by sympathetic black characters: "We had instructions from the network that if a black is shown in a bad light, we must also show a black in a good light."[32]

Gay people have not yet achieved the degree of social power and legitimacy which would permit them to demand the same self-censorship on the part of the media, and consequently we are still treated to gay villains and victims unbalanced by gay heroes or even just plain gay folks. As we have seen from Kathleen Montgo-mery's research, gay pressure can hope at most for a limited success: a story which offends neither minority nor mainstream sensibilities too much. Could we hope for much more? Probably not, since the numbers simply are not there to put sufficient pressure on the media – and numbers are the bottom line. We might exact concessions along the way, forcing some respect for our humanity, but we cannot expect the media to tell our stories for us, or allow us to do so through their channels.

The ultimate expression of independence for a minority audience struggling to free itself from the dominant culture's hegemony is to become the creators and not merely the consumers of media images. In recent years lesbian women and gay men have begun – although with difficulty – to gather the necessary resources with which to tell our own stories.

There have always been minority media in the United States; various immigrant groups supported newspapers, books, theater and occasionally movies in their native languages. But these immigrant voices were stilled as succeeding generations were assimilated into mainstream culture, losing touch with the language and culture of their grandparents. The black press has survived and occasionally flourished alongside the mainstream media, and black culture (music and dance in particular) has been the source of much inspiration and talent which have crossed over into the mainstream (sometimes in whiteface).

Since the 1970s a lesbian and gay alternative culture has offered a range of media sources and products – press, music, theater, pornography – which are unmistakably the product of gay people's sensibility. Here, too, there is the occasional cross-over, as when Harvey Fierstein's *Torch Song Trilogy* wound its way from off-off-Broadway to a Tony Award for best play on Broadway. But crossing-over is no guarantee of protection from the dominant culture. Even speaking in his own voice – quite literally, as when Fierstein starred in his play – the gay author may find that straight audiences do not see beyond their preconceptions. *Torch Song Trilogy* was reviewed in the *New York Times* by Walter Kerr, the "dean" of Broadway theater critics, and the review is both patronizing and simply wrong.[33] Much of the action in the third act centers on the fact that Arnold, the protagonist, has adopted a gay teenager, and on the "return" of his former lover who is in the process of leaving his wife. The play ends with clear intimations of an emerging gay "nuclear family" – with Arnold as mother, his returned lover as daddy, and their adopted gay son. What does Walter Kerr do with this? He misunderstands – or at least misrepresents – it so badly that I must assume bigotry blinded him to plot details so obvious no tyro critic could miss them. He implies that the adopted son is a "kept" boy Arnold has picked up. The former lover is described as "also sharing the flat, though not yet the boy." When the boy tells the former lover, "I'd be proud to call you daddy," Kerr detects "possible betrayal, sensual shiftings" – that is, he thinks the boy is seducing the man!

One clue to Kerr's stupidity – astounding in so veteran a critic – may be found in his comment about "this rambling and, because it can only move in circles, repetitive plot." Why, we might ask, can it only move in circles? The answer is not to be found in the theory of drama, but in the tired homophobic clichés of psychiatric theories about gay people. Kerr "knows" that we are all caught up in narcissistic repetition compulsions. The truth is, of course, that Kerr is the one who is handicapped by a repetition compulsion, sitting there on the aisle wrapped in the old miasmal mist.

When mainstream critics do not blame gay artists for things which they have themselves misread into the works they are reviewing, they may still find fault with them for not rising above their parochial concerns, that is, for addressing themselves to the concerns of their fellow gay people. In a letter to the *New York Times Book Review*,[34] justifying his negative review of Edmund White's *States of Desire: Travels in Gay America*, Paul Cowan assures us that,

> it's crucial to communicate across tribal lines. Good literature has always done that – it has transformed a particular subject into something universal. Mr. White didn't do that: in my opinion it's one of the reasons he failed to write a good book.

I'm tempted to say, aha, the old universalism ploy! Perhaps good literature has always transformed a particular subject into something universal. But, of course, there's always a double standard in the application of the universalism criterion.

In an essay entitled "Colonialist Criticism," the Nigerian writer Chinua Achebe decries those western critics who evaluate African literature on the basis of whether it overcomes "parochialism" and "achieves universality":

> It would never occur to them to doubt the universality of their own literature. In the nature of things, the work of a Western writer is automatically informed by universality. It is only others who must strive to achieve it.[35]

In the past decade lesbian and gay film makers have been able, with difficulty, to raise the money needed to produce independent documentaries and fictional films which have inaugurated a true alternative channel in the crucial media of movies and television. The pioneering documentary *Word is Out* (1977), and the more recent Oscar-winning *Life and Times of Harvey Milk*, among others, represent authentic examples of gay people speaking for ourselves, in our own words; although even here there have been compromises in order to meet the demands of the Public Broadcasting System – the only viable channel for independent documentaries in the United States.[36] And, even more recently and tentatively, there are the stirrings of lesbian and gay fiction films exhibited through mainstream (art) theaters and becoming accessible to a nationwide gay audience.

> There is, alternatively, a homosexual cinema. It neither concerns itself overtly with issues of gay politics nor does it present gay sexuality as society's perennial dirty secret. The key to gay films, whether they are made by heterosexuals or homosexuals, is that they do not view the existence of gay people as controversial.... These films may reflect the fear, agitation, and bigotry of a society confronted with such truth, but it is not their view that such emotions are rational or even important to explore.[37]

The products of the nascent lesbian/gay cinema find a powerful response among their primary audience, and can easily become cult films of a different sort from the midnight orphans of the mainstream industry. *Desert Hearts* is such a film. Made on a small budget collected in two and a half years of arduous grass-roots fund raising and based on a novel by lesbian author Jane Rule, *Desert Hearts* achieved both cross-over box-office success and a cult following among lesbians.

> "I've waited 25 years for this movie," says Pat, a 47-year-old secretary in San Francisco, California. "I'm sick of seeing only heterosexual love stories. *Desert Hearts* is a movie I can finally identify with. It's like when I was little, we only had "white dolls" to play with, as if all babies were white. Movie makers have done the same thing; they've generally ignored gays until the last few years. This movie is a positive step in making lesbian movies more acceptable to the general public. I've seen it 22 times and am still not tired of it."

> "I think that women are drawn to it, lesbians are drawn to it in the same way that black people were drawn to *Superfly*. It isn't so much the content. It's a matter of the identification with it and the way it's been presented," says screenplay writer Natalie Cooper. "I'm glad that it served – for anyone – no matter how small, something that could make people feel okay, instead of feeling peripheral or put down. Just to say, "Hey, I dig it and I love it; I do that, too." They can say, "This is our movie, this is our thing." It makes them feel, dare I say maybe, not proud but viable."[38]

Finally, then, the answer to the plight of the marginalized minority audience would seem to lie in the cultivation of alternative channels, even while we continue to press upon the media our claims for equitable and respectful treatment. But neither goal can be easily achieved, and each will require overcoming formidable obstacles.

Notes

1 George Gerbner and Larry Gross, "Living with Television," *Journal of Communication* 26, no. 2 (1976): 182.

2 George Gerbner, Larry Gross, Michael Morgan, and Nancy Signorielli, "Living with Television: The Dynamics of the Cultivation Process," in Jennings Bryant and Dolf Zillmann (eds.), *Perspectives on Media Effects* (Hillsdale, NJ: Lawrence Erlbaum Associates, 1986), pp. 17–40.

3 George Gerbner, Larry Gross, Michael Morgan, and Nancy Signorielli, "The "Mainstreaming" of America," *Journal of Communication* 30, no. 3 (1980): 10–29; George Gerbner, Larry Gross, Michael Morgan, and Nancy Signorielli, "Charting the Mainstream: Television's Contributions to Political Orientations," *Journal of Communication* 32, no. 2 (1982): 100–27; and Gerbner *et al.*, "Living with Television" (1986).

4 See George Gerbner, Larry Gross, Stewart Hoover, Michael Morgan, Nancy Signorielli, Harry Cotugno, and Robert Wuthnow, *Religion and Television* (University of Pennsylvania: The Annenberg School of Communications, 1984); and Stewart Hoover, "The 700 Club as Religion and as Television," unpublished Ph.D. dissertation, University of Pennsylvania, 1985.

5 Hoover, "The 700 Club," pp. 382f.

6 Murray Roth, "CBS Evaluates Turner Takeover: "Not a Snowball's Chance . . .","" *Variety*, April 24, 1985, p. 163.

7 See Larry Gross, "The Cultivation of Intolerance," in G. Melischek *et al.* (eds.), *Cultural Indicators: An International Symposium* (Vienna: Austrian Academy of Sciences, 1984), pp. 345–63.

8 Vito Russo, "A State of Being," *Film Comment* (April 1986): 32.

9 Vito Russo, *The Celluloid Closet: Homosexuality in the Movies* (New York: Harper & Row, 1981).

10 Kathleen Montgomery, "Gay Activists and the Networks," *Journal of Communication* 31, no. 3 (1981): 49–57.

11 Russo, "A State of Being," p. 32.

12 Andrea Weiss, "From the Margins: New Images of Gays in the Cinema," *Cineaste* (1986): 4–8.

13 William Henry, "That Certain Subject," *Channels* (April 1987): 43f.

14 Russo, *The Celluloid Closet*, p. 251.

15 Antonio Pasquali, "Latin America: Our Image or Theirs?," in *Getting the Message Across* (no editor listed) (Paris: The UNESCO Press, 1975), pp. 62f.

16 Andrew Hodges and David Hutter, *With Downcast Gays: Aspects of Homosexual Self-Oppression* (Toronto: Pink Triangle Press, 1977), p. 4.

17 Ahad Ha-Am (Asher Ginzberg), "Moses," in *Selected Essays of Ahad Ha-Am*, ed. Leon Simon (New York: Atheneum, 1970), p. 320.

18 Gregg Kilday, "Hollywood's Homosexuals," *Film Comment* (April 1986): 40.

19 Barry Adam, *The Survival of Domination: Inferiorization and Everyday Life* (New York: Elsevier, 1978), p. 89.

20 Samir Hachem, "Inside the Tinseled Closet," *The Advocate*, March 17, 1987, p. 48.

21 Raymond Williams, *Marxism and Literature* (Oxford: Oxford University Press, 1977), p. 111.

22 Thomas Morgan, "The Black Viewers' New Allure for the Networks," *New York Times*, December 1, 1986.

23 Eugene Michaud, "The Whole Left Is Watching," Ph.D. dissertation in progress, University of Pennsylvania, 1987 (personal communication).

24 Elizabeth Ellsworth, "Illicit Pleasures: Feminist Spectators and *Personal Best*," *Wide Angle* 8, no. 2 (1986): 54.

25 Jack Babuscio, "Camp and the Gay Sensibility," in Richard Dyer (ed.), *Gays and Film* (London: British Film Institute, 1977), p. 40.

26 Ibid., p. 45.

27 See ibid.; also Richard Dyer, *Heavenly Bodies: Film Stars and Society* (London: British Film Institute/Macmillan, 1987).

28 Derek Cohen and Richard Dyer, "The Politics of Gay Culture," in Gay Left Collective (eds.), *Homosexuality: Power and Politics* (London: Allison & Busby, 1980), pp. 177f.

29 See Dyer, *Heavenly Bodies*.

30 Bruce Austin, "Portrait of a Cult Film Audience: *The Rocky Horror Picture Show*," *Journal of Communication* 31, no. 2 (1981): 47.

31 Stephen Farber, "Minority Villains Are Touchy Network Topic," *New York Times*, February 29, 1985.

32 Ibid.

33 *New York Times*, June 27, 1982.

34 *New York Times Book Review*, September 3, 1980.

35 Chinua Achebe, "Colonialist Criticism," in *Morning Yet on Creation Day* (New York: Anchor Books, 1976), p. 11.

36 See Thomas Waugh, "Minority Self-Imaging in Oppositional Film Practice: Lesbian and Gay Documentary," in Larry Gross *et al.* (eds.), *Image Ethics* (New York: Oxford University Press, 1988).

37 Russo, "A State of Being," p. 34.

38 Jan Huston, "Fans Make *Desert Hearts* a Cult Classic," *Gay Community News*, January 25, 1987, p. 8.

22

Eating the Other: Desire and Resistance*

bell hooks

> This is theory's acute dilemma: that desire expresses itself most fully where only those absorbed in its delights and torments are present, that it triumphs most completely over other human preoccupations in places sheltered from view. Thus it is paradoxically in hiding that the secrets of desire come to light, that hegemonic impositions and their reversals, evasions, and subversions are at their most honest and active, and that the identities and disjunctures between felt passion and established culture place themselves on most vivid display.
>
> (Joan Cocks, *The Oppositional Imagination*)

Within current debates about race and difference, mass culture is the contemporary location that both publicly declares and perpetuates the idea that there is pleasure to be found in the acknowledgment and enjoyment of racial difference. The commodification of Otherness has been so successful because it is offered as a new delight, more intense, more satisfying than normal ways of doing and feeling. Within commodity culture, ethnicity becomes spice, seasoning that can liven up the dull dish that is mainstream white culture. Cultural taboos around sexuality and desire are transgressed and made explicit as the media bombards folks with a message of difference no longer based on the white supremacist assumption that "blondes have more fun." The "real fun" is to be had by bringing to the surface all those "nasty" unconscious fantasies and longings about contact with the Other embedded in the secret (not so secret) deep structure of white supremacy. In many ways it is a contemporary revival of interest in the "primitive," with a distinctly postmodern slant. As Marianna Torgovnick argues in *Gone Primitive: Savage Intellects, Modern Lives*:

> What is clear now is that the West's fascination with the primitive has to do with its own crises in identity, with its own need to clearly demarcate subject and object even while flirting with other ways of experiencing the universe.

* From bell hooks, *Black Looks: Race and Representation* (Boston, Mass.: South End Press, 1992), pp. 21–39.

Certainly from the standpoint of white supremacist capitalist patriarchy, the hope is that desires for the "primitive" or fantasies about the Other can be continually exploited, and that such exploitation will occur in a manner that reinscribes and maintains the *status quo*. Whether or not desire for contact with the Other, for connection rooted in the longing for pleasure, can act as a critical intervention challenging and subverting racist domination, inviting and enabling critical resistance, is an unrealized political possibility. Exploring how desire for the Other is expressed, manipulated, and transformed by encounters with difference and the different is a critical terrain that can indicate whether these potentially revolutionary longings are ever fulfilled.

Contemporary working-class British slang playfully converges the discourse of desire, sexuality, and the Other, evoking the phrase getting "a bit of the Other" as a way to speak about sexual encounter. Fucking is the Other. Displacing the notion of Otherness from race, ethnicity, skin-color, the body emerges as a site of contestation where sexuality is the metaphoric Other that threatens to take over, consume, transform *via* the experience of pleasure. Desired and sought after, sexual pleasure alters the consenting subject, deconstructing notions of will, control, coercive domination. Commodity culture in the United States exploits conventional thinking about race, gender, and sexual desire by "working" both the idea that racial difference marks one as Other and the assumption that sexual agency expressed within the context of racialized sexual encounter is a conversion experience that alters one's place and participation in contemporary cultural politics. The seductive promise of this encounter is that it will counter the terrorizing force of the *status quo* that makes identity fixed, static, a condition of containment and death. And that it is this willingness to transgress racial boundaries within the realm of the sexual that eradicates the fear that one must always conform to the norm to remain "safe." Difference can seduce precisely because the mainstream imposition of sameness is a provocation that terrorizes. And as Jean Baudrillard suggests in *Fatal Strategies*:

> Provocation – unlike seduction, which allows things to come into play and appear in secret, dual and ambiguous – does not leave you free to be; it calls on you to reveal yourself as you are. It is always blackmail by identity (and thus a symbolic murder, since you are never that, except precisely by being condemned to it).

To make one's self vulnerable to the seduction of difference, to seek an encounter with the Other, does not require that one relinquish forever one's mainstream positionality. When race and ethnicity become commodified as resources for pleasure, the culture of specific groups, as well as the bodies of individuals, can be seen as constituting an alternative playground where members of dominating races, genders, sexual practices affirm their power-over in intimate relations with the Other. While teaching at Yale, I walked one bright spring day in the downtown area of New Haven, which is close to campus and invariably brings one into contact with many of the poor black people who live nearby, and found myself walking behind a group of very blond, very white, jock type boys. (The downtown area was often talked about as an arena where racist domination of blacks by whites was contested on the sidewalks, as white people, usually male, often jocks, used their bodies to force black people off the sidewalk, to push our bodies aside, without ever looking at us or acknowledging our presence.) Seemingly unaware of my presence, these young men talked about their plans to fuck as many girls from other racial/ethnic groups as they could "catch" before graduation. They "ran" it down. Black girls were high on the list, Native American girls hard to find, Asian girls (all lumped into the same category), deemed easier to entice, were considered "prime targets." Talking about this overheard conversation with my students, I found that it was commonly accepted that one "shopped" for sexual partners in the same way one "shopped" for courses at Yale, and that race and ethnicity was a serious category on which selections were based.

To these young males and their buddies, fucking was a way to confront the Other, as well as a way to make themselves over, to leave behind white "innocence" and enter the world of "experience." As is often the case in this society, they were confident that non-white people had more life experience, were more worldly, sensual, and sexual because they were different. Getting a bit of the Other, in this case engaging in sexual encounters with non-white females, was considered a ritual of transcendence, a movement out into a world of difference that would transform, an acceptable rite of passage. The direct objective was not simply to sexually possess the Other; it was to be changed in some way by the encounter. "Naturally," the presence of the Other, the body of the Other, was seen as existing to serve the ends of white male desires. Writing about the way difference is recouped in the West in "The "Primitive" Unconscious of Modern Art, or White Skin, Black Masks," Hal Foster reminds readers that Picasso regarded the tribal objects he had acquired as "witnesses" rather than as "models." Foster critiques this positioning of the Other, emphasizing that this recognition was "contingent upon instrumentality": "In this way, through affinity and use, the primitive is sent up into the service of the Western tradition (which is then seen to have partly produced it)." A similar critique can be made of contemporary trends in inter-racial sexual desire and contact initiated by white males. They claim the body of the colored Other instrumentally, as unexplored terrain, a symbolic frontier that will be fertile ground for their reconstruction of the masculine norm, for asserting themselves as transgressive desiring subjects. They call upon the Other to be both witness and participant in this transformation.

For white boys to openly discuss their desire for colored girls (or boys) publicly announces their break with a white supremacist past that would have such desire articulated only as taboo, as secret, as shame. They see their willingness to openly name their desire for the Other as affirmation of cultural plurality (its impact on sexual preference and choice). Unlike racist white men who historically violated the bodies of black women/women of color to assert their position as colonizer/conqueror, these young men see themselves as non-racists, who choose to transgress racial boundaries within the sexual realm not to dominate the Other, but rather so that they can be acted upon, so that they can be changed utterly. Not at all attuned to those aspects of their sexual fantasies that irrevocably link them to collective white racist domination, they believe their desire for contact represents a progressive change in white attitudes towards non-whites. They do not see themselves as perpetuating racism. To them the most potent indication of that change is the frank expression of longing, the open declaration of desire, the need to be intimate with dark Others. The point is to be changed by this convergence of pleasure and Otherness. One dares – acts – on the assumption that the exploration into the world of difference, into the body of the Other, will provide a greater, more intense pleasure than any that exists in the ordinary world of one's familiar racial group. And even though the conviction is that the familiar world will remain intact even as one ventures outside it, the hope is that they will reenter that world no longer the same.

The current wave of "imperialist nostalgia" (defined by Renato Rosaldo in *Culture and Truth* as "nostalgia, often found under imperialism, where people mourn the passing of what they themselves have transformed" or as "a process of yearning for what one has destroyed that is a form of mystification") often obscures contemporary cultural strategies deployed not to mourn but to celebrate the sense of a continuum of "primitivism." In mass culture, imperialist nostalgia takes the form of reenacting and reritualizing in different ways the imperialist, colonizing journey as narrative fantasy of power and desire, of seduction by the Other. This longing is rooted in the atavistic belief that the spirit of the "primitive" resides in the bodies of dark Others whose cultures, traditions, and lifestyles may indeed be irrevocably changed by imperialism, colonization, and racist domination. The desire to make contact with those bodies deemed Other, with no apparent will to dominate, assuages the guilt of the past, even takes the form of a defiant gesture where one denies accountability and historical connection. Most importantly, it establishes a contemporary narrative where the suffering imposed by structures of domination on those designated Other is deflected by an emphasis on seduction and longing where the desire is not to make the Other over in one's image but to become the Other.

Whereas mournful imperialist nostalgia constitutes the betrayed and abandoned world of the Other as an accumulation of lack and loss, contemporary longing for the "primitive" is expressed by the projection onto the Other of a sense of plenty, bounty, a field of dreams. Commenting on this strategy in "Readings in Cultural Resistance," Hal Foster contends, "Difference is thus used productively; indeed, in a social order which seems to know no outside (and which must contrive its own transgressions to redefine its limits), difference is often fabricated in the interests of social control as well as of commodity innovation." Masses of young people dissatisfied by U.S. imperialism, unemployment, lack of economic opportunity, afflicted by the post-modern malaise of alienation, no sense of grounding, no redemptive identity, can be manipulated by cultural strategies that offer Otherness as appeasement, particularly through commodification. The contemporary crises of identity in the west, especially as experienced by white youth, are eased when the "primitive" is recouped *via* a focus on diversity and pluralism which suggests the Other can provide life-sustaining alternatives. Concurrently, diverse ethnic/racial groups can also embrace this sense of specialness, that histories and experience once seen as worthy only of disdain can be looked upon with awe.

Cultural appropriation of the Other assuages feelings of deprivation and lack that assault the psyches of radical white youth who choose to be disloyal to western civilization. Concurrently, marginalized groups, deemed Other, who have been ignored, rendered invisible, can be seduced by the emphasis on Otherness, by its commodification, because it offers the promise of recognition and reconciliation. When the dominant culture demands that the Other be offered as sign that progressive political change is taking place, that the American Dream can indeed be inclusive of difference, it invites a resurgence of essentialist cultural nationalism. The acknowledged Other must assume recognizable forms. Hence, it is not African American culture formed in resistance to contemporary situations that surfaces, but nostalgic evocation of a "glorious" past. And even though the focus is often on the ways that this past was "superior" to the present, this cultural narrative relies on stereotypes of the "primitive," even as it eschews the term, to evoke a world where black people were in harmony with nature and with one another. This narrative is linked to white western conceptions of the dark Other, not to a radical questioning of those representations.

Should youth of any other color not know how to move closer to the Other, or how to get in touch with the "primitive," consumer culture promises to show the way. It is within the commercial realm of advertising that the drama of Otherness finds expression. Encounters with Otherness are clearly marked as more exciting, more intense, and more threatening. The lure is the combination of pleasure and danger. In the cultural marketplace the Other is coded as having the capacity to be more alive, as holding the secret that will allow those who venture and dare to break with the cultural anhedonia (defined in Sam Keen's *The Passionate Life* as "the insensitivity to pleasure, the incapacity for experiencing happiness") and experience sensual and spiritual renewal. Before his untimely death, Michel Foucault, the quintessential transgressive thinker in the west, confessed that he had real difficulties experiencing pleasure:

> I think that pleasure is a very difficult behavior. It's not as simple as that to enjoy one's self. And I must say that's my dream. I would like and I hope I die of an overdose of pleasure of any kind. Because I think it's really difficult and I always have the feeling that I do not feel *the* pleasure, the complete total pleasure and, for me, it's related to death. Because I think that the kind of pleasure I would consider as *the* real pleasure, would be so deep, so intense, so overwhelming that I couldn't survive it. I would die.

Though speaking from the standpoint of his individual experience, Foucault voices a dilemma felt by many in the west. It is precisely that longing for *the* pleasure that has led the white west to sustain a romantic fantasy of the "primitive" and the concrete search for a real primitive paradise, whether that location be a country or a body, a dark continent or dark flesh, perceived as the perfect embodiment of that possibility.

Within this fantasy of Otherness, the longing for pleasure is projected as a force that can disrupt and subvert the will to dominate. It acts to both mediate and challenge. In Lorraine Hansberry's play *Les Blancs*, it is the desire to experience closeness and community that leads the white American journalist Charles to make contact and attempt to establish a friendship with Tshembe, the black revolutionary. Charles struggles to divest himself of white supremacist privilege, eschews the role of colonizer, and refuses racist exoticization of blacks. Yet he continues to assume that he alone can decide the nature of his relationship to a black person. Evoking the idea of a universal transcendent subject, he appeals to Tshembe by repudiating the role of oppressor, declaring, "I am a man who feels like talking." When Tshembe refuses to accept the familiar relationship offered him, refuses to satisfy Charles' longing for camaraderie and contact, he is accused of hating white men. Calling attention to situations where white people have oppressed other white people, Tshembe challenges Charles, declaring that "race is a device – no more, no less," that "it explains nothing at all." Pleased with this disavowal of the importance of race, Charles agrees, stating "race hasn't a thing to do with it." Tshembe then deconstructs the category "race" without minimizing or ignoring the impact of racism, telling him:

> I believe in the recognition of devices as *devices* – but I also believe in the reality of those devices. In one century men choose to hide their conquests under religion, in another under race. So you and I may recognize the fraudulence of the device in both cases, but the fact remains that a man who has a sword run through him because he will not become a Moslem or a Christian – or who is lynched in Mississippi or Zatembe because he is black – is suffering the utter reality of that device of conquest. And it is pointless to pretend that it doesn't *exist* – merely because it is a lie . . .

Again and again Tshembe must make it clear to Charles that subject to subject contact between white and black which signals the absence of domination, of an oppressor/oppressed relationship, must emerge through mutual choice and negotiation. That simply by expressing their desire for "intimate" contact with black people, white people do not eradicate the politics of racial domination as they are made manifest in personal interaction.

Mutual recognition of racism, its impact both on those who are dominated and those who dominate, is the only standpoint that makes possible an encounter between races that is not based on denial and fantasy. For it is the ever present reality of racist domination, of white supremacy, that renders problematic the desire of white people to have contact with the Other. Often it is this reality that is most masked when representations of contact between white and non-white, white and black, appear in mass culture. One area where the politics of diversity and its concomitant insistence on inclusive representation have had serious impact is advertising. Now that sophisticated market surveys reveal the extent to which poor and materially underprivileged people of all races/ethnicities consume products, sometimes in a quantity disproportionate to income, it has become more evident that these markets can be appealed to with advertising. Market surveys revealed that black people buy more Pepsi than other soft drinks and suddenly we see more Pepsi commercials with black people in them.

The world of fashion has also come to understand that selling products is heightened by the exploitation of Otherness. The success of Benetton ads, which with their racially diverse images have become a model for various advertising strategies, epitomize this trend. Many ads that focus on Otherness make no explicit comments, or rely solely on visual messages, but the recent fall *Tweeds* catalogue provides an excellent example of the way contemporary culture exploits notions of Otherness with both visual images and text. The catalogue cover shows a map of Egypt. Inserted into the heart of the country, so to speak, is a photo of a white male (an *Out of Africa* type) holding an Egyptian child in his arms. Behind them is not the scenery of Egypt as modern city, but rather shadowy silhouettes resembling huts and palm trees. Inside, the copy quotes Gustave Flaubert's comments from *Flaubert in Egypt*. For seventy-five pages Egypt becomes a landscape of dreams, and its darker-skinned people background, scenery to highlight whiteness, and the longing of whites to inhabit, if only for a time, the world of the Other. The front page copy declares:

> We did not want our journey to be filled with snapshots of an antique land. Instead, we wanted to rediscover our clothing in the context of a different culture. Was it possible, we wondered, to express our style in an unaccustomed way, surrounded by Egyptian colors, Egyptian textures, even bathed in an ancient Egyptian light?

Is this not imperialist nostalgia at its best – potent expression of longing for the "primitive"? One desires "a bit of the Other" to enhance the blank landscape of whiteness. Nothing is said in the text about Egyptian people, yet their images are spread throughout its pages. Often their faces are blurred by the camera, a strategy which ensures that readers will not become more enthralled by the images of Otherness than those of whiteness. The point of this photographic attempt at defamiliarization is to distance us from whiteness, so that we will return to it more intently.

In most of the "snapshots," all carefully selected and posed, there is no mutual looking. One desires contact with the Other even as one wishes boundaries to remain intact. When bodies contact one another, touch, it is almost always a white hand doing the touching, white hands that rest on the bodies of colored people, unless the Other is a child. One snapshot of "intimate" contact shows two women with their arms linked, the way close friends might link arms. One is an Egyptian woman identified by a caption that reads "with her husband and baby, Ahmedio A'bass, 22, leads a gypsy's life"; the second woman is a white-skinned model. The linked hands suggest that these two women share something, have a basis of contact and indeed they do, they resemble one another, look more alike than different. The message again is that "primitivism," though more apparent in the Other, also resides in the white self. It is not the world of Egypt, of "gypsy" life, that is affirmed by this snapshot, but the ability of white people to roam the world, making contact. Wearing pants while standing next to her dark "sister" who wears a traditional skirt, the white woman appears to be cross-dressing (an ongoing theme in *Tweeds*). Visually the image suggests that she and first world white women like her are liberated, have greater freedom to roam than darker women who live peripatetic lifestyles.

Significantly, the catalogue that followed this one focused on Norway. There the people of Norway are not represented, only the scenery. Are we to assume that white folks from this country are as at "home" in Norway as they are here so there is no need for captions and explanations? In this visual text, whiteness is the unifying feature – not culture. Of course, for *Tweeds* to exploit Otherness to dramatize "whiteness" while in Egypt, it cannot include darker-skinned models since the play on contrasts that is meant to highlight "whiteness" could not happen nor could the exploitation that urges consumption of the Other whet the appetite in quite the same way; just as inclusion of darker-skinned models in the Norway issue might suggest that the west is not as unified by whiteness as this visual text suggests. Essentially speaking, both catalogues evoke a sense that white people are homogeneous and share "white bread culture."

Those progressive white intellectuals who are particularly critical of "essentialist" notions of identity when writing about mass culture, race, and gender have not focused their critiques on white identity and the way essentialism informs representations of whiteness. It is always the non-white, or in some cases the non-heterosexual Other, who is guilty of essentialism. Few white intellectuals call attention to the way in which the contemporary obsession with white consumption of the dark Other has served as a catalyst for the resurgence of essentialist based racial and ethnic nationalism. Black nationalism, with its emphasis on black separatism, is resurging as a response to the assumption that white cultural imperialism and white yearning to possess the Other are invading black life, appropriating and violating black culture. As a survival strategy, black nationalism surfaces most strongly when white cultural appropriation of black culture threatens to decontextualize and thereby erase knowledge of the specific historical and social context of black experience from which cultural productions and distinct black styles emerge. Yet most white intellectuals writing critically about black culture do not see these constructive dimensions of black nationalism and tend to see it instead as naive essentialism, rooted in notions of ethnic purity that resemble white racist assumptions.

In the essay "Hip, and the Long Front of Color," white critic Andrew Ross interprets Langston Hughes' declaration ("You've taken my blues and gone – You sing 'em on Broadway – And you sing 'em in Hollywood Bowl – And you mixed 'em up with symphonies – And you fixed 'em – So they don't sound like me. Yet, you done taken my blues and gone.") as a "complaint" that "celebrates . . . folk purism." Yet Hughes' declaration can be heard as a critical comment on appropriation (not a complaint). A distinction must be made between the longing for ongoing cultural recognition of the creative source of particular African American cultural productions that emerge from distinct black experience, and essentialist investments in notions of ethnic purity that undergird crude versions of black nationalism.

Currently, the commodification of difference promotes paradigms of consumption wherein whatever difference the Other inhabits is eradicated, *via* exchange, by a consumer cannibalism that not only displaces the Other but denies the significance of that Other's history through a process of decontextualization. Like the "primitivism" Hal Foster maintains "absorbs the primitive, in part *via* the concept of affinity" contemporary notions of "crossover" expand the parameters of cultural production to enable the voice of the non-white Other to be heard by a larger audience even as it denies the specificity of that voice, or as it recoups it for its own use.

This scenario is played out in the film *Heart Condition* when Mooney, a white racist cop, has a heart transplant and receives a heart from Stone, a black man he has been trying to destroy because Stone has seduced Chris, the white call girl that Mooney loves. Transformed by his new "black heart," Mooney learns how to be more seductive, changes his attitudes towards race, and, in perfect Hollywood style, wins the girl in the end. Unabashedly dramatizing a process of "eating the Other" (in ancient religious practices among so called "primitive" people, the heart of a person may be ripped out and eaten so that one can embody that person's spirit or special characteristics), a film like *Heart Condition* addresses the fantasies of a white audience. At the end of the film, Mooney, reunited with Chris through marriage and surrounded by Stone's caring black kin, has become the "father" of Chris and Stone's bi-racial baby who is dark-skinned, the color of his father. Stone, whose ghost has haunted Mooney, is suddenly "history" – gone. Interestingly, this mainstream film suggests that patriarchal struggle over "ownership" (i.e., sexual possession of white women's bodies) is the linchpin of racism. Once Mooney can accept and bond with Stone on the phallocentric basis of their mutual possession and "desire" for Chris, their homosocial bonding makes brotherhood possible and eradicates the racism that has kept them apart. Significantly, patriarchal bonding mediates and becomes the basis for the eradication of racism.

In part, this film offers a version of racial pluralism that challenges racism by suggesting that the white male's life will be richer, more pleasurable, if he accepts diversity. Yet it also offers a model of change that still leaves a white supremacist capitalist patriarchy intact, though no longer based on coercive domination of black people. It insists that white male desire must be sustained by the "labor" (in this case the heart) of a dark Other. The fantasy, of course, is that this labor will no longer be exacted *via* domination, but will be given willingly. Not surprisingly, most black folks talked about this film as "racist." The young desirable handsome intelligent black male (who we are told *via* his own self-portrait is "hung like a shetland pony") must die so that the aging white male can both restore his potency (he awakens from the transplant to find a replica of a huge black penis standing between his legs) and be more sensitive and loving. Torgovnick reminds readers in *Gone Primitive* that a central element in the western fascination with primitivism is its focus on "overcoming alienation from the body, restoring the body, and hence the self, to a relation of full and easy harmony with nature or the cosmos." It is this conceptualization of the "primitive" and the black male as quintessential representative that is dramatized in *Heart Condition*. One weakness in Torgovnick's work is her refusal to recognize how deeply the idea of the "primitive" is entrenched in the psyches of everyday people, shaping contemporary racist stereotypes, perpetuating racism. When she suggests, "our own culture by and large rejects the association of blackness with rampant sexuality and irrationality, with decadence and corruption, with disease and death," one can only wonder what culture she is claiming as her own.

Films like *Heart Condition* make black culture and black life backdrop, scenery for narratives that essentially focus on white people. Nationalist black voices critique this cultural crossover, its decentering of black experience as it relates to black people, and its insistence that it is acceptable for whites to explore blackness as long as their ultimate agenda is appropriation. Politically "on the case" when they critique white cultural appropriation of black experience that reinscribes it within a "cool" narrative of white supremacy, these voices can not be dismissed as naive. They are misguided when they suggest that white cultural imperialism is best critiqued and resisted by black separatism, or when they evoke outmoded notions of ethnic purity that deny the way in which black people exist in the west, are western, and are at times positively influenced by aspects of white culture.

Steve Perry's essay "The Politics of Crossover" deconstructs notions of racial purity by outlining the diverse inter-cultural exchanges between black and white musicians, yet he seems unable to acknowledge that this reality does not alter the fact that white cultural imperialist appropriation of black culture maintains white supremacy and is a constant threat to black liberation. Even though Perry can admit that successful black crossover artists, such as Prince, carry the "crossover impulse" to the point where it "begins to be a denial of blackness," he is unable to see this as threatening to black people who are daily resisting racism, advocating ongoing decolonization, and in need of an effective black liberation struggle.

Underlying Perry's condescension, and at times contemptuous attitude towards all expressions of black nationalism, is a traditional leftist insistence on the primacy of class over race. This standpoint inhibits his capacity to understand the specific political needs of black people that are addressed, however inadequately, by essenti-alist-based black separatism. As Howard Winant clarifies in "Postmodern Racial Politics in the United States: Difference and Inequality," one must understand race to understand class because "in the postmodern political framework of the contem-porary United States, hegemony is determined by the articulation of race and class." And most importantly it is the "ability of the right to represent class issues in racial terms" that is "central to the current pattern of conservative hegemony." Certainly an essentialist-based black nationalism imbued with and perpetuating many racial stereotypes is an inadequate and ineffective response to the urgent demand that there be renewed and viable revolutionary black liberation struggle that would take radical politicization of black people, strategies of decolonization, critiques of capitalism, and ongoing resistance to racist domination as its central goals.

Resurgence of black nationalism as an expression of black people's desire to guard against white cultural appropriation indicates the extent to which the commodifica-tion of blackness (including the nationalist agenda) has been reinscribed and mar-keted with an atavistic narrative, a fantasy of Otherness that reduces protest to spectacle and stimulates even greater longing for the "primitive." Given this cultural context, black nationalism is more a gesture of powerlessness than a sign of critical resistance. Who can take seriously Public Enemy's insistence that the dominated and their allies "fight the power" when that declaration is in no way linked to a collective organized struggle. When young black people mouth 1960s black nationalist rheto-ric, don Kente cloth, gold medallions, dread their hair, and diss the white folks they hang out with, they expose the way meaningless commodification strips these signs of political integrity and meaning, denying the possibility that they can serve as a catalyst for concrete political action. As signs, their power to ignite critical consciousness is diffused when they are commodified. Communities of resistance are replaced by communities of consumption. As Stuart and Elizabeth Ewen emphasize in *Channels of Desire*:

> The politics of consumption must be understood as something more than what to buy, or even what to boycott. Consumption is a social relationship, the dominant relationship

in our society – one that makes it harder and harder for people to hold together, to create community. At a time when for many of us the possibility of meaningful change seems to elude our grasp, it is a question of immense social and political proportions. To establish popular initiative, consumerism must be transcended – a difficult but central task facing all people who still seek a better way of life.

Work by black artists that is overtly political and radical is rarely linked to an oppositional political culture. When commodified it is easy for consumers to ignore political messages. And even though a product like rap articulates narratives of coming to critical political consciousness, it also exploits stereotypes and essentialist notions of blackness (like black people have natural rhythm and are more sexual). The television show *In Living Color* is introduced by lyrics that tell listeners "do what you wanna do." Positively, this show advocates transgression, yet it negatively promotes racist stereotypes, sexism, and homophobia. Black youth culture comes to stand for the outer limits of "outness." The commercial nexus exploits the culture's desire (expressed by whites and blacks) to inscribe blackness as "primitive" sign, as wildness, and with it the suggestion that black people have secret access to intense pleasure, particularly pleasures of the body. It is the young black male body that is seen as epitomizing this promise of wildness, of unlimited physical prowess and unbridled eroticism. It was this black body that was most "desired" for its labor in slavery, and it is this body that is most represented in contemporary popular culture as the body to be watched, imitated, desired, possessed. Rather than a sign of pleasure in daily life outside the realm of consumption, the young black male body is represented most graphically as the body in pain.

Regarded fetishisticly in the psycho-sexual racial imagination of youth culture, the real bodies of young black men are daily viciously assaulted by white racist violence, black on black violence, the violence of overwork, and the violence of addiction and disease. In her introduction to *The Body in Pain*, Elaine Scarry states that "there is ordinarily no language for pain," that "physical pain is difficult to express; and that this inexpressibility has political consequences." This is certainly true of black male pain. Black males are unable to fully articulate and acknowledge the pain in their lives. They do not have a public discourse or audience within racist society that enables them to give their pain a hearing. Sadly, black men often evoke racist rhetoric that identifies the black male as animal, speaking of themselves as "endangered species," as "primitive," in their bid to gain recognition of their suffering.

When young black men acquire a powerful public voice and presence *via* cultural production, as has happened with the explosion of rap music, it does not mean that they have a vehicle that will enable them to articulate that pain. Providing narratives that are mainly about power and pleasure, that advocate resistance to racism yet support phallocentrism, rap denies this pain. True, it was conditions of suffering and survival, of poverty, deprivation, and lack that characterized the marginal locations from which breakdancing and rap emerged. Described as "rituals" by participants in the poor urban non-white communities where they first took place, these practices offered individuals a means to gain public recognition and voice. Much of the psychic pain that black people experience daily in a white supremacist context is caused by

dehumanizing oppressive forces, forces that render us invisible and deny us recognition. Michael H. (commenting on style in Stuart Ewen's book *All Consuming Images*)
also talks about this desire for attention, stating that breakdancing and rap are a
way to say "listen to my story, about myself, life, and romance." Rap music provides
a public voice for young black men who are usually silenced and overlooked. It
emerged in the streets – outside the confines of a domesticity shaped and informed
by poverty, outside enclosed spaces where young male bodies had to be contained and
controlled.

In its earliest stages, rap was "a male thing." Young black and brown males could
not breakdance and rap in cramped living spaces. Male creativity, expressed in rap and
dancing, required wide-open spaces, symbolic frontiers where the body could do its
thing, expand, grow, and move, surrounded by a watching crowd. Domestic space,
equated with repression and containment, as well as with the "feminine" was resisted
and rejected so that an assertive patriarchal paradigm of competitive masculinity and
its concomitant emphasis on physical prowess could emerge. As a result, much rap
music is riddled with sexism and misogyny. The public story of black male lives
narrated by rap music speaks directly to and against white racist domination, but
only indirectly hints at the enormity of black male pain. Constructing the black male
body as site of pleasure and power, rap and the dances associated with it suggest
vibrancy, intensity, and an unsurpassed joy in living. It may very well be that living on
the edge, so close to the possibility of being "exterminated" (which is how many
young black males feel) heightens one's ability to risk and make one's pleasure more
intense. It is this charge, generated by the tension between pleasure and danger, death
and desire, that Foucault evokes when he speaks of that *complete total pleasure* that is
related to death. Though Foucault is speaking as an individual, his words resonate in a
culture affected by anhedonia – the inability to feel pleasure. In the United States,
where our senses are daily assaulted and bombarded to such an extent that an
emotional numbness sets in, it may take being "on the edge" for individuals to feel
intensely. Hence the overall tendency in the culture is to see young black men as both
dangerous and desirable.

Certainly the relationship between the experience of Otherness, of pleasure and
death, is explored in the film *The Cook, the Thief, His Wife and Her Lover*, which
critiques white male imperialist domination even though this dimension of the movie
was rarely mentioned when it was discussed in this country. Reviewers of the film did
not talk about the representation of black characters, one would have assumed from
such writing that the cast was all white and British. Yet black males are a part of the
community of subordinates who are dominated by one controlling white man. After
he has killed her lover, his blonde white wife speaks to the dark-skinned cook, who
clearly represents non-white immigrants, about the links between death and pleasure.
It is he who explains to her the way blackness is viewed in the white imagination. The
cook tells her that black foods are desired because they remind those who eat them of
death, and that this is why they cost so much. When they are eaten (in the film, always
and only by white people), the cook as native informant tells us it is a way to flirt with
death, to flaunt one's power. He says that to eat black food is a way to say "death, I am
eating you" and thereby conquering fear and acknowledging power. White racism,

imperialism, and sexist domination prevail by courageous consumption. It is by eating the Other (in this case, death) that one asserts power and privilege.

A similar confrontation may be taking place within popular culture in this society as young white people seek contact with dark Others. They may long to conquer their fear of darkness and death. On the reactionary right, white youth may be simply seeking to affirm "white power" when they flirt with having contact with the Other. Yet there are many white youths who desire to move beyond whiteness. Critical of white imperialism and "into" difference, they desire cultural spaces where boundaries can be transgressed, where new and alternative relations can be formed. These desires are dramatized by two contemporary films, John Waters' *Hairspray* and the more recent film by Jim Jarmusch, *Mystery Train*. In *Hairspray*, the "cool" white people, working-class Traci and her middle-class boyfriend, transgress class and race boundaries to dance with black folks. She says to him as they stand in a rat-infested alley with winos walking about, "I wish I was dark-skinned." And he replies, "Traci, our souls are black even though our skin is white." Blackness – the culture, the music, the people – is once again associated with pleasure as well as death and decay. Yet their recognition of the particular pleasures and sorrows black folks experience does not lead to cultural appropriation but to an appreciation that extends into the realm of the political – Traci dares to support racial integration. In this film, the longing and desire whites express for contact with black culture is coupled with the recognition of the culture's value. One does not transgress boundaries to stay the same, to reassert white domination. *Hairspray* is nearly unique in its attempt to construct a fictive universe where white working class "undesirables" are in solidarity with black people. When Traci says she wants to be black, blackness becomes a metaphor for freedom, an end to boundaries. Blackness is vital not because it represents the "primitive" but because it invites engagement in a revolutionary ethos that dares to challenge and disrupt the *status quo*. Like white rappers MC Search and Prime Minister Pete Nice who state that they "want to bring forth some sort of positive message to black people, that there are white people out there who understand what this is all about, who understand we have to get past all the hatred," Traci shifts her positionality to stand in solidarity with black people. She is concerned about her freedom and sees her liberation linked to black liberation and an effort to end racist domination.

Expressing a similar solidarity with the agenda of "liberation," which includes freedom to transgress, Sandra Bernhard, in her new film *Without You I'm Nothing*, also associates blackness with this struggle. In the March issue of *Interview* she says that the movie has "this whole black theme, which is like a personal metaphor for being on the outside." This statement shows that Bernhard's sense of blackness is both problematic and complex. The film opens with her pretending she is black. Dressed in African clothing, she renders problematic the question of race and identity, for this representation suggests that racial identity can be socially constructed even as it implies that cultural appropriation falls short because it is always imitation, fake. Conversely, she contrasts her attempt to be a black woman in drag with the black female's attempt to imitate a white female look. Bernhard's film suggests that alternative white culture derives its standpoint, its impetus from black culture. Identifying herself with marginalized Others, Bernhard's Jewish heritage as well as her sexually ambiguous erotic practices are experiences that already place her outside the mainstream. Yet the film does not clarify the nature of her identification with black culture. Throughout the film, she places herself in a relationship of comparison and competition with black women, seemingly exposing white female envy of black women and their desire to "be" imitation black women; yet she also pokes fun at black females. The unidentified black woman who appears in the film, like a phantom, looking at herself in the mirror has no name and no voice. Yet her image is always contrasted with that of Bernhard. Is she the fantasy Other Bernhard desires to become? Is she the fantasy Other Bernhard desires? The last scene of the film seems to confirm that black womanhood is the yardstick Bernhard uses to measure herself. Though she playfully suggests in the film that the work of black women singers like Nina Simone and Diana Ross is derivative, "stolen" from her work, this inversion of reality ironically calls attention to the way white women have "borrowed" from black women without acknowledging the debt they owe. In many ways, the film critiques white cultural appropriation of "blackness" that leaves no trace. Indeed, Bernhard identifies that she had her artistic beginnings working in black clubs, among black people. Though acknowledging where she is coming from, the film shows Bernhard clearly defining an artistic performance space that only she as a white woman can inhabit. Black women have no public, paying audience for our funny imitations of white girls. Indeed, it is difficult to imagine any setting other than an all black space where black women could use comedy to critique and ridicule white womanhood in the way Bernhard mocks black womanhood.

Closing the scene shrouded in a cloak that resembles an American flag, Bernhard unveils her nearly nude body. The film ends with the figure of the black woman, who has heretofore only been in the background, foregrounded as the only remaining audience watching this seductive performance. As though she is seeking acknowledgment of her identity, her power, Bernhard stares at the black woman, who returns her look with a contemptuous gaze. As if this look of disinterest and dismissal is not enough to convey her indifference, she removes a tube of red lipstick from her purse and writes on the table "fuck Sandra Bernhard." Her message seems to be: "you may need black culture since without us you are nothing, but black women have no need of you." In the film, all the white women strip, flaunt their sexuality, and appear to be directing their attention to a black male gaze. It is this standpoint that the film suggests may lead them to ignore black women and only notice what black women think of them when we are "right up in their face."

Bernhard's film walks a critical tightrope. On one hand it mocks white appropriation of black culture, white desire for black (as in the scene where Bernhard with a blonde white girl persona is seen being "boned" by a black man whom we later find is mainly concerned about his hair – i.e., his own image) even as the film works as spectacle largely because of the clever ways Bernhard "uses" black culture and standard racial stereotypes. Since so many of the representations of blackness in the film are stereotypes it does not really go against the Hollywood cinematic grain. And like the *Tweeds* catalogue on Egypt, ultimately black people are reduced, as Bernhard declares in *Interview*, to "a personal metaphor." Blackness is the backdrop of Otherness she uses to insist on and clarify her status as Other, as cool, hip, and transgressive.

Even though she lets audiences know that as an entertainment "rookie" she had her start working in close association with black people, the point is to name where she begins to highlight how far she has come. When Bernhard "arrives," able to exploit Otherness in a big time way, she arrives alone, not in the company of black associates. They are scenery, backdrop, background. Yet the end of the film problematizes this leave-taking. Is Bernhard leaving black folks or has she been rejected and dismissed? Maybe it's mutual. Like her entertainment cohort Madonna, Bernhard leaves her encounters with the Other richer than she was at the onset. We have no idea how the Other leaves her.

When I began thinking and doing research for this piece, I talked to folks from various locations about whether they thought the focus on race, Otherness, and difference in mass culture was challenging racism. There was overall agreement that the message that acknowledgment and exploration of racial difference can be pleasurable represents a breakthrough, a challenge to white supremacy, to various systems of domination. The over-riding fear is that cultural, ethnic, and racial differences will be continually commodified and offered up as new dishes to enhance the white palate – that the Other will be eaten, consumed, and forgotten. After weeks of debating with one another about the distinction between cultural appropriation and cultural appreciation, students in my introductory course on black literature were convinced that something radical was happening, that these issues were "coming out in the open." Within a context where desire for contact with those who are different or deemed Other is not considered bad, politically incorrect, or wrong-minded, we can begin to conceptualize and identify ways that desire informs our political choices and affiliations. Acknowledging ways the desire for pleasure, and that includes erotic longings, informs our politics, our understanding of difference, we may know better how desire disrupts, subverts, and makes resistance possible. We cannot, however, accept these new images uncritically.

23

The Politics of Representation in Network Television*

Herman Gray

Along with the structural shifts, cultural discourses, and institutional transformations of the television industry, contemporary television representations of blackness are linked to the presence and admittedly limited influence of a small number of highly visible black producers, writers, directors, and on-screen talent in the entertainment industry. Within the institutional constraints and cultural traditions of a collaborative and producer-driven medium such as television, the successes of Bill Cosby, Oprah Winfrey, Stan Lathan, Arsenio Hall, Marla Gibbs, Keenen Ivory Wayans, Stanley Robertson, Kellie Goode, Dolores Morris, Suzanne de Passe, Topper Carew, Frank Dawson, Sherman Hemsley, Quincy Jones, Thomas Carter, Carl Franklin, Michael Warren, Debbie Allen, and Tim Reid increased their individual abilities at studios and the networks to shape the creation, direction, and tone of television representations of African Americans (Gunther 1990; Horowitz 1989; O'Connor 1990; Zook 1994).[1]

Of course, there is nothing particularly remarkable about the presence of black producers, writers, and directors in network television. Indeed, directors and producers Michael Moye, Thomas Carter, Suzanne de Passe, and others have been central to the production of such critically acclaimed programming as *Equal Justice* and *Lonesome Dove* (Gunther 1990).[2] What is remarkable, however, is that these critically and commercially successful shows have not necessarily been organized around black themes and black cultural sensibilities. Television clearly needs more of this kind of black presence.

At the other extreme are television shows that traffic heavily in themes and representations about blacks, but that, by and large, operate under the creative control and direction of white studio and network executives. Successful comedies such as *Sanford & Son*, Norman Lear/Bud Yorkin staples *The Jeffersons* and *Good Times*, and more recent shows such as *Amen* and *227* come immediately to mind. To be sure, these shows employed black writers and actors, and they drew their creative

* From Herman Gray, *Watching Race: Television and the Struggle for "Blackness"* (Minneapolis: University of Minnesota Press, 1995), pp. 70–92.

direction, look, and sensibility from African American culture. But ultimately, the
overall creative responsibility for these shows rested with white executive producers –
Bud Yorkin, Norman Lear, the Carsey-Werner Company, Irma Kalish, Ed Weinber-
ger, and Miller-Boyett Productions (Newcomb and Alley 1983).

In the final analysis, the creative vision of the white producers predominated even if
situations and themes they explored were drawn from African American culture
(Newcomb and Alley 1983; interviews with black writers from *227*, 1990). Although
the programs were shows about blacks (rather than black shows), there were clearly
boundaries concerning cultural representations, social themes, and professional conventions that they dared not transgress. As some of the black television writers from
227 explained to me, the nuances and sensibilities of African American culture that
many of them found funny and attempted to bring to particular scripts or scenes
became points of professional contention or were eliminated because white head
writers and producers thought otherwise.[3] Black writers seldom had the same veto
power over white characters, situations, and themes (interview with writers from *227*,
1990).

For many of the shows based on the situations and experiences of blacks, the
conventions of television production (especially collaborative writing) serve to discipline, contain, and ultimately construct a point of view. Not surprisingly, this point
of view constructs and privileges white middle-class audiences as the ideal viewers and
subjects of television stories. In the producer-driven medium of television, a paucity
of producers of color continues to be the rule. In a 1989 report issued by the
National Commission on Working Women, researcher Sally Steenland (1989) notes
that "minority producers constitute only 7 per cent of all producers working on
shows with minority characters. Minority female producers comprise only 2 per cent
of the total. Of 162 producers working on 30 shows containing minority characters,
only 12 are people of color, while 150 (93 per cent) are white. Of the 12 minority
producers, 8 are male and 4 are female" (p. 11).

African American writers, directors, and producers in the television industry must
still negotiate the rough seas of an institutional and cultural system tightly but subtly
structured by race and gender (Dates 1990).[4] It is all the more remarkable, then, that
a small number of visible and influential black executive producers, directors, and
writers forced open creative spaces within the productive apparatus of television. And
within this discursive and industrial space – between black invisibility and white-
authorized representations of blackness – black producers such as Cosby, Wayans,
Hall, and Jones have had some impact. Rather than simply placing blackness and
black themes in the service of the creative visions of white producers or inserting
blackness within existing aesthetic visions, these producers have helped to challenge
and transform conventional television treatments of blackness by introducing black
viewpoints and perspectives (Hampton 1989). In short, they have introduced different approaches and placed existing aesthetic and production conventions in the
service of blackness and African American cultural perspectives (Gunther 1990;
O'Connor 1990; Ressner 1990). By trying to construct and represent the experiences, nuances, and explicit concerns of African Americans, these producers offer not
only different stories, but alternative ways of negotiating and realizing them. Indeed,

Kristal Brent Zook (1994) argues quite convincingly that in the 1980s and 1990s television has been an especially important discursive and institutional space because it serves as a vehicle for intertextual and autobiographical dialogue for blacks.

In a business long criticized for the absence of people of color in decision-making positions and authority, efforts on the part of black executives to hire and train African Americans are, to say the least, hard to sustain.[5] In terms of hiring, training, and placement of black talent in all phases of the industry, Bill Cosby, Quincy Jones, and Keenen Ivory Wayans have been singled out. For example, Susan Fales, former executive producer of the *The Cosby Show* spinoff, *A Different World*, began her television career in television as an intern with *The Cosby Show* (interview with Susan Fales, 1990).

The impact of this small cohort of influential black producers occasionally, but all too rarely, reaches beyond the generic and thematic boundaries of situation comedy and the thematic dominance of streetwise masculinity that pervades so much of contemporary television representations of blacks. *The Women of Brewster Place, Lonesome Dove,* and *Motown 25: Yesterday, Today, Forever, Polly,* and *The Mary Thomas Story* were all projects created, engineered, or produced by black women: Oprah Winfrey (Harpo Productions), Suzanne de Passe (Motown), and Dolores Morris (Disney Television). As core members of *A Different World*'s production team, black women such as executive producer Susan Fales, director and writer Debbie Allen, and writers Neema Barnette and Yvette Lee were all responsible for the creative look, feel, and direction of the program. As Jacqueline Bobo (1991) points out, these and other black women tell stories about black women that are different from those told by others, and they tell those stories differently. Thus, these black women contribute to the more general project of "fleshing out their female characters to become more multi-dimensional and like actual women and . . . experimenting with important issues and themes" (Steenland 1987: 24).

Like their counterparts in cinema and literature, this recent cohort of black television producers has experienced growing visibility and success that has heightened the expectations of black audiences and critics. These heightened expectations have, in turn, produced conflict among and criticism from African Americans. For instance, heated public criticism has been directed toward Keenen Ivory Wayans, creator and former producer of *In Living Color*, for staging his irreverent humor at the expense of blacks; toward Arsenio Hall for his failure to place more blacks on the staff and technical crew of his late-night talk show; and toward Bill Cosby because his series often failed to address social issues facing black Americans (Braxton 1991; Christon 1989; Collins 1990; Dyson 1989; Fuller 1992; Gray 1989; Jhally and Lewis 1992).

The mere presence of a critical group of successful black producers, directors, and writers has, nevertheless, helped to bring different, often more complex, stories, themes, characters, and representations of blackness to commercial network television. Questions about the continuing presence of racism and sexism in the television industry as well as the social impact and cultural meaning of these stories are ongoing subjects of heated debate and study. The fact remains, however, that the variety and sheer number of stories about blacks proliferated in the 1980s to a degree perhaps unparalleled in the history of television (Siegel 1989a; Waters and Huck 1988).

The Historical and Discursive Formation of Television
Treatments of Blackness

Alone, the argument that television representation of blackness is primarily shaped by changing industrial and market conditions that enabled a small number of black producers, directors, and writers to tell stories about black life from the perspective of blacks is reductionist. To avoid such reductionism, I want to argue also for a reading of the social meaning and cultural significance of television's representations of blackness in terms of their political, historical, and aesthetic relationship to earlier generations of shows about blacks. I contend that contemporary television representations of blacks depend heavily on shows about families, the genre of (black) situation comedy, entertainment/variety programming, and the social issue traditions of Norman Lear (Allen 1987; Dates 1990; MacDonald 1983; Spigel 1992; Taylor 1989).

Ultimately, then, I argue that our contemporary moment continues to be shaped discursively by representations of race and ethnicity that began in the formative years of television (Lipsitz 1990b; Riggs 1991a; Spigel 1992; Winston 1982). The formative period of television and its representation of race and ethnicity in general and blacks in particular is central to my argument in two crucial ways: first, together with dominant representations of blacks in film, radio, the press, and vaudeville, this inaugural moment helped to shape the cultural and social terms in which representations of blacks appeared in mass media and popular culture (Dates 1990); second, as illustrated by Marlon Riggs's (1991a) documentary film, *Color Adjustment*, this formative period is a defining discursive and aesthetic moment that enabled and shaped the adjustments that black representations continue to make. It remains the moment against which all other television representations of blackness have reacted. And it is the defining moment with which subsequent representations, including those in the 1980s and beyond, remain in dialogue (Dates 1990; Riggs 1991b; Taylor 1991; Winston 1982).

In the early 1950s, programs such as *Amos 'n' Andy, Beulah, The Jack Benny Show,* and *Life with Father* presented blacks in stereotypical and subservient roles whose origins lay in eighteenth- and nineteenth-century popular forms (Cripps 1983; Dates 1990; Ely 1991; Winston 1982). Blacks appeared primarily as maids, cooks, "mammies," and other servants, or as con artists and deadbeats. These stereotypes were necessary for the representation and legitimation of a racial order built on racism and white supremacy. Media scholars and historians have clearly established the formative role of radio in the institutional and aesthetic organization of early television (Czitrom 1982). As Winston (1982), Dates and Barlow (1990), and Ely (1991) suggest, the networks, first with radio and later with television shows such as *Beulah, Amos 'n' Andy,* and *The Jack Benny Show*, played an active and crucial role in the construction and representation of blacks in American mass media.[6] In the televisual world of the early 1950s, the social and cultural rules of race relations between blacks and whites were explicit: black otherness was required for white subjectivity; blacks and whites occupied separate and unequal worlds; black labor was always in the service of white domesticity (*The Jack Benny Show, Life with Father, Beulah*); black humor was necessary for the amusement of whites.[7]

Culturally, because blackness served whiteness in this way, the reigning perspective of this world was always staged from a white subject position; when television did venture inside the separate and unfamiliar world of blacks – in, say, *Amos 'n' Andy* – viewers found comforting reminders of whiteness and the ideology of white supremacy that it served: here was the responsible, even sympathetic, black domestic in *Beulah*; there were the responsible but naive members of the world of *Amos 'n' Andy*. But seldom were there representations of the social competence and civic responsibilities that would place any of the black characters from these shows on equal footing with whites (Dates 1990: 204). Black characters who populated the television world of the early 1950s were happy-go-lucky social incompetents who knew their place and whose antics served to amuse and comfort culturally sanctioned notions of whiteness, especially white superiority and paternalism. These black folk could be trusted to manage white households, nurture white children, and "restore balance and normalcy to the [white] household" (Dates 1990: 262), but they could not be trusted with the social and civic responsibilities of full citizenship as equals with whites.

In the racially stratified and segregated social order of the 1950s United States, there was enough about these representations to both comfort and offend. So pervasive and secure was the discourse of whiteness that in their amusement whites were incapable of seeing these shows and the representations they presented as offensive. At the same time, of course, many middle-class blacks were so outraged by these shows, particularly *Amos 'n' Andy*, that the NAACP successfully organized and engineered a campaign in 1953 to remove the show from the air (Cripps 1983; Dates 1990; Ely 1991; Montgomery 1989). As racist and stereotypical as these representations were, the cultural and racial politics they activated were far from simple; many poor, working-class, and even middle-class blacks still managed to read against the dominant discourse of whiteness and find humor in the show. However, because of the charged racial politics between blacks and whites, as well as the class and cultural politics within black America, the tastes, pleasures, and voices in support of the show were drowned out by the moral outrage of middle-class blacks.[8] To be sure, although blacks and whites alike may have found the show entertaining and funny, these pleasures meant different things. They were situated in very different material and discursive worlds. The social issues, political positions, and cultural alliances that shows such as *Amos 'n' Andy* organized and crystallized, then, were powerful and far-reaching in their impact, so much so that I believe that contemporary representations remain in dialogue with and only now have begun to transcend this formative period.[9]

By the late 1950s and throughout the 1960s, the few representations of blacks that did appear on network television offered more benign and less explicitly stereotypical images of African Americans. Shows such as *The Nat "King" Cole Show* (1956–57), *I Spy* (1965–68), and *Julia* (1968–71) attempted to make blacks acceptable to whites by containing them or rendering them, if not culturally white, invisible.[10] In these shows the social and cultural "fact of blackness" was treated as a minor if not coincidental theme – present but contained. In the racially tense and stratified United States of the middle 1960s, Diahann Carroll and Bill Cosby lived and worked in mostly white worlds where whites dare not notice and blacks dare not acknowledge their blackness. Where the cultural and social "fact of blackness" was irrepressible, indeed, central to the aesthetics of a show, it had to be contained. (Whiteness also operated as the dominant and normative place of subjectivity both on and off the screen. In this racialized world of television common sense neither whites nor blacks had any need to acknowledge whiteness explicitly.)

This strategy of containment was used with Nat Cole, the elegant and sophisticated star of *The Nat "King" Cole Show*.[11] An accomplished jazz – read black – pianist, Cole was packaged and presented by NBC to foreground his qualities as a universally appealing entertainer. Cole was the host of a television variety show that emphasized his easy manner and polished vocal style, and the containment of his blackness was clearly aimed to quell white fears and appeal to liberal white middle-class notions of responsibility and good taste. In the social and cultural climate of the times, NBC thought it necessary to separate Cole from any association with the black jazz life (an association made larger than life with the sensational press coverage of Billie Holiday, Charlie Parker, Charles Mingus, and Miles Davis), equating black jazz artists with drugs, sex, rebellion, and social deviance. Despite this cautious strategy, the network's failure to secure national sponsors for the show, especially in the South, resulted in cancellation of *The Nat "King" Cole Show* after only one season. Sanitized and contained representations of blacks in the late 1950s and the 1960s developed in response to the stereotypical images that appeared in the early days of television. They constitute signal moments in discursive adjustment and readjustment of black representations in commercial television (MacDonald 1983; Montgomery 1989; Winston 1982).

Against this discursive backdrop as well as the social rebellions of the 1960s, the representations of black Americans that appeared throughout the 1970s were a direct response to social protest and petititions by blacks against American society in general and the media in particular for the general absence of black representations (MacDonald 1983; Montgomery 1989; Winston 1982). Beginning in 1972, television program makers and the networks produced shows that reached for "authentic" representations of black life within poor urban communities.[12] These programs were created as responses to angry calls by different sectors of the black community for "relevant" and "authentic" images of black people.

It is easy to see now that both the demand for relevant shows and the networks' responses were themselves profoundly influenced by the racial and cultural politics of the period. The new shows offered were designed to contain the anger and impatience of communities on the move politically; program makers, the networks, and "the community" never paused to examine critically the notions of relevance or authenticity. As a visible and polemical site of cultural debate, television moved away from its treatment of blacks in the previous decade. The television programs involving blacks in the 1970s were largely representations of what white liberal middle-class television program makers assumed (or projected) were "authentic" accounts of poor black urban ghetto experiences. *Good Times* (1974–79), *Sanford*

& Son (1972–77), and *What's Happening!!* (1976–79), for example, were all set in poor urban communities and populated by blacks who were often unemployed or underemployed. But more important, for the times, these black folk were good-humored and united in racial solidarity regardless (or perhaps because) of their condition. Ironically, despite the humor and social circumstances of the characters, these shows continued to idealize and quietly reinforce a normative white middle-class construction of family, love, and happiness. These shows implicitly reaffirmed the commonsense belief that such ideals and the values they promote are the rewards of individual sacrifice and hard work.

These themes appeared in yet another signal moment in commercial television representations of African Americans – in the hugely successful miniseries *Roots*. Inhabiting the televisual space explored three years earlier in the miniseries *The Autobiography of Miss Jane Pittman*, *Roots* distinguished itself commercially and thematically as one of the most-watched television shows in history. Based on Alex Haley's book of the same name, *Roots* presented the epic story of the black American odyssey from Africa through slavery to the twentieth century. It brought to millions of Americans, for the first time, the story of the horrors of slavery and the noble struggles of black Americans. This television representation of blacks remained anchored by familiar commitments to economic mobility, family cohesion, private property, and the notion of America as a land of immigrants held together by shared struggles of hardships and ultimate triumph.

There is little doubt that the success of *Roots* helped to recover and reposition television constructions and representations of African Americans and blackness from their historic labors in behalf of white racism and myths of white superiority. But the miniseries also contributed quite significantly to the transformation, in the popular imaginary, of the discourse of slavery and American race relations between blacks and whites. That is to say, with *Roots* the popular media discourse about slavery moved from one of almost complete invisibility (never mind structured racial subordination, human degradation, and economic exploitation) to one of ethnicity, immigration, and human triumph. This powerful television epic effectively constructed the story of American slavery from the stage of emotional identifications and attachments to individual characters, family struggles, and the realization of the American dream. Consequently, the social organization of racial subordination, the cultural reliance on human degradation, and the economic exploitation of black labor receded almost completely from the story. And, of course, this quality is precisely what made the television series such a huge success.

From the distance of some seventeen years, I also want to suggest another less obvious but powerful effect of *Roots*, especially for African American cultural struggles over the sign of blackness. My criticisms of the dominant labors of the series notwithstanding, I want to propose that for an entire generation of young blacks, *Roots* also opened – enabled, really – a discursive space in mass media and popular culture within which contemporary discourses of blackness developed and circulated. I think that it is possible to locate within the media discourse of blackness articulated by *Roots* some of the enabling conditions necessary for the rearticulation of the discourse of Afrocentric nationalism. In other words, I would place *Roots* in dialogue with the reactivation and renewed interest in black studies and the development of African-centered rap and black urban style, especially their contemporary articulation and expression in popular culture and mass media. It seems to me that *Roots* enabled and facilitated the circulation and saturation of the popular imaginary with television representation of Africa and blackness. Finally, relative to the televisual construction of African Americans and blackness in the 1950s and 1960s, *Roots* helped to alter slightly, even momentarily interrupt, the gaze of television's idealized white middle-class viewers and subjects. However minimal, with its cultural acknowledgment of black viewers and subjects, the miniseries enabled a temporary but no less powerful transitional space within which to refigure and reconstruct black television representations.[13]

In black-oriented situation comedies of the late 1970s and early 1980s, especially the long-running *The Jeffersons*, as well as *Benson, Webster, Diff'rent Strokes*, and *Gimme a Break*, black upward social mobility and middle-class affluence replaced black urban poverty as both setting and theme (Gray 1986).[14] Predictably, however, the humor remained. Even though these situation comedies were set in different kinds of "families" – single-parent households, homes with cross-racial adoptions – that were supposed to represent an enlightened approach to racial difference, in the end they too were anchored by and in dialogue with familiar themes and emblems of familial stability, individualism, and middle-class affluence (Gray 1986). Although blackness was explicitly marked in these shows, it was whiteness and its privileged status that remained unmarked and therefore hegemonic within television's discursive field of racial construction and representation (Kelley 1992). As with their predecessors from the 1950s and 1960s, blacks in the shows from the 1970s and early 1980s continued to serve as surrogate managers, nurturers, and objects of white middle-class fascination (Dates 1990; Steenland 1989). Furthermore, as conventional staples of the genre, they required unusual and unfamiliar situations (e.g., black children in white middle-class homes) for thematic structure and comedic payoff. In appearance, this generation of shows seems more explicit, if not about the subject of race, at least about cultural difference. However, because they continued to construct and privilege white middle-class viewers and subject positions, in the end they were often as benign and contained as shows about blacks from earlier decades.

The Cosby Moment

Discursively, in terms of television constructions of blackness, *The Cosby Show* is culturally significant because of the productive space it cleared and the aesthetic constructions of black cultural style it enabled. Pivotal to understanding the social position and cultural significance of contemporary television representations of blackness is what I shall call the Cosby moment. Like the miniseries *Roots, The Cosby Show* reconfigured the aesthetic and industrial spaces within which modern television representations of blacks are constructed.

Indeed, under Bill Cosby's careful guidance the show quite intentionally presented itself as a corrective to previous generations of television representations of black life.

In countless press interviews, Cosby voiced his frustrations with television's representation of blacks. Here is just one:

> Run down what you saw of black people on TV before the Huxtables. You had "Amos 'n' Andy," one of the funniest shows ever, people say. But who ever went to college? Who tried for better things? In "Good Times," J. J. Walker played a definite underachiever. In "Sanford & Son," you have a junk dealer living a few thousand dollars above the welfare level. "The Jeffersons" move uptown. He owns a dry-cleaning store, lives in an integrated neighborhood. Where are the sociological writings about this? (Quoted in Christon 1989: 45)

Positioning *The Cosby Show* in relation to the previous history of programs about blacks helps explain its upper-middle-class focus. More significantly, the show's discursive relationship to television's historical treatment of African Americans and contemporary social and cultural debates (about the black underclass, the black family, and black moral character) helps to explain its insistent recuperation of African American social equality (and competence), especially through the trope of the stable and unified black middle-class family (Dates 1990; Downing 1988; Dyson 1989; Fuller 1992; Jhally and Lewis 1992).

In *The Cosby Show*, blackness, although an element of the show's theme, character, and sensibility, was mediated and explicitly figured through home life, family, and middle-classness. Cosby explained the show's treatment of race: "It may seem I'm an authority because my skin color gives me a mark of a victim. But that's not a true label. I won't deal with the *foolishness* of racial overtones on the show. I base an awful lot of what I've done simply on what people will enjoy. I want to show a family that has a *good* life, not people to be jealous of" (quoted in Christon 1989: 7; emphasis added).[15] The Huxtable family is universally appealing, then, largely because it is a middle-class family that happens to be black (Dates 1990; Dyson 1989; Fuller 1992; Gray 1989; Greenly 1987; Jhally and Lewis 1992).

In an enactment of what Stuart Hall (1981b) calls the "politics of reversals" in black-oriented shows from the 1970s, the merger of race (blackness) and class (poverty) often provided little discursive and textual space for whites and many middle-class blacks to construct meaning for the shows that was not troubling and derisive. *The Cosby Show* strategically used the Huxtables' upper-middle-class status to invite audience identifications across race, gender, and class lines. For poor, working-, and middle-class African Americans, Asian Americans, latinos, and whites it was impossible simply to laugh at these characters and make their blackness an object of derision and fascination. Rather, blackness coexisted in the show on the same discursive plane as their upper-middle-class success (Dyson 1989; Jhally and Lewis 1992).

In this respect, *The Cosby Show* is critical to the development of contemporary television representations of blacks. The show opened to some whites and affirmed for many (though by no means all) blacks a vast and previously unexplored territory of diversity within blackness – that is, upper-middle-class life.[16] On the question of *The Cosby Show*'s importance to the representation of differences within blackness, Michael Dyson (1989) perceptively notes:

> *The Cosby Show* reflects the increasing diversity of African American life, including continuous upward social mobility by blacks, which provides access to new employment opportunities and expands the black middle class. Such mobility and expansion insures the development of new styles for blacks that radically alter and impact African American culture. *The Cosby Show* is a legitimate expression of one aspect of that diversity. Another aspect is the intra-racial class divisions and differentiation introduced as a result of this diversification of African American life. (p. 29)

Discursively, the show appropriated the genre of situation comedy and used it to offer a more complex representation of African American life than had been seen previously.

This ability to organize and articulate different audiences together successfully through televisual representations of upper-middle-class African Americans accounts for *The Cosby Show*'s popularity as well as the criticisms and suspicions it generated (Dyson 1989; Gray 1989; Jhally and Lewis 1992). If, to its credit, the program did not construct a monolithic and one-dimensional view of blackness, then, as Dyson points out, its major drawback was its unwillingness to build on the very diversity and complexity of black life that it brought to television. That is to say, the show seemed unwilling to critique and engage various aspects of black diversity that it visually represented. In particular, *The Cosby Show* often failed even to comment on the economic and social disparities and constraints facing millions of African Americans outside of the middle class.

The show seemed unable, or unwilling, to negotiate its universal appeals to family, the middle class, mobility, and individualism on the one hand and the particularities of black social, cultural, political, and economic realities on the other. While effectively representing middle-class blackness as one expression of black diversity, the show in turn submerged other sites, tensions, and points of difference by consistently celebrating mobility, unlimited consumerism, and the patriarchal nuclear family (Dyson 1989; Gray 1989). Notwithstanding its political and cultural desires, *The Cosby Show* seemed nevertheless underwritten by the racial politics of "unity," which comes at the cost of subordinating key differences within that unity. In the social climate of the Reagan and Bush years and amid debates about affirmative action and the urban underclass, the show as Dyson (1989) puts it,

> presented a black universe as the norm, feeling no need to announce the imposition of African American perspectives since they are assumed. Cosby has shown us that we need not construct the whole house of our life experience from the raw material of our racial identity. And that black folk are interested in issues which transcend race. *However, such coming of age progress should not lead to zero-sum social concerns so that to be aware of race-transcending issues replaces or cancels out concerns about the black poor or issues which generate interracial conflict.* (p. 30; emphasis added)

As Dyson suggests, *The Cosby Show*'s strategic stance on the "foolishness of racial overtones" has its limits. This was made painfully obvious in April 1992 with the entirely coincidental, but no less poignant, juxtaposition of the show's final episode with news coverage of the Los Angeles riots. The televisual landscape that evening dramatically illustrated that no matter how much television tries to manage and smooth them over, conflict, rage, and suspicion based on race and class are central elements of contemporary America. Next to the rage that produced pictures of Los Angeles burning, the representations and expressions of African American life and experience on *The Cosby Show* (and so much of contemporary television) seemed little more than soothing symbolic props required to affirm America's latest illusion of feel-good multiculturalism and racial cooperation.

Many of the same contradictions and labors of blackness found in the representations of African Americans on *The Cosby Show* were also present in other black-oriented shows that appeared in the aftermath of the show's success. *Amen, Homeroom, 227, Snoops, Family Matters*, and *True Colors* all provided familiar (and comfortable) renderings of black middle-class family life in the United States. The cultural traditions and social experiences and concerns of many African Americans, although much more explicit, nevertheless functioned in these programs as comedic devices, to stage the action or signal minor differences. Although often staged from a black normative universe, these shows seldom presented black subjectivities and cultural traditions as alternative perspectives on everyday life.[17] That is to say, as a cultural and experiential referent, blackness was seldom privileged or framed as a vantage point for critical insights, guides to action, or explanations for what happens to African American people in modern American society.

By contrast, *Frank's Place*, some of the programming on the Black Entertainment Television cable network, *A Man Called Hawk*, early programs on *The Arsenio Hall Show, Yo! MTV Raps, Pump It Up, Rap Street, A Different World*, and *In Living Color* often deployed race and class in different ways.[18] As I argue in the remaining chapters, these shows present visions and perspectives in which African American social locations and experiences are more central to the programs' structure and viewpoint. Of course, all of these shows operate squarely within the conventional and aesthetic boundaries of their particular genres – situation comedy, variety, talk, or whatever. But, as I suggest below, in significant respects these shows are different from the others, including *The Cosby Show*. At the same time, however, they are dependent on *Cosby* and the shows that preceded it for representations of black experiences in America. That is, how they construct black subjects can be read only against previous shows. In this respect, I regard *The Cosby Show* as a critically important moment, a transitional point, if you will, in the development of television representations of blacks. *The Cosby Show* and some of the innovative shows that followed it (e.g., *Frank's Place, Roc, A Man Called Hawk*) form part of a continuing discourse of adjustment and dialogue with the history of television representations of blacks.

The Cosby Show's most significant contribution to television's representations of blacks and the ongoing discursive adjustments that are central to such a project has been the way that it repositioned and recoded blackness and black (middle-class) subjectivity within television's own discursive and institutional practices. To be sure, the limitations and criticisms of the show, especially the cultural labors it performed in the rearticulation of a new, more "enlightened" racism, as well as the consolidation of Reaganism on the question of race and morality, must be registered (Gray 1993a;

Jhally and Lewis 1992; Miller 1988). However, coming as it did in the midst of neoconservative assaults, African American cultural debates, and the transformation of the television industry, the show has also had an enabling effect within television. Indeed, *The Cosby Show* itself became the subject of parody and imitation. In its last few seasons the show turned its thematic gaze away from its narrow preoccupation with familial domesticity to pressing social issues, including education and employment, affecting urban black youth.[19]

   For most of its run I remained ambivalent about *The Cosby Show*. As a regular viewer, on many occasions I found pleasures in the predictable humor and identified with the idealizations of family, mobility, and material security represented on the show. I took particular delight in the program's constant attempt to showcase black music and such musicians as John Birks (Dizzy) Gillespie, B. B. King, Mongo Santamaria, and Betty Carter. On the other hand, in my classes, at conferences, and in print I have criticized the show for its idealization of the middle class and its failure to address issues that confront a large number of African Americans. I have often regarded this ambivalence as my unwillingness to stake out a position on the show, to make up my mind. But this unwillingness, I am increasingly convinced, is part of the show's appeal, its complexity in an age of racial and cultural politics where the sign of blackness labors in the service of many different interests at once. As I have been arguing, *The Cosby Show* constructed and enabled new ways of representing African Americans' lives. But within black cultural politics of difference the strategy of staging black diversity within the limited sphere of domesticity and upper-middle-class affluence has its costs.

Discursive Practices and Contemporary Television Representations of Blackness

Having mapped the institutional and discursive history of commercial network television representations of blackness, I now want to suggest that contemporary images of African Americans are anchored by three kinds of discursive practices. I shall refer to these as assimilationist (invisibility), pluralist (separate but equal), and multiculturalist (diversity). In each of these discursive practices, I am interested in how the strategies of signification employed in representative television programs construct, frame, stage, and narrate general issues of race and, more specifically, black subjectivity and presence in contemporary U.S. society.

   These practices are historically and discursively related to one another and to contemporary social discourses about race. Thus, the dominance and primacy of a particular set of images and representations from each of these television constructions and representations of blackness are contingent on the social, technological, and institutional conditions in which they are situated. Through reruns, cable networks, syndication, and independent stations, viewers have virtually unlimited access to the complete body of television representations of blacks. Thus, these programs constitute a vital part of the contemporary television landscape and should be examined by media and television scholars in terms of the shifting meanings and pleasures they offer in our present moment (see Butsch 1990).

Assimilation and the discourse of invisibility

Assimilationist television discourses treat the social and political issues of black presence in particular and racism in general as individual problems. As complex social and political issues, questions of race, gender, class, and power are addressed through the treatment of racism and racial inequality as the results of prejudice (attitudes), and through the foregrounding of the individual ego as the site of social change and transformation. I consider shows assimilationist to the extent that the worlds they construct are distinguished by the complete elimination or, at best, marginalization of social and cultural difference in the interest of shared and universal similarity. These are noble aspirations, to be sure, but such programs consistently erase the histories of conquest, slavery, isolation, and power inequalities, conflicts, and struggles for justice and equality that are central features of U.S. society (see Lipsitz 1990b). Programs organized by such assumptions are framed almost entirely through codes and signifying practices that celebrate racial invisibility and color blindness (see Gray 1986). Beginning with *I Spy* and continuing with *Julia, Mission: Impossible*, and *Room 222*, these early shows integrated individual black characters into hegemonic white worlds void of any hint of African American traditions, social struggle, racial conflicts, and cultural difference.

Contemporary variations on this theme remain with us today. In the 1980s, assimilationist television representations of African Americans could be found in daytime soaps, advertising, and local and network new programs as well as in such prime-time shows as *Family Ties, The Golden Girls, Designing Women, L.A. Law*, and *Night Court*. Without a doubt, some of these shows, including *L.A. Law, The Golden Girls*, and *Designing Women*, featured episodes that explicitly addressed issues of contemporary racial politics, but I nonetheless maintain that where such themes were explicitly addressed they were underwritten and framed by assumptions that privilege individual cooperation and color blindness. In other words, at their best these shows acknowledged but nevertheless framed cultural distinctions and conflicts based on race in ways that ultimately appealed to visions of color blindness, similarity, and universal harmony. In terms of black participation (and inclusion), black characters' acceptance seemed to be inversely related to the degree of separation from black social life and culture. Unique individual black characters (such as Anthony in *Designing Women*) seemed to demonstrate the principle of racial exceptionalism. That is, they seemed to be appealing because of their uniqueness and their neatness of fit into a normative television universe.

Assimilationist programs construct a United States where the historic and contemporary consequences of structured social inequality and a culture deeply inflected and defined by racism are invisible and inconsequential to the lives of its citizens. Seldom on these shows is there ever any sustained engagement with the messiness, confusion, and tension caused by racism and inequality that punctuate the daily experience of so many members of our society. In these televisual worlds American racial progress is measured by the extent to which individual citizens, regardless of color, class, or gender, are the same and are treated equally within the existing social, economic, and cultural (and televisual) order. When they exist, race, class, and gender inequalities seem quite extraordinary, and they always seem to operate at the level of individual experience. Put differently, to the extent that these tensions and conflicts are addressed at all, they figure primarily through individual characters (white and black) with prejudiced attitudes, who then become the focus of the symbolic transformation required to restore narrative balance.

In keeping with television's conventional emphasis on character and dramatic action, assimilationist television discourses locate the origins and operation of prejudiced attitudes at the level of the individual, where they stem from deeply held fears, insecurities, and misunderstandings by individual whites who lack sufficient contact with blacks and other peoples of color. For blacks, on the other hand, they are expressed as the hurts and pains of exclusion that have inevitably hardened into victimization, anger, and irrationality. Typical examples from episodes of *Family Ties* and *The Golden Girls* used the presence of black neighbors and a potential romantic interest, respectively, to identify and draw out white prejudices and suspicions about blacks. In the end, misunderstandings and mistrust were revealed as the source of fear and suspicion. With television's conventional reliance on narrative resolution, once identified, such troubling issues as racial prejudice are easily resolved (or contained) in the space of thirty minutes.

One other characteristic defines shows embedded in an assimilationist discourse: the privileged subject position is necessarily that of the white middle class. That is to say, whiteness is the privileged yet unnamed place from which to see and make sense of the world. This very transparency contributes to the hegemonic status of this televisual construction of whiteness, placing it beyond critical interrogation. Indeed, relative to the hegemonic status that whiteness occupies in this discourse, blackness simply works to reaffirm, shore up, and police the cultural and moral boundaries of the existing racial order. From the privileged angle of their normative race and class positions, whites are portrayed as sympathetic advocates for the elimination of prejudice.

Pluralist or Separate-but-Equal Discourses

Separate-but-equal discourses situate black characters in domestically centered black worlds and circumstances that essentially parallel those of whites. Like their white counterparts, these shows are anchored by the normative ideals of individual equality and social inclusion. In other words, they maintain a commitment to universal acceptance into the transparent "normative" middle class. However, it is a separate-but-equal inclusion. In this television world, blacks and whites are just alike save for minor differences of habit and perspective developed from African American experiences in a homogeneous and monolithic black world. In this televisual black world, African Americans face the same experiences, situations, and conflicts as whites except for the fact that they remain separate but equal.

I have in mind such programs as *Family Matters, 227, Amen*, and *Fresh Prince of Bel Air*; earlier shows with predominantly black casts that currently run in syndication from previous seasons, such as *The Jeffersons, What's Happening!!, Sanford & Son*, and *That's My Mama*; as well as some of the programming featured on Black Entertainment Television.[20] What makes these shows pluralist and therefore different from the assimilationist shows is their explicit recognition of race (blackness) as the basis of cultural difference (expressed as separation) as a feature of US society.[21] As in so much of television, the social and historical contexts in which these acknowledged differences are expressed, sustained, and meaningful are absent. The particularity of black cultural difference is therefore articulated with(in) the dominant historical, cultural, and social discourses about American society. It is possible, then, to recognize, indeed celebrate, the presence of African Americans, latinos, Asians, Native Americans, and women and the particularly distinct tradition, experiences, and positions they represent without disrupting and challenging the dominant narratives about American society. In other words, race as the basis of inequality, conquest, slavery, subordination, exploitation, even social location is eliminated, as are the oppositions, struggles, survival strategies, and distinctive lifeways that result from these experiences. In this manner cultural difference and diversity can be represented, even celebrated, but in ways that confirm and authorize dominant social, political, cultural, and economic positions and relationships. From the separate-but-equal televisual world inaugurated by *Amos 'n' Andy*, a large number of black representations remain separate, even if they have gained, symbolically at least, a measure of equality.

Contemporary black-oriented shows and the representations they offer occupy a discursive space still marked by their relationship to an unnamed but nevertheless hegemonic order. Like assimilationist representations, pluralist representations are constructed from an angle of vision defined by that normative order. The assumptions organizing pluralist representations of black life offer variations and modifications of the representations in the assimilationist paradigm. These shows are also tethered to this hegemonic white middle-class universe in yet another way – through the conventional formulas, genres, codes, and practices that structure their representations. Hence, on the face of it, shows from *227* to *Family Matters* present themes, experiences, and concerns that seem, and in some instances are, "uniquely African American" – for example, the black church (*Amen*) and black women's friendships (*227* and, more recently, *Living Single*). Of course, the images of black life in these shows do represent one mode of black participation in American society. However, representations of blackness in these separate-but-equal worlds depend on an essential and universal black subject for their distinction from and similarity to the normative center. On programs such as *Amen, 227*, and *Family Matters*, black people live out simple and largely one-dimensional lives in segregated universes where they encounter the usual televisual challenges in the domestic sphere – social relations, child rearing, awkward situations, personal embarrassment, and romance.

Culturally, these shows construct a view of American race relations in which conflict, tension, and struggles over power, especially claims on blackness, depend on the logic of a cultural pluralism that requires a homogeneous, totalizing blackness, a blackness incapable of addressing the differences, tensions, and diversities among African Americans (and other communities of color).[22] Shows organized by such pluralist logic seldom, if ever, critique or engage the hegemonic character of (middle-class constructions of) whiteness or, for that matter, totalizing constructions of blackness.

Discursively, the problem of racial inequality is displaced by the incorporation of blacks into that great American stew where such cultural distinctions are minor issues that enrich the American cultural universe without noticeably disturbing the delicate balance of power, which remains unnamed, hidden, and invisible. Obscured are representations of diversity within and among African Americans, as well as the intraracial/ethnic alliances and tensions that also characterize post-civil rights race relations in the United States. Together with assimilationist discourses, these television programs effectively work for some viewers to produce pleasures and identifications precisely because their presence on commercial network television symbolically confirms the legitimacy and effectiveness of the very cultural pluralism on which America's official construction and representation of itself depend. Obscured in the process is the impact (and responses to it) of structured social inequality and the social hierarchies that are structured by it.

Multiculturalism/diversity

I argued earlier in this chapter that *The Cosby Show* reconfigured representations of African Americans in commercial network television. Although this program marked an aesthetic and discursive turn away from assimilationist and pluralist practices, key elements of both continued to structure and organize aspects of *The Cosby Show*, which remained rooted in both sets of discourses. In style and form, the show operated from the normative space of a largely black, often multicultural world that paralleled that of whites. It appealed to the universal themes of mobility and individualism, and it privileged the upper-middle-class black family as the site of social life.

At the same time, the show moved some distance away from these elements through its attempt to explore the interiors of black lives and subjectivities from the angle of African Americans. *The Cosby Show* constructed black Americans as the authors of and participants in their own notion of America and what it means to be American. This transitional moment was most evident in the show's use of blackness and African American culture as a kind of emblematic code of difference.

More central to the transition from assimilationist and pluralist discourses to an engagement with the cultural politics of difference, however, are *Frank's Place* and, more recently, *Roc* and *South Central*. The short-lived *Frank's Place* was coproduced by Tim Reid and Hugh Wilson and aired on the CBS television network during the 1987–88 season. The show was distinguished by its explicit construction and positioning of African American culture at the very center of its social and cultural universe. From this position the show examined everyday life from the perspective of working-class as well as middle-class blacks. It seldom, if ever, adjusted its perspective and its representation of African American cultural experiences to the gaze of an idealized white middle-class audience. The discursive practices that structured *Frank's*

Place (and *Roc*) are also distinguished by an innovative approach to television as a form – the program's explicit attention to African American themes, the use of original popular music from the African American musical tradition (i.e., blues), the blurring of genres (comedy/drama), the lack of closure and resolution, the setting and location, and the use of different visual and narrative strategies (e.g., a cinematic look and feel, lighting, and production style). (In the case of *Roc*, I would add to these the use of live/real-time production.)

In addition to *Frank's Place* I would count some of the very early seasons of *The Arsenio Hall Show*, *A Different World*, and *In Living Color* as representative programs that have explicitly engaged the cultural politics of diversity and multiculturalism within the sign of blackness. Television programs operating within this discursive space position viewers, regardless of race, class, or gender locations, to participate in black experiences from multiple subject positions. In these shows viewers encounter complex, even contradictory, perspectives and representations of black life in America. The guiding sensibility is neither integrationist nor pluralist, though elements of both may turn up. Unlike in assimilationist discourses, there are Black Subjects (as opposed to black Subjects), and unlike in pluralist discourses, these Black Subjects are not so total and monolithic that they become THE BLACK SUBJECT.

The issue of cultural difference and the problem of African American diversity and inclusion form the social ground from which these shows operate. As illustrated by *The Cosby Show*, the discourse of multiculturalism/diversity offers a view of what it means to be American from the vantage point of African Americans. But, unlike *The Cosby Show*, this is not a zero-sum game. The social and cultural terms in which it is possible to be black and American and to participate in the American experience are more open. Although these terms often continue to support a "normative" conception of the American universe (especially in its class and mobility aspirations), in other respects shows such as *Frank's Place* and *Roc* stretch this conception by interrogating and engaging African American cultural traditions, perspectives, and experiences.[23]

In shows that engage cultural politics of difference within the sign of blackness, black life and culture are constantly made, remade, modified, and extended. They are made rather than discovered, and they are dynamic rather than frozen (Hall 1989). Such programs create a discursive space in which subject positions are transgressive and contradictory, troubling, and pleasurable, as are the representations used to construct identity (see Lipsitz 1990b), a space that is neither integrationist nor pluralist – indeed, it is often both at the same time. Not surprisingly, black middle-class cultural perspectives and viewpoints continue to shape and define these shows; however, they are driven less by the hegemonic gaze of whiteness. (This gaze is detectable in the assimilationist attempt to silence cultural difference and in the pluralist attempt to claim that African American cultural experiences are parallel to white immigrant experiences.)

It is not that the representations that appear within this set of discursive practices and strategies simply offer a more culturally satisfying and politically progressive alternative to assimilationist and pluralist discourses. Indeed, they often do not. They do, however, represent questions of diversity within blackness more directly, explicitly, and frequently, and as central features of the programs. As I show in the chapters that follow, *A Different World, Frank's Place, Roc*, and *In Living Color* have consistently and explicitly examined issues of racism, apartheid, discrimination, nationalism, masculinity, color coding, desegregation, and poverty from multiple and complex perspectives within blackness.

In these shows, differences that originate from within African American social and cultural experiences have been not just acknowledged, but interrogated, even parodied as subjects of television. *In Living Color* and *A Different World*, for instance, have used drama, humor, parody, and satire to examine subjects as diverse as Caribbean immigrants, black fraternities, beauty contests, black gay men, the Nation of Islam, Louis Farrakhan, Jesse Jackson, Marion Barry, racial attitudes, hip-hop culture, and white guilt. The richness of African American cultural and social life as well as the experience of otherness that derives from subordinate status and social inequality are recognized, critiqued, and commented on. The racial politics that helps to structure and define U.S. society is never far from the surface.

Watching Television, Seeing Black

In many of the programs located in both pluralist and multiculturalist discourses, African American culture is central to the construction of black subjects as well as program content, aesthetic organization, setting, and narrative. These discourses, especially those that I regard as multiculturalist, operate at multiple levels of class, gender, region, color, and culture, and though fractured and selective, their dominant angle of vision, social location, and cultural context are African American (Fiske 1987; Hall 1980, 1989; Newcomb 1984). In all of the television representations of cultural difference there remains a contradictory character, one where the leaks, fractures, tensions, and contradictions in a stratified multicultural society continue to find expression.

Although contained within the larger hegemonic terms of the dominant American discourse on race and race relations driven by the narrative of inclusion, many of the shows circulating within these various discursive practices provide different representations of African Americans on commercial network television (Hall 1981b). Within commercial television representations of African American culture, the most compelling and powerful representations mark, displace, and disarticulate hegemonic and normative cultural assumptions and representations about America's racial order. At their best, such representations fully engage all aspects of African American life and, in the process, move cultural struggles within television and media beyond limited and narrow questions of positive/negative images, role models, and simple reversals to the politics of representation (Fregoso 1990; Hall 1989).

As I demonstrate in the remaining chapters, contemporary television representations of blackness require a sharper, more engaged analytic focus on the multilayered, dialogic, intertextual, and contradictory character of racial representations in commercial network television. I do not claim, of course, that these representations are inherently resistant or oppositional. The hegemonic terms and effects of racial repre-

sentation are no longer hidden, silenced, and beyond analytic and political interrogation. To make sense of television representations of blackness politically, we must
theorize and understand them in relation to other television representations and to
discourses beyond the television screen. The readings, affirmations, and interrogations that follow attempt just such a critical practice.

Notes ·

1   One of the very specific ways in which the presence of these limited spheres of individual
    influence has been expressed in the organization and production of television programs
    about blacks is through the use of black professionals as consultants and advisers in the
    development of programs featuring blacks. For an interesting discussion of this phenom-
    enon in the cases of women, Mexican Americans, and blacks in television, see Katheryn
    Montgomery's *Target Prime Time* (1989).
2   See Horowitz (1989) for a detailed discussion of the role of black film executives in the
    production of several commercially successful films in the 1980s.
3   In some instances, black actors and actresses exert some influence on the creative vision
    and direction of black representations. These actors and actresses, however, do not or may
    not choose to receive production and writing titles (interview with Marla Gibbs, 1990; see
    also Zook 1994).
4   My interview data confirm observations made by Gitlin (1983), Horowitz (1989), and
    Steenland (1987, 1989).
5   Black studio and network executives with whom I spoke reported that black executives are
    concentrated at the middle levels of the management structure, where they often have the
    power to stop a project, but few are positioned at the very top, where they can "green-
    light" a project (interviews with Stanley Robertson, Dolores Morris, and Frank Dawson,
    1990). See also Horowitz (1989).
6   See *Black Film Review* (1993) for a discussion of the crucial role of black filmmakers such
    as Oscar Micheaux in generating counter-representations of blacks.
7   Also, black women were big, loud, and dark, and fulfilled the role of the nurturing
    caretaker of the white home (e.g., *Beulah*).
8   In 1952, *Amos 'n' Andy* received an Emmy Award nomination (Ely 1991).
9   Many of the criticisms leveled at rap music and programs such as *In Living Color* have their
    roots in the black cultural politics of this period. Concerns about racial embarrassment,
    black perpetuation of stereotypes, and so on were as urgent, especially for the black middle
    class, then as they are now.
10 Another show from the period that followed this pattern for the social construction and
    representation of blackness was *Room 222*.
11 Other variety shows of the period featuring black hosts included *The Leslie Uggams
    Show* (1969), *The Flip Wilson Show* (1970–74), and *The New Bill Cosby Show*
    (1972–73).
12 In the early 1970s, *The Flip Wilson Show*, a comedy-variety show starring comedian Flip
    Wilson, enjoyed a four-year run. The show has been characterized as a breakthrough in
    commercial television because it was the first black-led variety show to rate consistently
    among the top-rated shows in television. This show included, among other things, the
    kind of black-based parody and humor that would reappear in the late 1980s with the
    explosion of black comedy and variety (see Kolbert 1993).

13 See Dates (1990: 257) for an inventory of black-oriented mini-series that aired following the commercial success of *Roots*.

14 *The Jeffersons* originally aired in 1975 and enjoyed a ten-year run. I place the series in relationship to these other programs because of the centrality of the mobility narrative in the show. Discursively, the series is important to the shows set in poverty because it serves to reinforce (rather than simply realize) the mobility myth.

15 African American writers from *227* told me that in the culture of the industry, black-oriented programs that explicitly attempt to address issues of inequality and racism or that seem to have a didactic function are regarded as "message shows." They also suggested that from the perspective of studios and the networks, such shows are perceived as risky and difficult to bring to the screen without stirring up trouble or offending some primary constituent (e.g., producers, networks, advertisers) in the production process (interviews with writers, 1990).

16 *The Arsenio Hall Show* is similar in this respect. The chatty format is really about the class and mobility aspirations of a new generation of young blacks and whites.

17 One of the executive producers at *227* described the show as a "reality-based show about a nice middle-class black family," therefore not a show with "messages or anything of that nature." She also conceded that the primary interest of the show is comedy (interview with Irma Kalish, 1990).

18 During the 1992–93 season, shows such as *Roc* and *Where I Live* continued this approach to programs about blacks.

19 Although designed to showcase the individual stars of the show, aesthetically *The Cosby Show*'s style also moved through subtle but noticeable changes, the most remarkable being the slow evolution of the show's opening strip over successive seasons. The background setting and theme music for the show's opening moved steadily from an empty blue screen (accompanied by jazz) background to a tropical island setting (accompanied by steel pans and Caribbean music) to a graffiti-filled wall on an urban street corner (accompanied by urban-based funk).

20 The continued circulation and availability of many of these older programs through reruns and cable are central to my claim that these programs are structured by pluralist discourses.

21 See Dates and Barlow (1990) for discussion of the formation, operation, and impact of black media organizations and black participation in mass media in the United States.

22 See Fregoso (1990: 264). The special issue of *Cultural Studies* published in October 1990 represents an important intervention by Chicana/o scholars on the issue of identity, racial politics, and cultural representation (Chabram and Fregoso 1990). See also Hall (1988).

23 Paul Gilroy (1991) has written rather persuasively about the cultural impress of blacks in England on the normative notions of what it means to be British, especially black and British. George Lipsitz (1990a) makes a similar argument.

References

Allen, Robert (ed.) (1987) *Channels of Discourse: Television and Contemporary Criticism.* Chapel Hill: University of North Carolina Press.

Bobo, Jacqueline (1991) "Black Women in Fiction and Non-Fiction: Images of Power and Powerlessness," *Wide Angle*, 13, nos. 3–4: 72–81.

Braxton, Greg (1991) "To Him Rap's No Laughing Matter," *Los Angeles Times*, July 14, Calendar, 4, 82, 84.

Butsch, Richard (1990) "Home Video and Corporate Plans: Capital's Limited Power to Manipulate Leisure," pp. 215–35 in Richard Butsch (ed.), *For Fun and Profit: The Transformation of Leisure into Consumption*. Philadelphia: Temple University Press.

Chabram, Angie C., and Rosa Linda Fregoso (eds.) (1990) "Chicana/o Cultural Representations: Reframing Alternative Critical Discourses" [special issue]. *Cultural Studies*, 4 (October).

Christon, Lawrence (1989) "The World According to the Cos," *Los Angeles Times*, December 10, Calendar, 6, 45–7.

Collins, Patricia Hill (1990) *Black Feminist Thought: Knowledge, Consciousness and the Politics of Empowerment*. New York: Routledge.

Cripps, Thomas (1983) "*Amos 'n' Andy* and the Debate over American Racial Integration," pp. 33–54 in John E. O'Connor (ed.), *American History, American Television: Interpreting the Video Past*. New York: Frederick Ungar.

Czitrom, Daniel (1982) *Media and the American Mind: From Morse to McLuhan*. Chapel Hill: University of North Carolina Press.

Dates, Jannette (1990) "Commercial Television," pp. 253–303 in Jannette Dates and William Barlow (eds.), *Split Image: African Americans in the Mass Media*. Washington, D.C.: Howard University Press.

Dates, Jannette, and William Barlow (eds) (1990) *Split Image: African Americans in the Mass Media*. Washington, D.C.: Howard University Press.

Downing, John (1988) "The Cosby Show and American Racial Discourse," pp. 46–74 in G. Smitherman-Donaldson and T. A. Van Dijk (eds.), *Discourse and Discrimination*. Detroit: Wayne State University Press.

Dyson, Michael (1989) "Bill Cosby and the Politics of Race," *Z Magazine*, September, 26–30.

Ely, Melvin Patrick (1991) *The Adventures of Amos 'n' Andy: A Social History of an American Phenomenon*. New York: Free Press.

Fiske, John (1987) *Television Culture*. London: Methuen.

Fregoso, Rosa Linda (1993) *The Bronze Screen: Chicana and Chicano Film Culture*. Minneapolis: University of Minnesota Press.

—— (1990) "*Born in East L.A.*: Chicano Cinema and the Politics of Representation." In Angie C. Chabram and Rosa Linda Fregoso (eds.) Chicana/o Cultural Representations: Reframing Alternative Critical Discourses [special issue], *Cultural Studies*, 4 (October): 264–81.

Fuller, Linda K. (1992) *The Cosby Show: Audiences, Impact, and Implication*. Westport, Conn.: Greenwood.

Gilrey, Paul (1991) *There Ain't No Black in the Union Jack: The Cultural Politics of Race and Nation*. Chicago: University of Chicago Press.

Gitlin, Todd (1983) *Inside Prime Time*. New York: Pantheon.

Gray, Herman (1993) "African American Political Desire and the Seductions of Contemporary Cultural Politics," *Cultural Studies*, 7: 364–74.

—— (1989) "Television, Black Americans and the American Dream," *Critical Studies in Mass Communication*, 6: 376–87.

—— (1986) "Television and the New Black Man: Black Male Images in Prime Time Situation Comedy," *Media, Culture and Society*, 8: 223–43.

Greenly, Andrew (1987) "Today's Morality Play: The Sitcom," *New York Times*, May 17, Arts and Leisure, 1, 40.

Gunther, Marc (1990) "Black Producers Add a Fresh Nuance," *New York Times*, August 26, Arts and Leisure, 25, 31.

Hall, Stuart (1989) "Cultural Identity and Cinematic Representation," *Framework*, 36: 68–82.

—— (1988) "Toad in the Garden: Thatcher among the Theorists." In Cary Nelson and Lawrence Grossberg (eds.), *Marxism and the Interpretation of Culture*. Urbana: University of Illinois Press.

——(1981a) "Notes on Deconstructing the Popular." In Raphael Samuel (ed.), *People's History and Socialist Theory*. London: Routledge & Kegan Paul.

——(1981b) "Whites of Their Eyes: Racist Ideology and the Media." In George Bridges and Rosalind Brunt (eds.), *Silver Linings*. London: Lawrence & Wishart.

——(1980) "Encoding/Decoding." In S. Hall et al. (eds.), *Culture, Media, Language*. London: Hutchinson.

Hampton, Henry (1989) "The Camera Lens as Two-Edged Sword," *New York Times*, January 15, H29, H37.

Horowitz, Jay (1989) "Hollywood's Dirty Little Secret," *Premiere*, March, 56, 59–64.

Jhally, Sut, and Justin Lewis (1992) *Enlightened Racism: The Cosby Show, Audiences, and the Myth of the American Dream*. Boulder, Col.: Westview.

Kelley, Robin (1992) "Notes on Deconstructing "the Folk,"" *American Historical Review*, 97: 1400–1406.

Kolbert, Elizabeth (1993) "From "Beulah" to Oprah: The Evolution of Black Images on TV," *New York Times*, January 15, B4.

Lipsitz, George (1990a) "Listening to Learn and Learning to Listen: Popular Culture, Cultural Theory, and American Studies," *American Quarterly*, 42: 615–37.

——(1990b) *Time Passages: Collective Memory and American Popular Culture*. Minneapolis: University of Minnesota Press.

MacDonald, J. Fred (1983) *Blacks and White TV: Afro-Americans in Television since 1948*. Chicago: Nelson-Hall.

Miller, Mark (1988) "Cosby Knows Best." In Mark Crispin Miller (ed.), *Boxed In: The Culture of TV*. Evanston, Ill.: Northwestern University Press.

Montgomery, Katheryn (1989) *Target Prime Time*. New York: Oxford University Press.

Newcomb, Horace (1984) "On the Dialogic Aspects of Mass Communication," *Critical Studies in Mass Communication*, 1: 34–50.

Newcomb, Horace, and Robert S. Alley (1983) *The Producer's Medium: Conversations with Creators of American TV*. New York: Oxford University Press.

O'Connor, John (1990) "On TV Less Separate, More Equal," *New York Times*, April 29, sec. 2, pp. 1, 35.

Ressner, Jeffrey (1990) "Off-Color TV," *Rolling Stone*, August 23, 50.

Riggs, Marlon (1991a) *Color Adjustment* (film). San Francisco: California Newsreel.

——(1991b) "Confessions of a Snap Queen." In Valerie Smith, C. Billops, and A. Griffin (eds.) [special issue], *Black American Literature Forum*, 25, no. 2.

Siegel, Ed (1989) "The Networks Go Ethnic," *Boston Globe*, September 16, Living/Arts, 7, 14.

Spigel, Lynn (1992) *Make Room for TV: Television and the Family Ideal in Postwar America*. Chicago: University of Chicago Press.

Steenland, Sally (1989) *Unequal Picture: Black, Hispanic, Asian, and Native American Characters on Television*. Washington, D.C.: National Commission on Working Women.

—— (1987) *Prime Time Power: Women Producers, Writers, and Directors in TV.* Washington, D.C.: National Commission on Working Women.

Taylor Clyde (1991) "The Rebirth of the Aesthetic in Cinema." In Manthia Diawara (ed.), Black Cinema [special issue], *Wide Angle*, 13, nos. 3–4, 12–30.

Taylor, Ella (1989) *Prime-Time Families: Television Culture in Postwar America.* Berkeley: University of California Press.

Waters, Harry F., and Janet Huck (1988) "TV's New Racial Hue," *Newsweek*, January 25, 52–4.

Winston, Michael R. (1982) "Racial Consciousness and the Evolution of Mass Communication in the United States," *Daedalus*, 111: 171–82.

Zook, Kristal Brent (1994) "How I Became the Prince of a Town Called Bel Air: Nationalist Desire in Black Television." Doctoral dissertation, University of California, Santa Cruz.

24

Under Western Eyes: Feminist Scholarship and Colonial Discourses*

Chandra Talpade Mohanty

Any discussion of the intellectual and political construction of "third world feminisms" must address itself to two simultaneous projects: the internal critique of hegemonic "Western" feminisms, and the formulation of autonomous, geographically, historically, and culturally grounded feminist concerns and strategies. The first project is one of deconstructing and dismantling; the second, one of building and constructing. While these projects appear to be contradictory, the one working negatively and the other positively, unless these two tasks are addressed simultaneously, "third world" feminisms run the risk of marginalization or ghettoization from both mainstream (right and left) and Western feminist discourses.

It is to the first project that I address myself. What I wish to analyze is specifically the production of the "third world woman" as a singular monolithic subject in some recent (Western) feminist texts. The definition of colonization I wish to invoke here is a predominantly *discursive* one, focusing on a certain mode of appropriation and codification of "scholarship" and "knowledge" about women in the third world by particular analytic categories employed in specific writings on the subject which take as their referent feminist interests as they have been articulated in the U.S. and Western Europe. If one of the tasks of formulating and understanding the locus of "third world feminisms" is delineating the way in which it resists and *works against* what I am referring to as "Western feminist discourse," an analysis of the discursive construction of "third world women" in Western feminism is an important first step.

Clearly Western feminist discourse and political practice is neither singular nor homogeneous in its goals, interests, or analyses. However, it is possible to trace a coherence of *effects* resulting from the implicit assumption of "the West" (in all its complexities and contradictions) as the primary referent in theory and praxis. My reference to "Western feminism" is by no means intended to imply that it is a

* From Chandra Talpade Mohanty, Ann Russo, and Lourdes Torres (eds.), *Third World Women and the Politics of Feminism* (Bloomington, Ind.: Indiana University Press, 1991), pp. 51–80.

monolith. Rather, I am attempting to draw attention to the similar effects of various textual strategies used by writers which codify Others as non-Western and hence themselves as (implicitly) Western. It is in this sense that I use the term *Western feminist*. Similar arguments can be made in terms of middle-class urban African or Asian scholars producing scholarship on or about their rural or working-class sisters which assumes their own middle-class cultures as the norm, and codifies working-class histories and cultures as Other. Thus, while this essay focuses specifically on what I refer to as "Western feminist" discourse on women in the third world, the critiques I offer also pertain to third world scholars writing about their own cultures, which employ identical analytic strategies.

It ought to be of some political significance, at least, that the term *colonization* has come to denote a variety of phenomena in recent feminist and left writings in general. From its analytic value as a category of exploitative economic exchange in both traditional and contemporary Marxisms (cf. particularly contemporary theorists such as Baran 1962, Amin 1977, and Gunder-Frank 1967) to its use by feminist women of color in the U.S. to describe the appropriation of their experiences and struggles by hegemonic white women's movements (cf. especially Moraga and Anzaldúa 1983; Smith 1983; Joseph and Lewis 1981; and Moraga 1984), colonization has been used to characterize everything from the most evident economic and political hierarchies to the production of a particular cultural discourse about what is called the "third world."[1] However sophisticated or problematical its use as an explanatory construct, colonization almost invariably implies a relation of structural domination, and a suppression – often violent – of the heterogeneity of the subject(s) in question.

My concern about such writings derives from my own implication and investment in contemporary debates in feminist theory, and the urgent political necessity (especially in the age of Reagan/Bush) of forming strategic coalitions across class, race, and national boundaries. The analytic principles discussed below serve to distort Western feminist political practices, and limit the possibility of coalitions among (usually white) Western feminists and working-class feminists and feminists of color around the world. These limitations are evident in the construction of the (implicitly consensual) priority of issues around which apparently *all* women are expected to organize. The necessary and integral connection between feminist scholarship and feminist political practice and organizing determines the significance and status of Western feminist writings on women in the third world, for feminist scholarship, like most other kinds of scholarship, is not the mere production of knowledge about a certain subject. It is a directly political and discursive *practice* in that it is purposeful and ideological. It is best seen as a mode of intervention into particular hegemonic discourses (for example, traditional anthropology, sociology, literary criticism, etc.); it is a political praxis which counters and resists the totalizing imperative of age-old "legitimate" and "scientific" bodies of knowledge. Thus, feminist scholarly practices (whether reading, writing, critical, or textual) are inscribed in relations of power – relations which they counter, resist, or even perhaps implicitly support. There can, of course, be no apolitical scholarship.

The relationship between "Woman" – a cultural and ideological composite Other constructed through diverse representational discourses (scientific, literary, juridical, linguistic, cinematic, etc.) – and "women" – real, material subjects of their collective histories – is one of the central questions the practice of feminist scholarship seeks to address. This connection between women as historical subjects and the re-presenta-tion of Woman produced by hegemonic discourses is not a relation of direct identity, or a relation of correspondence or simple implication.[2] It is an arbitrary relation set up by particular cultures. I would like to suggest that the feminist writings I analyze here discursively colonize the material and historical heterogeneities of the lives of women in the third world, thereby producing/re-presenting a composite, singular "third world woman" – an image which appears arbitrarily constructed, but nevertheless carries with it the authorizing signature of Western humanist discourse.[3]

I argue that assumptions of privilege and ethnocentric universality, on the one hand, and inadequate self-consciousness about the effect of Western scholarship on the "third world" in the context of a world system dominated by the West, on the other, characterize a sizable extent of Western feminist work on women in the third world. An analysis of "sexual difference" in the form of a cross-culturally singular, monolithic notion of patriarchy or male dominance leads to the construction of a similarly reductive and homogeneous notion of what I call the "third world differ-ence" – that stable, ahistorical something that apparently oppresses most if not all the women in these countries. And it is in the production of this "third world difference" that Western feminisms appropriate and "colonize" the constitutive complexities which characterize the lives of women in these countries. It is in this process of discursive homogenization and systematization of the oppression of women in the third world that power is exercised in much of recent Western feminist discourse, and this power needs to be defined and named.

In the context of the West's hegemonic position today, of what Anouar Abdel-Malek (1981) calls a struggle for "control over the orientation, regulation and decision of the process of world development on the basis of the advanced sector's monopoly of scientific knowledge and ideal creativity," Western feminist scholarship on the third world must be seen and examined precisely in terms of its inscription in these particular relations of power and struggle. There is, it should be evident, no universal patriarchal framework which this scholarship attempts to counter and resist – unless one posits an international male conspiracy or a monolithic, ahistorical power structure. There is, however, a particular world balance of power within which any analysis of culture, ideology, and socioeconomic conditions necessarily has to be situated. Abdel-Malek is useful here, again, in reminding us about the inherence of politics in the discourses of "culture":

> Contemporary imperialism is, in a real sense, a hegemonic imperialism, exercising to a maximum degree a rationalized violence taken to a higher level than ever before – through fire and sword, but also through the attempt to control hearts and minds. For its content is defined by the combined action of the military-industrial complex and the hegemonic cultural centers of the West, all of them founded on the advanced levels of development attained by monopoly and finance capital, and supported by the benefits of both the scientific and technological revolution and the second industrial revolution itself. (145–46)

Western feminist scholarship cannot avoid the challenge of situating itself and examining its role in such a global economic and political framework. To do any less would be to ignore the complex interconnections between first and third world economies and the profound effect of this on the lives of women in all countries. I do not question the descriptive and informative value of most Western feminist writings on women in the third world. I also do not question the existence of excellent work which does not fall into the analytic traps with which I am concerned. In fact I deal with an example of such work later on. In the context of an overwhelming silence about the experiences of women in these countries, as well as the need to forge international links between women's political struggles, such work is both pathbreaking and absolutely essential. However, it is both to the *explanatory potential* of particular analytic strategies employed by such writing, and to their *political effect* in the context of the hegemony of Western scholarship that I want to draw attention here. While feminist writing in the U.S. is still marginalized (except from the point of view of women of color addressing privileged white women), Western feminist writing on women in the third world must be considered in the context of the global hegemony of Western scholarship – i.e., the production, publication, distribution, and consumption of information and ideas. Marginal or not, this writing has political effects and implications beyond the immediate feminist or disciplinary audience. One such significant effect of the dominant "representations" of Western feminism is its conflation with imperialism in the eyes of particular third world women.[4] Hence the urgent need to examine the *political* implications of our *analytic* strategies and principles.

My critique is directed at three basic analytic principles which are present in (Western) feminist discourse on women in the third world. Since I focus primarily on the Zed Press Women in the Third World series, my comments on Western feminist discourse are circumscribed by my analysis of the texts in this series.[5] This is a way of focusing my critique. However, even though I am dealing with feminists who identify themselves as culturally or geographically from the "West," as mentioned earlier, what I say about these presuppositions or implicit principles holds for anyone who uses these methods, whether third world women in the West, or third world women in the third world writing on these issues and publishing in the West. Thus, I am not making a culturalist argument about ethnocentrism; rather, I am trying to uncover how ethnocentric universalism is produced in certain analyses. As a matter of fact, my argument holds for any discourse that sets up its own authorial subjects as the implicit referent, i.e., the yardstick by which to encode and represent cultural Others. It is in this move that power is exercised in discourse.

The first analytic presupposition I focus on is involved in the strategic location of the category "women" vis-à-vis the context of analysis. The assumption of women as an already constituted, coherent group with identical interests and desires, regardless of class, ethnic or racial location, or contradictions, implies a notion of gender or sexual difference or even patriarchy which can be applied universally and cross-culturally. (The context of analysis can be anything from kinship structures and the organization of labor to media representations.) The second analytical presupposition is evident on the methodological level, in the uncritical way "proof" of universality and cross-cultural validity are provided. The third is a more specifically political presupposition underlying the methodologies and the analytic strategies, i.e., the model of power and struggle they imply and suggest. I argue that as a result of the two modes – or, rather, frames – of analysis described above, a homogeneous notion of the oppression of women as a group is assumed, which, in turn, produces the image of an "average third world woman." This average third world woman leads an essentially truncated life based on her feminine gender (read: sexually constrained) and her being "third world" (read: ignorant, poor, uneducated, tradition-bound, domestic, family-oriented, victimized, etc.). This, I suggest, is in contrast to the (implicit) self-representation of Western women as educated, as modern, as having control over their own bodies and sexualities, and the freedom to make their own decisions.

The distinction between Western feminist re-presentation of women in the third world and Western feminist self-presentation is a distinction of the same order as that made by some Marxists between the "maintenance" function of the housewife and the real "productive" role of wage labor, or the characterization by developmentalists of the third world as being engaged in the lesser production of "raw materials" in contrast to the "real" productive activity of the first world. These distinctions are made on the basis of the privileging of a particular group as the norm or referent. Men involved in wage labor, first world producers, and, I suggest, Western feminists who sometimes cast third world women in terms of "ourselves undressed" (Michelle Rosaldo's [1980] term), all construct themselves as the normative referent in such a binary analytic.

"Women" as Category of Analysis, or: We Are All Sisters in Struggle

By women as a category of analysis, I am referring to the crucial assumption that all of us of the same gender, across classes and cultures, are somehow socially constituted as a homogeneous group identified prior to the process of analysis. This is an assumption which characterizes much feminist discourse. The homogeneity of women as a group is produced not on the basis of biological essentials but rather on the basis of secondary sociological and anthropological universals. Thus, for instance, in any given piece of feminist analysis, women are characterized as a singular group on the basis of a shared oppression. What binds women together is a sociological notion of the "sameness" of their oppression. It is at this point that an elision takes place between "women" as a discursively constructed group and "women" as material subjects of their own history.[6] Thus, the discursively consensual homogeneity of "women" as a group is mistaken for the historically specific material reality of groups of women. This results in an assumption of women as an always already constituted group, one which has been labeled "powerless," "exploited," "sexually harassed," etc., by feminist scientific, economic, legal, and sociological discourses. (Notice that this is quite similar to sexist discourse labeling women weak, emotional, having math anxiety, etc.) This focus is not on uncovering the material and ideological specificities that constitute a particular group of women as "powerless" in a particular context. It is, rather, on finding a variety of cases of "powerless" groups of women to prove the general point that women as a group are powerless.

In this section I focus on five specific ways in which "women" as a category of analysis is used in Western feminist discourse on women in the third world. Each of these examples illustrates the construction of "third world women" as a homogeneous "powerless" group often located as implicit *victims* of particular socioeconomic systems. I have chosen to deal with a variety of writers – from Fran Hosken, who writes primarily about female genital mutilation, to writers from the Women in International Development school, who write about the effect of development policies on third world women for both Western and third world audiences. The similarity of assumptions about "third world women" in all these texts forms the basis of my discussion. This is not to equate all the texts that I analyze, nor is it to equalize their strengths and weaknesses. The authors I deal with write with varying degrees of care and complexity; however, the *effect* of their representation of third world women is a coherent one. In these texts women are defined as victims of male violence (Fran Hosken); victims of the colonial process (Maria Cutrufelli); victims of the Arab familial system (Juliette Minces); victims of the economic development process (Beverley Lindsay and the [liberal] WID School); and finally, victims of *the* Islamic code (Patricia Jeffery). This mode of defining women primarily in terms of their *object status* (the way in which they are affected or not affected by certain institutions and systems) is what characterizes this particular form of the use of "women" as a category of analysis. In the context of Western women writing/studying women in the third world, such objectification (however benevolently motivated) needs to be both named and challenged. As Valerie Amos and Pratibha Parmar argue quite eloquently, "Feminist theories which examine our cultural practices as "feudal residues" or label us "traditional," also portray us as politically immature women who need to be versed and schooled in the ethos of Western feminism. They need to be continually challenged..." (1984, 7).

Women as Victims of Male Violence

Fran Hosken, in writing about the relationship between human rights and female genital mutilation in Africa and the Middle East, bases her whole discussion/condemnation of genital mutilation on one privileged premise: that the goal of this practice is "to mutilate the sexual pleasure and satisfaction of woman" (1981: 11). This, in turn, leads her to claim that woman's sexuality is controlled, as is her reproductive potential. According to Hosken, "male sexual politics" in Africa and around the world "share the same political goal: to assure female dependence and subservience by any and all means" (14). Physical violence against women (rape, sexual assault, excision, infibulation, etc.) is thus carried out "with an astonishing consensus among men in the world" (14). Here, women are defined consistently as the *victims* of male control – the "sexually oppressed."[7] Although it is true that the potential of male violence against women circumscribes and elucidates their social position to a certain extent, defining women as archetypal victims freezes them into "objects-who-defend-themselves," men into "subjects-who-perpetrate-violence," and (every) society into powerless (read: women) and powerful (read: men) groups of people. Male violence must be theorized and interpreted *within* specific societies, in order both to understand it better and to effectively organize to change it.[8] Sisterhood cannot be assumed on the basis of gender; it must be forged in concrete historical and political practice and analysis.

Women as Universal Dependents

Beverly Lindsay's conclusion to the book *Comparative Perspectives of Third World Women: The Impact of Race, Sex and Class* (1983: 298, 306) states: "dependency relationships, based upon race, sex and class, are being perpetuated through social, educational, and economic institutions. These are the linkages among Third World Women." Here, as in other places, Lindsay implies that third world women constitute an identifiable group purely on the basis of shared dependencies. If shared dependencies were all that was needed to bind us together as a group, third world women would always be seen as an apolitical group with no subject status. Instead, if anything, it is the *common context* of political struggle against class, race, gender, and imperialist hierarchies that may constitute third world women as a strategic group at this historical juncture. Lindsay also states that linguistic and cultural differences exist between Vietnamese and black American women, but "both groups are victims of race, sex, and class." Again black and Vietnamese women are characterized by their victim status.

Similarly, examine statements such as "My analysis will start by stating that all African women are politically and economically dependent" (Cutrufelli 1983: 13), "Nevertheless, either overtly or covertly, prostitution is still the main if not the only source of work for African women" (Cutrufelli 1983: 33). *All* African women are dependent. Prostitution is the only work option for African women as a *group*. Both statements are illustrative of generalizations sprinkled liberally through a recent Zed Press publication, *Women of Africa: Roots of Oppression*, by Maria Rosa Cutrufelli, who is described on the cover as an Italian writer, sociologist, Marxist, and feminist. In the 1980s, is it possible to imagine writing a book entitled *Women of Europe: Roots of Oppression*? I am not objecting to the use of universal groupings for descriptive purposes. Women from the continent of Africa can be descriptively characterized as "women of Africa." It is when "women of Africa" becomes a homogeneous sociological grouping characterized by common dependencies or powerlessness (or even strengths) that problems arise – we say too little and too much at the same time.

This is because descriptive gender differences are transformed into the division between men and women. Women are constituted as a group via dependency relationships vis-à-vis men, who are implicitly held responsible for these relationships. When "women of Africa" as a group (versus "men of Africa" as a group?) are seen as a group precisely because they are generally dependent and oppressed, the analysis of specific historical differences becomes impossible, because reality is always apparently structured by divisions – two mutually exclusive and jointly exhaustive groups, the victims and the oppressors. Here the sociological is substituted for the biological, in order, however, to create the same – a unity of women. Thus, it is not the descriptive potential of gender difference but the privileged positioning and explanatory potential of gender difference as the *origin* of oppression that I question. In using "women of Africa" (as an already constituted group of oppressed peoples) as a category of analysis, Cutrufelli denies any historical specificity to the location of women as subordinate, powerful, marginal, central, or otherwise, vis-à-vis particular social and power networks. Women are taken as a unified "powerless" group prior to the analysis in question Thus, it is then merely a matter of specifying the context *after the fact*. "Women" are now placed in the context of the family, or in the workplace, or within religious networks, almost as if these systems existed outside the relations of women with other women, and women with men.

The problem with this analytic strategy, let me repeat, is that it assumes men and women are already constituted as sexual-political subjects prior to their entry into the arena of social relations. Only if we subscribe to this assumption is it possible to undertake analysis which looks at the "effects" of kinship structures, colonialism, organization of labor, etc., on women, who are defined in advance as a group. The crucial point that is forgotten is that women are produced through these very relations as well as being implicated in forming these relations. As Michelle Rosaldo argues, "woman's place in human social life is not in any direct sense a product of the things she does (or even less, a function of what, biologically, she is) but the meaning her activities acquire through concrete social interactions" (1980: 400). That women mother in a variety of societies is not as significant as the value attached to mothering in these societies. The distinction between the act of mothering and the status attached to it is a very important one – one that needs to be stated and analyzed contextually.

Married Women as Victims of the Colonial Process

In Lévi-Strauss's theory of kinship structure as a system of the exchange of women, what is significant is that exchange itself is not constitutive of the subordination of women; women are not subordinate because of the *fact* of exchange, but because of the *modes* of exchange instituted, and the values attached to these modes. However, in discussing the marriage ritual of the Bemba, a Zambian matrilocal, matrilineal people, Cutrufelli in *Women of Africa* focuses on the fact of the marital exchange of women before and after Western colonization, rather than the value attached to this exchange in this particular context. This leads to her definition of Bemba women as a coherent group affected in a particular way by colonization. Here again, Bemba women are constituted rather unilaterally as victims of the effects of Western colonization.

Cutrufelli cites the marriage ritual of the Bemba as a multistage event "whereby a young man becomes incorporated into his wife's family group as he takes up residence with them and gives his services in return for food and maintenance" (43). This ritual extends over many years, and the sexual relationship varies according to the degree of the girl's physical maturity. It is only after she undergoes an initiation ceremony at puberty that intercourse is sanctioned, and the man acquires legal rights over her. This initiation ceremony is the more important act of the consecration of women's reproductive power, so that the abduction of an uninitiated girl is of no consequence, while heavy penalty is levied for the seduction of an initiated girl. Cutrufelli asserts that the effect of European colonization has changed the whole marriage system. Now the young man is entitled to take his wife away from her people in return for money. The implication is that Bemba women have now lost the protection of tribal laws. However, while it is possible to see how the structure of the traditional marriage contract (versus the postcolonial marriage contract) offered women a certain amount of control over their marital relations, only an analysis of the political significance of the actual practice which privileges an initiated girl over an uninitiated one, indicating a shift in female power relations as a result of this ceremony, can provide an accurate account of whether Bemba women were indeed protected by tribal laws *at all times*.

However, it is not possible to talk about Bemba women as a homogeneous group within the traditional marriage structure. Bemba women *before* the initiation are constituted within a different set of social relations compared to Bemba women *after* the initiation. To treat them as a unified group characterized by the fact of their "exchange" between male kin is to deny the sociohistorical and cultural specificities of their existence, and the differential *value* attached to their exchange before and after their initiation. It is to treat the initiation ceremony as a ritual with no political implications or effects. It is also to assume that in merely describing the *structure* of the marriage contract, the situation of women is exposed. Women as a group are positioned within a given structure, but there is no attempt made to trace the effect of the marriage practice in constituting women within an obviously changing network of power relations. Thus, women are assumed to be sexual-political subjects prior to entry into kinship structures.

Women and Familial Systems

Elizabeth Cowie (1978), in another context, points out the implications of this sort of analysis when she emphasizes the specifically political nature of kinship structures which must be analyzed as ideological practices which designate men and women as father, husband, wife, mother, sister, etc. Thus, Cowie suggests, women as women are not *located* within the family. Rather, it is *in* the family, as an effect of kinship structures, that women as women are *constructed*, defined within and by the group. Thus, for instance, when Juliette Minces (1980) cites *the* patriarchal family as the basis for "an almost identical vision of women" that Arab and Muslim societies have, she falls into this very trap (see especially p. 23). Not only is it problematical to speak of a vision of women shared by Arab and Muslim societies (i.e., over twenty different countries) without addressing the particular historical, material, and ideological power structures that construct such images, but to speak of the patriarchal family or the tribal kinship structure as the origin of the socioeconomic status of women is to again assume that women are sexual-political subjects prior to their entry into the family. So while on the one hand women attain value or status within the family, the assumption of a singular patriarchal kinship system (common to all Arab and Muslim societies) is what apparently structures women as an oppressed group in these societies! This singular, coherent kinship system presumably influences another separate and given entity, "women." Thus, all women, regardless of class and cultural differences, are affected by this system. Not only are *all* Arab and Muslim women seen to constitute a homogeneous oppressed group, but there is no discussion of the specific *practices* within the family which constitute women as mothers, wives, sisters, etc. Arabs and Muslims, it appears, don't change at all. Their patriarchal family is carried over from the times of the prophet Mohammed. They exist, as it were, outside history.

Women and Religious Ideologies

A further example of the use of "women" as a category of analysis is found in cross-cultural analyses which subscribe to a certain economic reductionism in describing the relationship between the economy and factors such as politics and ideology. Here, in reducing the level of comparison to the economic relations between "developed and developing" countries, any specificity to the question of women is denied. Mina Modares (1981), in a careful analysis of women and Shi'ism in Iran, focuses on this very problem when she criticizes feminist writings which treat Islam as an ideology separate from and outside social relations and practices, rather than a discourse which includes rules for economic, social, and power relations within society. Patricia Jeffery's (1979) otherwise informative work on Pirzada women in purdah considers Islamic ideology a partial explanation for the status of women in that it provides a justification for the purdah. Here, Islamic ideology is reduced to a set of ideas whose internalization by Pirzada women contributes to the stability of the system. However, the primary explanation for purdah is located in the control that Pirzada men have over economic resources, and the personal security purdah gives to Pirzada women.

By taking a specific version of Islam as *the* Islam, Jeffery attributes a singularity and coherence to it. Modares notes, " "Islamic Theology" then becomes imposed on a separate and given entity called "women." A further unification is reached: Women (meaning *all women*), regardless of their differing positions within societies, come to be affected or not affected by Islam. These conceptions provide the right ingredients for an unproblematic possibility of a cross-cultural study of women" (63). Marina Lazreg makes a similar argument when she addresses the reductionism inherent in scholarship on women in the Middle East and North Africa:

> A ritual is established whereby the writer appeals to religion as *the* cause of gender inequality just as it is made the source of underdevelopment in much of modernization theory. In an uncanny way, feminist discourse on women from the Middle East and North Africa mirrors that of theologians' own interpretation of women in Islam. . . .

The overall effect of this paradigm is to deprive women of self-presence, of being. Because women are subsumed under religion presented in fundamental terms, they are inevitably seen as evolving in nonhistorical time. They virtually have no history. Any analysis of change is therefore foreclosed.   (1988: 87)

While Jeffery's analysis does not quite succumb to this kind of unitary notion of religion (Islam), it does collapse all ideological specificities into economic relations, and universalizes on the basis of this comparison.

Women and the Development Process

The best examples of universalization on the basis of economic reductionism can be found in the liberal "Women in Development" literature. Proponents of this school seek to examine the effect of development on third world women, sometimes from self-designated feminist perspectives. At the very least, there is an evident interest in and commitment to improving the lives of women in "developing" countries. Scholars such as Irene Tinker and Michelle Bo Bramsen (1972), Ester Boserup (1970), and Perdita Huston (1979) have all written about the effect of development policies on women in the third world.[9] All three women assume "development" is synonymous with "economic development" or "economic progress." As in the case of Minces's patriarchal family, Hosken's male sexual control, and Cutrufelli's Western colonization, development here becomes the all-time equalizer. Women are affected positively or negatively by economic development policies, and this is the basis for cross-cultural comparison.

For instance, Perdita Huston (1979) states that the purpose of her study is to describe the effect of the development process on the "family unit and its individual members" in Egypt, Kenya, Sudan, Tunisia, Sri Lanka, and Mexico. She states that the "problems" and "needs" expressed by rural and urban women in these countries all center around education and training, work and wages, access to health and other services, political participation, and legal rights. Huston relates all these "needs" to the lack of sensitive development policies which exclude women as a group or category. For her, the solution is simple: implement improved development policies which emphasize training for women fieldworkers, use women trainees, and women rural development officers, encourage women's cooperatives, etc. Here again, women are assumed to be a coherent group or category prior to their entry into "the development process." Huston assumes that all third world women have similar problems and needs. Thus, they must have similar interests and goals. However, the interests of urban, middle-class, educated Egyptian housewives, to take only one instance, could surely not be seen as being the same as those of their uneducated, poor maids. Development policies do not affect both groups of women in the same way. Practices which characterize women's status and roles vary according to class. Women are constituted as women through the complex interaction between class, culture, religion, and other ideological institutions and frameworks. They are not "women" – a coherent group – solely on the basis of a particular economic system or policy. Such reductive cross-cultural comparisons result in the colonization of the specifics of daily existence and the complexities of political interests which women of different social classes and cultures represent and mobilize.

Thus, it is revealing that for Perdita Huston, women in the third world countries she writes about have "needs" and "problems," but few if any have "choices" or the freedom to act. This is an interesting representation of women in the third world, one which is significant in suggesting a latent self-presentation of Western women which bears looking at. She writes, "What surprised and moved me most as I listened to women in such very different cultural settings was the striking common-ality – whether they were educated or illiterate, urban or rural – of their most basic values: the importance they assign to family, dignity, and service to others" (1979: 115). Would Huston consider such values unusual for women in the West?

What is problematical about this kind of use of "women" as a group, as a stable category of analysis, is that it assumes an ahistorical, universal unity between women based on a generalized notion of their subordination. Instead of analytically *demonstrating* the production of women as socioeconomic political groups within particular local contexts, this analytical move limits the definition of the female subject to gender identity, completely bypassing social class and ethnic identities. What characterizes women as a group is their gender (sociologically, not necessarily biologically, defined) over and above everything else, indicating a monolithic notion of sexual difference. Because women are thus constituted as a coherent group, sexual difference becomes coterminous with female subordination, and power is automatically defined in binary terms: people who have it (read: men), and people who do not (read: women). Men exploit, women are exploited. Such simplistic formulations are historically reductive; they are also ineffectual in designing strategies to combat oppressions. All they do is reinforce binary divisions between men and women.

What would an analysis which did not do this look like? Maria Mies's work illustrates the strength of Western feminist work on women in the third world which does not fall into the traps discussed above. Mies's study of the lace makers of Narsapur, India (1982), attempts to carefully analyze a substantial household industry in which "housewives" produce lace doilies for consumption in the world market. Through a detailed analysis of the structure of the lace industry, production and reproduction relations, the sexual division of labor, profits and exploitation, and the overall consequences of defining women as "non-working housewives" and their work as "leisure-time activity." Mies demonstrates the levels of exploitation in this industry and the impact of this production system on the work and living conditions of the women involved in it. In addition, she is able to analyze the "ideology of the housewife," the notion of a woman sitting in the house, as providing the necessary subjective and sociocultural element for the creation and maintenance of a produc-tion system that contributes to the increasing pauperization of women, and keeps them totally atomized and disorganized as workers. Mies's analysis shows the effect of a certain historically and culturally specific mode of patriarchal organization, an organization constructed on the basis of the definition of the lace makers as "non-working housewives" at familial, local, regional, statewide, and international levels. The intricacies and the effects of particular power networks not only are emphasized, but they form the basis of Mies's analysis of how this particular group of women is situated at the center of a hegemonic, exploitative world market.

This is a good example of what careful, politically focused, local analyses can accomplish. It illustrates how the category of women is constructed in a variety of political contexts that often exist simultaneously and overlaid on top of one another. There is no easy generalization in the direction of "women" in India, or "women in the third world"; nor is there a reduction of the political construction of the exploitation of the lace makers to cultural explanations about the passivity or obedience that might characterize these women and their situation. Finally, this mode of local, political analysis which generates theoretical categories from within the situation and context being analyzed, also suggests corresponding effective strategies for organizing against the exploitation faced by the lace makers. Narsapur women are not mere victims of the production process, because they resist, challenge, and subvert the process at various junctures. Here is one instance of how Mies delineates the connections between the housewife ideology, the self-consciousness of the lace makers, and their interrelationships as contributing to the latent resistances she perceives among the women:

> The persistence of the housewife ideology, the self-perception of the lace makers as petty commodity producers rather than as workers, is not only upheld by the structure of the industry as such but also by the deliberate propagation and reinforcement of reactionary patriarchal norms and institutions. Thus, most of the lace makers voiced the same opinion about the rules of *purdah* and seclusion in their communities which were also propagated by the lace exporters. In particular, the *Kapu* women said that they had never gone out of their houses, that women of their community could not do any other work than housework and lace work etc. but in spite of the fact that most of them still subscribed fully to the patriarchal norms of the *gosha* women, there were also contradictory elements in their consciousness. Thus, although they looked down with contempt upon women who were able to work outside the house – like the untouchable *Mala* and *Madiga* women or women of other lower castes, they could not ignore the fact that these women were earning more money precisely because they were *not* respectable housewives but workers. At one discussion, they even admitted that it would be better if they could also go out and do coolie work. And when they were asked whether they would be ready to come out of their houses and work in one place in some sort of a factory, they said they would do that. This shows that the *purdah* and housewife ideology, although still fully internalized, already had some cracks, because it has been confronted with several contradictory realities.   (157)

It is only by understanding the *contradictions* inherent in women's location within various structures that effective political action and challenges can be devised. Mies's study goes a long way toward offering such analysis. While there are now an increasing number of Western feminist writings in this tradition,[10] there is also, unfortunately, a large block of writing which succumbs to the cultural reductionism discussed earlier.

Methodological Universalisms, or: Women's Oppression is a Global Phenomenon

Western feminist writings on women in the third world subscribe to a variety of methodologies to demonstrate the universal cross-cultural operation of male dominance and female exploitation. I summarize and critique three such methods below, moving from the simplest to the most complex.

First, proof of universalism is provided through the use of an arithmetic method. The argument goes like this: the greater the number of women who wear the veil, the more universal is the sexual segregation and control of women (Deardon 1975: 4–5). Similarly, a large number of different, fragmented examples from a variety of countries also apparently add up to a universal fact. For instance, Muslim women in Saudi Arabia, Iran, Pakistan, India, and Egypt all wear some sort of a veil. Hence, this indicates that the sexual control of women is a universal fact in those countries in which the women are veiled (Deardon 1975: 7, 10). Fran Hosken writes, "Rape, forced prostitution, polygamy, genital mutilation, pornography, the beating of girls and women, purdah (segregation of women) are all violations of basic human rights" (1981: 15). By equating purdah with rape, domestic violence, and forced prostitution, Hosken asserts its "sexual control" function as the primary explanation for purdah, whatever the context. Institutions of purdah are thus denied any cultural and historical specificity, and contradictions and potentially subversive aspects are totally ruled out.

In both these examples, the problem is not in asserting that the practice of wearing a veil is widespread. This assertion can be made on the basis of numbers. It is a descriptive generalization. However, it is the analytic leap from the practice of veiling to an assertion of its general significance in controlling women that must be questioned. While there may be a physical similarity in the veils worn by women in Saudi Arabia and Iran, the specific meaning attached to this practice varies according to the cultural and ideological context. In addition, the symbolic space occupied by the practice of purdah may be similar in certain contexts, but this does not automatically indicate that the practices themselves have identical significance in the social realm. For example, as is well known, Iranian middle-class women veiled themselves during the 1979 revolution to indicate solidarity with their veiled working-class sisters, while in contemporary Iran, mandatory Islamic laws dictate that all Iranian women wear veils. While in both these instances, similar reasons might be offered for the veil (opposition to the Shah and Western cultural colonization in the first case, and the true Islamicization of Iran in the second), the concrete *meanings* attached to Iranian women wearing the veil are clearly different in both historical contexts. In the first case, wearing the veil is both an oppositional and a revolutionary gesture on the part of Iranian middle-class women; in the second case, it is a coercive, institutional mandate (see Tabari 1980 for detailed discussion). It is on the basis of such context-specific differentiated analysis that effective political strategies can be generated. To assume that the mere practice of veiling women in a number of Muslim countries indicates the universal oppression of women through sexual segregation not only is analytically reductive, but also proves quite useless when it comes to the elaboration of oppositional political strategy.

Second, concepts such as reproduction, the sexual division of labor, the family, marriage, household, patriarchy, etc., are often used without their specification in local cultural and historical contexts. Feminists use these concepts in providing explanations for women's subordination, apparently assuming their universal applicability. For instance, how is it possible to refer to "the" sexual division of labor when the *content* of this division changes radically from one environment to the next, and from one historical juncture to another? At its most abstract level, it is the fact of the differential assignation of tasks according to sex that is significant; however, this is quite different from the *meaning* or *value* that the content of this sexual division of labor assumes in different contexts. In most cases the assigning of tasks on the basis of sex has an ideological origin. There is no question that a claim such as "women are concentrated in service-oriented occupations in a large number of countries around the world" is descriptively valid. Descriptively, then, perhaps the existence of a similar sexual division of labor (where women work in service occupations such as nursing, social work, etc., and men in other kinds of occupations) in a variety of different countries can be asserted. However, the concept of the "sexual division of labor" is more than just a descriptive category. It indicates the differential *value* placed on "men's work" versus "women's work."

Often the mere existence of a sexual division of labor is taken to be proof of the oppression of women in various societies. This results from a confusion between and collapsing together of the descriptive and explanatory potential of the concept of the sexual division of labor. Superficially similar situations may have radically different, historically specific explanations, and cannot be treated as identical. For instance, the rise of female-headed households in middle-class America might be construed as a sign of great independence and feminist progress, whereby women are considered to have *chosen* to be single parents, there are increasing numbers of lesbian mothers, etc. However, the recent increase in female-headed households in Latin America,[11] where women might be seen to have more decision-making power, is concentrated among the poorest strata, where life choices are the most constrained economically. A similar argument can be made for the rise of female-headed families among black and Chicana women in the U.S. The positive correlation between this and the level of poverty among women of color and white working-class women in the U.S. has now even acquired a name: the feminization of poverty. Thus, while it is possible to state that there is a rise in female-headed households in the U.S. and in Latin America, this rise cannot be discussed as a universal indicator of women's independence, nor can it be discussed as a universal indicator of women's impoverishment. The *meaning* of and *explanation* for the rise obviously vary according to the sociohistorical context.

Similarly, the existence of a sexual division of labor in most contexts cannot be sufficient explanation for the universal subjugation of women in the work force. That the sexual division of labor does indicate a devaluation of women's work must be shown through analysis of particular local contexts. In addition, devaluation of *women* must also be shown through careful analysis. In other words, the "sexual division of labor" and "women" are not commensurate analytical categories. Concepts such as the sexual division of labor can be useful only if they are generated through local, contextual analyses (see Eldhom, Harris, and Young 1977). If such concepts are assumed to be universally applicable, the resultant homogenization of class, race, religious, and daily material practices of women in the third world can create a false sense of the commonality of oppressions, interests, and struggles between and among women globally. Beyond sisterhood there are still racism, colonialism, and imperialism!

Finally, some writers confuse the use of gender as a superordinate category of organizing analysis with the universalistic proof and instantiation of this category. In other words, empirical studies of gender differences are confused with the analytical organization of cross-cultural work. Beverly Brown's (1983) review of the book *Nature, Culture and Gender* (Strathern and McCormack 1980) best illustrates this point. Brown suggests that nature:culture and female:male are superordinate categories which organize and locate lesser categories (such as wild/domestic and biology/technology) within their logic. These categories are universal in the sense that they organize the universe of a system of representations. This relation is totally independent of the universal substantiation of any particular category. Her critique hinges on the fact that rather than clarify the generalizability of nature:culture :: female:male as subordinate organization categories, *Nature, Culture and Gender* construes the universality of this equation to lie at the level of empirical truth, which can be investigated through fieldwork. Thus, the usefulness of the nature:culture :: female:male paradigm as a universal mode of the organization of representation within any particular sociohistorical system is lost. Here, methodological universalism is assumed on the basis of the reduction of the nature:culture :: female:male analytic categories to a demand for empirical proof of its existence in different cultures. Discourses of representation are confused with material realities, and the distinction made earlier between "Woman" and "women" is lost. Feminist work which blurs this distinction (which is, interestingly enough, often present in certain Western feminists' self-representation) eventually ends up constructing monolithic images of "third world women" by ignoring the complex and mobile relationships between their historical materiality on the level of specific oppressions and political choices, on the one hand, and their general discursive representations, on the other.

To summarize: I have discussed three methodological moves identifiable in feminist (and other academic) cross-cultural work which seeks to uncover a universality in women's subordinate position in society. The next and final section pulls together the previous sections, attempting to outline the political effects of the analytical strategies in the context of Western feminist writing on women in the third world. These arguments are not against generalization as much as they are for careful, historically specific generalizations responsive to complex realities. Nor do these arguments deny the necessity of forming strategic political identities and affinities. Thus, while Indian women of different religions, castes, and classes might forge a political unity on the basis of organizing against police brutality toward women (see Kishwar and Vanita 1984), an *analysis* of police brutality must be contextual. Strategic coalitions which construct oppositional political identities for themselves are based on generalization and provisional unities, but the analysis of these group identities cannot be based on universalistic, ahistorical categories.

The Subject(s) of Power

This last section returns to an earlier point about the inherently political nature of feminist scholarship, and attempts to clarify my point about the possibility of detecting a colonialist move in the case of a hegemonic first–third world connection in scholarship. The nine texts in the Zed Press Women in the Third World series that I have discussed[12] focused on the following common areas in examining women's "status" within various societies: religion, family/kinship structures, the legal system, the sexual division of labor, education, and finally, political resistance. A large number of Western feminist writings on women in the third world focus on these themes. Of course the Zed texts have varying emphases. For instance, two of the studies, *Women of Palestine* (Downing 1982) and *Indian Women in Struggle* (Omvedt 1980), focus explicitly on female militance and political involvement, while *Women in Arab Society* (Minces 1980) deals with Arab women's legal, religious, and familial status. In addition, each text evidences a variety of methodologies and degrees of care in making generalizations. Interestingly enough, however, almost all the texts assume "women" as a category of analysis in the manner designated above.

Clearly this is an analytical strategy which is neither limited to these Zed Press publications nor symptomatic of Zed Press publications in general. However, each of the particular texts in question assumes "women" have a coherent group identity within the different cultures discussed, prior to their entry into social relations. Thus, Omvedt can talk about "Indian women" while referring to a particular group of women in the State of Maharashtra, Cutrufelli about "women of Africa," and Minces about "Arab women" as if these groups of women have some sort of obvious cultural coherence, distinct from men in these societies. The "status" or "position" of women is assumed to be self-evident, because women as an already constituted group are *placed* within religious, economic, familial, and legal structures. However, this focus whereby women are seen as a coherent group across contexts, regardless of class or ethnicity, structures the world in ultimately binary, dichotomous terms, where women are always seen in opposition to men, patriarchy is always necessarily male dominance, and the religious, legal, economic, and familial systems are implicitly assumed to be constructed by men. Thus, both men and women are always apparently constituted whole populations, and relations of dominance and exploitation are also posited in terms of whole peoples – wholes coming into exploitative relations. It is only when men and women are seen as different categories or groups possessing different *already constituted* categories of experience, cognition, and interests as *groups* that such a simplistic dichotomy is possible.

What does this imply about the structure and functioning of power relations? The setting up of the commonality of third world women's struggles across classes and cultures against a general notion of oppression (primarily the group in power – i.e., men) necessitates the assumption of what Michel Foucault (1980: 135–45) calls the "juridico-discursive" model of power, the principal features of which are "a negative relation" (limit and lack), an "insistence on the rule" (which forms a binary system), a "cycle of prohibition," the "logic of censorship," and a "uniformity" of the apparatus functioning at different levels. Feminist discourse on the third world which assumes a homogeneous category – or group – called women necessarily operates through the setting up of originary power divisions. Power relations are structured in terms of a unilateral and undifferentiated source of power and a cumulative reaction to power. Opposition is a generalized phenomenon created as a response to power – which, in turn, is possessed by certain groups of people.

The major problem with such a definition of power is that it locks all revolutionary struggles into binary structures – possessing power versus being powerless. Women are powerless, unified groups. If the struggle for a just society is seen in terms of the move from powerless to powerful for women as a *group*, and this is the implication in feminist discourse which structures sexual difference in terms of the division between the sexes, then the new society would be structurally identical to the existing organization of power relations, constituting itself as a simple *inversion* of what exists. If relations of domination and exploitation are defined in terms of binary divisions – groups which dominate and groups which are dominated – surely the implication is that the accession to power of women as a group is sufficient to dismantle the existing organization of relations? But women as a group are not in some sense essentially superior or infallible. The crux of the problem lies in that initial assumption of women as a homogeneous group or category ("the oppressed"), a familiar assumption in Western radical and liberal feminisms.[13]

What happens when this assumption of "women as an oppressed group" is situated in the context of Western feminist writing about third world women? It is here that I locate the colonialist move. By contrasting the representation of women in the third world with what I referred to earlier as Western feminisms' self-presentation in the same context, we see how Western feminists alone become the true "subjects" of this counterhistory. Third world women, on the other hand, never rise above the debilitating generality of their "object" status.

While radical and liberal feminist assumptions of women as a sex class might elucidate (however inadequately) the autonomy of particular women's struggles in the West, the application of the notion of women as a homogeneous category to women in the third world colonizes and appropriates the pluralities of the simultaneous location of different groups of women in social class and ethnic frameworks; in doing so it ultimately robs them of their historical and political *agency*. Similarly, many Zed Press authors who ground themselves in the basic analytic strategies of traditional Marxism also implicitly create a "unity" of women by substituting "women's activity" for "labor" as the primary theoretical determinant of women's situation. Here again, women are constituted as a coherent group not on the basis of "natural" qualities or needs but on the basis of the sociological "unity" of their role in domestic production and wage labor (see Haraway 1985, esp. p. 76). In other words, Western feminist discourse, by assuming women as a coherent, already constituted group which is placed in kinship, legal, and other structures, defines third world women as subjects *outside* social relations, instead of looking at the way women are constituted *through* these very structures.

Legal, economic, religious, and familial structures are treated as phenomena to be judged by Western standards. It is here that ethnocentric universality comes into play. When these structures are defined as "underdeveloped" or "developing" and women are placed within them, an implicit image of the "average third world woman" is produced. This is the transformation of the (implicitly Western) "oppressed woman" into the "oppressed third world woman." While the category of "oppressed woman" is generated through an exclusive focus on gender difference, "the oppressed third world woman" category has an additional attribute – the "third world difference!" The "third world difference" includes a paternalistic attitude toward women in the third world.[14] Since discussions of the various themes I identified earlier (kinship, education, religion, etc.) are conducted in the context of the relative "underdevelopment" of the third world (which is nothing less than unjustifiably confusing development with the separate path taken by the West in its development, as well as ignoring the directionality of the first–third world power relationship), third world women as a group or category are automatically and necessarily defined as religious (read "not progressive"), family-oriented (read "traditional"), legal minors (read "they-are-still-not-conscious-of-their-rights"), illiterate (read "ignorant"), domestic (read "backward"), and sometimes revolutionary (read "their-country-is-in-a-state-of-war; they-must-fight!"). This is how the "third world difference" is produced.

When the category of "sexually oppressed women" is located within particular systems in the third world which are defined on a scale which is normed through Eurocentric assumptions, not only are third world women defined in a particular way prior to their entry into social relations, but since no connections are made between first and third world power shifts, the assumption is reinforced that the third world just has not evolved to the extent that the West has. This mode of feminist analysis, by homogenizing and systematizing the experiences of different groups of women in these countries, erases all marginal and resistant modes and experiences.[15] It is significant that none of the texts I reviewed in the Zed Press series focuses on lesbian politics or the politics of ethnic and religious marginal organizations in third world women's groups. Resistance can thus be defined only as cumulatively reactive, not as something inherent in the operation of power. If power, as Michel Foucault has argued recently, can really be understood only in the context of resistance,[16] this misconceptualization is both analytically and strategically problematical. It limits theoretical analysis as well as reinforces Western cultural imperialism. For in the context of a first/third world balance of power, feminist analyses which perpetrate and sustain the hegemony of the idea of the superiority of the West produce a corresponding set of universal images of the "third world woman," images such as the veiled woman, the powerful mother, the chaste virgin, the obedient wife, etc. These images exist in universal, ahistorical splendor, setting in motion a colonialist discourse which exercises a very specific power in defining, coding, and maintaining existing first/third world connections.

To conclude, then, let me suggest some disconcerting similarities between the typically authorizing signature of such Western feminist writings on women in the third world, and the authorizing signature of the project of humanism in general – humanism as a Western ideological and political project which involves the necessary recuperation of the "East" and "Woman" as Others. Many contemporary thinkers, including Foucault (1978, 1980), Derrida (1974), Kristeva (1980), Deleuze and Guattari (1977), and Said (1978), have written at length about the underlying anthropomorphism and ethnocentrism which constitute a hegemonic humanistic problematic that repeatedly confirms and legitimates (Western) Man's centrality. Feminist theorists such as Luce Irigaray (1981), Sarah Kofman (see Berg 1982), and Helene Cixous (1981) have also written about the recuperation and absence of woman/women within Western humanism. The focus of the work of all these thinkers can be stated simply as an uncovering of the political *interests* that underlie the binary logic of humanistic discourse and ideology whereby, as a valuable recent essay puts it, "the first (majority) term (Identity, Universality, Culture, Disinterested-ness, Truth, Sanity, Justice, etc.), which is, in fact, secondary and derivative (a construction), is privileged over and colonizes the second (minority) term (differ-ence, temporality, anarchy, error, interestedness, insanity, deviance, etc.), which is in fact, primary and originative" (Spanos 1984). In other words, it is only insofar as "Woman/Women" and "the East" are defined as *Others*, or as peripheral, that (Western) Man/Humanism can represent him/itself as the center. If is not the center that determines the periphery, but the periphery that, in its boundedness, determines the center. Just as feminists such as Kristeva and Cixous deconstruct the latent anthropomorphism in Western discourse, I have suggested a parallel strategy in this essay in uncovering a latent ethnocentrism in particular feminist writings on women in the third world.[17]

As discussed earlier, a comparison between Western feminist self-presentation and Western feminist re-presentation of women in the third world yields significant results. Universal images of "the third world woman" (the veiled woman, chaste virgin, etc.), images constructed from adding the "third world difference" to "sexual difference," are predicated upon (and hence obviously bring into sharper focus) assumptions about Western women as secular, liberated, and having control over their own lives. This is not to suggest that Western women *are* secular, liberated, and in control of their own lives. I am referring to a *discursive* self-presentation, not necessarily to material reality. If this were a material reality, there would be no need for political movements in the West. Similarly, only from the vantage point of the West is it possible to define the "third world" as underdeveloped and economically dependent. Without the overdetermined discourse that creates the *third* world, there would be no (singular and privileged) first world. Without the "third world woman," the particular self-presentation of Western women mentioned above would be problematical. I am suggesting, then, that the one enables and sustains the other. This is not to say that the signature of Western feminist writings on the third world has the same authority as the project of Western humanism. However, in the context of the hegemony of the Western scholarly establishment in the production and dissemination of texts, and in the context of the legitimating impera-tive of humanistic and scientific discourse, the definition of "the third world woman" as a monolith might well tie into the larger economic and ideological praxis of "disin-terested" scientific inquiry and pluralism which are the surface manifestations of a latent economic and cultural colonization of the "non-Western" world. It is time to move beyond the Marx who found it possible to say: They cannot represent them- selves; they must be represented.

Notes

This essay would not have been possible without S. P. Mohanty's challenging and careful reading. I would also like to thank Biddy Martin for our numerous discussions about feminist theory and politics. They both helped me think through some of the arguments herein.

1   Terms such as *third* and *first world* are very problematic both in suggesting oversimplified similarities between and among countries labeled thus, and in implicitly reinforcing existing economic, cultural, and ideological hierarchies which are conjured up in using such termi- nology. I use the term "*third world*" with full awareness of its problems, only because this is the terminology available to us at the moment. The use of quotation marks is meant to suggest a continuous questioning of the designation. Even when I do not use quotation marks, I mean to use the term critically.

2   I am indebted to Teresa de Lauretis for this particular formulation of the project of feminist theorizing. See especially her introduction in de Lauretis, *Alice Doesn't: Feminism, Semio- tics, Cinema* (Bloomington: Indiana University Press, 1984); see also Sylvia Wynter, "The Politics of Domination," unpublished manuscript.

3   This argument is similar to Homi Bhabha's definition of colonial discourse as strategically creating a space for a subject people through the production of knowledges and the exercise of power. The full quote reads: "[colonial discourse is] an apparatus of power....an apparatus that turns on the recognition and disavowal of racial/cultural/historical differ- ences. Its predominant strategic function is the creation of a space for a subject people through the production of knowledges in terms of which surveillance is exercised and a complex form of pleasure/unpleasure is incited. It (i.e. colonial discourse) seeks authoriza- tion for its strategies by the production of knowledges by coloniser and colonised which are stereotypical but antithetically evaluated" (1983: 23).

4   A number of documents and reports on the UN International Conferences on Women, Mexico City, 1975, and Copenhagen, 1980, as well as the 1976 Wellesley Conference on Women and Development, attest to this. Nawal el Saadawi, Fatima Mernissi, and Mallica Vajarathon (1978) characterize this conference as "American-planned and organized," situating third world participants as passive audiences. They focus especially on the lack of self-consciousness of Western women's implication in the effects of imperialism and racism in their assumption of an "international sisterhood." A recent essay by Valerie Amos and Pratibha Parmar (1984) characterizes as "imperial" Euro-American feminism which seeks to establish itself as the only legitimate feminism.

5   The Zed Press Women in the Third World series is unique in its conception. I choose to focus on it because it is the only contemporary series I have found which assumes that "women in the third world" are a legitimate and separate subject of study and research. Since 1985, when this essay was first written, numerous new titles have appeared in the Women in the Third World series. Thus, I suspect that Zed has come to occupy a rather privileged position in the dissemination and construction of discourses by and about third world women. A number of the books in this series are excellent, especially those which deal directly with women's resistance struggles. In addition, Zed Press consistently publishes

progressive feminist, antiracist, and antiimperialist texts. However, a number of the texts written by feminist sociologists, anthropologists, and journalists are symptomatic of the kind of Western feminist work on women in the third world that concerns me. Thus, an analysis of a few of these particular works in this series can serve as a representative point of entry into the discourse I am attempting to locate and define. My focus on these texts is therefore an attempt at an internal critique: I simply expect and demand more from this series. Needless to say, progressive publishing houses also carry their own authorizing signatures.

6   Elsewhere I have discussed this particular point in detail in a critique of Robin Morgan's construction of "women's herstory" in her introduction to *Sisterhood is Global: The International Women's Movement Anthology* (New York: Anchor Press/Doubleday, 1984). See my "Feminist Encounters: Locating the Politics of Experience," *Copyright* 1, "Fin de Siecle 2000," 30–44, especially 35–7.

7   Another example of this kind of analysis is Mary Daly's (1978) *Gyn/Ecology.* Daly's assumption in this text, that women as a group are sexually victimized, leads to her very problematic comparison between the attitudes toward women witches and healers in the West, Chinese footbinding, and the genital mutilation of women in Africa. According to Daly, women in Europe, China, and Africa constitute a homogeneous group as victims of male power. Not only does this label (sexual victims) eradicate the specific historical and material realities and contradictions which lead to and perpetuate practices such as witch hunting and genital mutilation, but it also obliterates the differences, complexities, and heterogeneities of the lives of, for example, women of different classes, religions, and nations in Africa. As Audre Lorde (1983) pointed out, women in Africa share a long tradition of healers and goddesses that perhaps binds them together more appropriately than their victim status. However, both Daly and Lorde fall prey to universalistic assumptions about "African women" (both negative and positive). What matters is the complex, historical range of power differences, commonalities, and resistances that exist among women in Africa which construct African women as "subjects" of their own politics.

8   See Eldhom, Harris, and Young (1977) for a good discussion of the necessity to theorize male violence within specific societal frameworks, rather than assume it as a universal fact.

9   These views can also be found in differing degrees in collections such as Wellesley Editorial Committee, ed., *Women and National Development: The Complexities of Change* (Chicago: University of Chicago Press, 1977), and *Signs*, Special Issue, "Development and the Sexual Division of Labor," 7, no. 2 (Winter 1981). For an excellent introduction of WID issues, see ISIS, *Women in Development: A Resource Guide for Organization and Action* (Philadelphia: New Society Publishers, 1984). For a politically focused discussion of feminism and development and the stakes for poor third world women, see Gita Sen and Caren Grown, *Development Crises and Alternative Visions: Third World Women's Perspectives* (New York: Monthly Review Press, 1987).

10 See essays by Vanessa Maher, Diane Elson and Ruth Pearson, and Maila Stevens in Kate Young, Carol Walkowitz, and Roslyn McCullagh, eds., *Of Marriage and the Market: Women's Subordination in International Perspective* (London: CSE Books, 1981); and essays by Vivian Mota and Michelle Mattelart in June Nash and Helen I. Safa, eds., *Sex and Class in Latin America: Women's Perspectives on Politics, Economics and the Family in the Third World* (South Hadley, Mass.: Bergin and Garvey, 1980). For examples of excellent, self-conscious work by feminists writing about women in their own historical and geographical locations, see Marnia Lazreg (1988) on Algerian women, Gayatri Chakravorty Spivak's "A Literary Representation of the Subaltern: A Woman's Text from

the Third World," in her *In Other Worlds: Essays in Cultural Politics* (New York: Methuen, 1987), 241–68, and Lata Mani's essay "Contentious Traditions: The Debate on SATI in Colonial India," *Cultural Critique* 7 (Fall 1987), 119–56.

11   Olivia Harris, "Latin American Women – An Overview," in Harris, ed., *Latin American Women* (London: Minority Rights Group Report no. 57, 1983), 4–7. Other MRG Reports include Ann Deardon (1975) and Rounaq Jahan (1980).

12   List of Zed Press publications: Patricia Jeffery, *Frogs in a Well: Indian Women in Purdah* (1979); Latin American and Caribbean Women's Collective, *Slaves of Slaves: The Challenge of Latin American Women* (1980); Gail Omvedt, *We Shall Smash This Prison: Indian Women in Struggle* (1980); Juliette Minces, *The House of Obedience: Women in Arab Society* (1980); Bobby Siu, *Women of China: Imperialism and Women's Resistance, 1900–1949* (1981); Ingela Bendt and James Downing, *We Shall Return: Women in Palestine* (1982); Maria Rosa Cutrufelli, *Women of Africa: Roots of Oppression* (1983); Maria Mies, *The Lace Makers of Narsapur: Indian Housewives Produce for the World Market* (1982); Miranda Davis, ed., *Third World/Second Sex: Women's Struggles and National Liberation* (1983).

13   For succinct discussions of Western radical and liberal feminisms, see Hester Eisenstein, *Contemporary Feminist Thought* (Boston: G. K. Hall & Co., 1983), and Zillah Eisenstein, *The Radical Future of Liberal Feminism* (New York: Longman, 1981).

14   Amos and Parmar describe the cultural stereotypes present in Euro-American feminist thought: "The image is of the passive Asian woman subject to oppressive practices within the Asian family with an emphasis on wanting to "help" Asian women liberate themselves from their role. Or there is the strong, dominant Afro-Caribbean woman, who despite her "strength" is exploited by the "sexism" which is seen as being a strong feature in relationships between Afro-Caribbean men and women" (9). These images illustrate the extent to which *paternalism* is an essential element of feminist thinking which incorporates the above stereotypes, a paternalism which can lead to the definition of priorities for women of color by Euro-American feminists.

15   I discuss the question of theorizing experience in my "Feminist Encounters" (1987) and in an essay coauthored with Biddy Martin, "Feminist politics: What's Home Got to Do with It?" in Teresa de Lauretis, ed., *Feminist Studies/Critical Studies* (Bloomington: Indiana University Press, 1986), 191–212.

16   This is one of M. Foucault's (1978, 1980) central points in his reconceptualization of the strategies and workings of power networks.

17   For an argument which demands a *new* conception of humanism in work on third world women, see Marnia Lazreg (1988). While Lazreg's position might appear to be diametrically opposed to mine, I see it as a provocative and potentially positive extension of some of the implications that follow from my arguments. In criticizing the feminist rejection of humanism in the name of "essential Man," Lazreg points to what she calls an "essentialism of difference" within these very feminist projects. She asks: "To what extent can Western feminism dispense with an ethics of responsibility when writing about different women? The point is neither to subsume other women under one's own experience nor to uphold a separate truth for them. Rather, it is to allow them to *be* while recognizing that what they are is just as meaningful, valid, and comprehensible as what we are.... Indeed, when feminists essentially deny other women the humanity they claim for themselves, they dispense with any ethical constraint. They engage in the act of splitting the social universe into us and them, subject and objects" (99–100).

This essay by Lazreg and an essay by S. P. Mohanty (1989) entitled "Us and Them: On the Philosophical Bases of Political Criticism" suggest positive directions for self-conscious cross-cultural analyses, analyses which move beyond the deconstructive to a fundamentally productive mode in designating overlapping areas for cross-cultural comparison. The latter essay calls not for a "humanism" but for a reconsideration of the question of the "human" in a posthumanist context. It argues that (1) there is no necessary "incompatibility between the deconstruction of Western humanism" and such "a positive elaboration" of the human, and moreover that (2) such an elaboration is essential if contemporary political-critical discourse is to avoid the incoherences and weaknesses of a relativist position.

References

Abdel-Malek, Anouar. 1981. *Social Dialectics: Nation and Revolution.* Albany: State University of New York Press.

Amin, Samir. 1977. *Imperialism and Unequal Development.* New York: Monthly Review Press.

Amos, Valerie, and Pratibha Parmar. 1984. "Challenging Imperial Feminism." *Feminist Review* 17: 3–19.

Baran, Paul A. 1962. *The Political Economy of Growth.* New York: Monthly Review Press.

Berg, Elizabeth. 1982. "The Third Woman." *Diacritics* (Summer): 11–20.

Bhabha, Homi. 1983. "The Other Question – The Stereotype and Colonial Discourse." *Screen* 24, no. 6: 23.

Boserup, Ester. 1970. *Women's Role in Economic Development.* New York: St. Martin's Press; London: Allen and Unwin.

Brown, Beverly. 1983. "Displacing the Difference – Review, *Nature, Culture and Gender.*" *m/f* 8: 79–89.

Cixous, Helene. 1981. "The Laugh of the Medusa." In Marks and De Courtivron (1981).

Cowie, Elizabeth. 1978. "Woman as Sign." *m/f* 1: 49–63.

Cutrufelli, Maria Rosa. 1983. *Women of Africa: Roots of Oppression.* London: Zed Press.

Daly, Mary, 1978. *Gyn/Ecology: The Metaethics of Radical Feminism.* Boston: Beacon Press.

Deardon, Ann, ed. 1975. *Arab Women.* London: Minority Rights Group Report no. 27.

de Lauretis, Teresa. 1984. *Alice Doesn't: Feminism, Semiotics, Cinema.* Bloomington: Indiana University Press.

——1986. *Feminist Studies Critical Studies.* Bloomington: Indiana University Press.

Deleuze, Giles, and Felix Guattari. 1977. *Anti-Oedipus: Capitalism and Schizophrenia.* New York: Viking.

Derrida, Jacques. 1974. *Of Grammatology.* Baltimore. Johns Hopkins University Press.

Eisenstein, Hester. 1983. *Contemporary Feminist Thought.* Boston: G. K. Hall and Co.

Eisenstein, Zillah. 1981. *The Radical Future of Liberal Feminism.* New York: Longman.

Eldhom, Felicity, Olivia Harris, and Kate Young. 1977. "Conceptualising Women." *Critique of Anthropology: "Women's Issue",* no. 3.

el Saadawi, Nawal, Fatima Mernissi, and Mallica Vajarathon. 1978. "A Critical Look at the Wellesley Conference." *Quest* 4, no. 2 (Winter): 101–107.

Foucault, Michel. 1978. *History of Sexuality: Volume One.* New York: Random House.

—— 1980. *Power/Knowledge.* New York: Pantheon.

Gunder-Frank, Audre. 1967. *Capitalism and Underdevelopment in Latin America.* New York: Monthly Review Press.

Haraway, Donna. 1985. "A Manifesto for Cyborgs: Science, Technology and Socialist Feminism in the 1980s." *Socialist Review* 80 (March/April): 65–108.

Harris, Olivia, 1983a. "Latin American Women – An Overview." In Harris (1983b).

—— 1983b. *Latin American Women*. London: Minority Rights Group Report no. 57.

Hosken, Fran. 1981. "Female Genital Mutilation and Human Rights." *Feminist Issues* 1, no. 3.

Huston, Perdita. 1979. *Third World Women Speak Out*. New York: Praeger.

Irigaray, Luce. 1981. "This Sex Which Is Not One" and "When the Goods Get Together." In Marks and De Courtivron (1981).

Jahan, Rounaq, ed. 1980. *Women in Asia*. London: Minority Rights Group Report no. 45.

Jeffery, Patricia. 1979. *Frogs in a Well: Indian Women in Purdah*. London: Zed Press.

Joseph, Gloria, and Jill Lewis. 1981. *Common Differences: Conflicts in Black and White Feminist Perspectives*. Boston: Beacon Press.

Kishwar, Madhu, and Ruth Vanita. 1984. *In Search of Answers: Indian Women's Voices from Manushi*. London: Zed Press.

Kristeva, Julia. 1980. *Desire in Language*. New York: Columbia University Press.

Lazreg, Marnia. 1988. "Feminism and Difference: The Perils of Writing as a Woman on Women in Algeria." *Feminist Issues* 14, no. 1 (Spring): 81–107.

Lindsay, Beverley, ed. 1983. *Comparative Perspectives of Third World Women: The Impact of Race, Sex and Class*. New York: Praeger.

Lorde, Audre. 1983. "An Open Letter to Mary Daly." In Moraga and Anzaldua (1983), 94–7.

Marks, Elaine, and Isabel De Courtivron. 1981. *New French Feminisms*. New York: Schocken Books.

Mies, Maria. 1982. *The Lace Makers of Narsapur: Indian Housewives Produce for the World Market*. London: Zed Press.

Minces, Juliette. 1980. *The House of Obedience: Women in Arab Society*. London: Zed Press.

Modares, Mina. 1981. "Women and Shi'ism in Iran." *m/f* 5 and 6: 61–82.

Mohanty, Chandra Talpade. 1987. "Feminist Encounters: Locating the Politics of Experience." *Copyright* 1, "Fin de Siecle 2000," 30–44.

Mohanty, Chandra Talpade, and Biddy Martin. 1986. "Feminist Politics: What's Home Got to Do with It?" In de Lauretis (1986).

Mohanty, S. P. 1989. "Us and Them: On the Philosophical Bases of Political Criticism." *Yale Journal of Criticism* 2 (March): 1–31.

Moraga, Cherríe. 1984. *Loving in the War Years*. Boston: South End Press.

Moraga, Cherríe, and Gloria Anzaldúa, eds. 1983. *This Bridge Called My Back: Writings by Radical Women of Color*. New York: Kitchen Table Press.

Morgan, Robin, ed. 1984. *Sisterhood Is Global: The International Women's Movement Anthology*. New York: Anchor Press/Doubleday; Harmondsworth: Penguin.

Nash, June, and Helen I. Safa, eds. 1980. *Sex and Class in Latin America: Women's Perspectives on Politics, Economics and the Family in the Third World*. South Hadley, Mass.: Bergin and Garvey.

Rosaldo, M. A. 1980. "The Use and Abuse of Anthropology: Reflections on Feminism and Cross-Cultural Understanding." *Signs* 53: 389–417.

Said, Edward. 1978. *Orientalism*. New York: Random House.

Sen, Gita, and Caren Grown. 1987. *Development Crises and Alternative Visions: Third World Women's Perspectives*. New York: Monthly Review Press.

Smith, Barbara, ed. 1983. *Home Girls: A Black Feminist Anthology*. New York: Kitchen Table Press.

Spanos, William V. 1984. "Boundary 2 and the Polity of Interest: Humanism, the "Center Elsewhere" and Power." *Boundary* 2 12, no. 3/13, no. 1 (Spring/Fall).

Spivak, Gayatri Chakravorty. 1987. *In Other Worlds: Essays in Cultural Politics.* London and New York: Methuen.

Strathern, Marilyn, and Carol McCormack, eds. 1980. *Nature, Culture and Gender.* Cambridge: Cambridge University Press.

Tabari, Azar, 1980. "The Enigma of the Veiled Iranian Women." *Feminist Review* 5:19–32.

Tinker, Irene, and Michelle Bo Bramsen, eds. 1972. *Women and World Development.* Washington, D.C.: Overseas Development Council.

Young, Kate, Carol Walkowitz, and Roslyn McCullagh, eds. 1981. *Of Marriage and the Market: Women's Subordination in International Perspective.* London: CSE Books.

25

Hybrid Cultures, Oblique Powers*

Néstor García Canclini

From the Public Space to Teleparticipation

Perceiving that the cultural transformations generated by the latest technologies and by changes in symbolic production and circulation were not the exclusive respons-ibility of the communications media induced a search for more comprehensive notions. As the new processes were associated with urban growth, it was thought that the city could become the unity that would give coherence and analytical consistency to the studies.

Undoubtedly, urban expansion is one of the causes that intensified cultural hybrid-ization. What does it mean for Latin American cultures that countries that had about 10 percent of their population in the cities at the beginning of the century now concentrate 60 to 70 percent in urban agglomerations? We have gone from societies dispersed in thousands of peasant communities with traditional, local, and homo-geneous cultures – in some regions, with strong indigenous roots, with little com-munication with the rest of each nation – to a largely urban scheme with a heterogeneous symbolic offering renewed by a constant interaction of the local with national and transnational networks of communication.

Manuel Castells already observed in his book *La cuestión urbana* that the dizzying development of cities, in making visible under this name multiple dimensions of social change, made it comfortable to attribute to them the responsibility of vaster processes (Castells, 1973: 93). Something similar occurred to what happened with the mass media. The megalopolis was accused of engendering anonymity; it was imagined that neighborhoods produce solidarity, the suburbs crime, and that green spaces relax . . .

Urban ideologies attributed to *one* aspect of the transformation, produced by the intercrossing of many forces of modernity, the "explanation" of all its knots and crises. Since that book by Castells, much evidence has accumulated showing that "urban society" is not sharply opposed to the "rural world" and that the predominance of secondary relations over primary ones and of heterogeneity over homogeneity (or the

* From Néstor García Canclini, *Hybrid Cultures: Strategies for Entering and Leaving Modernity,* trans. Christopher L. Chiappari and Silva L. Lopes (Minneapolis: University of Minnesota Press, 1995), pp. 207–63.

opposite, according to the school) is not due only to the population concentration in the cities.

The urbanization predominant in contemporary societies is intertwined with serialization and anonymity in production, with restructurings of immaterial communication (from mass media to the telematic) that modify the connections between the private and public. How can we explain the fact that many changes in thinking and taste in urban life coincide with those in the peasantry, if not because the commercial interactions of the latter with the cities and the reception of electronic media in rural houses connects them daily with modern innovations?

Inversely, living in a big city does not imply becoming dissolved in the massive and the anonymous. The violence and public insecurity, the incomprehensibility of the city (who knows all the neighborhoods of a capital city?), lead us to search for selective forms of sociability in domestic intimacy and in trusting encounters. Popular groups seldom leave their spaces, whether peripheral or centrally located; middle- and upper-class sectors increase the bars on their windows and close and privatize the streets of their neighborhoods. For everyone radio and television, and for some the computer connected to basic services, bring them information and entertainment at home.

Living in cities, writes Norbert Lechner in his study on daily life in Santiago (1982), has become "isolating a space of one's own." In contrast to what Habermas observed in early periods of modernity, the public sphere is no longer the place of rational participation from which the social order is determined. It was like that, in part, in Latin America during the second half of the nineteenth century and the first half of the twentieth. It is enough to record the role of the "press, theater, and the patrician salons in conformity with a Creole elite"; first for restricted sectors, then broader ones, liberalism assumed that the public will should be constituted as "the result of the discussion and publicity of individual opinions" (Lechner, 1982: Part 2, 73–74).

Studies of the formation of popular neighborhoods in Buenos Aires in the first half of the century recorded that the microsocial structures of urbanism – the club, the café, the neighborhood society, the library, the political committee – organized the identity of the migrants and Creoles by linking immediate life with the global transformations that were being sought by society and the state. Reading and sports, militancy and neighborhood sociability were united in a utopian continuity with national political movements (Gutiérrez and Romero, 1985).

This is coming to an end, partly due to changes in the staging of politics; I am referring to the mix of bureaucratization and "mass mediatization." The masses, called upon since the 1960s to express themselves in the streets and to form unions, were being subordinated in many cases to bureaucratic formations. The last decade presents frequent caricatures of that movement: populist leaderships without economic growth and without surplus to distribute, end up overwhelmed by a perverse mixture of reconversion and recession and sign tragic pacts with the speculators of the economy (Alan García in Peru, Carlos Andrés Pérez in Venezuela, Carlos Menem in Argentina). The massive use of the city for political theatricalization is reduced; economic measures and requests for the collaboration of the people are announced on television. Marches and rallies in streets and squares are occasional or have minor effect. In the three countries cited, as in others, public demonstrations generated by the impoverishment of the majority sometimes adopt the form of disarticulated explosions, attacks on shops and supermarkets, on the margin of the organic paths to political representation.

The city's loss of meaning is in direct relation to the difficulties of political parties and unions in calling people to collective tasks that do not produce income or are of doubtful economic gain. The lesser visibility of macrosocial structures, their subordination to nonmaterial and different circuits of communication that mediatize personal and group interactions, is one of the causes for the decline in the credibility of all-encompassing social movements, such as the parties that concentrated the entirety of labor demands and civic representation. The emergence of multiple demands, enlarged in part by the growth of cultural protests and those relating to the quality of life, raises a diversified spectrum of organizations to speak for them: urban, ethnic, youth, feminist, consumer, ecological movements, and so on. Social mobilization, in the same way as the structure of the city, is fragmented in processes that are more and more difficult to totalize.

The efficacy of these movements depends, in turn, on the reorganization of the public space. Their actions have a low impact when they are limited to using traditional forms of communication (oral, of artisanal production, or in written texts that circulate from person to person). Their power grows if they act in mass networks: not only the urban presence of a demonstration of one or two hundred thousand persons, but – even more – their capacity to interfere with the normal functioning of a city and find support, for that very reason, in the electronic information media. Then, sometimes, the sense of the urban is restored and the massive ceases to be a vertical system of diffusion to become a larger expression of local powers, a complementing of the fragments.

At a time when the city or the public sphere is occupied by actors that technically calculate their decisions and technobureaucratically organize the attention to the demands, according to criteria of revenue and efficiency, polemical subjectivity – or simply subjectivity – retreats to the private sphere. The market reorders the public world as a stage for consumption and dramatization of the signs of status. The streets are saturated with cars, people rushing to fulfill work obligations or to a programmed recreation activity, almost always according to its economic yield.

A separate organization of "free time," which turns it into a prolongation of work and money, contributes to this reformulation of the public. From working breakfasts to work, to business lunches, to work, to seeing what is on television at home, and some days to socially productive dinners. The free time of the popular sectors, compelled by underemployment and wage deterioration, is even less free in having to be busy with a second or third job, or in looking for them.

Collective identities find their constitutive stage less and less in the city and in its history, whether distant or recent. Information about unforeseen social vicissitudes is received in the home and commented upon among family or with close friends. Almost all sociability, and reflection about it, is concentrated in intimate exchanges. Since information on price increases, what the governor did, and even the accidents that happened the previous day in our own city reach us through the media, these become the dominant constituents of the "public" meaning of the city, those that simulate integrating a disintegrated imaginary urban sphere.

Although this is the trend, it would be unjust not to point out that sometimes the mass media also contribute to overcoming fragmentation. To the degree they inform us about the common experiences of urban life – social conflicts, pollution, which streets have traffic jams at what hours – they establish networks of communication and make it possible to apprehend the social, collective meaning of what happens in the city. On a broader scale, it may be affirmed that radio and television, in placing in relation to each other diverse historical, ethnic, and regional patrimonies and diffusing them massively, coordinate the multiple temporalities of different spectators.

The investigations of these processes should articulate the integrating and disintegrating effects of television with other processes of unification and atomization generated by the recent changes in urban development and the economic crisis. The groups that get together now and then to analyze collective questions – parents at school, workers at their workplace, neighborhood organizations – tend to act and think as self-referential and often sectored groups because economic pressure forces them down the economic ladder. This has been studied chiefly by sociologists in the southern cone, where military dictatorships suspended political parties, unions, and other mechanisms of grouping, mobilization, and collective cooperation. The repression attempted to reshape the public space by reducing social participation to the insertion of each individual in the benefits of consumption and financial speculation.[1] Up to a point, the media became the great mediators and mediatizers, and therefore substitutes for other collective interactions.

The dictatorships made this transformation more radical. But in the last decade, when other Latin American governments have shared this neoconservative policy, its effects have been generalized. "To appear in public" is today to be seen by many people scattered in front of the family television set or reading the newspaper in their home. Political leaders and intellectuals accentuate their conditions as theatrical actors, their messages are distributed if they are "news," and "public opinion" is something measurable by opinion polls. The citizen becomes a client, a "public consumer."

"Urban culture" is restructured by giving up its leading role in the public space to electronic technologies. Given that almost everything in the city "happens" thanks to the fact that the media say so, and in seeming to occur the way the media want it to, there is an accentuation of social mediatization and of the weight of the stagings, and political actions are constituted as so many images of the political. Thus Eliseo Verón (1985), pushing things to the extreme, asserts that participating today means having relations with an "audiovisual democracy" in which the real is produced by the images created in the media.

I would put it in somewhat different terms. More than an absolute substitution of urban life by the audiovisual media, I perceive a *game of echoes*. The commercial advertising and political slogans that we see on television are those that we reencounter in the streets, and vice versa: the ones are echoed in the others. To this circularity of the communicational and the urban are subordinated the testimonies of history and the public meaning constructed in longtime experiences.

Historical Memory and Urban Conflicts

From mass culture to technoculture, from urban space to teleparticipation. In observing this trend, we run the risk of relapsing into the linear historical perspective and suggesting that communicational technologies *substitute for* the inheritance of the past and public interactions.

It is necessary to reintroduce the question of the modern and postmodern uses of history. I am going to do so with the most challenging and apparently most solemn reference: monuments. What meaning do they conserve or renew in the midst of the transformations of the city and in competition with transitory phenomena like advertising, graffiti, and political demonstrations?

There was a time when monuments, along with schools and museums, were a legitimizing stage of the traditional cultured. Their gigantic size or distinguished placement contributed to exalting them. "Why are there no statues in short sleeves?" the Argentine television program *La noticia rebelde* asked the architect Osvaldo Giesso, director of the Cultural Center of the city of Buenos Aires. To give a long, drawn-out response would require considering the statues together with the rhetoric of textbooks, the ritualism of civic ceremonies, and the other self-consecrating liturgies of power. One would also have to analyze how the monumentalist aesthetic that governs most historic spaces in Latin America was initiated as an expression of authoritarian social systems in the pre-Columbian world. Spanish and Portuguese colonial expansionism was superimposed on them because of the need to compete with the grandiloquence of indigenous architecture by means of neoclassical giganticism and baroque exuberance. Finally, it would be necessary to analyze how the processes of independence and construction of our nations engendered enormous buildings and murals, portraits of heroes, and calendars of historical events, all designed to establish an iconography representative of the size of the utopias.

What do monuments claim to say within contemporary urban symbolism? In revolutionary processes with broad popular participation, public rites and monumental constructions express the historic impulse of mass movements. They are part of the struggle for a new visual culture in the midst of the stubborn persistence of signs of the old order, such as occurred with the first postrevolutionary Mexican muralism and with Russian graphic art in the twenties and Cuban graphic art in the sixties. But when the new movement becomes the system, the projects for change follow the route of bureaucratic planning more than that of participative mobilization. When social organization is stabilized, ritualism becomes sclerotic.

To show the type of tensions that are established between historical memory and the visual scheme of modern cities, I will analyze a group of monuments. It is a small selection from the abundant documentation on monuments of Mexico assembled by Paolo Gori and Helen Escobedo (1989).[2] I am going to begin with a group of sculptures that represent the founding of Tenochtitlán and are located a short distance from the Zócalo in Mexico City.

These examples suffice to show the changes the most solid commemorations of patrimony suffer. Monuments often contain several styles and references to diverse historical and artistic periods. Another hybridization is added later in interacting with urban growth, advertising, graffiti, and modern social movements. The iconography of national traditions (Juárez) is used as a resource for struggling against those who, in the name of other traditions (those of Catholicism that condemn abortion), oppose modernity.

These images suggest diverse ways in which traditions and the monuments that consecrate them are reutilized today. Certain heroes of the past survive in the middle of conflicts that unfold in any modern city between systems of political and commercial signs, traffic signals, and social movements.

Modern development attempted to distribute objects and signs in specific places: commodities in current use, in shops; objects of the past, in history museums; those that claim to be valuable for their aesthetic meaning, in art museums. At the same time, the messages emitted by commodities, historical works, and artistic works, and those that indicate how to use them, circulate through schools and the mass media. A rigorous classification of *things* and of the *languages* that speak about them sustains the systematic organization of the social *spaces* in which they should be consumed. This order structures the life of consumers and prescribes behaviors and modes of perceiving that are appropriate for each situation. To be cultured in a modern city consists in knowing how to distinguish between what is purchased for use, what is commemorated, and what is enjoyed symbolically. The social system requires living in a compartmentalized way.

Nevertheless, urban life transgresses this order all the time. In the movement of the city, commercial interests are crossed with historical, aesthetic, and communicational ones. The semantic struggles to neutralize each other, to perturb the message of the others or change its meaning, and to subordinate the rest to its own logic are stagings of the conflicts between social forces: between the market, history, the state, advertising, and the popular struggle for survival.

While historical objects in museums are removed from history and their intrinsic meaning is frozen in an eternity where nothing will ever happen, monuments open to the urban dynamic facilitate the interaction of memory with change and the revitalization of heroes thanks to propaganda or transit: they continue struggling with the social movements that survive them. In Mexico's museums, the heroes of independence are distinguished by their relation to those of the Reform and the revolution; in the street their meaning is renewed in dialoguing with present contradictions. Without display windows or guards to protect them, urban monuments are happily exposed to their being inserted into contemporary life by graffiti or a popular demonstration. Although sculptors resist abandoning the formulas of classical realism in representing the past or making heroes in short sleeves, monuments are kept up-to-date by the "irreverences" of the citizens.

Graffiti, commercial posters, social and political demonstrations, monuments – languages that represent the main forces operating in the city. Monuments are almost always works with which political power consecrates the founding persons and events of the state. Commercial posters seek to synchronize daily life with the interests of economic power. Graffiti (like the posters and political events of the oppositions) express popular criticism of the imposed order. That is why the publicity announcements that hide or contradict the monuments, and the graffiti written over other graffiti, are so significant. At times the proliferation of announcements drowns out historical identity and dissolves memory in the anxious perception of the novelties that are incessantly renewed by advertising. On the other hand, the authors of spontaneous legends are saying that monuments are inadequate for expressing how the city moves. Is not the need to politically reinscribe monuments evidence of the distance between a state and a people, or between history and the present?

Decollecting

This difficulty in including what we earlier totalized under the formula "urban culture," or with the notions of cultured, popular, and massive, presents the problem of whether the organization of culture can be explained by reference to *collections* of symbolic goods. The disarticulation of the urban also puts into doubt the possibility of cultural systems' finding their key in the relations of the population with a certain type of *territory* and history that would, in a peculiar sense, prefigure the behaviors of each group. The next step in this analysis must be to work with the (combined) processes of *decollecting* and *deterritorialization*.

The formation of specialized collections of high art and folklore was a device in modern Europe, and later in Latin America, for ordering symbolic goods in separate groups and hierarchizing them. A certain type of paintings, music, and books belonged to those who were cultured, even though they did not have them in their houses and even though it was through access to museums, concert halls, and libraries. To know their order was already a way of possessing them that distinguished them from those who did not know how to relate to that order.

The history of art and literature was formed on the basis of collections that were housed in museums and libraries when these were buildings for keeping, exhibiting, and consulting collections. Today art museums exhibit Rembrandt and Bacon in one room, popular objects and industrial design in the following ones, and beyond those are happenings, performances, installations, and body art by artists who no longer believe in the works and refuse to produce collectible objects. Public libraries continue to exist in a more traditional mode, but any intellectual or student works much more in his or her private library, where books are mixed with journals, newspaper clippings, fragmentary bits of information that will be moved often from one shelf to another and whose use requires them to be spread out on several tables and on the floor. The situation of the cultural worker today is what Benjamin glimpsed in that pioneering text in which he described the sensations of moving and unpacking his library among the disorder of the boxes, "the floor strewn with scattered papers," the loss of the order that connected those objects with a history of knowledge, making him feel that the mania of collecting "is no longer of our time" (Benjamin, 1969: 59–66).

On the other hand, there was a repertory of folklore, of the objects of peoples or classes that had different customs and therefore other collections. Folklore was born from collecting, as we saw in an earlier chapter. It was formed when collectors and folklorists moved to archaic societies, investigated and preserved the containers used for cooking, the clothing, and the masks used in ritual dancing, and then gathered them together in museums. The containers, masks, and textiles are now found equalized under the name of "handicrafts" in urban markets. If we want to buy the best designs, we no longer go to the mountains or the forests where the Indians who produce them live, because the pieces of diverse ethnic groups are mixed together in shops in the cities.

The aggregate of works and messages that used to structure visual culture and provide the grammar of reading the city diminished their efficacy in the urban space as well. There is no homogeneous architectural system and the distinguishing profiles of neighborhoods are being lost. The lack of urban regulation, and the cultural hybridity of buildings and users intermix styles from various eras in a single street. The interaction of the monuments with advertising and political messages situates the organization of memory and visual order in heteroclite networks.

The agony of collections is the clearest symptom of how the classifications that used to distinguish the cultured from the popular, and both from the massive, are disappearing. Cultures no longer are grouped in fixed and stable wholes, and therefore the possibility disappears of being cultured by knowing the repertory of "the great works," or of being popular because one manages the meaning of the objects and messages produced by a more or less closed community (an ethnic group, a neighborhood, a class). Now these collections renew their composition and their hierarchy with the fashions; they are crossed all the time and, to top it all off, each user can make his or her own collection. The technologies of reproduction permit each person to set up a repertory of records and cassettes in his or her home that combine the cultured with the popular, including those who already do this in the structure of their works: Piazzola, who mixes the tango with jazz and classical music, and Caetano Veloso and Chico Buarque, who appropriate at once the experimentation of the concrete poets, Afro-Brazilian traditions, and post-Webernian musical experimentation.

In addition, there is a proliferation of reproduction devices that we cannot define as either cultured or popular. In them collections are lost, and images and contexts – along with the semantic and historical references that used to bind together their meanings – are destructed.

Photocopiers. Books are unbound; anthologies approach authors incapable of being dealt with in symposia; new bindings group together chapters of diverse volumes following the logic not of intellectual production but of their uses: to prepare for an exam, to follow the tastes of a professor, to pursue sinuous itineraries absent in the routine classifications of bookstores and libraries. This fragmentary relation with books leads us to lose the structure in which the chapters are inserted; we descend, Monsiváis once wrote, into the "Xerox grade of reading." It is also true that the freer handling of texts, their reduction to notes, as desacralized as the tape-recorded class – which sometimes never passes to the written page because it is transferred directly to the screen of a computer – induces more fluid links among the texts and among students and knowledge.

Videocassette recorders. One forms his or her personal collection by mixing football games and Fassbinder films, North American series, Brazilian soap operas, and a debate over the foreign debt – what the channels broadcast when we are watching them, when we are working, or when we are sleeping. The recording may be immediate or delayed and with the possibility of erasing, rerecording, and verifying how it turned out. The video recorder resembles television and the library, says Jean Franco: "it permits the juxtaposition of very different topics starting from an arbitrary system and directed to communities that transcend the limits between races, classes, and sexes" (1987: 56). In truth, the video recorder goes farther than the library. It reorders a series of traditional or modern oppositions: between the national and the foreign, leisure and work, news and entertainment, politics and fiction. It also intervenes in sociability by allowing us to not miss a social or family gathering because we are watching a program and by promoting networks for borrowing and exchanging cassettes.

Videos. This is the most intrinsically postmodern genre. Intergenre: it mixes music, image, and text. Transtemporal: it gathers together melodies and images of various epochs and freely cites deeds out of context; it takes up what was done by Magritte and Duchamp, but for mass audiences. Some works take advantage of the versatility of video to create works that are brief but dense and systematic: *Fotoromanza* by Antonioni, *Thriller* by John Landis, *All Night Long* by Bob Rafelson, for example. But in most cases all action is given in fragments; it does not ask us to concentrate or to look for a continuity. There is no history to speak of. Not even art history or the media matter: images are plundered from everywhere and in any order. In a two-minute video, the German singer Falco summarizes the story of *The Black Vampire* by Fritz Lang; Madonna dresses like Marilyn Monroe, copying the choreography of *Gentleman Prefer Blondes* and the facial expressions of Betty Boop: "Those who remember love the homage and the nostalgia. Those who have no memory of it or who were not born yet also love it as their eyes follow the treat that is being sold to them as something brand-new" (McAllister, 1989: 21–23). There is no interest in indicating what is new and what comes from before. To be a good spectator one has to abandon oneself to the rhythm and enjoy the ephemeral sights. Even the videos that present a story downplay or ironize it by means of parodying montages and abrupt accelerations. This training in a fleeting perception of the real has had so much success that it is not limited to discotheques or a few entertainment programs on television; in the United States and Europe there are channels that broadcast them twenty-four hours a day. There are business, political, music, advertising, and educational videos that are replacing the business manual, the pamphlet, the theatrical spectacle, and the more or less reasoned staging of politics in electoral meetings. They are cold, indirect dramatizations that do not require the personal presence of interlocutors. The world is seen as a discontinuous effervescence of images, art as fast food. This ready-to-think culture allows us to de-think historical events without worrying about understanding them. In one of his films Woody Allen made fun of what he had understood by speed-reading *War and Peace*: "It talks about Russia," he concluded. *Le Nouvel Observateur* says seriously that it finds a new way of reinterpreting the student revolts of 1968 using this aesthetic: they were a "revolt clip: hot montage of shock images, rupture of rhythm, cutoff ending" (1987: 43).

Video games. These are like the participative version of videos. When they take the place of movies – not only in the public's free time but in the space of the movie theaters that close for lack of viewers – the operation of cultural displacement is clear. From contemporary cinema they take the most violent aspects: war scenes, car and motorcycle races, karate and boxing matches. They familiarize directly with the sensuality and efficacy of technology; they provide a mirror-screen where power itself and the fascination of battling with the big forces of the world are staged by taking advantage of the latest techniques and without the risk of direct confrontations. They dematerialize and disembody danger, giving us only the pleasure of winning out over others, or the possibility, in being defeated, that the only thing lost is coins in a machine.

As studies on the effects of television established long ago, these new technological resources are not neutral, nor are they omnipotent. Their simple formal innovation implies cultural changes, but the final sign depends on the uses different actors assign to them. We cite them here because they crack the orders that used to classify and distinguish cultural traditions; they weaken historical meaning and the macrostructural conceptions to the benefit of intense and sporadic relations with isolated objects, with their signs and images. Some postmodern theorists argue that this predominance of immediate and dehistoricized relations is coherent with the collapse of the great metaphysical narratives.

Actually, there are no reasons to lament the decomposition of rigid collections that, by separating the cultured, the popular, and the massive, promoted inequalities. Nor do we think that there are prospects for restoring the classic order of modernity. We see in the irreverent crossings occasions for relativizing religious, political, national, ethnic, and artistic fundamentalisms that absolutize certain patrimonies and discriminate against the rest. But we wonder if extreme discontinuity as a perceptive habit, the diminution of opportunities for understanding the reelaboration of the subsistent meanings of some traditions and for intervening in their change, do not reinforce the unconsulted power of those who continue to be concerned with understanding and managing the great networks of objects and meanings; the transnationals and the states.

Among the decollecting and dehierarchizing strategies of the cultural technologies must be included the existing asymmetry in production and use between the central and the dependent countries and between consumers of different classes within the same society. The possibilities for taking advantage of technological innovations and adapting them to their own productive and communicational needs are unequal in the central countries – generators of inventions, with high investment in renovating their industries, goods, and services – and in Latin America, where investments are frozen because of the debt and austerity policies, where scientists and technicians work with ridiculous budgets or have to emigrate, and where control of the more modern cultural media is highly concentrated and depends a great deal on outside programming.

Of course it is not a question of returning to the paranoid denunciations and conspiratorial conceptions of history that accused the modernization of quotidian and mass culture of being an instrument of the powerful in order to better exploit.

The question is to understand how the dynamic itself of technological development remodels society and coincides with or contradicts social movements. There are different kinds of technologies, each with various possibilities for development and articulation with the others. There are social sectors with diverse cultural capitals and dispositions for appropriating them with different meanings: decollecting and hybridization are not the same for the adolescents from the popular classes who go to public video-game parlors as they are for those from the middle and upper classes who have the games at home. The meanings of the technologies are constructed according to the ways they are institutionalized and socialized.

The technological remodeling of social practices does not always contradict traditional cultures and modern arts. It has extended, for example, the use of patrimonial goods and the field of creativity. Just as video games trivialize historical battles and some videos trivialize experimental art trends, computers and other uses of video make it easy to obtain data, visualize graphics and innovate them, simulate the use of pieces and information, and reduce the distance between conception and execution, knowledge and application, information and decision. This multiple appropriation of cultural patrimonies opens up original possibilities for experimentation and communication with democratizing uses, as is appreciated in the use some popular movements make of video.

But new technologies not only promote creativity and innovation; they also reproduce known structures. The three most frequent uses of video – consumption of commercial movies, porno films, and the recording of family events – repeat audio-visual practices initiated by photography and the Super 8. On the other hand, video art – explored mainly by painters, musicians, and poets – reaffirms the difference and the hermetism in a way similar to that of art galleries and movie clubs.

The coexistence of these contradictory uses reveals that the interactions of new technologies with previous culture makes them part of a much bigger project than the one they unleashed or the one they manage. One of these changes of long standing that technological intervention makes more evident is the reorganization of the links between groups and symbolic systems; the decollections and hybridizations no longer permit a rigid linking of social classes to cultural strata. Although many works remain within the minority or popular circuits for which they were made, the prevailing trend is for all sectors to mix into their tastes objects whose points of origin were previously separated. I do not want to say that this more fluid and complex circulation has evaporated class differences. I am only saying that the reorganization of the cultural stagings and the constant crossings of identities require that we ask ourselves in a different way about the orders that systematize the material and symbolic relations among groups.

Deterritorializing

The most radical inquiries into what it means to be entering and leaving modernity are by those who assume the tensions between deterritorialization and reterritorialization. With this I am referring to two processes: the loss of the "natural" relation of culture to geographical and social territories and, at the same time, certain relative, partial territorial relocalizations of old and new symbolic productions.

In order to document this transformation of contemporary cultures I will analyze first the transnationalization of symbolic markets and migrations. Then I propose to explore the aesthetic meaning of this change by following the strategies of some impure arts.

1.   There was a method of associating the popular with the national that, as we noted in earlier chapters, nourished the modernization of Latin American cultures. Carried out first in the form of colonial domination, then as industrialization and urbanization under metropolitan models, modernity seemed to be organized in politicoeconomic and cultural antagonisms: colonizers versus colonized, cosmopolitanism versus nationalism. The last pair of opposites was the one handled by dependency theory, according to which everything was explained by the confrontation between imperialism and national popular cultures.

Studies of economic and cultural imperialism served to get to know some devices used by the international centers of scientific, artistic, and communicational production that conditioned, and still condition, our development. But this model is insufficient for understanding current power relations. It does not explain the planetary functioning of an industrial, technological, financial, and cultural system whose headquarters is not in a single nation but in a dense network of economic and ideological structures. Nor does it take into account the need of metropolitan nations to make their borders flexible and integrate their economies and their educational, technological, and cultural systems, as is occurring in Europe and North America.

The persistent inequality between what the dependency theorists called the First and the Third Worlds maintains with relative effect some of their postulates. But although the decisions and benefits of the exchanges may be concentrated in the bourgeoisie of the metropolises, new processes make the asymmetry more complex: the decentralization of corporations, the planetary simultaneity of information, and the adaptation of certain international forms of knowledge and images to the knowledge and habits of each community. The delocalization of symbolic products by electronics and telematics, and the use of satellites and computers in cultural diffusion, also impede our continuing to see the confrontations of peripheral countries as frontal combats with geographically defined nations.

The Manichaeism of those oppositions becomes even less realistic in the eighties and nineties when several dependent countries are registering a notable increase in their cultural exports. In Brazil, the advance of massification and industrialization of culture did not imply – contrary to what tended to be said – a greater dependency on foreign production. Statistics reveal that in the last several years its cinematography and the proportion of national films on the screens grew: from 13.9 percent in 1971 to 35 percent in 1982. Books by Brazilian authors, which accounted for 54 percent of publishing production in 1973, rose to 70 percent in 1981. Also, more national records and cassettes are listened to, while imported music declines. In 1972, 60 percent of television programming was foreign; in 1983, it fell to 30 percent. At the same time that this trend toward nationalization and autonomy is occurring in cultural production, Brazil is becoming a very active agent in the Latin American market of symbolic goods by exporting soap operas. As it also succeeds in broadly penetrating the central countries, it became the seventh world producer of television and advertising, and the sixth in records. Renato Ortiz, from whom I take these data, concludes that they went "from defense of the national popular to exportation of the international popular" (1988: 182–206).

Although this trend does not occur in the same way in all Latin American countries, there are similar aspects in those of more modern cultural development that reestablish the articulations between the national and the foreign. Such changes do not eliminate the question of how distinct classes benefit from and are represented in the culture produced in each country, but the radical alteration of the stagings of production and consumption – as well as the character of the goods that are presented – questions the "natural" association of the popular with the national and the equally a priori opposition with the international.

2.   Multidirectional migrations are the other factor that relativizes the binary and polar paradigm in the analysis of intercultural relations. Latin American internationalization is accentuated in the last few decades, when migrations not only include writers, artists, and exiled politicians as happened since last century, but settlers from all social layers. How do we include in the one-directional schema of imperialist domination the new flows of cultural circulation opened up by the transplants of Latin Americans to the United States and Europe, from the least-developed countries to the most prosperous ones of our continent, from poor regions to urban centers? Are there two million South Americans who, according to the most conservative statistics, left Argentina, Chile, Brazil, and Uruguay in the seventies because of ideological persecution and economic suffering? It is not accidental that the most innovative reflection on deterritorialization is unfolding in the principal area of migrations on the continent – the border between Mexico and the United States.

From both sides of that border, intercultural movements show their painful face: the underemployment and uprooting of peasants and indigenous people who had to leave their lands in order to survive. But a very dynamic cultural production is also growing there. If there are more than 250 Spanish-language radio and television stations in the United States, more than fifteen hundred publications in Spanish, and a high interest in Latin American literature and music, it is not only because there is a market of twenty million "Hispanics," or 8 percent of the US population (38 percent in New Mexico, 25 percent in Texas, and 23 percent in California). It is also due to the fact that so-called Latin culture produces films like *Zoot Suit* and *La Bamba*, the songs of Rubén Blades and Los Lobos, aesthetically and culturally advanced theaters like that of Luis Valdez, and visual artists whose quality and aptitude for making popular culture interact with modern and postmodern symbolism incorporates them into the North American mainstream.[3]

Whoever is familiar with these artistic movements knows that many are rooted in the everyday experiences of the popular sectors. So that no doubts remain about the transclass extent of the phenomenon of deterritorialization, it is useful to refer to the anthropological investigations on migrants. Roger Rouse studied the inhabitants of

Aguililla, a rural town in southwestern Michoacán, apparently only accessible by a dirt road. Its two main activities continue to be agriculture and raising livestock for subsistence, but the emigration that began in the forties was such an incentive that almost all families there now have members who live or have lived abroad. The declining local economy is sustained by the flow of dollars sent from California, especially from Redwood City, that nucleus of microelectronics and post-industrial North American culture in Silicon Valley, where the Michoacanos work as laborers and in services. Most stay for brief periods in the United States, and those who remain longer maintain constant relations with their place of origin. There are so many outside of Aguililla, and so frequent are their connections with those who remain there, that one can no longer conceive of the two wholes as separate communities:

> Through the constant migration back and forth and the growing use of telephones, the residents of Aguililla tend to be reproducing their links with people that are two thousand miles away as actively as they maintain their relations with their immediate neighbors. Still more, and more generally, through the continuous circulation of people, money, commodities, and information, the diverse settlements have intermingled with such force that they are probably better understood as forming only one community dispersed in a variety of places. (Rouse, 1988: 1–2)

Two conventional notions of social theory collapse in the face of these "crossed economies, meaning systems that intersect, and fragmented personalities." One of these is that of "community," employed both for isolated peasant populations and for expressing the abstract cohesion of a compact national state, in both cases definable by relation to a specific territory. It was assumed that the links between the members of those communities would be more intense inside than outside of their space, and that the members treat the community as the principal medium to which they adjust their actions. The second image is the one that opposes center and periphery, also an "abstract expression of an idealized imperial system," in which the gradations of power and wealth would be distributed concentrically: most in the center and a progressive decrease as we move toward surrounding zones. The world functions less and less in this way, says Rouse; we need "an alternative cartography of social space" based instead on the notions of "circuit" and "border."

It also should not be assumed, he adds, that this reordering only includes those on the margins. He notes a similar disarticulation in the economy of the United States, previously dominated by autonomous blocks of capital. In the central area of Los Angeles, 75 percent of the buildings now belong to foreign capital; in all urban centers combined, 40 percent of the population consists of ethnic minorities from Asia and Latin America, and "it is calculated that this number will approach 60 percent in the year 2010" (Rouse, 1988: 2). There is an "implosion of the third world in the first," according to Renato Rosaldo (n.d.: 9); "the notion of an authentic culture as an autonomous internally coherent universe is no longer sustainable" in either of these two worlds, "except perhaps as a "useful fiction" or a revealing distortion" (Rosaldo, 1989: 217).

When, in the last few years of his life, Michel de Certeau taught in San Diego, he used to say that in California the mix of immigrants from Mexico, Colombia, Norway, Russia, Italy, and the eastern United States made him think that "life consists of constantly crossing borders." Roles are taken and changed with the same versatility as cars and houses:

> This mobility rests on the postulate that one is not identified either by birth, by family, by professional status, by friendships or love relationships, or by property. It seems as if all identity defined by status and place (of origin, of work, of residence, etc.) were reduced, if not swept away, by the velocity of all movements. It is known that there is no identity document in the United States; it is replaced by the driver's license and the credit card, that is, by the capacity to cross space and by participation in a game of fiduciary contracts between North American citizens. (Certeau, 1981: 10–18)[4]

During the two periods during which I studied the intercultural conflicts on the Mexican side of the border, in Tijuana, in 1985 and 1988, several times I thought that this city is, along with New York, one of the biggest laboratories of postmodernity.[5] In 1950 it had no more than sixty thousand inhabitants; today there are more than a million, with migrants from almost all regions of Mexico (mainly Oaxaca, Puebla, Michoacán, and the Federal District) who have settled there over the years. Some go daily into the United States to work; others cross the border during the planting and harvesting seasons. Even those who stay in Tijuana are linked to commercial exchanges between the two countries, to North American *maquiladoras* located on the Mexican border, or to tourist services for the three or four million people from the United States who arrive in this city every year.

From the beginning of this century until fifteen years ago, Tijuana was known for a casino (abolished during the Cárdenas government), cabarets, dance halls, and liquor stores where North Americans came to elude their country's prohibitions on sex, gambling, and alcohol. The recent installation of factories, modern hotels, cultural centers, and access to wide-ranging international information has made it into a modern, contradictory, cosmopolitan city with a strong definition of itself.

In interviews we did of primary, secondary, and university students, and of artists and cultural promoters from all social layers, there was no theme more central for their self-definition than border life and intercultural contacts. One of our research techniques was to ask them to name the most representative places of life and culture in Tijuana in order to photograph them later; we also took pictures of other scenes that seemed to condense the city's meaning (publicity posters, casual encounters, graffiti) and selected fifty photos to show to fourteen groups from various economic and cultural levels. Two-thirds of the images they judged most representative of the city, and about which they spoke with the greatest emphasis, were those that linked Tijuana with what lies beyond it: Revolution Avenue, its shops and tourist centers, the minaret that bears witness to where the casino was, the parabolic antennas, the legal and illegal passages on the border, the neighborhoods where those from different parts of the country are concentrated, the tomb of the Unknown Soldier, "lord of the émigrés," to whom they go to ask that he arrange their "papers" or to thank him for their not having been caught by *la migra* (or Immigration).

The multicultural character of the city is expressed in the use of Spanish, English, and also indigenous languages in the neighborhoods and *maquiladoras*, or among those who sell crafts downtown. This pluralism diminishes when we move from private interactions to public languages, that is, those of radio, television, and urban advertising, where English and Spanish predominate and coexist "naturally."

Along with the poster that recommends the disco club and the radio station that plays "rock in your language," another announces a Mexican liqueur in English. Music and alcoholic beverages – two symbols of Tijuana – coexist under this linguistic duality. "The other choice" is explicitly the liqueur, but the contiguity of the messages makes it possible that it also refers to rock in Spanish. The ambivalence of the image, which the interviewees considered analogous to life in the city, also allows us to conclude – following the order of reading – that the other choice is English.

The uncertainty generated by the bilingual, bicultural, and binational oscillations has its equivalence in the relations with its own history. Some of the photos were chosen precisely because they allude to the simulated character of a good portion of Tijuana culture. The Hot Water Tower, burned in the 1960s with the intention of forgetting the casino it represented, was rebuilt a few years ago and now is exhibited with pride on magazine covers and in advertising; but in pointing out to the interviewees that the current tower is in a different location than the original one, they argue that the change is a way of displacing and relocating the past.

On several corners of Revolution Avenue there are zebras. In reality they are painted burros. They are there so that North American tourists can be photographed with a landscape behind them in which images from various regions of Mexico are crowded together: volcanoes, Aztec figures, cacti, the eagle with the serpent. "Faced with the lack of other types of things, as there are in the south where there are pyramids, there is none of that here ... as if something had to be invented for the gringos," they said in one of the groups. In another group, they pointed out that "it also refers to the myth that North Americans bring with them, that it has something to do with crossing the border into the past, into the wilderness, into the idea of being able to ride horseback."

One interviewee told us: "The wire that separates Mexico from the United States could be the main monument of culture on the border."

In arriving at the beach "the line" falls and leaves a transit zone, used at times by undocumented migrants. Every Sunday the fragmented families on both sides of the border gather for picnics.

Where the borders move, they can be rigid or fallen; where buildings are evoked in another place than the one they represent, every day the spectacular invention of the city itself is renewed and expanded. The simulacrum comes to be a central category of culture. Not only is the "authentic" relativized. The obvious, ostentatious illusion – like the zebras that everyone knows are fake or the hiding games of illegal migrants that are "tolerated" by the United States police – becomes a resource for defining identity and communicating with others.

To these hybrid and simulated products, border artists and writers add their own intercultural laboratory. The following is from a radio interview with Guillermo Gómez-Peña, editor of the bilingual journal *La línea quebrada/The broken line*, with offices in Tijuana and San Diego:

> REPORTER: If you love our country so much, as you say you do, why do you live in California?
>
> GÓMEZ-PEÑA: I am de-Mexicanizing myself in order to Mexicomprehend myself...
>
> REPORTER: What do you consider yourself, then?
>
> GÓMEZ-PEÑA: Post-Mexica, pre-Chicano, pan-Latino, land-crossed, Art American...it depends on the day of the week or the project in question.

Several Tijuana periodicals are dedicated to reworking the definitions of identity and culture taking the border experience as their starting point. *La línea quebrada*, which is the most radical, says that it expresses a generation that grew up "watching *charro* and science-fiction movies, listening to cumbias and Moody Blues songs, building altars and filming in Super 8, reading *El Corno Emplumado* and *Art Forum*." Since they live in the interval, "in the crack between the two worlds," and since they are "the ones who didn't go because we didn't fit, the ones who still don't arrive or don't know where to arrive," they decide to assume all possible identities:

> When they ask me my nationality or ethnic identity, I cannot respond with one word, since my "identity" has multiple repertories: I am Mexican but also Chicano and Latin American. On the border they call me "chilango" or "mexiquillo"; in the capital "pocho" or "norteño," and in Europe "sudaca." Anglo-Saxons call me "Hispanic" or "Latino," and Germans have more than once confused me with being Turkish or Italian.

With a phrase that would please a migrant as much as a young rocker, Gómez-Peña explains that "our deepest generational feeling is that of the loss that arises from the departure." But there are also things that they have gained: "a view of culture that is more experimental, that is, multifocal and tolerant" (Gómez-Peña, 1987: 3–5).[6]

Other artists and writers from Tijuana question the euphemized view of the contradictions and the uprooting they perceive in the *La línea quebrada* group. They reject the celebration of the migrations often caused by poverty in the place from which people migrate, and which is repeated in their new destination. There is no lack of those who, despite not having been born in Tijuana, contest this parodic and detached insolence in the name of their fifteen or twenty years in the city: "people who have arrived recently and want to discover us and tell us who we are."

Both in this polemic and in other manifestations of strong emotions in referring to the photos of Tijuana, we saw a complex movement that we would call *reterritorialization*. The same people who praise the city for being open and cosmopolitan want to fix signs of identification and rituals that differentiate them from those who are just passing through, who are tourists, or...anthropologists curious to understand intercultural crossings.

The editors of the other Tijuana journal, *Esquina baja*, devoted a long time to explaining to us why they wanted, in addition to having an organ in which to express themselves,

> to generate an audience of readers, a local journal of quality in all aspects, such as design and presentation...in order to counteract a bit that centrist trend that exists in the country, because what there is in the provinces does not succeed in transcending, and is minimized, if it does not first pass through the fine sieve of the Federal District.

We find something similar in the vehemence with which everyone rejected the "missionary" criteria for cultural activities favored by the central government. Against the national programs designed to "affirm Mexican identity" on the northern border, Baja Californians argue that they are as Mexican as the rest, though in a different way. About the "threat of North American cultural penetration" they say that, in spite of the geographic and communicational proximity to the United States, the daily commercial and cultural exchanges make them live inequality intensely and therefore have a less idealized image of those who receive a similar influence in the capital via television messages and imported consumer goods.

Deterritorialization and reterritorialization. In the exchanges of traditional symbols with international communications circuits, culture industries, and migrations, questions about identity and the national, the defense of sovereignty, and the unequal appropriation of knowledge and art do not disappear. The conflicts are not erased, as neoconservative postmodernism claims. They are placed in a different register, one that is multifocal and more tolerant, and the autonomy of each culture is rethought – sometimes – with smaller fundamentalist risks. Nevertheless, the chauvinist critiques of "those from the center" sometimes engender violent conflicts: acts of aggression against recently arrived migrants and discrimination in school and at work.

The intense crossings and the instability of traditions, bases of the valorizing opening, may also be – in conditions of labor competition – a source of prejudice and confrontation. Therefore, the analysis of the advantages or inconveniences of deterritorialization should not be reduced to the movements of ideas or cultural codes, as is frequently the case in the bibliography on postmodernity. Their meaning is also constructed in connection with social and economic practices, in struggles for local power, and in the competition to benefit from alliances with external powers.

Oblique Powers

This crossing of some postmodern transformations of the symbolic market and of everyday culture contributes to understanding the failure of certain ways of doing politics that are based on two principles of modernity: the autonomy of symbolic processes and the democratic renewal of the cultured and the popular. Likewise, it can help us explain the generalized success of neoconservative politics and the lack of socializing or more democratic alternatives adapted to the level of technological development and the complexity of the social crisis. In addition to the economic advantages of the neoconservative groups, their action is facilitated by their having better captured the sociocultural meaning of the new structures of power.

Starting from what we have been analyzing, a key question returns: the cultural reorganization of power. It is a question of analyzing *what the political consequences are of moving from a vertical and bipolar conception of sociopolitical relations to one that is decentered and multidetermined.*

It is understandable that there is resistance to this displacement. The Manichaean and conspiratorial representations of power find partial justification in some contemporary processes. The central countries use technological innovations to accentuate the asymmetry and inequality between them and the dependent countries. The hegemonic classes take advantage of industrial reconversion to reduce workers' employment, cut back the power of the unions, and commercialize goods – among which are educational and cultural ones – about which, after historic struggles, agreement had been reached that they were public services. It would seem that the big groups in which power is concentrated are the ones that subordinate art and culture to the market, the ones that discipline work and daily life.

A broader view allows us to see other economic and political transformations, supported by long-lasting cultural changes, that are giving a different structure to the conflicts. The crossings between the cultured and the popular render obsolete the polar representation between both modalities of symbolic development, and therefore revitalize the political opposition between hegemonics and subalterns, conceived as if it were a question of totally distinct and always opposed groups. What we know today about the intercultural operations of the mass media and new technologies, and about the reappropriation that makes of them diverse receivers, distances us from the theses about the omnipotent manipulation of the big metropolitan consortia. The classic paradigms with which domination was explained are incapable of taking into account the dissemination of the centers, the multipolarity of social initiatives, the plurality of references – taken from diverse territories – with which artists, artisans, and the mass media assemble their works.

The increase in processes of hybridization makes it evident that we understand very little about power if we only examine confrontations and vertical actions. Power would not function if it were exercised only by bourgeoisie over proletarians, whites over indigenous people, parents over children, the media over receivers. Since all these relations are *interwoven* with each other, each one achieves an effectiveness that it would never be able to by itself. But it is not simply a question of some forms of domination being superimposed on others and thereby being strengthened. What gives them their efficacy is the obliqueness that is established in the fabric. How can we discern where ethnic power ends and where family power begins, or the borders between political and economic power? Sometimes it is possible, but what is most important is the shrewdness with which the cables are mixed, and secret orders passed and responded to affirmatively.

Hegemonic, subaltern: heavy words that helped us to name the divisions between people but not to include movements of affection and participation in solidary or complicit activities in which hegemonic and subaltern groups are needed. Those who work on the border in constant relation with the tourism, factories, and language of the United States look strangely at those who consider them to be absorbed by the empire. For the protagonists of those relations, the interferences of English in their speech (to a certain extent equivalent to the infiltration of Spanish in the South of the United States) express the indispensable transactions in which everyday exchanges happen.

It is not necessary to look at those transactions as phenomena exclusive to zones of dense interculturalism. The ideological dramatization of social relations tends to exalt so much the oppositions that it ends by not seeing the rites that unite and connect them; it is a sociology of gratings, not of what is said through them or when they are not there. The most rebellious popular sectors and the most combative leaders satisfy their basic needs by participating in a system of consumption that they do not choose. They cannot invent the place where they work, the transportation that brings them there, nor the school where they educate their children, nor their food, nor their clothes, nor the media that supply them with daily information. Even protests against that order are made using a language they do not choose and demonstrating in streets or squares that were made by others. However many transgressive uses they make of the language, the streets, and the squares, the resignification is temporary and does not cancel the weight of the habits whereby we reproduce the sociocultural order, inside and outside of ourselves.

These realities – so obvious, but usually omitted in the ideological dramatization of conflicts – become clearer when nonpolitical behaviors are observed. Why do the popular sectors support those who oppress them? Medical anthropologists observe that in the face of health problems, the usual conduct of subaltern groups is not to attack the exploitation that makes it difficult for them to receive adequate care, but rather to accommodate themselves to the uses of the illness by private medicine or to take advantage as much as possible of deficient state services. This is not due to a lack of consciousness about their health needs, about the oppression that weighs them down, nor about the inadequacy or speculative cost of the services. Even when radical means of action are available for confronting inequality, they opt for intermediate solutions. The same thing happens in other scenarios. In the face of the economic crisis, they demand better salaries and at the same time limit their own consumption. Against political hegemony, the transaction consists, for example, in accepting personal relations in order to obtain individual benefits; in the ideological realm, in incorporating and positively valuing elements produced outside of their own group (criteria of prestige, hierarchies, designs, and functions of objects). The same combination of scientific and traditional practices – going to the doctor or to the healer – is a transactional way of taking advantage of the resources of both medicines, whereby the users reveal a conception that is more flexible than that of the modern medical system, so attached to allopathy, and of many anthropologists and folklorists who idealize the autonomy of traditional practices. From the perspective of the users, both therapeutic modalities are complementary and function as repertoires of resources starting from which they effect transactions between hegemonic and popular knowledge.[9]

The hybridizations described throughout this book bring us to the conclusion that today all cultures are border cultures. All the arts develop in relation to other arts:

handicrafts migrate from the countryside to the city; movies, videos, and songs that recount events of one people are interchanged with others. Thus cultures lose the exclusive relation with their territory, but they gain in communication and knowledge.

There is yet another way in which the obliquity of the symbolic circuits allows us to rethink the links between culture and power. The search for mediations and diagonal ways for managing conflicts gives cultural relations a prominent place in political development. When we do not succeed in changing whoever governs, we satirize him or her in Carnival dances, journalistic humor, and graffiti. Against the impossibility of constructing a different order, we establish masked challenges in myths, literature, and comic strips. The struggle between classes or ethnic groups is, most of the time, a metaphorical struggle. Sometimes, starting from metaphors, new transformative practices slowly or unexpectedly invade the picture.

At every border there are rigid wires and fallen wires. Exemplary actions, cultural rodeos, rites are ways of going beyond the limits wherever possible. I think of the cunning of undocumented migrants in the United States, of the parodic rebelliousness of Colombian and Argentine graffiti. I remember the Mothers of the Plaza de Mayo walking every Thursday in a cyclical ritualism, holding photos of their disappeared children like icons, until they succeeded years later in having some of the guilty condemned to prison.

But the frustrations of human rights organizations make us reflect also on the role of culture as a symbolic expression for sustaining a demand when political paths are closed. The day the Argentine Congress approved the Law of Ending (Ley de Punto Final), which absolved hundreds of torturers and murderers, two formerly disappeared persons put themselves into narrow booths, handcuffed and blindfolded, in front of the legislative palace, with posters that said "The end means returning to this" – the ritual repetition of disappearance and confinement as the only way of preserving memory of them when political failure seemed to eliminate them from the social horizon.

This limited symbolic effectiveness leads to that fundamental distinction for defining relations between the cultural and political fields that we analyzed in the preceding chapter: the difference between *action* and *acting*. A chronic difficulty in the political valorization of cultural practices is to understand them as actions – that is, as effective interventions in the material structures of society. Certain sociologizing readings also measure the utility of a mural or a film by its capacity to perform and generate immediate and verifiable modifications. It is hoped that the spectators respond to the supposed "conscientizing" actions with "consciousness-raising" and "real changes" in their conduct. As this almost never happens, one reaches pessimistic conclusions about the efficacy of artistic messages.

Cultural practices are performances more than actions. They represent and simulate social actions but only sometimes operate as an action. This happens not only in cultural activities that are expressly organized and acknowledged as such; ordinary behaviors too, whether grouped in institutions or not, employ simulated action and symbolic performance. Presidential discourses in the face of a conflict that cannot be resolved with the available resources, the criticism of governmental performance by political organizations without the power to reverse it, and, of course, the verbal rebellions of the common citizen are performances that are more understandable for the theatrical gaze than for that of "pure" politics. Anthropology informs us that this is not due to the distance that crises put between ideals and acts but to the constitutive structure of the articulation between the political and the cultural in any society. Perhaps the greatest interest for politics in taking into account the symbolic problematic lies not in the sure efficacy of certain goods or messages but in the fact that the theatrical and ritual aspects of the social make evident what there is of the oblique, the simulated, and the deferred in any interaction.

Notes

1 On Chile, see Lechner's *Notas sobre la vida cotidiana* and Brunner's *Un espejo trizado Ensayos sobre cultura y politicas*, especially the first part. With respect to Argentina, see Landi (1984).

2 The photos of this series of monuments were taken by Paolo Gori. The book that he did with Helen *Eurobolo* is entitled *Mexican Monuments: Strange Encounters* (1980). A more extensive analysis of the problems treated here can be found in my article "Monuments, Billboards, and Graffiti," included in that volume. I am grateful to the Institute of Aesthetic Research of the National University of Mexico for having facilitated my access to photos by Gori that were not included in the book, and that were donated by the author to that institution.

3 Two historians of Chicano art, Shifra M. Goldman and Tomás Ybarra-Frausto, have documented this cultural production and reflected upon it in an original way (1985). See, for example, the introductions to their book *Arte Chicago: A Comprehensive Annotated Bibliography of Chicago Art, 1965–1981*: see also the articles by both of them in Rodriguez Prampolini.

4 It should be clarified that the conception of life as a constant crossing of borders, although it remains adequate, is not as easy as Michel de Certeau pronounces it when it is a question of "second-class" North American citizens – for example, blacks, Puerto Ricans, and Chicanos.

5 The report of this investigation can be read in García Canclini and Safa, *Tijuana: la also de toda la genri*: photos by Lourdes Grobet. Jennifer Metcalfe, Federico Rosas, and Ernesto Bermejillo collaborated in the study.

6 With respect to the intercultural hybridization among rockers, *cholos*, and punks who produce magazines, records, and cassettes with information and music from various continents – see Valenzuela (1998).

7 The second slogan involves a play on words that does not translate into English without losing the effect of the original Spanish: "Dios no cumple. Ni años." But the free translation given here captures more or less the sentiment of the original. – *Trans.*

8 This affirmation, like others I cite from Fontanarrosa, was obtained in a personal interview with him in Rosario, Argentina, on 18 March 1988.

9 I am using here the investigations carried out by Menéndez and Módena, who extensively analyze the practices of transaction.

References

Baudrillard, Jean (1981) *For a Critique of the Political Economy of the Sign*, trans. Charles Levin. St. Louis, Mo.: Telos Press.

Benjamin, Walter (1969) "Unpacking My Library: A Talk about Book Collecting." In *Illuminations*, trans. Harry Zohn. New York: Schocken Books.

Brunner, José Joaquín (1988) *Un espejo trizado. Ensayos sobre cultura y políticas culturales*. Santiago: FLACSO.

Castells, Manuel (1973) *La cuestión urbana*, 2nd edn. Mexico: Siglo.

Certeau, Michel de (1981) "Californie, un théâtre de passants," *Autrement*, 31 (April).

Franco, Jean (1987) "Recibir a los bárbaros: ética y cultura de masas," *Nexos*, 115 (July), Mexico.

Goldman, Shifra M., and Tomás Ybarra-Frausto (1985) *Arte Chicano: A Comprehensive Annotated Bibliography of Chicano Art, 1965–1981*. Berkeley: Chicano Studies Library and Publications Unit, University of California.

Gómez-Peña, Guillermo (1987) "Wacha ese border, son," *La Jornada Semanal*, 162 (October 27).

Gori, Paolo, and Helen Escobedo (eds) (1989) *Mexican Monuments: Strange Encounters*. New York: Abbeville Press.

Gutiérrez, Leandro H., and Luis Alberto Romero (1985) "La cultura de los sectores populares porteños," *Espacios* 2. Universidad de Buenos Aires.

Landi, Oscar (1984) "Cultura y política en la transición democrática." In *Proceso, crisis y transición democrática*, vol. 1, ed. Oskar Oszlak. Buenos Aires: Centro Editor de América Latina.

Le Nouvel Observateur (1987), January 9–15: 43.

Lechner, Norbert (1982) *Notas sobre la vida cotidiana: habitar, trabajar, consumir*, vol. 1, part 1. Santiago: FLACSO.

Lyotard, Jean-François (1993) *The Postmodern Explained: Correspondence 1982–1985*, translation edited by Julian Pefanis and Morgan Thomas. Minneapolis: University of Minnesota Press.

McAllister, Ricardo (1989) "Videoclips. La estética del parpadeo," *Crisis*, Mexico: 67 (January–February), Buenos Aires.

Menéndez, Eduardo (1981) *Poder, estratificación y salud*. Mexico: Ediciones de la Casa Chata.

Módena, María Eugenia (1990) *Madres, médicos y curanderos: diferencia cultural e identidad ideológica*. Mexico: CIESAS.

Ortiz, Renato (1988) *A moderna tradição brasileira*. São Paulo: Brasiliense.

Rosaldo, Renato (1989) *Culture and Truth: The Remaking of Social Analysis*. Boston, Mass.: Beacon Press.

——(n.d.) *Ideology, Place, and People without Culture*. Stanford University, Department of Anthropology.

Rouse, Roger (1988) "Mexicano, Chicano, Pocho. La migración mexicana y el espacio social del posmodernismo," *Página Uno*, supplement to *Unomásuno* (December 31).

Sarlo, Beatriz (1988) *Una modernidad periférica: Buenos Aires 1920 y 1930*. Buenos Aires: Nueva Visión.

Valenzuela, José Manuel (1988) *A la brava ese! Cholos, punks, chavos banda*. Tijuana: Colegio de la Frontera Norte.

Verón, Eliseo (1985) "Discurso político y estrategia de la imagen. Entrevista de Rodolfo Fogwill," *Espacios*, 3 (December): 59–65.

Part V

The Postmodern Turn and New Media

Introduction to Part V

Postmodernism lives. Legions of detractors and years of intellectual debate have done nothing to arrest its expansion or reduce its impact, and scores of usurpers have failed miserably in stultifying its scope. Despite or because of being profanely ambivalent and ambiguous, rejoicing in consumption and celebrating obsessions, ignoring consistency and avoiding stability, favoring illusions and pleasure, postmodernism is the only possible contemporary answer to a century worn out by the rise and fall of modern ideologies, the pervasion of capitalism, and an unprecedented sense of personal responsibility and individual impotence.

(Celeste Olalquiaga)

The essays in this section represent diverse theoretical positions on the contested and complex terrain of the "postmodern." The term is diverse and contradictory, and the essays in this section often offer conflicting interpretations of postmodern culture and media.[1] Ranging from Baudrillard's vision of a fragmented and hyperreal society of simulation to Jameson's Marxist analysis of postmodernism as the cultural logic of capitalism, to analyses of younger scholars who advocate the postmodern turn, these essays advance differing perspectives on a cultural and theoretical shift that has significantly transformed the ways we think about media culture and society.

French theorist Jean Baudrillard was one of the first to theorize a postmodern break in history.[2] In his studies of simulations and simulacra, from which we excerpt in *KeyWorks*, he distinguishes between modernity as an era of history organized around production, opposed to postmodernity as a stage of history organized around simulations – by which he means models or images, as when situation comedies on television simulate real families and life, or virtual reality games simulate the real.

For Baudrillard, the relationship implicit in the modernist idea of an original and a copy becomes transposed and disrupted in a postmodern period where referents and signifiers are no longer logically linked; rather, duplications represent the "real" in the postmodern world. By Baudrillard's definition, "simulacrum," a copy without an original, is manifested in Disneyland, which he discusses as a simulation of an idealized America. On his reading, Disneyland provides a hyperreal model of the United States that is more-real-than-real, generating role models, ideals, and an image of a perfect world. For Baudrillard, Disneyland is also a replica of a fantasy that serves to draw attention away from the Disneylike character of the rest of America. Likewise, he claims that the Watergate scandal was not a scandal but rather, in his view, a normal outcome of the "monstrous unprincipled enterprise" of contemporary American politics. The Watergate Affair for Baudrillard serves to deflect attention from the fact that American political life is itself corrupt to the core, that capital in "its instantaneous cruelty, its incomprehensible ferocity, its fundamental immorality – this is what is scandalous, unaccountable for" (1983: 28–9).

The Baudrillardian simulacrum displaces and renders obsolete the idea of an "original." This society of simulacra is hyperreal – seemingly more real than any original – modeled on simulations and ideals that are then reproduced in actual existence; hence, the simulation or model comes to structure and constitute everyday life. In this original situation, simulations in the postmodern world replace and become reality, so that women undergo extensive cosmetic surgery to emulate the airbrushed and digitally manipulated models in the pages of magazines, and televised re-enactments of crimes are accepted as news stories. This is a world in which power is not ideological but simulated, created through signs and models; it is a world in which there is no "subject," but rather a vortex of simulation created by constant implosions of images, information, and messages.

Fredric Jameson in his famous article "Postmodernism, or the Cultural Logic of Late Capitalism" (1984), from which we excerpt here, interprets postmodernism as a type of cultural form appropriate to the contemporary stage of global capitalism.[3] In his groundbreaking essay, Jameson claims that postmodern culture manifests "the emergence of a new kind of flatness or depthlessness, a new kind of superficiality in the most literal sense – perhaps the supreme formal feature of all the postmodernisms" (1991: 9). Existentially, he identifies the "waning of affect" within fragmented postmodern selves devoid of the expressive energies characteristic of modernism. Such one-dimensional postmodern texts and selves put in question the continued relevance of hermeneutic depth models such as the Marxian model of essence and appearance; true and false consciousness; the Freudian model of latent and manifest meanings; the existentialist model of authentic and inauthentic existence; and the semiotic model of signifier and signified.

The models of postmodernity and postmodern culture advanced by Baudrillard and Jameson have been immensely influential in cultural studies. One version involves an appropriation of the collapse of high into low culture, of depth onto surface, and the audience into the text, such that distinctions within media culture and between texts, audiences, and contexts are increasingly difficult to make; in its more extreme versions, the postmodern turn in cultural studies excludes the very possibility of progressive or critical encoding or decoding of cultural texts, or production of alternative cultures. This version of postmodern cultural criticism thus signifies the death of hermeneutics: in place of what Paul Ricoeur (1970) termed a "hermeneutics of suspicion" and the hermeneutical reading of cultural symbols and texts emerges a postmodern view that there is nothing behind the surface of texts, no depth or multiplicity of meanings for critical inquiry to discover and explicate. This version of postmodern cultural criticism thus renounces hermeneutics and tends to privilege the medium over the message, style over substance, and form over content. For postmodern theorists such as Baudrillard, as for McLuhan, "the medium is the message" and the rise to cultural dominance of media culture is symptomatic of far-reaching social and cultural changes.

A more affirmative version of postmodern cultural theory and media theory celebrates the new culture in emphasis on the appearance, look, style, variety, and diversity of contemporary culture. Other theorists see potential for promoting new oppositional types of cultural analysis and politics in the field of the postmodern. Hal Foster (1983) distinguishes between a conservative postmodernism of quotation and pastiche of past cultural forms contrasted to a postmodernism of resistance which champions art works that engage in social criticism and subversion. Indeed, many feminists, people of color, gays and lesbians, multiculturalists, postcolonialists and others have developed diverse forms of postmodern cultural studies which stress otherness and marginality, valorizing the culture and practices of individuals and groups excluded from mainstream culture, and thus generating a cultural studies of the margins and oppositional voices. Nestor Garcia Canclini (1995), for instance, describes the "hybrid cultures" and "oblique powers" of forms of popular art in Latin America, including monuments, graffiti, comic books, and songs, while Jésus Martín-Barbero describes how local groups and individuals assimilate media culture to construct their own popular forms.

In the Prologue to her book *Megalopolis* which we include in this section, Celeste Olalquiaga situates her work within postmodernism and indicates the importance of its major themes for understanding contemporary culture. Drawing on many of the major theorists collected in this text, Olalquiaga indicates the close affinities between postmodernism and today's media culture, with its insatiable lust to appropriate, assimilate, and regurgitate images, fashions, hits, and pleasures. For Olalquiaga, kitsch (mass art said to be in bad taste), popular culture, and postmodernism all exhibit "irreverent recycling, a taste for iconography and the artificial, a pleasure in color, gloss, melodrama, and overdetermination," leading her to conclude that "postmodernism is kitsch, kitsch is postmodern *avant la lettre*, or both" (1992: p. xiv).

Angela McRobbie, in an essay "Feminism, Postmodernism, and the 'Real Me,'" which appears below in *KeyWorks*, wants to appropriate postmodernism for an activist feminist theory. She begins by noting that there are three approaches to postmodernism in today's conjuncture: those who simply affirm and celebrate it; those who completely reject it; and those who wish to avoid the excesses of a completely affirmative and highly rhetorical postmodernism for a "remorseless critique of modernity" combined with "a looking to those accounts of postmodernity as a way of finding a place from which to speak and a space from which to develop that critique of the places and the spaces of exclusion inside modernity." Herself a major participant in the development of British cultural studies, McRobbie cites Stuart Hall as a positive example of a productive appropriation of postmodernism. She emphasizes Hall's positioning of himself on "the other side of modernity," seeing "turbulence and savagery," while others perceive order and reason. From this perspective, the postmodern turn validates the discourses of those marginalized or oppressed within modern societies to speak and articulate experiences, positions, and perspectives suppressed in the canonical culture and master theories of the modern era.

McRobbie herself wants to use postmodernism for feminism, arguing that post-modern discourses put in question notions of "the real me," essentialist notions of the self that suggest there is a natural, unified and hidden essence that we should discover and realize. Such notions, McRobbie suggests, smuggle in conventional concepts of conformity and fixity, and cover over the ability to create more hybri-dized, complex, and unconventional selves that should be seen as contingent, flexible, and subject to further change and development. Such conceptions, McRobbie sug-gests, help women – and others! – to question the standard models of femininity (or masculinity we would add) and to construct novel conceptions of their potential and possible lives.

In a study of "Postmodern Virtualities," Mark Poster highlights the importance of perceiving the implications of new media, communication, and information technol-ogies. A scholar of French postmodern theory and new technologies, Poster proposes theorizing how new communication media are producing innovative and alternative forms of culture and subjectivity. Citing the proliferation of new information and communication technology, Poster argues against limited understanding of these phenomena as mere instruments that can be used by existing subjects and institutions. Rather, for Poster, the emergent media and technology are novel envir-onments that create new realms of experience such as virtual reality and innovative forms of communication and subjectivity. Just as books created an individual rational subject in the modern era of print culture, in the multimedia era, Poster claims, alternative forms of cultural identity and experience are emerging in the virtual communities, cyberspaces, and relations of the booming and expanding cyberculture.

For Poster and theorists such as Sherry Turkle (1995), computer technologies thus create novel identities, social relations, and realms of experience such as cyberspace, as well as new forms of communication within the new technoculture. Many postmo-dern theorists, such as Baudrillard and Poster, however, arguably exaggerate the rupture with the past, failing to note both the continuities and the ways that the novelties they evoke are rooted in the dynamics of modernity (e.g., that the new technoculture is a part of an emergent stage of capitalism and integrally connected with globalization). Poster argues in his earlier book *Mode of Information* (1990), for example, that the mode of production is now transcended in importance by the mode of information as a fundamental principle of organizing society, just as Baudrillard argues that simulation is now the organizing principle of contemporary society and not political economy. We would argue, by contrast, that the modes of production and information are intertwined within an emergent stage of capitalism and that we need both cultural analysis and political economy to make sense of this situation. Hence, while Poster highlights the importance of perceiving the connection of postmodernity with new media and subjectivities, he does not link these phenomena with the restructuring of capital and globalization, and thus severs linkage between cultural analysis and political economy.

There is in fact a type of technological determinism in many variants of postmodern theory. Baudrillard and Poster both erase political economy and are overly determini-st in descriptions of the forms of subjectivity and culture that the new technologies are producing. For Baudrillard, we are thrown into a novel world of simulation and hyperreality where the modern subject dissolves and implodes in a precession of simulacra. Reality, meaning, identity, and a wide range of modern categories dissolve for Baudrillard in what he describes as a "catastrophe of modernity." Poster perceives more positive potential in the new technologies, as well as the need for innovative cultural and political practices to promote a more democratic and egalitarian future. But there is a covert determinism in assuming that new technologies automatically generate alternative subjectivities and identities. It is for us too linear and reductive to claim that modern technology and culture produces one type of (rational, autonomous, centered, and stable) subject, while the rapidly proliferating and mutating cyberculture produces multiple, hybridized, and flexible subjects. While Poster claims that the "second media age" of more interactive computer technology is responsible for generating the new subjectivities he valorizes, in fact earlier media such as film, radio, and television were already producing more fragmented, decentered, and hybridized subjects and presumably, we would argue, the features of a critical and autonomous rational modern subjectivity are still possible and valuable today.

Furthermore, just as there are extremely affirmative and celebratory embracings of postmodern theory, contrasted to passionate critiques and denunciations, so too are there positive and affirmative celebrations of the new media and technologies, as well as skeptical and critical perspectives. Hence, while Poster, Turkle, and myriad champions of the cyberculture see promising developments within new media and cultural spaces, some critics are skeptical, resisting claims concerning the emancipatory or novel features of new media and stressing by contrast the ways that capitalism is colonizing and controlling new media and how they are new sources of profitability, domination, and social control (see Goulding, 1998; Robins and Webster, 1999; and Schiller, 1999).

We would propose that there are both democratizing and empowering aspects and uses of new technologies, as well as more troubling features, such as threats to privacy and democracy and the empowering of corporations over individuals. Moreover, there are both continuities and discontinuities with previous technologies and modes of social organization. On the whole, we would maintain that we are in a novel cultural space between the modern and the postmodern with highly complex conflicts between new and previous forms of culture, technology, and subjectivity. While we would agree that technological revolution and the global restructuring of capitalism are dramatically transforming our world, we believe that older modern theories and methods, as well as new postmodern ones, are valuable in helping us meet the challenges and changes of the contemporary era, and that there are negative and positive features in this turbulent transformation.

In any case, media and culture are more important than ever today and so the contemporary student and citizen needs to become media and computer literate – indeed multimedia literate with new literacies for the present age (see Kellner, 1998; Hammer and Kellner, 1999). The texts we have assembled in this concluding section provide some access to the brave new cultural and technological worlds that we are inhabiting and dramatize the need for new understandings and approaches to culture and society if we are to survive the exigencies of the new millennium.

Notes

1   For an overview of postmodern theory and debates, see Best and Kellner (1991, 1997, and forthcoming).
2   See Baudrillard (1983a, 1983b, 1993, and 1994); for an overview of Baudrillard see Kellner (1989 and 2000).
3   On Jameson, see the essays collected in Kellner (1989b) and Homer (1998).

References

Baudrillard, Jean (1983a) *Simulations.* New York: Semiotext (e).

——(1983b) *In the Shadow of the Silent Majorities.* New York: Semiotext (e).

——(1983c) "The Ecstacy of Communication:" In *The Anti-Aesthetic,* ed. Hal Foster. Washington: Bay Press.

——(1993) *Symbolic Exchange and Death.* London: Sage.

——(1994) *Simulacra and Simulation.* Ann Arbor: University of Michigan Press.

Best, Steven, and Kellner, Douglas (1987) "(Re)Watching Television: Notes Toward a Political Criticism." *Diacritics* (Summer): 97–113.

——(1991) *Postmodern Theory: Critical Interrogations.* London and New York: Macmillan and Guilford Press.

——(1997) *The Postmodern Turn.* New York: Guilford Press.

——(forthcoming) *The Postmodern Adventure.* New York: Guilford Press.

Golding, Peter (1998) "Worldwide Wedge: Division and Contradiction in the Global Information Infrastructure." In Daya Kishan Thussu (Ed.), *Electronic Empires: Global Media and Local Resistance.* London: Arnold.

Hammer, Rhonda and Douglas Kellner (1999) "Multimedia Pedagogical Curriculum for the New Millennium," *Journal of Adolescent & Adult Literacy,* vol. 42, no. 7 (April): 522–6, and longer version forthcoming in *Journal of Religious Education* (2000).

Homer, Sean (1998) *Fredric Jameson: Marxism, Hermeneutics, Postmodernism.* Cambridge: Polity Press.

Jameson, Fredric (1984). "Postmodernism, or the Cultural Logic of Late Capitalism," *New Left Review,* 146 (July–August): 53–92.

Kellner, Douglas (1989a) *Jean Baudrillard: From Marxism to Postmodernism and Beyond.* Cambridge and Palo Alto: Polity Press and Stanford University Press.

——(ed.) (1989b) *Postmodernism/Jameson/Critique,* Washington, D.C.: Maisonneuve.

——(1998) "Multiple Literacies and Critical Pedagogy in a Multicultural Society," *Educational Theory,* vol. 48, no. 1: 103–122.

McRobbie, Angela (1985) "Feminism, Postmodernism, and the 'Real Me.'" In *Postmodernism and Popular Culture,* 61–74. New York and London: Routledge.

Olalquiaga, Celeste (1992) "Prologue." In *Megalopolis,* xi–xxi. Minneapolis: University of Minnesota Press.

Poster, Mark (1990) *Mode of Information.* Palo Alto, Cal.: Stanford University Press.

——(1995) "Postmodern Virtualities." In *Cyberspace, Cyberbodies, Cyberpunk,* 79–95, edited by Mike Featherstone and Rogers Burrows. London: Sage.

Robins, Kevin and Frank Webster (1999) *Times of the Technoculture.* New York: Routledge.

Ricoeur, Paul (1970) *Freud and Philosophy: An Essay on Interpretation.* New Haven: Yale University Press.

Schiller, Dan (1999) *Digital Capitalism.* Cambridge, Mass.: MIT Press.

Turkle, Sherry (1995) *Life on the Screen: Identity in the Age of the Internet.*

26

The Precession of Simulacra*

Jean Baudrillard

> The simulacrum is never what hides the truth – it is truth that hides the fact that there is none.
>   The simulacrum is true.
>
> (Ecclesiastes)

If once we were able to view the Borges fable in which the cartographers of the Empire draw up a map so detailed that it ends up covering the territory exactly (the decline of the Empire witnesses the fraying of this map, little by little, and its fall into ruins, though some shreds are still discernible in the deserts – the metaphysical beauty of this ruined abstraction testifying to a pride equal to the Empire and rotting like a carcass, returning to the substance of the soil, a bit as the double ends by being confused with the real through aging) – as the most beautiful allegory of simulation, this fable has now come full circle for us, and possesses nothing but the discrete charm of second-order simulacra.[1]

Today abstraction is no longer that of the map, the double, the mirror, or the concept. Simulation is no longer that of a territory, a referential being, or a substance. It is the generation by models of a real without origin or reality: a hyperreal. The territory no longer precedes the map, nor does it survive it. It is nevertheless the map that precedes the territory – *precession of simulacra* – that engenders the territory, and if one must return to the fable, today it is the territory whose shreds slowly rot across the extent of the map. It is the real, and not the map, whose vestiges persist here and there in the deserts that are no longer those of the Empire, but ours. *The desert of the real itself.*

In fact, even inverted, Borges's fable is unusable. Only the allegory of the Empire, perhaps, remains. Because it is with this same imperialism that present-day simulators attempt to make the real, all of the real, coincide with their models of simulation. But it is no longer a question of either maps or territories. Something has disappeared: the sovereign difference, between one and the other, that constituted the charm of abstraction. Because it is difference that constitutes the poetry of the map and the

---

* From Jean Baudrillard, *Simulacra and Simulation*, trans. Sheila Faria Glaser (Ann Arbor, Mich.: University of Michigan Press, 1994), pp. 1–42.

charm of the territory, the magic of the concept and the charm of the real. This imaginary of representation, which simultaneously culminates in and is engulfed by the cartographer's mad project of the ideal coextensivity of map and territory, disappears in the simulation whose operation is nuclear and genetic, no longer at all specular or discursive. It is all of metaphysics that is lost. No more mirror of being and appearances, of the real and its concept. No more imaginary coextensivity: it is genetic miniaturization that is the dimension of simulation. The real is produced from miniaturized cells, matrices, and memory banks, models of control – and it can be reproduced an indefinite number of times from these. It no longer needs to be rational, because it no longer measures itself against either an ideal or negative instance. It is no longer anything but operational. In fact, it is no longer really the real, because no imaginary envelops it anymore. It is a hyperreal, produced from a radiating synthesis of combinatory models in a hyperspace without atmosphere.

By crossing into a space whose curvature is no longer that of the real, nor that of truth, the era of simulation is inaugurated by a liquidation of all referentials – worse: with their artificial resurrection in the systems of signs, a material more malleable than meaning, in that it lends itself to all systems of equivalences, to all binary oppositions, to all combinatory algebra. It is no longer a question of imitation, nor duplication, nor even parody. It is a question of substituting the signs of the real for the real, that is to say of an operation of deterring every real process via its operational double, a programmatic, metastable, perfectly descriptive machine that offers all the signs of the real and short-circuits all its vicissitudes. Never again will the real have the chance to produce itself – such is the vital function of the model in a system of death, or rather of anticipated resurrection, that no longer even gives the event of death a chance. A hyperreal henceforth sheltered from the imaginary, and from any distinction between the real and the imaginary, leaving room only for the orbital recurrence of models and for the simulated generation of differences.

The Divine Irreference of Images

To dissimulate is to pretend not to have what one has. To simulate is to feign to have what one doesn't have. One implies a presence, the other an absence. But it is more complicated than that because simulating is not pretending: "Whoever fakes an illness can simply stay in bed and make everyone believe he is ill. Whoever simulates an illness produces in himself some of the symptoms" (Littré). Therefore, pretending, or dissimulating, leaves the principle of reality intact: the difference is always clear, it is simply masked, whereas simulation threatens the difference between the "true" and the "false," the "real" and the "imaginary." Is the simulator sick or not, given that he produces "true" symptoms? Objectively one cannot treat him as being either ill or not ill. Psychology and medicine stop at this point, forestalled by the illness's henceforth undiscoverable truth. For if any symptom can be "produced," and can no longer be taken as a fact of nature, then every illness can be considered as simulatable and simulated, and medicine loses its meaning since it only knows how to treat "real" illnesses according to their objective causes. Psychosomatics evolves in a dubious manner at the borders of the principle of illness. As to psychoanalysis, it transfers the symptom of the organic order to the unconscious order: the latter is new and taken for "real" more real than the other – but why would simulation be at the gates of the unconscious? Why couldn't the "work" of the unconscious be "produced" in the same way as any old symptom of classical medicine? Dreams already are.

Certainly, the psychiatrist purports that "for every form of mental alienation there is a particular order in the succession of symptoms of which the simulator is ignorant and in the absence of which the psychiatrist would not be deceived." This (which dates from 1865) in order to safeguard the principle of a truth at all costs and to escape the interrogation posed by simulation – the knowledge that truth, reference, objective cause have ceased to exist. Now, what can medicine do with what floats on either side of illness, on either side of health, with the duplication of illness in a discourse that is no longer either true or false? What can psychoanalysis do with the duplication of the discourse of the unconscious in the discourse of simulation that can never again be unmasked, since it is not false either?[2]

What can the army do about simulators? Traditionally it unmasks them and punishes them, according to a clear principle of identification. Today it can discharge a very good simulator as exactly equivalent to a "real" homosexual, a heart patient, or a madman. Even military psychology draws back from Cartesian certainties and hesitates to make the distinction between true and false, between the "produced" and the authentic symptom. "If he is this good at acting crazy, it's because he is." Nor is military psychology mistaken in this regard: in this sense, all crazy people simulate, and this lack of distinction is the worst kind of subversion. It is against this lack of distinction that classical reason armed itself in all its categories. But it is what today again outflanks them, submerging the principle of truth.

Beyond medicine and the army, favored terrains of simulation, the question returns to religion and the simulacrum of divinity: "I forbade that there be any simulacra in the temples because the divinity that animates nature can never be represented." Indeed it can be. But what becomes of the divinity when it reveals itself in icons, when it is multiplied in simulacra? Does it remain the supreme power that is simply incarnated in images as a visible theology? Or does it volatilize itself in the simulacra that, alone, deploy their power and pomp of fascination – the visible machinery of icons substituted for the pure and intelligible Idea of God? This is precisely what was feared by Iconoclasts, whose millennial quarrel is still with us today.[3] This is precisely because they predicted this omnipotence of simulacra, the faculty simulacra have of effacing God from the conscience of man, and the destructive, annihilating truth that they allow to appear – that deep down God never existed, that only the simulacrum ever existed, even that God himself was never anything but his own simulacrum – from this came their urge to destroy the images. If they could have believed that these images only obfuscated or masked the Platonic Idea of God, there would have been no reason to destroy them. One can live with the idea of distorted truth. But their metaphysical despair came from the idea that the image didn't conceal anything at all, and that these images were in essence not images, such as an original model would have made them, but perfect simulacra, forever radiant with their own fascination. Thus this death of the divine referential must be exorcised at all costs.

One can see that the iconoclasts, whom one accuses of disdaining and negating images, were those who accorded them their true value, in contrast to the iconolaters who only saw reflections in them and were content to venerate a filigree God. On the other hand, one can say that the icon worshipers were the most modern minds, the most adventurous, because, in the guise of having God become apparent in the mirror of images, they were already enacting his death and his disappearance in the epiphany of his representations (which, perhaps, they already knew no longer represented anything, that they were purely a game, but that it was therein the great game lay – knowing also that it is dangerous to unmask images, since they dissimulate the fact that there is nothing behind them).

This was the approach of the Jesuits, who founded their politics on the virtual disappearance of God and on the worldly and spectacular manipulation of consciences – the evanescence of God in the epiphany of power – the end of transcendence, which now only serves as an alibi for a strategy altogether free of influences and signs. Behind the baroqueness of images hides the éminence grise of politics.

This way the stake will always have been the murderous power of images, murderers of the real, murderers of their own model, as the Byzantine icons could be those of divine identity. To this murderous power is opposed that of representations as a dialectical power, the visible and intelligible mediation of the Real. All Western faith and good faith became engaged in this wager on representation: that a sign could refer to the depth of meaning, that a sign could be exchanged for meaning and that something could guarantee this exchange – God of course. But what if God himself can be simulated, that is to say can be reduced to the signs that constitute faith? Then the whole system becomes weightless, it is no longer itself anything but a gigantic simulacrum – not unreal, but a simulacrum, that is to say never exchanged for the real, but exchanged for itself, in an uninterrupted circuit without reference or circumference.

Such is simulation, insofar as it is opposed to representation. Representation stems from the principle of the equivalence of the sign and of the real (even if this equivalence is utopian, it is a fundamental axiom). Simulation, on the contrary, stems from the utopia of the principle of equivalence, *from the radical negation of the sign as value*, from the sign as the reversion and death sentence of every reference. Whereas representation attempts to absorb simulation by interpreting it as a false representation, simulation envelops the whole edifice of representation itself as a simulacrum.

Such would be the successive phases of the image:

it is the reflection of a profound reality;
it masks and denatures a profound reality;
it masks the *absence* of a profound reality;
it has no relation to any reality whatsoever: it is its own pure simulacrum.

In the first case, the image is a *good* appearance – representation is of the sacramental order. In the second, it is an evil appearance – it is of the order of maleficence. In the third, it plays at being an appearance – it is of the order of sorcery. In the fourth, it is no longer of the order of appearances, but of simulation.

The transition from signs that dissimulate something to signs that dissimulate that there is nothing marks a decisive turning point. The first reflects a theology of truth and secrecy (to which the notion of ideology still belongs). The second inaugurates the era of simulacra and of simulation, in which there is no longer a God to recognize his own, no longer a Last Judgment to separate the false from the true, the real from its artificial resurrection, as everything is already dead and resurrected in advance.

When the real is no longer what it was, nostalgia assumes its full meaning. There is a plethora of myths of origin and of signs of reality – a plethora of truth, of secondary objectivity, and authenticity. Escalation of the true, of lived experience, resurrection of the figurative where the object and substance have disappeared. Panic-stricken production of the real and of the referential, parallel to and greater than the panic of material production: this is how simulation appears in the phase that concerns us – a strategy of the real, of the neoreal and the hyperreal that everywhere is the double of a strategy of deterrence.

Ramses, or the Rosy-Colored Resurrection

Ethnology brushed up against its paradoxical death in 1971, the day when the Philippine government decided to return the few dozen Tasaday who had just been discovered in the depths of the jungle, where they had lived for eight centuries without any contact with the rest of the species, to their primitive state, out of the reach of colonizers, tourists, and ethnologists. This at the suggestion of the anthropologists themselves, who were seeing the indigenous people disintegrate immediately upon contact, like mummies in the open air.

In order for ethnology to live, its object must die; by dying, the object takes its revenge for being "discovered" and with its death defies the science that wants to grasp it.

Doesn't all science live on this paradoxical slope to which it is doomed by the evanescence of its object in its very apprehension, and by the pitiless reversal that the dead object exerts on it? Like Orpheus, it always turns around too soon, and, like Eurydice, its object falls back into Hades.

It is against this hell of the paradox that the ethnologists wished to protect themselves by cordoning off the Tasaday with virgin forest. No one can touch them anymore: as in a mine the vein is closed down. Science loses precious capital there, but the object will be safe, lost to science, but intact in its "virginity." It is not a question of sacrifice (science never sacrifices itself, it is always murderous), but of the simulated sacrifice of its object in order to save its reality principle. The Tasaday, frozen in their natural element, will provide a perfect alibi, an eternal guarantee. Here begins an antiethnology that will never end and to which Jaulin, Castaneda, Clastres are various witnesses. In any case, the logical evolution of a science is to distance itself increasingly from its object, until it dispenses with it entirely: its autonomy is only rendered even more fantastic – it attains its pure form.

The Indian thus returned to the ghetto, in the glass coffin of the virgin forest, again becomes the model of simulation of all the possible Indians *from before ethnology*. This model thus grants itself the luxury to incarnate itself beyond itself in the "brute" reality of these Indians it has entirely reinvented – Savages who are indebted to ethnology for still being Savages: what a turn of events, what a triumph for this science that seemed dedicated to their destruction!

Of course, these savages are posthumous: frozen, cryogenized, sterilized, protected *to death*, they have become referential simulacra, and science itself has become pure simulation. The same holds true at Cruesot, at the level of the "open" museum where one museumified in situ, as "historical" witnesses of their period, entire working-class neighborhoods, living metallurgic zones, an entire culture, men, women, and children included – gestures, languages, customs fossilized alive as in a snapshot. The museum, instead of being circumscribed as a geometric site, is every-where now, like a dimension of life. Thus ethnology, rather than circumscribing itself as an objective science, will today, liberated from its object, be applied to all living things and make itself invisible, like an omnipresent fourth dimension, that of the simulacrum. *We are all Tasadays*, Indians who have again become what they were – simulacral Indians who at last proclaim the universal truth of ethnology.

We have all become living specimens in the spectral light of ethnology, or of antiethnology, which is nothing but the pure form of triumphal ethnology, under the sign of dead differences, and of the resurrection of differences. It is thus very naive to look for ethnology in the Savages or in some Third World – it is here, everywhere, in the metropolises, in the White community, in a world completely cataloged and analyzed, then *artificially resurrected under the auspices of the real*, in a world of simulation, of the hallucination of truth, of the blackmail of the real, of the murder of every symbolic form and of its hysterical, historical retrospection – a murder of which the Savages, noblesse oblige, were the first victims, but that for a long time has extended to all Western societies.

But in the same breath ethnology grants us its only and final lesson, the secret that kills it (and which the Savages knew better than it did): the vengeance of the dead.

The confinement of the scientific object is equal to the confinement of the mad and the dead. And just as all of society is irremediably contaminated by this mirror of madness that it has held up to itself, science can't help but die contaminated by the death of this object that is its inverse mirror. It is science that masters the objects, but it is the objects that invest it with depth, according to an unconscious reversion, which only gives a dead and circular response to a dead and circular interrogation.

Nothing changes when society breaks the mirror of madness (abolishes the asy-lums, gives speech back to the insane, etc.) nor when science seems to break the mirror of its objectivity (effacing itself before its object, as in Castaneda, etc.) and to bend down before the "differences." The form produced by confinement is followed by an innumerable, diffracted, slowed-down mechanism. As ethnology collapses in its classical institution, it survives in an antiethnology whose task it is to reinject the difference fiction, the Savage fiction everywhere, to conceal that it is this world, ours, which has again become savage in its way, that is to say, which is devastated by difference and by death.

In the same way, with the pretext of saving the original, one forbade visitors to enter the Lascaux caves, but an exact replica was constructed five hundred meters from it, so that everyone could see them (one glances through a peephole at the authentic cave, and then one visits the reconstituted whole). It is possible that the memory of the original grottoes is itself stamped in the minds of future generations, but from now on there is no longer any difference: the duplication suffices to render both artificial.

In the same way science and technology were recently mobilized to save the mummy of Ramses II, after it was left to rot for several dozen years in the depths of a museum. The West is seized with panic at the thought of not being able to save what the symbolic order had been able to conserve for forty centuries, but out of sight and far from the light of day. Ramses does not signify anything for us, only the mummy is of an inestimable worth because it is what guarantees that accumulation has meaning. Our entire linear and accumulative culture collapses if we cannot stockpile the past in plain view. To this end the pharaohs must be brought out of their tomb and the mummies out of their silence. To this end they must be exhumed and given military honors. They are prey to both science and worms. Only absolute secrecy assured them this millennial power – the mastery over putrefaction that signified the mastery of the complete cycle of exchanges with death. *We* only know how to place our science in service of *repairing* the mummy, that is to say restoring a *visible* order, whereas embalming was a mythical effort that strove to immortalize a *hidden* dimension.

We require a visible past, a visible continuum, a visible myth of origin, which reassures us about our end. Because finally we have never believed in them. Whence this historic scene of the reception of the mummy at the Orly airport. Why? Because Ramses was a great despotic and military figure? Certainly. But mostly because our culture dreams, behind this defunct power that it tries to annex, of an order that would have had nothing to do with it, and it dreams of it because it exterminated it by exhuming it *as its own past.*

We are fascinated by Ramses as Renaissance Christians were by the American Indians, those (human?) beings who had never known the word of Christ. Thus, at the beginning of colonization, there was a moment of stupor and bewilderment before the very possibility of escaping the universal law of the Gospel. There were two possible responses: either admit that this Law was not universal, or exterminate the Indians to efface the evidence. In general, one contented oneself with converting them, or even simply discovering them, which would suffice to slowly exterminate them.

Thus it would have been enough to exhume Ramses to ensure his extermination by museumification. Because mummies don't rot from worms: they die from being transplanted from a slow order of the symbolic, master over putrefaction and death, to an order of history, science, and museums, our order, which no longer masters anything, which only knows how to condemn what preceded it to decay and death and subsequently to try to revive it with science. Irreparable violence toward all secrets, the violence of a civilization without secrets, hatred of a whole civilization for its own foundation.

And just as with ethnology, which plays at extricating itself from its object to better secure itself in its pure form, *demuseumification* is nothing but another spiral in artificiality. Witness the cloister of Saint-Michel de Cuxa, which one will repatriate at great cost from the Cloisters in New York to reinstall it in "its original site." And everyone is supposed to applaud this restitution (as they did "the experimental campaign to take back the sidewalks" on the Champs Elysees!). Well, if the exportation of the cornices was in effect an arbitrary act, if the Cloisters in New York are an artificial mosaic of all cultures (following a logic of the capitalist centralization of value), their reimportation to the original site is even more artificial: it is a total simulacrum that links up with "reality" through a complete circumvolution.

The cloister should have stayed in New York in its simulated environment, which at least fooled no one. Repatriating it is nothing but a supplementary subterfuge, acting as if nothing had happened and indulging in retrospective hallucination.

In the same way, Americans flatter themselves for having brought the population of Indians back to pre-Conquest levels. One effaces everything and starts over. They even flatter themselves for doing better, for exceeding the original number. This is presented as proof of the superiority of civilization: it will produce more Indians than they themselves were able to do. (With sinister derision, this overproduction is again a means of destroying them: for Indian culture, like all tribal culture, rests on the limitation of the group and the refusal of any "unlimited" increase, as can be seen in Ishi's case. In this way, their demographic "promotion" is just another step toward symbolic extermination.)

Everywhere we live in a universe strangely similar to the original – things are doubled by their own scenario. But this doubling does not signify, as it did traditionally, the imminence of their death – they are already purged of their death, and better than when they were alive; more cheerful, more authentic, in the light of their model, like the faces in funeral homes.

The Hyperreal and the Imaginary

Disneyland is a perfect model of all the entangled orders of simulacra. It is first of all a play of illusions and phantasms: the Pirates, the Frontier, the Future World, etc. This imaginary world is supposed to ensure the success of the operation. But what attracts the crowds the most is without a doubt the social microcosm, the *religious*, miniaturized pleasure of real America, of its constraints and joys. One parks outside and stands in line inside, one is altogether abandoned at the exit. The only phantasmagoria in this imaginary world lies in the tenderness and warmth of the crowd, and in the sufficient and excessive number of gadgets necessary to create the multitudinous effect. The contrast with the absolute solitude of the parking lot – a veritable concentration camp – is total. Or, rather: inside, a whole panoply of gadgets magnetizes the crowd in directed flows – outside, solitude is directed at a single gadget: the automobile. By an extraordinary coincidence (but this derives without a doubt from the enchantment inherent to this universe), this frozen, childlike world is found to have been conceived and realized by a man who is himself now cryogenized: Walt Disney, who awaits his resurrection through an increase of 180 degrees centigrade.

Thus, everywhere in Disneyland the objective profile of America, down to the morphology of individuals and of the crowd, is drawn. All its values are exalted by the miniature and the comic strip. Embalmed and pacified. Whence the possibility of an ideological analysis of Disneyland (L. Marin did it very well in *Utopiques, jeux d'espace* [Utopias, plays of space]): digest of the American way of life, panegyric of American values, idealized transposition of a contradictory reality. Certainly. But this masks something else and this "ideological" blanket functions as a cover for a *simulation of the third order*: Disneyland exists in order to hide that it is the "real" country, all of "real" America that *is* Disneyland (a bit like prisons are there to hide that it is the social in its entirety, in its banal omnipresence, that is carceral). Disneyland is presented as imaginary in order to make us believe that the rest is real, whereas all of Los Angeles and the America that surrounds it are no longer real, but belong to the hyperreal order and to the order of simulation. It is no longer a question of a false representation of reality (ideology) but of concealing the fact that the real is no longer real, and thus of saving the reality principle.

The imaginary of Disneyland is neither true nor false, it is a deterrence machine set up in order to rejuvenate the fiction of the real in the opposite camp. Whence the debility of this imaginary, its infantile degeneration. This world wants to be childish in order to make us believe that the adults are elsewhere, in the "real" world, and to conceal the fact that true childishness is everywhere – that it is that of the adults themselves who come here to act the child in order to foster illusions as to their real childishness.

Disneyland is not the only one, however. Enchanted Village, Magic Mountain, Marine World: Los Angeles is surrounded by these imaginary stations that feed reality, the energy of the real to a city whose mystery is precisely that of no longer being anything but a network of incessant, unreal circulation – a city of incredible proportions but without space, without dimension. As much as electrical and atomic power stations, as much as cinema studios, this city, which is no longer anything but an immense scenario and a perpetual pan shot, needs this old imaginary like a sympathetic nervous system made up of childhood signals and faked phantasms.

Disneyland: a space of the regeneration of the imaginary as waste-treatment plants are elsewhere, and even here. Everywhere today one must recycle waste, and the dreams, the phantasms, the historical, fairylike, legendary imaginary of children and adults is a waste product, the first great toxic excrement of a hyperreal civilization. On a mental level, Disneyland is the prototype of this new function. But all the sexual, psychic, somatic recycling institutes, which proliferate in California, belong to the same order. People no longer look at each other, but there are institutes for that. They no longer touch each other, but there is contactotherapy. They no longer walk, but they go jogging, etc. Everywhere one recycles lost faculties, or lost bodies, or lost sociality, or the lost taste for food. One reinvents penury, asceticism, vanished savage naturalness: natural food, health food, yoga. Marshall Sahlins's idea that it is the economy of the market, and not of nature at all, that secretes penury, is verified, but at a secondary level: here, in the sophisticated confines of a triumphal market economy is reinvented a penury/sign, a penury/simulacrum, a simulated behavior of the underdeveloped (including the adoption of Marxist tenets) that, in the guise of ecology, of energy crises and the critique of capital, adds a final esoteric aureole to the triumph of an esoteric culture. Nevertheless, maybe a mental catastrophe, a mental implosion and involution without precedent lies in wait for a system of this kind, whose visible signs would be those of this strange obesity, or the incredible co-existence of the most bizarre theories and practices, which correspond to the im-probable coalition of luxury, heaven, and money, to the improbable luxurious materialization of life and to undiscoverable contradictions.

Political Incantation

Watergate. The same scenario as in Disneyland (effect of the imaginary concealing that reality no more exists outside than inside the limits of the artificial perimeter): here the scandal effect hiding that there is no difference between the facts and their denunciation (identical methods on the part of the CIA and of the *Washington Post* journalists). Same operation, tending to regenerate through scandal a moral and political principle, through the imaginary, a sinking reality principle.

The denunciation of scandal is always an homage to the law. And Watergate in particular succeeded in imposing the idea that Watergate *was* a scandal – in this sense it was a prodigious operation of intoxication. A large dose of political morality reinjected on a world scale. One could say along with Bourdieu: "The essence of every relation of force is to dissimulate itself as such and to acquire all its force only because it dissimulates itself as such," understood as follows: capital, immoral and without scruples, can only function behind a moral superstructure, and whoever revives this public morality (through indignation, denunciation, etc.) works spontan-eously for the order of capital. This is what the journalists of the *Washington Post* did.

But this would be nothing but the formula of ideology, and when Bourdieu states it, he takes the "relation of force" for the *truth* of capitalist domination, and he himself *denounces* this relation of force as *scandal* – he is thus in the same determi-nistic and moralistic position as the *Washington Post* journalists are. He does the same work of purging and reviving moral order, an order of truth in which the veritable symbolic violence of the social order is engendered, well beyond all the relations of force, which are only its shifting and indifferent configuration in the moral and political consciences of men.

All that capital asks of us is to receive it as rational *or* to combat it in the name of rationality, to receive it as moral *or* to combat it in the name of morality. Because *these are the same*, which *can be thought of in another way*: formerly one worked to dissimulate scandal – today one works to conceal that there is none.

Watergate is not a scandal, this is what must be said at all costs, because it is what everyone is busy concealing, this dissimulation masking a strengthening of morality, of a moral panic as one approaches the primitive (*mise en*) *scène* of capital: its instantan-eous cruelty, its incomprehensible ferocity, its fundamental immorality – that is what is scandalous, unacceptable to the system of moral and economic equivalence that is the axiom of leftist thought, from the theories of the Enlightenment up to

Communism. One imputes this thinking to the contract of capital, but it doesn't give a damn – it is a monstrous unprincipled enterprise, nothing more. It is "enlightened" thought that seeks to control it by imposing rules on it. And all the recrimination that replaces revolutionary thought today comes back to incriminate capital for not following the rules of the game. "Power is unjust, its justice is a class justice, capital exploits us, etc." – as if capital were linked by a contract to the society it rules. It is the Left that holds out the mirror of equivalence to capital hoping that it will comply, comply with this phantasmagoria of the social contract and fulfill its obligations to the whole of society (by the same token, no need for revolution: it suffices that capital accommodate itself to the rational formula of exchange).

Capital, in fact, was never linked by a contract to the society that it dominates. It is a sorcery of social relations, it is a *challenge to society*, and it must be responded to as such. It is not a scandal to be denounced according to moral or economic rationality, but a challenge to take up according to symbolic law.

Möbius-Spiraling Negativity

Watergate was thus nothing but a lure held out by the system to catch its adversaries – a simulation of scandal for regenerative ends. In the film, this is embodied by the character of "Deep Throat," who was said to be the éminence grise of the Republicans, manipulating the left-wing journalists in order to get rid of Nixon – and why not? All hypotheses are possible, but this one is superfluous: the Left itself does a perfectly good job, and spontaneously, of doing the work of the Right. Besides, it would be naive to see an embittered good conscience at work here. Because manipulation is a wavering causality in which positivity and negativity are engendered and overlap, in which there is no longer either an active or a passive. It is through the *arbitrary* cessation of this spiraling causality that a principle of political reality can be saved. It is through the *simulation* of a narrow, conventional field of perspective in which the premises and the consequences of an act or of an event can be calculated, that a political credibility can be maintained (and of course "objective" analysis, the struggle, etc.). If one envisions the entire cycle of any act or event in a system where linear continuity and dialectical polarity no longer exist, in a field *unhinged by simulation*, all determination evaporates, every act is terminated at the end of the cycle having benefited everyone and having been scattered in all directions.

Is any given bombing in Italy the work of leftist extremists, or extreme-right provocation, or a centrist *mise-en-scène* to discredit all extreme terrorists and to shore up its own failing power, or again, is it a police-inspired scenario and a form of blackmail to public security? All of this is simultaneously true, and the search for proof, indeed the objectivity of the facts does not put an end to this vertigo of interpretation. That is, we are in a logic of simulation, which no longer has anything to do with a logic of facts and an order of reason. Simulation is characterized by a *precession of the model*, of all the models based on the merest fact – the models come first, their circulation, orbital like that of the bomb, constitutes the genuine magnetic field of the event. The facts no longer have a specific trajectory, they are born at the intersection of models, a single fact can be engendered by all the models at once. This anticipation, this precession, this short circuit, this confusion of the fact with its model (no more divergence of meaning, no more dialectical polarity, no more negative electricity, implosion of antagonistic poles), is what allows each time for all possible interpretations, even the most contradictory – all true, in the sense that their truth is to be exchanged, in the image of the models from which they derive, in a generalized cycle.

The Communists attack the Socialist Party as if they wished to shatter the union of the Left. They give credence to the idea that these resistances would come from a more radical political need. In fact, it is because they no longer want power. But do they not want power at this juncture, one unfavorable to the Left in general, or unfavorable to them within the Union of the Left – or do they no longer want it, by definition? When Berlinguer declares: "There is no need to be afraid to see the Communists take power in Italy," it simultaneously signifies:

that there is no need to be afraid, since the Communists, if they come to power, will change nothing of its fundamental capitalist mechanism;

that there is no risk that they will ever come to power (because they don't want to) – and even if they occupy the seat of power, they will never exercise it except by proxy;

that in fact, power, genuine power no longer exists, and thus there is no risk whoever seizes power or seizes it again;

but further: I, Berlinguer, am not afraid to see the Communists take power in Italy – which may seem self-evident, but not as much as you might think, because

it could mean the opposite (no need for psychoanalysis here): *I am afraid* to see the Communists take power (and there are good reasons for that, even for a Communist).

All of this is simultaneously true. It is the secret of a discourse that is no longer simply ambiguous, as political discourses can be, but that conveys the impossibility of a determined position of power, the impossibility of a determined discursive position. And this logic is neither that of one party nor of another. It traverses all discourses without them wanting it to.

Who will unravel this imbroglio? The Gordian knot can at least be cut. The Möbius strip, if one divides it, results in a supplementary spiral without the reversibility of surfaces being resolved (here the reversible continuity of hypotheses). Hell of simulation, which is no longer one of torture, but of the subtle, maleficent, elusive twisting of meaning[4] – where even the condemned at Burgos are still a gift from Franco to Western democracy, which seizes the occasion to regenerate its own flagging humanism and whose indignant protest in turn consolidates Franco's regime by uniting the Spanish masses against this foreign intervention? Where is the truth of all that, when such collusions admirably knot themselves together without the knowledge of their authors?

Conjunction of the system and of its extreme alternative like the two sides of a curved mirror, a "vicious" curvature of a political space that is henceforth magnetized, circularized, reversibilized from the right to the left, a torsion that is like that of the evil spirit of commutation, the whole system, the infinity of capital folded back on its own surface: transfinite? And is it not the same for desire and the libidinal space? Conjunction of desire and value, of desire and capital. Conjunction of desire and the law, the final pleasure as the metamorphosis of the law (which is why it is so widely the order of the day): only capital takes pleasure, said Lyotard, before thinking that *we* now take pleasure in capital. Overwhelming versatility of desire in Deleuze, an enigmatic reversal that brings desire "revolutionary in itself, and as if involuntarily, wanting what it wants," to desire its own repression and to invest in paranoid and fascist systems? A malign torsion that returns this revolution of desire to the same fundamental ambiguity as the other, the historical revolution.

All the referentials combine their discourses in a circular, Möbian compulsion. Not so long ago, sex and work were fiercely opposed terms; today both are dissolved in the same type of demand. Formerly the discourse on history derived its power from violently opposing itself to that of nature, the discourse of desire to that of power – today they exchange their signifiers and their scenarios.

It would take too long to traverse the entire range of the operational negativity of all those scenarios of deterrence, which, like Watergate, try to regenerate a moribund principle through simulated scandal, phantasm, and murder – a sort of hormonal treatment through negativity and crisis. It is always a question of proving the real through the imaginary, proving truth through scandal, proving the law through transgression, proving work through striking, proving the system through crisis, and capital through revolution, as it is elsewhere (the Tasaday) of proving ethnology through the dispossession of its object – without taking into account:

the proof of theater through antitheater;
the proof of art through antiart;
the proof of pedagogy through antipedagogy;
the proof of psychiatry through antipsychiatry, etc.

Everything is metamorphosed into its opposite to perpetuate itself in its expurgated form. All the powers, all the institutions speak of themselves through denial, in order to attempt, by simulating death, to escape their real death throes. Power can stage its own murder to rediscover a glimmer of existence and legitimacy. Such was the case with some American presidents: the Kennedys were murdered because they still had a political dimension. The others, Johnson, Nixon, Ford, only had the right to phantom attempts, to simulated murders. But this aura of an artificial menace was still necessary to conceal that they were no longer anything but the mannequins of power. Formerly, the king (also the god) had to die, therein lay his power. Today, he is miserably forced to feign death, in order to preserve the *blessing* of power. But it is lost.

To seek new blood in its own death, to renew the cycle through the mirror of crisis, negativity, and antipower: this is the only solution-alibi of every power, of every institution attempting to break the vicious circle of its irresponsibility and of its fundamental nonexistence, of its already seen and of its already dead.

The Strategy of the Real

The impossibility of rediscovering an absolute level of the real is of the same order as the impossibility of staging illusion. Illusion is no longer possible, because the real is no longer possible. It is the whole *political* problem of parody, of hypersimulation or offensive simulation, that is posed here.

For example: it would be interesting to see whether the repressive apparatus would not react more violently to a simulated holdup than to a real holdup. Because the latter does nothing but disturb the order of things, the right to property, whereas the former attacks the reality principle itself. Transgression and violence are less serious because they only contest the *distribution* of the real. Simulation is infinitely more dangerous because it always leaves open to supposition that, above and beyond its object, *law and order themselves might be nothing but simulation.*

But the difficulty is proportional to the danger. How to feign a violation and put it to the test? Simulate a robbery in a large store: how to persuade security that it is a simulated robbery? There is no "objective" difference: the gestures, the signs are the same as for a real robbery, the signs do not lean to one side or another. To the established order they are always of the order of the real.

Organize a fake holdup. Verify that your weapons are harmless, and take the most trustworthy hostage, so that no human life will be in danger (or one lapses into the criminal). Demand a ransom, and make it so that the operation creates as much commotion as possible – in short, remain close to the "truth," in order to test the reaction of the apparatus to a perfect simulacrum. You won't be able to do it: the network of artificial signs will become inextricably mixed up with real elements (a policeman will really fire on sight; a client of the bank will faint and die of a heart attack; one will actually pay you the phony ransom), in short, you will immediately find yourself once again, without wishing it, in the real, one of whose functions is precisely to devour any attempt at simulation, to reduce everything to the real – that is, to the established order itself, well before institutions and justice come into play.

It is necessary to see in this impossibility of isolating the process of simulation the weight of an order that cannot see and conceive of anything but the real, because it cannot function anywhere else. The simulation of an offense, if it is established as such, will either be punished less severely (because it has no "consequences") or punished as an offense against the judicial system (for example if one sets in motion a police operation "for nothing") – but *never as simulation* since it is precisely as such that no equivalence with the real is possible, and hence no repression either. The challenge of simulation is never admitted by power. How can the simulation of virtue be punished? However, as such it is as serious as the simulation of crime. Parody renders submission and transgression equivalent, and that is the most serious crime, because it *cancels out the difference upon which the law is based.* The established order can do nothing against it, because the law is a simulacrum of the second order, whereas simulation is of the third order, beyond true and false, beyond equivalences, beyond rational distinctions upon which the whole of the social and power depend. Thus, *lacking the real*, it is there that we must aim at order.

This is certainly why order always opts for the real. When in doubt, it always prefers this hypothesis (as in the army one prefers to take the simulator for a real madman). But this becomes more and more difficult, because if it is practically impossible to isolate the process of simulation, through the force of inertia of the real that surrounds us, the opposite is also true (and this reversibility itself is part of the apparatus of simulation and the impotence of power): namely, it is *now impossible to isolate the process of the real*, or to prove the real.

This is how all the holdups, airplane hijackings, etc. are now in some sense simulation holdups in that they are already inscribed in the decoding and orchestration rituals of the media, anticipated in their presentation and their possible consequences. In short, where they function as a group of signs dedicated exclusively to their recurrence as signs, and no longer at all to their "real" end. But this does not make them harmless. On the contrary, it is as hyperreal events, no longer with a specific content or end, but indefinitely refracted by each other (just like so-called historical events: strikes, demonstrations, crises, etc.),[5] it is in this sense that they cannot be controlled by an order that can only exert itself on the real and the rational, on causes and ends, a referential order that can only reign over the referential, a determined power that can only reign over a determined world, but that cannot do anything against this indefinite recurrence of simulation, against this nebula whose weight no longer obeys the laws of gravitation of the real, power itself ends by being dismantled in this space and becoming a simulation of power (disconnected from its ends and its objectives, and dedicated to the *effects of power* and mass simulation).

The only weapon of power, its only strategy against this defection, is to reinject the real and the referential everywhere, to persuade us of the reality of the social, of the gravity of the economy and the finalities of production. To this end it prefers the discourse of crisis, but also, why not? that of desire. "Take your desires for reality!" can be understood as the ultimate slogan of power since in a nonreferential world, even the confusion of the reality principle and the principle of desire is less dangerous than contagious hyperreality. One remains among principles, and among those power is always in the right.

Hyperreality and simulation are deterrents of every principle and every objective, they turn against power the deterrent that it used so well for such a long time. Because in the end, throughout its history it was capital that first fed on the destructuration of every referential, of every human objective, that shattered every ideal distinction between true and false, good and evil, in order to establish a radical law of equivalence and exchange, the iron law of its power. Capital was the first to play at deterrence, abstraction, disconnection, deterritorialization, etc., and if it is the one that fostered reality, the reality principle, it was also the first to liquidate it by exterminating all use value, all real equivalence of production and wealth, in the very sense we have of the unreality of the stakes and the omnipotence of manipulation. Well, today it is this same logic that is even more set against capital. And as soon as it wishes to combat this disastrous spiral by secreting a last glimmer of reality, on which to establish a last glimmer of power, it does nothing but multiply the *signs* and accelerate the play of simulation.

As long as the historical threat came at it from the real, power played at deterrence and simulation, disintegrating all the contradictions by dint of producing equivalent signs. Today when the danger comes at it from simulation (that of being dissolved in the play of signs), power plays at the real, plays at crisis, plays at remanufacturing artificial, social, economic, and political stakes. For power, it is a question of life and death. But it is too late.

Whence the characteristic hysteria of our times: that of the production and reproduction of the real. The other production, that of values and commodities, that of the belle epoque of political economy, has for a long time had no specific meaning. What every society looks for in continuing to produce, and to overproduce, is to restore the real that escapes it. That is why *today this "material" production is that of the hyperreal itself*. It retains all the features, the whole discourse of traditional production, but it is no longer anything but its scaled-down refraction (thus hyperrealists fix a real from which all meaning and charm, all depth and energy of representation have vanished in a hallucinatory resemblance). Thus everywhere the hyperrealism of simulation is translated by the hallucinatory resemblance of the real to itself.

Power itself has for a long time produced nothing but the signs of its resemblance. And at the same time, another figure of power comes into play: that of a collective demand for *signs* of power – a holy union that is reconstructed around its disappearance. The whole world adheres to it more or less in terror of the collapse of the political. And in the end the game of power becomes nothing but the *critical* obsession with power – obsession with its death, obsession with its survival, which increases as it disappears. When it has totally disappeared, we will logically be under the total hallucination of power – a haunting memory that is already in evidence everywhere, expressing at once the compulsion to get rid of it (no one wants it anymore, everyone unloads it on everyone else) and the panicked nostalgia over its loss. The melancholy of societies without power: this has already stirred up fascism, that overdose of a strong referential in a society that cannot terminate its mourning.

With the extenuation of the political sphere, the president comes increasingly to resemble that *Puppet of Power* who is the head of primitive societies (Clastres).

All previous presidents pay for and continue to pay for Kennedy's murder as if they were the ones who had suppressed it – which is true phantasmatically, if not in fact. They must efface this defect and this complicity with their simulated murder. Because, now it can only be simulated. Presidents Johnson and Ford were both the object of failed assassination attempts which, if they were not staged, were at least perpetrated by simulation. The Kennedys died because they incarnated something: the political, political substance, whereas the new presidents are nothing but caricatures and fake film – curiously, Johnson, Nixon, Ford, all have this simian mug, the monkeys of power.

Death is never an absolute criterion, but in this case it is significant: the era of James Dean, Marilyn Monroe, and the Kennedys, of those who really died simply because they had a mythic dimension that implies death (not for romantic reasons, but because of the fundamental principle of reversal and exchange) – this era is long gone. It is now the era of murder by simulation, of the generalized aesthetic of simulation, of the murder-alibi – the allegorical resurrection of death, which is only there to sanction the institution of power, without which it no longer has any substance or an autonomous reality.

These staged presidential assassinations are revealing because they signal the status of all negativity in the West: political opposition, the "Left," critical discourse, etc. – a simulacral contrast through which power attempts to break the vicious circle of its nonexistence, of its fundamental irresponsibility, of its "suspension." Power floats like money, like language, like theory. Criticism and negativity alone still secrete a phantom of the reality of power. If they become weak for one reason or another, power has no other recourse but to artificially revive and hallucinate them.

It is in this way that the Spanish executions still serve as a stimulant to Western liberal democracy, to a dying system of democratic values. Fresh blood, but for how much longer? The deterioration of all power is irresistibly pursued: it is not so much the "revolutionary forces" that accelerate this process (often it is quite the opposite), it is the system itself that deploys against its own structures this violence that annuls all substance and all finality. One must not resist this process by trying to confront the system and destroy it, because this system that is dying from being dispossessed of its death expects nothing but that from us: that we give the system back its death, that we revive it through the negative. End of revolutionary praxis, end of the dialectic. Curiously, Nixon, who was not even found worthy of dying at the hands of the most insignificant, chance, unbalanced person (and though it is perhaps true that presidents are assassinated by unbalanced types, this changes *nothing*: the leftist penchant for detecting a rightist conspiracy beneath this brings out a false problem – the function of bringing death to, or the prophecy, etc., against power has always been fulfilled, from primitive societies to the present, by demented people, crazy people, or neurotics, who nonetheless carry out a social function as fundamental as that of presidents), was nevertheless ritually put to death by Watergate. Watergate is still a mechanism for the ritual murder of power (the American institution of the presidency is much more thrilling in this regard than the European: it surrounds itself with all the violence and vicissitudes of primitive powers, of savage rituals). But already impeachment is no longer assassination: it happens via the Constitution. Nixon has nevertheless arrived at the goal of which all power dreams: to be taken seriously enough, to constitute a mortal enough danger to the group to be one day relieved of his duties, denounced, and liquidated. Ford doesn't even have this opportunity anymore: a simulacrum of an already dead power, he can only accumulate against himself the signs of reversion through murder – in fact, he is immunized by his impotence, which infuriates him.

In contrast to the primitive rite, which foresees the official and sacrificial death of the king (the king or the chief is nothing without the promise of his sacrifice), the modern political imaginary goes increasingly in the direction of delaying, of concealing for as long as possible, the death of the head of state. This obsession has accumulated since the era of revolutions and of charismatic leaders: Hitler, Franco, Mao, having no "legitimate" heirs, no filiation of power, see themselves forced to perpetuate themselves indefinitely – popular myth never wishes to believe them dead. The pharaohs already did this: it was always one and the same person who incarnated the successive pharaohs.

Everything happens as if Mao or Franco had already died several times and had been replaced by his double. From a political point of view, that a head of state remains the same or is someone else doesn't strictly change anything, so long as they resemble each other. For a long time now a head of state – *no matter which one* – is nothing but the simulacrum of himself, and *only that gives him the power and the quality to govern*. No one would grant the least consent, the least devotion to a *real* person. It is to his double, he being always already *dead*, to which allegiance is given. This myth does nothing but translate the persistence, and at the same time the deception, of the necessity of the king's sacrificial death.

We are still in the same boat: no society knows how to mourn the real, power, the *social itself*, which is implicated in the same loss. And it is through an artificial revitalization of all this that we try to escape this fact. *This situation will no doubt end up giving rise to socialism.* Through an unforeseen turn of events and via an irony that is no longer that of history, it is from the death of the social that socialism will emerge, as it is from the death of God that religions emerge. A twisted advent, a perverse event, an unintelligible reversion to the logic of reason. As is the fact that power is in essence no longer present except to conceal that there is no more power. A simulation that can last indefinitely, because, as distinct from "true" power – which is, or was, a structure, a strategy, a relation of force, a stake – it is nothing but the object of a social *demand*, and thus as the object of the law of supply and demand, it is no longer subject to violence and death. Completely purged of a *political* dimension, it, like any other commodity, is dependent on mass production and consumption. Its spark has disappeared, only the fiction of a political universe remains.

The same holds true for work. The spark of production, the violence of its stakes no longer exist. The whole world still produces, and increasingly, but subtly work has become something else: a need (as Marx ideally envisioned it but not in the same sense), the object of a social "demand," like leisure, to which it is equivalent in the course of everyday life. A demand exactly proportional to the loss of a stake in the work process.[6] Same change in fortune as for power: the *scenario* of work is there to conceal that the real of work, the real of production, has disappeared. And the real of the strike as well, which is no longer a work stoppage, but its alternate pole in the ritual scansion of the social calendar. Everything occurs as if each person had, after declaring a strike, "occupied" his place and work station and recommenced production, as is the norm in a "self-managed" occupation, exactly in the same terms as before, all while declaring himself (and in virtually being) permanently on strike.

This is not a dream out of science fiction: everywhere it is a question of doubling the process of work. And of a doubling of the process of going on strike – striking incorporated just as obsolescence is in objects, just as crisis is in production. So, there is no longer striking, nor work, but both simultaneously, that is to say something else: a *magic of work*, a trompe l'oeil, a scenodrama (so as not to say a melodrama) of production, a collective dramaturgy on the empty stage of the social.

It is no longer a question of the ideology of work – the traditional ethic that would obscure the "real" process of work and the "objective" process of exploitation – but of the scenario of work. In the same way, it is no longer a question of the ideology of power, but of the *scenario* of power. Ideology only corresponds to a corruption of reality through signs; simulation corresponds to a short circuit of reality and to its duplication through signs. It is always the goal of the ideological analysis to restore the objective process, it is always a false problem to wish to restore the truth beneath the simulacrum.

This is why in the end power is so much in tune with ideological discourses and discourses on ideology, that is they are discourses of *truth* – always good for countering the mortal blows of simulation, even and especially if they are revolutionary.

The End of the Panopticon

It is still to this ideology of lived experience – exhumation of the real in its fundamental banality, in its radical authenticity – that the American TV verité experiment attempted on the Loud family in 1971 refers: seven months of uninterrupted shooting, three hundred hours of nonstop broadcasting, without a script or a screenplay, the odyssey of a family, its dramas, its joys, its unexpected events, nonstop – in short, a "raw" historical document, and the "greatest television performance, comparable, on the scale of our day-to-day life, to the footage of our landing on the moon." It becomes more complicated because this family fell apart during the filming: a crisis erupted, the Louds separated, etc. Whence that insoluble controversy: was TV itself responsible? What would have happened *if TV hadn't been there?*

More interesting is the illusion of filming the Louds *as if TV weren't there*. The producer's triumph was to say: "They lived as if we were not there." An absurd, paradoxical formula – neither true nor false: utopian. The "as if *we* were not there" being equal to "as if *you* were there." It is this utopia, this paradox that fascinated the twenty million viewers, much more than did the "perverse" pleasure of violating someone's privacy. In the "verité" experience it is not a question of secrecy or perversion, but of a sort of frisson of the real, or of an aesthetics of the hyperreal, a frisson of vertiginous and phony exactitude, a frisson of simultaneous distancing and magnification, of distortion of scale, of an excessive transparency. The pleasure of an excess of meaning, when the bar of the sign falls below the usual waterline of meaning: the nonsignifier is exalted by the camera angle. There one sees what the real never was (but "as if you were there"), without the distance that gives us perspectival space and depth vision (but "more real than nature"). Pleasure in the microscopic simulation that allows the real to pass into the hyperreal. (This is also somewhat the case in porno, which is fascinating more on a metaphysical than on a sexual level.)

Besides, this family was already hyperreal by the very nature of its selection: a typical ideal American family, California home, three garages, five children, assured social and professional status, decorative housewife, upper-middle-class standing. In a way it is this statistical perfection that dooms it to death. Ideal heroine of the American way of life, it is, as in ancient sacrifices, chosen in order to be glorified and to die beneath the flames of the medium, a modern *fatum*. Because heavenly fire no longer falls on corrupted cities, it is the camera lens that, like a laser, comes to pierce lived reality in order to put it to death. "The Louds: simply a family who agreed to deliver themselves into the hands of television, and to die by it," the director will say. Thus it is a question of a sacrificial process, of a sacrificial spectacle offered to twenty million Americans. The liturgical drama of a mass society.

TV verité. A term admirable in its ambiguity, does it refer to the truth of this family or to the truth of TV? In fact, it is TV that is the truth of the Louds, it is TV that is true, it is TV that renders true. Truth that is no longer the reflexive truth of the mirror, nor the perspectival truth of the panoptic system and of the gaze, but the manipulative truth of the test that sounds out and interrogates, of the laser that touches and pierces, of computer cards that retain your preferred sequences, of the genetic code that controls your combinations, of cells that inform your sensory universe. It is to this truth that the Loud family was subjected by the medium of TV, and in this sense it amounts to a death sentence (but is it still a question of truth?).

End of the panoptic system. The eye of TV is no longer the source of an absolute gaze, and the ideal of control is no longer that of transparency. This still presupposes an objective space (that of the Renaissance) and the omnipotence of the despotic gaze. It is still, if not a system of confinement, at least a system of mapping. More subtly, but always externally, playing on the opposition of seeing and being seen, even if the panoptic focal point may be blind.

Something else in regard to the Louds. "You no longer watch TV, it is TV that watches you (live)," or again: "You are no longer listening to Don't Panic, it is Don't Panic that is listening to you" – a switch from the panoptic mechanism of surveillance (*Discipline and Punish* [Surveiller et punir]) to a system of deterrence, in which the distinction between the passive and the active is abolished. There is no longer any imperative of submission to the model, or to the gaze "YOU are the model!" "YOU are the majority!" Such is the watershed of a hyperreal sociality, in which the real is confused with the model, as in the statistical operation, or with the medium, as in the Louds' operation. Such is the last stage of the social relation, ours, which is no longer one of persuasion (the classical age of propaganda, of ideology, of publicity, etc.) but one of deterrence: "YOU are information, you are the social, you are the event, you are involved, you have the word, etc." An about-face through which it becomes impossible to locate one instance of the model, of power, of the gaze, of the medium itself, because *you* are always already on the other side. No more subject, no more focal point, no more center or periphery: pure flexion or circular inflexion. No more violence or surveillance: only "information," secret virulence, chain reaction, slow implosion, and simulacra of spaces in which the effect of the real again comes into play.

We are witnessing the end of perspectival and panoptic space (which remains a moral hypothesis bound up with all the classical analyses on the "objective" essence of power), and thus to the *very abolition of the spectacular*. Television, for example in the case of the Louds, is no longer a spectacular medium. We are no longer in the society of the spectacle, of which the situationists spoke, nor in the specific kinds of alienation and repression that it implied. The medium itself is no longer identifiable as such, and the confusion of the medium and the message (McLuhan)[7] is the first great formula of this new era. There is no longer a medium in the literal sense: it is now intangible, diffused, and diffracted in the real, and one can no longer even say that the medium is altered by it.

Such a blending, such a viral, endemic, chronic, alarming presence of the medium, without the possibility of isolating the effects – spectralized, like these advertising laser sculptures in the empty space of the event filtered by the medium – dissolution of TV in life, dissolution of life in TV – indiscernible chemical solution: we are all Louds doomed not to invasion, to pressure, to violence and blackmail by the media and the models, but to their induction, to their infiltration, to their illegible violence.

But one must watch out for the negative turn that discourse imposes: it is a question neither of disease nor of a viral infection. One must think instead of the media as if they were, in outer orbit, a kind of genetic code that directs the mutation of the real into the hyperreal, just as the other micromolecular code controls the passage from a representative sphere of meaning to the genetic one of the pro-grammed signal.

It is the whole traditional world of causality that is in question: the perspectival, determinist mode, the "active," critical mode, the analytic mode – the distinction between cause and effect, between active and passive, between subject and object, between the end and the means. It is in this sense that one can say: TV is watching us, TV alienates us, TV manipulates us, TV informs us... In all this, one remains dependent on the analytical conception of the media, on an external active and effective agent, on "perspectival" information with the horizon of the real and of meaning as the vanishing point.

Now, one must conceive of TV along the lines of DNA as an effect in which the opposing poles of determination vanish, according to a nuclear contraction, retrac-tion, of the old polar schema that always maintained a minimal distance between cause and effect, between subject and object: precisely the distance of meaning, the gap, the difference, the smallest possible gap (PPEP!),[8] irreducible under pain of reabsorption into an aleatory and indeterminate process whose discourse can no longer account for it, because it is itself a determined order.

It is this gap that vanishes in the process of genetic coding, in which indeterminacy is not so much a question of molecular randomness as of the abolition, pure and simple, of the *relation*. In the process of molecular control, which "goes" from the DNA nucleus to the "substance" that it "informs," there is no longer the traversal of an effect, of an energy, of a determination, of a message. "Order, signal, impulse, message": all of these attempt to render the thing intelligible to us, but by analogy, retranscribing in terms of inscription, of a vector, of decoding, a dimension of which we know nothing – it is no longer even a "dimension," or perhaps it is the fourth (which is defined, however, in Einsteinian relativity by the absorption of the distinct poles of space and time). In fact, this whole process can only be understood in its negative form: nothing separates one pole from another anymore, the beginning from the end; there is a kind of contraction of one over the other, a fantastic telescoping, a collapse of the two traditional poles into each other: *implosion* – an absorption of the radiating mode of causality, of the differential mode of determina-tion, with its positive and negative charge – an implosion of meaning. *That is where simulation begins.*

Everywhere, in no matter what domain – political, biological, psychological, mediatized – in which the distinction between these two poles can no longer be maintained, one enters into simulation, and thus into absolute manipulation – not into passivity, but into *the indifferentiation of the active and the passive*. DNA realizes this aleatory reduction at the level of living matter. Television, in the case of the Louds, also reaches this *indefinite* limit in which, vis-à-vis TV, they are neither more nor less active or passive than a living substance is vis-à-vis its molecular code. Here and there, a single nebula whose simple elements are indecipherable, whose truth is indecipherable.

The Orbital and the Nuclear

The apotheosis of simulation: the nuclear. However, the balance of terror is never anything but the spectacular slope of a system of deterrence that has insinuated itself from *the inside* into all the cracks of daily life. Nuclear suspension only serves to seal the trivialized system of deterrence that is at the heart of the media, of the violence without consequences that reigns throughout the world, of the aleatory apparatus of all the choices that are made for us. The most insignificant of our behaviors is regulated by neutralized, indifferent, equivalent signs, by zero-sum signs like those that regulate the "strategy of games" (but the true equation is elsewhere, and the unknown is precisely that variable of simulation which makes of the atomic arsenal itself a hyperreal form, a simulacrum that dominates everything and reduces all "ground-level" events to being nothing but ephemeral scenarios, transforming the life left us into survival, into a stake without stakes – not even into a life insurance policy: into a policy that already has no value).

It is not the direct threat of atomic destruction that paralyzes our lives, it is deterrence that gives them leukemia. And this deterrence comes from that fact that *even the real atomic clash is precluded* – precluded like the eventuality of the real in a system of signs. The whole world pretends to believe in the reality of this threat (this is understandable on the part of the military, the gravity of their exercise and the discourse of their "strategy" are at stake), but it is precisely at this level that there are no strategic stakes. The whole originality of the situation lies in the improbability of destruction.

Deterrence precludes war – the archaic violence of expanding systems. Deterrence itself is the neutral, implosive violence of metastable systems or systems in involution. There is no longer a subject of deterrence, nor an adversary nor a strategy – it is a planetary structure of the annihilation of stakes. Atomic war, like the Trojan War, will not take place. The risk of nuclear annihilation only serves as a pretext, through the sophistication of weapons (a sophistication that surpasses any possible objective to such an extent that it is itself a symptom of nullity), for installing a universal security system, a universal lockup and control system whose deterrent effect is not at all aimed at an atomic clash (which was never in question, except without a doubt in the very initial stages of the cold war, when one still confused the nuclear apparatus with conventional war) but, rather, at the much greater probability of any real event, of anything that would be an event in the general system and upset its balance. The balance of terror is the terror of balance.

Deterrence is not a strategy, it circulates and is exchanged between nuclear protagonists exactly as is international capital in the orbital zone of monetary speculation
whose fluctuations suffice to control all global exchanges. Thus the *money of destruction* (without any reference to *real* destruction, any more than floating capital has a
real referent of production) that circulates in nuclear orbit suffices to control all the
violence and potential conflicts around the world.

What is hatched in the shadow of this mechanism with the pretext of a maximal,
"objective," threat, and thanks to Damocles' nuclear sword, is the perfection of
the best system of control that has ever existed. And the progressive satellization
of the whole planet through this hypermodel of security.

The same goes for *peaceful* nuclear power stations. Pacification does not distinguish
between the civil and the military: everywhere where irreversible apparatuses of
control are elaborated, everywhere where the notion of security becomes omnipotent, everywhere where the *norm* replaces the old arsenal of laws and violence (including war), it is the system of deterrence that grows, and around it grows the historical,
social, and political desert. A gigantic involution that makes every conflict, every
finality, every confrontation contract in proportion to this blackmail that interrupts,
neutralizes, freezes them all. No longer can any revolt, any story be deployed
according to its own logic because it risks annihilation. No strategy is possible any
longer, and escalation is only a puerile game given over to the military. The political
stake is dead, only simulacra of conflicts and carefully circumscribed stakes
remain.

The "space race" played exactly the same role as nuclear escalation. This is why the
space program was so easily able to replace it in the 1960s (Kennedy/Khrushchev), or
to develop concurrently as a form of "peaceful coexistence." Because what, ultimately, is the function of the space program, of the conquest of the moon, of the
launching of satellites if not the institution of a model of universal gravitation, of
satellization of which the lunar module is the perfect embryo? Programmed microcosm, where *nothing can be left to chance*. Trajectory, energy, calculation, physiology,
psychology, environment – nothing can be left to contingencies, this is the total
universe of the norm – the Law no longer exists, it is the operational immanence of
every detail that is law. A universe purged of all threat of meaning, in a state of asepsis
and weightlessness – it is this very perfection that is fascinating. The exaltation of the
crowds was not a response to the event of landing on the moon or of sending a man
into space (this would be, rather, the fulfillment of an earlier dream), rather, we are
dumbfounded by the perfection of the programming and the technical manipulation,
by the immanent wonder of the programmed unfolding of events. Fascination with
the maximal norm and the mastery of probability. Vertigo of the model, which unites
with the model of death, but without fear or drive. Because if the law, with its aura of
transgression, if order, with its aura of violence, still taps a perverse imaginary, the
norm fixes, fascinates, stupefies, and makes every imaginary involute. One no longer
fantasizes about the minutiae of a program. Just watching it produces vertigo. The
vertigo of a world without flaws.

Now, it is the same model of programmatic infallibility, of maximum security and
deterrence that today controls the spread of the social. There lies the true nuclear

fallout: the meticulous operation of technology serves as a model for the meticulous operation of the social. Here as well, *nothing will be left to chance,* moreover this is the essence of socialization, which began centuries ago, but which has now entered its accelerated phase, toward a limit that one believed would be explosive (revolution), but which for the moment is translated by an inverse, *implosive,* irreversible process: the generalized deterrence of chance, of accident, of transversality, of finality, of contradiction, rupture, or complexity in a sociality illuminated by the norm, doomed to the descriptive transparency of mechanisms of information. In fact, the spatial and nuclear models do not have their own ends: neither the discovery of the moon, nor military and strategic superiority. Their truth is to be the models of simulation, the model vectors of a system of planetary control (where even the superpowers of this scenario are not free – the whole world is satellized).[9]

Resist the evidence: in satellization, he who is satellized is not who one might think. Through the orbital inscription of a spatial object, it is the planet earth that becomes a satellite, it is the terrestrial principle of reality that becomes eccentric, hyperreal, and insignificant. Through the orbital instantiation of a system of control like peaceful coexistence, all the terrestrial microsystems are satellized and lose their autonomy. All energy, all events are absorbed by this eccentric gravitation, everything condenses and implodes toward the only micromodel of control (the orbital satellite), as conversely, in the other, biological, dimension, everything converges and implodes on the molecular micromodel of the genetic code. Between the two, in this forking of the nuclear and the genetic, in the simultaneous assumption of the two fundamental codes of deterrence, every principle of meaning is absorbed, every deployment of the real is impossible.

The simultaneity of two events in the month of July 1975 illustrated this in a striking manner: the linkup in space of the two American and Soviet supersatellites, apotheosis of peaceful coexistence – the suppression by the Chinese of ideogrammatic writing and conversion to the Roman alphabet. The latter signifies the "orbital" instantiation of an abstract and modelized system of signs, into whose orbit all the once unique forms of style and writing will be reabsorbed. The satellization of language: the means for the Chinese to enter the system of peaceful coexistence, which is inscribed in their heavens at precisely the same time by the linkup of the two satellites. Orbital flight of the Big Two, neutralization and homogenization of every-one else on earth.

Yet, despite this deterrence by the orbital power – the nuclear or molecular code – events continue at ground level, misfortunes are even more numerous, given the global process of the contiguity and simultaneity of data. But, subtly, they no longer have any meaning, they are no longer anything but the duplex effect of simulation at the summit. The best example can only be that of the war in Vietnam, because it took place at the intersection of a maximum historical and "revolutionary" stake, and of the installation of this deterrent authority. What meaning did this war have, and wasn't its unfolding a means of sealing the end of history in the decisive and culminating historic event of our era?

Why did this war, so hard, so long, so ferocious, vanish from one day to the next as if by magic?

Why did this American defeat (the largest reversal in the history of the USA) have no internal repercussions in America? If it had really signified the failure of the planetary strategy of the United States, it would necessarily have completely disrupted its internal balance and the American political system. Nothing of the sort occurred.

Something else, then, took place. This war, at bottom, was nothing but a crucial episode of peaceful coexistence. It marked the arrival of China to peaceful coexistence. The nonintervention of China obtained and secured after many years, China's apprenticeship to a global modus vivendi, the shift from a global strategy of revolution to one of shared forces and empires, the transition from a radical alternative to political alternation in a system now essentially regulated (the normalization of Peking–Washington relations): this was what was at stake in the war in Vietnam, and in this sense, the USA pulled out of Vietnam but won the war.

And the war ended "spontaneously" when this objective was achieved. That is why it was deescalated, demobilized so easily.

This same reduction of forces can be seen on the field. The war lasted as long as elements irreducible to a healthy politics and discipline of power, even a Communist one, remained unliquidated. When at last the war had passed into the hands of regular troops in the North and escaped that of the resistance, the war could stop: it had attained its objective. The stake is thus that of a political relay. As soon as the Vietnamese had proved that they were no longer the carriers of an unpredictable subversion, one could let them take over. That theirs is a Communist order is not serious in the end: it had proved itself, it could be trusted. It is even more effective than capitalism in the liquidation of "savage" and archaic precapitalist structures.

Same scenario in the Algerian war.

The other aspect of this war and of all wars today: behind the armed violence, the murderous antagonism of the adversaries – which seems a matter of life and death, which is played out as such (or else one could never send people to get themselves killed in this kind of thing), behind this simulacrum of fighting to the death and of ruthless global stakes, the two adversaries are fundamentally in solidarity against something else, unnamed, never spoken, but whose objective outcome in war, with the equal complicity of the two adversaries, is total liquidation. Tribal, communitarian, precapitalist structures, every form of exchange, of language, of symbolic organization, that is what must be abolished, that is the object of murder in war – and war itself, in its immense, spectacular death apparatus, is nothing but the medium of this process of the terrorist rationalization of the social – the murder on which sociality will be founded, whatever its allegiance, Communist or capitalist. Total complicity, or division of labor between two adversaries (who may even consent to enormous sacrifices for it) for the very end of reshaping and domesticating social relations.

"The North Vietnamese were advised to countenance a scenario for liquidating the American presence in the course of which, of course, one must save face."

This scenario: the extremely harsh bombardments of Hanoi. Their untenable character must not conceal the fact that they were nothing but a simulacrum to enable the Vietnamese to seem to countenance a compromise and for Nixon to make the Americans swallow the withdrawal of their troops. The game was already won, nothing was objectively at stake but the verisimilitude of the final montage.

The moralists of war, the holders of high wartime values should not be too discouraged: the war is no less atrocious for being only a simulacrum – the flesh suffers just the same, and the dead and former combatants are worth the same as in other wars. This objective is always fulfilled, just like that of the charting of territories and of disciplinary sociality. What no longer exists is the adversity of the adversaries, the reality of antagonistic causes, the ideological seriousness of war. And also the reality of victory or defeat, war being a process that triumphs well beyond these appearances.

In any case, the pacification (or the deterrence) that dominates us today is beyond war and peace, it is that at every moment war and peace are equivalent. "War is peace," said Orwell. There also, the two differential poles implode into each other, or recycle one another – a simultaneity of contradictions that is at once the parody and the end of every dialectic. Thus one can completely miss the truth of a war: namely, that it was finished well before it started, that there was an end to war at the heart of the war itself, and that perhaps it never started. Many other events (the oil crisis, etc.) *never started*, never existed, except as artificial occurrences – abstract, ersatz, and as artifacts of history, catastrophes and crises destined to maintain a historical investment under hypnosis. The media and the official *news service* are only there to maintain the illusion of an actuality, of the reality of the stakes, of the objectivity of facts. All the events are to be read backward, or one becomes aware (as with the Communists "in power" in Italy, the retro, posthumous rediscovery of the gulags and Soviet dissidents like the almost contemporary discovery, by a moribund ethnology, of the lost "difference" of Savages) that all these things arrived too late, with a history of delay, a spiral of delay, that they long ago exhausted their meaning and only live from an artificial effervescence of signs, that all these events succeed each other without logic, in the most contradictory, complete equivalence, in a profound indifference to their consequences (but this is because there are none: they exhaust themselves in their spectacular promotion) – all "newsreel" footage thus gives the sinister impression of kitsch, of retro and porno at the same time – doubtless everyone knows this, and no one really accepts it. The reality of simulation is unbearable – crueler than Artaud's Theater of Cruelty, which was still an attempt to create a dramaturgy of life, the last gasp of an ideality of the body, of blood, of violence in a system that was already taking it away, toward a reabsorption of all the stakes without a trace of blood. For us the trick has been played. All dramaturgy, and even all real writing of cruelty has disappeared. Simulation is the master, and we only have a right to the retro, to the phantom, parodic rehabilitation of all lost referentials. Everything still unfolds around us, in the cold light of deterrence (including Artaud, who has the right like everything else to his revival, to a second existence as the *referential* of cruelty).

This is why nuclear proliferation does not increase the risk of either an atomic clash or an accident – save in the interval when the "young" powers could be tempted to make a nondeterrent, "real" use of it (as the Americans did in Hiroshima – but precisely only they had a right to this "use value" of the bomb, all of those who have acquired it since will be deterred from using it by the very fact of possessing it). Entry into the atomic club, so prettily named, very quickly effaces (as unionization does in the working world) any inclination toward violent intervention. Responsibility, control, censure, self-deterrence always grow more rapidly than the forces or the weapons at our disposal: this is the secret of the social order. Thus the very possibility of paralyzing a whole country by flicking a switch *makes* it so that the electrical engineers will never use this weapon: the whole myth of the total and revolutionary strike crumbles at the very moment when the means are available – but alas *precisely because* those means are available. Therein lies the whole process of deterrence.

It is thus perfectly probable that one day we will see nuclear powers export atomic reactors, weapons, and bombs to every latitude. Control by threat will be replaced by the more effective strategy of pacification through the bomb and through the possession of the bomb. The "little" powers, believing that they are buying their independent striking force, will buy the virus of deterrence, of their own deterrence. The same goes for the atomic reactors that we have already sent them: so many neutron bombs knocking out all historical virulence, all risk of explosion. In this sense, the nuclear everywhere inaugurates an accelerated process of *implosion*, it freezes everything around it, it absorbs all living energy.

The nuclear is at once the culminating point of available energy and the maximization of energy control systems. Lockdown and control increase in direct proportion to (and undoubtedly even faster than) liberating potentialities. This was already the aporia of the modern revolution. It is still the absolute paradox of the nuclear. Energies freeze in their own fire, they deter themselves. One can no longer imagine what project, what power, what strategy, what subject could exist behind this enclosure, this vast saturation of a system by its own forces, now neutralized, unusable, unintelligible, nonexplosive – except for the possibility of *an explosion toward the center*, of an *implosion* where all these energies would be abolished in a catastrophic process (in the literal sense, that is to say in the sense of a reversion of the whole cycle toward a minimal point, of a reversion of energies toward a minimal threshold).

Notes

1   Cf. J. Baudrillard, "L'ordre des simulacres" (The order of simulacra), in *L'échange symbolique et la mort* (Symbolic exchange and death) (Paris: Gallimard, 1976).
2   A discourse that is itself not susceptible to being resolved in transference. It is the entanglement of these two discourses that renders psychoanalysis interminable.
3   Cf. M. Perniola, *Icônes, visions, simulacres* (Icons, visions, simulacra), 39.
4   This does not necessarily result in despairing of meaning, but just as much in the improvisation of meaning, of nonmeaning, of many simultaneous meanings that destroy each other.
5   Taken together, the energy crisis and the ecological *mise-en-scène* are themselves a *disaster movie*, in the same style (and with the same value) as those that currently comprise the golden days of Hollywood. It is useless to laboriously interpret these films in terms of their relation to an "objective" social crisis or even to an "objective" phantasm of disaster. It is in another sense that it must be said that it is *the social itself that*, in contemporary discourse, *is organized along the lines of a disaster-movie script*. (Cf. M. Makarius, *La stratégie de la catastrophe* [The strategy of disaster], 115.)

6   To this flagging investment in work corresponds a parallel decline in the investment in consumption. Goodbye to use value or to the prestige of the automobile, goodbye amorous discourses that neatly opposed the object of enjoyment to the object of work. Another discourse takes hold that is a *discourse of work on the object of consumption* aiming for an active, constraining, puritan reinvestment (use less gas, watch out for your safety, you've gone over the speed limit, etc.) to which the characteristics of automobiles pretend to adapt. Rediscovering a stake through the transposition of these two poles. Work becomes the object of a need, the car becomes the object of work. There is no better proof of the lack of differentiation among all the stakes. It is through the same slippage between the "right" to vote and electoral "duty" that the divestment of the political sphere is signaled.

7   The medium/message confusion is certainly a corollary of that between the sender and the receiver, thus sealing the disappearance of all dual, polar structures that formed the discursive organization of language, of all determined articulation of meaning reflecting Jakobson's famous grid of functions. That discourse "circulates" is to be taken literally: that is, it no longer goes from one point to another, but it traverses a cycle that *without distinction* includes the positions of transmitter and receiver, now unlocatable as such. Thus there is no instance of power, no instance of transmission – power is something that circulates and whose source can no longer be located, a cycle in which the positions of the dominator and the dominated are exchanged in an endless reversion that is also the end of power in its classical definition. The circularization of power, of knowledge, of discourse puts an end to any localization of instances and poles. In the psychoanalytic interpretation itself, the "power" of the interpreter does not come from any outside instance but from the interpreted himself. This changes everything, because one can always ask of the traditional holders of power where they get their power from. Who made you duke? The king. Who made you king? God. Only God no longer answers. But to the question: who made you a psychoanalyst? the analyst can well reply: You. Thus is expressed, by an inverse simulation, the passage from the "analyzed" to the "analysand," from passive to active, which simply describes the spiraling effect of the shifting of poles, the effect of circularity in which power is lost, is dissolved, is resolved in perfect manipulation (it is no longer of the order of directive power and of the gaze, but of the order of tactility and commutation). See also the state/family circularity assured by the fluctuation and metastatic regulation of the images of the social and the private (J. Donzelot, *La police des familles* [The policing of families]).

    Impossible now to pose the famous question: "From what position do you speak?" – "How do you know?" "From where do you get your power?" without hearing the immediate response: "But it is *of* you (from you) that I speak" – meaning, it is you who are speaking, you who know, you who are the power. Gigantic circumvolution, circumlocution of the spoken word, which is equal to a blackmail with no end, to a deterrence that cannot be appealed of the subject presumed to speak, leaving him without a reply, because to the question that he poses one ineluctably replies: but *you are* the answer, or: your question is already an answer, etc. – the whole strangulatory sophistication of intercepting speech, of the forced confession in the guise of freedom of expression, of trapping the subject in his own interrogation, of the precession of the reply to the question (all the violence of interpretation lies there, as well as that of the conscious or unconscious management of the "spoken word" [*parole*]).

    This simulacrum of the inversion or the involution of poles, this clever subterfuge, which is the secret of the whole discourse of manipulation and thus, today, in every domain, the secret of any new power in the erasure of the scene of power, in the assumption of all words from which has resulted this fantastic silent majority characteristic of our time – all of this started without a doubt in the political sphere with the democractic simulacrum, which today is the substitution for the power of God with the power of the people as the source of power, and of power as *emanation* with power as *representation*. Anti-Copernican revolution: no transcendental instance either of the sun or of the luminous sources of power and knowledge – everything comes from the people and everything returns to them. It is with this magnificent recycling that the universal simulacrum of manipulation, from the scenario of mass suffrage to the present-day phantoms of opinion polls, begins to be put in place.

8   PPEP is an acronym for smallest possible gap, or "plus petit écart possible." – [Trans.]
9   Paradox: all bombs are clean: their only pollution is the system of security and of control they radiate *as long as they don't explode.*

27

Postmodernism, or the Cultural Logic of Late Capitalism*

Fredric Jameson

The last few years have been marked by an inverted millennarianism, in which premonitions of the future, catastrophic or redemptive, have been replaced by senses of the end of this or that (the end of ideology, art, or social class; the 'crisis' of Leninism, social democracy, or the welfare state, etc., etc.): taken together, all of these perhaps constitute what is increasingly called postmodernism. The case for its existence depends on the hypothesis of some radical break or *coupure*, generally traced back to the end of the 1950s or the early 1960s. As the word itself suggests, this break is most often related to notions of the waning or extinction of the hundred-year-old modern movement (or to its ideological or aesthetic repudiation). Thus, abstract expressionism in painting, existentialism in philosophy, the final forms of representation in the novel, the films of the great *auteurs*, or the modernist school of poetry (as institutionalized and canonized in the works of Wallace Stevens): all these are now seen as the final, extraordinary flowering of a high modernist impulse which is spent and exhausted with them. The enumeration of what follows then at once becomes empirical, chaotic, and heterogeneous: Andy Warhol and pop art, but also photo-realism, and beyond it, the 'new expressionism'; the moment, in music, of John Cage, but also the synthesis of classical and 'popular' styles found in composers like Phil Glass and Terry Riley, and also punk and new wave rock (the Beatles and the Stones now standing as the high-modernist moment of that more recent and rapidly evolving tradition); in film, Godard, post-Godard and experimental cinema and video, but also a whole new type of commercial film (about which more below); Burroughs, Pynchon, or Ishmael Reed, on the one hand, and the French *nouveau roman* and its succession on the other, along with alarming new kinds of literary criticism, based on some new aesthetic of textuality or *écriture*... The list might be extended indefinitely; but does it imply any more fundamental change or break than the periodic style- and fashion-changes determined by an older high-modernist imperative of stylistic innovation?[1]

* From Fredric Jameson, "Postmodernism, or the Cultural Logic of Late Capitalism," *New Left Review*, vol. 146 (July–August 1984), pp. 53–92.

The Rise of Aesthetic Populism

It is in the realm of architecture, however, that modifications in aesthetic production are most dramatically visible, and that their theoretical problems have been most centrally raised and articulated; it was indeed from architectural debates that my own conception of postmodernism – as it will be outlined in the following pages – initially began to emerge. More decisively than in the other arts or media, postmodernist positions in architecture have been inseparable from an implacable critique of architectural high modernism and of the so-called International Style (Frank Lloyd Wright, Le Corbusier, Mies), where formal criticism and analysis (of the high-modernist transformation of the building into a virtual sculpture, or monumental 'duck', as Robert Venturi puts it) are at one with reconsiderations on the level of urbanism and of the aesthetic institution. High modernism is thus credited with the destruction of the fabric of the traditional city and of its older neighbourhood culture (by way of the radical disjunction of the new Utopian high-modernist building from its surrounding context); while the prophetic elitism and authoritarianism of the modern movement are remorselessly denounced in the imperious gesture of the charismatic Master.

Postmodernism in architecture will then logically enough stage itself as a kind of aesthetic populism, as the very title of Venturi's influential manifesto, *Learning from Las Vegas*, suggests. However we may ultimately wish to evaluate this populist rhetoric, it has at least the merit of drawing our attention to one fundamental feature of all the postmodernisms enumerated above: namely, the effacement in them of the older (essentially high-modernist) frontier between high culture and so-called mass or commercial culture, and the emergence of new kinds of texts infused with the forms, categories and contents of that very Culture Industry so passionately denounced by all the ideologues of the modern, from Leavis and the American New Criticism all the way to Adorno and the Frankfurt School. The postmodernisms have in fact been fascinated precisely by this whole 'degraded' landscape of schlock and kitsch, of TV series and Reader's Digest culture, of advertising and motels, of the late show and the grade-B Hollywood film, of so-called paraliterature with its airport paperback categories of the gothic and the romance, the popular biography, the murder mystery and science-fiction or fantasy novel: materials they no longer simply 'quote', as a Joyce or a Mahler might have done, but incorporate into their very substance.

Nor should the break in question be thought of as a purely cultural affair: indeed, theories of the postmodern – whether celebratory or couched in the language of moral revulsion and denunciation – bear a strong family resemblance to all those more ambitious sociological generalizations which, at much the same time, bring us the news of the arrival and inauguration of a whole new type of society, most famously baptized 'post-industrial society' (Daniel Bell), but often also designated consumer society, media society, information society, electronic society or 'high tech', and the like. Such theories have the obvious ideological mission of demonstrating, to their own relief, that the new social formation in question no longer obeys the laws of classical capitalism, namely the primacy of industrial production and the omnipresence of class struggle. The Marxist tradition has therefore resisted them with vehemence, with the signal exception of the economist Ernest Mandel, whose book *Late Capitalism* sets out not merely to anatomize the historic originality of this new society (which he sees as a third stage or moment in the evolution of capital), but also to demonstrate that it is, if anything, a *purer* stage of capitalism than any of the moments that preceded it. I will return to this argument later; suffice it for the moment to emphasize a point I have defended in greater detail elsewhere,[2] namely that every position on postmodernism in culture – whether apologia or stigmatization – is also at one and the same time, and *necessarily*, an implicitly or explicitly political stance on the nature of multinational capitalism today.

Postmodernism as Cultural Dominant

A last preliminary word on method: what follows is not to be read as stylistic description, as the account of one cultural style or movement among others. I have rather meant to offer a periodizing hypothesis, and that at a moment in which the very conception of historical periodization has come to seem most problematical indeed. I have argued elsewhere that all isolated or discrete cultural analysis always involves a buried or repressed theory of historical periodization; in any case, the conception of the 'genealogy' largely lays to rest traditional theoretical worries about so-called linear history, theories of 'stages', and teleological historiography. In the present context, however, lengthier theoretical discussion of such (very real) issues can perhaps be replaced by a few substantive remarks.

One of the concerns frequently aroused by periodizing hypotheses is that these tend to obliterate difference, and to project an idea of the historical period as massive homogeneity (bounded on either side by inexplicable 'chronological' metamorphoses and punctuation marks). This is, however, precisely why it seems to me essential to grasp 'postmodernism' not as a style, but rather as a cultural dominant: a conception which allows for the presence and coexistence of a range of very different, yet subordinate features.

Consider, for example, the powerful alternative position that postmodernism is itself little more than one more stage of modernism proper (if not, indeed, of the even older romanticism); it may indeed be conceded that all of the features of postmodernism I am about to enumerate can be detected, full-blown, in this or that preceding modernism (including such astonishing genealogical precursors as Gertrude Stein, Raymond Roussel, or Marcel Duchamp, who may be considered outright postmodernists, *avant la lettre*). What has not been taken into account by this view is, however, the social position of the older modernism, or better still, its passionate repudiation by an older Victorian and post-Victorian bourgeoisie, for whom its forms and ethos are received as being variously ugly, dissonant, obscure, scandalous, immoral, subversive and generally 'anti-social'. It will be argued here that a mutation in the sphere of culture has rendered such attitudes archaic. Not only are Picasso and Joyce no longer ugly; they now strike us, on the whole, as rather 'realistic'; and this is the result of a canonization and an academic institutionalization of the modern movement generally, which can be traced to the late 1950s. This is indeed surely one of the most plausible explanations for the emergence of postmodernism itself, since the younger generation of the 1960s will now confront the formerly oppositional modern movement as a set of dead classics, which 'weigh like a nightmare on the brains of the living', as Marx once said in a different context.

As for the postmodern revolt against all that, however, it must equally be stressed that its own offensive features – from obscurity and sexually explicit material to psychological squalor and overt expressions of social and political defiance, which transcend anything that might have been imagined at the most extreme moments of high modernism – no longer scandalize anyone and are not only received with the greatest complacency but have themselves become institutionalized and are at one with the official culture of Western society.

What has happened is that aesthetic production today has become integrated into commodity production generally: the frantic economic urgency of producing fresh waves of ever more novel-seeming goods (from clothing to airplanes), at ever greater rates of turnover, now assigns an increasingly essential structural function and position to aesthetic innovation and experimentation. Such economic necessities then find recognition in the institutional support of all kinds available for the newer art, from foundations and grants to museums and other forms of patronage. Architecture is, however, of all the arts that closest constitutively to the economic, with which, in the form of commissions and land values, it has a virtually unmediated relationship: it will therefore not be surprising to find the extraordinary flowering of the new postmodern architecture grounded in the patronage of multinational business, whose expansion and development is strictly contemporaneous with it. That these two new phenomena have an even deeper dialectical interrelationship than the simple one-to-one financing of this or that individual project we will try to suggest later on. Yet this is the point at which we must remind the reader of the obvious, namely that this whole global, yet American, postmodern culture is the internal and superstructural expression of a whole new wave of American military and economic domination throughout the world: in this sense, as throughout class history, the underside of culture is blood, torture, death and horror.

The first point to be made about the conception of periodization in dominance, therefore, is that even if all the constitutive features of postmodernism were identical and continuous with those of an older modernism – a position I feel to be demonstrably erroneous but which only an even lengthier analysis of modernism proper could dispel – the two phenomena would still remain utterly distinct in their meaning and social function, owing to the very different positioning of postmodernism in the economic system of late capital, and beyond that, to the transformation of the very sphere of culture in contemporary society.

More on this point at the conclusion of the present essay. I must now briefly address a different kind of objection to periodization, a different kind of concern about its possible obliteration of heterogeneity, which one finds most often on the Left. And it is certain that there is a strange quasi-Sartrean irony – a 'winner loses' logic – which tends to surround any effort to describe a 'system', a totalizing dynamic, as these are detected in the movement of contemporary society. What happens is that the more powerful the vision of some increasingly total system or logic – the Foucault of the prisons book is the obvious example – the more powerless the reader comes to feel. Insofar as the theorist wins, therefore, by constructing an increasingly closed and terrifying machine, to that very degree he loses, since the critical capacity of his work is thereby paralysed, and the impulses of negation and revolt, not to speak of those of social transformation, are increasingly perceived as vain and trivial in the face of the model itself.

I have felt, however, that it was only in the light of some conception of a dominant cultural logic or hegemonic norm that genuine difference could be measured and assessed. I am very far from feeling that all cultural production today is 'postmodern' in the broad sense I will be conferring on this term. The postmodern is however the force field in which very different kinds of cultural impulses – what Raymond Williams has usefully termed 'residual' and 'emergent' forms of cultural production – must make their way. If we do not achieve some general sense of a cultural dominant, then we fall back into a view of present history as sheer heterogeneity, random difference, a coexistence of a host of distinct forces whose effectivity is undecidable. This has been at any rate the political spirit in which the following analysis was devised: to project some conception of a new systemic cultural norm and its reproduction, in order to reflect more adequately on the most effective forms of any radical cultural politics today.

The exposition will take up in turn the following constitutive features of the postmodern: a new depthlessness, which finds its prolongation both in contemporary 'theory' and in a whole new culture of the image or the simulacrum; a consequent weakening of historicity, both in our relationship to public History and in the new forms of our private temporality, whose 'schizophrenic' structure (following Lacan) will determine new types of syntax or syntagmatic relationships in the more temporal arts; a whole new type of emotional ground tone – what I will call 'intensities' – which can best be grasped by a return to older theories of the sublime; the deep constitutive relationships of all this to a whole new technology, which is itself a figure for a whole new economic world system; and, after a brief account of postmodernist mutations in the lived experience of built space itself, some reflections on the mission of political art in the bewildering new world space of late multinational capital.

The Deconstruction of Expression

'Peasant Shoes'

We will begin with one of the canonical works of high modernism in visual art, Van Gogh's well-known painting of the peasant shoes, an example which as you can imagine has not been innocently or randomly chosen. I want to propose two ways of reading this painting, both of which in some fashion reconstruct the reception of the work in a two-stage or double-level process.

I first want to suggest that if this copiously reproduced image is not to sink to the level of sheer decoration, it requires us to reconstruct some initial situation out of which the finished work emerges. Unless that situation – which has vanished into the past – is somehow mentally restored, the painting will remain an inert object, a reified end-product, and be unable to be grasped as a symbolic act in its own right, as praxis and as production.

This last term suggests that one way of reconstructing the initial situation to which the work is somehow a response is by stressing the raw materials, the initial content, which it confronts and which it reworks, transforms, and appropriates. In Van Gogh, that content, those initial raw materials, are, I will suggest, to be grasped simply as the whole object world of agricultural misery, of stark rural poverty, and the whole rudimentary human world of backbreaking peasant toil, a world reduced to its most brutal and menaced, primitive and marginalized state.

Fruit trees in this world are ancient and exhausted sticks coming out of poor soil; the people of the village are worn down to their skulls, caricatures of some ultimate grotesque typology of basic human feature types. How is it then that in Van Gogh such things as apple trees explode into a hallucinatory surface of colour, while his village stereotypes are suddenly and garishly overlaid with hues of red and green? I will briefly suggest, in this first interpretative option, that the willed and violent transformation of a drab peasant object world into the most glorious materialization of pure colour in oil paint is to be seen as a Utopian gesture: as an act of compensation which ends up producing a whole new Utopian realm of the senses, or at least of that supreme sense – sight, the visual, the eye – which it now reconstitutes for us as a semi-autonomous space in its own right – part of some new division of labour in the body of capital, some new fragmentation of the emergent sensorium which replicates the specializations and divisions of capitalist life at the same time that it seeks in precisely such fragmentation a desperate Utopian compensation for them.

There is, to be sure, a second reading of Van Gogh which can hardly be ignored when we gaze at this particular painting, and that is Heidegger's central analysis in *Der Ursprung des Kunstwerkes*, which is organized around the idea that the work of art emerges within the gap between Earth and World, or what I would prefer to translate as the meaningless materiality of the body and nature and the meaning-endowment of history and of the social. We will return to that particular gap or rift later on; suffice it here to recall some of the famous phrases, which model the process whereby these henceforth illustrious peasant shoes slowly recreate about themselves the whole missing object-world which was once their lived context. 'In them,' says Heidegger, 'there vibrates the silent call of the earth, its quiet gift of ripening corn and its enigmatic self-refusal in the fallow desolation of the wintry field.' 'This equipment,' he goes on, 'belongs to the *earth* and it is protected in the *world* of the peasant woman . . . Van Gogh's painting is the disclosure of what the equipment, the pair of peasant shoes, *is* in truth . . . This entity emerges into the unconcealment of its being', by way of the mediation of the work of art, which draws the whole absent world and earth into revelation around itself, along with the heavy tread of the peasant woman, the loneliness of the field path, the hut in the clearing, the worn and broken instruments of labour in the furrows and at the hearth. Heidegger's account needs to be completed by insistence on the renewed materiality of the work, on the transformation of one form of materiality – the earth itself and its paths and physical objects – into that other materiality of oil paint affirmed and foregrounded in its own right and for its own visual pleasures; but has nonetheless a satisfying plausibility.

'Diamond Dust Shoes'

At any rate, both of these readings may be described as *hermeneutical*, in the sense in which the work in its inert, objectal form, is taken as a clue or a symptom for some vaster reality which replaces it as its ultimate truth. Now we need to look at some shoes of a different kind, and it is pleasant to be able to draw for such an image on the recent work of the central figure in contemporary visual art. Andy Warhol's *Diamond Dust Shoes* evidently no longer speaks to us with any of the immediacy of Van Gogh's footgear: indeed, I am tempted to say that it does not really speak to us at all. Nothing in this painting organizes even a minimal place for the viewer, who confronts it at the turning of a museum corridor or gallery with all the contingency of some inexplicable natural object. On the level of the content, we have to do with what are now far more clearly fetishes, both in the Freudian and in the Marxian sense (Derrida remarks, somewhere, about the Heideggerian *Paar Bauernschube*, that the Van Gogh footgear are a heterosexual pair, which allows neither for perversion nor for fetishization). Here, however, we have a random collection of dead objects, hanging together on the canvas like so many turnips, as shorn of their earlier life-world as the pile of shoes left over from Auschwitz, or the remainders and tokens of some incomprehensible and tragic fire in a packed dancehall. There is therefore in Warhol no way to complete the hermeneutic gesture, and to restore to these oddments that whole larger lived context of the dance hall or the ball, the world of jetset fashion or of glamour magazines. Yet this is even more paradoxical in the light of biographical information: Warhol began his artistic career as a commercial illustrator for shoe fashions and a designer of display windows in which various pumps and slippers figured prominently. Indeed, one is tempted to raise here – far too prematurely – one of the central issues about postmodernism itself and its possible political dimensions: Andy Warhol's work in fact turns centrally around commodification, and the great billboard images of the Coca-Cola bottle or the Campbell's Soup can, which explicitly foreground the commodity fetishism of a transition to late capital, *ought* to be powerful and critical political statements. If they are not that, then one would surely want to know why, and one would want to begin to wonder a little more seriously about the possibilities of political or critical art in the postmodern period of late capital.

But there are some other significant differences between the high modernist and the postmodernist moment, between the shoes of Van Gogh and the shoes of Andy Warhol, on which we must now very briefly dwell. The first and most evident is the emergence of a new kind of flatness or depthlessness, a new kind of superficiality in the most literal sense – perhaps the supreme formal feature of all the postmodernisms to which we will have occasion to return in a number of other contexts.

Then we must surely come to terms with the role of photography and the photographic/negative in contemporary art of this kind: and it is this indeed which confers its deathly quality on the Warhol image, whose glacéd x-ray elegance mortifies the reified eye of the viewer in a way that would seem to have nothing to do with death or the death obsession or the death anxiety on the level of content. It is indeed as though we had here to do with the inversion of Van Gogh's Utopian gesture: in the earlier work, a stricken world is by some Nietzschean fiat and act of the will transformed into the stridency of Utopian colour. Here, on the contrary, it is as though the external and coloured surface of things – debased and contaminated in advance by their assimilation to glossy advertising images – has been stripped away to reveal the deathly black-and-white substratum of the photographic negative which subtends them. Although this kind of death of the world of appearance becomes thematized in certain of Warhol's pieces – most notably, the traffic accidents or the electric chair series – this is not, I think, a matter of content any longer but of some more fundamental mutation both in the object world itself – now become a set of texts or simulacra – and in the disposition of the subject.

The waning of affect

All of which brings me to the third feature I had in mind to develop here briefly, namely what I will call the waning of affect in postmodern culture. Of course, it would be inaccurate to suggest that all affect, all feeling or emotion, all subjectivity, has vanished from the newer image. Indeed, there is a kind of return of the repressed in *Diamond Dust Shoes*, a strange compensatory decorative exhilaration, explicitly designated by the title itself although perhaps more difficult to observe in the reproduction. This is the glitter of gold dust, the spangling of gilt sand, which seals the surface of the painting and yet continues to glint at us. Think, however, of Rimbaud's magical flowers 'that look back at you', or of the august premonitory eye-flashes of Rilke's archaic Greek torso which warn the bourgeois subject to change his life: nothing of that sort here, in the gratuitous frivolity of this final decorative overlay.

The waning of affect is, however, perhaps best initially approached by way of the human figure, and it is obvious that what we have said about the commodification of objects holds as strongly for Warhol's human subjects, stars – like Marilyn Monroe – who are themselves commodified and transformed into their own images. And here too a certain brutal return to the older period of high modernism offers a dramatic shorthand parable of the transformation in question. Edvard Munch's painting *The Scream* is of course a canonical expression of the great modernist thematics of alienation, anomie, solitude and social fragmentation and isolation, a virtually programmatic emblem of what used to be called the age of anxiety. It will here be read not merely as an embodiment of the expression of that kind of affect, but even more as a virtual deconstruction of the very aesthetic of expression itself, which seems to have dominated much of what we call high modernism, but to have vanished away – for both practical and theoretical reasons – in the world of the postmodern. The very concept of expression presupposes indeed some separation within the subject, and along with that a whole metaphysics of the inside and the outside, of the wordless pain within the monad and the moment in which, often cathartically, that 'emotion' is then projected out and externalized, as gesture or cry, as desperate communication and the outward dramatization of inward feeling. And this is perhaps the moment to say something about contemporary theory, which has among other things been committed to the mission of criticizing and discrediting this very hermeneutic model of the inside and the outside and of stigmatizing such models as ideological and metaphysical. But what is today called contemporary theory – or better still, theoretical discourse – is also, I would want to argue, itself very precisely a post-modernist phenomenon. It would therefore be inconsistent to defend the truth of its theoretical insights in a situation in which the very concept of 'truth' itself is part of the metaphysical baggage which poststructuralism seeks to abandon. What we can at least suggest is that the poststructuralist critique of the hermeneutic, of what I will shortly call the depth model, is useful for us as a very significant symptom of the very postmodernist culture which is our subject here.

Overhastily, we can say that besides the hermeneutic model of inside and outside which Munch's painting develops, there are at least four other fundamental depth models which have generally been repudiated in contemporary theory: the dialectical one of essence and appearance (along with a whole range of concepts of ideology or false consciousness which tend to accompany it); the Freudian model of latent and manifest, or of repression (which is of course the target of Michel Foucault's program-matic and symptomatic pamphlet *La Volonté de savoir*); the existential model of authenticity and inauthenticity, whose heroic or tragic thematics are closely related to that other great opposition between alienation and disalienation, itself equally a casualty of the poststructural or postmodern period; and finally, latest in time, the great semiotic opposition between signifier and signified, which was itself rapidly unravelled and deconstructed during its brief heyday in the 1960s and 70s. What replaces these various depth models is for the most part a conception of practices, discourses and textual play, whose new syntagmatic structures we will examine later on: suffice it merely to observe that here too depth is replaced by surface, or by multiple surfaces (what is often called intertextuality is in that sense no longer a matter of depth).

Nor is this depthlessness merely metaphorical: it can be experienced physically and literally by anyone who, mounting what used to be Raymond Chandler's Beacon Hill from the great Chicano markets on Broadway and 4th St. in downtown Los Angeles, suddenly confronts the great free-standing wall of the Crocker Bank Center (Skid-more, Owings and Merrill) – a surface which seems to be unsupported by any volume, or whose putative volume (rectangular, trapezoidal?) is ocularly quite unde-cidable. This great sheet of windows, with its gravity-defying two-dimensionality, momentarily transforms the solid ground on which we climb into the contents of a stereopticon, pasteboard shapes profiling themselves here and there around us. From all sides, the visual effect is the same: as fateful as the great monolith in Kubrick's *2001* which confronts its viewers like an enigmatic destiny, a call to evolutionary mutation. If this new multinational downtown (to which we will return later in another context) effectively abolished the older ruined city fabric which it violently replaced, cannot something similar be said about the way in which this strange new surface in its own peremptory way renders our older systems of perception of the city somehow archaic and aimless, without offering another in their place?

Euphoria and self-annihilation

Returning now for one last moment to Munch's painting, it seems evident that *The Scream* subtly but elaborately deconstructs its own aesthetic of expression, all the while remaining imprisoned within it. Its gestural content already underscores its own failure, since the realm of the sonorous, the cry, the raw vibrations of the human throat, are incompatible with its medium (something underscored within the work by the homunculus' lack of ears). Yet the absent scream returns more closely towards that even more absent experience of atrocious solitude and anxiety which the scream was itself to 'express'. Such loops inscribe themselves on the painted surface in the form of those great concentric circles in which sonorous vibration becomes ultimately visible, as on the surface of a sheet of water – in an infinite regress which fans out from the sufferer to become the very geography of a universe in which pain itself now speaks and vibrates through the material sunset and the landscape. The visible world now becomes the wall of the monad on which this 'scream running through nature' (Munch's words) is recorded and transcribed: one thinks of that character of Lautréamont who, growing up inside a sealed and silent membrane, on sight of the monstrousness of the deity, ruptures it with his own scream and thereby rejoins the world of sound and suffering.

All of which suggests some more general historical hypothesis: namely, that concepts such as anxiety and alienation (and the experiences to which they correspond, as in *The Scream*) are no longer appropriate in the world of the postmodern. The great Warhol figures – Marilyn herself, or Edie Sedgewick – the notorious burn-out and self-destruction cases of the ending 1960s, and the great dominant experiences of drugs and schizophrenia – these would seem to have little enough in common anymore, either with the hysterics and neurotics of Freud's own day, or with those canonical experiences of radical isolation and solitude, anomie, private revolt, Van Gogh-type madness, which dominated the period of high modernism. This shift in the dynamics of cultural pathology can be characterized as one in which the alienation of the subject is displaced by the fragmentation of the subject.

Such terms inevitably recall one of the more fashionable themes in contemporary theory – that of the 'death' of the subject itself = the end of the autonomous bourgeois monad or ego or individual – and the accompanying stress, whether as some new moral ideal or as empirical description, on the *decentring* of that formerly centred subject or psyche. (Of the two possible formulations of this notion – the historicist one, that a once-existing centred subject, in the period of classical capitalism and the nuclear family, has today in the world of organizational bureaucracy dissolved; and the more radical poststructuralist position for which such a subject never existed in the first place but constituted something like an ideological mirage – I obviously incline towards the former; the latter must in any case take into account something like a 'reality of the appearance'.)

We must add that the problem of expression is itself closely linked to some conception of the subject as a monad-like container, within which things are felt which are then expressed by projection outwards. What we must now stress, however, is the degree to which the high-modernist conception of a unique *style*, along with the accompanying collective ideals of an artistic or political vanguard or *avant-garde*, themselves stand or fall along with that older notion (or experience) of the so-called centred subject.

Here too Munch's painting stands as a complex reflexion on this complicated situation: it shows us that expression requires the category of the individual monad, but it also shows us the heavy price to be paid for that precondition, dramatizing the unhappy paradox that when you constitute your individual subjectivity as a self-sufficient field and a closed realm in its own right, you thereby also shut yourself off from everything else and condemn yourself to the windless solitude of the monad, buried alive and condemned to a prison-cell without egress.

Postmodernism will presumably signal the end of this dilemma, which it replaces with a new one. The end of the bourgeois ego or monad no doubt brings with it the end of the psychopathologies of that ego as well – what I have generally here been calling the waning of affect. But it means the end of much more – the end for example of style, in the sense of the unique and the personal, the end of the distinctive individual brushstroke (as symbolized by the emergent primacy of mechanical repro-duction). As for expression and feelings or emotions, the liberation, in contemporary society, from the older *anomie* of the centred subject may also mean, not merely a liberation from anxiety, but a liberation from every other kind of feeling as well, since there is no longer a self present to do the feeling. This is not to say that the cultural products of the postmodern era are utterly devoid of feeling, but rather that such feelings – which it may be better and more accurate to call 'intensities' – are now free-floating and impersonal, and tend to be dominated by a peculiar kind of euphoria to which I will want to return at the end of this essay.

The waning of affect, however, might also have been characterized, in the narrower context of literary criticism, as the waning of the great high-modernist thematics of time and temporality, the elegiac mysteries of *durée* and of memory (something to be understood fully as a category of literary criticism associated as much with high modernism as with the works themselves). We have often been told, however, that we now inhabit the synchronic rather than the diachronic, and I think it is at least empirically arguable that our daily life, our psychic experience, our cultural languages, are today dominated by categories of space rather than by categories of time, as in the preceding period of high modernism proper.

The Postmodern and the Past

Pastiche eclipses parody

The disappearance of the individual subject, along with its formal consequence, the increasing unavailability of the personal *style*, engender the well-nigh universal prac-tice today of what may be called pastiche. This concept, which we owe to Thomas Mann (in *Doktor Faustus*), who owed it in turn to Adorno's great work on the two paths of advanced musical experimentation (Schoenberg's innovative planification,

Stravinsky's irrational eclecticism), is to be sharply distinguished from the more readily received idea of parody.

This last found, to be sure, a fertile area in the idiosyncracies of the moderns and their 'inimitable' styles: the Faulknerian long sentence with its breathless gerundives, Lawrentian nature imagery punctuated by testy colloquialism, Wallace Stevens' inveterate hypostasis of nonsubstantive parts of speech ('the intricate evasions of as'), the fateful, but finally predictable, swoops in Mahler from high orchestral pathos into village accordeon sentiment, Heidegger's meditative-solemn practice of the false etymology as a mode of 'proof'... All these strike one as somehow 'characteristic', insofar as they ostentatiously deviate from a norm which then reasserts itself, in a not necessarily unfriendly way, by a systematic mimicry of their deliberate eccentricities.

Yet, in the dialectical leap from quantity to quality, the explosion of modern literature into a host of distinct private styles and mannerisms has been followed by a linguistic fragmentation of social life itself to the point where the norm itself is eclipsed: reduced to a neutral and reified media speech (far enough from the Utopian aspirations of the inventors of Esperanto or Basic English), which itself then becomes but one more idiolect among many. Modernist styles thereby become postmodernist codes: and that the stupendous proliferation of social codes today into professional and disciplinary jargons, but also into the badges of affirmation of ethnic, gender, race, religious, and class-fraction adhesion, is also a political phenomenon, the problem of micropolitics sufficiently demonstrates. If the ideas of a ruling class were once the dominant (or hegemonic) ideology of bourgeois society, the advanced capitalist countries today are now a field of stylistic and discursive heterogeneity without a norm. Faceless masters continue to inflect the economic strategies which constrain our existences, but no longer need to impose their speech (or are henceforth unable to); and the postliteracy of the late capitalist world reflects, not only the absence of any great collective project, but also the unavailability of the older national language itself.

In this situation, parody finds itself without a vocation; it has lived, and that strange new thing pastiche slowly comes to take its place. Pastiche is, like parody, the imitation of a peculiar mask, speech in a dead language: but it is a neutral practice of such mimicry, without any of parody's ulterior motives, amputated of the satiric impulse, devoid of laughter and of any conviction that alongside the abnormal tongue you have momentarily borrowed, some healthy linguistic normality still exists. Pastiche is thus blank parody, a statue with blind eyeballs: it is to parody what that other interesting and historically original modern thing, the practice of a kind of blank irony, is to what Wayne Booth calls the 'stable ironies' of the 18th century.

It would therefore begin to seem that Adorno's prophetic diagnosis has been realized, albeit in a negative way: not Schoenberg (the sterility of whose achieved system he already glimpsed) but Stravinsky is the true precursor of the postmodern cultural production. For with the collapse of the high-modernist ideology of style – what is as unique and unmistakable as your own fingerprints, as incomparable as your own body (the very source, for an early Roland Barthes, of stylistic invention and innovation) – the producers of culture have nowhere to turn but to the past: the imitation of dead styles, speech through all the masks and voices stored up in the imaginary museum of a now global culture.

'Historicism' effaces history

This situation evidently determines what the architecture historians call 'historicism', namely the random cannibalization of all the styles of the past, the play of random stylistic allusion, and in general what Henri Lefebvre has called the increasing primacy of the 'neo'. This omnipresence of pastiche is, however, not incompatible with a certain humour (nor is it innocent of all passion) or at least with addiction – with a whole historically original consumers' appetite for a world transformed into sheer images of itself and for pseudo-events and 'spectacles' (the term of the Situationists). It is for such objects that we may reserve Plato's conception of the 'simulacrum' – the identical copy for which no original has ever existed. Appropriately enough, the culture of the simulacrum comes to *life* in a society where exchange-value has been generalized to the point at which the very memory of use-value is effaced, a society of which Guy Debord has observed, in an extraordinary phrase, that in it 'the image has become the final form of commodity reification' (*The Society of the Spectacle*).

The new spatial logic of the simulacrum can now be expected to have a momentous effect on what used to be historical time.

The past is thereby itself modified: what was once, in the historical novel as Lukács defines it, the organic genealogy of the bourgeois collective project – what is still, for the redemptive historiography of an E. P. Thompson or of American 'oral history', for the resurrection of the dead of anonymous and silenced generations, the retrospective dimension indispensable to any vital reorientation of our collective future – has meanwhile itself become a vast collection of images, a multitudinous photographic simulacrum. Guy Debord's powerful slogan is now even more apt for the 'prehistory' of a society bereft of all historicity, whose own putative past is little more than a set of dusty spectacles. In faithful conformity to poststructuralist linguistic theory, the past as 'referent' finds itself gradually bracketed, and then effaced altogether, leaving us with nothing but texts.

The nostalgia mode

Yet it should not be thought that this process is accompanied by indifference: on the contrary, the remarkable current intensification of an addiction to the photographic image is itself a tangible symptom of an omnipresent, omnivorous and well-nigh libidinal historicism. The architects use this (exceedingly polysemous) word for the complacent eclecticism of postmodern architecture, which randomly and without principle but with gusto cannibalizes all the architectural styles of the past and combines them in overstimulating ensembles. Nostalgia does not strike one as an altogether satisfactory word for such fascination (particularly when one thinks of the pain of a properly modernist nostalgia with a past beyond all but aesthetic retrieval), yet it directs our attention to what is a culturally far more generalized manifestation of the process in commercial art and taste, namely the so-called 'nostalgia film' (or what the French call 'la mode rétro').

These restructure the whole issue of pastiche and project it onto a collective and social level, where the desperate attempt to appropriate a missing past is now refracted through the iron law of fashion change and the emergent ideology of the 'generation'. *American Graffiti* (1973) set out to recapture, as so many films have attempted since, the henceforth mesmerizing lost reality of the Eisenhower era: and one tends to feel that for Americans at least, the 1950s remain the privileged lost object of desire – not merely the stability and prosperity of a pax Americana, but also the first naive innocence of the countercultural impulses of early rock-and-roll and youth gangs (Coppola's *Rumble Fish* will then be the contemporary dirge that laments their passing, itself, however, still contradictorily filmed in genuine 'nostalgia film' style). With this initial breakthrough, other generational periods open up for aesthetic colonization: as witness the stylistic recuperation of the American and the Italian 1930s, in Polanski's *Chinatown* and Bertolluci's *Il Conformista* respectively. What is more interesting, and more problematical, are the ultimate attempts, through this new discourse, to lay siege either to our own present and immediate past, or to a more distant history that escapes individual existential memory.

Faced with these ultimate objects – our social, historical and existential present, and the past as 'referent' – the incompatibility of a postmodernist 'nostalgia' art language with genuine historicity becomes dramatically apparent. The contraction propels this model, however, into complex and interesting new formal inventiveness: it being understood that the nostalgia film was never a matter of some old-fashioned 'representation' of historical content, but approached the 'past' through stylistic connotation, conveying 'pastness' by the glossy qualities of the image, and '1930s-ness' or '1950s-ness' by the attributes of fashion (therein following the prescription of the Barthes of *Mythologies*, who saw connotation as the purveying of imaginary and stereotypical idealities, 'Sinité', for example, as some Disney-EPCOT 'concept' of China).

The insensible colonization of the present by the nostalgia mode can be observed in Lawrence Kazdan's elegant film, *Body Heat*, a distant 'affluent society' remake of James M. Cain's *The Postman Always Rings Twice*, set in a contemporary Florida small town not far from Miami. The word 'remake' is, however, anachronistic to the degree to which our awareness of the pre-existence of other versions, previous films of the novel as well as the novel itself, is now a constitutive and essential part of the film's structure: we are now, in other words, in 'intertextuality' as a deliberate, built-in feature of the aesthetic effect, and as the operator of a new connotation of 'pastness' and pseudo-historical depth, in which the history of aesthetic styles displaces 'real' history.

Yet from the outset a whole battery of aesthetic signs begin to distance the officially contemporary image from us in time: the art deco scripting of the credits, for example, serves at once to programme the spectator for the appropriate 'nostalgia' mode of reception (art deco quotation has much the same function in contemporary architecture, as in Toronto's remarkable Eaton Centre). Meanwhile, a somewhat different play of connotations is activated by complex (but purely formal) allusions to the institutions of the star system itself. The protagonist, William Hurt, is one of a new generation of film 'stars' whose status is markedly distinct from that of the preceding generation of male superstars, such as Steve McQueen or Jack Nicholson (or even, more distantly, Brando), let alone of earlier moments in the evolution of the institutions of the star. The immediately preceding generation projected its various roles through, and by way of, well-known 'off-screen' personalities, who often connoted rebellion and non-conformism. The latest generation of starring actors continues to assure the conventional functions of stardom (most notably, sexuality) but in the utter absence of 'personality' in the older sense, and with something of the anonymity of character acting (which in actors like Hurt reaches virtuouso proportions, yet of a very different kind from the virtuosity of the older Brando or Olivier). This 'death of the subject' in the institution of the star, however, opens up the possibility of a play of historical allusions to much older roles – in this case to those associated with Clark Gable – so that the very style of the acting can now also serve as a 'connotator' of the past.

Finally, the setting has been strategically framed, with great ingenuity, to eschew most of the signals that normally convey the contemporaneity of the United States in its multinational era: the small-town setting allows the camera to elude the high-rise landscape of the 1970s and 80s (even though a key episode in the narrative involves the fatal destruction of older buildings by land speculators); while the object world of the present-day – artifacts and appliances, even automobiles, whose styling would at once serve to date the image – is elaborately edited out. Everything in the film, therefore, conspires to blur its official contemporaneity and to make it possible for you to receive the narrative as though it were set in some eternal Thirties, beyond real historical time. The approach to the present by way of the art language of the simulacrum, or of the pastiche of the stereotypical past, endows present reality and the openness of present history with the spell and distance of a glossy mirage. But this mesmerizing new aesthetic mode itself emerged as an elaborated symptom of the waning of our historicity, of our lived possibility of experiencing history in some active way: it cannot therefore be said to produce this strange occultation of the present by its own formal power, but merely to demonstrate, through these inner contradictions, the enormity of a situation in which we seem increasingly incapable of fashioning representations of our own current experience.

The fate of 'real history'

As for 'real history' itself – the traditional object, however it may be defined, of what used to be the historical novel – it will be more revealing now to turn back to that older form and medium and to read its postmodern fate in the work of one of the few serious and innovative Left novelists at work in the United States today, whose books are nourished with history in the more traditional sense, and seem, so far, to stake out successive generational moments in the 'epic' of American history. E. L. Doctorow's *Ragtime* gives itself officially as a panorama of the first two decades of the century; his most recent novel, *Loon Lake*, addresses the Thirties and the Great Depression; while *The Book of Daniel* holds up before us, in painful juxtaposition, the two great moments of the Old Left and the New Left, of Thirties and Forties Communism and the radicalism of the 1960s (even his early Western may be said to fit into this scheme and to designate in a less articulated and formally self-conscious way the end of the frontier of the late nineteenth century).

The Book of Daniel is not the only one of these three major historical novels to establish an explicit narrative link between the reader's and the writer's present and the older historical reality which is the subject of the work; the astonishing last page of *Loon Lake*, which I will not disclose, also does this in a very different way; while it is a matter of some interest to note that the first sentence of the first version of *Ragtime* positions us explicitly in our own present, in the novelist's house in New Rochelle, New York, which will then at once become the scene of its own (imaginary) past in the 1900s. This detail has been suppressed from the published text, symbolically cutting its moorings and freeing the novel to float in some new world of past historical time whose relationship to us is problematical indeed. The authenticity of the gesture, however, may be measured by the evident existential fact of life that there no longer does seem to be any organic relationship between the American history we learn from the schoolbooks and the lived experience of the current multinational, high-rise, stagflated city of the newspapers and of our own daily life.

A crisis in historicity, however, inscribes itself symptomally in several other curious formal features within this text. Its official subject is the transition from a pre-World-War I radical and working-class politics (the great strikes) to the technological invention and new commodity production of the 1920s (the rise of Hollywood and of the image as commodity): the interpolated version of Kleist's *Michael Kohlhaas*, the strange tragic episode of the Black protagonist's revolt, may be thought to be a moment related to this process. My point, however, is not some hypothesis as to the thematic coherence of this decentred narrative; but rather just the opposite, namely the way in which the kind of reading this novel imposes makes it virtually impossible for us to reach and to thematize those official 'subjects' which float above the text but cannot be integrated into our reading of the sentences. In that sense, not only does the novel resist interpretation, it is organized systematically and formally to short-circuit an older type of social and historical interpretation which it perpetually holds out and withdraws. When we remember that the theoretical critique and repudiation of interpretation as such is a fundamental component of poststructuralist theory, it is difficult not to conclude that Doctorow has somehow deliberately built this very tension, this very contradiction, into the flow of his sentences.

As is well known, the book is crowded with real historical figures – from Teddy Roosevelt to Emma Goldman, from Harry K. Thaw and Sandford White to J. Pierpont Morgan and Henry Ford, not to speak of the more central role of Houdini – who interact with a fictive family, simply designated as Father, Mother, Older Brother, and so forth. All historical novels, beginning with Scott himself, no doubt in one way or another involve a mobilization of previous historical knowledge, generally acquired through the schoolbook history manuals devised for whatever legitimizing purpose by this or that national tradition – thereafter instituting a narrative dialectic between what we already 'know' about The Pretender, say, and what he is then seen to be concretely in the pages of the novel. But Doctorow's procedure seems much more extreme than this; and I would argue that the designation of both types of characters – historical names or capitalized family roles

– operates powerfully and systematically to reify all these characters and to make it impossible for us to receive their representation without the prior interception of already-acquired knowledge or doxa – something which lends the text an extra-ordinary sense of déjà-vu and a peculiar familiarity one is tempted to associate with Freud's 'return of the repressed' in 'The Uncanny', rather than with any solid historiographic formation on the reader's part.

Loss of the radical past

Meanwhile, the sentences in which all this is happening have their own specificity, which will allow us a little more concretely to distinguish the moderns' elaboration of a personal style from this new kind of linguistic innovation, which is no longer personal at all but has its family kinship rather with what Barthes long ago called 'white writing'. In this particular novel, Doctorow has imposed upon himself a rigorous principle of selection in which only simple declarative sentences (predomin-antly mobilized by the verb 'to be') are received. The effect is, however, not really one of the condescending simplification and symbolic carefulness of children's literature, but rather something more disturbing, the sense of some profound subterranean violence done to American English which cannot, however, be detected empirically in any of the perfectly grammatical sentences with which this work is formed. Yet other more visible technical 'innovations' may supply a clue to what is happening in the language of *Ragtime*: it is for example well known that the source of many of the characteristic effects of Camus' novel *L'Etranger* can be traced back to that author's wilful decision to substitute, throughout, the French tense of the 'passé composé' for the other past tenses more normally employed in narration in that language. I will suggest that it is *as if* something of that sort were at work here (without committing myself further to what is obviously an outrageous leap): it is, I say, *as though* Doctorow had set out systematically to produce the effect or the equivalent, in his language, of a verbal past tense we do not possess in English, namely the French preterite (or *passé simple*), whose 'perfective' movement, as Émile Benveniste taught us, serves to separate events from the present of enunciation and to transform the stream of time and action into so many finished, complete, and isolated punctual event-objects which find themselves sundered from any present situation (even that of the act of storytelling or enunciation).

E. L. Doctorow is the epic poet of the disappearance of the American radical past, of the suppression of older traditions and moments of the American radical tradition: no one with left sympathies can read these splendid novels without a poignant distress which is an authentic way of confronting our own current political dilemmas in the present. What is culturally interesting, however, is that he has had to convey this great theme formally (since the waning of the content is very precisely his subject), and, more than that, has had to elaborate his work by way of that very cultural logic of the postmodern which is itself the mark and symptom of his dilemma. *Loon Lake* much more obviously deploys the strategies of the pastiche (most notably in its reinvention of Dos Passos); but *Ragtime* remains the most peculiar and stunning monument to the aesthetic situation engendered by the disappearance of the historical referent. This historical novel can no longer set out to represent the historical past; it can only 'represent' our ideas and stereotypes about that past (which thereby at once becomes 'pop history'). Cultural production is thereby driven back inside a mental space which is no longer that of the old monadic subject, but rather that of some degraded collective 'objective spirit': it can no longer gaze directly on some putative real world, at some reconstruction of a past history which was once itself a present; rather, as in Plato's cave, it must trace our mental images of that past upon its confining walls. If there is any realism left here, therefore, it is a 'realism' which is meant to derive from the shock of grasping that confinement, and of slowly becoming aware of a new and original historical situation in which we are condemned to seek History by way of our own pop images and simulacra of that history, which itself remains forever out of reach.

The Breakdown of the Signifying Chain

The crisis in historicity now dictates a return, in a new way, to the question of temporal organization in general in the postmodern force field, and indeed, to the problem of the form that time, temporality and the syntagmatic will be able to take in a culture increasingly dominated by space and spatial logic. If, indeed, the subject has lost its capacity actively to extend its pro-tensions and re-tensions across the temporal manifold, and to organize its past and future into coherent experience, it becomes difficult enough to see how the cultural productions of such a subject could result in anything but 'heaps of fragments' and in a practice of the randomly heterogeneous and fragmentary and the aleatory. These are, however, very precisely some of the privileged terms in which postmodernist cultural production has been analysed (and even defended, by its own apologists). Yet they are still privative features; the more substantive formulations bear such names as textuality, *écriture*, or schizophrenic writing, and it is to these that we must now briefly turn.

I have found Lacan's account of schizophrenia useful here, not because I have any way of knowing whether it has clinical accuracy, but chiefly because – as description rather than diagnosis – it seems to me to offer a suggestive aesthetic model. (I am obviously very far from thinking that any of the most significant postmodernist artists – Cage, Ashbery, Sollers, Robert Wilson, Ishmael Reed, Michael Snow, Warhol or even Beckett himself – are schizophrenics in any clinical sense.) Nor is the point some culture-and-personality diagnosis of our society and its art, as in culture critiques of the type of Christopher Lasch's influential *The Culture of Narcissism*, from which I am concerned radically to distance the spirit and the methodology of the present remarks: there are, one would think, far more damaging things to be said about our social system than are available through the use of psychological categories.

Very briefly, Lacan describes schizophrenia as a breakdown in the signifying chain, that is, the interlocking syntagmatic series of signifiers which constitutes an utterance or a meaning. I must omit the familial or more orthodox psychoanalytic background to this situation, which Lacan transcodes into language by describing the Oedipal rivalry in terms, not so much of the biological individual who is your rival for the mother's attention, but rather of what he calls the Name-of-the-Father, paternal authority now considered as a linguistic function. His conception of the signifying chain essentially presupposes one of the basic principles (and one of the great discoveries) of Saussurean structuralism, namely the proposition that meaning is not a one-to-one relationship between signifier and signified, between the materiality of language, between a word or a name, and its referent or concept. Meaning on the new view is generated by the movement from Signifier to Signifier: what we generally call the Signified – the meaning or conceptual content of an utterance – is now rather to be seen as a meaning-effect, as that objective mirage of signification generated and projected by the relationship of Signifiers among each other. When that relationship breaks down, when the links of the signifying chain snap, then we have schizophrenia in the form of a rubble of distinct and unrelated signifiers. The connection between this kind of linguistic malfunction and the psyche of the schizophrenic may then be grasped by way of a two-fold proposition: first, that personal identity is itself the effect of a certain temporal unification of past and future with the present before me; and second, that such active temporal unification is itself a function of language, or better still of the sentence, as it moves along its hermeneutic circle through time. If we are unable to unify the past, present and future of the sentence, then we are similarly unable to unify the past, present and future of our own biographical experience or psychic life.

With the breakdown of the signifying chain, therefore, the schizophrenic is reduced to an experience of pure material Signifiers, or in other words of a series of pure and unrelated presents in time. We will want to ask questions about the aesthetic or cultural results of such a situation in a moment; let us first see what it feels like: 'I remember very well the day it happened. We were staying in the country and I had gone for a walk alone as I did now and then. Suddenly, as I was passing the school, I heard a German song; the children were having a singing lesson. I stopped to listen, and at that instant a strange feeling came over me, a feeling hard to analyse but akin to something I was to know too well later – a disturbing sense of unreality. It seemed to me that I no longer recognized the school, it had become as large as a barracks; the singing children were prisoners, compelled to sing. It was as though the school and the children's song were set apart from the rest of the world. At the same time my eye encountered a field of wheat whose limits I could not see. The yellow vastness, dazzling in the sun, bound up with the song of the children imprisoned in the smooth stone school-barracks, filled me with such anxiety that I broke into sobs. I ran home to our garden and began to play "to make things seem as they usually were," that is, to return to reality. It was the first appearance of those elements which were always present in later sensations of unreality: illimitable vastness, brilliant light, and the gloss and smoothness of material things.'[3]

In our present context, this experience suggests the following remarks: first, the breakdown of temporality suddenly releases this present of time from all the activities and the intentionalities that might focus it and make it a space of praxis; thereby isolated, that present suddenly engulfs the subject with undescribable vividness, a materiality of perception properly overwhelming, which effectively dramatizes the power of the material – or better still, the literal – Signifier in isolation. This present of the world or material signifier comes before the subject with heightened intensity, bearing a mysterious charge of affect, here described in the negative terms of anxiety and loss of reality, but which one could just as well imagine in the positive terms of euphoria, the high, the intoxicatory or hallucinogenic intensity.

'China'

What will happen in textuality or schizophrenic art is strikingly illuminated by such clinical accounts, although in the cultural text, the isolated Signifier is no longer an enigmatic state of the world or an incomprehensible yet mesmerizing fragment of language, but rather something closer to a sentence in free-standing isolation. Think, for example, of the experience of John Cage's music, in which a cluster of material sounds (on the prepared piano for example) is followed by a silence so intolerable that you cannot imagine another sonorous chord coming into existence, and cannot imagine remembering the previous one well enough to make any connection with it if it does. Some of Beckett's narratives are also of this order, most notably *Watt*, where a primacy of the present sentence in time ruthlessly disintegrates the narrative fabric that attempts to reform around it. My example will, however, be a less sombre one, a text by a younger San Francisco poet whose group or school – so-called Language Poetry or the New Sentence – seems to have adopted schizophrenic fragmentation as its fundamental aesthetic.

> China
> We live on the third world from the sun. Number three. Nobody tells us what to do
> The people who taught us to count were being very kind.
> It's always time to leave.
> If it rains, you either have your umbrella or you don't.
> The wind blows your hat off.
> The sun rises also.
> I'd rather the stars didn't describe us to each other; I'd rather we do it for ourselves.
> Run in front of your shadow.
> A sister who points to the sky at least once a decade is a good sister.
> The landscape is motorized.
> The train takes you where it goes.
> Bridges among water.
> Folks straggling along vast stretches of concrete, heading into the plane.
> Don't forget what your hat and shoes will look like when you are nowhere
>   to be found.
> Even the words floating in air make blue shadows.
> If it tastes good we eat it.
> The leaves are falling. Point things out.
> Pick up the right things.
> *Hey guess what?* What? *I've learned how to talk.* Great.
> The person whose head was incomplete burst into tears.
> As it fell, what could the doll do? Nothing.
> Go to sleep.
> You look great in shorts. And the flag looks great too.

Everyone enjoyed the explosions.
Time to wake up.
But better get used to dreams.

                              (Bob Perelman from *Primer*, This Press, Berkeley)

Many things could be said about this interesting exercise in discontinuities: not the least paradoxical is the reemergence here across these disjoined sentences of some more unified global meaning. Indeed, insofar as this is in some curious and secret way a political poem, it does seem to capture something of the excitement of the immense, unfinished social experiment of the New China – unparalleled in world history – the unexpected emergence, between the two super-powers, of 'number three', the freshness of a whole new object world produced by human beings in some new control over their collective destiny, the signal event, above all, of a collectivity which has become a new 'subject of history' and which, after the long subjection of feudalism and imperialism, again speaks in its own voice, for itself as though for the first time.

I mainly wanted to show, however, the way in which what I have been calling schizophrenic disjunction or *écriture*, when it becomes generalized as a cultural style, ceases to entertain a necessary relationship to the morbid content we associate with terms like schizophrenia, and becomes available for more joyous intensities, for precisely that euphoria which we saw displacing the older affects of anxiety and alienation.

Consider, for example, Jean-Paul Sartre's account of a similar tendency in Flaubert: 'His sentence' (Sartre tells us about Flaubert) 'closes in on the object, seizes it, immobilizes it, and breaks its back, wraps itself around it, changes into stone and petrifies its object along with itself. It is blind and deaf, bloodless, not a breath of life; a deep silence separates it from the sentence which follows; it falls into the void, eternally, and drags its prey down into that infinite fall. Any reality, once described, is struck off the inventory.' (*What is Literature?*)

Yet I am tempted to see this reading as a kind of optical illusion (or photographic enlargement) of an unwittingly genealogical type: in which certain latent or subordinate, properly postmodernist features of Flaubert's style are anachronistically foregrounded. Yet it affords another interesting lesson in periodization, and in the dialectical restructuring of cultural dominants and subordinates. For these features, in Flaubert, were symptoms and strategies in that whole posthumous life and resentment of praxis which is denounced (with increasing sympathy) throughout the three thousand pages of Sartre's *Family Idiot*. When such features become themselves the cultural norm, they shed all such forms of negative affect and become available for other, more decorative uses.

But we have thereby not fully exhausted the structural secrets of Perelman's poem, which turns out to have little enough to do with that referent called China. The author has in fact related how, strolling through Chinatown, he came across a book of photographs whose idiogrammatic captions remained a dead letter to him (or perhaps one should say, a material signifier). The sentences of the poem in question are then Perelman's own captions to those pictures, their referents another image, another absent text; and the unity of the poem is no longer to be found within its language, but outside itself, in the bound unity of another, absent book. There is here a striking parallel to the dynamics of so-called photorealism, which looked like a return to representation and figuration after the long hegemony of the aesthetics of abstraction, until it became clear that its objects were not to be found in the 'real world' either, but were themselves photographs of that real world, this last now transformed into images, of which the 'realism' of the photorealist painting is now the simulacrum.

Collage and radical difference

This account of schizophrenia and temporal organization might, however, have been formulated in a different way, which brings us back to Heidegger's notion of a gap or rift, albeit in a fashion that would have horrified him. I would like, indeed, to characterize the postmodernist experience of form with what will seem, I hope, a paradoxical slogan: namely the proposition that 'difference relates'. Our own recent criticism, from Macherey on, has been concerned to stress the heterogeneity and profound discontinuities of the work of art, no longer unified or organic, but now virtual grab-bag or lumber room of disjoined subsystems and random raw materials and impulses of all kinds. The former work of art, in other words, has now turned out to be a text, whose reading proceeds by differentiation rather than by unification. Theories of difference, however, have tended to stress disjunction to the point at which the materials of the text, including its words and sentences, tend to fall apart into random and inert passivity, into a set of elements which entertain purely external separations from one another.

In the most interesting postmodernist works, however, one can detect a more positive conception of relationship which restores its proper tension to the notion of differences itself. This new mode of relationship through difference may sometimes be an achieved new and original way of thinking and perceiving; more often it takes the form of an impossible imperative to achieve that new mutation in what can perhaps no longer be called consciousness. I believe that the most striking emblem of this new mode of thinking relationships can be found in the work of Nam June Paik, whose stacked or scattered television screens, positioned at intervals within lush vegetation, or winking down at us from a ceiling of strange new video stars, recapitulate over and over again prearranged sequences or loops of images which return at dysynchronous moments on the various screens. The older aesthetic is then practised by viewers, who, bewildered by this discontinuous variety, decide to concentrate on a single screen, as though the relatively worthless image sequence to be followed there had some organic value in its own right. The postmodernist viewer, however, is called upon to do the impossible, namely to see all the screens at once, in their radical and random difference; such a viewer is asked to follow the evolutionary mutation of David Bowie in *The Man Who Fell to Earth*, and to rise somehow to a level at which the vivid perception of radical difference is in and of itself a new mode of grasping what used to be called relationship: something for which the word *collage* is still only a very feeble name.

The Hysterical Sublime

Now we need to complete this exploratory account of postmodernist space and time with a final analysis of that euphoria or those intensities which seem so often to characterize the newer cultural experience. Let us stress again the enormity of a transition which leaves behind it the desolation of Hopper's buildings or the stark Midwest syntax of Sheeler's forms, replacing them with the extraordinary surfaces of the photorealist cityscape, where even the automobile wrecks gleam with some new hallucinatory splendour. The exhilaration of these new surfaces is all the more para-doxical in that their essential content – the city itself – has deteriorated or disinte-grated to a degree surely still inconceivable in the early years of the 20th century, let alone in the previous era. How urban squalor can be a delight to the eyes, when expressed in commodification, and how an unparalleled quantum leap in the aliena-tion of daily life in the city can now be experienced in the form of a strange new hallucinatory exhilaration – these are some of the questions that confront us in this moment of our inquiry. Nor should the human figure be exempted from investiga-tion, although it seems clear that for the newer aesthetic the representation of space itself has come to be felt as incompatible with the representation of the body: a kind of aesthetic division of labour far more pronounced than in any of the earlier generic conceptions of landscape, and a most ominous symptom indeed. The privileged space of the newer art is radically anti-anthropomorphic, as in the empty bathrooms of Doug Bond's work. The ultimate contemporary fetishization of the human body, however, takes a very different direction in the statues of Duane Hanson – what I have already called the simulacrum, whose peculiar function lies in what Sartre would have called the *derealization* of the whole surrounding world of everyday reality. Your moment of doubt and hesitation as to the breath and warmth of these polyester figures, in other words, tends to return upon the real human beings moving about you in the museum, and to transform them also for the briefest instant into so many dead and flesh-coloured simulacra in their own right. The world thereby momentarily loses its depth and threatens to become a glossy skin, a stereoscopic illusion, a rush of filmic images without density. But is this now a terrifying or an exhilarating experi-ence?

It has proved fruitful to think such experience in terms of what Susan Sontag once, in an influential statement, isolated as 'camp'. I propose a somewhat different cross-light on it, drawing on the equally fashionable current theme of the 'sublime', as it has been rediscovered in the works of Edmund Burke and Kant; or perhaps, indeed, one might well want to yoke the two notions together in the form of something like a camp or 'hysterical' sublime. The sublime was for Burke, as you will recall, an experience bordering on terror, the fitful glimpse, in astonishment, stupor and awe, of what was so enormous as to crush human life altogether: a description then refined by Kant to include the question of representation itself – so that the object of the sublime is now not only a matter of sheer power and of the physical incommensur-ability of the human organism with Nature, but also of the limits of figuration and the incapacity of the human mind to give representation to such enormous forces. Such forces Burke, in his historical moment at the dawn of the modern bourgeois state, was only able to conceptualize in terms of the divine; while even Heidegger continues to entertain a fantasmatic relationship with some organic precapitalist peasant landscape and village society, which is the final form of the image of Nature in our own time.

Today, however, it may be possible to think all this in a different way, at the moment of a radical eclipse of Nature itself: Heidegger's 'field path' is after all irredeemably and irrevocably destroyed by late capital, by the green revolution, by neocolonialism and the megalopolis, which runs its superhighways over the older fields and vacant lots, and turns Heidegger's 'house of being' into condominiums, if not the most miserable unheated rat-infested tenement buildings. The *other* of our society is in that sense no longer Nature at all, as it was in precapitalist societies, but something else which we must now identify.

The apotheosis of capitalism

I am anxious that this other thing should not overhastily be grasped as technology per se, since I will want to show that technology is here itself a figure for something else. Yet technology may well serve as adequate shorthand to designate that enormous properly human and anti-natural power of dead human labour stored up in our machinery, an alienated power, what Sartre calls the counterfinality of the practico-inert, which turns back on and against us in unrecognizable forms and seems to constitute the massive dystopian horizon of our collective as well as our individual praxis.

Technology is, however, on the Marxist view the result of the development of capital, rather than some primal cause in its own right. It will therefore be appropriate to distinguish several generations of machine power, several stages of technological revolution within capital itself. I here follow Ernest Mandel who outlines three such fundamental breaks or quantum leaps in the evolution of machinery under capital: 'The fundamental revolutions in power technology – the technology of the produc-tion of motive machines by machines – thus appears as the determinant moment in revolutions of technology as a whole. Machine production of steam-driven motors since 1848; machine production of electric and combustion motors since the 90s of the 19th century; machine production of electronic and nuclear-powered apparatuses since the 40s of the 20th century – these are the three general revolutions in technology engendered by the capitalist mode of production since the "original" industrial revolution of the later 18th century' (*Late Capitalism*, p. 18).

The periodization underscores the general thesis of Mandel's book *Late Capital-ism*, namely that there have been three fundamental moments in capitalism, each one marking a dialectical expansion over the previous stage: these are market capitalism, the monopoly stage or the stage of imperialism, and our own – wrongly called postindustrial, but what might better be termed multinational capital. I have already pointed out that Mandel's intervention in the postindustrial involves the proposition that late or multinational or consumer capitalism, far from being inconsistent with Marx's great 19th-century analysis, constitutes on the contrary the purest form of capital yet to have emerged, a prodigious expansion of capital into hitherto uncommodified areas. This purer capitalism of our own time thus eliminates the enclaves of precapitalist organization it had hitherto tolerated and exploited in a tributary way: one is tempted to speak in this connection of a new and historically original penetration and colonization of Nature and the Unconscious: that is, the destruction of precapitalist third world agriculture by the Green Revolution, and the rise of the media and the advertising industry. At any rate, it will also have been clear that my own cultural periodization of the stages of realism, modernism and post-modernism is both inspired and confirmed by Mandel's tripartite scheme.

We may speak therefore of our own age as the Third (or even Fourth) Machine Age; and it is at this point that we must reintroduce the problem of aesthetic representation already explicitly developed in Kant's earlier analysis of the sublime – since it would seem only logical that the relationship to, and representation of, the machine could be expected to shift dialectically with each of these qualitatively different stages of technological development.

It is appropriate therefore to recall the excitement of machinery in the preceding moment of capital, the exhilaration of futurism most notably, and of Marinetti's celebration of the machine gun and the motor car. These are still visible emblems, sculptural nodes of energy which give tangibility and figuration to the motive ener-gies of that earlier moment of modernization. The prestige of these great streamlined shapes can be measured by their metaphorical presence in Le Corbusier's buildings, vast Utopian structures which ride like so many gigantic steamshipliners upon the urban scenery of an older fallen earth. Machinery exerts another kind of fascination in artists like Picabia and Duchamp, whom we have no time to consider here; but let me mention, for the sake of completeness, the ways in which revolutionary or communist artists of the 1930s also sought to reappropriate this excitement of machine energy for a Promethean reconstruction of human society as a whole, as in Fernand Leger and Diego Rivera.

What must then immediately be observed is that the technology of our own moment no longer possesses this same capacity for representation: not the turbine, nor even Sheeler's grain elevators or smokestacks, not the baroque elaboration of pipes and conveyor belts nor even the streamlined profile of the railroad train – all vehicles of speed still concentrated at rest – but rather the computer, whose outer shell has no emblematic or visual power, or even the casings of the various media themselves, as with that home appliance called television which articulates nothing but rather implodes, carrying its flattened image surface within itself.

Such machines are indeed machines of reproduction rather than of production, and they make very different demands on our capacity for aesthetic representation than did the relatively mimetic idolatry of the older machinery of the futurist moment, of some older speed-and-energy sculpture. Here we have less to do with kinetic energy than with all kinds of new reproductive processes; and in the weaker productions of postmodernism the aesthetic embodiment of such processes often tends to slip back more comfortably into a mere thematic representation of content – into narratives which are *about* the processes of reproduction, and include movie cameras, video, tape recorders, the whole technology of the production and reproduction of the simulacrum. (The shift from Antonioni's modernist *Blowup* to DePalma's postmodernist *Blowout* is here paradigmatic.) When Japanese architects, for example, model a building on the decorative imitation of stacks of cassettes, then the solution is at best a thematic and allusive, although often humorous, one.

Yet something else does tend to emerge in the most energetic postmodernist texts, and it is the sense that beyond all thematics or content the work seems somehow to tap the networks of reproductive process and thereby to afford us some glimpse into a post-modern or technological sublime, whose power or authenticity is documented by the success of such works in evoking a whole new postmodern space in emergence around us. Architecture therefore remains in this sense the privileged aesthetic language; and the distorting and fragmenting reflexions of one enormous glass surface to the other can be taken as paradigmatic of the central role of process and reproduction in postmodernist culture.

As I have said, however, I want to avoid the implication that technology is in any way the 'ultimately determining instance' either of our present-day social life or of our cultural production: such a thesis is of course ultimately at one with the post-Marxist notion of a 'post-industrialist' society. Rather, I want to suggest that our faulty representations of some immense communicational and computer network are themselves but a distorted figuration of something even deeper, namely the whole world system of present-day multinational capitalism. The technology of contemporary society is therefore mesmerizing and fascinating, not so much in its own right, but because it seems to offer some privileged representational shorthand for grasping a network of power and control even more difficult for our minds and imaginations to grasp – namely the whole new decentred global network of the third stage of capital itself. This is a figural process presently best observed in a whole mode of contemporary entertainment literature, which one is tempted to characterize as 'high tech paranoia', in which the circuits and networks of some putative global computer hook-up are narratively mobilized by labyrinthine conspiracies of autonomous but deadly interlocking and competing information agencies in a complexity often beyond the capacity of the normal reading mind. Yet conspiracy theory (and its garish narrative manifestations) must be seen as a degraded attempt – through the figuration of advanced technology – to think the impossible totality of the contemporary world system. It is therefore in terms of that enormous and threatening, yet only dimly perceivable, other reality of economic and social institutions that in my opinion the postmodern sublime can alone be adequately theorized.

Post-Modernism and the City

Now, before I try to offer a somewhat more positive conclusion, I want to sketch the analysis of a full-blown postmodern building – a work which is in many ways uncharacteristic of that postmodern architecture whose principal names are Robert Venturi, Charles Moore, Michael Graves, and more recently Frank Gehry, but which to my mind offers some very striking lessons about the originality of postmodernist space. Let me amplify the figure which has run through the preceding remarks, and make it even more explicit: I am proposing the motion that we are here in the presence of something like a mutation in built space itself. My implication is that we ourselves, the human subjects who happen into this new space, have not kept pace with that evolution; there has been a mutation in the object, unaccompanied as yet by any equivalent mutation in the subject; we do not yet possess the perceptual equipment to match this new hyperspace, as I will call it, in part because our perceptual habits were formed in that older kind of space I have called the space of high modernism. The newer architecture therefore – like many of the other cultural products I have evoked in the preceding remarks – stands as something like an imperative to grow new organs, to expand our sensorium and our body to some new, as yet unimaginable, perhaps ultimately impossible, dimensions.

The Bonaventura Hotel

The building whose features I will very rapidly enumerate in the next few moments is the Bonaventura Hotel, built in the new Los Angeles downtown by the architect and developer John Portman, whose other works include the various Hyatt Regencies, the Peachtree Center in Atlanta, and the Renaissance Center in Detroit. I have mentioned the populist aspect of the rhetorical defence of postmodernism against the elite (and Utopian) austerities of the great architectural modernisms: it is generally affirmed, in other words, that these newer buildings are popular works on the one hand; and that they respect the vernacular of the American city fabric on the other, that is to say, that they no longer attempt, as did the masterworks and monuments of high modernism, to insert a different, a distinct, an elevated, a new Utopian language into the tawdry and commercial sign-system of the surrounding city, but rather, on the contrary, seek to speak that very language, using its lexicon and syntax as that has been emblematically 'learned from Las Vegas'.

On the first of these counts, Portman's *Bonaventura* fully confirms the claim: it is a popular building, visited with enthusiasm by locals and tourists alike (although Portman's other buildings are even more successful in this respect). The populist insertion into the city fabric is, however, another matter, and it is with this that we will begin. There are three entrances to the *Bonaventura*, one from Figueroa, and the other two by way of elevated gardens on the other side of the hotel, which is built into the remaining slope of the former Beacon Hill. None of these is anything like the old hotel marquee, or the monumental porte-cochère with which the sumptuous buildings of yesteryear were wont to stage your passage from city street to the older interior. The entryways of the *Bonaventura* are as it were lateral and rather backdoor affairs: the gardens in the back admit you to the sixth floor of the towers, and even there you must walk down one flight to find the elevator by which you gain access to the lobby. Meanwhile, what one is still tempted to think of as the front entry, on Figueroa, admits you, baggage and all, onto the second-storey shopping balcony, from which you must take an escalator down to the main registration desk. More about these elevators and escalators in a moment. What I first want to suggest about these curiously unmarked ways-in is that they seem to have been imposed by some new category of closure governing the inner space of the hotel itself (and this over and above the material constraints under which Portman had to work). I believe that, with a certain number of other characteristic postmodern buildings, such as the *Beaubourg* in Paris, or the Eaton Centre in Toronto, the *Bonaventura* aspires to being a total space, a complete world, a kind of miniature city (and I would want to add that to this new total space corresponds a new collective practice, a new mode in which individuals move and congregate, something like the practice of a new and historically original kind of hyper-crowd). In this sense, then, ideally the mini-city of Portman's *Bonaventura* ought not to have entrances at all, since the entryway is always the seam that links the building to the rest of the city that surrounds it: for it does not wish to be a part of the city, but rather its equivalent and its replacement or substitute. That is, however, obviously not possible or practical, whence the deliberate downplaying and reduction of the entrance function to its bare minimum. But this disjunction from the surrounding city is very different from that of the great monuments of the International Style: there, the act of disjunction was violent, visible, and had a very real symbolic significance – as in Le Corbusier's great *pilotis* whose gesture radically separates the new Utopian space of the modern from the degraded and fallen city fabric which it thereby explicitly repudiates (although the gamble of the modern was that this new Utopian space, in the virulence of its Novum, would fan out and transform that eventually by the very power of its new spatial language). The *Bonaventura*, however, is content to 'let the fallen city fabric continue to be in its being' (to parody Heidegger); no further effect, no larger protopolitical Utopian transformation, is either expected or desired.

This diagnosis is to my mind confirmed by the great reflective glass skin of the *Bonaventura*, whose function I will now interpret rather differently than I did a moment ago when I saw the phenomenon of reflexion generally as developing a thematics of reproductive technology (the two readings are however not incompatible). Now one would want rather to stress the way in which the glass skin repels the city outside; a repulsion for which we have analogies in those reflector sunglasses which make it impossible for your interlocutor to see your own eyes and thereby achieve a certain aggressivity towards and power over the Other. In a similar way, the glass skin achieves a peculiar and placeless dissociation of the *Bonaventura* from its neighbourhood: it is not even an exterior, inasmuch as when you seek to look at the hotel's outer walls you cannot see the hotel itself, but only the distorted images of everything that surrounds it.

Now I want to say a few words about escalators and elevators: given their very real pleasures in Portman, particularly these last, which the artist has termed 'gigantic kinetic sculptures' and which certainly account for much of the spectacle and the excitement of the hotel interior, particularly in the Hyatts, where like great Japanese lanterns or gondolas they ceaselessly rise and fall – given such a deliberate marking and foregrounding in their own right, I believe one has to see such 'people movers' (Portman's own term, adapted from Disney) as something a little more than mere functions and engineering components. We know in any case that recent architectural theory has begun to borrow from narrative analysis in other fields, and to attempt to see our physical trajectories through such buildings as virtual narratives or stories, as dynamic paths and narrative paradigms which we as visitors are asked to fulfil and to complete with our own bodies and movements. In the *Bonaventura*, however, we find a dialectical heightening of this process: it seems to me that the escalators and elevators here henceforth replace movement but also and above all designate themselves as new reflexive signs and emblems of movement proper (something which will become evident when we come to the whole question of what remains of older forms of movement in this building, most notably walking itself). Here the narrative stroll has been underscored, symbolized, reified and replaced by a transportation machine which becomes the allegorical signifier of that older promenade we are no longer allowed to conduct on our own: and this is a dialectical intensification of the auto-referentiality of all modern culture, which tends to turn upon itself and designate its own cultural production as its content.

I am more at a loss when it comes to conveying the thing itself, the experience of space you undergo when you step off such allegorical devices into the lobby or atrium, with its great central column, surrounded by a miniature lake, the whole positioned between the four symmetrical residential towers with their elevators, and surrounded by rising balconies capped by a kind of greenhouse roof at the sixth level. I am tempted to say that such space makes it impossible for us to use the language of volume or volumes any longer, since these last are impossible to seize. Hanging streamers indeed suffuse this empty space in such a way as to distract systematically and deliberately from whatever form it might be supposed to have; while a constant busyness gives the feeling that emptiness is here absolutely packed, that it is an element within which you yourself are immersed, without any of that distance that formerly enabled the perception of perspective or volume. You are in this hyperspace up to your eyes and your body; and if it seemed to you before that that suppression of depth I spoke of in postmodern painting or literature would necessarily be difficult to achieve in architecture itself, perhaps you may now be willing to see this bewildering immersion as the formal equivalent in the new medium.

Yet escalator and elevator are also in this context dialectical opposites; and we may suggest that the glorious movement of the elevator gondolas is also a dialectical compensation for this filled space of the atrium – it gives us the chance at a radically different, but complementary, spatial experience, that of rapidly shooting up through the ceiling and outside, along one of the four symmetrical towers, with the referent, Los Angeles itself, spread out breathtakingly and even alarmingly before us. But even this vertical movement is contained: the elevator lifts you to one of those revolving cocktail lounges, in which you, seated, are again passively rotated about and offered a contemplative spectacle of the city itself, now transformed into its own images by the glass windows through which you view it.

Let me quickly conclude all this by returning to the central space of the lobby itself (with the passing observation that the hotel rooms are visibly marginalized: the corridors in the residential sections are low-ceilinged and dark, most depressingly functional indeed; while one understands that the rooms are in the worst of taste). The descent is dramatic enough, plummeting back down through the roof to splash down in the lake; what happens when you get there is something else, which I can only try to characterize as milling confusion, something like the vengeance this space takes on those who still seek to walk through it. Given the absolute symmetry of the four towers, it is quite impossible to get your bearings in this lobby; recently, colour coding and directional signals have been added in a pitiful and revealing, rather desperate attempt to restore the coordinates of an older space. I will take as the most dramatic practical result of this spatial mutation the notorious dilemma of the shopkeepers on the various balconies: it has been obvious, since the very opening of the hotel in 1977, that nobody could ever find any of these stores, and even if you located the appropriate boutique, you would be most unlikely to be as fortunate a second time; as a consequence, the commercial tenants are in despair and all the merchandise is marked down to bargain prices. When you recall that Portman is a businessman as well as an architect, and a millionaire developer, an artist who is at one and the same time a capitalist in his own right, one cannot but feel that here too something of a 'return of the repressed' is involved.

So I come finally to my principal point here, that this latest mutation in space – postmodern hyperspace – has finally succeeded in transcending the capacities of the individual human body to locate itself, to organize its immediate surroundings perceptually, and cognitively to map its position in a mappable external world. And I have already suggested that this alarming disjunction point between the body and its built environment – which is to the initial bewilderment of the older modernism as the velocities of space craft are to those of the automobile – can itself stand as the symbol and analogue of that even sharper dilemma which is the incapacity of our minds, at least at present, to map the great global multinational and decentred communicational network in which we find ourselves caught as individual subjects.

The new machine

But as I am anxious that Portman's space not be perceived as something either exceptional or seemingly marginalized and leisure-specialized on the order of Disney-land, I would like in passing to juxtapose this complacent and entertaining (although bewildering) leisure-time space with its analogue in a very different area, namely the space of postmodern warfare, in particular as Michael Herr evokes it in his great book on the experience of Vietnam, called *Dispatches*. The extraordinary linguistic innovations of this work may still be considered postmodern, in the eclectic way in which its language impersonally fuses a whole range of contemporary collective idiolects, most notably rock language and Black language: but the fusion is dictated by problems of content. This first terrible postmodernist war cannot be told in any of the traditional paradigms of the war novel or movie – indeed that breakdown of all previous narrative paradigms is, along with the breakdown of any shared language through which a veteran might convey such experience, among the principal subjects of the book and may be said to open up the place of a whole new reflexivity. Benjamin's account of Baudelaire, and of the emergence of modernism from a new experience of city technology which transcends all the older habits of bodily perception, is both singularly relevant here, and singularly antiquated, in the light of this new and virtually unimaginable quantum leap in technological alienation: 'He was a moving-target-survivor subscriber, a true child of the war, because except for the rare times when you were pinned or stranded the system was geared to keep you mobile, if that was what you thought you wanted. As a technique for staying alive it seemed to make as much sense as anything, given naturally that you were there to begin with and wanted to see it close; it started out sound and straight but it formed a cone as it progressed, because the more you moved the more you saw, the more you saw the more besides death and mutilation you risked, and the more you risked of that the more you would have to let go of one day as a "survivor". Some of us moved around the war like crazy people until we couldn't see which way the run was taking us anymore, only the war all over its surface with occasional, unexpected penetration. As long as we could have choppers like taxis it took real exhaustion or depression near shock or a dozen pipes of opium to keep us even apparently quiet, we'd still be running around inside our skins like something was after us, ha ha, La Vida Loca. In the months after I got back the hundreds of helicopters I'd flown in began to draw together until they'd formed a collective metachopper, and in my mind it was the sexiest thing going; saver-destroyer, provider-waster, right hand-left hand, nimble, fluent, canny and human; hot steel, grease, jungle-saturated canvas webbing, sweat cooling and warming up again, cassette rock and roll in one ear and door-gun fire in the other, fuel, heat, vitality and death, death itself, hardly an intruder.'[4]

In this new machine, which does not, like the older modernist machinery of the locomotive or the airplane, represent motion, but which can only be represented *in motion*, something of the mystery of the new postmodernist space is concentrated.

The Abolition of Critical Distance

The conception of postmodernism outlined here is a historical rather than a merely stylistic one. I cannot stress too greatly the radical distinction between a view for which the postmodern is one (optional) style among many others available, and one which seeks to grasp it as the cultural dominant of the logic of late capitalism: the two approaches in fact generate two very different ways of conceptualizing the phenomenon as a whole, on the one hand moral judgements (about which it is indifferent whether they are positive or negative), and on the other a genuinely dialectical attempt to think our present of time in History.

Of some positive moral evaluation of postmodernism little needs to be said: the complacent (yet delirious) camp-following celebration of this aesthetic new world (including its social and economic dimension, greeted with equal enthusiasm under the slogan of 'post-industrial society') is surely unacceptable – although it may be somewhat less obvious the degree to which current fantasies about the salvational nature of high technology, from chips to robots – fantasies entertained not only by left as well as right governments in distress but also by many intellectuals – are essentially of a piece with more vulgar apologies for postmodernism.

But in that case it is also logical to reject moralizing condemnations of the post-modern and of its essential triviality, when juxtaposed against the Utopian 'high seriousness' of the great modernisms: these are also judgements one finds both on the Left and on the radical Right. And no doubt the logic of the simulacrum, with its transformation of older realities into television images, does more than merely replicate the logic of late capitalism; it reinforces and intensifies it. Meanwhile, for political groups which seek actively to intervene in history and to modify its otherwise passive momentum (whether with a view towards channeling it into a socialist transformation of society or diverting it into the regressive reestablishment of some simpler fantasy past), there cannot but be much that is deplorable and reprehensible in a cultural form of image addiction which, by transforming the past visual mirages, stereotypes or texts, effectively abolishes any practical sense of the future and of the collective project, thereby abandoning the thinking of future change to fantasies of sheer catastrophe and inexplicable cataclysm – from visions of 'terrorism' on the social level to those of cancer on the personal. Yet if postmodernism is a historical phenomenon, then the attempt to conceptualize it in terms of moral or moralizing judgements must finally be identified as a category-mistake. All of which becomes more obvious when we interrogate the position of the cultural critic and moralist: this last, along with all the rest of us, is now so deeply immersed in postmodernist space, so deeply suffused and infected by its new cultural categories, that the luxury of the old-fashioned ideological critique, the indignant moral denunciation of the other, becomes unavailable.

The distinction I am proposing here knows one canonical form in Hegel's differentiation of the thinking of individual morality or moralizing (*Moralität*) from that whole very different realm of collective social values and practices (*Sittlichkeit*). But it finds its definitive form in Marx's demonstration of the materialist dialectic, most notably in those classic pages of the *Manifesto* which teach the hard lesson of some more genuinely dialectical way to think historical development and change. The topic of the lesson is, of course, the historical development of capitalism itself and the deployment of a specific bourgeois culture. In a well-known passage, Marx powerfully urges us to do the impossible, namely to think this development positively *and* negatively all at once; to achieve, in other words, a type of thinking that would be capable of grasping the demonstrably baleful features of capitalism along with its extraordinary and liberating dynamism simultaneously, within a single thought, and without attenuating any of the force of either judgement. We are, somehow, to lift our minds to a point at which it is possible to understand that capitalism is at one and the same time the best thing that has ever happened to the human race, and the worst. The lapse from this austere dialectical imperative into the more comfortable stance of the taking of moral positions is inveterate and all too human: still, the urgency of the subject demands that we make at least some effort to think the cultural evolution of late capitalism dialectically, as catastrophe and progress all together.

Such an effort suggests two immediate questions, with which we will conclude these reflexions. Can we in fact identify some 'moment of truth' within the more evident 'moments of falsehood' of postmodern culture? And, even if we can do so, is there not something ultimately paralysing in the dialectical view of historical development proposed above; does it not tend to demobilize us and to surrender us to passivity and helplessness, by systematically obliterating possibilities of action under the impenetrable fog of historical inevitability? It will be appropriate to discuss these two (related) issues in terms of current possibilities for some effective contemporary cultural politics and for the construction of a genuine political culture.

To focus the problem in this way is of course immediately to raise the more genuine issue of the fate of culture generally, and of the function of culture specifically, as one social level or instance, in the postmodern era. Everything in the previous discussion suggests that what we have been calling postmodernism is inseparable from, and unthinkable without the hypothesis of, some fundamental mutation of the sphere of culture in the world of late capitalism, which includes a momentous modification of its social function. Older discussions of the space, function or sphere of culture (most notably Herbert Marcuse's classic essay on 'The Affirmative Character of Culture') have insisted on what a different language would call the 'semi-autonomy' of the cultural realm: its ghostly, yet Utopian, existence, for good or ill, above the practical world of the existent, whose mirror image it throws back in forms which vary from the legitimations of flattering resemblance to the contestatory indictments of critical satire or Utopian pain.

What we must now ask ourselves is whether it is not precisely this 'semi-autonomy' of the cultural sphere which has been destroyed by the logic of late capitalism. Yet to argue that culture is today no longer endowed with the relative autonomy it once enjoyed as one level among others in earlier moments of capitalism (let alone in pre-capitalist societies), is not necessarily to imply its disappearance or extinction. On the contrary: we must go on to affirm that the dissolution of an autonomous sphere of culture is rather to be imagined in terms of an explosion: a prodigious expansion of culture throughout the social realm, to the point at which everything in our social life – from economic value and state power to practices and to the very structure of the psyche itself – can be said to have become 'cultural' in some original and as yet untheorized sense. This perhaps startling proposition is, however, substantively quite consistent with the previous diagnosis of a society of the image or the simulacrum, and a transformation of the 'real' into so many pseudo-events.

It also suggests that some of our most cherished and time-honoured radical conceptions about the nature of cultural politics may thereby find themselves outmoded. However distinct those conceptions may have been – which range from slogans of negativity, opposition, and subversion to critique and reflexivity – they all shared a single, fundamentally spatial, presupposition, which may be resumed in the equally time-honoured formula of 'critical distance'. No theory of cultural politics current on the Left today has been able to do without one notion or another of a certain minimal aesthetic distance, of the possibility of the positioning of the cultural act outside the massive Being of capital, which then serves as an Archimedean point from which to assault this last. What the burden of our preceding demonstration suggests, however, is that distance in general (including 'critical distance' in particular) has very precisely been abolished in the new space of postmodernism. We are submerged in its henceforth filled and suffused volumes to the point where our now postmodern bodies are bereft of spatial coordinates and practically (let alone theoretically) incapable of distantiation; meanwhile, it has already been observed how the prodigious new expansion of multinational capital ends up penetrating and colonizing those very pre-capitalist enclaves (Nature and the Unconscious) which offered extraterritorial and Archimedean footholds for critical effectivity. The short-hand language of 'cooptation' is for this reason omnipresent on the Left; but offers a most inadequate theoretical basis for understanding a situation in which we all, in one way or another, dimly feel that not only punctual and local countercultural forms of cultural resistance and guerrilla warfare, but also even overtly political interventions like those of *The Clash*, are all somehow secretly disarmed and reabsorbed by a system of which they themselves might well be considered a part, since they can achieve no distance from it.

What we must now affirm is that it is precisely this whole extraordinarily demoralizing and depressing original new global space which is the 'moment of truth' of postmodernism. What has been called the postmodernist 'sublime' is only the moment in which this content has become most explicit, has moved the closest to the surface of consciousness, as a coherent new type of space in its own right – even though a certain figural concealment or disguise is still at work here, most notably in the high-technological thematics in which the new spatial content is still dramatized and articulated. Yet the earlier features of the postmodern which were enumerated above can all now be seen as themselves partial (yet constitutive) aspects of the same general spatial object.

The argument for a certain authenticity in these otherwise patently ideological productions depends on the prior proposition that what we have now been calling postmodern (or multinational) space is not merely a cultural ideology or fantasy, but has genuine historical (and socio-economic) reality as a third great original expansion of capitalism around the globe (after the earlier expansions of the national market and the older imperialist system, which each had their own cultural specificity and generated new types of space appropriate to their dynamics). The distorted and unreflexive attempts of newer cultural production to explore and to express this new space must then also, in their own fashion, be considered as so many approaches to the representation of (a new) reality (to use a more antiquated language). As paradoxical as the terms may seem, they may thus, following a classic interpretive option, be read as peculiar new forms of realism (or at least of the mimesis of reality), at the same time that they can equally well be analysed as so many attempts to distract and to divert us from that reality or to disguise its contradictions and resolve them in the guise of various formal mystifications.

As for that reality itself, however – the as yet untheorized original space of some new 'world system' of multinational or late capitalism (a space whose negative or baleful aspects are only too obvious), the dialectic requires us to hold equally to a positive or 'progressive' evaluation of its emergence, as Marx did for the newly unified space of the national markets, or as Lenin did for the older imperialist global network. For neither Marx nor Lenin was socialism a matter of returning to small (and thereby less repressive and comprehensive) systems of social organization; rather, the dimensions attained by capital in their own times were grasped as the promise, the framework, and the precondition for the achievement of some new and more comprehensive socialism. How much the more is this not the case with the even more global and totalizing space of the new world system, which demands the invention and elaboration of an internationalism of a radically new type? The disastrous realignment of socialist revolution with the older nationalisms (not only in Southeast Asia), whose results have necessarily aroused much serious recent Left reflexion, can be adduced in support of this position.

The need for maps

But if all this is so, then at least one possible form of a new radical cultural politics becomes evident: with a final aesthetic proviso that must quickly be noted. Left cultural producers and theorists – particularly those formed by bourgeois cultural traditions issuing from romanticism and valorizing spontaneous, instinctive or unconscious forms of 'genius' – but also for very obvious historical reasons such as Zhdanovism and the sorry consequences of political and party interventions in the arts – have often by reaction allowed themselves to be unduly intimidated by the repudiation, in bourgeois aesthetics and most notably in high modernism, of one of the age-old functions of art – namely the pedagogical and the didactic. The teaching function of art was, however, always stressed in classical times (even though it there mainly took the form of *moral* lessons); while the prodigious and still imperfectly understood work of Brecht reaffirms, in a new and formally innovative and original way, for the moment of modernism proper, a complex new conception of the relationship between culture and pedagogy. The cultural model I will propose similarly foregrounds the cognitive and pedagogical dimensions of political art and culture, dimensions stressed in very different ways by *both* Lukács *and* Brecht (for the distinct moments of realism and modernism, respectively).

We cannot, however, return to aesthetic practices elaborated on the basis of historical situations and dilemmas which are no longer ours. Meanwhile, the conception of space that has been developed here suggests that a model of political culture appropriate to our own situation will necessarily have to raise spatial issues as its fundamental organizing concern. I will therefore provisionally define the aesthetic of such new (and hypothetical) cultural form as an aesthetic of *cognitive mapping*.

In a classic work, *The Image of the City*, Kevin Lynch taught us that the alienated city is above all a space in which people are unable to map (in their minds) either their own positions or the urban totality in which they find themselves: grids such as those of Jersey City, in which none of the traditional markers (monuments, nodes, natural boundaries, built perspectives) obtain, are the most obvious examples. Disalienation in the traditional city, then, involves the practical reconquest of a sense of place, and the construction or reconstruction of an articulated ensemble which can be retained in memory and which the individual subject can map and remap along the moments of mobile, alternative trajectories. Lynch's own work is limited by the deliberate restriction of his topic to the problems of the city form as such; yet it becomes extraordinarily suggestive when projected outwards onto some of the larger national and global spaces we have touched on here. Nor should it be too hastily assumed that his model – while it clearly raises very central issues of representation as such – is in any way easily vitiated by the conventional poststructuralist critiques of the 'ideology of representation' or mimesis. The cognitive map is not exactly mimetic, in that older sense; indeed the theoretical issues it poses allow us to renew the analysis of representation on a higher and much more complex level.

There is, for one thing, a most interesting convergence between the empirical problems studied by Lynch in terms of city space and the great Althusserian (and

Lacanian) redefinition of ideology as 'the representation of the subject's *Imaginary* relationship to his or her *Real* conditions of existence'. Surely this is exactly what the cognitive map is called upon to do, in the narrower framework of daily life in the physical city: to enable a situational representation on the part of the individual subject to that vaster and properly unrepresentable totality which is the ensemble of the city's structure as a whole.

Yet Lynch's work also suggests a further line of development insofar as cartography itself constitutes its key mediatory instance. A return to the history of this science (which is also an art) shows us that Lynch's model does not yet in fact really correspond to what will become map-making. Rather, Lynch's subjects are clearly involved in pre-cartographic operations whose results traditionally are described as itineraries rather than as maps; diagrams organized around the still subject-centred or existential journey of the traveller, along which various significant key features are marked – oases, mountain ranges, rivers, monuments and the like. The most highly developed form of such diagrams is the nautical itinerary, the sea chart or *portulans*, where coastal features are noted for the use of Mediterranean navigators who rarely venture out into the open sea.

Yet the compass at once introduces a new dimension into sea charts, a dimension that will utterly transform the problematic of the itinerary and allow us to pose the problem of a genuine cognitive mapping in a far more complex way. For the new instruments – compass, sextant and theodolite – do not merely correspond to new geographic and navigational problems (the difficult matter of determining longitude, particularly on the curving surface of the planet, as opposed to the simpler matter of latitude, which European navigators can still empirically determine by ocular inspection of the African coast); they also introduce a whole new coordinate – that of relationship to the totality, particularly as it is mediated by the stars and by new operations like that of triangulation. At this point, cognitive mapping in the broader sense comes to require the coordination of existential data (the empirical position of the subject) with unlived, abstract conceptions of the geographic totality.

Finally, with the first globe (1490) and the invention of the Mercator projection around the same period, yet a third dimension of cartography emerges, which at once involves what we would today call the nature of representational codes, the intrinsic structures of the various media, the intervention, into more naive mimetic conceptions of mapping, of the whole new fundamental question of the languages of representation itself: and in particular the unresolvable (well-nigh Heisenbergian) dilemma of the transfer of curved space to flat charts; at which point it becomes clear that there can be no true maps (at the same time in which it also becomes clear that there can be scientific progress, or better still, a dialectical advance, in the various historical moments of map-making).

Social cartography and symbol

Transcoding all this now into the very different problematic of the Althusserian definition of ideology, one would want to make two points. The first is that the Althusserian concept now allows us to rethink these specialized geographical and cartographic issues in terms of social space, in terms, for example, of social class and national or international context, in terms of the ways in which we all necessarily *also* cognitively map our individual social relationship to local, national and international class realities. Yet to reformulate the problem in this way is also to come starkly up against those very difficulties in mapping which are posed in heightened and original ways by that very global space of the postmodernist or multinational moment which has been under discussion here. These are not merely theoretical issues, but have urgent practical political consequences: as is evident from the conventional feelings of First World subjects that existentially (or 'empirically') they really do inhabit a 'post-industrial society', from which traditional production has disappeared and in which social classes of the classical type no longer exist – a conviction which has immediate effects on political praxis.

The second observation to be proposed is that a return to the Lacanian under-pinnings of Althusser's theory can afford some useful and suggestive methodological enrichments. Althusser's formulation remobilizes an older and henceforth classical Marxian distinction between science and ideology, which is still not without value for us. The existential – the positioning of the individual subject, the experience of daily life, the monadic 'point of view' on the world to which we are necessarily, as biological subjects, restricted – is in Althusser's formula implicitly opposed to the realm of abstract knowledge, a realm which as Lacan reminds us is never positioned in or actualized by any concrete subject but rather by that structural void called 'le sujet supposé savoir', 'the subject supposed to know', a subject-place of knowledge; what is affirmed is not that we cannot know the world and its totality in some abstract or 'scientific' way – Marxian 'science' provides just such a way of knowing and con-ceptualizing the world abstractly, in the sense in which, e.g. Mandel's great book offers a rich and elaborated *knowledge* of that global world system, of which it has never been said here that it was unknowable, but merely that it was unrepresentable, which is a very different matter. The Althusserian formula in other words designates a gap, a rift, between existential experience and scientific knowledge: ideology has then the function of somehow inventing a way of articulating those two distinct dimen-sions with each other. What a historicist view of this 'definition' would want to add is that such coordination, the production of functioning and living ideologies, is dis-tinct in different historical situations, but above all, that there may be historical situations in which it is not possible at all – and this would seem to be our situation in the current crisis.

But the Lacanian system is three-fold and not dualistic. To the Marxian-Althusserian opposition of ideology and science correspond only two of Lacan's tripartite functions, the Imaginary and the Real, respectively. Our digression on cartography, however, with its final revelation of a properly representational dialectic of the codes and capacities of individual languages or media, reminds us that what has until now been omitted was the dimension of the Lacanian Symbolic itself.

An aesthetic of cognitive mapping – a pedagogical political culture which seeks to endow the individual subject with some new heightened sense of its place in the global system – will necessarily have to respect this now enormously complex repre-sentational dialectic and to invent radically new forms in order to do it justice. This is not, then, clearly a call for a return to some older kind of machinery, some older and more transparent national space, or some more traditional and reassuring perspectival or mimetic enclave: the new political art – if it is indeed possible at all – will have to hold to the truth of postmodernism, that is to say, to its fundamental object – the world space of multinational capital – at the same time at which it achieves a break-through to some as yet unimaginable new mode of representing this last, in which we may again begin to grasp our positioning as individual and collective subjects and regain a capacity to act and struggle which is at present neutralized by our spatial as well as our social confusion. The political form of postmodernism, if there ever is any, will have as its vocation the invention and projection of a global cognitive mapping, on a social as well as a spatial scale.

Notes

1   The present essay draws on lectures and on material previously published in *The Anti-Aesthetic*, edited by Hal Foster (Port Townsend, Washington: Bay Press, 1983) and in *Amerika Studien/American Studies* 29/1 (1984).
2   In 'The Politics of Theory', *New German Critique*, 32, Spring/Summer 1984.
3   Marguerite Séchehaye, *Autobiography of a Schizophrenic Girl*, trans. by G. Rubin-Rabson, New York, 1968, p. 19.
4   Michael Herr, *Dispatches*, New York, 1978, pp. 8–9

28

Prologue from *Megalopolis**

Celeste Olalquiaga

Postmodernism lives. Legions of detractors and years of intellectual debate have done nothing to arrest its expansion or reduce its impact and scores of usurpers have failed miserably in stultifying its scope. Despite or because of being profanely ambivalent and ambiguous, rejoicing in consumption and celebrating obsessions, ignoring consistency and avoiding stability, favoring illusions and pleasure, postmodernism is the only possible contemporary answer to a century worn out by the rise and fall of modern ideologies, the pervasion of capitalism, and an unprecedented sense of personal responsibility and individual impotence.

Whether one likes it or not, postmodernism is a state of things. It is primarily determined by an extremely rapid and freewheeling exchange to which most responses are faltering, impulsive, and contradictory. What is at stake is the very constitution of being – the ways we perceive ourselves and others, the modes of experience that are available to us, the women and men whose sensibilities are shaped by urban exposure.

At the risk of being thrown to the lions, I admit that in general I find the debate about postmodernism monotonous, verbose, and self-referential. It is either reduced exclusively to art or caught up in a web of academic disquisitions, neither of which is of much interest to people outside those worlds. Furthermore, the postmodern debate is often tied into a right-or-wrong kind of argumentation that drains postmodernism of two of its most important features: versatility and the emptying of hierarchies. Consequently, instead of discussing in this prologue the main literature about postmodernism, I will look at those texts that have shaped *Megalopolis* in one way or another.

Walter Benjamin, a lyrical critic in the age of modern capitalism, is perhaps the most influential thinker for the kind of cultural study practiced here. Benjamin's work is fundamental for any complex reading of city life, and his splendid writing is a continuous source of inspiration. Benjamin's understanding of allegory and melancholy, as well as his privileging of random looking, fragmentary insights, and imagery, together with a nonjudgmental attitude toward mass culture, anticipated the postmodern gaze.[1]

---

* From Celeste Olalquiaga, *Megalopolis: Contemporary Cultural Sensibilities* (Minneapolis: University of Minnesota Press, 1992), pp. xi–xxi.

One could say, following Deleuze and Guattari, that Benjamin's method is "rhyzomatic" in that it abandons dualism and linear thinking in favor of multiple associations at different semiotic levels.[2] In this way Benjamin can, for example, map the conflicts of a nascent modernity through Baudelaire's poetry or describe the dramatic reconstitution of perception in the distracted flounderings of that exemplary urbanite, the *flâneur*, whose main pleasure was to get lost in the crowds so as to observe the world in peaceful anonymity. Benjamin moves swiftly between philosophy and street signs, personal memories and literary tropes, inaugurating a way of looking at things whose full recognition is still due, as the academic reticence toward interdisciplinary cultural studies clearly shows.

At the heart of this reticence lies a deeply rooted belief that culture, unless it is manifested in one of the liberal arts, is not a proper object of intellectual attention. At best, cultural phenomena qualify for statistical proof of the determining power of "real" discourses (i.e., for progressive thought, the intricate web of class, race, and gender) whose autonomy and hegemony are seldom questioned. Such epistemological bias wipes out of existence the whole realm of what Michel de Certeau called "the practice of everyday life,"[3] dragging in its wake the understanding of popular culture and, however contradictorily, since it was adopted as an academic fad, of its most ardent redeemer, postmodernism.[4]

Feminists in particular have been quick to point out the reasons behind this common segregation. Theorists like Tania Modleski and Angela McRobbie stress popular culture's subversive potential, indicating how threatening it can ultimately prove to discourses that rely (at times by means of analytical study) on the promotion of class, gender, or race privilege to maintain their stronghold.[5] After all, popular culture, postmodernism, and cultural studies advocate each in its own conflictive way for the emergence of experiences that have been for too long relegated to an intellectual backyard. Furthermore, until very recently the prevailing notion of cultural imperialism assumed a passive spectatorship, ignoring all kinds of creative reception and paradoxically encouraging all sorts of suspicious paternalisms.

It is precisely to such an unacknowledged dynamic reception that Modleski turns in her analyses of genre films, for example, in her discussion of their liberating and pleasurable effects in Manuel Puig's novel-turned-film *The Kiss of the Spider Woman*. Similarly, McRobbie affirms the importance of appropriation, (mis)quotation, and recycling for black urban music, and Donna Haraway underlines the implicit breaking down of hierarchy in technological interface, tracing it in popular science fiction literature.[6] In Latin America, where a jaded notion of cultural imperialism still helps to maintain the official fictions of national identity, theorists like Néstor García-Canclini are describing the multiple spectator strategies used to meaningfully integrate otherwise arid and abstract discourses. García-Canclini's study of museum goers' sentimental enjoyment of high art, for instance, discovers an unwillingly insubordinate public reaction under an apparently reverential behavior.[7]

What is so threatening about popular culture is not, as has been often affirmed, its supposed mechanical or passive traits, but rather, as Modleski suggests, the enjoyment with which it is integrated into daily practice. The ready pleasure of "trash" magazines and Hollywood films clashes head-on with the aesthetic pleasure worshiped by high-art followers – classicists and modernists alike. Obviously, this aesthetic pleasure is founded on a sophisticated sense of taste whose exquisite sensibility is granted and guaranteed by an education that in turn is made possible by money. Never mind that Benjamin exposed the demise of uniqueness and originality half a century ago in his famous essay on art in the age of mechanical reproduction.[8] No matter how anachronistic, these Romantic notions are still revered today, as is that other stubborn myth, male genius – which goes to show how postmodernism's flattening of history in one eternal present that contains all pasts and futures is indeed an accurate rendition of historical linearity as yet another ideological construct.

Kitsch is, as I contend in chapter 3 [Olalquiaga 1992], one of the best examples of how such aesthetic and intellectual segregations work and of how they paradoxically contain the seeds of their own destruction. For kitsch, generally understood as bad taste or a poor imitation of art and therefore always banished to the margins of artistic practice, does exactly what that practice fears so much: it gathers its motifs randomly and eclectically, fragmenting the cohesion and continuity so cherished by high art, and then dares to re-present them in the most blunt, figurative, and sentimental ways, much to the delight of its "uneducated" consumers and the distress of critics. Kitsch and postmodernism's sharing of an irreverent recycling, a taste for iconography and the artificial, a pleasure in color, gloss, melodrama, and overdetermination, lead me to believe that either postmodernism is kitsch, kitsch is postmodern *avant la lettre*, or both.

While some feminists have been eager to defend the subversive features of postmodernism, claiming that its lack of respect for all kinds of boundaries – that is, historical in the disruption of continuous time, geographical in the enormous exchange between countries and the constant shifting of political and ethnic frontiers, physical in the confusion between the body and electronic apparatuses – opens up new grounds for cultural negotiation, it is precisely the extent of this negotiation that has become the touchstone of postmodernity's legitimacy. Much of the postmodern debate revolves around how social power is articulated and distributed in postmodernism, whose mere existence then becomes contingent on whether it can be qualified as emancipatory or alienating.

This debate became most apparent in the early 1980s, when two European philosophers closed ranks: in one corner, Jean-François Lyotard defended postmodernism's disruption of systemic order as an anarchic force; in the opposite corner, Jürgen Habermas claimed that such disruption only conceals or encourages totalitarian forms of control.[9] Such a discussion attributes to postmodernism an intrinsic function that is, at the very least, controversial, given that postmodernism is a state of things, not a structured and coherent ideology. Postmodernism is then conflated with those discourses that attempt to derive a meaning from it, being perceived alternately as revolutionary, fascistic, hedonistic, or redemptive. Simply put, postmodernism, as popular culture before it, becomes what each interpretation needs it to be, with the theory comfortably sitting in for its object of inquiry.[10] The relativity of such dogmatic positions is apparent in a similar discussion on technology, which Haraway lucidly turns around by proposing how technology can provide destabilizing strategies. In so doing, she shatters the sterile duality that doomed technology to either unquestionable progress or unavoidable social control.

Habermas contributed to this great postmodern divide in more ways than one, refusing to accept postmodernism as substantially different from modernism.[11] Habermas's belief in the healing powers of what he considers the unrealized enlightenment project of modernity denies postmodernism its basic take on that project – that it failed to deliver. And while many of postmodernism's most salient features (disillusionment in what have been called the master narratives of modernity, an unashamed nostalgia for other times, a melancholic overtone) derive from this implicit cultural acknowledgment, others (i.e., the aforementioned eclecticism and breaking down of boundaries) do not hinge at all on modernism, but rather on the plurality and difference it so adamantly tried to purify.

This preoccupation with the origins (in the end, a question of paternity) only succeeds in further confusing the issue of where to go from here. In this respect, I find Marshall McLuhan's lack of demagoguery refreshing. From the 1960s on, McLuhan concentrated on describing the ways in which technology and mass media were transforming culture and speculating, quite accurately as it turns out, on the state of things to come. McLuhan not only refused to be programmatic, he also declined the historiographical genre, favoring instead an image-ridden and fragmentary language that is closer to the phenomena he talks about. He became at once an academic pariah and a best-selling author.[12]

In other words, the postmodern debate has not transcended what Umberto Eco dubbed a couple of decades ago "apocalittici e integrati," referring to the raging polemic about mass media's goods and evils.[13] In the United States this has taken on several nuances of its own, in particular a very postmodern schizophrenia whereby theorists simultaneously love and hate postmodernism. Perhaps its most interesting representative is that peculiar cosmic prophet Jean Baudrillard, the mere mention of whose name produces among debaters an effect similar to that of Moses on the Red Sea. Personally, I confess to an ambiguous relationship, since despite being influenced by Baudrillard's gaze and believing that simulation is fundamental to the understanding of postmodernism, I disagree completely with his final analysis on the disappearance of the referent.[14]

To me, as to several of the theorists mentioned earlier (Deleuze, Haraway), the postmodern flattening of meaning does not imply its disappearance but rather a shifting of registers that allows the formation of new ways of signifying. The flattening of meaning is the exhaustion of certain features that were believed to be intrinsic to it – depth (moving along vertical paradigms that grant a hierarchical position as opposed to moving along a more integrative horizontality), linear causality, univocality – but which turned out to be dispensable when put to the test of new formations or new modes of analyses. This can be clearly appreciated in the extremely hybrid character of contemporary cultural identities, which cannot be defined according to national origin or other types of inherent belonging, but rather by the intricate and extensive web of relationships that different individuals and groups establish in their daily practice and in their imaginary enactments. Or, as Chantal Mouffe says, referring to the postmodern political subject in her inspiring essay on radical democracy, "a subject constructed at the point of intersection of a multiplicity of subject-positions."[15]

So, when Stuart Hall states that "the world dreams itself to be American,"[16] he is referring to the idiosyncratic vision that each culture has of what "being American" is, as well as to the multifarious ways in which American imagery is appropriated and, more often than not, subverted by the mere fact of becoming an icon. A typical example of this process happened recently in Caracas, where the telecommunications system's acute malfunctioning was popularly confronted by the fad of carrying cellular phone look-alike handbags. Such a parody of the uneven fate of transferred high tech in the Third World is underscored by Venezuelans' intact belief in the United States as still representing the most sophisticated technological life-style available. This kind of recycling is far from the contestatory silence Baudrillard attributes to majorities: as opposed to a mute or passive resistance, the ability of collectivities to flex cultural material can be quite eloquent, as long as one is willing to pay attention to these articulations instead of lamenting the waning of conventional discursive arrangements and the loss of a stable referent.

Another figure relevant to the postmodern debate in the United States is Fredric Jameson, mainly because of his pivotal essay on postmodernism as the cultural counterpart of late capitalism, the phase corresponding to high technology and multinational capital.[17] One of the most troubling premises of this proposal is the degree of causality attributed to capitalism in the formation and transformation of culture. As Modleski, among others, points out, subordinating postmodernism to capitalism reduces the complexities of cultural processes and ignores other important forces at play in their production. Among these, the relevance of flexible and adaptational strategies by collectivities that are either marginalized from or struggling within mainstream hegemony is considerable. The current redefinition of the political sphere by nonpartisan groups and the growing importance and influence of hybrid or deterritorialized cultural identities are among the most radical illustrations of this kind of negotiation, as I argue in chapter 5 [Olalquiaga 1992]. Hence the importance of acknowledging that difference has been fundamental to the constitution and life of postmodernism so far.[18]

There can be no doubt, however, about postmodernism's intrinsic relation to capitalism, since the contemporary flattening of meaning has its most explicit antecedent in the shift from use to exchange value. In this sense, one could say that postmodernism is capitalism's currency, more than its cultural logic. Yet to consider that exchange value terminally cancels use value reinforces the tenet of a mechanical and passive reception. Instead, conceiving how consumption allows reinfusing semiotic value onto the commodity (activating it as a sign susceptible to multiple uses) does not deny the dramatic effects of commodity fetishism (i.e., the fragmentation and alienation of subjectivity), but acknowledges how a dynamic, creative consumption is made possible at many levels.

Paradoxically, it might be precisely capitalism's emptying of a univocal and monological use value that enabled the eventual breaking down of conventional ways of meaning formation.[19] By neutralizing the established relationship between an object and its means of production (or, semiotically, between the signifier and the signified) and redefining production in the flat language of market exchange, capitalism deflated uniqueness in favor of its own conventions. In so doing, it unwittingly destabilized a process (on which it nevertheless continued to rely) that grants legitimacy on the grounds of endemic belonging (birth) and seniority (tradition), and in terms of property rights. Thus, the waning of use value can still be lamented as the loss of the "natural," "organic," "unmediated" way of relating to things and experience, the apparent diversity and specificity of original use lost to the homogenizing (however undemocratic) language of exchange value.

Such a fall from grace is almost one with the loss of the aura of originality in the face of mechanical reproduction – a process lucidly analyzed by Benjamin and that, once again, remits us to the paradigms of the popular culture polemic, that is, to a hierarchy of goodness with exclusivity at the top. For the purposes of this prologue, however, what matters is that the process of exchange in itself had until recently a very limited appeal in daily life, where it always appeared under the pragmatic guise of enabling consumption of and access to necessary or fetishized experiences. So, although it suspended use value as a form of immanent meaning, capital did not sit in its place as a stable referent (except in the case of financial speculation in real estate, bonds, art collections, etc.) but rather reached out to an affective investment outside itself.

Postmodernism terminates this arrangement by taking commodity fetishism to the extreme and declaring it the explicit object of its discursive practice rather than hiding it behind a coherent system of meaning. Avoiding a rationale for consumption based on functionality (that is, on possible use), postmodernism sponsors consumption as an autonomous practice. The act of consuming is reedemed as an open-ended possibility of satisfaction, and the interchangeability of commodities is increased to the maximum, as their value is established by circulatory speed and pervasiveness. Constant and unmediated consumption, then, displaces purpose to the point that commodity fetishism becomes an icon, continually replaying its own fragmentation, alienation, and deterritorialization. As a result, postmodernism successfully empties all present and former referential meanings (those that allude to a permanent and unequivocal signification), fracturing the coherence of the discourses that contained them (history, religion, science, etc.). Attempting to reconstitute those meanings at this point is an exercise in nostalgia. The challenge lies in how to take advantage of this suspension of disbelief in order to elicit an entirely different set of meaningful formations. The purpose of this book is to describe how such an apparently finite project as postmodernism, understood as the glorification of consumption, does in fact enable the articulation of novel and often contradictory experiences.

The breaking down of traditional referentiality is manifested in what have become the postmodern trademarks, namely quotation, recycling, pastiche, and simulation. These are indicative not only of the loss of conventional boundaries between production and consumption, but also of an unprecedented mediation in our mode of consuming, which converts all elements of experience into mobile texts that can be transformed at random. Such a distanced reception, indifferent to notions of belonging or loyalty to origins (that is, no longer bound by use value), is best described as a vicarious sensibility (understanding by sensibility a collective disposition toward certain cultural practices): one where experience is lived indirectly, through the intercession of a third party, so to speak, that acts as both its catalyst and its buffer.

Given that all experience is subject to the mediation of a "trained" way of perceiving things (through the structuring power of language in interaction with diverse social ideologies),[20] what I mean here by vicariousness is the indirect impression of those personal events that are usually thought to be lived directly – physical sensation, for example. In contemporary urban experience, feelings, emotions, and sensations are more effectively called upon by media imagery or high-tech simulacra than through direct exposure, a condition Jameson described as the "waning of affect."[21] This is where the impact of late capitalism may be measured, for it is through the agency of high technology that the forsaken relationship between subject and object knows its most radical split, that is, where vicariousness can best be appreciated. In sum, if modern vicarious experience can be conventionally traced back to the kind of confusion Madame Bovary and Don Quijote developed between themselves and the characters of the literature they so loved to read, then postmodern vicarious experience must be acknowledged as a permanent state of existential displacement supported by a technology that has become second nature to us.

Concretely, high technology has induced a confusion between spatial and temporal boundaries, collapsing the conventions that formerly distinguished fantasy from reality and creating a third, quite polemical, cognitive space: that of simulation. As I argue in chapter 1 [Olalquiaga 1992], contemporary culture is caught between the referential and simulative modes of experience. In the former, meaning is produced by indexicality, where signs derive signification from a system of implicit categories and hierarchies that in turn rely on tradition to exercise either affirmative or subversive functions. In simulation, perception is formulated through media (mainly visual images) that discard all types of categorical distinctions – temporal, geographical, and even physical (in the conflation of the organic with the technological) – leaving signs to look at each other intertextually for signification. Simulation enables us to understand, for instance, how contemporary collective memory is made up of television programs instead of a shared notion of history.

The downfall of established referentiality, which can be traced back to the process of commodity fetishism and most recently to recycling strategies for cultural survival, is furthered by the simultaneous disillusionment in modernity's dream of progress. Despite its reversals by the two world wars and the countereffects of industrialism, this dream managed to survive until the 1950s, when it irredeemably began to fade. The failure of modernism's utopic aspirations dislocated the human-centered Romantic belief on which the twentieth century started, leaving in its place a skepticism that can barely muster notions of direction or identity. Without a future to look forward to and with a past whose beliefs modernism itself discredited as stale and insufficient, what remained after the 1950s was a present loaded with a sense of temporal emptiness.

The fragmentation, intertextuality, and massive commodification of everyday life that began with modernity once had a function that has now been totally lost. Modernization strove to create a better world, but belief in a better world is now exhausted, and only its formal mechanisms remain. In the same way that the ruins of the world's fairs, which once grandiosely represented this belief, have aged, so too has modernism, leaving only the dusty shells of its dreams behind. In the midst of this obsolescence, however, new ways of life emerge, more skeptical of those visions that represent the world as moving in only one direction. I believe this moment of new life emerging from the ruins of decaying dreams has been properly called postmodernism.

Highly reminiscent of the continuous metamorphosis of life and death, the paradoxical postmodern condition will be discussed here in [Olalquiaga 1992] in the following urban tendencies: the referential emptiness left by high technology and its replenishment with iconographies that belong to other times and other peoples (chapter 3, on kitsch); the replacement of time by a space saturated with temporal allusions (chapter 2, on the retro fashion); the conversion of a postindustrial melancholia fascinated with decay into an iconography that parodies, and often transforms into a political tool, that melancholy (chapter 4, on organic and technological ruins, and chapter 5, on Latin American postindustrial pop).

It is perhaps to the disconcerting quality of postmodernism's continuous transformation of time into space, emptiness into saturation, body into electronics, and absence into presence that one can attribute the premature claim of postmodernism's demise and explain why, like the phoenix, it always emerges stronger from the ashes of such fatuous fires. It is certainly because of that metamorphic quality that I rely in this book on the narrative figure of allegory to describe certain trends in postmodern sensibility. For allegory, as proposed by Benjamin, represents a continuous movement toward an unattainable origin, a movement marked by the awareness of a loss that it attempts to compensate with a baroque saturation and the obsessive reiteration of fragmented memories.[22] Like the myriad experiences of a long journey to a mythic homeland that, in comparison, will prove barren and empty, *Megalopolis* stands and was written for those cities whose greatness emerges from the interstices of their own ruins.

Notes

1   See Walter Benjamin, "Allegory and Trauerspiel," *The Origin of German Tragic Drama*, trans. John Osborne (London: New Left Books, 1977): 159–235: "Central Park," *New German Critique*, 34 (Winter 1985): 32–58: *Charles Baudelaire: A Lyric Poet in the Era of High Capitalism*, trans. Harry Zohn (London: Verso, 1983): "The Work of Art in the Age of Mechanical Reproduction," *Illuminations*, trans. Harry Zohn (London: Jonathan Cape, 1970): 219–53. For a thoroughly researched description of the evolution of Benjamin's thinking and work see Susan Buck-Morss, *The Dialectics of Seeing: Walter Benjamin and the Arcades Project* (Cambridge, Mass.: MIT Press, 1989).

2   Gilles Deleuze and Félix Guattari, *Rhizome (Introduction)* (Paris: Editions de Minuit, 1976). Semiotics studies culture as a system of signs, analyzing how those signs constitute meaning. See Roland Barthes, *Mythologies* (Paris: Editions du Seuil, 1957) and "Semiology and the Urban," in M. Gottdiener and Alexandros Ph. Lagopoulos (eds), *The City and the Sign: An Introduction to Urban Semiotics* (New York: Columbia University Press, 1986): 87–98; Umberto Eco, *Il Segno* (Milan: ISEDI, 1973) and *Tratado de Semiotica General* (Barcelona: Lumen, 1977); Kaja Silverman, *The Subject of Semiotics* (New York: Oxford University Press, 1983).

3   Michel de Certeau, *The Practice of Everyday Life* (Berkeley: University of California Press, 1984).

4   By popular culture I mean the multiple ways in which vast numbers of people relate to urban life and events – a definition that includes mass culture but excludes folk art.

5   Angela McRobbie, "Postmodernism and Popular Culture," in Lisa Appignanesi (ed.), *Postmodernism*, ICA Documents, vol. 4 (London: Free Association Books, 1986): 165–79. Tania Modleski, "Femininity as Masquerade: A Feminist Approach to Mass Culture," in Colin MacCabe (ed.), *High Theory/Low Culture: Analysing Popular Television and Film* (New York: St. Martin's Press, 1986): 37–53; "The Terror of Pleasure: The Contemporary Horror Film and Postmodern Theory," in Modleski (ed.), *Studies in Entertainment: Critical Approaches to Mass Culture* (Bloomington: Indiana University Press, 1986): 155–67.

6   Donna Haraway, "A Manifesto for Cyborgs: Science, Technology, and Socialist Feminism in the 1980s," in her *Primate Visions: Gender, Race, and Nature in the World of Modern Science* (New York: Routledge, 1989).

7   Néstor García Canclini, *Culturas híbridas: Estrategias para entrar y salir de la modernidad* (Mexico City: Grijalbo, forthcoming).

8   Walter Benjamin, "The Work of Art in the Age of Mechanical Reproduction."

9   Jean-François Lyotard, *The Postmodern Condition: A Report on Knowledge*, trans. Geoff Bennington and Brian Massumi (Minneapolis: University of Minnesota Press, 1984); Jürgen Habermas, "Modernity – An Incomplete Project," trans. Seyla Ben-Habib, in Hal Foster (ed.), *The Anti-Aesthetic: Essays on Postmodern Culture* (Port Townsend, Washington: Bay Press, 1983): 3–15. For a critical survey on the postmodern debate see Andreas Huyssen, "Mapping the Postmodern," *New German Critique*, 33 (Fall 1984): 5–52. Thanks to Andreas Huyssen for his support during the writing of this book.

10 Michel de Certeau, *Practice of Everyday Life*, 96.

11 See Chantal Mouffe's lucid discussion on this topic in her "Radical Democracy: Modern or Postmodern?" in Andrew Ross (ed.), *Universal Abandon? The Politics of Postmodernism* (Minneapolis: University of Minnesota Press, 1988): 31–45.

12 Gerald E. Stearn (ed.), *McLuhan: Hot and Cool: A Critical Symposium with a Rebuttal by Marshall McLuhan* (New York: Dial Press, 1967).

13 Umberto Eco, *Apocalípticos e integrados ante la cultura de masas*, trans. Andres Boglar (Barcelona: Lumen, 1968).

14 Jean Baudrillard, "The Ecstasy of Communication," trans. John Johnston, in Foster, *The Anti-Aesthetic*, 126–34, and *Simulations*, trans. Paul Foss, Paul Patton, and John Johnston (New York: Semiotext[e], 1983).

15 Chantal Mouffe, "Radical Democracy," in Andrew Ross (ed.), *Universal Abandon?*, 35.

16 Quoted in Andrew Ross (ed.), *Universal Abandon?*, xii.

17 Fredric Jameson, "Postmodernism; or, the Cultural Logic of Late Capitalism," *New Left Review*, 146 (July–August 1984): 53–92.

18 It does seem overzealous, however, to attribute to feminism the primacy of difference, as Andreas Huyssen and Craig Owens do when they claim feminism plays a founding role in postmodernism. For if difference is a practice of inclusion that integrates discordant elements, it is as constitutive of feminism as of the other discourses mentioned here that exercise a similar politics; it is in feminism, however, that difference is best articulated theoretically. See Craig Owens, "The Discourse of Others: Feminists and Postmodernism," in Foster, *The Anti-Aesthetic*, 57–82; Andreas Huyssen, "Mass Culture as Woman: Modernism's Other," in Modleski, *Studies in Entertainment*, 188–208; and Laura Kipnis,

"Feminism: The Political Conscience of Postmodernism?" in Ross (ed.), *Universal Abandon?*, 149–166.

19 I am following Mikhail Bakhtin's distinction between a monological textuality with a univocal and centered meaning, and a dialogical textuality that is pluralistic and inter-textual. See Michael Holquist (ed.), *The Dialogic Imagination: Four Essays by M. M. Bakhtin* (Austin: University of Texas Press, 1981).

20 I am privileging a Lacanian psychoanalytic reading of the structuring of the social. For a brilliant reading of Lacan, see Silverman, *The Subject of Semiotics*.

21 Frederic Jameson, "Postmodernism," in *New Left Review* (July–August 1984): 61–2.

22 See also Joel Fineman, "The Structure of Allegorical Desire," *October*, 12 (1980): 46–66.

29

Feminism, Postmodernism and the 'Real Me'*

Angela McRobbie

A three-way split has developed recently around postmodernism. There are those who refuse to admit that postmodernism engages with anything that modernism is not better able to explain and who also defend the values of modernism as they relate to both intellectual work and political analysis. This grouping has established itself as a counterbalance to those others who from such a 'reasonable' standpoint display what are viewed as the excesses of postmodernism. Allowing even for predictable negative typecasting in a debate which has become as heated as this, the image of these postmodernists remains particularly flimsy and marked by what Butler (1992) describes as a kind of slur of infantilism or at least youthful aberration. The third path is occupied by the postcolonialists and there is in this work both a notion of what Gilroy (1993), drawing on Bauman, labels 'the counter-cultures of modernity' and at the same time a remorseless critique of modernity and a looking to those accounts of postmodernity as a way of finding a place from which to speak and a space from which to develop that critique of the places and the spaces of exclusion inside modernity.

The question which will be asked in this chapter is what does this three-way divide mean for women? And how does feminism define itself in an intellectual world now characterized by shifting borders, boundaries and identities? To begin to answer this question it is necessary to look first at how two strands of this debate, the pro-modernist and the postcolonialist, put on the agenda quite separate issues as central to our understanding of contemporary society. These usefully set a framework for going on to consider the place of feminism in this new conceptualization of the social. But in engaging with the feminists who have taken up a strongly post-modernist position, the reader should be warned that these writers have been criticized for 'taking leave of their senses'. To enter their discourse is therefore to display a willingness to consciously explore the other side, the under-side of contemporary critical theory, a realm of thinking which is frequently charged with

* From Angela McRobbie, *Postmodernism and Popular Culture* (London and New York: Routledge, 1985), pp. 61–74.

the abandonment not just of reason, but also of the subject, good sense and politics. In this process of searching around in the landscape of post-feminism, as well as postmodernism and postcoloniality, the question of who 'we' intellectuals are these days and what role we have to play in feminist politics is constantly forced into prominence.

Postmodernists: Guilty of Playing with Politics

My starting-point is to suggest that the provocative stance adopted in language by a figure like Lyotard (1984), which results in his being charged with playfulness, is a deliberate strategy, a way of positioning himself within a certain kind of rhetorical mode which allows him to develop his critique. Gregor McLennan (1992a: 18) has recently expressed his antipathy to this way of thinking as follows: 'The contemporary world, in spite of patches of surface civilisation, remains too ravaged by oppression, ignorance and malnutrition for privileged intellectuals to trade in seriousness for the sparkling interplay of language games.' Contrary to this position it can be argued that postmodernism represents neither an absence of seriousness, nor a kind of political immorality or irresponsibility. It works as a critique because it forces precisely this kind of response, either urgently (and perhaps defensively) to redefine and defend the political and intellectual formation of modernity, or else, having subjected to scrutiny the great pillars of thinking which have supported the project of modernity, to stand back and ask 'What's going on?' (as the great soul singer Marvin Gaye put it).

Postmodernism is a concept for understanding social change. It seems feeble to suggest it, but maybe the reason for the hostility to the concept in Britain lies at least partly in the abysmal fate of social science research and intellectual work in general in the UK during and after the Thatcher years, where the nature of these constraints inevitably produced defensive political and intellectual responses. Sociology as well as 'society' itself became such redundant categories that there was little opportunity to investigate what the new theoretical vocabulary might look like in practice. Thus while there has been a debate about 'new ways of living' and about post-Fordism as well as one on fragmentation and identity, there has been little opportunity to examine in any depth the lived 'condition of postmodernity'. As a result the really engaged debate on how best to understand this refiguring of society was never able to take place. What happened instead was either a rejection and retrenchment which none the less involved re-examining the premises and the assumptions upon which the intellectual edifice of modernity was based, or else a process of translating some of the categories of French or American postmodernism into the cultural politics of contemporary Britain. This latter can best be seen in the emergence of 'New Times' (Hall and Jacques, 1989) politics in the late 1980s and early 1990s with its interest in consumerism, identity, ethnicity, and with the critique of essentialism, be it in relation to gender (Riley, 1988), class (Laclau, 1991) or ethnicity (McRobbie, 1985; Bhabha, 1990).

Finding the 'Real Me'

The notion of the 'real me' suggests the fictive unity of the self and the essentialism entailed in the search for such a person. What is being questioned in this phrase as used by Stuart Hall (1992) is the possibility of ever finding a 'real me'. One of the issues that will be explored here is what remains when we do away with the real me. How do we construct what I would define as a sufficiently focused 'social self' in order to be effective in politics? And who can such a politics now claim to represent? Who, therefore, is the discursive 'I' which speaks or writes, to whom and with what purpose? This question will be returned to in the final part of this chapter. But, for the moment, I would want to signal postmodernity as marking a convergence of a number of discourses each of which opens up new possibilities for positioning the self. Many would argue that feelings of dislocation or turbulence, and experiences of fragmentation and crises of identity were as much part of the experience of modernity as they now are of postmodernity (Berman, 1984). But what is distinctive about the discourses considered in the following pages is the respect for difference which they display, not, as some might see it, a 'simple' celebration of difference, but rather a rigorous thinking through of what 'living with difference' (Mercer, 1990) might entail. In addition I think there is a brave and necessary inclusion in the new intellectual agenda of difference, a different kind of language, one which insists on the interplay between intellectual boundaries and borders and also one which recognizes the importance of what have been the hidden dimensions of subjectivity, those which arise from positionalities which, within modernism, had no legitimate place, i.e. that of the black woman, that of the mother, the daughter, that of the feminist intellectual, the feminist teacher.

This kind of work is reflected in Carolyn Steedman's *Landscape for a Good Woman* (1985) which pulls together strands of social history and personal psychoanalysis producing a remarkable text where the oblique search for the 'real me' through the joint guidance of history and psychoanalysis produces instead a layered, mysterious, unresolved self, a fictive daughter, whose positionality as daughter within a particular configuration of class, culture and family, has required that 'she' produce 'this' book. Feminism, in Steedman's case, also requires a necessary interdisciplinarity of intellectual work which problematizes its own foundations. It may well be that it is this which makes such work, as well as that produced by postcolonialist writers including Trinh T. Min-ha (1989), Homi Bhabha (1990) and Gayatri Chakravorty Spivak (1992), appear unruly and truculent and poetically disrespectful of the boundaries which have guarded and guaranteed the old rules of academia. It is partly this 'game' of academic convention and the defence of disciplinary boundaries as guarantors of academic authorship and identity, which underpins recent altercations between those who defend modernity and those who move in some 'other' direction.

In the recent volume which is part of the new Open University social science course, *Modernity and Its Futures*, we find an interesting version of the debate for and against postmodernism being played out by Gregor McLennan (1992b) and Stuart Hall (1992). Neither author wholly defends one against the other. But as McLennan veers towards modernity, Stuart Hall leans towards the exploration of fragmented subjectivity. In the following pages a reading of these debates will be suggested as a means of establishing a framework for considering recent work in feminist theory.

Critical Embrace: Modernity and its Critique

In some ways the embracing of modernity as a critical concept in contemporary political thinking is a way of decentring Marxism by showing it to belong to a broader philosophical project. Thus, while Stuart Hall shows how modernity and its focus on 'man' and the unified subject was itself undermined by Freud (the unconscious), by Marx himself (production and labour rather than exchange, the market and free will), later by structuralism (which opposed the transparency of meaning) and more recently by the social movements (including those of gender, sexual identity and ethnicity), so also could we say that the interest in modernity can be seen as a way of both relocating Marx in a less universalistic mode (a kind of process of downgrading or relativizing) and of looking to find something in modernity which can be used to ward off the encroaching chaos of postmodernity. Feminist intellectuals (with a few exceptions) have tended either to argue for the necessity of some of those great modernist values: truth, objectivity, reason (Nicholson, 1990), or else they have argued against the assumed invisibility of women found in much of the recent writing on modernity (Bowlby, 1992; Nava, 1992).

Gregor McLennan reminds us that the Enlightenment gave rise to the idea of social betterment, of improving and making better the society in which we live. The development of the social sciences was part of this project. Are these 'foundations of modern thought' now obsolete? Or do they only need to be revised? The first of these questions implies that postmodernity blows everything away, the second that the existing vocabulary merely needs updating. McLennan opts for modifying modernity. He pitches the 'overhauling' Lyotard against the more 'reasonable' Habermas (1985). For Lyotard the Enlightenment promised science as pure knowledge and as narrative-free practice, but that picture of pure knowledge was in itself part of a very powerful story which helped legitimize capitalist exploitation. Therefore, beware of the meta-narratives. Knowledge is not pure or in the mind but moves in a game. Habermas, in contrast, sees the Enlightenment as an ideal not a reality. It poses questions of morality, science and art as separate from myth and primitivity. To abandon the commitment to reason and rationality is to embrace despair and conservatism. We can retain hope of objectivity in universals (the good life, the better society) without having 'naive expectations'. Enter the theory of communicative action/reason.

For McLennan relativism is the issue. Does cultural relativism lead to cognitive relativism, that is, we cannot understand therefore we give up and go home? Relativism encourages indifference, he suggests. It means that arguments about what is good and true cannot be engaged in and across cultures. Critics of this position (the rest, the others) would, McLennan agrees, say that what is being defended here 'is the culture and society of western science and philosophy'. He says in defence of this position that some values can be shared cross-culturally. And if this is not possible and if knowledge has such little import then why carry on doing academic work at all? Modernity did not promise one kind of progress but many. There was always a radicalized strand within modernity.

McLennan argues his position on the grounds that there is communicative action across cultures. There are still universals; for example, the possibility of democracy. One problem is that he takes the postmodernity critique as a kind of intellectual earthquake. He responds truculently. It is one or the other. If there is no logic, no reason, then we all shut up shop or embrace mysticism or unreason or madness. But this mode of argumentation based on pitching two binary opposites against each other need not always be the most useful way of proceeding. The tendency is to feel the necessity of coming down strongly in favour of one or the other, or, as McLennan does in a later piece, more measuredly, to bring together the 'better elements of Enlightenment sociology' with 'the undoubted insights of "post" currents. Not...in order to form some bland and convenient theoretical convergence but rather to generate a series of productive and taxing tensions' (McLennan, 1992a: 20). What this restrained mode cannot afford to do is to look beyond the 'reasonable' frame of reference within which the debate is conducted. Why not? What happens when we challenge this kind of management of reason, when we suggest that the tensions are more usefully explored when they remain aggressively outside and deeply uncomfortable with this kind of 'convergence'?

Stuart Hall: Working in a World of Shifting Boundaries

Stuart Hall travels down a different road. What he is interested in exploring are the new worldly identities which have come into being, sweeping away, as capitalism itself does, the old nation-states which were the bearers of modernity and the givers of identity and 'nationality'. Instead we live in a world of moving boundaries, a world in which borders are crossed, new sub-nationalisms and transnationalisms are embraced. For Hall it is the struggle to explain which is important. What he turns his attention to are those aspects of modernity which incorporated subjection and subordination in the language of social advance, exploration, development, civilization. This more open-ended approach avoids the either/ors which define the terms of McLennan's argument. Instead it adopts a strategy of unsettlement and an embracing of the idea of difference and hybridity. What is also unsettled and differentiated is the 'real me'. This approach is also quite different from Jameson's (1984) and Harvey's (1989), as well as McLennan's, in that we see no sign of a return to the values or ethics of modernism being proposed. It is focused around the 'new ethnicities' and it looks out for the connections among subjugated people which emerge from within the tracks of the metacommunications networks of the new global order.

Hall's contribution is significant also in that it does not prioritize an exclusively academic mode as the means of producing knowledge and understanding. Postcolonialist writing acknowledges the work found in and produced by the intersection of art and popular culture. Culture is a broad site of learning, and perhaps we learn best and are most open to ideas when the barriers between the discipline and the academy and the experiences of everyday life are broken down. There is a sense in which Stuart Hall is here speaking from the other side, from the space of difference. Where those who espoused modernity and its ideals saw vision and order and reason and achievement he sees turbulence and savagery. Included in Hall's essay is a quote from Salman Rushdie responding to the review of his book *The Satanic Verses*, 'A bit of this and a bit of that is how newness enters the world. It is the great possibility that mass migration gives the world' (Hall, 1992: 311; quoting Rushdie). If, therefore, post-colonialist experience shares anything in common with the postmodern experience, then it must be a postmodernism which is much more than an overstylized posture adopted by those who can afford to abandon politics. Instead it is a way of marking out a new set of convergences and divergences round certain critical questions about the society in which we live.

Towards a Feminist Postmodernism

In her contribution to *Beyond Equality and Difference*, Rosi Braidotti (1992) rejects the defence of theoretical reason, the unity of the subject and even of equality (equal to whom, she asks?) as 'domination', Enlightenment concepts, which have been part of an apparatus of regulation and subordination hidden under the great achievements of rationality and knowledge. This marks her out immediately as a postmodern feminist. The question that has to be asked, she suggests, is that of how we think, what is it to think? What does it mean if reason and truth are unsettled from their secure places in the foundationalist discipline of philosophy? She thus opens up for debate not only the possibility of other ways of thinking, but also the question of on whose behalf do we think as critical feminist intellectuals? What is the responsibility of the feminist intellectual? Is it not, in part, to think about thinking and thus to unveil some of the power relations caught up in the category of knowledge?

These questions which she is asking from a feminist viewpoint, happen to coincide with the critique of western thinking by subaltern discourses. So the whole status of thinking and of thought is called into question. Let us move out of a dualistic logic, she continues: male versus female, women equal to men. 'Feminists propose that reason does not sum up the totality of or even what is best in the human capacity for thinking' (Braidotti, 1992: 181). Do we therefore learn to think differently as a 'female feminist subject'? The postmodern subject, argues Braidotti, is a subject in process, organized by a will to know and a desire to speak. The crisis of subjectivity produced by postmodernity 'offers many positive openings' (Braidotti, 1992: 183). This crisis emerged in the dying moments of modernity through Freud, for example, with his insistence of the non-coincidence of the subject with consciousness, and then later with Foucault's account of the self as the product of discourse. Much thought, she reminds us, following Freud, is pre-rational, unconscious matter. Rationality rests on premises about thinking which are themselves nonrational. And desire 'is that which being the a-priori condition for thinking is in excess of the thinking process itself' (Braidotti, 1992: 184). For Braidotti the enunciation of a philosophical stance rests, therefore, on a non-philosophical disposition to represent the self, to inscribe the subject in language. How then do we rethink subjectivity and the body as an 'interface of will with desire', that is, the will to know and the desire to say?

Such an emphasis on desire inevitably runs the risk of positing desire as the source of a new essentialism. This is particularly the case when desire coincides not just with language but also with sexuality which is then taken, as Foucault (1984) has pointed out, as representing the truth of the body and of the self. Or is it rather, as Braidotti argues, that in western culture the sexed body dominates over the other levels of experience? It is how we are known, how we come to know. In language we are sexed and this process of being sexed is one of the key modalities of power inscribed in each of our bodies: 'Sexuality is the dominant discourse of power in the West' (Braidotti, 1992: 185).

It is therefore a point of contestation. What, the feminist critic might ask, *is* the female body, what is it for, for whom? And to follow in this vein the feminist cultural critic might ask, is it because Madonna constructs herself exactly along this axis of *all body* that she unnerves and disrupts the axis of power which prefers to remain hidden? She pulls it all off the top shelf of the newsagent's, brings it – sex, power, pornography, the body – to the surface and leaves us to respond. It could be suggested that by placing her body on precisely those lines of classification, for example, as the site of sex, as the truth of femininity, and also as the property of the female self, something that can and does give pleasure quite autonomously from the regulative discourses within which it is more traditionally placed, the image of Madonna is disruptive. It is too much about sexuality to exist comfortably within the commercial machine, even where that machine is already linked with excessive sexual imagery (i.e. pop), or where it is licensed to shock. Instead of simply rejecting the essentialism which equates woman with body, Braidotti argues that (like Madonna) we must revisit the sites of assumed essentialism and work through them. We should explore the boundaries by going back to them.

But if we no longer know what woman is, if we are all good anti-essentialists, and if we take into account the critique by black feminists of white feminism's universalism, how do we move from analysing the implications for power of the borders and boundaries, to actively redefining the bonds through which a politics remains viable? Like all of the postmodern feminists being considered here, Braidotti puts the possibility of a communicative bond between women as the basis for politics on the agenda. This takes the form for feminist intellectuals of a kind of accountability, a recognition of the relations of responsibility between a writer and her readers and, it could be added, between a teacher and her students. Feminist thinking should, then, attempt to represent and analyse what it is to be female. In one decisive way, this breaks down the barriers between art, fiction, culture and the academic disciplines in much the way that Stuart Hall suggests (Hall, 1992). By far the most visible example of this force for breaking down barriers is the success and achievement of black women's writing over the last few years, not just for the community of women it brings into being as readers, but also because it *is* simultaneously art, history, literature, sociology, politics, biography, autobiography and also popular culture. At the opposite end of the same spectrum but 'doing' in her own theoretical work very much the same kind of thing, we could also place Gayatri Chakravorty Spivak.

Coming from the high end of deconstruction, and bringing to this practice a feminist postcolonialist critique, Spivak works within the discourse of theory but so transforms it as to make it an entirely different kind of practice. It becomes an interrogative, interweaving, reflective poetics. For Spivak the community of women can only come after the recognition of difference between women, and after the raising of some key questions about who is talking to whom, and why, all points which she returns to in her contribution to *Feminists Theorise the Political* (Spivak, 1992).

This is a similar position to that described by Judith Butler, who also engages with a notion of the community of women. In articulating women, from a feminist perspective, such a category is immediately broken and it is the breaking that is the important point (Butler, 1992). Who is not spoken to in feminism? In addition, who was the 'subject' of feminism, but is no more? How has feminism opened itself out to speak to many female subjects and yet still engages with only a few? Butler sees these as crucial questions and illustrates them by referring to the old centrality of the mother as one of the primary stable subjects of feminist discourse. But this figure of the mother is not a biologically defined and stable category. She herself shifts and changes, just as feminism also does. As her children grow up and move away she no longer defines herself primarily through that particular mode of subjectivity. So the subjects of feminism change, feminism itself changes, particularly as it becomes subject to criticism by black women and, as the society within which feminism exists also undergoes quite dramatic changes, this too has an impact on what feminism is and can be. We could also add to Butler's questions the important one of how under such conditions feminism, or what remains of it, can hope to reproduce itself among a generation of younger women? What space away from feminism do young women need in order to disconnect from the historical experience of their mothers or their teachers and then find their own way towards feminism, redefining it in the process for themselves? These questions of how feminism continues and seeks to extend itself while recognizing different histories, experiences and identities are therefore crucial. Can it continue, can it still call itself feminism? What must it do to be able to legitimately address women?

As well as laying the ground for developing post-feminism theoretically, Judith Butler also takes issue with the slightly ridiculing tones frequently adopted to make light of postmodernism. As though in direct engagement with Gregor McLennan she disputes the assumption that there 'must' be a foundation and a stable subject to have a politics. She sees this as authoritarian, the use of the 'must' clause. Postmodernism does not mean that we have to do away with the subject but rather we ask after the process of its construction. The value of postmodernism therefore is that, like deconstruction, it shows clearly how arguments bury opposition. Its disorderly force is rude and impertinent in that it shows where power resides, hidden and quiet and displeased at being exposed. Demonstrating these ruses does not mean descending into unruly chaos. Rather it allows for open debate and dispute about boundaries and disciplines and what constitutes a study, what is knowledge. 'A social theory committed to democratic contestation within a post-colonialist horizon needs to find a way to bring into question the foundations it is compelled to lay down' (Butler, 1992: 8).

Thus even minimal foundations need scrutinizing. Within feminism there is a need to speak as and for women but no sooner is this done than it is objected to. This is the point at which things move. Women then become 'an undesignatable field of wills'. The dispute *is* the ground of feminist theory. The category of women has to be released from the anchoring which feminism felt it needed. 'What women signify has been taken for granted too long.... We have to instead break from the list of meanings and expand the possibilities of what it is to be a woman' (Butler, 1992: 16). Sex imposes a uniformity on bodies for the purposes of reproductive sexuality. This is also an act of violence. Therefore there must be a redefining, an invention of new categories. (We could add to this the question of whether this is already happening, with the emergence of the 'single mother' as a sign of these expanded possibilities of being female, a category which marks a changed society and a changed mode of familial organization.)

Jane Flax (1992a) completes the assault on the male modernists who defend reason by saying how comforting it is to believe that reason will triumph and bail us all out. How often has it? Admittedly, it is frightening to think that without truth, pure power might prevail. Feminists are as prone to this wishful thinking that reason will win through as anybody else. But, says Flax, this failure to face up to the limits of reason, truth and knowledge is predicted on fear of letting go and of thinking outside the safety of inherited assumptions about thought. 'They fear what will emerge in disrupted places if they are not in feminist control. They believe innocent clean knowledge is available somewhere for our discovery and use' (Flax, 1992b: 457). Flax prefers desire, fantasy and power. 'What we really want is power in the world not an innocent truth' (1992b: 458). Many feminists are fearful of losing what they have gained by embracing or being seen to embrace postmodernity. But this being made insecure is productive and it coincides with being made insecure by the critique of women of colour. 'At its best postmodernity invites us to engage in a continual process of dis-illusionment with the grandiose fantasies that have brought us to the brink of annihilation' (Flax, 1992b: 460). Feminist postmodernism does not eliminate the subject or the self but finds it in operation as a series of bit parts in the concrete field of social relations. Politics must therefore imply subjectivities in process, interacting and debating.

This idea of, as Stuart Hall puts it, becoming rather than being, continues the mode of argument that all of these feminist writers adopt, that is, to avoid binary oppositions and to dispute the value of terms like equality, and relativism, as the other of a discourse of absolutism (men, universalism) which they are committed to questioning. What emerges from this work is a desire to hold on to the notion of a meaningful feminist politics by interrogating rather than assuming the relations between who is talking to whom. In subjecting some of the big questions and concepts to critical scrutiny these feminist writers are not taking leave of their senses but rather are asking questions about how we learn, how we think and write. This has the effect of realigning the disciplines, rearranging the furniture of intellectual life. It allows for a certain interdisciplinary licence.

In the absence of a 'real me', what I would describe as a social self (the female feminist subject as Braidotti labels her) none the less emerges, marked by a set of constraints and dispositions. This social self participates in intimacy, in communality and communication. She also uses desire and will in order to understand the process of subjection. The feminist social self, it might be suggested, is an amalgam of fragmented identities formed in discourse and history and called into being both by the experiences of femininity and by the existence and availability of a feminist discourse whether that comes in the form of books, education, mass media, or through friends, politics and community. This, I think, is what Butler and the other feminist writers discussed here mean by the communicative aspect of female experience.

Unmasking the 'Real Me'

But while little work has been done on what is left behind when the myth of the 'real me' is revealed, deconstructing the 'real me' has involved showing it to be a social and political requirement, a form of enforcement, a means of regulating legitimate ways of being, legitimate ways of understanding the self and the world. The 'real "respectable" me' is also the product of a certain kind of psychoanalytical violence where desire is also constrained and endlessly defined in culture around the tropes of heterosexuality. Not being at one with this 'real me' has produced much pain and suffering and has required, on the part of gay men and lesbian women, enormous effort to construct different kinds of subjectivity. But if the 'real me' is a mask, a fiction which transcends discourse as an essence, how then, once we have dislodged this kind of self, can we talk about women, about identity, or indeed of feminism as mobilizing political categories? Once again Gayatri Spivak shows how, for white western feminists, there is still instant recourse to a language where feminism is pursued unalert to the limits of its efficacy and unwilling to be constantly interrogating who is the subject of its address. It is her attentiveness to the consequences of being designated a subaltern subject as she moves with her passport through the boundaries and barriers of nation-states and is inevitably questioned as to her professional status as teacher, as a person 'here' to give a paper, that makes her ever alert to the question of power. In her contribution to *Feminists Theorise the Political* Spivak 1992: 56) asks, 'What is it to write for you? What is it to teach? What is it to learn? What is it to assume that one already knows the meaning of the words "something is taught by me and something is learned by others"?'

The value of the work of these feminist writers lies in their interrogating of the ground rules, the boundaries and the barriers which define feminist theory and politics and which simultaneously have to be broken, have to be trespassed on. In this postmodern field what we find is not, however, a scene of catastrophe, the cost of questioning reason, the punishment for risking rationality. The riposte to white feminists that they were not speaking and could not speak on behalf of 'all women', has prompted a reassessment of the feminist self and who she is, and is speaking to and about. At the same time this particular fragmentation of the feminist subject is confirmed through the global and postmodern critique of the European Enlightenment. It is not so much a question of what is left behind, what fragments of the disassembled self can be picked up and put together again, but rather how might the continual process of putting oneself together be transformed to produce the empowerment of subordinate groups and social categories. This might mean living with fragmentation, with the reality of inventing the self rather than endlessly searching for the self. But abandoning the 'real me' need not mean resignation, despair, or simply being reconciled to the loss of wholeness.

Living along the fault-lines of the postmodern condition might also give us some reasons to feel cheerful. We might modestly be aware of our limited successes, in putting feminism (with all the limits that word implies) into the webs of popular discourses about gender and sexuality. The appearance of new feminist discourses, not just in the academy but also in women's magazines, for example, and in some other spaces within the commercial mass media, tells us that feminism now has some control over constructions of the feminine, as Charlotte Brunsdon has recently suggested (1992). But this fact should not be viewed as unproblematic success. There remains the question of what sort of feminism is found in these spaces and to whom is it speaking?

This kind of question challenges, by necessity, the process of reproducing feminism. Just as a feminist 'real me' was perhaps a necessary fiction in the early 1970s, so also was it necessary then to believe in the reproduction of feminism as part of the process of politicization. That such an attempt can backfire is not just about 'backlash' but more productively about other younger women (like black women) disputing their being represented by feminists, just as much as they might take issue with their being represented in advertising, or in popular culture, or in the tabloid press. Thus, once again, politics occurs in the act of breaking away from the claim to be represented. New, emergent or otherwise excluded identities emerge from this discourse of rejection and repudiation. 'This is not us', they are saying. And in saying so there is also a question of who indeed 'they' are.

While this might create a crisis for the (white) feminist movement and for the feminist intellectuals who came into being in the 1970s, such a crisis is no bad thing. In the process of being challenged, older feminist identities are also revised. And what remains is remembered, perhaps even in a 'passion of remembrance' (Blackwood and Julien, 1985).

The passage of feminism into the 1990s should not be seen, in conclusion, as a process of political dismemberment, leaving behind a sadly dispersed band of individuals dotted about the globe but found mostly in the universities of the western world and defining themselves as 'feminist writers' or 'feminist intellectuals'. Nor should it be understood, after postmodernism, as a politics of difference based simply on pluralism, on everyone going their own way. In short the strength of feminism lies in its ability to create discourse, to dispute, to negotiate the boundaries and the barriers, and also to take issue with the various feminisms which have sprung into being. The value of the contribution to new feminist theory by Butler and Scott in *Feminists Theorise the Political*, Bock and James in *Beyond Equality and Difference*, and Hall, Held and McGrew in *Modernity and Its Futures* (all 1992) lies first in their rejection that there could be or should be 'one voice', second in their willingness to take risks by exploring the relatively unnavigated political continent which lies 'beyond equality and difference', third in their engagement with the politics of difference as characterized not by pluralism but by lines of connection and of disconnection, and fourth by their abandonment of the search for the 'real me' in favour, to use Judith Butler's words again, 'of expanding the possibilities of what it means to be a woman'.

References

Berman, Marshall (1984) *All That Is Solid Melts into Air: The Experience of Modernity*, London: Verso.

Bhabha, Homi (1990) 'DissemiNation: time, narrative and the margins of the modern nation', in H. Bhabha (ed.) *Nation and Narration*, London: Routledge, pp. 15–48.

Blackwood, Maureen and Julien, Isaac (dirs) (1985) *The Passion of Remembrance*, Sankofa Films.

Bowlby, Rachel (1992) *Still Crazy After All These Years*, London: Routledge.

Braidotti, Rosi (1992) 'On the feminist female subject or from she-self to she-other', in G. Bock and S. James (eds) *Beyond Equality and Difference: Citizenship, Feminist Politics and Female Subjectivity*, London: Routledge, pp. 176–92.

Brunsdon, Charlotte (1992) 'Pedagogies of the feminine: feminist teaching and women's genres', *Screen* 32, 4: 364–82.

Butler, Judith (1992) 'Contingent foundations: feminism and the question of "postmodernism"', in J. Butler and J. W. Scott (eds) *Feminists Theorise the Political*, London: Routledge, pp. 3–22.

Flax, Jane (1992a) 'Beyond equality: gender, justice and difference', in G. Bock and S. James (eds) *Beyond Equality and Difference: Citizenship, Feminist Politics and Female Subjectivity*, London: Routledge, pp. 192–209.

Flax, Jane, (1992b) 'The end of innocence', in J. Butler and J. W. Scott (eds) *Feminists Theorise the Political*, London: Routledge, pp. 445–64.

Foucault, Michel (1984) *The History of Sexuality*, vol. 1, Harmondsworth, Mx: Penguin.

Gilroy, Paul (1993) *The Black Atlantic*, London: Verso.

Habermas, Jürgen (1985) 'Modernity: an incomplete project', in H. Foster (ed.) *Postmodern Culture*, London: Pluto Press, pp. 3–15.

Hall, Stuart (1992) 'The question of cultural identity', in S. Hall, D. Held and D. McGrew (eds) *Modernity and Its Futures*, Oxford: Polity Press, pp. 273–327.

Hall, Stuart and Jacques, Martin (1989) *New Times: The Changing Face of Politics in the 1990s*, London: Lawrence & Wishart.

Harvey, David (1989) *The Condition of Postmodernity*, Oxford: Blackwell.

Jameson, Fredric (1984) 'Postmodernism, or the cultural logic of capital', *New Left Review* 146: 53–92.

Laclau, Ernesto (1991) *Reflections on the New Revolutions of Our Times*, London: Verso.

Lyotard, Jean-François (1984) *The Postmodern Condition*, Manchester: Manchester University Press.

McLennan, Gregor (1992a) 'Sociology after postmodernism', inaugural address, Faculty of Social Sciences Occasional Papers, Massey University, Palmers Bag, New Zealand, pp. 1–22.

McLennan, Gregor (1992b) 'The Enlightenment project, revisited', in S. Hall, D. Held and D. McGrew (eds) *Modernity and Its Futures*, Oxford: Polity Press, pp. 327–79.

McRobbie, Angela (1985) 'Strategies of vigilance: an interview with Gayatri Chakravorty Spivak', *Block* 10: 5–9.

Mercer, Kobena (1990) 'Welcome to the jungle', in J. Rutherford (ed.) *Identity*, London: Lawrence & Wishart, pp. 43–71.

Min-ha, Trinh T. (1989) *Woman, Native, Other*, Bloomington, IN: Indiana University Press.

Nava, Mica (1992) *Changing Cultures: Feminism, Youth, Consumerism*, London: Sage.

Nicholson, Linda J. (ed.) (1990) *Feminism/Postmodernism*, New York: Routledge.

Riley, Denise (1988) *'Am I That Name?': Feminism and the Category of 'Women' in History*, London: Macmillan.

Spivak, Gayatri Chakravorty (1992) 'French feminism revisited', in J. Butler and J. W. Scott (eds) *Feminists Theorise the Political*, London: Routledge, pp. 54–86.

Steedman, Carolyn (1985) *Landscape for a Good Woman*, London: Virago.

30

Postmodern Virtualities*

Mark Poster

Introduction

On the eve of the 21st century there have been two innovative discussions about the general conditions of life: one concerns a possible 'postmodern' culture and even society; the other concerns broad, massive changes in communications systems. Postmodern culture is often presented as an alternative to existing society which is pictured as structurally limited or fundamentally flawed. New communications systems are often presented as a hopeful key to a better life and a more equitable society. The discussion of postmodern culture focuses to a great extent on an emerging new individual identity or subject position, one that abandons what may in retrospect be the narrow scope of the modern individual with its claims to rationality and autonomy. The discourse surrounding the new communications systems attends more to the imminent technical increase in information exchange and the ways this advantage will redound to already existing individuals and already existing institutions.
  My purpose in this essay is to bring these two discussions together, to enact a confrontation between them so that the advantages of each may redound to the other, while the limitations of each may be revealed and discarded. My contention is that a critical understanding of the new communications systems requires an evaluation of the type of subject it encourages, while a viable articulation of postmodernity must include an elaboration of its relation to new technologies of communication.
  For what is at stake in these technical innovations, I contend, is not simply an increased 'efficiency' of interchange, enabling new avenues of investment, increased productivity at work and new domains of leisure and consumption, but a broad and extensive change in the culture, in the way identities are structured. If I may be allowed a historical analogy: the technically advanced societies are at a point in their history similar to that of the emergence of an urban, merchant culture in the midst of feudal society in the Middle Ages. At that point practices of the exchange of com-

* From Mark Poster, *Cyberspace/Cyberbodies/Cyberpunk*, eds. Mike Featherstone and Roger Burrows (Thousand Oaks, Sage, 1995), pp. 79–95.

modities required individuals to act and speak in new ways,[1] ways drastically different from the aristocratic code of honor with its face-to-face encounters based on trust for one's word and its hierarchical bonds of interdependency. Interacting with total strangers, sometimes at great distances, the merchants required written documents guaranteeing spoken promises and an 'arm's length distance' attitude even when face-to-face with the other, so as to afford a 'space' for calculations of self-interest. A new identity was constructed, gradually and in a most circuitous path to be sure, among the merchants, in which a coherent, stable sense of individuality was grounded in independent, cognitive abilities. In this way the cultural basis for the modern world was begun, one that eventually would rely upon print media to encourage and disseminate these urban forms of identity.

In the 20th century, electronic media are supporting an equally profound transformation of cultural identity. Telephone, radio, film, television, the computer and now their integration as 'multimedia' reconfigure words, sounds and images so as to cultivate new configurations of individuality. If modern society may be said to foster an individual who is rational, autonomous, centered and stable (the 'reasonable man' of the law, the educated citizen of representative democracy, the calculating 'economic man' of capitalism, the grade-defined student of public education), then perhaps a postmodern society is emerging which nurtures forms of identity different from, even opposite to those of modernity. And electronic communications technologies significantly enhance these postmodern possibilities. Discussions of these technologies, as we shall see, tend often to miss precisely this crucial level of analysis, treating them as enhancements for already formed individuals to deploy to their advantage or disadvantage.[2]

The Communications 'Superhighway'

One may regard the media from a purely technical point of view, to the extent that is possible, evaluating them in relation to their ability to transmit units of information. The question to ask then is how much information with how little noise may be transmitted at what speed and over what distance to how many locations? Until the late 1980s technical constraints limited the media's ability in these terms. To transmit a high quality image over existing (twisted pair copper wire) phone lines took about ten minutes using a 2400-baud modem or two minutes using a 9600-baud modem. Given these specifications it was not possible to send 'real time' 'moving' images over the phone lines. The great limitation, then, of the first electronic media age is that images could only be transmitted from a small number of centers to a large number of receivers, either by air or by coaxial cable. Until the end of the 1980s an 'economic' scarcity existed in the media highways that encouraged and justified, without much thought or consideration, the capitalist or nation-state exploitation of image transmission. Since senders needed to build their own information roads by broadcasting at a given frequency or by constructing (coaxial) wire networks, there were necessarily few distributors of images. The same economies of technology, it might be noted in passing, applied to processes of information production.

Critical theorists such as Benjamin, Enzensberger and McLuhan[3] envisioned the democratic potential of the increased communication capacity of radio, film and television. While there is some truth to their position, the practical model for a more radical communications potential during the first media age was rather the telephone. What distinguishes the telephone from the other great media is its decentralized quality and its universal exchangeability of the positions of sender and receiver. Anyone can 'produce' and send a message to anyone else in the system and, in the advanced industrial societies, almost everyone is in the system. These unique qualities were recognized early on by both defenders and detractors of the telephone.

In the recent past the only technology that imitates the telephone's democratic structure is the Internet, the government funded electronic mail, database and general communication system.[4] Until the 1990s, even this facility has been largely restricted to government, research and education institutions, some private industry and individuals who enroll in private services (Compuserve, Prodigy) which are connected to it. In the last few years Internet has gained enormously in popularity and by the mid-1990s boasts 30 million users around the world (Cooke and Lehrer, 1993). But Internet and its segments use the phone lines, suffering their inherent technical limitations. Technical innovations in the late 1980s and early 1990s, however, are making possible the drastic reduction of earlier constraints. The digital encoding of sound, text and image, the introduction of fiber-optic lines replacing copper wire, the ability to transmit digitally encoded images and the subsequent ability to compress this information, the vast expansion of the frequency range for wireless transmission, innovations in switching technology and a number of other advances have so enlarged the quantity and types of information that may soon be able to be transmitted that a qualitative change, to allude to Engels' dialectical formula, in the culture may also be imminent.

Information superhighways are being constructed that will enable a vast increase in the flow of communications. The telephone and cable companies are estimating the change to be from a limit of 60 or so one-way video/audio channels to one of 500 with limited bidirectionality. But this kind of calculation badly misses the point. The increase in transmission capacity (both wired and wireless) will be so great that it will be possible to transmit any type of information (audio, video or text) from any point in the network to any other point or points, and to do so in 'real time', in other words quickly enough so that the receiver will see or record at least 24 frames of video per second with an accompanying audio frequency range of 20 to 20,000 Hertz. The metaphor of the 'superhighway' only attends to the movement of information, leaving out the various kinds of cyberspace on the Internet, meeting places, work areas and electronic cafés in which this vast transmission of images and words becomes places of communicative relation. The question that needs to be raised is 'will this technological change provide the stimulus for the installation of new media different enough from what we now have to warrant the periodizing judgment of a second electronic media age?' If that is the case, how is the change to be understood?

A discourse on the new communications technology is in process of formation, one which is largely limited by the vision of modernity. The importance of the information superhighway is now widely recognized, with articles appearing in periodicals from the specialized zines (*Wired* and *Mondo 2000*) to general journals (*Time, Forbes* and *The Nation*). Essays on the new technology vary from breathless enthusiasm to wary caution to skepticism. Writing in *Time*, Philip Elmer-Dewitt (1993: 52) forecasts: 'The same switches used to send a TV show to your home can also be used to send a video from your home to any other – paving the way for video phones. . . . The same system will allow anybody with a camcorder to distribute videos to the world . . . '. Key to the new media system are not only the technical advances mentioned above but also the merger of existing communication technologies. Elmer-Dewitt continues, ' . . . the new technology will force the merger of television, telecommunications, computers, consumer electronics, publishing and information services into a single interactive information industry' (1993: 52–3). Other observers emphasize the prospects of wireless technology. Writing in *Forbes*, George Gilder (1993: 107) predicts the spread of this system:

> . . . the new minicell replaces a rigid structure of giant analog mainframes with a system of wireless local area networks . . . these wide and weak [replacing broadcasting based on 'long and strong'] radios can handle voice, data and even video at the same time . . . the system fulfills the promise of the computer revolution as a spectrum multiplier . . . [the new system will] banish once and for all the concept of spectrum scarcity.

Whether future communications media employ wired, wireless or some combination of the two, the same picture emerges of profound transformation.

Faced with this gigantic combination of new technology, integration of older technologies, creation of new industries and expansion of older ones, commentators have not missed the political implications. In *Tikkun*, David Bollier underlines the need for a new set of policies to govern and regulate the second media age in the public interest. President Bill Clinton and Vice-President Al Gore have already drawn attention to the problem, stressing the need for broad access to the superhighway, but also indicating their willingness to make the new developments safe for the profit motive. For them the main issue at stake is the strength of the United States in relation to other nations (read especially Japan) and the health of the industries involved. Bollier (1993: 22) points to wider concerns, such as strengthening community life, supporting families and invigorating the democratic process.[5] At this point I want to note that Bollier understands the new media entirely within the framework of *modern* social institutions. The 'information superhighway' is for him a transparent tool that brings new efficiencies but by itself changes nothing. The media merely redound to the benefit of or detract from familiar institutions – the family, the community, the state.

If Bollier presents a liberal or left-liberal agenda for politics confronted by the second media age, Mitchell Kapor, former developer of Lotus 1–2–3, offers a more radical interpretation. He understands better than Bollier that the information superhighway opens qualitatively new political opportunities because it creates new loci of speech:

> the crucial political question is 'Who controls the switches?' There are two extreme choices. Users may have indirect, or limited control over when, what, why, and from whom they get information and to whom they send it. That's the broadcast model today,

and it seems to breed consumerism, passivity, crassness, and mediocrity. Or, users may have decentralized, distributed, direct control over when, what, why, and with whom they exchange information. That's the Internet model today, and it seems to breed critical thinking, activism, democracy, and quality. We have an opportunity to choose now.   (Kapor, 1993: 5)

With Kapor, the interpretation of the new media returns to the position of Enzensberger: socialist or radical democratic control of the media results in more freedom, more enlightenment, more rationality; capitalist or centralist control results in oppression, passivity, irrationality. Kapor's reading of the information superhighway remains within the binaries of modernity. No new cultural formations of the self are imagined or even thought possible. While the political questions raised by Bollier and Kapor are valid and raise the level of debate well beyond its current formation, they remain limited to the terms of discussion that are familiar in the landscape of modernity.

The political implications of the Internet for the fate of the nation-state and the development of a global community also requires attention. The dominant use of English on the Internet suggests the extension of American power as does the fact that e-mail addresses in the US alone do not require a country code. The Internet normalizes American users. But the issue is more complex. In Singapore, English serves to *enable* conversations between hostile ethnic groups, being a neutral 'other'. Of course, vast inequalities of use exist, changing the democratic structure of the Internet into an occasion for further wrongs to the poorer populations. Even within the high-use nations, wealthy white males are disproportionate users. Yet technologies sometimes spread quickly and the Internet is relatively cheap. Only grassroots political mobilization on this issue will ensure wide access (Tehranian, forthcoming).

In some ways the Internet undermines the territoriality of the nation-state: messages in cyberspace are not easily delimited in Newtonian space, rendering borders ineffective. In the Teale–Homolka trial of early 1994, a case of multiple murders including sexual assault and mutilation, the Canadian government was unable to enforce an information blackout because of Usenet postings in the United States being available in Canada (Turner, 1994). In order to combat communicative acts that are defined by one state as illegal, nations are being compelled to coordinate their laws, putting their vaunted 'sovereignty' in question. So desperate are national governments, confronted by the disorder of the Internet, that schemes to monitor all messages are afoot, such as the American government's idea to monopolize encryption with a 'Clipper Chip' or the FBI's insistence on building surveillance mechanisms into the structure of the information superhighway (Hotz, 1993: 22). Nation-states are at a loss when faced with a global communication network. Technology has taken a turn that defines the character of power of modern governments.

The effortless reproduction and distribution of information is greeted by modern economic organizations, the corporations, with the same anxiety that plagues nation-states. Audio taping was resisted by the moguls of the music industry; video taping by Hollywood; modems by the telephone industry giants. Property rights are put in doubt when information is set free of its material integument to move and to multiply in cyberspace with few constraints. The response of our captains of industry is the absurd one of attempting vastly to extend the principle of property by promulgating new 'intellectual property laws', flying in the face of the advance in the technologies of transmission and dissemination. The problem for capitalism is how to contain the word and the image, to bind them to proper names and logos when they flit about at the speed of light and procreate with indecent rapidity, not arborially, to use the terms of Deleuze and Guattari, as in a centralized factory, but rhyzomically, at any decentered location. If that were not enough to daunt defenders of modern notions of property, First Amendment issues are equally at risk. Who, for example, 'owns' the rights to and is thereby responsible for the text on Internet bulletin boards: the author, the system operator, the community of participants? Does freedom of speech extend to cyberspace, as it does to print? How easy will it be to assess damages and mete out blame in a communicative world whose contours are quite different from those of face-to-face speech and print? These and numerous other fundamental questions are raised by Internet communications for institutions, laws and habits that developed in the very different context of modernity.

Reality Problematized

Before turning to the issue of the cultural interpretation of the second media age, we need to consider a further new technology, that of virtual reality. The term 'virtual' was used in computer jargon to refer to situations that were near substitutes. For example, virtual memory means the use of a section of a hard disk to act as something else, in this case, random access memory. 'Virtual reality' is a more dangerous term since it suggests that reality may be multiple or take many forms.[6] The phrase is close to that of 'real time', which arose in the audio recording field when splicing, multiple-track recording and multiple-speed recording made possible 'other times' to that of clock time or phenomenological time. In this case, the normal or conventional sense of 'time' had to be preserved by the modifier 'real'. But again the use of the modifier only draws attention to non-'reality' of clock time, its non-exclusivity, its insubstantiality, its lack of foundation. The terms 'virtual reality' and 'real time' attest to the force of the second media age in constituting a simulational culture. The mediation has become so intense that the things mediated can no longer even pretend to be unaffected. The culture is increasingly simulational in the sense that the media often changes the things that it treats, transforming the identity of originals and referentialities. In the second media age 'reality' becomes multiple.

Virtual reality is a computer-generated 'place' which is 'viewed' by the participant through 'goggles' but which responds to stimuli from the participant or participants. A participant may 'walk' through a house that is being designed for him or her to get a feel for it before it is built. Or she may 'walk' through a 'museum' or 'city' whose paintings or streets are computer-generated but the position of the individual is relative to their actual movement, not to a predetermined computer program or 'movie'. In addition, more than one individual may experience the same virtual reality at the same time, with both persons' 'movements' affecting the same 'space'. What is more, these individuals need not be in the same physical location but may be communicating information to the computer from distant points through modems. Further 'movements' in virtual reality are not quite the same as movements in 'old reality': for example, one can fly or go through walls since the material constraints of earth need not apply. While still in their infancy, virtual reality programs attest to the increasing 'duplication', if I may use this term, of reality by technology. But the duplication incurs an alternation: virtual realities are fanciful imaginings that, in their difference from real reality, evoke play and discovery, instituting a new level of imagination. Virtual reality takes the imaginary of the word and the imaginary of the film or video image one step farther by placing the individual 'inside' alternative worlds. By directly tinkering with reality, a simulational practice is set in place which alters forever the conditions under which the identity of the self is formed.

Already transitional forms of virtual reality are in use on the Internet. MUDs or Multi User Domains have a devoted following. These are conferences of sorts in which participants adopt roles in a neo-medieval adventure game. Although the game is played textually, that is, moves are typed as sentences, it is highly 'visual' in the sense that complex locations, characters and objects interact continuously. In a variant of a MUD, LambdaMOO, a database contains 'objects' as 'built' by participants to improve upon the sense of reality. As a result, a quasi-virtual reality is created by the players. What is more, each player adopts a fictional role that may be different from their actual gender and indeed this gender may change in the course of the game, drastically calling into question the gender system of the dominant culture as a fixed binary. At least during the fictional game, individuals explore imaginary subject positions while in communication with others. In LambdaMOO, a series of violent 'rapes' by one character caused a crisis among the participants, one that led to special conferences devoted to the issue of punishing the offender and thereby better defining the nature of the community space of the conference. This experience also cautions against depictions of cyberspace as utopia: the wounds of modernity are borne with us when we enter this new arena and in some cases are even exacerbated. Nonetheless, the makings of a new cultural space are also at work in the MUDs. One participant argues that continuous participation in the game leads to a sense of involvement that is somewhere between ordinary reality and fiction (Dibbell, 1993).[7] The effect of new media such as the Internet and virtual reality, then, is to multiply the kinds of 'realities' one encounters in society.

The Postmodern Subject

The information superhighway and virtual reality are communications media that enrich existing forms of consumer culture. But they also depart or may depart from what we have known as the mass media or the 'culture industry' in a number of crucial ways. I said 'may depart' because neither of these technologies has been fully constituted as cultural practices; they are emergent communication systems whose features are yet to be specified with some permanence or finality. One purpose of this essay is to suggest the importance of some form of political concern about how these technologies are being actualized. The technical characteristics of the information superhighway and virtual reality are clear enough to call attention to their potential for new cultural formations. It is conceivable that the information superhighway will be restricted in the way the broadcast system is. In that case, the term 'second media age' is unjustified. But the potential of a decentralized communications system is so great that it is certainly worthy of recognition. Examples from the history of the installation and dissemination of communications technologies are instructive. Carolyn Marvin points out that the telephone was, at the outset, by no means the universal, decentralized network it became. The phone company was happy to restrict the use of the instrument to those who registered. It did not understand the social or political importance of the universality of participation, being interested mainly in income from services provided. Also the example of Telefon Hirmondó, a telephone system in Budapest in the period before the First World War, is worth recalling. The Hungarians used the telephone as a broadcast system, with a published schedule of programming. They also restricted narrowly the dissemination of the technology to the ruling class. The process by which the telephone was instituted as a universally disseminated network in which anyone is able to call anyone else occurred in a complex, multi-leveled historical articulation in which the technology, the economic structure, the political institutions, the political culture and the mass of the population each played interacting roles (Marvin, 1988: 222ff). A similarly complex history will no doubt accompany the institution of the information superhighway and virtual reality.

In *The Mode of Information* (Poster, 1990) I argued that electronic communications constitute the subject in ways other than that of the major modern institutions. If modernity or the mode of production signifies patterned practices that elicit identities as autonomous and (instrumentally) rational, postmodernity or the mode of information indicates communication practices that constitute subjects as unstable, multiple and diffuse. The information superhighway and virtual reality will extend the mode of information to still further applications, greatly amplifying its diffusion by bringing more practices and more individuals within its pattern of formation. No doubt many modern institutions and practices continue to exist and indeed dominate social space. The mode of information is an emergent phenomenon that affects small but important aspects of everyday life. It certainly does not blanket the advanced industrial societies and has even less presence in less developed nations. The information superhighway and virtual reality may be interpreted through the poststructuralist lens I have used here in relation to the cultural issue of subject constitution. If that is done, the question of the mass media is seen not simply as that of sender/receiver, producer/consumer, ruler/ruled. The shift to a decentralized network of communications makes senders receivers, producers consumers, rulers ruled, upsetting the logic of understanding of the first media age. The step I am suggesting is at least temporarily to abandon that logic and adopt a poststructuralist cultural analysis of modes of subject constitution. This does not answer all the questions opened by the second media age, especially the political ones which at the moment are extremely difficult. But it permits the recognition of an emergent postmodernity and a tentative approach to a political analysis of that cultural system; it permits the beginning of a line of thought that confronts the possibility of a new age, avoiding the continued, limiting, exclusive repetition of the logics of modernity.

Subject constitution in the second media age occurs through the mechanism of interactivity. A technical term referring to two-way communications, 'interactivity' has become, by dint of the advertising campaigns of telecommunications corporations, desirable as an end in itself so that its usage can float and be applied in countless contexts having little to do with telecommunications. Yet the phenomenon of communicating at a distance through one's computer, of sending and receiving digitally encoded messages, of being 'interactive' has been the most popular application of the Internet. Far more than making purchases or obtaining information electronically, communicating by computer claims the intense interest of countless thousands (Dery, 1993). The use of the Internet to simulate communities far outstrips its function as retail store or reference work. In the words of Howard Rheingold (1993: 61), an enthusiastic Internet user, 'I can attest that I and thousands of other cybernauts know that what we are looking for, and finding in some surprising ways, is not just information but instant access to ongoing relationships with a large number of other people.' Rheingold terms the network of relations that come into existence on Internet bulletin boards 'virtual communities'. Places for 'meeting' on the Internet, such as 'the Well' frequented by Rheingold, provide 'areas' for 'public' messages, which all subscribers may read, and private 'mailbox' services for individual exchanges.

The understanding of these communications is limited by modern categories of analysis. For example, many have interpreted the success of 'virtual communities' as an indication that 'real' communities are in decline. Internet provides an alternative, these critics contend, to the real thing (Rheingold, 1993: 62). But the opposition 'virtual' and 'real' community contains serious difficulties. In the case of the nation, generally regarded as the strongest group identification in the modern period and thus perhaps the most 'real' community of this era, the role of the imaginary has been fundamental (Anderson, 1983). Pre-electronic media like the newspaper were instrumental in disseminating the sign of the nation and interpellating the subject in relation to it. In even earlier types of community, such as the village, kinship and residence were salient factors of determination. But identification of an individual or family with a specific group was never automatic, natural or given, always turning, as Jean-Luc Nancy (1991: xxxviii) argues, on the production of an 'essence' which reduces multiplicity into fixity, obscuring the political process in which 'community' is constructed: ' . . . the thinking of community as essence . . . is in effect the closure of the political'.[8] He rephrases the term community by asking the following question: 'How can we be receptive to the *meaning* of our multiple, dispersed, mortally fragmented existences, which nonetheless only make sense by existing in common?' (1991: xi). Community for him then is paradoxically the absence of 'community'. It is rather the matrix of fragmented identities, each pointing toward the other, which he chooses to term 'writing'.

Nancy's critique of community in the older sense is crucial to the understanding of the construction of self in the Internet. For his part, Nancy has chosen to deny the significance of new communications technologies, as well as new subaltern subject positions in his understanding of community:

> The emergence and our increasing consciousness of decolonized communities has not
> profoundly modified [the givens of community], nor has today's growth of unpreced-
> ented forms of being-in-common – through channels of information as well as through
> what is called the 'multiracial society' – triggered any genuine renewal of the question of
> community.   (Nancy, 1991: 22)

Nancy denies the relation I am drawing between a postmodern constitution of the
subject and bidirectional communications media. The important point however is
that in order to do so he first posits the subject as 'multiple, dispersed, mortally
fragmented' in an ontological statement. To this extent he removes the question of
community from the arena of history and politics, the exact purpose of his critique
of the essentialist community in the first place. While presenting an effective
critique of the essentialist community Nancy reinstates the problem at the level of
the subject by ontologizing its inessentialism. My preference is rather to specify the
historical emergence of the decentered subject and explore its links with new communications situations.

We may now return to the question of the Internet and its relation to a 'virtual
community'. To restate the issue: the Internet and virtual reality open the possibility
of new kinds of interactivity such that the idea of an opposition of real and unreal
community is not adequate to specify the differences between modes of bonding,
serving instead to obscure the manner of the historical construction of forms of
community. In particular, this opposition prevents asking the question of the forms
of identity prevalent in various types of community. The notion of a real community,
as Nancy shows, presupposes the fixed, stable identities of its members, the exact
assumption that Internet communities put into question. Observers of participants in
Internet 'virtual communities' repeat in near unanimity that long or intense experience with computer-mediated electronic communication is associated with a certain
fluidity of identity. Rheingold foresees huge cultural changes as the effect of Internet
use on the individual: '. . . are relationships and commitments as we know them even
possible in a place where identities are fluid? . . . We reduce and encode our identities
as words on a screen, decode and unpack the identities of others' (1993: 61). In
bulletin boards like the Well, people connect with strangers without much of the
social baggage that divides and alienates. Without visual cues about gender, age,
ethnicity and social status, conversations open up in directions that otherwise might
be avoided. Participants in these virtual communities often express themselves with
little inhibition and dialogues flourish and develop quickly. Yet Rheingold attributes
the conviviality of the Well and the extravagant identity transformations of MUDs to
'the hunger for community that has followed the disintegration of traditional communities around the world' (1991: 62). Even for this advocate of new communications technologies the concept of a real community regulates his understanding of the
new interactivity. While there may be some truth to a perspective that sees 'virtual
communities' as compensations for the loss of real communities, I prefer to explore
the new territory and define its possibilities.

Another aspect to understanding identity in virtual communities is provided by
Stone. Her studies of electronic communication systems suggest that participants

code 'virtual' reality through categories of 'normal' reality. They do so by communicating to each other as if they were in physical common space, as if this space were inhabited by bodies, were mappable by Cartesian perspective, and by regarding the interactions as events, as fully significant for the participants' personal histories (Stone, 1992: 618). While treatment of new media by categories developed in relation to earlier ones is hardly new, in this case the overlap serves to draw closer together the two types of ontological status. Virtual communities derive some of their verisimilitude from being treated as if they were plain communities, allowing members to experience communications in cyberspace as if they were embodied social interactions. Just as virtual communities are understood as having the attributes of 'real' communities, so 'real' communities can be seen to depend on the imaginary: what makes a community vital to its members is their treatment of the communications as meaningful and important. Virtual and real communities mirror each other in chiasmic juxtaposition.

Narratives in Cyberspace

Electronic mail services and bulletin boards are inundated by stories. Individuals appear to enjoy relating narratives to those they have never met and probably never will meet. These narratives often seem to emerge directly from peoples' lives but many no doubt are inventions. The appeal is strong to tell one's tale to others, to many, many others. One observer suggests the novelty of the situation:

> technology is breaking down the notion of few-to-many communications. Some communicators will always be more powerful than others, but the big idea behind cyber-tales is that for the first time the many are talking to the many. Every day, those who can afford the computer equipment and the telephone bills can be their own producers, agents, editors and audiences. Their stories are becoming more and more idiosyncratic, interactive and individualistic, told in different forums to diverse audiences in different ways. (Katz, 1994)

This explosion of narrativity depends upon a technology that is unlike print and unlike the electronic media of the first age: it is cheap, flexible, readily available, quick. It combines the decentralized model of the telephone and its numerous 'producers' of messages with the broadcast model's advantage of numerous receivers. Audio (Internet Talk Radio) and video (the World-Wide Web using Mosaic) are being added to text, enhancing considerably the potentials of the new narratives. There is now a 'World-Wide Web' which allows the simultaneous transmission of text, images and sound, providing hypertext links as well. The implications of the Web are astounding: film clips and voice readings may be included in 'texts' and 'authors' may indicate their links as 'texts'. In addition, other related technologies produce similar decentralizing effects. Such phenomena as 'desktop broadcasting', widespread citizen camcorder 'reporting', and digital film-making are transgressing the constraints of broadcast oligopolies (*Mondo 2000*, 1993: 34 and 106).

The question of narrative position has been central to the discussion of postmodernity. Jean-François Lyotard has analyzed the change in narrative legitimation structures of the premodern, modern and postmodern epochs. Lyotard (1984) defines the postmodern as an 'incredulity' toward metanarratives, especially that of progress and its variants deriving from the Enlightenment. He advocates a turn to the 'little story' which validates difference, extols the 'unpresentable' and escapes the overbearing logic of instrumentality that derives from the metanarrative of progress. Any effort to relate second media age technologies with the concept of the postmodern must confront Lyotard's skepticism about technology. For Lyotard, it must be recalled, technology itself is fully complicit with *modern* narrativity. For example, he warns of the dangers of 'a generalized computerization of society' in which the availability of knowledge is politically dangerous:

> The performativity of an utterance . . . increases proportionally to the amount of information about its referent one has at one's disposal. Thus the growth of power, and its self-legitimation, are now taking the route of data storage and accessibility, and the operativity of information.   (Lyotard, 1984: 47)

Information technologies are thus complicit with new tendencies toward totalitarian control, not toward a decentralized, multiple 'little narrativity' of postmodern culture.

The question may be raised, then, of the narrative structure of second media age communications: does it or is it likely to promote the proliferation of little narratives or does it invigorate a developing authoritarian technocracy? Lyotard describes the narrative structure of tribal, premodern society as stories that first legitimate institutions, second contain many different forms of language, third are transmitted by senders who are part of the narrative and have heard it before and listeners who are possible senders, fourth construct a nonlinear temporality that foreshortens the past and the present, rendering each repetition of the story strangely concurrent and, most importantly, fifth authorize everyone as a narrator. Modern society, Lyotard argues derives its legitimacy from narratives about science. Within science, language first does not legitimate institutions, second contains the single language form of denotation, third does not confirm addressee as possible sender, fourth gains no validity by being reported, and fifth constructs 'diachronic' temporality. These contrasting characteristics may serve, as Lyotard wishes, to indicate the 'pragmatics' of language. It would be interesting to analyze the role of technologies in the premodern and modern cases, and especially the change, within the modern, from print to broadcast media.

In any case, for Lyotard, the postmodern little narrative refunctions the premodern language game but only in limited ways. Like the tribal myth, the little narrative insists on 'the heteromorphous nature of language games' (1984: 66); in short, it validates difference. Unlike older narrative forms, the little narrative emphasizes the role of invention, the indication of the unknown and the unexpected. Lyotard looks to certain developments in the natural sciences for his examples of such postmodern narratives, but we may turn to the Internet and to the developing technology of virtual reality. As we have seen, the Internet seems to encourage the proliferation of stories, local narratives without any totalizing gestures and it places senders and addressees in symmetrical relations. Moreover, these stories and their performance consolidate the 'social bond' of the Internet 'community', much like the premodern narrative. But invention is central to the Internet, especially in MUDs and virtual reality: the production of the unknown or paralogy, in Lyotard's term, is central to second media age communications. In particular the relation of the utterance to representation is not limited to denotation as in the modern language game of science, and indeed the technology encourages a lightening of the weight of the referent. This is an important basis for the instability of identity in electronic communications, leading to the insertion of the question of the subject and its construction. In this spirit, Katherine Hayles (1993a: 175) defines the 'revolutionary potential' of virtual reality as follows: 'to expose the presuppositions underlying the social formations of late capitalism and to open new fields of play where the dynamics have not yet rigidified and new kinds of moves are possible'.

For the new technologies install the 'interface', the face between the faces; the face that insists that we remember that we have 'faces', that we have sides that are present at the moment of utterance, that we are not present in any simple or immediate way. The interface has become critical to the success of the Internet. To attain wide appeal, the Internet must not simply be efficient, useful or entertaining: it must present itself in an agreeable manner. The enormous problem for interface design is the fear and hostility humans nourish toward machines and toward a dim recognition of a changing relation toward them, a sharing of space and an interdependence (Springer, 1991). The Internet interface must somehow appear 'transparent', that is to say, appear not to be an interface, not to come between two alien beings and also seem fascinating, announcing its novelty and encouraging an exploration of the difference of the machinic. The problem of the Internet then is not simply 'technological' but para-machinic: to construct a boundary between the human and the machinic that draws the human into the technology, transforming the technology into 'used equipment' and the human into a 'cyborg', into one meshing with machines.[9]

In Wim Wenders' recent film, *Until the End of the World*, (1991) several characters view their own dreams on videotape, becoming so absorbed in what they see that they forget to eat and sleep. The characters sit transfixed before their viewing devices, ignoring everyone around them, disregarding all relations and affairs. Limited to the microworld of their own dreams, the characters are lost in a narcissistic stupor. And yet their total absorption is compelling. Visual representations of the unconscious – no doubt Wenders has film itself in mind – are irresistible compared to everyday reality, a kind of hyperreality.

One can imagine that virtual reality devices will become as compelling as the dream videos in Wenders' film. Virtual reality machines should be able to allow the particpant to enter imagined worlds with convincing verisimilitude, releasing immense potentials for fantasy, self-discovery and self-construction. When groups of individuals are able to interact in the same virtual space the possibilities are even more difficult to conceive. One hesitates to suggest that these experiences are commensurate with something that has been termed community. Yet there is every reason to think that virtual reality technologies will develop rapidly and will eventually enable participation through the Internet. Connected to one's home computer one will experience an audiovisual 'world' generated from a node somewhere in the Internet and this will include other participants in the same way that today one can communicate with others on bulletin boards in videotext. If such experiences become commonplace, just as viewing television is today, then surely reality will have been multiplied. The continued Western quest for making tools may at that point retrospectively be reinterpreted in relation to its culmination in virtual reality. From the club that extends and replaces the arm to virtual reality in cyberspace, technology has evolved to mime and to multiply, to multiplex and to improve upon the real.

Notes

1 See Agnew (1986) for an analysis of the formation of this subject position and its particular relation to the theater. Habermas (1989) offers a 'public sphere' of coffee houses, salons and other agora-like locations, as the arena of the modern subject, while Weber (1958) looks to Calvinist religion for the roots of the same phenomenon.
2 See, for example, the discussion of new 'interactive' technologies in the *New York Times* on 19 December 1993. In 'The Uncertain Promises of Interactivity', Calvin Sims restricts future innovations to movies on demand, on-line information services, interactive shopping, 'participatory programming', video games and conferencing systems for business. He omits electronic mail and its possible expansion to sound and image in networked virtual reality systems.
3 I have not discussed the work of Marshall McLuhan simply for lack of space and also because it is not as directly related to traditions of critical social theory as is Benjamin's, Enzensberger's and Baudrillard's. Also of interest is Kittler (1990a, 1990b).
4 For an excellent essay on the economics of the Internet and its basic structural features see Hal Varian, 'Economic FAQs About the Internet', which is available on the Internet at listserver@essential.org (send message: subscribe tap-info [your name]).
5 See also the cautionary tone of Herbert Schiller (1993).
6 Many writers prefer the term 'artificial reality' precisely because they want to underscore the privilege of real reality. Needless to say this substitution will not cure the problem.
7 I am indebted to Rob King for making me aware of this piece.
8 See also the response by Blanchot (1988).
9 Hayles (1993b: 69–91) interprets these 'different configurations of embodiment, technology and culture' through the binary pattern/randomness rather than presence/absence.

References

Agnew, J. C. (1986) *Worlds Apart: The Market and the Theatre in Anglo-American Thought, 1550–1750*. New York: Cambridge University Press.

Anderson, B. (1983) *Imagined Communities: Reflections on the Origin and Spread of Nationalism*. New York: Verso.

Blanchot, M. (1988) *The Unavowable Community*, trans. Pierre Joris. Barrytown, NY: Station Hill Press.

Bollier, D. (1993) 'The Information Superhighway: Roadmap for Renewed Public Purpose', *Tikkun* 8(4): 20–2.

Cooke, K. and D. Lehrer (1993) 'The Whole World is Talking', *The Nation* 12 July: 89–90.

Dery, M. (ed.) (1993) 'Flame Wars: The Discourse of Cyberculture', *South Atlantic Quarterly* 92(4).

Dibbell, J. (1993) 'A Rape in Cyberspace', *The Village Voice* 21 December: 36–42.

Elmer-Dewitt, P. (1993) 'Take a Trip into the Future on the Electronic Superhighway', *Time* 12 April: 50–8.

Gilder, G. (1993) 'Telecosm: The New Rule of Wireless', *Forbes ASAP* 29 March: 96, 98–104, 106–9.

Habermas, J. (1989) *The Structural Transformation of the Public Sphere*, trans. Thomas Burger. Cambridge, MA: MIT Press.

Hayles, K. (1993a) 'The Seductions of Cyberspace', in V. Conley (ed.) *Rethinking Technologies*. Minneapolis: University of Minnesota Press.

Hayles, K. (1993b) 'Virtual Bodies and Flickering Signifiers', *October* 66: 69–91.

Hotz, R. L. (1993) 'Computer Code's Security Worries Privacy Watchdogs', *Los Angeles Times* 4 October: A3, A22.

Kapor, M. (1993) 'Where Is the Digital Highway Really Heading?: The Case for a Jeffersonian Information Policy', *Wired* 1(3): 53–9, 94.

Katz, J. (1994) 'The Tales They Tell in Cyber-Space Are a Whole Other Story', *Los Angeles Times* 23 January: A1, A30.

Kittler, F. (1990a) 'Gramophone, Film, Typewriter', *October* 41: 101–18.

Kittler, F. (1990b) *Discourse Networks: 1800/1900*, trans. Michael Metteer. Stanford: Stanford University Press.

Lyotard, J. F. (1984) *The Postmodern Condition: A Report on Knowledge*, trans. Geoff Bennington and Brian Massumi. Minneapolis: University of Minnesota Press.

Marvin, C. (1988) *When Old Technologies Were New: Thinking About Electric Communication in the Late Nineteenth Century*. New York: Oxford.

Mondo 2000 (1993) No. 11.

Nancy, J. L. (1991) *The Inoperative Community*, trans. Peter Conner et al. Minneapolis: University of Minnesota Press.

Poster, M. (1990) *The Mode of Information*. Oxford: Polity Press.

Rheingold, H. (1993) 'A Slice of Life in My Virtual Community', in L. Harasim (ed.) *Global Networks: Computers and International Communication*. Cambridge: MIT Press.

Schiller, H. (1993) 'The "Information Highway": Public Way or Private Road?', *The Nation* July 12.

Springer, C. (1991) 'The Pleasure of the Interface', *Screen* 32(3): 303–23.

Stone, A. R. (1992) 'Virtual Systems', in *Incorporations*, ed. Jonathan Crary and Stanford K. Winter. Cambridge: MIT Press.

Tehranian, M. (forthcoming) 'World With/Out Wars: Moral Spaces and the Ethics of Transnational Communication', *The Public* (Ljubljana).

Turner, C. (1994) 'Courts Gag Media at Sensational Canada Trial', *Los Angeles Times* May 15: A4.

Weber, M. (1958) *The Protestant Ethic and the Spirit of Capitalism*, trans. Talcott Parsons. New York: Macmillan.

Index